THE PSYCHOLOGY
OF READING

THE PSYCHOLOGY OF READING

KEITH RAYNER
ALEXANDER POLLATSEK
University of Massachussetts

LEA LAWRENCE ERLBAUM ASSOCIATES, PUBLISHERS
Hillsdale, New Jersey   Hove, UK

Originally published in 1989.

Lawrence Erlbaum Associates, Inc., Publishers
365 Broadway
Hillsdale, New Jersey 07642

Library of Congress Cataloging-in-Publication Data

Rayner, Keith
  The psychology of reading.
  Bibliography.
  Includes index.
  1. Reading, Psychology of. I. Pollatsek,
Alexander.   II. Title.
BF456.R2R33   1989   418   88-22419

ISBN 0-8058-1872-3

Books published by Lawrence Erlbaum Associates are printed
on acid-free paper, and their bindings are chosen
for strength and durability.

Printed in the United States of America

10 9 8 7 6 5 4 3 2

Contents

Preface

Reading is a highly complex skill that is a prerequisite to success in our society. In a society such as ours, where so much information is communicated in written form, it is important to investigate this essential behavior. In the past 15 years, a great deal has been learned about the reading process from research by cognitive psychologists. This book is our attempt to summarize that work and to put it into a coherent framework. For the most part, our emphasis is on the *process* of reading. We are most interested in how readers go about extracting information from the printed page and comprehending the text. We will not be quite so concerned about the *product* of reading (or what people remember from what they have read). Nor will we be centrally concerned with issues about how to teach children to read. Each of these issues is addressed in the book (the product of reading in Chapter 8 and learning to read in Chapters 9 and 10), but the major focus is on the moment-to-moment processes that a reader engages in during reading.

We have written this book for advanced undergraduates and beginning level graduate students, though we would hope that our colleagues in cognitive psychology who are interested in the process of reading will find the work useful to them. We have also tried to write the book so that it is fairly accessible to students who do not have backgrounds in psychology. The book is divided into five sections. In Part One, we provide an overview of some relevant background information that should be particularly important to readers who do not have a background in cognitive psychology. In this first section, we present an analysis of writing systems and also discuss how readers recognize words. Part Two, "Skilled Reading of Text," deals with the work of the eyes during reading and with the role of inner speech in reading. In Part Three, "Understanding Text," we focus on how readers comprehend text. Part Four deals with learning to read and various types of reading disability. In Part Five, we discuss speedreading and individual differences and then attempt to tie the major ideas of the book together by discussing models of the reading process.

We have written this book so that the instructor need not cover all of it in a course. Chapters 3 through 8 form the core of the book and subsequent chapters presuppose reading them. Chapter 1, however, can be omitted or skimmed by students who have had an undergraduate course in cognitive psychology, and Chapter 2 can be omitted or skimmed by students with a background in linguistics. Chapters 9 and 10, Chapter 11, and Chapter 12, however, form three separate units, any of which (or all) could be omitted without disturbing continuity. Chapter 13 provides a brief overview and summation of the book.

The initial drafts of most of the chapters in this book were written while the first author was on sabbatical leave at the Department of Experimental Psychology at the University of Oxford and while the second author was on sabbatical leave at the Department of Psychology at the University of Oregon. We gratefully acknowledge the hospitality of those two departments. Some of the final work on the book was completed while the first author was a Fellow at the Netherlands Institute for Advanced Study. Appreciation is expressed to that institution as well as our home institution, the University of Massachusetts. We also thank our editors at Prentice Hall, first John Isley and then Susan Finnemore, for their assistance and gentle prodding in encouraging us to complete the manuscript. Karen Winget's technical editing is also much appreciated. The book was also helped greatly by reviews of the entire manuscript that were provided by James Juola and Paul van den Broek, and by reviews of parts of the book provided by Morti Gernsbacher, Simon Garrod, and Chuck Perfetti.

We hope that the citations throughout this book point to the intellectual debt we owe to other researchers. We would especially like to thank our colleagues at the University of Massachusetts to whom we owe a great intellectual debt. UMass is an excellent place for researchers interested in reading and language to work. We thank our colleagues Jim Chumbley, Susan Duffy, Lyn Frazier, Jerry Myers, and Arnie Well for their comments on various chapters. In addition, their work on reading-related issues has very much influenced our thinking. We have also been very influenced in our thinking by Dave Balota, Harry Blanchard, Albrecht Inhoff, John Henderson, Bob Morrison, and Susan Lima (who were recently either graduate students or postdoctoral fellows with us). Our work and conversations with other former graduate students (Pat Carroll, Susan Ehrlich, Fernanda Ferreira, Ed O'Brien, Fran Pirozzolo, and Maria Slowiaczek) will be apparent in the book and we also thank them. A number of current graduate students at the University of Massachusetts read a draft of the entire book and provided us with comments; accordingly, we thank Janey Barnes, Susan Boyce, Marica DeVincenzi, Barbara Greene, Robin Morris, Sara Sereno, Mikiko Shinjo, Gale Sinatra, Kevin Stone, Ted Trobaugh, and Janice Wright. Mary-Lou Reid and Mary-Ann Palmieri provided excellent secretarial assistance to us and, as former school teachers, also tried to always remind us of the practical implications of research on reading. We owe a debt of gratitude to our own mentors in graduate school (George McConkie and Robert Bjork) for getting us started in our work. In addition, we would like to acknowledge a debt to Tom Carr. Many of his ideas from previous collaborations and conversations have found their way into the book (especially Chapter 3). Finally, and most importantly, we thank Chuck Clifton for his help in many ways. He read (as a reviewer for Prentice-Hall) the entire volume, provided us with excellent comments and was always available to discuss various issues that were puzzling us.

Both the National Science Foundation and the National Institute of Child Health and Human Development have been very generous in supporting our research on reading and we are pleased to acknowledge their support.

We owe a particular debt of gratitude to our families. As we found out, writing a book is an exhausting and time-consuming endeavor. Our families saw less of us during the time that we were working on this book, and we have made many promises that we will be freer with our time for the next little while. We hope to deliver on our promises, but as some measure of our appreciation for their support we are happy to dedicate this book to Susan, Ashley, and Jonathan and to Harriet, Shura, and David. We would also like to dedicate the book to our parents and express a deep sense of regret that Frank Pollatsek did not live to see it.

THE PSYCHOLOGY
OF READING

PART ONE
BACKGROUND INFORMATION

In the first three chapters of this book, we will present some information that will be necessary for you to understand many of the points that we will stress in later chapters. In Chapter 1, some key concepts from cognitive psychology will be introduced that will be used throughout the book. Cognitive psychology is the branch of experimental psychology that studies how the mind functions and is structured, and in the past 20 years many cognitive psychologists have been studying how the mind works during reading. In Chapter 1, we will introduce many of the basic conceptual tools that cognitive psychologists use when they study mental processes in general and reading in particular.

In Chapter 2, an overview of the different writing systems that have been used or are in use throughout the world will be presented. As in Chapter 1, we will also use Chapter 2 to introduce some key concepts from linguistics and psychology. Since the rest of the book will be dealing with the processes that result when readers attempt to decipher the black marks on the page, it is essential that we have some knowledge of the stimulus that is the starting point for all those processes. In addition, it is important to discuss the significant characteristics of different writing systems—partly to gain some insight into written English and partly to clear up misconceptions about many writing systems.

Note that we used the term *processes* a few times in the preceding sentences. This book is primarily about *how* the mind processes information during reading. We will have virtually nothing to say about motivational and emotional issues during reading. Our focus in the book will be on the reading process for skilled readers who are motivated to read. We assume that such skilled and motivated reading characterizes much of reading, and as you shall see, it is enough of a challenge to explain it. However, beginning reading and certain kinds of reading disabilities will be the focus of Part 4.

Chapter 3 is one of the most important chapters in the book because there we will discuss how words are identified. In that chapter, we will describe some of the work cognitive psychologists have done to understand how isolated words are perceived, recognized, and understood. Some researchers are critical of this work and suggest that identifying words in isolation is quite different from normal fluent reading. The position we adopt (and will justify at various points in the book) is that skilled reading involves a number of component processes, and that these component processes can be studied. That is not to say we believe that reading is merely identifying individual words and stringing the meaning of the words together; the process of comprehending text is much more complex than that. However, a moment's reflection should make it clear that for reading to proceed at all efficiently, we must be able to recognize and understand the meaning of most—if not all—the individual words we encounter.

The first section of the book thus will primarily provide you with the background information necessary to understand the process of reading. In the subsequent sections, this background information will be used to help you understand the complex information-processing activities that occur when you read and understand text.

CHAPTER ONE
INTRODUCTION AND PRELIMINARY INFORMATION

Reading is a complex skill that is pretty much taken for granted by those who can do it. In the early-seventies (when cognitive psychologists became very interested in studying reading), one of the authors (then a graduate student) got into an elevator in the engineering department at a famous university in the United States with a copy of Smith's book *Understanding Reading* (1971) under his arm. A bright young freshman engineering student upon seeing the book was quick to remark, "Oh, reading, I learned how to do that 15 years ago." That remark is pretty consistent with most people's attitudes about reading. While those who can do it fluently take it for granted, its complexity is more apparent to those who are having trouble. Reading is sometimes difficult for children to learn (particularly in comparison to the ease with which they learn to speak), and illiterate adults find learning to read agonizingly frustrating.

Anyone reading this book is likely to be familiar with 30,000 or more words, and can generally recognize most of them within a fraction of a second. A skilled reader can do this despite the fact that the letters which make up the words are often printed in different typefonts. In the case of handwritten letters, a reader can still read and comprehend despite rather dramatic differences in style and legibility. In being able to read and identify words in spite of all this variability, a skilled reader is able to perform a feat that is well beyond the capability of the most powerful computer programs available today. But this is not all. Skilled readers can identify words that have different meanings in different contexts. Consider the use of the word *boxer* in the following two sentences:

John knew the boxer was angry when he started barking at him. (1.1)

John knew the boxer was angry when he started yelling at him. (1.2)

These two sentences are identical except for a single word which makes clear the appropriate meaning of the word *boxer*. The less common meaning for *boxer* is a dog. Since dogs bark and people don't, however, *boxer* in Sentence 1.1 clearly refers to a dog. Likewise, in Sentence 1.2 the fact that the *boxer* is yelling leads us to believe that the sentence is referring to a person. If you are observant, you may have noticed that there are actually two ambiguities in sentences 1.1 and 1.2. Not only is the word *boxer* ambiguous but also the pronoun *he*. In 1.1, *he* would be interpreted as the *boxer* because of *barking,* but in 1.2, *he* could either be *John* or *the boxer*. There is some bias, however, in sentences like 1.1 and 1.2 to associate the pronoun with the most recent antecedent. Other factors can change the bias; in 1.3, *he* is most likely *John,* but in 1.4, *he* is most likely *the boxer*.

The boxer hit John because he started yelling at him. (1.3)

The boxer hit John and then he started yelling at him. (1.4)

The point of this discussion is that we can easily understand the meaning of these different sentences despite the fact that individual words have more than one meaning and pronouns occasionally have unclear antecedents. Coupled with this fact is the observation that we can easily understand puns, idioms, and metaphors. For example, in Sentence 1.5

John thought the billboard was a wart on the landscape. (1.5)

none of us would believe the literal meaning of the word *wart* was intended. We quite easily understand the sentence to mean that the billboard was ugly and spoiled the scene. Just as we can easily comprehend the metaphor in sentence 1.5, the idiomatic nature of sentence 1.6

John hit the nail on the head with his answer. (1.6)

presents a difficulty only for nonnative readers of English who attempt a literal interpretation of the sentence and find it nonsensical. Thus, skilled readers are very good at combining the meanings of individual words to derive the meaning of sentences and paragraphs, as well as short passages and books. Readers can draw inferences by relying upon what they already know to help understand text, and from reading words they can form images of scenes and appreciate poetry.

We have been arguing that the feats of a skilled reader are truly impressive. Very powerful computers, despite tremendous memory capacity, cannot do what a skilled reader can do; such machines (or more specifically the programs that run them), would fail on many of the tasks we have mentioned that a skilled reader handles almost effortlessly. How do skilled readers accomplish this complex task? And how is the skill acquired? These are the central questions of this book. For the most part, we will focus on the skilled reader in attempting to explain the process of reading. Our primary rationale is that we must understand the skill itself before we can understand how it is acquired, and our primary orientation in this book is a cognitive-psychology–information-processing point of view (i.e., understanding the component mechanisms underlying reading). In the remainder of this chapter, we will attempt to place the rest of the book into perspective. We will do this by first discussing how researchers have historically viewed reading. Then we will present an overview of the human information-processing system, discussing what types of processing mechanisms may be involved in reading.

HISTORICAL OVERVIEW OF READING RESEARCH

The roots of cognitive psychology, the branch of experimental psychology that studies how the mind works, can be traced to the establishment of Wundt's laboratory in Leipzig in 1879. Workers in Wundt's laboratory were keenly interested in questions related to memory and to language processing. Shortly thereafter, there was considerable interest in the process of reading which reached its apex with the publication of Huey's (1908) *The Psychology and Pedagogy of Reading*. A perusal of the chapters in the first part of his book (that part dealing with the psychology of reading) will reveal that the chapters bear a remarkable similarity to the topics covered in the present volume and most other contemporary books dealing with the psychology of reading. Huey and his contemporaries were interested in eye movements in reading, the nature of the perceptual span (how much information can be perceived during a fixation of the eye), word-recognition processes, inner speech, reading comprehension, and reading rate. Huey's marvelously cogent and concise description of his findings and those of his contemporaries prior to 1908 is still a joy to read. Many of the basic facts we know about eye movements during reading were discovered by Huey and contemporaries using cumbersome and seemingly archaic techniques in comparison to the sophisticated devices currently available to record eye movements during reading. Yet their discoveries have stood the test of time and have held up when replicated using more accurate recording systems. A contemporary of Huey, Emile Javal, the French oculist, first noted that during reading our eyes do not move smoothly across the page as our phenomenological impressions would imply. Rather our eyes make a series of jumps (or *saccades* in French) along the line. Between the jumps the eyes remain relatively still, for about a quarter of a second, in what is referred to as a *fixation*. A large number of experiments were carried out by Huey and his contemporaries to understand the work of the eyes in reading.

In order to study how much information can be perceived in a single eye fixation, the tachistoscope was devised. The t-scope (as it is often called) is a device that allows an experimenter to control how much information is presented to a subject, as well as the duration of the exposure. By varying the amount of information available in the t-scope and by presenting it for a duration brief enough to preclude any eye movement, early researchers hoped to infer the size of the *perceptual span* or the area of effective vision during a fixation. Huey's book also describes classic experiments by Cattell (1886) and by Erdmann and Dodge (1898) on word recognition, and two full chapters in the book are devoted to the role of inner speech in reading. Huey's observations on inner speech and word-recognition processes are lucid, and amazingly relevant to current issues.

Work related to the cognitive processes involved in reading continued for a few years after the publication of Huey's book. However, serious work by psychologists on the reading process pretty much came to a halt a few years after 1913. In that year, the behaviorist revolution in experimental psychology began. According to behaviorist doctrine, the only things worthy of study by experimental psychologists were activities that could be seen, observed, and measured. Since cognitive processes involved in skilled reading cannot be observed and directly measured, interest in reading waned between 1920 and 1960. While Buswell and Tinker carried out some well-known investigations of eye movements during reading, their work, for the most part, dealt with purely peripheral components of reading. Attempts to relate the activity of the eye to the activity of the mind were virtually nonexistent.

In essence, work on the cognitive processes associated with reading came to a standstill in the 1920s and did not begin again until the 1960s. Small wonder that when Huey's book was republished in 1968 it seemed so relevant. Not much had been learned about reading in the 60 years between the initial publication of the work and its second appearance. We hasten to point out that in addition to the work on eye movements during reading by researchers such as Buswell and Tinker, some work on reading did continue during the interval in question. But most of it was conducted in education schools where the primary focus is generally on more applied aspects of reading. Thus, there was work on the most appropriate method to teach reading, and many of the standardized reading tests still in existence today were developed during that period. However, work on the mental processes associated with reading was almost nonexistent.

Today, we find many psychologists interested in reading. Why has this change taken place? The primary reason appears to have been the failure of behaviorism to account for language processing in any reasonable way. The promise of behaviorism was always that if psychologists could understand the laws of learning and behavior in simple tasks (like knee jerks and eye blinks), those laws could be generalized to more complex tasks like language processing. In 1957, B. F. Skinner decided it was high time that the behaviorists produced on this promise, and he published *Verbal Behavior* which was an account of language from a behaviorist viewpoint. The linguist Noam Chomsky (1959) wrote a scathing review not only of the book but of behaviorism in general.

In essence, Chomsky argued that behaviorist principles could not account for language learning or language processes in general. Around that same time, he also published *Syntactic Structures* (1957), which was a radical departure from traditional linguistic theory. In that work, he suggested that the study of language and the mind are intimately related and presented an elegant theory of grammar. Many psychologists, disillusioned with behaviorism, became very interested in Chomsky's theories of language processing. After a hiatus of more than 40 years, work on cognitive processes was underway. (There were a number of other factors that contributed to the reemergence of the study of cognitive processes around 1960, but they are beyond the scope of our current discussion.) Out of the burgeoning interest in language processes in general, interest in the reading process began once again around 1970. Since the mid-1960s a number of scholarly journals dealing with cognitive processes and human experimental psychology have been founded, and each issue of these journals generally contains at least one article related to reading. In addition, a number of textbooks dealing with reading have appeared in the last 5 or 6 years. Clearly, there is now considerable interest among cognitive psychologists in studying reading.

It is important to note that cognitive psychologists studying reading approach the issue from slightly different perspectives. Some have a background rooted in perception research and see the study of word recognition, for example, as a means to study perceptual processes or pattern recognition using well-defined stimuli. Others approach the study of reading with a background in memory processes and verbal learning theory. They tend to approach the study of reading by examining comprehension processes. Still others are interested in reading in and of itself, because they believe, as Huey pointed out 80 years ago, that to understand what the mind does during reading would be "the acme of a psychologist's achievements, since it would be to describe very many of the most intricate workings of the human mind, as well as to unravel the tangled story of the most remarkable specific performance that civilization has learned."

It is our contention that this diversity of interests and backgrounds is healthy and can easily be accommodated within the information processing approach because it views reading as a highly complex process relying on a number of subprocesses. Indeed, most of the breakthroughs have come from researchers working on different subcomponents of the reading process and there have been few global insights that have been the key to answering many of the questions about a complex skill like reading. While it is clear that the information obtained by cognitive psychologists needs to be put together into a unified framework, the present state of the art justifies an emphasis on the different component processes of a complex skill.

Critics of the information-processing approach often argue that attempts to isolate component processes of reading result in tasks very much unlike reading. For example, to study word-recognition processes, cognitive psychologists often present a word for a very brief duration (say 50 milliseconds, which is one-twentieth of a second). A subject in such an experiment may be asked to pronounce the word or make some type of decision about it (Is it a word? Does it belong to a certain category of things? Is it larger than a breadbox?) In making decisions about the word, subjects push one button for a "yes" response and another for a "no" response. Admittedly, these tasks are unlike reading. Yet to respond appropriately, subjects may well be using the same processing mechanisms that they use during reading. Perhaps an analogy will help. Suppose we're interested in studying walking. If we study the motor responses that people make when they take two steps, critics may say, "But that's not walking. When you walk you go a long way." True, but are the motor responses any different when you take two steps? Undoubtedly not. What cognitive psychologists strive to do is set up experiments in which the same processing mechanisms are used in the task derived as in reading. Sometimes we're more successful than other times. In this book, we will place the greatest weight on those experiments that most closely match the task of reading.

It is important to point out that the primary methodology of the cognitive psychologist is empirical experimentation. Theories and models of processes such as reading are also critically important because they help to formulate the kinds of research questions to be asked. Theories often arise from informal observations and intuitions as well as experiments. The ultimate test of a theory, however, is an experiment in which contrasting theoretical positions are tested against each other. With these points in mind, we now turn to a description of the human information processing system.

OVERVIEW OF THE HUMAN INFORMATION-PROCESSING SYSTEM

In this section, we will present an overview of the human information-processing system. However, we caution you that not all cognitive psychologists would agree with the notion of distinct stages. Indeed, the best way to describe the human information-processing system is quite controversial (see Craik and Lockhart 1972; Broadbent 1984). Consisting of three distinct stages (sensory store, short-term memory, and long-term memory), the type of model we will present is rather controversial at the moment, as is the assumption that the system is more or less passive. We will overlook such controversies because our primary intention is to give the flavor of the information-processing approach and to introduce terminology that virtually all cognitive psychologists use. In addition, some of the controversy over details is peripheral to understanding reading.

Figure 1.1 shows an example of a typical stage model of the human information-processing system. It consists of three stages and each stage has distinct functions and characteristics. However, prior to examining such a system, we must discuss something about the initial sensory registration of printed words by the eyes and subsequent pattern recognition processes.

The Retina and Visual Acuity

Vision depends on a pair of specialized organs (the eyes) whose neural receptors can be thought of as being part of the brain which has extended outside of the cortex. Patterns of light falling on the sensory neurons in the retina result in the sensation of seeing. When you look at a page of text (like the one you are currently reading), you are not able to see all of the words on the page equally well. This is because of *acuity limitations*. In terms of acuity, a horizontal line of text falling on the retina can be divided into three regions: foveal, parafoveal, and peripheral. The foveal area subtends about 2 degrees of visual angle around your fixation point; the parafoveal area subtends about 10 degrees of visual angle around fixation (4 degrees to the left and to the right beyond the foveal region); the peripheral area includes everything on the line of text beyond the parafoveal region. Acuity is greatest in the center of vision (the fovea) and drops off markedly in the parafovea and even more so in the periphery. This is because of the anatomical structure of the retina.

The retina is composed of two types of receptors called *rods* and *cones*. The fovea consists almost entirely of cones, and with distance from the fovea, the density of cones decreases and the density of rods increases.

FIGURE 1-1 An overview of the human information-processing system.

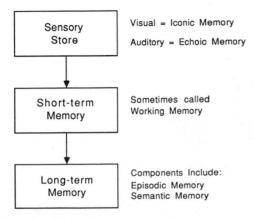

Thus, the peripheral region of the retina is composed entirely of rods. The parafovea contains a mixture of rods and cones. These two types of receptors serve dramatically different functions. The cones are specialized for processing detail and for acuity. In addition to permitting fine discrimination of detail, cones also serve in the discrimination of wavelengths or hue. The rods, on the other hand, are specialized for detecting movement and permit discrimination of brightness or shades of gray. The rods are particularly important for night vision; when you enter a dark room, at first you cannot "see" anything. However, after a short while (unless the room is totally dark) your rods adapt and you can see.

The most important point to be gleaned from the description of rods and cones is that the acuity necessary for discriminating fine detail (as is necessary in reading) is available only in the center of vision. A simple experiment can demonstrate this quite clearly. If you were asked to look into a tachistoscope and tell us the word (or letter) that appeared there, your accuracy in doing so would decrease as the stimulus was presented further from your point of fixation. The stimuli are presented briefly enough (about 150 milliseconds or less) so that it is virtually impossible for you to move your eyes to look directly at it. Figure 1.2 shows how performance in such a task would depend upon how close to fixation the stimulus was presented. In the figure, we have also plotted the relative distribution of rods and cones in the retina. Note that the accuracy function in our experiment is very similar to the distribution of cones in the retina. The purpose of this demonstration is to convince you that in order to discriminate the fine details of letters and words as we read, we must move our eyes to place the fovea over that part of the text we want to read.

FIGURE 1-2 Relative frequency of the density of cones (solid line) and rods (dashed line) across the visual field. Dotted line shows the accuracy of identifying a target word exposed briefly to the left or right of fixation.

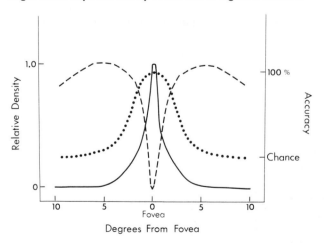

Pattern Recognition Processes

After we move our eyes to place the fovea on the word or words that we want to read, pattern recognition begins. Actually, the pattern-recognition process for a word may have begun on the prior fixation when the word was in parafoveal vision, as we shall see in Chapter 4. What we are concerned with in this section is how the brain goes about recognizing the letters and words which must be processed for us to read. To take a simple example, how do we recognize the printed letter *A?* Two major theories of pattern recognition have been proposed. The first *template-matching theory,* suggests that we have stored in our brains a representation of every pattern that we can recognize. Thus, we recognize the letter *A* by comparing the pattern of excitation from the cells in the retina to a template stored in memory. If there is a match between the representation and the stimulus, the letter *A* is perceived.

While template-matching theory works quite well in computer pattern-recognition devices that read letters and digits in highly constrained contexts, such as the digits that specify the code number for your checking account, it is well known (Neisser 1967; Crowder 1982) that such a system would fail to recognize instances of the letter *A* that were slightly deviant with respect to shape, size, or orientation as Figure 1.3 shows. The major problem for the theory in its most rigid form is that it suggests that we have a template for every variation of every pattern we are able to recognize. The simple pattern for the letter *A,* for example, can appear in a number of different typefonts and handwriting variations. Yet we are able to recognize it quite easily. It seems unwieldy to think that we have so many patterns stored in our head.

One way to make the template-matching theory more workable is to assume that before comparisons of new input to those stored take place, the input is "cleaned up" or normalized. The normalization process would separate essential information in the stimulus from most nonessential information. For example, variations in size could be taken care of before comparisons to a template occurred by transforming all images to a standard size. Accounting for variations in orientation prior to the matching process also seems quite reasonable. It is somewhat harder to understand how the normalization process would fill in missing gaps and eliminate fuzzy squiggles (as in handwriting) that are irrelevant to recognizing the pattern as the letter *A.*

While the normalization process gives plausibility to the template-matching theory, the second theory, *feature-detection theory,* is more parsimonious in accounting for how the pattern-recognition process deals with such variation and is generally considered to be a more viable account. The starting point for feature-detection theory is the idea that there are many common elements for letters (consisting of horizontal, vertical oblique, and curved lines) and that we analyze these component elements in recognizing a pattern. The letters *C* and *G* and the letters *O* and *Q,* for

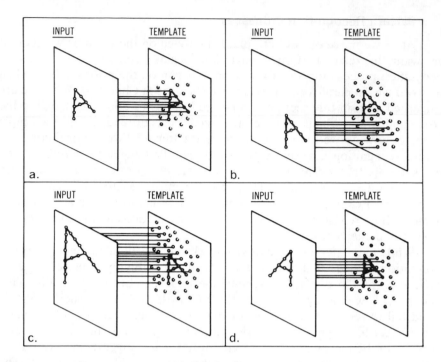

FIGURE 1-3 Illustration of the difficulties with a simple template-matching system for character recognition. (After Neisser 1967, with permission of Prentice-Hall.)

example, have a great deal of similarity and featural overlap. The distinguishing feature between the *C* and *G* is the horizontal line that is present in the *G,* but not in the *C*. The distinguishing feature between the *O* and *Q* is the oblique line present in the *Q* but absent in the *O*. According to feature-detection theory, when a letter is analyzed the first step is to prepare a list of its features and this list is compared with the list stored in memory. This process then is *analytical* in that we put together the different elements of the pattern until recognition occurs. Template-matching theory, on the other hand, is more of a *holistic* process. As we implied, the feature-detection theory is considerably less cumbersome because the analytic processes rely on a small number of features that are common to all typefonts (the distinguishing feature for *C* versus *G* remains invariant over different typefonts and handwriting styles), as opposed to having a different template for each style of print.

What type of evidence is there for feature-detection theory? Three types of evidence are consistent with the theory: (1) physiological data from animals, (2) stabilized image research, and (3) visual search data.

The best known physiological evidence in favor of feature detection theory comes from work by Hubel and Wiesel (1962) on the visual system of the cat. Using electrical recordings, Hubel and Wiesel were able to examine the rate of firing of individual cells in the visual system as a function of what the cat was looking at. The most important finding from their work for our purposes is that they demonstrated that cortical cells in the visual system fired differentially depending on the stimulus. Line, edge, and slit detectors, as well as more complex detectors, were all discovered. It is easy to generalize from these results (although it should be done cautiously) and suggest that there are also feature detectors in humans specialized for firing when the various horizontal, vertical, oblique, and curved lines making up the letters of our alphabet fall in front of our eyes.

The stabilized image experiments use sophisticated technology to hold an image fixed or stabilized on the retina; to whatever extent the eyes move, the presented stimulus moves a corresponding amount in the same direction. In contrast, even when we are asked to hold our eyes very still in normal vision, there is a slight movement or tremor of the eyes (called *nystagmus*). Apparently, the nystagmus is important for perception because under stabilized image conditions perception gradually blanks out so that the observer no longer sees the stimulus. What is interesting is that perception of the stabilized image does not blank out instantaneously. Instead, it is gradual, and lines sharing the same orientation disappear at the same time as depicted in Figure 1.4. The manner in which the stimulus fades is further support for feature-detection theory, since the units fading out appear to be features of the objects.

FIGURE 1-4 **Perceptual fragmentation in "stopped images." The figures at the left are stimulus patterns; the others are typical products of fragmentation. (From Pritchard 1961, with permission of Scientific American).**

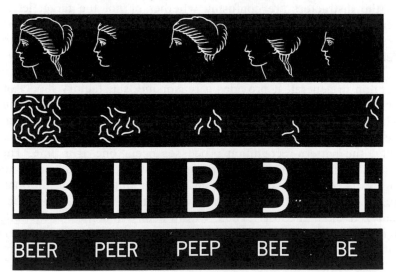

STANDARD CONDITION TARGET = Z	NONCONFUSABLE CONDITION TARGET = Z	CONFUSABLE CONDITION TARGET = Z
RYVMKF	CBSOGS	VMWNMW
PTHSHG	UBSQQQ	WYLKWV'
GTVCBH	BQOUDG	XMWLLY
HUIRYD	SCDOBC	YXZWXL
KIREGD	CZOQUS	NMWYMN
GBZTBN	DUBCCD	YNLXLI
POLKRF	DOQUCB	MNWXMH
FTIEWR	CCOQOU	LYXWLT
. . .	. . .	. . .
. . .	. . .	. . .

FIGURE 1-5 Neisser's visual search task. A display is exposed and the subject must scan vertically, from top to bottom, until finding a target item. Time to reach the target is recorded as a function of the position of the target.

The third line of evidence for feature-detection theory is the work on visual search originated by Neisser (1967). Figure 1.5 shows sample stimuli in the task. You are asked to find the target letter Z. It turns out that the letter Z is much easier to find (subjects are over twice as fast) in the middle column than in either of the other columns. The reason, of course, is that the distractor letters in the middle column are all letters that are quite dissimilar to the target and do not share many features with it. Template-matching theory would suggest that there should be no difference between the columns because the number of matches that must be made would be equivalent in each. However, feature-detection theory can account for the result, since virtually the same set of feature-detector cells would be firing when the distractors are confusing whether or not the target letter was present. On the other hand, when the target is embedded in dissimilar letters, the cells that fire for the letter Z will only fire when the target is present.

While there are criticisms of feature detection as a theory of object perception in general, it provides a reasonably satisfactory model of how letters and words are processed. One issue that we have not discussed, which will become relevant in a later chapter, is whether pattern recognition processes occur in a *serial* or *parallel* manner. If information is analyzed serially, the pattern-recognition processes occur one at a time. Thus, in Neisser's visual-search task, feature analysis would occur for one letter and when it was complete would begin on the next, and so on. If information is analyzed in parallel, the sensory information from various spatial locations is analyzed simultaneously. Thus, within acuity limits, all of the letters in each row in Figure 1.5 would be analyzed at once. The experiments on word identification that we will discuss in Chapter 3 also argue for parallel processing.

In this section we have argued that the pattern-recognition processes that operate on print can best be conceptualized in terms of feature-analytic processes. We return now to a more detailed examination of the information-processing system depicted in Figure 1.1.

The Sensory Store

The lowest level in the information-processing system is generally referred to as the *sensory store*. For auditory information, the store is referred to as *echoic memory* (see Cowan 1984 for a discussion). For visual information, the store is referred to as *iconic memory*. Iconic memory is considered to be a temporary memory store in which much of the information physically available in the stimulus is still available after the display has gone off.

In one of the most widely cited experiments in cognitive psychology, Sperling (1960) demonstrated the existence of a visual sensory store. He presented subjects with three rows of 4 letters each for a brief duration (say 50 milliseconds or one-twentieth of a second). In a control condition, subjects were instructed to report as many of the letters as possible, and the average number of letters reported was 4.5. In the experimental conditions, Sperling used a partial report technique in which he cued subjects as to which row they should report. Thus if after the display went off, subjects heard a high pitch tone they were to report the top row, a medium tone the middle row, and a low pitch the bottom row. The tone was presented at various delays after the disappearance of the letters from the screen. Sometimes the tone occurred simultaneously with the offset of the letters and sometimes it occurred up to a second after the letters disappeared.

Sperling's reasoning was that if we have an iconic memory (though he did not call it such), we should be able to use the cue to "read out" the letters from the cued row. If the tone actually occurred prior to the onset of the letters, then we would be able to use that information to focus on the relevant row. Sperling's question was whether or not we can use the cue to examine information after it has physically disappeared from before our eyes. If so, then we must have an iconic memory in which all or most of the information present in the stimulus is still available. In fact, what Sperling found was that subjects could report on average 3.3 letters from the array, which means they must have had approximately 10 letters available in their memory system. Since the subject had no way of knowing beforehand which row was going to be signaled, it must be the case that subjects could get roughly 3.3 letters from any of the rows.

Keep in mind that when subjects in the control condition were asked to report as many letters from the display as they could, they averaged 4.5 letters. How do we account for the discrepancy between the cued partial report trials and the whole report condition? If we assume that iconic memory has a large capacity (say 10 letters from a 3-by-4 array) and that the rate at which people can "read out" letters is slow (say 3 to 5 letters in a quarter of a second), then the discrepancy can be explained. If the letters are taken from the whole display, performance is limited by the read-out process. On the other hand, if the tone cues the subject that only one row is relevant, then the subject has time to read out most of that row.

Since Sperling's demonstration, there have been literally hundreds of experiments investigating the characteristics of iconic memory. This research has revealed that the primary characteristics of iconic memory are that (1) the memory has a large capacity, (2) it has a duration of roughly a quarter of a second, (3) it is precategorical, (4) it is interfered with by new information, and (5) the read-out rate is relatively slow.

The current status of iconic memory is highly debatable (see Coltheart 1980a; Haber 1983; Turvey 1977). Some workers in the field are now arguing that it is an *epiphenomenon* (i.e., a phenomenon that occurs but is of no real functional significance) of the highly sterile and controlled experimental laboratory; after all, when does a stimulus appear before our eyes for a fraction of a second only to disappear completely? Such individuals tend to argue that iconic memory, like our appendix, has no functional utility. Others argue that all biological mechanisms are adaptive, and just because we do not know for certain what function the icon serves, does not mean it does not have a role in processing.

With respect to reading, it is not at all clear what function iconic memory might serve. Clearly, subjects in iconic-memory experiments are not reading in the sense that we would normally think of reading. In reading, the stimulus does not disappear from in front of our eyes after only a brief exposure (unless perhaps we try reading in a lightning storm). At one time, it was thought that something similar to an iconic memory played a role in integrating visual information across the eye movements we make during reading. We will discuss that idea in some detail in Chapter 4, but to anticipate that discussion a bit, the available evidence argues against such a conclusion. Indeed, the fact that we make eye movements so frequently is a problem for the utility of iconic memory in reading. Recall that the duration of iconic memory is roughly a quarter of a second, which is about the rate at which we make eye movements. Given that information in iconic memory is disrupted by new information and that eye movements occur at the rate they do, plus the fact that the information we want to read is available to us continuously (we can always look back with our eyes), it does not seem that iconic memory plays any role in reading.

At this point, you may be asking yourself: if iconic memory plays no role in reading why was it discussed in such detail? Indeed, why was it discussed at all? There are two reasons why we troubled to present the details of iconic memory. First, our primary purpose in Part 1 is to present an overview of the human information-processing system. Numerous information-processing models of the reading process (Mackworth 1972; Massaro

1975; Mitchell 1982; Gough 1972) have used the concept of iconic memory as the initial stage of registration of visual information during reading. Recall that we argued that at this point we are not so concerned about the extent to which the different stages are accurate and useful in understanding reading; they are presented to give you a flavor for the approach. Which brings us to our second reason for discussing iconic memory in such detail: the notion of *buffers* (or temporary storage units) in information processing turns out to be highly useful. Actually, the icon is little more than a buffer in which information is held for some later processing activity. The short life of the icon in fact suggests that the visual features of the print are of little use once the eye is no longer looking at them. As we shall see later, the notion of a buffer has been very useful in various types of research related to the reading process. By discussing iconic memory in such detail, we hope you will have a sense for how such a concept may be useful in designing experiments and theorizing about reading.

To summarize, iconic memory is the initial stage in an information-processing model. Although highly transient, it has a large capacity. We have also argued that its usefulness for understanding reading is limited since the stimulus is always available to us in reading. However, the concept of a bufferlike store has been useful in experiments related to the reading process.

Short-Term Memory

According to the standard view of the information-procesing system, due to the transient nature of iconic memory we need to get information registered by the sense organs into a more permanent structure. The structure is *short-term memory* (STM). Considerable information is lost before it can be transferred to STM because the read-out rate from iconic memory is quite slow. A certain amount of information, however, is transferred to STM, which it turns out has problems of its own. First, and most importantly, it has a limited capacity. The capacity of STM is about 7 plus or minus 2 items (Miller 1956). Notice that we said "items," not letters, words, or digits. Indeed, we can learn to short-circuit to some extent the limited capacity of short-term memory by various types of *chunking strategies*. If the number 967835241 is presented to you orally and you treat each individual digit as an item you will have a difficult time recalling it in the same order. Quite simply, for most people, STM will be overloaded. You will, however, be able to recall the number with 100 percent accuracy if you treat it as three 3-digit numbers (967-835-241). Another way that we deal with the capacity limitation of STM is through a process called *rehearsal*. When you look up a telephone number in the phone book, you often find yourself repeating it (often silently, but sometimes aloud) so that you won't forget it. In other words, you rehearse the number over and over. Such a strategy is another way to hold information in short-term memory.

Notice we said that you often repeat the number over to yourself silently. For a long time, it was considered that STM was exclusively an acoustic store. That is, even information coming in the visual modality was assumed to be recoded into acoustic or auditory information. The reason for this was that the kinds of errors that subjects made in recalling information in STM tended to be acoustically, not visually, related to the information actually presented. We now know that there are visual and semantic codes in STM. Still, for linguistic stimuli, STM is primarily acoustic as evidenced by the fact that we try and remember phone numbers from the telephone book by rehearsing them subvocally. This aspect of STM turns out to be particularly important for understanding the role of subvocal or inner speech in reading.

The fact that we engage in various strategies (some of them unconscious) to short-circuit the limited capacity of STM has led some workers to refer to it as *working memory* (Baddeley and Hitch 1974). That is, STM can be considered a flexible workspace whose limited capacity can be allocated to either storage or processing. Information in STM can remain there as long as it is being worked on. Working memory, in the sense of a flexible workspace for processing, is also heavily involved in reading. Words are integrated in this memory, and as we shall see later, comprehension processes are initiated here.

To summarize, STM has a limited capacity. Using rehearsal, however, we can hold items there for long periods of time. We also develop efficient strategies for dealing with the limited capacity. Short-term memory is also primarily acoustic. Whereas iconic memory was argued to have limited usefulness in understanding reading processes, the characteristics of STM are important in understanding inner speech in reading and comprehension processes.

Long-Term Memory

The rate at which we can set up programs to transfer information from STM to long-term memory is relatively slow in relation to the rate at which new information enters STM, so that considerable information is lost. However, it is generally believed that once information enters *long-term memory* (LTM) it is stored there permanently. Patients under a local anesthetic whose brains have been electrically stimulated can remember things they long since thought they had forgotten and even relive memories of events that occurred a long while in the past (Penfield and Roberts 1959). Information in LTM is not organized in a haphazard fashion. Indeed, LTM is highly organized and much of the material that we cannot retrieve has been mislaid, not lost. The major problem with LTM is getting the appropriate retrieval key to access information stored there. This is not surprising given the vast amount of new information we process and store in LTM each day. In addition, there is evidence that the new information we learn interferes with our ability to retrieve previously stored information. Conversely, information already stored in LTM can interfere with retrieving newly learned information.

Most cognitive psychologists now believe that it is appropriate to think of two types of long-term memory: *episodic memory* and *semantic memory* (Tulving 1972). Episodic memory is the memory for sequences of events in your life. Semantic memory, which is more important for understanding reading, contains general knowledge you have. A part of semantic memory that is important for reading is the *lexicon*. The lexicon, which like LTM itself is highly organized, contains the meanings of the 30,000 or more words that you know. The goal of most reading is to understand something new and to store the gist of it in LTM. To do so involves processing the meanings of the words we know, or accessing our lexicon in LTM. Further, to understand idioms, metaphors, and the like, we have to use general world knowledge that we have stored there. And when authors are a bit vague, we must make inferences based on what we already know to understand their point.

Selection of Information

An issue that relates to the conceptual framework which we have presented is how information is selected to be passed on to the next stage of processing. In vision, of course, the eyes are a major device for selection. You point your eyes at those stimuli you want to process and ignore others. As we discussed earlier, this overt selection process is not all-or-none. While stimuli seen in extrafoveal vision are processed less well than those in foveal vision, they are processed.

However, pointing the eyes is not the only selectional mechanism in vision. In our discussion of Sperling's experiments, we tacitly assumed that there was a selection process which could help "read out" the appropriate row of letters. A great deal of recent research has documented the reality of such a covert mechanism of spatial attention. In essence, even when they do not move their eyes, human and animal subjects can respond to visual stimuli more quickly and accurately when they are cued as to where in extrafoveal vision these stimuli will be (Posner 1980). Furthermore, the locus of this attentional system in the brain is becoming increasingly well understood. We will return to these selectional issues in Chapters 4 and 5.

In contrast to the above attentional mechanisms, the processes by which information is selected to go to LTM (or is made more retrievable from LTM) are less well understood. Clearly, factors such as your motivation to remember the material, the length of time it is in STM, and the meaningfulness of the material all affect how well you will remember it later. We will touch on these issues again when we discuss memory for discourse in Chapter 8.

The Concept of Processing Stages

An assumption of the model we have outlined above is that there are discrete processing stages. That is, it is assumed that information is processed in one stage and, only when that processing is completed, is the information shipped on to the next stage. This assumption underlies a great deal of cognitive psychology because processing will be much easier to study if it can be broken down into simpler components.

Sternberg (1969) proposed a widely used test to determine whether such a stage notion is valid. The test assumes that the dependent variable used to study mental processing is response time, or the time between the presentation of a stimulus and the time to execute a response. We can best explain the idea with an example from Sternberg's experiment. He used a memory search task, in which subjects were initially given a *memory set* (1 to 6 digits) to hold in memory, and then they had to indicate if a *probe* digit (which was presented visually) was in the memory set. His finding was that the time to determine whether the probe digit matched one of the items in the memory set increased as the memory set got bigger. In fact, the time increased by about 40 milliseconds (msec) with each additional memory set item, suggesting that it took subjects 40 msec to compare each additional memory item with the probe.

Thus, a measurable search process appears to be occurring in STM. What would happen if the probe digit was presented in "visual noise" (i.e., it was embedded in a lot of random dots so that it was harder to see)? If we view the process of identifying the digit as a stage prior to searching STM, then the digit should take longer to identify when presented in noise, but the rate of search in STM should be unaffected since the identification stage would be complete regardless of whether the digit was "clean" or "noisy." In contrast, if identification and search are not discrete stages so that visual noise is still part of the item being compared to the memory set items, one would expect that the search time per item would increase. In fact, Sternberg obtained the former result—overall times increased with a "noisy" probe digit but memory search times did not—and concluded that identification of the digit was a stage prior to STM search. The basic logic of this experiment has been used widely in cognitive psychology and will come up again at several points in the book.

The Reality of Information-Processing Models

If this is your first exposure to information processing, you may be asking yourself to what extent the different structures presented in the model have been localized in the brain. The answer is that, for the most part, they haven't. Neurophysiologists working on brain functions have found chemical changes in the brains of animals during learning stages that could correspond to STM functions. In addition, studies of brain localization have revealed different functions of different parts of the cortex (especially language functions). However, there is not likely to be an anatomical division between STM and LTM. Nor have we localized the lexicon in the cortex.

In fact, the concept of the mind is a rather abstract entity. The mind is the concept that we can think of as being the executor responsible for cognitive activity, which presumably can be ultimately explained in terms of the structure and function of the brain. The task of the cognitive psychologist is to learn how the mind is structured and functions. If it were possible, perhaps an ideal way to study reading would be to open up a reader's brain and observe what kinds of activities and changes occurred during reading. But we cannot do this. Thus, cognitive psychologists are forced to infer characteristics of how the mind works in skilled cognitive tasks, like reading, on the basis of various types of evidence that we can accumulate. In a sense then, a cognitive psychologist is like a detective searching for clues to how the mind works. The type of structures presented in Figure 1.1 and elsewhere in this book serve as a convenient way of hypothesizing about how the mind works and then summarizing what we know. Throughout this book, we will present evidence accumulated by cognitive psychologists about how the mind works in reading, and we will frequently use diagrams to present the information-processing flow, such as in Figure 1.1, to summarize what we know. But it would be a mistake to think of these structures as necessarily mapping directly onto parts of the brain.

Brain Function and Reading

In the prior section we differentiated between the brain and the mind. While much of our focus will be on how the mind works in reading, we also know that there are specific brain functions related to reading. In this section, we briefly review some of them.

Information registered on the retina is transmitted to the visual cortex. The cerebral cortex of human beings is divided into two hemispheres that have different but complementary functions. Some functions are bilaterally represented in the brain. For example, there is a visual area at the back of both of the hemispheres. However, some areas, particularly those associated with language processing, seem to be localized almost exclusively in only one hemisphere. For most people, regions of the left hemisphere are responsible for language processing. Regions of the right hemisphere, on the other hand, are specialized for non-verbal, spatial processing. In some left-handed people the functions of the two hemispheres of the brain may be reversed. The two hemispheres are connected by a bundle of nerve fibers called the corpus callosum.

We know about the different functions of the two hemispheres from two types of evidence. First, experiments on normal subjects often take advantage of the fact that information seen in the left half of the visual field of either eye arrives initially in the right hemisphere and things seen in the right half of the visual field arrive initially in the left hemisphere. Material presented to the center of vision is simultaneously available to both hemispheres of the brain. (With respect to the left and right ears, a similar pattern holds as for the presentation of visual information.) From experiments in which stimuli are briefly presented in the left or right visual field, we know that words are processed more efficiently when presented in the right visual field (implying left-hemisphere processing), whereas faces and pictures are processed more efficiently when presented in the left visual field. From such experiments, it is often argued that the left hemisphere operates in a serial and analytic fashion and the right hemisphere operates in a parallel and holistic fashion, although there is no compelling reason for this conclusion. The second way we know about the functions of the two hemispheres is from research on both brain-damaged patients, who have one of the two hemispheres missing (from birth or because of brain injury), and "split-brain" patients, who have had the corpus callosum severed as a treatment for epilepsy. With respect to language, the basic evidence is that if certain regions of the left hemisphere are damaged language functions are impaired, but right-hemispheric damage does not produce language impairment. For the "split-brain" patients, the evidence is that linguistic information put into the left hemisphere is processed normally, whereas there is little comprehension of linguistic information put into the right hemisphere. Recently, a great deal about the reading process has been learned by examination of patients with brain damage (and known lesion sites). In Chapter 11, we will review the evidence obtained from such patients. We will omit the details of the physiology (such as the location of language-specific sites) here and in Chapter 11 since such information adds little to our understanding of reading.

WHAT IS READING?

In this chapter so far, we have presented preliminary information necessary to understand how cognitive psychologists think about reading. This brings us to a critical question. What do we mean by "reading"? It is obvious that to many people, reading is an all-encompassing activity that can take on different forms. For example, when you look at a map, are you reading? When you proofread a paper, are you reading? When you look at a computer program to find your programming error, are you reading? When you scan a newspaper for the latest results of the stock market, are you reading? We will take the conservative view that none of these activities are what we have in mind as reading. It is also obvious that when you read a novel on a 5-hour airplane trip, you may at times be reading slightly differently than when you read this book. Four hours into your trip you find that you are only half way through the book, so you start skipping over sections which seem redundant looking only for relevant and new information so you can finish it before reaching your destination. You would have a difficult time understanding a textbook if you read in such a fashion, yet we can generally skim most novels and still understand the story. In our chapter on speed reading, we will discuss skimming and the adjustments the reader makes under such conditions. However, apart from that chapter, we will focus on the rather careful type of skilled reading that occurs when you read to comprehend a textbook, a newspaper article, or a narrative.

It would be easy at this point to get into a lengthy argument about what is and is not reading. We do not wish to do so. We hope it is clear what we have in mind by reading. If forced to provide a definition of reading, we would probably say *reading is the ability to extract visual information from the page and comprehend the meaning of the text.* By focusing on the careful reading of a newspaper article, for example, we do not wish to imply that the other activities mentioned are not interesting. Our bias is that activities such as proofreading and skimming probably involve strategies and processes that are different from normal silent reading. At places, we will examine such tasks. However, our central concern is how people read during normal silent reading.

This brings us to a second critical question. What is the best way to study reading? The answer to the question depends on which aspect of the reading process you are interested in studying. We mentioned earlier that cognitive psychologists interested in word recognition generally present isolated words to people in a tachistoscope and ask them to make some kind of judgment about, or response, to that word. We shall discuss such tasks in detail in Chapter 3. Other researchers interested in the role of inner speech in reading have devised clever techniques to determine its role in understanding written language. If researchers are interested in how much of the text the reader comprehends, then they would want to examine how well readers can answer questions about the content of the text. Techniques used to study inner speech and comprehension will be discussed in chapters 6 and 8, respectively.

If the goal is to study the cognitive processes that occur during (normal silent) reading of text on a moment-to-moment basis, then any technique that has readers do something different, such as read words in isolation or read text out loud, may significantly distort the component process in silent reading one wishes to study, such as word identification or the role of acoustic codes in reading. While it is plausible that the components of reading do not change radically from task to task, there is no guarantee. Thus, the relevance of any technique is an open question if we don't know how the processes work during silent reading.

This brings us to eye-movement recording, the primary technique used to study cognitive processes during actual silent reading. Recording of eye movements has a long history in experimental psychology as noted earlier in this chapter. However, it has only been of late that eye-movement data have been widely used to infer moment-to-moment cognitive processes during reading. It is now fairly clear that where readers look and how long they look there provides valuable information about the mental processes associated with understanding a given word or set of words (Just and Carpenter 1980; Rayner 1978a). Eye-movement recording can be accomplished in a variety of ways, but often involves shining onto the eye a beam of invisible (infrared) light that is reflected back from the cornea or retina to a sensing device. With this methodology, readers are free to look at any part of the text for as long as they wish. As mentioned above, the technique also has a great deal of ecological validity in that subjects in eye-movement experiments are actually engaged in the task that we wish to study, namely reading.

This is not to say that eye-movement recording is free from criticism. In order to distinguish movements of the eyes from movements of the head, it is often necessary to stabilize the head. This is often done by using a bitebar (which consists of dental compound that is very soft when a subject bites into it but quickly hardens to provide a dental impression that keeps the head still). In other cases, forehead rests are used, and subjects generally read from a display placed directly in front of them. Some critics have suggested that the rigid constraints on head movement, plus the fact that in reading—outside of the eye-movement laboratory—we often look down at the text (rather than straight ahead), will lead to different reading strategies. It has even been suggested that the mere fact that our eye movements are being recorded will make us conscious of them and lead us to do something different when we read under such circumstances. Our impression is that these concerns are all ill founded. Indeed, Tinker (1939) demonstrated quite some time ago that the reading rate and comprehension of subjects in a soft easy chair with a book did not differ from the reading rate obtained in the eye-movement laboratory.

Both of the authors have been subjects in experiments using eye-movement recordings. Our firm impression is that reading in the eye-movement laboratory is virtually the same as reading outside of it, and it is definitely our sense and intuition that this latter technique provides a much better approximation of reading, itself, than any other technique. But we do not want to argue that eye-movement recording is the only way to study skilled reading. Many of the techniques mentioned throughout this book provide useful information, but the best type of evidence will be converging data, in which information obtained from a number of the techniques converge on the same answer to a given question. Our intention is to use converging evidence from a number of sources to understand reading, but our greatest emphasis will be on the data obtained while the subject is reading connected text, rather than simply being engaged in one of the clever tasks cognitive psychologists have devised.

MODELS OF READING

While there are many facts about reading that have been learned by cognitive psychologists, many people often find cognitive psychology somewhat frustrating because there is often conflicting evidence on a single issue. There are many reasons why this may be the case, including the fact that our experiments are sometimes not very good. But another reason is that cognitive psychologists often have different *models* or *theories* of how some mental process works. What are models and theories? Let's borrow from Carr (1982) in defining these two concepts. A *theory* is a set of principles (assumptions or rules or laws) that together constitutes a verbal or mathematical description of an interesting phenomenon, and an explanation of how or why the phenomenon happens. A theory defines the important characteristics of a phenomenon that are then included in a model of the phenomenon. A *model* represents a description of the major working parts of a real-life process (such as reading). The description captures the most important characteristics of each part's operation, though it might leave out large amounts of detail. Currently, there are a number of models of the reading process that, in our opinion, vary in the extent to which they capture important aspects of the skill.

We shall not attempt to describe various models of reading here. Rather, let us simply characterize these models as being primarily (1) *bottom up,* (2) *top down,* or (3) *interactive.* Incidentally, these three types of models are characteristic not only of the reading process but of the descriptions of most of the tasks and phenomena that cognitive psychologists typically investigate. Some books on reading (Just and Carpenter 1987; Smith 1971) present their audience with a model of reading and then interpret relevant evidence within the framework of that model. Some books on reading (Crowder 1982; Downing and Leong 1982; Gibson and Levin 1975) manage to avoid presenting a model of reading altogether and present only the facts as interpreted by the authors (in some cases the rationale is that a single model cannot capture the complexities of reading or the varieties of types of reading). Other books (Mitchell 1982; Perfetti 1985; Taylor and Taylor 1983) present evidence first, and then on the basis of the evidence describe a model of the reading process. We will adopt this latter strategy and present you with the facts as we see them. There is a danger in presenting the model first and then fitting the facts to the model because such a strategy often makes it sound as though we know more than we really do. We also suspect that researchers often become committed to a particular model of the reading process and that the model itself then becomes more important than the data collected.

We feel that most of these models are little more than general frameworks which provide some biases about which aspects of reading are really important. Our discussion of models will indicate many of our biases and provide the "bare bones" of a general framework. This framework will acquire more detail as we progress through the book. In the final chapter, we will briefly summarize the framework that has evolved throughout the book.

Bottom-up models (Gough 1972) stress that most information flows in a passive manner through the human information-processing system. The major idea is that this flow of information is very fast and that knowledge we have stored in memory has little impact on how the processing takes place. In contrast, proponents of top-down models (Goodman 1970; Smith 1971) feel that the passive flow of information through the processing system is relatively slow because there are numerous bottlenecks (places where the architecture of the system forces us to slow down). Accordingly, to short-circuit the bottlenecks these models stress that we rely heavily on information stored in memory (general information that we have about the world) to help speed up our processing. The primary way in which readers short-circuit the information-processing bottlenecks is to formulate hypotheses about what they will next read. This view of reading, often referred to as the *hypothesis-testing model,* was once very popular. However, evidence now suggests that the visual processing of text is very fast and that the extent to which readers engage in hypothesis testing or guessing behaviors seems to play a minimal role in the process of reading. We will return to this issue at various points throughout the chapters that follow. For now, let us simply state that a bottom-up view of reading more accurately character-izes the available evidence. That is not to say we do not think that top-down processes play no role in reading. They clearly do. Perhaps our model of the reading process can best be described as a bottom-up model in which the reader gets some help from top-down processes.

We have told you briefly what bottom-up and top-down models are, but we have not yet mentioned interactive models. Interactive models (Just and Carpenter 1980; McClelland 1986; Rumelhart 1976) allow for all sorts of communications between top-down and bottom-up processes. Proponents claim that these models are very good in accounting for the data on reading processes. Critics argue that while these models may be able to account for lots of data, they are unconstrained and hence do not predict very well what the outcome of any particular experiment might be. In contrast, the major virtue of most bottom-up models is that they are very good at making clear predictions about performance measures.

The view of reading that we will be presenting will largely be a bottom-up view, but with some influences from top-down processes. Notice that we have used the word *process* a number of times in this discussion. Elsewhere in this book, we will make a distinction between the *process* of reading and the *product* of reading. The product of reading is the information that gets stored in memory; it is what gets comprehended during reading. The major emphasis in this book is on the process rather than the product of reading (though the latter will be discussed in Chapter 8) because, from our point of view, the most important thing to understand about reading is the process. This is a bias that not everyone would agree with. For example, educators would undoubtedly argue that knowing the best way to teach children to read is more important than understanding the process of skilled reading. While we appreciate their opinion, our sense is that if we can understand the process of skilled reading, we may well be able to provide useful information to educators about what they are trying to teach. In essence, we believe that understanding the process of skilled reading should provide firm conclusions about how to instruct novices to become skilled in the task. Our discussion in chapters 9 and 10 will highlight some of the ways that we believe research has made clear how children should be instructed to learn to read.

Some cognitive psychologists who study the product of reading would also want to argue with us concerning our bias towards understanding the process of reading. To their way of thinking, what people remember from what they read may be more important than how they go about the chore of reading. However, our response to such a point is that understanding the process by which some mental structure is created almost logically entails understanding that structure. In contrast, understanding what gets stored in memory may not reveal much about the processes that created the structure. Thus, understanding what is in memory as a result of reading discourse may not be unique to reading; essentially the same structures may be created when people listen to discourse. We are not saying that understanding the product of reading and how that product gets remembered is not important. It's just that reading is a remarkable skill that must be understood—quite apart from issues like general comprehension skills and intelligence.

CHAPTER TWO
WRITING SYSTEMS

Perhaps the place to start our detailed discussion of reading is at the beginning of the reading process: the printed (or written) page. A careful analysis of the information contained in the squiggles on the page will help in understanding the task that confronts the reader. In the course of this analysis, we will introduce several linguistic concepts—relating to both spoken and written language—that are necessary for a meaningful discussion of reading. A general discussion of writing systems will also help to put the task of reading English in a broader context.

Before plunging into a discussion of writing systems, we might hazard a definition of what *writing* is. At first the exercise seems silly, since we all know what "writing" means. One definition is that writing "is the 'fixing' of spoken language in a permanent or semi-permanent form" (Diringer 1962, p. 13). It seems that such a definition is too broad, since we wouldn't want to count a tape or phonograph recording of speech as writing, even though it may serve roughly the same function as a written transcript. Somehow, we feel that writing implies that the record is to be perceived by the eyes. What about Braille? Most people would call that a writing system, so that the eyes aren't necessary. Will any code do? For example, is listening to Morse code "reading"? We doubt that most people would accept that, so inherent in writing is some sort of spatially arranged message that is usually perceived by the eyes, but could be perceived by a tactile sense. (While reading systems for the blind, such as Braille, are certainly writing systems, they fall beyond the scope of this book since the perceptual system for encoding the message is so different from ordinary reading.)

The major problem in defining writing comes in trying to determine whether we agree with the requirement that writing "fixes" speech, and if so, what we mean by it. Some people find that requirement too restrictive, and deem as writing any visual message that conveys meaning. That definition seems too loose because most people would probably not call a painting such as the *Mona Lisa* writing, but would reserve the term *writing* for graphic displays that are understood as a code for a spoken message. There is disagreement, however, about how literal a transcription of the spoken word the graphic display has to be in order to count as writing.

Consider the following: There is a picture of Christopher Columbus followed by a picture of three ships followed by 80 suns followed by a picture of an island. Most people in our culture would probably be able to deduce that these pictures stand for a narrative about Columbus (or some explorer) sailing across the ocean, taking many days to do so, and discovering land. Is such a representation writing? This appears to be a borderline case. Some people would classify it as writing and others wouldn't. To those who would accept it as writing, the necessary features are that there is an *ordered sequence* of written symbols from which the gist of a spoken message can be obtained. However, others who use the term more restrictively would require that the sequence of symbols give a word-for-word translation of the spoken message.

As we will see, virtually all modern writing systems and most of those in the past that have survived satisfy the more restrictive definition, so that most writing systems are designed to give verbatim representations of spoken language. Whether the process of reading does in fact involve such a decoding into spoken language or a more direct translation into "meaning" is a subject of much controversy, which we will discuss in later chapters.

While the code for speech provided by most writing systems is word for word, it is not complete. Even though some inflection and phrasing is captured by punctuation, much of the inflection and stress in speech is lost, so that the precise meaning of a written message may be unclear (e.g., was Mr. X's comment in the novel meant to be sarcastic?). To get a feeling of how much detail is lost, think of how difficult it is to read a line from a play as it would be said by the character speaking the line.

Even though some of the subtleties of speech are lost in writing, the message is basically intelligible if the words are preserved. Thus, the word is a fundamental unit in language. Moreover, if a writing system is to transcribe words accurately, then it seems likely that the fundamental units in that writing system can be no bigger than the word. In fact, this is the case for all true writing systems. With this in mind, the focus in this chapter is on how writing systems represent words.

POSSIBLE PRINCIPLES OF REPRESENTATION

Logographic

If one is trying to devise a code in which the reader can decipher every word, one possible system is to have a visual symbol represent each word. That is, have a picture of a dog represent a dog or a picture of a foot represent a foot. This system is sometimes called a *logography* (Gelb 1963). In order for the system to be practical, the pictures would have to be fairly schematic so that people other than talented artists could write and also so that the task of writing did not take a ridiculous amount of time. (Some systems of writing, such as hieroglyphics, used what were probably deliberately complex symbols; the purpose of such symbols was to represent religious messages and the reading and writing of such symbols was often restricted to a priestly caste and considered a magical ability.)

Such a pictorial system runs into problems. The first is one of discrimination: A core vocabulary in the spoken language is at least 2,000 words and it is hard to draw that many discriminable pictures. (In fact, no written language uses appreciably more than 1,000 basic symbols.) Second, pictures work well for concrete nouns, but less well for other parts of speech. If one uses a picture to represent a verb such as *standing* with a picture of a man standing, the chances are that it will be hard to discriminate that from the symbol to represent *man*. Often, logographic systems use the same symbol to represent two such words and rely on context to allow the reader to determine which meaning is intended. Similarly, abstract nouns can be represented by pictures, such as representing *day* by a picture of the sun. There are some abstract nouns such as *democracy* and *vacuum* that would try the ingenuity of the symbol designer, and most *function words* (i.e., articles, prepositions, pronouns, and conjunctions) are virtually impossible to represent pictorially.

One solution to the problem of representing abstract concepts with pictures is to allow some words to be represented by arbitrary symbols, as with our use of numerals to represent numbers or with % and &. However, extensive use of such arbitrary symbols would probably tax the reader's— and writer's—memory. A second solution is to relax the principle of one picture per word and allow more than one picture to represent a word. For example, one could represent *god* by two symbols: a picture of a man and a picture of stars. One could represent *sun* by a picture of a sun, but represent *day* by a picture of a sun followed by a picture of a clock to signify that the word is a unit of time. One could represent *ran* by a picture of a man running followed by a picture of a clock to represent past tense. (This solution would still have trouble with words such as *of* and *but*.)

This latter solution involves analyzing words into component units of meaning such as *ran* = action of running + past tense or *day* = unit of time measured by the sun. Thus, the 100,000 or so words in a language may be built out of a more manageably sized set of atoms of meaning (perhaps a thousand or so). Linguists use the term *morpheme* to denote certain subword units of meaning. However, the term is reserved for when the analysis into component meanings is transparent. Thus, BOYS would be decomposed into *boy* + plural and RAN would be decomposed into *run* + past tense even though the decomposition is not reflected in units in the surface form of speech or writing. However, the obscure and idiosyncratic analysis of *day* above is not a morphemic decomposition. Even so, the question of whether a word can be broken into component morphemes—and what the appropriate decompositions are—is sometimes controversial. This suggests that words are the natural unit in the language rather than the morpheme. However, the definiition of *word* in the spoken language is also not without its problems. The problem is illustrated by the fact that we are often unsure whether combinations such as HEADSTAND are written as one word or two or hyphenated. Defining words as sequences of letters that are written without intervening spaces would be unsatisfactory, since there would be no principled way of knowing whether something was a word or not. Most compound words started out as two words and evolved through frequency of usage to being written without a space. However, some linguists (e.g., Selkirk 1982) have attempted a more principled definition so that some compounds written with a space (e.g., PUNCH CARD) are words.

Giving a detailed argument for the necessity of both words and morphemes as linguistic units would be beyond the scope of this discussion. However, even a superficial analysis suggests that neither is the more "natural." In two-syllable words such as FOOTSTOOL or BENDING, the morpheme is the basic unit in the speech stream (a syllable) and the decision to call those two syllables a word is based on relatively abstract criteria about which reasonable people may disagree. In contrast, in our previous example of RAN, the natural unit in the speech stream is the word, and the morphemes are the more abstact units. That most logographic systems use symbols to represent both words and morphemes is testimony to the reality of both units of analysis.

Before going on, we should mention a strength of such a system: One doesn't have to know the spoken language in order to decipher it. As long as one knows what the symbols mean, one can decode the written language.

Syllabic

One way out of the difficulties posed by a logographic system is to relax the requirement that a picture has to be related to the meaning of a word or of a word part. For example, we might find it hard to come up with a symbol for the word LABEL, so that we might represent it with the symbol for "lay" (such as a picture of a person lying down) and the picture for "bell." We now allow the picture for "bell" to stand for the sound /bell/ regardless of whether that sound is related to the meaning of the word BELL. Using meaningful pictures to sound out words is sometimes known as the "rebus principle," and you have probably encountered it in puzzles, comic books, or newspapers. It is of course not necessary that the sound units represented by pictures be single syllables. In fact, in many writing systems, there are some such pictures for single syllables and some for two-syllable units (Gelb 1963).

If one goes to a system where a character stands for a unit of sound, then the question naturally arises as to whether one needs to make the character look like something. If a character is to represent the sound /lay/ regardless of its meaning, why bother with a picture that represents one of its meanings? Why not just have an arbitrary symbol, which could be much easier to draw, stand for the syllable /lay/? The answer depends somewhat on the number of syllables (or possibly longer units) that one needs to represent. How many syllables are there in the language? Consider a language like English. There are roughly 25 consonant sounds and 10 vowel sounds. Syllables are possible with a consonant vowel (CV) such as /ba/ or /lay/, a vowel consonant (VC) such as /ad/, or a consonant vowel consonant (CVC) such as /bat/. If one restricted oneself to CVCs, there would be roughly $25 \times 10 \times 25$, or 6,250, syllables if all combinations were possible. Not all are, but a reasonable fraction are, so that in most languages there are a thousand or so syllables. On the other hand, some languages like Japanese have only about 100 syllables because the syllables are mostly of one form (in Japanese, they are CVs).

If one needed to represent only 100 or so syllables by symbols, then using arbitrary characters to represent them seems feasible, but if there are 10 times that many syllables, it does not. One solution would be to use 100 or so syllable signs and to use 1 sign to represent several syllables. For example, one sign could stand for /ba/, /bi/, and /bu/, or one sign could stand for /du/ and /tu/. (We already took advantage of this in our LABEL example, since the second syllable's pronunciation is only approximately that of BELL.) In such a system, there would clearly be times where there are ambiguities and two distinct words would have the same written form. If the way the symbols are chosen is reasonably clever, then the number of ambiguous words may not be ridiculous, and the ambiguities that occur usually may be made clear by the context. Of course, even in the spoken language, there are words that sound the same—such as *bank,* which can mean a business or the edge of a river—that also have to be clarified.

A second solution to the problem for having fewer symbols than syllables is to bend what the symbols stand for. For example, one might represent the syllable /bam/ by two signs, one representing /ba/ and the second /am/. One could even go further and represent /clam/ by symbols for /ca/, /la/, and /am/. Real languages have tended to use both of these solutions, once it was decided not to bother with creating symbols that were pictorial. The second solution, however, stretches the principle of a symbol per syllable, since the symbols often stand for smaller units. In fact, as we will see, the distinction between languages based on the syllable and alphabetic languages is often fuzzy.

Phonemic

We all know that letters represent smaller units in spoken language than the syllable. While the syllable needed no formal definition for the preceding section to make sense, this smaller unit, the *phoneme,* is not nearly as self-evident. One might think at first that a phoneme is the smallest unit that one could say in isolation. However, there are some phonemes (the "stop consonants": *b, p, d, t, g,* and *k*) that cannot be said alone. They need some vowel sound either before or after them to be uttered. However, the idea of phonemes being the smallest sound unit in the speech stream is essentially correct. (We should hasten to point out that the principle of a letter representing a phoneme is an extreme simplification of the "alphabetic principle." We will elaborate on that point in detail below.)

There is a somewhat fussy distinction we need to make. Not all distinguishable speech sounds in the language are distinct phonemes—only those that the language cares about. For example, the /k/ sound in KEEP and COOL is different. If you pay attention to where your tongue is when you make the two /k/ sounds, you will note that it is in a different place, and in fact the sound coming out of your mouth is different in the two cases. These distinguishable speech sounds are known as *allophones*. We could represent the /k/ sound in KEEP by *k* and the /k/ sound in COOL by @. The reason we don't use two symbols to represent the two sounds (and most English speakers are unaware of the distinction until it is pointed out to them) is that the distinction never needs to be made in English. That is, there are never two words that differ only by this distinction: there would never be two words only differing by that sound and thus we do not need @ to distinguish KEEP and @EEP. Thus the phoneme is a category: all the allophones that are not distinguished by the language are in the same phoneme. This categorization changes from language to language. Some languages distinguish the two /k/ sounds above and so these sounds are separate phonemes in those languages (and represented by different letters). Conversely, /l/ and /r/ are not separate phonemes in Japanese. The great advantage of representing phonemes over representing larger units is that there are a smaller number of them. There are fewer than 100 phonemes used in all human languages and a typical language like English employs about 40 of them (see Figure 2.1). The limit to the number of phonemes is probably a combination of the limit on the different positions the mouth can assume while talking and a limit to the fineness of discrimination possible when perceiving a rapid and continuous message such as typical speech.

Several comments are in order. The first is that a majority of phonemes are consonants. This fact is reflected by the English alphabet, which contains 21 symbols for consonants and 5 symbols for vowels. The second is that the relation between alphabetic symbols and phonemes is not simple. Some phonemes are represented by more than one letter such as /sh/, /ch/, and /th/, even though the phonemes are not combinations of the component sounds (e.g., /sh/ is not /s/ + /h/. On the other hand, certain letters

PHONETIC SYMBOLS USED IN ENGLISH

CONSONANTS		VOWELS		COMBINATIONS AND DIPHTHONGS	
Symbol	Example	Symbol	Example	Symbol	Example
p	*p*ill	i	s*ea*t	ǰ	*j*ar
b	*b*ill	I	s*i*t	ʍ	*wh*ere
d	*d*one	ɛ	s*e*t	ay	b*i*te
t	*t*on	e	ba*i*t	æw	ab*ou*t
g	*g*ale	æ	s*a*t	ɔy	to*y*
k	*k*ale	u	b*oo*t		
m	*m*ail	U	p*u*t		
n	*n*ail	ʌ	b*u*t		
ŋ	ri*ng*	o	c*oa*t		
s	*s*ing	ɔ	c*au*ght		
z	*z*ing	a	c*o*t		
f	*f*at	ə	sof*a*		
v	*v*at	ɨ	m*a*rry		
θ	*th*in				
ð	*th*en				
š	*sh*in				
ž	mea*s*ure				
č	*ch*in				
l	*l*ate				
r	*r*ate				
y	*y*et				
w	*w*et				
h	*h*it				

FIGURE 2-1 The standard phonetic symbols used to represent sounds in English. The consonants and vowels listed are clearly basic phonemes, while the sounds represented in the last column could be viewed as combinations of phonemes. Throughout the book, however, we will represent sound in a more informal way, using diagonal slashes together with a (hopefully) unambiguous pronunciation to indicate the sound intended (e.g., /dawg/ to represent the sound of "dog").

represent combinations of phonemes. For example, in English, *j* stands for /d/ + /zh/ and *x* stands for /k/ + /s/. Second, while English may be extreme in this respect, letters can represent more than one phoneme as in most alphabetic languages, particularly in the case of vowels.

Thus, while the ideal of the alphabet is to represent each phoneme by a letter, the correspondence is usually not straightforward. There are several possible reasons for this. The first is economy. Since there are usually fewer letters than phonemes in a language, it may be easier to have some ambiguities in the representation of the sound than to use a larger set of symbols which would necessitate finer visual discriminations and also probably slow down the writing process. Second is the matter of variation in the speech signal, both between speakers and in different contexts for the same individual. These differences are most obvious with vowels. Between individuals, there are substantial differences in how vowels are pronounced (most notably with different dialects) and the inventors of alphabets may have decided that they wanted to ignore many of those differences (e.g., I is pronounced /aye/ in some dialects of English but /ah/ in others). Secondly, words are pronounced differently in different contexts (e.g., THE is pronounced /thuh/ or /thee/ depending on whether the word following it has an initial consonant or vowel sound). Third, and perhaps most important, the makers of alphabets may not have really understood what phonemes are. The type of analysis needed to uncover the basic phonemes of a language requires a high level of awareness of the sound actually coming out of the speaker's mouth. This requires the very difficult task of ignoring the meaning of the speech (as in the "thuh"-"thee" example above).

We need to define one more term before proceeding. If languages usually represent more than one phoneme by a letter, then it would make sense to represent similar letters with the same phoneme. One system invented by linguists to characterize differences among phonemes is *distinctive features*. Distinctive features can perhaps be best explained by an example. The *stop consonants* (*b, p, d, t,* [hard] *g,* and *k*) all share the distinctive feature of *stopping:* they are all produced by the mouth briefly cutting off the flow of air. They are distinguished from each other by two other distinctive features, *voicing* and *place of articulation*. Voicing refers to whether the vocal cords vibrate during the consonantal sound or not: The vocal cords vibrate for the voiced consonants, *b, d,* and g, but not for the voiceless ones, *p, t,* and *k* (place your hand on your voice box while pronouncing the six sounds to confirm this). Place of articulation refers to where the sound is cut off: *b* and *p* are cut off in the front of the mouth, *d* and *t* in the middle, and *g* and *k* in the back.

The basic idea, of course, is that the distinctive features capture the structure of phonemes. If two phonemes share many distinctive features, they are similar. In general, the economies of representation in alphabetic languages can be explained by distinctive features (especially with respect to vowels). Long and short vowels, which differ by only one distinctive feature, are commonly represented by a single letter. Similarly, "th" in English represents two phonemes (as in *this* and *thin*) that differ only by voicing. Other economies seem more arbitrary, however, such as hard and soft *g,* which are quite different phonemes.

You may have wondered whether a writing system could be based on distinctive features. If a set of distinctive features defines a phoneme, then, in principle, one could represent language by using a set of symbols for the set of distinctive features. One reason why most languages do not represent distinctive features may be that such an enterprise calls for even more careful analysis of language than a phonemic representation, and it is not clear that a really satisfactory set of distinctive features exists for vowels. A second reason that writing systems usually stop at the phoneme may be that not too much economy will be achieved by a distinctive feature representation over a phonemic representation, since the number of symbols required for a phonemic representation (about 25 to 40) does not seem to place much of a burden on the reader. However, there is a writing system, Hangul (part of the written Korean language), in which distinctive features are important. We will discuss Hangul later in the chapter.

To summarize, the last widely used principle for writing is to attempt to represent each phoneme of the spoken language by a written symbol, which we call a letter. While there are a few languages (e.g., Finnish) where this principle is closely approximated, most alphabetic languages only roughly approximate it. We have speculated a bit on why this is so, and will come back to the issue several times later in the chapter when we discuss specific writing systems.

The fact that alphabetic languages only loosely use the "alphabetic principle"—representing a phoneme by a letter—brings us perhaps to the most important point about writing systems in general. We have seen that there are several units that writing systems could use as the basis for representation: word, morpheme, syllable, subsyllable (e.g., consonant-vowel combinations), phoneme, or even distinctive feature. In principle, one could construct a writing system in which only one of the units was represented. *In practice, however, no writing system is completely pure and many are complex mixtures.*

A BRIEF HISTORY OF WRITING

Inventions of Writing

No one knows when humans acquired the power of speech, but it is generally assumed that spoken language of some sort evolved at least 100,000 years ago and perhaps much earlier than that. Homo erectus (i.e., "Java Man" and "Peking Man"), whose brain was not much different from ours, appears at least 1 million years ago. It is generally agreed that the ability to speak was the result of an evolutionary change in the brain. Certain areas of the human brain associated with speech are markedly larger than in ape brains. Furthermore, in most humans, there is lateral asymmetry in the control of speech functions: certain areas of the left cerebral cortex are specialized for language, suggesting a unique genetic programming. While there are some hints of such asymmetry in chimpanzees, the differences between humans and apes appear to be essentially qualitative.

In contrast, writing is a relatively recent human activity. Moreover, the ability to read and write was not produced by a biological change but by a cultural change. The only essential prerequisite to be able to read and write for a human capable of spoken language is to belong to a literate culture. (However, reading involves other abilities, such as visual perception, and it may tax language abilities more heavily than spoken language. We will discuss these issues more fully in chapters 9–11.)

Writing is arguably the most important invention in human history. The opportunity for human knowledge to build on other knowledge is severely limited without the medium of writing. Not only does writing allow a permanence to human thought but also a complexity and scope to human expression that seems barely possible without it. The first great "knowledge explosion" in Egypt, the Near East, India, China, and Greece is clearly due, in large part, to the invention of writing.

The earliest known artifacts that could be considered writing by the loosest definition are the famous and extraordinarily beautiful 20,000-year-old "cave paintings" in southern France and northern Spain. The pictures, mostly of animals but with some human figures, possibly tell some sort of story or may merely be pictures with expressive, magical, or religious purpose. Other assorted pictures have been found antedating the rise of the great civilizations of the Near East, but the earliest artifacts that are clearly writing date from about only 5,500 years ago in Mesopotamia.

Why did writing develop so late? We can conjecture that there are cultural reasons. The society had to be rich enough to allow some people the leisure time to develop a writing system and allow sufficient numbers of people the leisure to learn it. Moreover, there must have been things that seemed worth writing down. The first civilizations that exploited large-scale irrigation agriculture seem obvious places where there was sufficient leisure to create the opportunity to write. However, it is not clear exactly how writing evolved in these cultures. The oldest writing of anything that appears to resemble sentences (found in what is now Iraq) appeared to be for the unromantic purpose of recording business transactions, while the earliest writing found in other cultures was for different purposes (e.g., descriptions of the exploits of kings). However, we have no guarantee that the artifacts that we have are representative of the writings of the civilization. Moreover, we have only a few clues about the immediate precursors of these writings and the significance of these clues is far from clear (see Gelb 1963).

Sumerian and Cuneiform The oldest Sumerian writings, dating from about 3500 BC, have not been fully decoded. They appear to be pictographic and perhaps as primitive a writing system as the Christopher Columbus example given earlier. The writing system developed quite rapidly (at least from our distant perspective). Other artifacts that are only slightly later not only use a single conventional symbol as a sun to represent "sun," "time," and "day," but also use the symbol for an arrow (pronounced /ti/) to represent both "arrow" and "life" (Diringer 1962; Gelb 1963). Thus, quite early in the history of language, a complete reliance on symbols to represent meaning pictorially was abandoned; at least some symbols represented a particular sound.

Around 3200 BC, another important development occurred. Since clay was an easily obtainable material in the region, more and more of the writing was done on clay. Apparently to speed the writing process, the symbols were pressed into the wet clay with a short stylus (rather than scratched).

This meant that the symbols were composed of short line segments rather than the smooth curves that would be natural for pictorial representations. A typical symbol would be made by about 3 to 10 line segments, and hence be an extremely stylized version of the pictorial symbol that it evolved from. (If the examples of symbols such as in the top of Figure 2.2 are representative, it is doubtful that someone not versed in the writing system could guess the meaning of more than 10 percent of the symbols.) Because there was uneven pressure applied to the tool when making the line segments, they were wedge-shaped (i.e., thicker at one end than the other). This feature was captured by the name of the writing system, *cuneiform,* which means ''wedge-shaped.''

Thus, in only about 300 years, the writing system evolved from primitive picture writing, which could probably only transmit the gist of a message, to a fairly stylized system in which symbols represented meanings in a relatively abstract way and in which there was some reliance on the principle that a symbol represents a sound rather than a meaning. We will see that this story is universal: Complete reliance on pictures to represent meaning is usually a brief stage, which soon develops into a system that uses symbols to represent sounds as well as meanings. As we have hinted in the first section of this chapter, these changes make sense. Drawing recognizable pictures of each word in the language is clearly impossible. The use of

FIGURE 2-2 (A, Below) Examples of the evolution from pictographic symbols to the more abstract cuneiform writing of Classic Assyrian. [Adapted from Diringer (1962), with permission of Thames and Hudson (London).] (B, Facing page) Photograph of the "Rosetta Stone," the key to deciphering hieroglyphic and hieratic writing. The top is written in hieroglyphic, the middle in hieratic, and the bottom in Greek. The same content is written in each of the three systems. (Reprinted with permission from THE BETTMAN ARCHIVE.)

Meaning	Original Pictograph	Pictograph Rotated To Position Of Cuneiform	Early Cuneiform	Classic Assyrian
Earth				
Mountain				
Food				
To Eat				
Fish				
Barley Grain				
Sun Day				

A

Der Stein von Rosetta. (¼ der wirklichen Größe.)

Inschrift eines Dekretes zu Ehren des Ptolemäus Epiphanes in hieroglyphischer und demotischer Abfassung, nebst grie   Übersetzung.

several pictures to represent a word meaning helps, but is so cumbersome that the writers and readers will quickly think of other solutions. These solutions involve making the symbols more schematic, or not tied to meaning, or both.

At first, it appears that the Sumerians used the same symbol to stand for several words related in meaning or several words with identical pronunciation and hoped that the correct meaning would be deduced from context, much as English-speaking readers would know that *chest* means a box rather than a part of the body when reading "He put the jewels in the chest." Two methods were developed in the writing system, however, to help in deciphering the symbols. One was the use of *determinatives* (Diringer 1962), which were unpronounced symbols that indicated the word class (e.g., bird, country, number, plural noun). The second system was to introduce a pronunciation hint. Thus, if a symbol could stand for several words related in meaning but having different sounds (such as sun, day, time), one might follow the symbol with a second symbol, called a *phonetic complement,* that stood for the syllable /ime/ so that the two syllables together would be interpreted as "word which means something like sun and sounds like /ime/, so it must be *time.*" These two additions to the writing system were fairly universally used in systems that used symbols to stand for the meanings of words (and still are used in Chinese).

The cuneiform system of writing was adopted by several groups speaking different languages. The Akkadians (also known as the Babylonians and Assyrians), whose language spread throughout the Middle East, adopted the cuneiform system around 2500 BC. By 1700 BC, the writing appeared to be relatively codified with between 600 and 700 symbols. About half the symbols stood for meanings and the other half stood for sounds. There is some disagreement among scholars (cf. Diringer 1962; Gelb 1963) as to whether all the sound representations were syllabic or whether some stood for phonemes as well. Cuneiform writing also spread to other groups—to the Elamites around 2500 BC and much later (circa 500 BC) to the Persians. In the Elamite system, there were only about 100 symbols, most standing for syllables, and in the Persian there were only 41 symbols which all stood for syllables.

Cuneiform, like all of the ancient languages, was a complete mystery until about 200 years ago. The Persian adaptation was fortunate from our standpoint since Persian is an Indo-European language related to our own. Even so, it first had to be deduced that the characters in the Persian cuneiform writing stood for syllables before the syllables were decoded. The decoding of the Persian writing system took about 80 years and was the key to fairly rapid progress in deciphering the Babylonian writing system and then the other forms of cuneiform, including the original Sumerian system. Few of the ancient languages have been fully decoded, however.

Egyptian   The original Egyptian writing, *hieroglyphic* writing (meaning "holy carving", is almost as old as the Sumerian, dating from about

3000 BC. It is not known whether the Egyptian writing system was in some way derived from the Sumerian or invented independently. Almost from the earliest examples, there is a strong reliance on representing sound. There were symbols that stood for meanings (logographs), symbols that stood for sounds (single or double syllables), symbols that were phonetic complements (gave a clue to the pronunciation of a word), and determinatives (gave the category of the word).

The name "hieroglyphic" was given by later people, since the writing was mostly used for holy or monumental writing and it was usually written on stone (at least in the collection of artifacts). However, it was sometimes written for other purposes and on materials such as wood or papyrus. The symbols were very elaborate and beautiful (see Fig. 2.2B), but not well suited for mundane purposes such as business transactions. Hence, a second system, called *hieratic* writing developed, starting only a little later than hieroglyphic writing. It was more or less a cursive form of hieroglyphics written with a brush-pen. The characters, however, were somewhat simplified and (as in cuneiform) the forms became less and less related to the meanings they represented. Many of the symbols were joined as in our cursive writing. A third version (also cursive) called *demotic* writing (i.e., writing of the people) appeared about 700 BC. It employed even simpler and more abstract versions of the symbols.

It was possible to decipher the ancient Egyptian writings because public decrees from this later period were often written in hieroglyphics, demotics, and Greek, which had become the dominant language of the area. The hieroglyphic writing was probably used to emphasize the sacred nature of the decree. A piece of such a document, the famed Rosetta Stone (see Figure 2.2B), discovered in 1799, helped in the deciphering of both ancient scripts using the Greek as a key. Coptic, the last stage of the ancient Egyptian language, was known to the decipherers.

Chinese The earliest Chinese writings, dating from 1500BC, are significantly more recent than those of the Near East. The forms are sufficiently different from modern Chinese that originally the writings could not be understood. Even today the writings have not been completely deciphered, though there is no dispute about the meanings of about a quarter of the symbols. One interesting feature is that at least some of the symbols represent sound (as phonetic complements). This has led experts to believe that these artifacts are not the beginning of the writing system and that there are older, more pictorial, writings which are lost or undiscovered, or that the writing system was an adaptation of the writing from the Near East. At present, there is no good evidence to choose among these possibilities.

Over time, the form of the symbols changed (especially with the invention of the brush in the third century BC and paper in the second century AD), but the structure of the written language has changed little since the oldest writings. The form has also changed little since AD 100. We will return to discuss Chinese later in the chapter. Two points are worth emphasizing, however: (1) The characters in Chinese, while having their origins in pictures, are often abstract, and not obviously identifiable to someone who hasn't been taught the meaning. (2) The system is not merely one in which there is a symbol per word (or morpheme); sound is represented in the system as well.

Other original writing systems   Ancient writings have been discovered in the Indus Valley (now in Pakistan) that are dated somewhere between 2500 and 3000 BC. There is no indication that the writing system was borrowed from any other. No writings dating from the period 2500 BC to 1000 BC have been found so it is hard to know the historical significance of these early writings. The symbols are pictographic but have not been decoded, so little has been discovered about the system. (As there are about 300 symbols, it is unlikely that the principle is completely syllabic.)

The writings of the great civilizations of the New World, especially the Mayan and Aztec, are the subject of great controversy, largely because they have also been barely deciphered. The fact that they have not been seems to be largely the result of racism or "culturalism:" variants of the languages represented are spoken today and people continued to write in the Mayan script (for example) until about 200 years ago. However, the Spanish had no interest in the native culture and even went to great lengths to destroy much of the writing.

Enough was preserved by the Spanish to know the Mayan symbols for units of time. Thus the meaning of some of the texts, which were calendars, is clear. These calendars are extraordinarily accurate in determining the length of the year. However, so little of the written language has been decoded that there is little certainty about the writing system. For example, Diringer (1962) claims that the Mayan and Aztec written languages were essentially in the same stage as the second stages of Egyptian and Sumerian languages (i.e., containing some syllabic signs), while Gelb (1963) views them as systems more primitive than "true writing" (roughly at about the Christopher Columbus level mentioned earlier).

The Development of the Alphabet

Most of us have been taught in school that the alphabet was invented only once and it was invented by the Phoenicians. This teaching is essentially true since all alphabetic writing systems can be traced to the Phoenicians. However, there is controversy about whether that system is a true alphabetic system since it did not represent vowel sounds. The first writing system that is unambiguously alphabetic, in the sense of attempting to represent each phoneme with a letter, is the Greek.

The alphabet was not the inspiration of one person, but rather a gradual development. As we have seen, almost the earliest writing systems employed some kind of sound principle, and by 2000 BC both the Egyptian and cuneiform systems had developed many symbols to represent syllables. As we hinted in the introduction, the difference between a *syllabary* (a writing system based on the syllable) and an alphabet (a writing system based on the phoneme) is not that clear.

All known syllabaries contain about 100 symbols. (It is not clear whether this is a practical limitation imposed on the writer or reader.) Since the Near Eastern spoken languages (like our own) contained far more syllables than that, symbols had to represent more than one syllable. The two standard principles for grouping syllables were discussed earlier. The first was to use a symbol to stand for a set of syllables that shared the same consonant sounds. For example, there would be one symbol for /bat/, /bit/, /bet/, /but/, /bot/, /boot/ . . . or one syllable for /ta/, /ti/, /tu/, /toe/. The second system was that the syllables represented by the same symbol would share a vowel sound and have different (but similar) consonant sounds. For example, one symbol would stand for /tak/ and /tag/ and /taq/ (*q* stands for a related consonant sound not in English). In Babylonian cuneiform writing, both systems of multiple representation were used, although the second principle (preserving the vowel sound and making the consonant sound ambiguous) predominates. However, in the Egyptian system, the first principle was universally used. The cuneiform system also represented some syllables by joining the two symbols: so that /ral/ would be /ra/ plus /al/.

In retrospect, we can see elements of the alphabet in both systems of writing. In the Egyptian system, a symbol that represented all syllables that were *t* plus a vowel is quite close to representing the phoneme *t*. In addition, the representation of a single syllable in cuneiform by two syllables indicates that units smaller than the syllable were being represented in the writing system. However, as indicated earlier, syllabic representation was only one principle in both the cuneiform and Egyptian writing systems; there were also characters to represent meaning as well. There were several other such writing systems in the Near East at this time (2000 BC to 1000 BC).

The first system that appears to have completely dispensed with both logographic signs and representation of syllables containing more than one consonant appeared in Phoenicia (modern Lebanon and Syria) about 1300 BC. This system had roughly 25 to 30 symbols, each one corresponding to a consonantal sound. There is controversy among scholars about whether the Phoenician system (and related systems) should be called alphabetic or syllabary. The details of this controversy need not concern us, since the essential character of the system is clear: (a) all the symbols represented consonantal sounds (which could be combined into a syllable containing more than one consonant) (b) vowel sounds were only occasionally represented, so that representation of the phonemic principle in the writing system was incomplete.

While the Phoenician writings discovered are the oldest, there are similar, roughly contemporaneous, writings throughout the area of various other Semitic languages (including Hebrew). The similarity of the writing makes it clear that there was extensive contact among the people of the area. It is not at all unlikely that a new discovery would indicate that some other group invented the system before the Phoenicians. They were, however, the first great sailors and traders, and were instrumental in exporting the system to the rest of the world. All known alphabetic systems are derived from this system.

The alphabetic principle thus seems to have evolved in two stages: first the consonants were represented and later, with the Greeks, the vowels were represented. Why is this so? One possibility is that this progression was inevitable since most of the information in discourse is carried by the consonants, *s ths phrs sggsts*. However, there are indications that this development also had its roots in the particular language. Remember that the Egyptian system also did not represent vowel sounds (as contrasted with the Babylonian cuneiform). The ancient Egyptian language and Semitic languages shared the feature that, for a large number of words, the consonants represent the basic meaning and the vowels indicate the form. Thus, the sequence of consonants *k, t,* and *b* (which we might indicate by "k*t*b") indicate something about writing which can appear in many forms: for example, *katab* ("he wrote"), *kaytib* ("writer"), *kitb* ("book"). While other languages sometimes use this principle (e.g., *ring, rang, rung* in English), it is much more fundamental in these languages. Thus, in these languages, it is not merely that the meaning of the message can be deciphered from a representation of the consonants, but that the essence of the meaning is often represented by the consonants.

The fact that the alphabetic principle was not independently invented again suggests that this two-stage development, if not absolutely necessary, made the creation of an alphabetic system much easier. One possibility is that potential inventors of an alphabetic system in other language systems would feel that they would have to represent all the aspects of the sound (including accent and stress) and find such a task overwhelming (this would be especially true in a tonal language such as Chinese). A second possibility is that these spoken Semitic languages, in which the structure of the form is represented directly in the structure of the underlying meaning—consonants represent the base meanings and vowels the grammatical form—helped the writers of that language to be more analytical about the sounds of the language and thus to be more aware of the phonemic units. As we will see in chapters 9 and 10, the concept of a phoneme is relatively abstract and certainly not obvious to children or other people learning to read.

There is much uncertainty about the parentage of these Semitic "alphabets." The fact that vowels are not represented suggests that they were derived from the Egyptian system, which had about the same number of symbols to represent syllables of the consonant-vowel form. However, neither the names nor forms of the symbols are clearly related to the Egyptian (or any other system), so there is no clear consensus among scholars about the evolution from a mixed logographic-syllabic system to the consonantal system of the Phoenicians and others.

In contrast to the uncertainty about the parentage of the Phoenician writing system, the story of its subsequent evolution is reasonably clear. The

Greeks adapted the Phoenician symbols for their language. However, there were some symbols left over that did not correspond to letters in the Greek language; these were used for the vowels. What is somewhat less clear is whether the representation of vowels evolved gradually (many of the symbols used for vowels represented "soft," and hence somewhat vowel-like, consonant sounds in the Semitic languages), or whether some scribe had a blinding flash of insight about vowels and then used the leftover symbols to represent them.

All of the European writing systems are derived from the Greek alphabet. New letters have been invented to represent sounds not represented in the Greek and the visual forms have changed a bit. However, the basic system is virtually the same as it was more than 2,000 years ago. The two modern European writing systems of importance besides the Greek are the Roman, used in English and most western European countries, and Cyrillic, used in eastern European countries, where the Russian Orthodox religion was predominant. (Serbo-Croatian, the most common language in Yugoslavia, is today written in both alphabets.)

The other major writing systems that are alphabetic derive from the Semitic scripts (such as Phoenician and Hebrew) through the Aramaic language, which became the dominant language in the Near East by around 500 BC. The Semitic writing systems were increasingly used to represent the spoken language and replaced cuneiform. The Aramaic script (which was only slightly changed from the Hebrew script) was in turn adapted to represent both the Arabic language and the languages of India. These scripts, in turn, were widely disseminated throughout much of southern Asia to places as far as the Philippine Islands and to much of northern Africa.

Many of these systems that are more directly based on the Semitic writing system (most notably modern Hebrew and Arabic) still incompletely represent vowels. While there are characters to represent some vowels, the vowel symbol is often omitted and sometimes marked by a *diacritic,* a mark above or below an adjoining consonant. In this sense, many of these scripts are not fully alphabetic.

Some Comments about "Progress"

Throughout this section we have discussed the evolution of writing systems. In fact, for much of the world, writing started out with picture writing, moved to a form of sound representation (usually syllabic), and then moved to an alphabetic system. In fact, no culture has moved the opposite way; i.e., abandoned a syllabic system for a logographic one or abandoned an alphabetic system for a syllabic one. Thus in an evolutionary sense, the alphabet is "fittest:" It has won out where it has competed. While some of the use of alphabetic systems can certainly be traced to armed conquest (most notably those of Christianity and Islam), many adoptions of the alphabet cannot (for example, the Turkish adoption of a Roman alphabet in the twentieth century). This suggests that there may be some sense in which an alphabetic writing system is better (at least for those spoken languages that have adopted the alphabetic system).

However, such a conclusion must be tempered with two observations. The first is that it is not clear exactly why it is better. For example, there is no good evidence that alphabetic languages can be read faster than nonalphabetic languages like Chinese. While there is some suggestion that alphabetic languages are easier to learn to read than Chinese, the data are largely anecdotal, and there are other nonalphabetic writing systems like Japanese that appear to present no problem in mastering reading. Thus, the superiority of alphabetic systems may be more related to the technology of writing and printing. Writing of nonalphabetic languages may take longer (Taylor 1981), printing of nonalphabetic languages is definitely harder, and constructing and using dictionaries of alphabetic languages are definitely easier.

The second observation is that the alphabetic system may be fittest for languages that have adopted the system, but may be less fit for languages that have not. Thus, nonalphabetic writing systems in use today may not be anachronisms, but serve to represent those spoken languages as well as an alphabetic system could. We will briefly consider a few representative nonalphabetic contemporary writing systems (together with a few alphabetic ones) to illustrate the variety of writing systems in use today.

SOME CURRENT WRITING SYSTEMS

Logography: Chinese

The Chinese writing system (and variants of it) is the only important logographic system in common use today. Hence, it is worth discussing in some detail. However, as we shall see, the common view of Chinese as "picture writing" is a gross oversimplification.

There is also confusion about the number of characters one would need in a language like Chinese. A language like English has several hundred thousand words, so that it is sometimes assumed that Chinese needs that many characters. However, the number of words is fewer in Chinese, since many of our words are inflected forms (e.g., *word-words, bring-brings-brought*), whereas Chinese does not use inflections. A more important reason why hundreds of thousands of characters are not needed in Chinese is that a character represents a morpheme (which is also a syllable) rather than a word. For example, *Beijing,* which means "north capital," is represented by two characters, one for "north" (*bei*) and one for "capital" (*jing*). While a very complete dictionary (the K'anghsi dictionary of 1716) has 40,000 characters, a dictionary of about 8,000 characters suffices for most purposes (Martin 1972). One estimate (Liu, Chang, and Wang 1975, cited in Taylor 1981) is that there are about 40,000 words in daily use in Taiwan, but only about 4,500 characters.

One feature of the spoken Chinese language should be emphasized: It is tonal. That is, a vowel sound can be spoken with several pitch contours (e.g., rising, falling, rising-falling) which change the basic meaning of the syllable. (In English, such changes would only convey subtleties such as emphasis.) Thus there are many more syllables in Chinese than in a nontonal language. This makes it unlikely that a workable syllabary (with arbitrary characters) is feasible for Chinese. The number of syllables is still much fewer than the number of morphemes (and characters), so there is homophony in Chinese (as in most written languages).

Characters have been usually classified into six types (Taylor 1981). In the first type, *pictographs,* the character is a representation of an object. However, this representation is often highly stylized (see Figure 2.3). For example, the character for "sun" (which was originally represented as a circle with a dot in the center) is now represented as a rectangle with a

FIGURE 2-3 (Top) Six categories of Chinese Characters (Bottom) An example of a Chinese sentence. (From Taylor 1981, with permission of Academic Press.)

Category	Example	
Pictograph	⊙ 日	sun
	☽ 月	moon
Simple Ideograph	⸗ 上	above
	⸗ 下	below
Compound Ideograph	日, 月 → 明	bright (sun, moon)
	女, 子 → 好	good (woman, child)
Analogous or Derived	网	fish net; extended to any network, cobweb
Phonetic loan	米 } 來 } /lai/	wheat ↓ come
Semantic – phonetic compound	女, 馬 → 媽	(woman) /nu/ + (horse) /ma/ = (nurse) /ma/

你	知道	準確	的	時間	嗎
you	know	correct	(suffix)	time	(particle

horizontal line through it. In a *simple ideograph,* the character represents the idea. For example, the characters for "above" and "below" show a line with something above and below it, respectively, or "middle" is represented by a quadrilateral with a vertical line through the middle. In *compound ideographs,* the character is composed of two or more simple pictographs or ideographs. For example, "bright" is composed of the characters for sun and moon, and "good" by the characters for woman and child. In *phonetic loans,* words from other languages are spelled with Chinese characters using the rebus principle. A fifth category, *analogous,* uses characters in a roughly metaphorical way, such as the character for a "fish net" is used to describe "networks." In the last type, *semantic-phonetic compounds,* the character is composed of two characters, one which represents the approximate meaning and the other the approximate sound. Thus, *nurse* (pronounced /ma/) is written as woman (pronounced /nu/) plus horse (pronounced /ma/). The basic idea is that the character means "woman that sounds like /ma/. (The phonetic complement often is only similar in pronunciation to the syllable.) The characters that constitute complex characters are sometimes written adjacently but compressed and sometimes in quite complex and overlapping spatial arrangements.

The above classification scheme makes clear that the characters are not the smallest unit, since many characters are composed of several other characters. Some of these basic building blocks, called *radicals,* have a special status. A radical is the basic semantic determiner for a character (such as the character for "woman" in the *nurse* example above). The dictionaries arrange characters according to their radicals, and all the words in the K'anghsi dictionary can be organized by 214 radicals.

The key, therefore, to learning what seems like a bewildering number of characters is not so much that they are pictures, but that they are structured. One estimate is that only about 5 percent of the characters are simple ideographs or pictographs, and about 90 percent are phonetic compounds (Alleton 1970, cited in Martin 1972). (The simple characters are encountered more than 5 percent of the time, however, since they tend to represent common words.) Thus for the most part, Chinese is not "picture writing:" many of the characters are highly stylized and not really pictures of the morphemes, and a principle of sound coding is involved in representing much of the language.

Syllabaries: Japanese and Korean

The Japanese and Korean writing systems are interesting because they make extensive use of syllabaries, and in fact either could be written totally within the respective syllabary system and be comprehensible. However, both systems are hybrids and also use characters derived from the Chinese writing system, even though neither spoken language is similar to Chinese (or to each other). Let us consider the two in turn.

Japanese   The Japanese language has little relation to Chinese except that there are some vocabulary items in Japanese of Chinese origin. In addition to profound differences in both vocabulary and linguistic structure, a marked surface difference between the languages is that Japanese is not tonal. In fact, there are only about 100 syllables in Japanese (fewer than in most western languages), since there are no consonant clusters and almost all the syllables are of the consonant-vowel form. One obvious consequence of a language with a small number of syllables is that if all morphemes are represented by single syllables, there would be an unacceptable number of homophones. Therefore it should come as no surprise that in Japanese, morphemes are often more than one syllable, and most words are polysyllabic. (Because of the simple syllabic structure in Japanese, however, there are still a large number of homophones.) Thus, in an attempt to borrow the Chinese writing system to represent Japanese, one could either create a system that consistently uses a character to represent a morpheme or consistently uses a character to represent a syllable, but one would have to abandon the Chinese system of representing both simultaneously. In fact, as we shall see, the Japanese written language is a mixture of systems embodying the two principles.

The Japanese system that in fact evolved is a mixture of two different systems (see Figure 2.4). In the first system, called *Kanji,* the symbols are a subset of the Chinese characters and have the same meanings as in Chinese. (Thus one character represents a morpheme.) Kanji is used to represent the roots of content words (i.e., nouns, verbs, adjectives, and adverbs). The system is complicated in that a character can have several different "readings" (i.e., pronunciations). Some of the readings are related to the original Chinese pronunciations (*On* readings) and others to Japanese roots (*Kun* readings). However, there can be more than one reading of each type so that there are often five or so readings for a single Kanji character. (The meanings of all the readings are related, however.) The number of Kanji characters is smaller than in Chinese: there are 1,850 "official" characters and about 1,000 "unofficial" ones in common use.

The second system, called *Kana,* uses characters that are simplifications of Chinese characters. The Kana characters form a syllabary: One character represents a syllable. There are 46 basic Kana characters together with two diacritical markings (see Figure 2.4). The diacritical markings change the features of the consonant sound (e.g., whether it is pronounced /ha/, /ba/, or /pa/). Since, as mentioned earlier, Japanese has a relatively small number of syllables (there are no consonant clusters and only one consonant, /nj/, is used at the end of the syllable), the approximately 100 Kana symbols are capable of representing any syllable in the language. Hence, Japanese could, in principle, be written using only Kana. However, the system is a hybrid. The roots of content words are represented by the Kanji, with two different forms of Kana serving two different purposes. One form, *Katakana* (*kata,* "fragment;" *kana,* "borrowed name"), is used to

Sound	Katakana	Kanji	Hiragana	Add (")	Sound: voiced	Add (°)	Semi voiced	
ha	ハ	八波	は	ば	ba	ぱ	pa	
hi	ヒ	比	ひ	び	bi	ぴ	pi	
f,hu	フ	不	ふ	ぶ	bu	ぷ	pu	take both (") & (°)
he	ヘ	３部	へ	べ	be	ぺ	pe	
ho	ホ	保	ほ	ぼ	bo	ぽ	po	
ka	カ	加	か	が	ga			
ki	キ	幾	き	ぎ	gi			
ku	ク	久	く	ぐ	gu			take only (")
ke	ケ	介計	け	げ	ge			
ko	コ	己	こ	ご	go			
na	ナ	奈	な					
ni	ニ	仁	に					
nu	ヌ	奴	ぬ					take neither (") nor (°)
ne	ネ	祢	ね					
no	ノ	乃	の					

鶏肉とベーコンは 1.5cm の角に切る。

chicken　　　　　BACON　　　　　　　　　　　　cube　　cut

FIGURE 2-4 **(Top) Katakana and Hiragana symbols. (Bottom) An example of a Japanese sentence taken from a cookbook illustrating use of Kanji, both types of Kana and Roman characters as well. (From Taylor 1981, with permission of Academic Press.)**

represent "loan words" from other languages (such as *baseball*). The other, *Hiragana* (*hiri,* "cursive"; *gana,* "borrowed name") is used to represent grammatical prefixes and suffixes, function words, and some content words. The Hiragana characters are basically cursive versions of the Katakana characters, although for a few pairs there is little resemblance between them. In English, script and printed forms sometimes also differ markedly, as with capital *A* and capital *Q*.

One estimate (Taylor 1981) is that 65 percent of the characters in normal text are Hiragana, 30 percent are Kanji, 4 percent are Katakana, and 1 percent are Arabic numerals and Roman letters. However, it seems that a greater part of the meaning is conveyed by the Kanji than that estimate represents. At first it might appear that such a hybrid system would be very hard to read. However, reading rates in Japanese (see Chapter 4) are comparable to those in English. Furthermore, literacy rates in Japan are among the highest in the world, suggesting that learning the Japanese writing system presents no more—and perhaps less—difficulty than an alphabetic one. One interesting aspect of Japanese reading instruction is that children are started out on the Kana (Hiragana) symbols and only introduced to the Kanji symbols gradually. The lower rates reported on reading problems in Japanese have suggested to some people (e.g., Rozin and Gleitman 1977) that using a syllabary might be the best way to introduce children to reading even in cultures with alphabetic languages.

Korean The Korean written language is, in basic outline, like the Japanese system. In South Korea, 1,300 Chinese characters represent the roots of most content words (as with Kanji) and a sound-based system, called *Hangul* (meaning "great letters"), represents the rest (as with Kana). (North Korea, however, has totally eliminated the Chinese characters.) Hangul is worth discussing briefly because of a unique feature. It does not merely represent syllables by arbitrary characters; instead, it is composed of components that represent phonemes and articulatory features. There are five basic consonant symbols that indicate the shape of part of the mouth when making the articulation (e.g., an L-shaped symbol represents the shape of the point of the tongue when it makes an /n/ sound). The 19 consonant symbols are derived from these basic symbols by adding strokes to represent distinctive feature changes. A long horizontal or vertical bar, together with a short bar or two, represents a vowel sound. The system is a syllabary, however, in that the symbols for the phonemes are not linearly arrayed as in a standard alphabetic language but packaged into "blocks" which represent syllables. (There are rules that dictate the relative positions of the phoneme symbols.) Hangul syllable characters look, to the Western eye, roughly like Chinese characters, although they are less curved (see Figure 2.5).

Thus, Hangul is unique in that it is, at the same time, an alphabetic system and a syllabary. A simple syllabary would have probably been unworkable in Korean, since it has a few thousand syllables (in contrast to the 100 or so syllables of Japanese). It was invented relatively recently (in the fifteenth century) under the direction of the emperor. As in Japan, literacy is high and reading problems are low (although such data are often unreliable) suggesting that Hangul is a good writing system. The scholars who created it decided on the system after studying various alphabetic systems. Whether it represents an improvement over standard alphabetic systems is unclear.

ㄱ /g/ : the root of the tongue as it closes the throat passage and touches the soft palate.

ㄴ /n/ : the shape of the point of the tongue as it touches the ridge behind the teeth.

ㅅ /s/ : upper (╱) and lower (╲) tooth get together

ㅎ /h/ : unobstructed throat passage in producing /o/ is joined by two strokes.

ㅁ /m/ : the shape of the closed mouth.

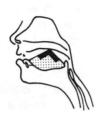
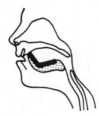

Position	Articulation manner					
	Basic symbols					Doubled
	Continuant	(Add)	Stop (Add)	Aspirated	Lateral	Tense
Velar			ㄱ ‾	ㅋ		ㄲ
Lingual	ㄴ	‾	ㄷ ‾	ㅌ	ㄹ	ㄸ
Bilabial	ㅁ	ˌˌ	ㅂ ˌˌ	ㅽ → ㅍ		ㅃ
Sibilant	ㅅ	‾	ㅈ ˋ	ㅊ		ㅉ, ㅆ
Glottal	ㅇ		ᅳ	ㅎ		

Complexity level[c]	Linearly arranged				Packaged in block[d]	Syllable	Morpheme (native)
	C	V	C	C			
I		ㅏ			아	V/a/	suffix; ah
I	ㄷ	ㅏ			다	CV/da/	all
II		ㅏ	ㄹ		말	VC/al/	egg
II	ㄷ	ㅏ	ㄹ		달	CVC/dal/	moon
III	ㄷ	ㅏ	ㄹ	ㄱ	닭	CVCC/dalg/	hen

FIGURE 2-5 (Top) Illustration of how Hangul represents the articulation of five basic consonants. (Middle) Illustration of how basic Hangul consonant symbols are elaborated to produce other consonant symbols. (Bottom) Illustration of the packaging of Hangul syllable blocks in three complexity levels. (From Taylor 1980 and Taylor 1981, with permission from Plenum Press and Academic Press.)

English and Other Alphabetic Systems

There are many alphabetic systems with interesting features. We will focus on English, since it is the language of this book as well as being the most widely used alphabetic language. Most readers of English know only too well that the representation of sound by the alphabet is only approximate. However, only some of the ways in which it falls short are sheer perversity. Let us consider what the options are for alphabetic languages.

A widely known language, Spanish, is quite regular in its spelling rules. One indication of the commitment in Spanish to a close relation of spelling to sound is the fact that *ch, ll, ñ,* and *rr* are called "letters." In the case of *ch, ll,* and *rr,* this means that the combination is not merely a blend of the other two. (*Ch* is pronounced approximately as in English, *ll* as either /ly/ or /y/ depending on the dialect, and *rr* as a more trilled sound than the single *r.*) A few consonants have more than one sound (*c* is either hard or soft as in English and *g* is either hard *g* or an /h/ sound.) However, the rules are totally regular: soft before *e* or *i,* hard before everything else. (*G* also has a third sound in the middle of two vowels.) The vowels each have a long and a short sound, and fairly simple rules allow one to determine which. Combined vowels indicate certain soft consonant sounds. For example, *ue* is pronounced /way/, which is approximately how the two component vowel sounds /oo/ and /ay/ would be pronounced if done quickly. *U,* however, has other functions as well. First, it always appears after *q* (as in English) and it has a special function after *g.* When it appears after a *g* and before an *e* or *i,* it is not pronounced, but merely indicates that the *g* is hard as in *guerra* (and an umlaut over the *u* is needed to indicate that the *u* is to be actually pronounced as in *vergüenza*). In addition, there are rules that indicate where stress is to be placed, and if a word violates the rule an accent is placed on the vowel of the stressed syllable.

Thus while Spanish is phonetic in the sense that one can sound out a Spanish word reliably knowing the rules, the rules one applies are more complex than the simplest alphabetic procedure of a single letter representing a single phoneme. Moreover, misspelling an unknown word in Spanish is possible, since more than one letter can stand for a single sound (e.g., *s* and *c* can both represent /s/ sounds in many dialects and *g* and *j* can both represent /h/ sounds). However, there is a language (Finnish) in which the principle of one letter for each phoneme is even more closely approximated. In Finnish, there is one letter for each consonant sound (and vice versa) and a reasonably literal representation of vowel sounds (although vowel sounds undergo subtle transformations in various contexts). While the simplicity of the structure of the spelling rules in Finnish is fairly rare, there are several other languages (e.g., Italian, Serbo-Croatian, Hungarian) in which the relation between spelling and sound is about as simple as Spanish. This raises the obvious question of why English spelling is so complex if other languages can manage with simpler spelling systems.

There are essentially four components to the answer. The first is that much of the apparent "irregularity" of English is not really irregularity, but applications of rules similar to the ones discussed so far. For example, *c* and *g* are hard or soft depending on the following vowel, certain clusters of letters are really single letters such as *ch, sh, th, ph,* and silent *e* lengthens the vowel sound preceding it (similar to the *u* following a *g* in Spanish which is not pronounced but changes the pronunciation of the *g*).

The second is historical. Spelling of English was codified relatively early for European languages and it was codified at a time when the pronunciation was changing. Thus at one time, *bough, rough, through,* and *though* all had the same final consonant sound. The spoken language changed, but the written language was frozen to reflect the sounds at an earlier time. In addition, since English is a composite of Germanic and Romance languages, different spelling systems come into play. One example is the pronunciation of *g*. Since *g* is always hard in Germanic languages, there are many exceptions to the "*g* soft before *e* and *i*" rule (which comes from the Romance languages) which are of Germanic origin (e.g., *girl, gift*). In addition, there are certain eccentricities, such as replacing *i* with *y* at the ends of words that reflect scribal practice (the *y* was thought to look nicer at the end).

The third component is that the structure of English spelling is different from that of Spanish and Finnish in that (in many cases) the spelling is meant to indicate the morphemic structure of the word rather than the pronunciation. Thus, the spelling of VINEYARD indicates that it has something to do with vines at the expense of representing the pronunciation of the *i* as long instead of short. Two general examples of this principle are pluralization—*s* represents the plural regardless of whether it is pronounced /s/ (TOPS) or /z/ (BINS)—and past tense—*ed* represents the past regardless of whether it is pronounced /ed/ (RELATED), /t/ (BASED), or /d/ (SPELLED). Another general example is with derived words such as COURAGEOUS or ROTATION. In English, pairs such as COURAGE-COURAGEOUS are spelled similarly, even though the vowel sounds in the stem change and the consonant sounds change in pairs such as ROTATE-ROTATION. In contrast to English, a language like Spanish will conceal the morphological relation between words to indicate the correct pronunciation. Thus, as a rule, morphemically related words in English are spelled alike to indicate their related meaning, while in a phonetically based language like Spanish, representing morphemic relationships is secondary to representing the sound.

There have been some claims that the system in English is close to optimal in reflecting the underlying morphological structure by a system of subtle rules (Chomsky and Halle 1968). While the claim may be justified in certain limited sets of vocabulary, there are too many inconsistencies in its application to take the claim seriously. In sets like PIN-PINNING and PINE-PINING, the spelling somewhat obscures the morphemic relationship in order to preserve the sound rules (long *i* before a single medial consonant or final *e*; short *i* before a double medial consonant or final consonant). Other examples that are similar to the usual Spanish procedure are PICNIC-PICNICKing and PANIC-PANICKing. Moreover, derivations do not always preserve the spelling of the morpheme as in PRONOUNCE-PRONUNCIATION.

The fourth way in which English spelling is designed to represent meaning apart from sound is different spelling for homophones such as THEIR-THERE and CITE-SITE. Here the written language is making a distinction that the spoken language does not. Of course, different spellings for homophones is not limited to English: it is common in logographic languages such as Chinese and the Kanji system in Japanese and in many alphabetic languages. While rarer in languages such as Spanish, variances do occur (e.g., *sí* meaning "yes" is written with an accent over the *i* to distinguish it from *si* meaning "if ").

Alphabetic languages are sometimes classified as having a "shallow" or "deep" orthography depending on whether the rules of spelling merely represent the sound (as in Spanish) or the morphemic structure as well (as in English), respectively. The above discussion indicates that the distinction is not absolute, since most alphabetic languages embody both principles to some extent.

SOME GENERAL COMMENTS ABOUT WRITING SYSTEMS

Direction of Writing

Writers of English are so used to the direction of writing being left to right that they forget that a left-to-right order is by no means universal. In fact, languages have used almost all conceivable systems to order print on the page. English and other contemporary European languages that use alphabets are all written from left to right with the order of the lines of print going from top to bottom. In contrast, Hebrew, Arabic, and other Semitic languages are written from right to left, but with the lines of print also going from top to bottom. In Chinese, the traditional organization of print was in columns, with a column being read from top to bottom and the columns read from right to left. Now, however, in the People's Republic of China, a horizontal system predominates with the direction of print going from left to right. Japanese can be written vertically in the traditional Chinese order or horizontally in either order (although the left-to-right order is far more prevalent). Historically, languages have been written in various directions. The Egyptian writing was originally vertical, but later was right to left, while cuneiform was left to right. The early alphabetic writings in both Greek and Roman, while always in rows, were by no means uniform as to direction, going from left to right, right to left, or using a more creative solution, called *boustrephedon:* one line of writing would be from left to right with the next right to left, with the direction of the characters reversed as well! (*Boustrephedon* means "as the ox plows.")

What is one to make of all this nonuniformity? It clearly suggests that the direction of print is relatively arbitrary, although there do appear to be two constraints. First, in going vertically across the page (either within a line or between lines), the direction is virtually always top to bottom, suggesting that there is something natural about the top being the starting place. Second, for alphabetic languages, the print is always organized in rows rather than columns. The organization of writing into rows rather than columns makes sense from what is known of visual perception, since there is good acuity further out from the center of fixation in the horizontal direction than in the vertical direction. Thus, if it is important to see a great deal of text along the line, row organization would be preferred over column organization. The fact that Chinese used vertical organization of the lines of text suggests that it is not important (or possible) to see a great deal of text at one time in Chinese.

It is surprising that left-to-right order is not more preferred for writing, since when writing right-handed (as over 90 percent of most populations do) the hand can assume a more natural position and not smear what has been written if it were written in ink. However, two factors may explain why right to left is used as much as it is. The first is that writing systems may have evolved when the standard writing may not have been with ink, but rather with such nonsmearable methods such as carving on stone or wood. (The fact that cuneiform was left to right may not have been an accident, since it was written in wet clay, where the smearing may have been a problem.) The second is that the order may have been codified in a writing system, and then other writing systems derived from it may have adopted the same order. Thus, the Semitic languages may have copied the Egyptian order and the Japanese and Korean the Chinese order.

It would be hard to determine experimentally if the order of the print mattered to the reader. Comparing across languages (such as comparing reading speed in Hebrew and English) would be of little value, since there are many differences between the two languages besides the order of print (but see Albert 1975). Since Chinese has been written in both a vertical and horizontal format, it would seem like the best opportunity to study the effect of the writing system independent of language differences. However, a study by Shen (1927) found a difference in favor of the vertical system, while a more modern study (Sun, Morita, and Stark 1985) found a big difference in favor of horizontal print. The difference between the findings probably reflects the fact that the vertical format predominated 60 years ago (and thus the readers had much more experience with it), while the horizontal format predominates in the People's Republic today.

More generally, if we compare across two sets of readers to test whether differences in the writing system matter, it is hard to eliminate linguistic or cultural differences, or both, in the comparison. If we compare individuals, it is hard to be sure that the familiarity with the writing systems is equated. Thus, we are unlikely to get a definitive answer to the question of whether the order of print matters. The fact that languages have used different orders and there appears to be no gross difference in reading speeds in readers of different languages suggests that there is no optimal order. The only exception may be that alphabetic languages work better in rows than columns because visual acuity is better in the horizontal direction. (However, since all alphabetic languages have a common source, the reason that they are all horizontally organized may merely be historical.)

Punctuation and Spacing

In English and other alphabetic languages, word boundaries are indicated by spaces, sentence boundaries by periods, and clause and many phrase boundaries are indicated by commas, parentheses, semicolons, and other punctuation markers, but morpheme boundaries are only occasionally marked by hyphens. In contrast, in most logographic languages, morpheme boundaries are clearly marked, while nothing else may be. In Chinese, all characters are equally spaced, so that it is often not clear what grouping of characters constitutes a word. In Japanese, because of the mixing of the logographic and syllabic characters, words and morphemes are both marked pretty well. A content word might be marked by more than one Kanji character, but then its wordness would be indicated because the surrounding characters would be Kana (which look quite different). On the other hand, the morphemic structure of a word is revealed not only by the series of Kanji characters, but inflections are marked by a Kana symbol adjacent to the Kanji root. It is still the case in Japanese that word boundaries are not consistently marked. The written languages derived from Chinese originally did not use punctuation either, so that morphemes were the only consistently marked unit. However, punctuation to indicate phrases and other larger units is now fairly commonly used, and in some systems spaces are sometimes used to indicate word boundaries.

We should emphasize, however, that the system of punctuation in alphabetic languages is not straightforward. For example, as any writer knows, the rules for the use of commas are not codified. Commas do not mark all phrase boundaries (presumably only those where the speaker takes a relatively long pause) and furthermore indicate other things as well (such as enumeration).

Another aspect of syntax that is usually only haphazardly marked in writing is the part of speech of a word. In Japanese, content words and function words are indicated by the Kanji-Kana distinction (although content words are written in Kana as well). In English, we indicate proper nouns (and their adjectival forms) by capitalization while in German all nouns are capitalized.

The above discussion makes clear that writing systems have been mainly designed to ensure that the written language has been captured at the level of the word or morpheme. Some higher order units, such as sentences, are now fairly consistently marked in most writing systems, but much of the higher order structure of the spoken language is not consistently indicated.

Is There a Best System of Writing?

The answer obviously depends on what you mean by "best." The history of writing suggests a clear evolutionary trend. Cultures started out with picture writing in which the symbols were arranged as if in a picture, rather than in a definite sequence. These systems evolved to a logographic system, which in turn evolved to syllabic systems and finally to alphabetic systems. While not all cultures have evolved to alphabetic systems, the order seems fixed: there are no recorded instances where a culture has moved backwards in the sequence. Such an evolutionary argument suggests that alphabets are "fitter" (in the Darwinian sense) than syllabaries, which in turn are fitter than logographic systems. However, if we are to take the evolutionary argument seriously, we have to remember that fitness is always defined in terms of the ecological niche of the organism (or culture).

There are many dimensions on which one can evaluate a writing system. For example, one advantage of a logographic system is that the same writing system can be used to represent different languages or dialects, as opposed to a sound-based system. (The distinction between a language and a dialect is not clear: one common definition is that a language is a "dialect with an army.") Historically, the Chinese writing system was used to represent a large number of dialects that were not mutually intelligible. The phonetic complements would be useful if the morphemes were pronounced roughly in the same way (as in French, Spanish, and Italian). On the other hand, a logography is much harder to codify (dictionaries are much harder to organize and use) and to produce (writing Chinese appears to be much slower than writing alphabetic languages and printing is far more difficult). Thus, a major selective pressure for the evolution away from logographies may have been to make writing and printing easier.

The advantage of alphabetic systems over syllabaries appears to be that, for many languages, the number of symbols needed to represent each syllable unambiguously is too great for either the writer or reader, or both. However, for a language like Japanese, it is not clear that an alphabetic system would be an improvement over Kana, since the number of syllables is so small.

There is little in the above discussion to suggest that a major contributor to the evolution of the alphabet was the ease of reading. The only possible exception is the evolution to the alphabet from the Middle-Eastern syllabic systems, which ambiguously marked syllables and perhaps had an unacceptably high level of ambiguity. The ambiguity in the syllabic systems does not pose as obvious a problem in the ease of writing as it does in the reading.

The evolutionary argument suggests, in fact, that each writing system has evolved to be fittest in its own particular niche and that no existing writing system is better at representing its spoken language than any other. Languages like Spanish may have shallow orthographies because the relationship between the morpheme and the sound is more transparent than in English, which may need a deeper orthography. Certainly, there is no reliable evidence that there are any marked differences among writing systems either in how rapidly they can be read by skilled readers or in how easily they can be learned by beginning readers. (We will touch on these issues later in the book.) On the other hand, we should not blindly accept each writing system in use to be optimal to represent the spoken language. There are undoubtedly many aspects of each written language that represent the debris of history and tradition that are irrelevant to current writers and readers. In addition, the ecological niches change. For example, the advantages of the current Chinese writing system over an alphabetic system may have outweighed the disadvantages several hundred years ago in their culture. However, now, when many more people are literate, the ease of printing, typing, and doing word-processing in an alphabetic language may outweigh the disadvantages (and the large effort needed to convert from one system to the other) and cause a transformation in the Chinese writing system.

CHAPTER THREE
WORD PERCEPTION

The question of how words are identified is clearly central to understanding reading. It has also been a major focus of research in cognitive psychology for the last 15 years. Much has been learned—not only facts but also a greater awareness of what the issues really are. However, there are some areas where our ability both to ask and answer questions is limited.

While laypeople undoubtedly differ in how they believe that word identification occurs and what its place is in the total process of reading, let us attempt a sketch of one commonsense view that emphasizes learning to read in order to raise some questions and indicate where the discussion will lead. Many people think that the question of how children learn to read their native language is central to understanding the reading process, including skilled reading. As we hope to show in this chapter, a naive version of this developmental perspective gives a misleading picture of skilled reading. However, we would like to present such a perspective to raise some important questions about reading. Some will be pretty much resolved in this chapter, but many will recur throughout the book.

When one starts out from a developmental perspective, it appears that recognizing the printed word is the central problem of reading. Presumably, the six-year-old child has a well-developed system for language understanding, and the major thing to be learned is how to plug the squiggles that are on the page into that system. If the child can learn to access the words of the spoken language from the written representation, then he or she should be able to understand the written representation. This suggests one central question about reading: *Is word recognition all that needs to be learned?*

If one looks at the beginning reader, this process of trying to identify written words is extremely effortful, and in fact some children fail to learn to do it fluently. In contrast, their processing of more complex speech than they are attempting to read appears to be relatively effortless and "biologically programmed." (Biologically programmed in the sense that all people without significant brain damage appear to be able to comprehend spoken language well.) While the adult (or even older child) can decode words with far less effort than the beginning reader, it might seem from this perspective that the processing of words is the "bottleneck" in the reading process: That is, in order to read, an "unnatural" and effortful step, visual word identification, has to be grafted onto a "natural" language understanding system designed by evolution. This leads to a second general question: *Is identifying words effortful and the rest of the reading process "automatic"?*

In addition to suggesting that word processing is effortful and the rest of the reading process is "automatic," this view also suggests that identifying words (especially with an alphabetic writing system) is largely a process of going from the letters to the appropriate sounds. While the previous chapter has made clear that the relationship in most alphabetic systems is more complex than going from individual letters to individual units of sounds, it would appear that if the beginning reader has the general idea of the alphabetic principle, he or she can go from the print to a sound, and for most words, the sound will be close enough to that in the spoken language to be able to access the correct meaning. This leads to a third question: *Are words identified by accessing the sound and then the meaning?*

If we think of the translation from letters to sound, we might think that reading is a letter-by-letter process (albeit fast). That is, the letters in a word might be processed *serially* (i.e., one at a time) from left to right in order to identify a word. This view is also concordant with the usual introspection that one's attention seems to sweep across the page smoothly from left to right. This leads to a fourth question: *Are letters in words processed serially or are words processed as wholes?*

Clearly, as readers become more proficient in reading, they become more fluent at identifying words. What exactly has been learned? A fifth question is: *Do skilled readers learn to apply the "rules of spelling" in a fluent way or do they learn specific associations between visual patterns and the sound and/or meaning of the word?*

Lastly, beginning readers seem to be aided quite a bit by having context for decoding the words. It is often more difficult for them to identify words in isolation than in a story. Especially if one believes that word identification is the bottleneck step in reading, this suggests that context may play a large role in reading. In fact, several writers (e.g., Goodman 1970) have suggested that reading is a sophisticated guessing game whereby the reader develops hypotheses about what is going to come up on the printed page and then tests these hypotheses by sampling the display. In such views, the process of reading words in isolation is only marginally related to that of reading words in text. This leads to a sixth question: *Does context radically affect the process of word identification?*

While the picture of reading presented above—associated with the naive layperson—is intuitively reasonable, most of it is incorrect as a theory of the skilled reader. In addition, while the reading process is far less well understood for beginning readers, much of it may be incorrect for them as well. In fact, much of what we know about word identification in skilled readers can be summarized by the following statements. (While not all people in the area would agree with them, most would.)

1. Word recognition is relatively automatic, and "higher order processes," such as constructing the correct syntactic structure, relating word meanings, and fitting the text into what the reader understands about the world, are what takes most of the reader's processing capacity.
2. Word recognition is not merely converting letters to sounds and then sounds to meaning. In fact, a defensible position is that converting to sound is largely irrelevant to the identification of words (although we believe otherwise). Most researchers do believe, however, that conversion to sound does play a part in the reading process after word identification—largely for its ability to aid short-term memory.
3. Words are not processed serially letter by letter. The letters in common short words appear to be processed *in parallel* (i.e., at the same time), although words are not learned as visual templates. Longer words may be processed differently, although not much is known about how they are processed.
4. Words are processed pretty much the same way in isolation as in text. While context somewhat affects the speed of processing words, its effects are surprisingly small.

(What is known about the other two questions—what people learn when they learn to read and whether they use rules of spelling in reading—is not easily summarized in a sentence or two. The latter question will be discussed in the present chapter and the former in chapters 9 and 10.)

The fourth point has important methodological implications, since it justifies the use of experiments in which words in isolation are identified to illuminate how words are processed in reading. Since context does have some effect, however, findings with isolated words can not be assumed to be perfect indicators of how word identification operates in reading text. While we will briefly allude in this chapter to how words are processed in context, we need to explain quite a bit of information about eye movements (in chapters 4 and 5) in order to discuss words in context. Chapters 4 through 8 will discuss how words in context are processed, although that issue is a major focus of Chapter 7. Since it is more difficult to study how words are processed in reading text (both because it requires more sophisticated equipment and because the experimenter has far less control over the situation), historically, most of the research on word perception has been on isolated words. Thus, isolated words will be our focus for this chapter.

How Long Does it Take to Identify a Word?

Before going on to discuss the questions raised earlier in detail, we will introduce the issues and familiarize you with the techniques used to get at those issues by asking the naive question of how long it takes to identify a word.

Response-time methods Let's start with something simple. We present a subject a word on some sort of visual display and measure how long it takes the subject to say the word aloud. If we can precisely control when the presentation of the word began and can precisely measure when the subject begins making the response, we would have a measure of something relevant. But is this measure the time to identify a word? What prevents us from concluding that it is?

First, we have measured the time it takes for something to emerge from the subject's mouth. What we are interested in, however, is the time that it took for the subject's brain to achieve a state that we call "identification." After the subject has identified the word, several other processes must take place for a response to occur: (a) the subject must decide what response is called for in the experiment—in this case, it is saying the name of the word; (b) the subject must retrieve the motor program for executing the response; (c) the command must be sent down nerve pathways to the mouth; (d) the muscles of the mouth and throat must execute the command. All of those processes take time. Thus the time we have measured is the time it takes to identify the word plus some excess baggage that we might want to simplify and call "decision time" and "response-execution time." This problem is clearly not unique to the naming task we have selected; it would be true of any response of the subject to a word.

In fact, it takes practiced subjects about 400 milliseconds (msec) to name common words. Thus we might feel that such an experiment would at least allow us to say that people identify a word in less than 400 msec. However, there is another basic problem facing us: What exactly do we mean by "identifying a word"? In reading, the important thing is getting to the meaning of the word. When the subject has named the word, does he or she necessarily know the meaning? The answer is clearly no. We can clearly name words that we do not know the meaning of and there are people with brain damage who can name a lot of words and nonwords and appear to have no idea of the meaning of what they are reading. Thus, naming (or more properly getting to the name of a word in memory) does not necessarily mean that its meaning has been accessed. Perhaps, however, for normal people reading words they know the meaning of, both of these events occur at roughly the same time. That seems reasonable, but it is by no means a foregone conclusion. In fact, one of the central questions of word processing is how those two events—accessing the name of a word and accessing the meaning of a word—are related.

Perhaps there is a better task for getting at whether the person has accessed the meaning of a word. Let's try a *categorization* task, such as asking the subject to judge whether the word is an animal or not. We would be certain then that the subject has accessed the meaning. However, to achieve that goal, we may have paid a big price. The naming task is relatively easy and effortless. While there is a decision stage, the decision of executing the vocal response /dawg/ when we see DOG seems natural, relatively quick, and relatively constant across words. However, the categorization task seems less so. In judging whether a word is an animal, subjects are relatively slow to respond "yes" to STARFISH and relatively slow to respond "no" to BACTERIA or even to ROSE, but quite quick to respond "no" to STONE. It is clear that the decision stage in the categorization task is much more intrusive: subjects need to do mental work after they have identified the meaning of the word in order to decide if it is in the appropriate category. In spite of all this, subjects can usually make these category decisions for relatively common instances within about 700 msec, so that we can really be sure that words are identified within about that time.

Is there no other simpler task that allows us to be sure that the subject has processed the meaning but doesn't involve an extensive decision stage afterwards? Unfortunately, no one has been clever enough to come up with one. One attempt to measure the time to identify a word that has been widely used is *lexical decision*. In the lexical-decision task, the subject is shown a letter string and asked to decide if it is a word or not. (Obviously, nonwords are used as well.) This task appears to be a bit simpler (and faster) than the categorization task. Moreover, we know that subjects must, in some sense, have identified the word when they know it is a word. However, we can't be at all sure that subjects know the meaning of a word at the moment that they know it is a word.

Brief presentation methods Perhaps methods that time the subject's response are not the best way. Instead one can think of timing the presentation. If we flashed a word briefly on the screen (let's say for 60 msec), and if the subject could still identify it (e.g., name it and give a synonym), would that mean that it only took the subject 60 msec to identify a word? (Note that here we do not necessarily time the subject's response; the time pressure is solely produced by the brief exposure.) There are several problems with making that conclusion. The first is that even though the stimulus is only physically present for 60 msec, the visual representation lasts longer than that. This is the phenomenon of *iconic memory* discussed in Chapter 1. The data on iconic memory suggest that the visual image would last for at least about 250 msec, although it would be fading over that interval.

Can we defeat iconic persistence? A procedure designed to do that is *masking.* After the presentation of the stimulus, a *pattern mask,* usually consisting of bits and pieces of letters or letterlike forms is presented in the same location. That is, the subject sees the word for 60 msec followed immediately by the mask. Subjectively the word looks like it disappears when the mask comes on. In spite of this, subjects with a little practice, which gets them used to this mildly bizarre situation, can identify words if they are exposed for about 60 msec (Adams 1979).

Does this demonstrate that it takes about 60 msec to identify a word? Well, it does seem to demonstrate that it takes at least that long, since you need a 60 msec dose of visual information to do it. However, masking is a complex phenomenon which is still far from understood. Even though the stimulus looks like it disappears after the mask comes on, the information may still be there for further processing. One possibility is that after 60 msec or so, the visual information from the masked stimulus is transferred to some kind of short-term memory where the mask cannot disrupt it so that the word identification processes can still operate on the information; however, information in this buffer need not lead to conscious perception. While this explanation may strike the reader as rather baroque, it is not at all far fetched. However, there is no compelling reason to accept such an explanation, so let's assume that the visual information (in some sense) disappears after 60 msec.

We must keep in mind that 60 msec is the time the stimulus is on, or, more importantly, the time before the mask appears. However, that doesn't mean that only 60 msec has elapsed between when the stimulus has come on and when the mask (in some fashion or other) tells the brain to let go of the first stimulus. We know it takes some time for the nerve impulses to travel from the eye, through the optic nerve, and into those regions of the brain that identify visual stimuli. (The exact regions are still not known, but there is some evidence that it is in areas known as "secondary visual cortex," [Petersen et al. 1988].) To pick a simple number, let's say that it takes about 50 msec. Thus, the word presented is moving up the visual pathways to the pattern-recognition system and the mask is following it 60 msec later. If the mask takes as long as the stimulus to get to those centers and interrupt processing of the stimulus, then the mask will arrive there 110 msec after the stimulus was presented. That is, the brain might only process the stimulus for 60 msec, but the total time elapsed between when the word appears and when the brain is forced by the mask to stop processing it would be 110 msec.

Assuming that the subject can identify the word, 60 msec plus this neural transmission time (assumed to be 50 msec in the above argument) would be a good estimate of how long it takes to process a word. How long, in fact, does neural transmission take? No one knows for sure, although 50 to 70 msec is probably not an unreasonable guess. (One other complication is that the masking stimulus' disrupting effect is likely to be transmitted to the brain a bit more quickly than the visual information about the word.) The bottom line, therefore, is that 60 msec is a lower-bound estimate for how long it takes to identify a word, although we should expect that it takes appreciably more time than that.

Estimates from reading text   Perhaps we are making it all too complicated and artificial. Why don't we examine real reading? The typical college student reads at about 300 words per minute or 5 words per second. That means that words in text are, on average, processed in about a fifth of a second or 200 msec. There are several problems with this. The first is that there is time used up in reading that has little to do with word identification. If one is reading difficult text (and text can be difficult even without unusual or technical words), reading can be slowed down to one-half that speed or less. Thus, it is clear that reading is more than word identification. On the other hand, we can't be sure that the reader is really identifying every word. He or she may guess at individual words or even phrases, and it is very difficult to test whether all the words in the text have been identified. In spite of everything, we do seem to be converging on an estimate. The reaction time studies demonstrated that word identification probably takes less than 400 msec, the experiments with brief presentations demonstrated that it takes at least 60 msec, and the estimate from reading suggests a number something like 200 msec.

Physiological methods   Perhaps we are wasting time with indirect methods. What about examining the brain itself to see when a word is recognized? The first problem is clearly that we have to study humans to study reading, and ethics prevent us from opening the skull to answer our question. Even if we could, we wouldn't know how to recognize "word identification" in the brain. We don't know for sure where it is and we also don't know whether we are looking for a pattern of increased electrical activity, decreased electrical activity, or some other, subtler change of state in the brain.

While there are several methods that can be used for studying human brain states without surgery, only one method at present, *evoked potentials,* is adequate for studying the time course of the processing of incoming stimuli. This method uses electrodes taped to the scalp and measures relatively gross electrical activity in the brain. The method is very imprecise for determining where the electrical activity is coming from. The signal is also very "noisy" so that the records from many trials have to be averaged in order to draw any conclusions. These records of electrical activity have certain relatively well-defined peaks that occur at certain approximate times after the stimulus is presented (although there is dispute about whether these peaks really are the same across tasks and subjects). If we forget about these disputes for the moment, there are several peaks of interest (e.g., Kutas and Hillyard 1980; Van Petten and Kutas 1987). One that occurs at about 300 to 400 msec appears to be the one that corresponds to making a decision about what response to select (see Figure 3.1). This is not what we are interested

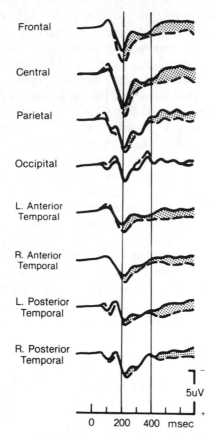

FIGURE 3-1 Average evoked potentials to function and content words taken at several locations on the scalp. As can be seen in the graph, there is some indication that some of the functions differ at about 100–150 msec, indicating that the brain can discriminate these classes of words that quickly. (From Kutas and Hillyard 1983, with permission of the Psychonomic Society and the author.)

in; we are looking for something before that. There is a peak at 50 to 100 msec, but it appears to be associated more with the detection that "something has happened" rather than identification of a particular stimulus. The "negative peak" at about 150 to 200 msec appears to be a reasonable guess as something that might be associated with stimulus identification. For example, the size of this peak differs when an auditory stimulus is attended to than when it is not (Hillyard et al. 1973). However, from the data at hand, it is definitely not clear what this peak represents. At one extreme, it could be representing a relatively early stage of stimulus processing such as the recognition that the stimulus is a sequence of letters. At the other extreme, it could represent a relatively late stage of processing such as a reaction to the identification of a word rather than the identification of the word itself.

However, it is suggestive that the estimates from these records also indicate a time something like 150 to 200 msec for word identification.

What then can we conclude from all the above methods? We are certain that 700 msec (categorization reaction time) is too slow for an estimate of the time to access the meaning of a printed word. We are pretty sure, but not certain, that 400 msec (naming time) is also too slow for an estimate. We are also pretty sure that 60 msec is too fast an estimate and that something like 150 msec is about right, although we shouldn't be too surprised if word identification took place in as little as 100 msec or as much as 200 msec after the word is first sensed by the eye.

Before going back to the questions raised at the beginning of the chapter, let us conclude this introduction by considering the question of whether the speed of identifying a word is influenced by the frequency of the word in the language. The frequency of the word is usually measured by taking some corpus of text that is assumed to be representative and actually counting the number of times that a particular word appears. The frequency count for American English that is the current standard is that of Francis and Kucera (1982). To give you some feel for frequency counts, words such as IRK, JADE, COVE, VANE, and PROD have counts of 2 to 5 per million, while words like CAT, COAT, GREET, and SQUARE all have frequencies greater than 30 per million.

The difference in lexical decision time between a high-frequency word such as COAT and a low-frequency word such as COVE is about 100 msec; however, the difference in naming times is considerably less, about 30 msec (Balota and Chumbley 1984). Clearly, both of these differences can not be estimates of how much longer it takes to identify a low-frequency word than to identify a high-frequency word. In reading, the difference in "fixation time" (i.e., the time the reader looks at a word) between high-frequency words and low-frequency words is also something like 30 msec (Inhoff and Rayner 1986). Thus, 30 msec seems like a better guess as the effect of frequency on the time to identify a word. (However, the effect may be appreciably bigger for *really* low-frequency words.) It should be pointed out that high-frequency words tend to be short and low-frequency words tend to be longer; however, the frequency effects reported above are obtained when the high- and low-frequency words are equated for the number of letters.

Let us now return to the questions raised at the beginning of the chapter. Our discussion of the time it took to access a word had several goals in mind. First, we wanted you to see how questions have to be sharpened in order to be answerable. For example, terms like *word identification* are not precise enough. Second, we wanted to introduce you to the experimental tools that we have available for answering questions about word processing. Third, we wanted to carry through an argument fully enough to see what sorts of "answers" we usually have. Each technique has its own problems, but if enough techniques appear to converge on a common answer, we can have a reasonable degree of confidence in our conclusion. (Sometimes we are luckier than others: techniques may converge or they may not.) Fourth, we wanted to give you one piece of the data that suggests that words in isolation are processed pretty much the same way as words in text: the times we estimated for word identification are not radically different in the two cases. (Rest assured that we will return to fully document this assertion later in the chapter and in Chapter 7.)

Is Word Processing Automatic?

The claim was made earlier that, perhaps contrary to intuition, the identification of the meaning of a printed word was a relatively automatic process and the part of reading that was using up most of the time and effort was likely to be the higher-order processes: those processes that put the meanings of words together so that sentence structure can be grasped, the meaning of sentences and paragraphs can be understood, and the intention and tone of the author can be comprehended.

Actually, the claim is a bit of an overstatement, since the case for the automaticity of word processing is not air-tight. However, the basic point will be seen to be valid: identifying the meanings of words is a rapid process for the skilled reader and is definitely not the "bottleneck" in reading. As we will see, this issue is important, since it shapes one's overall model of the reading process. For example, several influential models of reading view word identification as the hard and unnatural step and therefore assume that readers heavily depend on context to identify words (e.g., Goodman 1970; Smith 1971). On the other hand, context is likely not to be important in determining how quickly and accurately words are identified if identifying words is automatic.

You may be getting impatient by now and wondering what on earth we mean by "automatic". To the layperson, the word *automatic* connotes something that is rapid, involuntary, and effortless. We will adopt Posner and Snyder's (1975) three criteria for automaticity that somewhat formalize this intuition: (1) the person may be *unaware* of the process; (2) the execution of the process is not under the *conscious control* of the subject— that is, the subject's intention to perform the task may be irrelevant to whether it is done; (3) the process takes *no processing capacity*—that is, it uses no resources that other mental operations might also use. These criteria are offered as a tentative definition in order to structure discussion. However it may be too much to ask of word identification to satisfy all three criteria. The criteria may be too strict: Perhaps no process (with the possible exception of some reflexes) satisfies all three.

Is identification of words unconscious? How could we possibly identify the meaning of a word and be unaware of it? Consider the following experimental situation. A word is flashed briefly and is followed by a pattern mask, as described earlier, but the word is exposed for only about 20 msec before the pattern mask appears. (Remember, something like a 50 to 60 msec exposure is needed for the subject to be able to identify the word 100 percent of the time.) If the experimental situation is arranged carefully—the pattern is an effective mask, the word and mask are about the same brightness—subjects will say that they can't see the word, and they will be unable to perform above chance when asked to report whether or not a word was presented prior to the mask, but the meaning of the word will be identified.

How could we test to see that a word has been processed if the reader is unaware of its meaning? We need a subtler test than asking the subject to report the word. Let us assume that DOG is the word that is flashed briefly. One possibility is to present two words that can be clearly seen (let's say DOG and BOY) a short time after and ask the subject to choose which of the two was the briefly exposed word. Subjects are also at chance level on this test of recognition memory, so we still have no evidence that subjects have identified the word (Balota 1983).

As experimenters, we need to be even more devious, which necessitates explaining an experimental procedure known as *priming* (Meyer and Schvaneveldt 1971). For the moment, we will forget about brief exposures. In a priming experiment, the experimenter shows two words in sequence, the *prime* and then the *target*. The sequence might be the words DOG and CAT. The experimenter is primarily interested in how quickly the second word, the target, is processed. In particular, is CAT processed any more rapidly when a related word such as DOG precedes it than when an unrelated word such as FAN precedes it? If we measure the response time to judge that CAT is a word (the *lexical-decision* task), in fact subjects will usually be about 30 to 50 msec faster to respond "yes" when DOG is the prime for CAT than when FAN (an unrelated word) is. A similar, but somewhat smaller, effect can be obtained when the subject names the target. The precise interpretation of the priming effect is still hotly debated (see Chapter 7). However, for our present purposes, the important thing is that the priming effect demonstrates that the meaning of the prime has been processed, since the speed of processing the target is dependent on the meaning of the prime.

Now let's return to our situation where DOG is flashed for approximately 20 msec followed by a mask. Instead of asking subjects what they saw, we ask them to make a lexical decision on another letter string about 500 msec later. Amazingly enough, subjects will be faster to judge that CAT is a word when preceded by DOG than when preceded by FAN even though they have no awareness of seeing the priming word. Thus, the meaning of the priming word has been identified, since the time to judge the target is influenced by whether the prime is related to it in meaning, even though the subject is unaware of identifying the prime. While this phenomenon of "unconscious priming" is somewhat controversial, it has been replicated many times (e.g., Marcel 1983; Balota 1983; Fowler et al. 1981; Carr et al. 1982). Moreover, the size of the priming effect is usually unaffected by whether the subject can identify the target stimulus or not (e.g., Balota 1983; Carr et al. 1982).

We have been a bit vague about what "awareness" means, and this has been a subject of controversy. The standard criterion is that the subject is at chance level if asked to say the word. However, one experimenter (Marcel 1983) has reported priming even when the subject is no better than chance at distinguishing between whether a priming stimulus preceded the mask or nothing preceded the mask. While not all researchers are convinced that priming can be obtained even when the subject is totally unaware that a stimulus was present (Holender 1986; Cheesman and Merikle 1984), it is clear that the meaning of a word can be "looked up" by its visual representation without the conscious experience of perceiving the word. Thus, the identification of the meaning of visual words is automatic according to the first criterion outlined above.

Is intention to process a word important? In some sense, the experiments discussed above may have already made the point: the word's meaning is processed even though the subject is unaware of that fact. However, since the subject is trying to do well in the experiment and trying to see everything as well as possible, perhaps the subject is intending to process the stimulus (even if unaware of having processed it), and that is important for the meaning being extracted. Would subjects extract the meaning in the above priming experiments even if they were trying not to? We don't know for sure since the experiment has not been carefully done. However, there is clear evidence that the meaning of a word is extracted when the subject is trying hard *not* to process it. The standard experiment that demonstrates this is one in which subjects see a printed word written in colored ink and are supposed to name the color of the ink. One of the most interesting conditions is when the subject sees a color name such as RED printed in green ink. In such a case, the time to make the correct response, "green," is very slow compared to when the subject says "green" to a green color patch.

This phenomenon, which is commonly called the "Stroop effect" after its discoverer (Stroop 1935), is not a transient phenomenon. It is a large effect—subjects are usually about 200 msec slower to say "green" to RED written in green ink than to a green color patch—and it only decreases a bit with extended practice (Dyer 1973). Subjects know that the word is interfering, but they can't avoid processing it. A similar effect is obtained when subjects see the word CAT in the middle of a line drawing of a dog and attempt to name the line drawing (Rayner and Posnansky 1978). However, while this phenomenon tells us that something about the word is processed, we don't know for sure that it is its meaning. Perhaps it is only that the word form accesses the motor program to name the word.

One way to test whether the meaning of the word has been accessed is to compare the size of the interference effect when the word is a competing color word such as RED and when it is an unrelated word such as ANT. In fact, while both words interfere with saying "green," the interference effect is substantially greater for RED than for ANT (Klein 1964). Thus, it appears that the interference has two components: (1) since unrelated words interfere, there is competition between the name of the word and the name of the ink; (2) since color names interfere more, the meaning of the word competes with the meaning of the color. A second finding that reinforces this conclusion is that an associate of a competing color name such as BLOOD interferes with saying "green" more than an unrelated word such as ANT does (Dyer 1973).

Thus, the Stroop effect demonstrates that both the name and meaning of a word are processed by skilled readers even when they are trying hard *not* to process them. So we see that identifying words is automatic both in the sense that it may go on without awareness and in that it goes on even when the subject is trying not to do it. The evidence for the third aspect of automaticity—not requiring limited capacity—is not nearly as clear cut.

Does word identification take processing capacity? Before plunging ahead to answer this question, we need to discuss briefly what one means by "processing capacity," and how one would test for it. In our discussion of cognitive psychology in Chapter 1, we briefly touched upon the concept of "limited capacity." Most theories of cognition assume (either explicitly or tacitly) that many cognitive acts need some sort of attentive process and there is a finite amount of this attention which limits how much information can be processed at a time. Some processes, such as the normal control of breathing, are assumed not to need any attentional processing, while others, such as the processing of discourse, are assumed to need attentional processing, since it is very difficult to process two conversations at once.

The basic test for whether a process requires attentional capacity seems simple: A process can be assumed not to require attention if it can be done at the same time as another process and not interfere with it; accordingly, the process probably uses some attentional capacity if it interferes in some way with the performance of the other task. For example, if it were true that one could multiply two-digit numbers in one's head as rapidly while driving a car as while sitting in an easy chair, then one would want to conclude that either driving or mental arithmetic (or both) did not take any limited capacity. On the other hand, if the mental arithmetic slowed down during driving or more errors were made, then one would conclude that both tasks were using a pool of limited capacity or resources. Put simply, the test of limited capacity is usually whether two things can be done at the same time as well as one.

We will assume that a process demonstrates no need for capacity if it doesn't slow down or interfere with other processes. However, it is not necessarily the case that interference is due to limited resources being shared. To see this, let us return to the Stroop task. We found that it took longer to say "green" to RED printed in green ink than to say "green" to a green color patch. Does that mean that processing the form (RED) and the color (green) each used processing resources? This conclusion seems unlikely: the interference is different when the word was RED than when it was ANT, and it is not clear why it should take more resources to identify RED than to identify ANT. Moreover, if the subject sees GREEN in green ink, then the naming time is even faster than for the color patch (Hintzman et al. 1972).

Thus, interference is not necessarily the result of competition for attentional resources. It could result from a competition between two incompatible responses. A reasonable explanation of the Stroop effect is that both the color and form of the printed word are identified without needing any capacity, but after both are processed, they produce responses that compete with each other. (It is possible that settling this response competition does require limited capacity, but that is a side issue here.)

However, Keele (1972) has claimed that a variation of the Stroop task does argue that processing the meaning of the color and form do not require the same limited capacity. Instead of asking for a vocal response, Keele had subjects press keys to indicate the color of the ink (one key for red, one for green, one for yellow, and one for blue). He found an interference effect for competing color words but none for neutral words. Thus, the key-press task appears to have eliminated the interference caused by activating two names, but not the interference caused by activating two conflicting meanings.

Keele's argument is the following. The interference effect with color names demonstrates that the meaning of the word has been processed at least up to the level of knowing whether it is a color word or not; however, since there is no interference for neutral words such as ANT compared to the baseline condition, one can conclude that processing the word took no resources. The first part of the argument is valid, but the second is problematic. In the first place, the baseline in Keele's experiment was a repeated colored nonsense pattern, which he assumed took no capacity to process. But there is no reason to assume that processing resources were not needed to process the nonsense form. The problem, however, transcends the particular experiment. Even if a color patch were used, one could still argue that processing resources were needed to process its form. In addition, it is possible that the lack of interference observed could be because processing the color takes no resources.

While Keele's results are not conclusive, they are consistent with the hypothesis that processing a printed word does not require limited capacity. It would be more conclusive if we could demonstrate that two printed words could be processed as quickly as one. How could we test this? What we need is a task that presents the same response requirements when two words are presented as when one is, so that differences between the two (if observed) could be ascribed to the greater difficulty of identifying two words. (Naming clearly won't work.) One task that has been employed is *visual search*. The subject is presented with one or more words and asked to determine whether, for example, there is an animal name present (Karlin and Bower 1976; Pollatsek, Well, and Gott 1978). Thus, the response—a key press to indicate "yes" or "no"—is identical in all cases. The response time to decide whether the name of an animal is in the visual display takes longer the more words there are in the display (in fact, about 200 msec per word). Thus, it appears that processing words does take capacity.

However, the process that takes capacity may not be the identification of the meaning of the words; it may be the subsequent step needed to decide whether a word is in the experimentally specified category. Can we determine which? There is a similar experiment involving letters and digits. The subject is presented with from 1 to 6 characters and asked to respond whether a digit is present. In this task, the time to detect a digit when there are 5 letters present is virtually the same as when there are no letters present (Egeth, Jonides, and Wall 1972). Thus, it appears that subjects can process the meaning of 6 characters and, furthermore, categorize them as letters and digits as rapidly as it takes to process 1. The letter-digit experiment thus indicates that categorization per se does not necessarily take capacity. However, the categorization of characters as letters and digits could easily be more automatic than the categorization of words.

Unfortunately, there is no clear solution here at present, so let's try to remember what we know. First, if we look at the Stroop data, we know that the meaning of the word is processed along with the color, and as far as we can tell, accessing the meaning of the word does not take away resources from processing the color (or vice versa). If we look at the search data, we get the opposite picture: categorizing two words takes more time than categorizing one, so that some process associated with categorizing appears to take resources. The letter-digit data argue that the process that requires limited resources may not be categorization, although we don't know for sure.

Thus the available data don't allow us to conclude with any certainty that word processing is automatic in the sense that it takes no capacity. However, we have abundant data that, even if it takes resources to process a word, it doesn't take the processor with limited resources much time. First consider our discussion of recognizing words followed by masks. In those experiments, something like a 50 to 60 msec interval between word and mask was sufficient for recognizing words. Although one had to consider neural transmission time if one wanted to know how long it took to recognize a word after it was presented, the neural transmission time is irrelevant if one wants to know how long the central word-processing mechanism is actually involved in identifying a word. Thus, we would estimate that time to be about 60 msec. Similar estimates come from two other sources.

The first is an experiment that used a masking procedure, but while subjects were reading text (Rayner et al. 1981). When subjects read text, their eye movements were monitored (see chapters 4 and 5), and each time the eye came to rest, the text was exposed for a fixed amount of time until a mask came on, obliterating the text. Thus, on each fixation, the subject had only a limited amount of time to see the text. In spite of this, when the mask appeared 50 msec after the start of each fixation, subjects could not only read the text, but their reading rate was only slowed by about 15 percent compared to normal reading. This suggests that only a little over 50 msec is needed to identify a word.

A second line of evidence comes from the technique known as *rapid serial visual presentation,* which has the catchy abbreviation RSVP. In this technique, subjects see words appear one after the other in the same place on a video screen. The finding is that subjects can comprehend material even when it is presented at rates of 12 to 15 words per second (Forster 1970; Potter, Kroll, and Harris 1980). Inferences about time are a bit indirect with this technique, since subjects have some time to piece the material together after the sentence is finished and fill in details even if all words were not processed. Nevertheless, there is evidence that most words are processed (e.g., it makes a difference if words like *the* are presented or not) so that the subject does appear to be processing a word in about 70 to 80 msec or so (and doing at least some higher-order processing as well).

Thus, while we can't be completely sure that the identification of a word is completely automatic for a skilled reader, it appears to take at most about 60 to 70 msec of mental activity. Since the average skilled reader reads even the simplest text at about 300 words a minute, or about 200 msec per word, it thus appears that identifying the meaning of words takes at most something like one-third of the mental processing needed for reading. Even this estimate may overstate how much resources word identification takes: while word identification takes some time, it doesn't necessarily take resources away from other processes.

How Does the Processing of Words Relate to the Processing of Letters?

Physically, the description of a word (especially a printed word) seems obvious. If a two-year-old girl gave you a book and asked you to show her what a word was, your task would be quite simple. You would explain that the words were the physical entities between the spaces, and you could go on to explain that the letters were the little units inside words that were separated by the smaller spaces. (The task of explaining what letters are would be substantially more difficult with handwriting.) Other units, such as syllables, are not physically marked in any clear way, so that you would not be able to demonstrate what a syllable "looks like" to the child.

All of the above underscores what may seem obvious; words are units of meaning and so delineating them is important. Moreover, since English is an alphabetic language, delineating the letters is also important in the orthography. In an alphabetic language, it seems obvious that letters must be natural units in the *perception* of words. However, when one starts thinking hard about the question, it is not so obvious that letters are used as units in the perception of printed words, especially for skilled readers. Since the process of word recognition for skilled readers is so fast and automatic, it is possible that the process of letter identification is bypassed. In fact, Smith (1971) has claimed that skilled readers identify English words pretty much the same way they identify a picture: they recognize the word as a visual pattern through visual features and the fact that it is composed of letters is irrelevant to the perception of a word. That seems like a pretty extreme position, yet it is not easy to refute without experimental data.

The position at the other extreme also has its adherents (e.g., Gough 1972). Gough claimed not only that letters are used to recognize words but that words are read letter-by-letter serially from left to right, and the reader encodes the word as the sequence of letters. While this view has been criticized as being unfeasible because the processing would be too slow, experimental data suggest that letters can be scanned at about 10 msec per letter (Sperling 1963). Thus, the typical reading rate of 300 words per minute is not inconsistent with such a scanning process.

As you might suspect, we believe the truth to be in between these two extremes. In the remainder of this section we will describe two experiments that we believe rule out these extreme views, and then we will propose a relatively simple model of word processing that is consistent with these two experiments. The remainder of the chapter will then use the framework of this model to discuss word perception.

Ruling out the serial letter-by-letter model An obvious conse-quence of the assumption that letters are processed serially in order to perceive a word is that a single letter should be processed more quickly than a word. Sperling's (1963) experiment cited previously gives one estimate of the time to process each letter. He found (roughly) that if an array of unrelated letters was exposed for 10 msec (followed by a pattern mask) 1 letter could be reported, 2 letters could be reported given a 20 msec exposure, 3 letters reported given a 30 msec exposure, and 4 letters given a 40 msec exposure. (After this, short-term memory limitations came into play, and not many more than 4 letters could be reported even with longer exposure durations.) This experiment suggests that random letters are processed serially at the rate of 10 msec per letter.

If letters in words were also processed serially, what would one predict for the time to identify a word? Since words are not composed of unrelated letters, then one might expect that processing a 4-letter word would require less time than processing all 4 letters of an unrelated letter string. For example, if the first letter of the word was a *T*, then the reader might expect the second letter to be an *H* or an E, and if it were, processing time for the second letter could be shortened by this expectation. But, and this is the important point, the serial letter-by-letter model of word processing predicts that it should take longer to process words than individual letters because processing the letters after the first letter will take some time, even if each of these letters is processed more rapidly than the first.

More than 100 years ago, Cattell (1886) tested this prediction by briefly exposing words and letters and asking subjects to report what they saw. In fact, subjects were better able to report the words than the letters! His experiment has several flaws, however. First, there was no mask presented after the words or letters, so that while the words and letters physically disappeared, the iconic representation (see Chapter 1) of the stimuli undoubtedly remained. Thus there may not have been much time pressure in encoding the visual information, and the errors observed may have been largely failures of short-term memory. Second, there was no control for guessing. Subjects may not have actually seen all the letters of a word but been able to guess fairly well from seeing a part of a word what the whole word was.

These factors would not explain why words were reported more accurately than letters, however. The first merely states that the icon may have lasted long enough to allow adequate time for both words and letters to be encoded. The second argues again why there may not have been much of a difference between words and letters. To explain why words were actually better than letters, one needs another factor. The one generally posited is that *words are more memorable than letters*. First of all, the words used in these experiments were usually concrete nouns, which should be more meaningful than letters. Second, in an experiment with many trials, the words are changed from trial to trial, whereas letters would have to be repeated. It could become very confusing to keep track of which letters were seen on which trials.

Cattell's experiment lay dormant until the cognitive psychology revolution of the 1960s, when Reicher (1969) replicated the experiment, attempting to remove possible artifacts (see also Johnston 1978; Johnston and McClelland 1974; Wheeler 1970). First, he used a pattern mask to control the effective stimulus presentation time. Second, he changed the task slightly to eliminate guessing as an explanation and to minimize the effect of memory. He presented a *target stimulus* (either a word such as *WORD,* a letter such as *D,* or a scrambled version of the word such as *ORWD).* The target stimulus was followed by the pattern mask and 2 probe letters, 1 above the critical letter of the target word and the other below it (see Figure 3.2). In this example, the probe letters would be *D* and *K,* and they would appear above and below where the *D* had been in either *WORD, ORWD,* or *D.* The

FIGURE 3-2 Sample displays from the experiment by Reicher (1969).

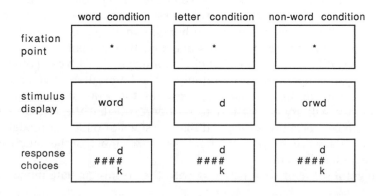

letters were chosen so that either would spell a word when combined with the other letters of the display (in this case, *word* or *work*). Thus, knowing or assuming that the target stimulus was a word would not allow the subject to perform above chance (50 percent correct) in the experiment.

Reicher found that the critical letter in the target word was reported more accurately than the same letter in isolation. He also found that the letter in isolation was reported with about the same accuracy as the letter in the nonword *ORWD*. Thus, Cattell's phenomenon appears to be real: letters in words are actually identified more accurately than letters in isolation. The phenomenon forces one of two conclusions. First, the serial model can't be correct if the errors in the experiment are due to limited encoding time forced by the mask, since it should take longer to encode 4 letters than 1. Alternatively, the serial model could be salvaged if one argued that the mask did not really impose perceptual difficulties and that the differences in the experiment were due to errors in short-term memory. While subsequent experiments have demonstrated that memory (in some sense) plays a part in the "word-superiority" effect (Mezrich 1973; Hawkins et al. 1976), there are several reasons to believe that Reicher's result is perceptual. First, the exposure duration is critical: Performance is about 100 percent even for the 4-letter nonwords (Adams 1979) if the target stimulus is exposed for 80 msec before the mask appears. Thus short-term memory, in some simple sense, can't be the limiting factor in these experiments. Second, the phenomenon that is probably most devastating for the serial model is that the *D* in the random string of letters *ORWD* is identified as accurately as the *D* in isolation. Since this condition should pose memory difficulties at least as great as the isolated letter condition, it would appear that there is no way that the serial model could explain why the target letters are reported equally accurately in the two conditions.

Words are not visual templates   Reicher's experiment rules out the hypothesis that letters in words are processed serially, but what does it establish? One possibility is that the letters are processed in parallel and then are wired up to word detectors that automatically "fire" when the letters do so (see Figure 3.3). An attractive feature of this model is that it explains why letters in nonwords are processed as well as letters in isolation. However, it appears not to be able to explain why letters in words are actually processed better than letters in isolation. The other possibility is that skilled readers develop special templates for words and that they actually process words and letters by different systems that have nothing to do with each other (with the word system operating more rapidly). The latter alternative appears to be more attractive since it directly explains the word-superiority effect. However, we will argue (not just to be perverse) that the visual template model is almost certainly wrong and that versions of the other model can in fact explain the word-superiority effect (as well as much of the data from the word processing literature).

To get a sense of what is wrong with the visual-template model, let us

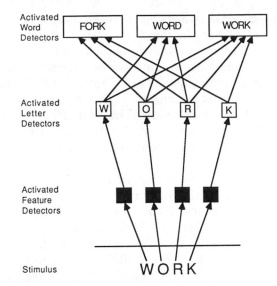

FIGURE 3-3 Schematic model of a parallel model of word identification. In each position, letter features are identified, which in turn lead to the identification of letters and then the word. In this diagram, several words are activated, but the appropriate word, WORK, is activated most strongly, since it receives activation from all four component letter detectors. The model will subsequently be made more complex.

consider what it would mean if the perception of a word did not go through the perception of its component letters. It would mean that there is some sort of visual template of the word DOG that would be compared against all visual patterns and if they were sufficiently similar to the visual template, then the visual pattern would be recognized as "dog." However, there is a problem here. We can recognize *dog* if it is written as *dog,* "DOG," and in innumerable different typefaces (including fairly strange ones used on computer screens). It is hard to see how one template or model could be used for all of these different varieties of typefaces. There are several ways one could attempt to salvage the model. First, one could postulate that there are separate templates for each variety of *dog* one encounters. Alternatively, one could posit that there are collections of "features" that define each word. Neither alternative seems very attractive in explaining how someone would be able to recognize words in a new typeface. In general, if the typeface is fairly novel the reader experiences initial difficulty, but then after a little while can read it about as well as a familiar typeface. One could say that a word printed in the novel typeface was close enough to the template of the word or had enough critical features so that it could be recognized. After sufficient experience, presumably the template would be altered or the critical features adjusted so that word would be recognized in the new typeface.

The problem with either of these explanations is the following. The reader has read several pages of the new typeface and has gotten used to it, *but has not encountered the word* lion *yet.* Both these models would predict (contrary to what would happen) that *lion* in the new typeface would present difficulties because its template (or critical features) have not yet become adjusted, since the perception of each word is separate from the perception of other words and the perception of its component letters. In contrast, the model that says that words are processed through their component letters would have no trouble with this kind of learning. Either a new template is learned for each letter in the new typeface or the critical features of the letters are adjusted when one encounters the new typeface, and once that happens, any combination of those letters should be perceived with little difficulty. (That is basically the alphabetic principle.)

Perhaps the clearest demonstration of this ability to overcome novel forms of words involves the use of text written in AlTeRnAtInG cAsE sUcH aS tHiS (Smith, Lott, and Cronnell 1969). In fact, given a little practice, readers encounter surprisingly little difficulty with such text and can read it as fast as normal text when the sizes of all the letters are equated and only a little slower than normal when the text looks like the above. The Smith et al. result could be criticized because measuring reading rate may not be a sufficiently sensitive measure of processing difficulties; if the text is easy enough, subjects may be able to guess words and letters in the alternating case condition well enough to get by. However, Coltheart and Freeman (1974) demonstrated that lexical decision times for words written in alternating case were only 12 msec slower than for words written in lower case.

How would these "whole word" theories attempt to explain this result? The template theory seems totally inadequate, since most subjects clearly have not encountered words in that form before. Smith, who espouses the feature theory, argued that the features for recognizing words are independent of the case of the letters. This seems pretty far-fetched, as it is hard to see what features certain upper and lower case letters such as *A,* and *a, R* and *r,* or *D* and *d* have in common. On the other hand, if the perception of words goes through the component letters, it is easy to see how the case manipulation poses little difficulty. (What we would have to add to the model is some explanation of why there was any difficulty with the alternating case text.) The fact that the case of the letters appears to be largely irrelevant to the perception of words has led to the widespread acceptance that word identification proceeds largely through case- and font-independent *abstract letter identities* (Besner, Coltheart, and Davelaar 1984; Coltheart 1981; Evett and Humphreys 1981; Rayner, McConkie and Zola 1980). It also leads to the conclusion that *word shape* is not an important cue for word identification (see Paap, Newsome, and Noel 1984, for corroborating evidence).

A model of word perception Let's briefly assess the argument so far. The experiments in tachistoscopic word recognition appear to rule out the hypothesis that letters in words (or even in nonwords) are processed serially. Second, it appears unlikely that the rapid perception of words is due to a visual template or set of features for each word (there will be additional evidence in a while against template theories). This appears to leave as the only reasonable contender the hypothesis that letters in words are processed in parallel and the encoding of a word goes through the component abstract letters. Since words are perceived better than either individual letters or strings of unrelated letters, however, one needs to say more than that letters are processed in parallel: In some way, the encoding of letters must be mutually facilitative.

Let us start out with a proof by blatant assertion: There are computer simulations of such a parallel encoding model that in fact can predict the word-superiority effect (McClelland and Rumelhart 1981; Paap et al. 1982; Rumelhart and McClelland 1982). While we make no claims that this type of model must be the way that the brain perceives words, it is at least plausible and is reasonably consistent with what we know about word perception. (However, it will need to be complicated as we will discuss later.) It is not easy to explain how such a model can explain the word-superiority effect, so if the following does not satisfy you, we recommend either going to the originals or taking our word for it. We will use the Paap et al. model, since it is somewhat easier to see how it works.

As can be seen in Figure 3.4, the model is quite simple. At the first stage of analysis there are visual features such as horizontal lines, edges, and corners. These feed into letter detectors at the second level of analysis and the letter detectors, in turn, feed into word detectors. (To simplify things, we leave out another level which would distinguish between case- and font-dependent letter detectors for *A, a,* a, and *a* which would all feed into a single abstract *A* detector.) The detectors work pretty much the way that individual neurons (nerve cells) work: if there is enough activity in the neurons feeding into a neuron, the neuron itself will become active. Thus, an *A* would be recognized in a given location if the features that constitute one of these representations of an *A* (such as horizontal lines, slanted lines, acute angle pointing up) are excited by the visual input. (Novel typefaces would presumably be learned either by creating new detectors for each of the letters or by modifying the features of one of the old detectors to be able to recognize the new ones as well.)

An important aspect of the model is that the activation is not all-or-none. If four features of a capital *A* are active, then the *A* detector is more active than if three features are, which in turn would produce more *A* activity than if two *A* features are active. The same applies at the word level. The *dog* detector would not need activity from all of the *d, o,* and *g* detectors to start its activity: there would be some activity in the *dog* detector given any activity in the component letters, and the more activity in the component letters, the more activity in *dog*. (Obviously, the word detector would have to know the spatial position of the component letters to be able to distinguish *dog* from *god*.)

Let us return to the word-superiority effect. Recall that the subject is briefly presented with a word or letter followed by a mask and errors are

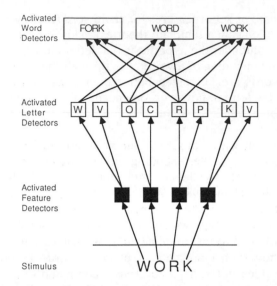

FIGURE 3-4 **Schematic model of a parallel model of word identification. As in the previous figure, there are three stages, feature detectors, letter detectors, and word detectors. However, in this version, more than one detector is activated at each level (e.g., *W* and *V* in the first letter position and several word detectors are activated). In a more realistic model, even more letter and word detectors would be activated. Moreover, what is not shown in the figure is that the activation for the detectors would not be equal: the detector for what is actually presented would get the highest activation, and the amount of activation for the other detectors would depend on their visual similarity to what was actually presented. In the model, only excitatory connections are shown. However, most such models would have inhibitory connections as well (e.g., evidence for *K* in the last position would inhibit firing of the detector for *WORD*).**

made. Thus, not all the visual features have been adequately processed. For the purposes of the argument, let us assume that a particular exposure duration sets the level of visual information so that each letter detector is only excited to 50 percent of its maximum level and the word detector is excited to a higher level (let's say 80 percent of its maximum level). How? Because of the redundancy of words: only a small fraction of the possible combinations of letters are words in the language. Thus, even a hint of *w, o, r,* and *k* may make the stimulus much more likely to be WORK than any other word (see Figure 3.4). In the Paap et al. model, letters are identified by reading off either the letter-detector activation directly or the word-detector activation. Since letters in isolation would have to be identified solely on the basis of letter-detector activity and letters in words can be identified either on the basis of word-detector or letter-detector activity, letters in words will be identified more accurately than letters in isolation even though the letter-detection level comes before the word-detection level!

We have sketched how the model explains the word-superiority effect. We have glossed over complexities, the major one being how the decision is actually made on what letter is actually in a given spatial position. The decision is complex since it must pay attention to activity at both the letter- and word-detector levels and it must also sort out competing activity (e.g., if a K is present, the "K" detector would be active, but so would the "H" and "N" detectors, since those letters share visual features with K). You may still find the explanation baffling, in that it is still hard to see how the letter in the word can be identified better than the letter in isolation *even when guessing has been controlled*. You may just have to take our word for it that such a model can in fact predict such a result. The model even makes good quantitative predictions about the size of the difference between identification of letters in words and letters in isolation.

There is a point that must be emphasized: The data we have been discussing are the percentage of correct identifications in a forced-choice between 2 letters. As the model makes clear (see Figure 3.4), letter identification is quite indirectly related to the activation of words and the activation of letters. Moreover, so far neither we nor Paap et al. have committed ourselves to what in the model would correspond to "perception of a word" or "perception of a letter." The simplest possibility is that the word (or letters) is perceived if the excitation in a particular detector exceeds a certain threshold, let's say 75 percent. That assumption leads to what may sound like an absurd prediction, namely that a word could be perceived before its component letters are perceived. However, the prediction may not be absurd. First, misspellings of words are sometimes (incorrectly) identified as the correctly spelled word and the reader is unaware of the misspelling (Ehrlich and Rayner 1981). Hence, the "word" is in some sense perceived before the component letters. Similarly, words can be misperceived (i.e., perceived as other words). Perhaps more strikingly, one can often be aware that a string such as "diffrence" is misspelled but take a while to discover what is wrong. All three examples suggest that perception of words and letters are somewhat independent processes (We will come back to these phenomena when we discuss the effects of context on word perception and proofreading in chapters 7 and 12.)

WORDS, SUBWORD UNITS, AND SOUND

We will assume for the rest of the book that the Paap et al. model gives an essentially correct picture of the relationship between word and letter identification: The letters in a word are processed in parallel and lead to identification of the word. But is the access to words that simple? In the simple model presented so far, each word is represented as a unit as in a mental *lexicon* or dictionary and access to each *lexical entry* or word detector in the lexicon is by a *direct visual route* in which the only psychologically real subword units are letters. In such a model, all other information about the word, such as its meaning, pronunciation, and etymology, is available only when the lexical entry has been accessed (just as the information about the pronunciation and meaning of WORK is found when the reader gets to the entry for "work" in a dictionary). Are rare words processed in the same way? What about words that the reader has never seen before? If the reader encounters something like MARD, does it have to be read letter by letter as if it was a random letter string or do its wordlike properties make it easier to perceive?

The issues are complex, and there is no definite answer to many of the questions. While the Paap et al. model in fact does a remarkably good job of handling a lot of data, we believe that there are phenomena that suggest that it is too simple and that there are other processes involved in the identification of words. In particular, we want to argue that a process in which the reader also uses the letters of a word to access the sound and then the meaning is also important in word recognition. That is, we believe that there are two routes to the lexicon—the *direct route* (exemplified by the Paap et al. model) and an *indirect route* (going through sound)—that are used by skilled readers to access the meaning of a word. While the central issue in word processing is how the meaning of a word is identified, it will be simpler to introduce the issues involved by asking how the pronunciation of a word is performed. We will even make a second detour initially to discuss how *pseudowords* (nonwords, like MAFER, that look like words) are pronounced. It will take a while, but we will return to the central issue—how we access a word's meaning.

The simplest possibility for how words are pronounced is that the "motor program" to pronounce the word is stored at the word detector or lexical entry. (An equivalent metaphor is that there is a direct link or pathway from the word detector to the motor program.) But how would such a model predict that a pseudoword such as MARD is pronounced? It would appear to require a totally different mechanism unless you posit that all conceivable words (even those never seen such as MARD) also have lexical entries. Since that alternative seems unlikely (and has not been seriously entertained), a more analytic mechanism is needed. Such a mechanism either would have to apply some rules of English pronunciation to novel letter strings or would have to be able to apply analogical rules from known words to novel strings.

Thus it appears that there is a sharp discontinuity between how words and nonwords are processed. What would a system such as that of Paap et al. do when it encountered a nonword? Would it first try to process the letter string as a word, and only when it decided that no word detector was sufficiently activated, would it then engage these other mechanisms for processing nonwords? If so, it would seem that processing a nonword should take a lot more time than processing a word. The facts of the matter are quite different, however. In the Reicher task, there is not only a word-superiority effect but a pseudoword-superiority effect! Letters in pseudowords like MARD are processed more accurately than letters in isolation (Baron and Thurston 1973; Hawkins et al. 1976). In most experiments, letters in words are processed a bit more accurately than letters in pseudowords, but there are several experiments in which there is no difference between the two (e.g., Baron and Thurston, but see Carr, Davidson, and Hawkins 1978). While it takes somewhat longer to pronounce pseudowords than words, it is still a very rapid process: The difference is 200 msec for unpracticed subjects but appreciably less for practiced subjects (Baron and Strawson 1976).

In many ways, this efficient processing of pseudowords should not be surprising. The organism should be equipped to deal with all plausible stimuli about as efficiently as ones actually encountered. This raises the possibility that we were wrong before and that words and nonwords are in fact processed by the same machinery. How can that be, since nonwords can't be processed by the same machinery that we have put forward to describe the encoding of words? We will argue that the way to resolve this paradox is that there are two sets of machinery used to process both words and nonwords, and thus our picture of word perception is incomplete. We will take a somewhat indirect route by first considering how nonwords would be processed.

Processing of pseudowords   Since we have discussed the Reicher paradigm in some detail, we will consider the pseudoword-superiority effect before going on to the more complex question of how pseudowords (and words) are pronounced. One's immediate reaction to the pseudoword-superiority effect is that it would be impossible for a model such as that of Paap et al. to explain. However, as we shall see, the Paap et al. model was in fact constructed largely to explain the pseudoword-superiority effect! (On the other hand, the pseudoword-superiority effect certainly goes against the word-as-visual-template model.)

So far, the Paap et al. model could not explain how letters in pseudowords are identified almost as accurately as letters in words, but it can if one mechanism is added. As we will see, a similar mechanism will be added to explain pronunciation. The mechanism is as follows. When a letter string appears, it excites not only the lexical entry which is identical to it but its "neighbors" as well. Thus the stimulus WORK excites the lexical entry "work" as well as "word," "wore," "fork," and possibly other lexical entries that are visually similar (see Figure 3.4). The question of how *similarity* is defined is complex: The similarity of the stimulus and the word detector would undoubtedly depend on the number of letters that they had in common in the same positions and the visual similarity of the letters that differed, and might also depend on the position of the difference (e.g., a difference between the stimulus and the lexical entry in the first letter position might be more important than a difference in a later position). However similarity is defined (let us assume, for simplicity, that it merely depends on the number of letters in common), the more similar the letter string to the lexical entry, the greater the excitation. Thus, WORK would be identified correctly, since the excitation would be greatest for "work."

What about MARD? Even though it has no lexical entry, it has neighbors like "card," "ward," "mark," "mare," and "maid," and each of

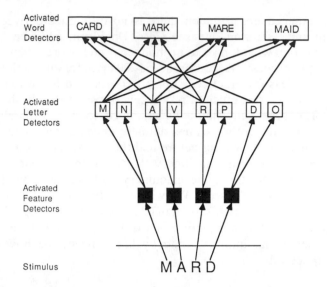

FIGURE 3-5   **The same mechanism as in Figure 3-4 in the process of identifying a pseudoword. As in Figure 3-4, only some of the activated letter and word detectors are shown. What is also not shown in the model is an additional stage, which would "poll" the activated word detectors to find the most popular letters at each letter position (see text). There are more complex versions of this model, in which there are "letter cluster detectors" as well (e.g., a detector for WO in the initial position). As subsequent discussion will indicate, these additional detectors are needed in order to account for all of the phenomena involving pseudowords.**

these entries would be excited to an appreciable degree (see Figure 3-5). To explain how a letter is detected, we need to make another assumption, namely that the subject can read letters off the lexical entries by polling them letter by letter. In the above example, most of the excited lexical entries would "vote" for *m* in the first position, *a* in the second position, *r* in the third position, and *d* in the fourth position, so that the letters of the pseudoword MARD could be read off of the word detectors. (The "read off" process would be in parallel, though). In the model, letters in real words are read off the word detectors in the same sort of way, so that there is some "noise" from the wrong votes of neighbors. However, it is still probably difficult to believe that this process would in fact lead to almost as accurate letter identification for pseudowords as for real words, so you will have to take our word that the model can in fact predict such a result. (The McClelland and Rumelhart model has a slightly different metaphor; it postulates feedback from the word detectors to the letter detectors, but this seems equivalent to the process of reading the letters off the word detectors described above.)

It thus seems that the direct lexical-entry model, if suitably modified, has a lot more flexibility and power than it appeared to at first. Note that while there are no subword units in the model other than letters, the process of "reading the letters off the word detectors" is analytic: the polling of the word detectors is letter by letter. This point will become even more important when we next consider how words (and pseudowords) are pronounced.

PRONOUNCING WORDS AND NONWORDS

When one thinks of pronouncing words and nonwords, it appears that there must be two different mechanisms involved. First, let us consider *irregular words,* those whose pronunciation could not be derived from applying any general knowledge of English pronunciation, e.g., ONE, TWO, CHOIR, WOMEN. In the case of ONE, for example, it appears that when the string is pronounced /won/, it must be because the lexical entry for the word has been accessed which in turn allows access to information about how to pronounce it (e.g., an auditory image, a motor program). A pseudoword such as MARD, however, can't be pronounced this way, unless one wants to postulate lexical entries for all conceivable words. It thus appears that a different system, perhaps a set of rules, allows a person to pronounce this or any new wordlike string of letters. In the case of MARD, the rules would be relatively simple: the three consonants can all be pronounced by general rules for the pronunciation of those consonants; the pronunciation of the vowel would be a bit more complex, however, since one would have to know the rule that makes *A* sound like /ah/ when followed by an *R*. Following this analysis, it would appear that *regular words* (i.e., those whose pronunciation is given by rules of English), such as TREE, could be pronounced by either of these mechanisms: the direct lexical access of pronunciation or the rule-generated system. It should be kept in mind that the rules that we are talking about are for the most part unconscious; the reader does not consciously apply them when pronouncing strings of letters in about half a second and may not even have conscious access to some of them upon longer reflection.

If this commonsense analysis were correct, what would we predict about the difficulty, or speed, or both, of pronouncing regular words, irregular words, and pseudowords? While the assumptions so far would not make any predictions about the relative ease of pronouncing irregular words and pseudowords, we might expect that irregular words are pronounced more quickly since the *direct lexical route* (i.e., the one in which the pronunciation is stored in the lexicon) would be faster than the rule system because the rules might be complex. This is in fact the case. What about regular vs. irregular words? The model we have outlined so far would predict that regular words are pronounced faster *if the rule system is used in the pronunciation of words*. There are two possible mechanisms for this: (1) The pronunciation of irregular words such as ONE could be slowed down by conflict—that is, the lexical system generates the pronunciation /won/, the rule system generates the pronunciation /own/, and there is conflict as in the Stroop paradigm discussed earlier; (2) The pronunciation of regular words could be speeded up by having two independent mechanisms generate the same pronunciation, and thus the response would be strengthened relative to responses that had only one mechanism feed into them. Needless to say, either or both of these hypotheses could be true.

In fact, a reliable finding (Baron and Strawson 1976; Seidenberg et al. 1984a) is that regular words are pronounced more rapidly than irregular words, so that it appears that both mechanisms are operative in the pronunciation of words. (If only the direct lexical mechanism were operative, then there would be no difference between regular and irregular words.) Moreover, there is little difference in naming time between regular and irregular words if they are frequent in the language, whereas there are clear differences between the two if they are less frequent in the language (Seidenberg et al. 1984a). That makes sense in terms of the dual-mechanism explanation. The indirect mechanism should be little influenced by the frequency in the language since it is based on "rules." However, the direct look-up should be faster for high-frequency words than for low-frequency words. Thus for high-frequency words, the direct route is fast enough to make the indirect route irrelevant. For lower-frequency words, the two routes are of more comparable speed; thus low-frequency regular words should be faster than low-frequency irregular words since there are two ways to access the sound.

This argument has failed to convince many researchers (e.g., Glushko 1979; Humphreys and Evett 1985) that there is in fact a rule-governed system that can access the pronunciations of words in time to affect fluent naming of words for reasons we will discuss presently. However, there are two issues that are often confused in this controversy that must be separated: (1) Are there two systems involved in word pronunciation? (2) If so, is the system that is not the direct lexical route a rule-governed system? We feel that most of the criticism is related to point (2) and not to (1).

One reason that the antagonists of a rule-governed system are unhappy with postulating such a system is that it is far from clear how to specify the rules of pronouncing English. For example, is the word DUMB regular or irregular? If it is regular, many of the rules would have to be fairly context-specific (e.g., "B is silent after M"). If one didn't allow such rules, then the pronunciation of B would be independent of context, and the silent B would be irregular. We probably need such contextual rules in our system to handle certain common things such as the ubiquitous "silent e," which is not itself pronounced but lengthens the sound of the previous vowel (e.g., FATE vs. FAT). However, how do the rules deal with COMB, COMBING, and COMBINE? We could call either COMBING or COMBINE irregular, which seems unsatisfactory, since neither seems irregular. If we stay within a rule framework, however, we now have to postulate more complex rules: the B in COMBING is silent because it is part of the syllable COMB, whereas the B in COMBINE is pronounced because it is in a different syllable than the M. Presumably, we would need a rule that knows that ING in COMBING is a suffix and for COMBINE knows that COM is a prefix.

(The task of figuring out that COM is a prefix is made more difficult by the fact that BINE isn't a word.) For longer words, there are also difficult questions about how to construct general rules for assigning stress to syllables without creating tons of irregular words.

In sum, if we postulate a rule system for generating pronunciations, we have one of two options. Either we can postulate simple general rules (Coltheart 1978; Simon and Simon 1973), in which case a large percentage of English words will be irregular (50 percent by the most extreme count) or we can postulate very complex rules that seem more consonant with our intuitions about regularity (Venezky 1970) so that few words (5 percent) are irregular. However, no one has proposed a rule system that is particularly satisfactory, so that if we accept the existence of a rule system, we are largely accepting an article of faith. Moreover, as the above example indicates, such a system will likely have to have information about specific lexical information (e.g., ING is a suffix, COM is a prefix, BINE is a stem that can be combined with prefixes).

The critics of a rule system propose that a lexical system looking quite a bit like that of Paap et al. can handle the pronunciation of both words and nonwords. Let's see how it works. First, consider a nonword such as MARD. It excites a neighborhood of lexical entries as before, such as "ward," "card," "mart," "mark," "maid," "mare." Each of these lexical entries excites, in turn, the pronunciation of that word. The pronunciation of MARD is then generated by polling each unit of sound (phonemes) in turn. Thus, most of the neighbors vote for an /m/ sound in the first position, an /ah/ sound in the second, and so on. Thus, according to the model, the apparently rule-governed behavior of generating pronunciations to novel strings is not due to abstract rules but to computations of knowledge contained in the lexicon (Brooks 1977). This type of model has been termed an *analogical model,* since the pronunciation of the novel string is purportedly generated by analogy with known words. We are not completely happy with the term since it does not really capture the type of computation done on the lexicon to derive a pronunciation. However, for lack of a better term, we will refer to these models as analogical models.

This is in fact a very clever system for producing rulelike behavior, but (a) is there evidence for it? (b) does it really work? The strongest evidence for such a model is that there appear to be lexical influences on the pronunciation of nonwords (Glushko 1979). That is, a nonword such as BINT, which has word neighbors that are inconsistent in their pronunciation (e.g., PINT, HINT, MINT), takes longer to pronounce than one such as TADE whose neighbors are consistent. Similar effects are found with words (e.g., Glushko 1979). Words whose pronunciation is regular but that have irregular neighbors (e.g., GAVE which has HAVE as a neighbor) take longer to pronounce than those that have no irregular neighbors (e.g., COAT). Proponents of a rule system could argue that these effects are produced by differential strengths of rules: rules that are consistently applied are stronger than those that are not.

The problem with the simple analogical system described above is that it doesn't really work. One difficulty is that nonwords such as JOOV are easy to pronounce in spite of the fact that they have no near neighboring words (Coltheart 1981): There is no word beginning with JOO and none ending with OOV. To generate a pronunciation with such a model, one has to postulate that words such as GROOVE and JOIN are neighbors, but this stretches the idea of neighbor quite a bit. In addition, the analogical mechanism would have to be quite clever in knowing how to "line up" the appropriate elements so that the extra phoneme in GROOVE is taken care of. There would be similar problems in pronouncing most longer nonwords such as MARDTORK or anything from "Jabberwocky," which would have virtually no word neighbors. Accordingly, the analogical model actually proposed by Glushko was complicated by expanding the lexicon to include bits and pieces of words. In his model, virtually all subsets of words were in the lexicon (e.g., the "lexicon" would include WOR . . . , WO . . . , . . . ORK, W . . . , . . . RK, in addition to WORK), and all of these units would have pronunciations attached. When a word or nonword appears, all of these units (both the word and subword units) are activated and a pronunciation is somehow computed from all of these firing units.

As you have probably surmised, such a model seems pretty close to a rule model. It is not too different to say that the A in MARDTORK is pronounced /ah/ because of a rule indicating that A followed by R is pronounced that way and to say that there are lots of ". . . AR . . ." entries excited which dictate the pronunciation /ahr/. Since neither model has been worked out in enough detail, it is hard to say whether they are just two different metaphors for thinking about "rules" or whether there is a principled difference between them. In either case, it is clear that the way that the human figures out the pronunciation of a new nonword is a very complex computation. Our present sympathies go with the analogical system, since it is a more satisfying explanation of the phenomenon than one in which complex rules are stored but are not open to consciousness (sometimes even after reflection). In addition, the notion of "rules" suggests some sort of serial combination process which is unlikely to be able to operate in the brief time span of word identification.

Some of the analogue theories have pushed the claim a bit too far, in our opinion, in arguing that there is really only one system that handles all pronunciation (Glushko 1981; Humphreys and Evett 1985), even the pronunciation of words. In the one-system view, when a word such as ONE is encountered, the lexical entries for ONE, all its parts, and all its neighbors' parts are all excited and the pronunciation is based on that total input. To account for the fact that ONE is pronounced correctly nearly all the time, the theory would have to postulate that the excitation of the item itself is enough stronger than the excitation of the neighbors, so that the conflicting pronunciations of the neighbors can only slow down but not overrule the pronunciation offered by the lexical entry "one." The important thing to keep in mind is that according to this view, the direct connection between a stimulus and its "own" lexical entry has no special status: it is only stronger than all the others.

This one-system view is problematic for several reasons. First of all, it would seem difficult to explain why instructions could change the output. If asked to pronounce HAVE, some would say /hahve/, but if asked to pronounce it according to the "rules of English," they could easily switch and say /hayve/. The most problematic result for such a view is that there are people with brain damage who seem to have selective damage for either the direct lexical route or the rule/analogy route. People termed *surface dyslexics* can come up with a pronunciation for virtually all words and nonwords (although understanding little); however, they mispronounce many irregular words by "regularizing" them, such as pronouncing IS-LAND /izland/ (Marshall and Newcombe 1973). Thus, it appears that their problem is parsimoniously explained by postulating that the rule/analogy system is intact while the direct system is damaged. (It is not fully damaged, since not all irregular words are regularized.) On the other hand, *phonemic dyslexics* pronounce most words correctly, but are virtually unable to pronounce nonwords (Coltheart 1981). Their problem is parsimoniously explained by saying that their direct system is relatively intact but their rule-analogy system is almost completely damaged. The proponents of the single-system view argue that since the data from these patients are a bit more complicated than is presented here, it is not completely conclusive evidence for two systems. For most people including ourselves, however, the evidence is conclusive enough that the burden of proof is on the single-system theorists to show why the two-system theory is wrong. (We will discuss the dyslexic data again in Chapter 11.)

To summarize this long, but necessary, discussion of pronunciation, it appears that there are two systems active in pronouncing words: a direct lexical system, in which the pronunciation of words is looked up in the appropriate lexical entry, and a rule/analogy system, whereby the pronunciation of a word or nonword is generated either by a system of rules or by a complex computation on a set of lexical and sublexical neighbors, or perhaps a combination of both. Both the direct lexical system and the rule/analogy system appear to be operative at all times, since the pronunciation of regular words takes less time than the pronunciation of irregular words.

ARE WORDS ACCESSED THROUGH THEIR SOUND?

If we consider Figure 3.6, which summarizes our discussion of the previous section, we see that both the direct lexical and rule/analogy systems are active in determining how a string of letters is pronounced. We now consider the related question of which systems are involved when printed words access the lexicon. The central question of this section is raised by path 2-4

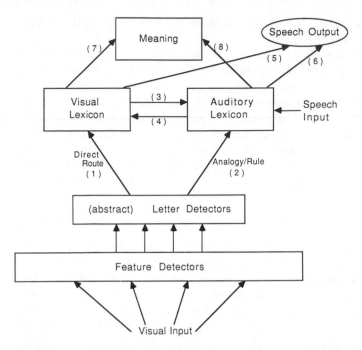

FIGURE 3-6 **Model of word recognition. Encoding of meaning would involve cooperative use of paths 1-7 and 2-8. Lexical decision would involve paths 1 and 2-4, although signals from the auditory lexicon would interfere with certain responses (as with pseudohomophones). Naming words would primarily involve routes 1-5 and 2-6, while naming pseudowords would primarily involve route 2-6. The analogy/rule route would include letter cluster detectors (or some equivalent) not shown in Figure 3-5.**

in the figure: Namely, does the rule/analogy system succeed in generating a pronunciation of a word in time for the sound generated to aid in lexical access? According to one extreme view (Gough 1972), the rule system is the only route by which lexical access occurs. (This can't be true, however, since readers would be unable to discriminate THERE from THEIR.) However, perhaps the most common view today is the opposite extreme: virtually all lexical access is by the direct visual route; the route going through rules (or analogies) to sound and then to the lexical entry plays a minor role, if any, in the access of word meanings. That position is reasonable, but not the only one possible. Let us consider the evidence.

The test of whether the rule/analogy system is involved in lexical access has focused on two empirical questions. The first is whether (as with pronunciation) the time to access the meaning of a regularly spelled word is less than that for an irregularly spelled word. If the rule system were involved, then one would expect a difference, since the rule system should be able to access the lexical entry for regular words but not for irregularly spelled words. The second is whether lexical entries are activated either by homophones or *pseudohomophones* (i.e., nonwords which when pronounced have the same sound as a real word such as PHOCKS). In fact, both questions have usually been examined with the lexical decision task: the former by testing whether the response time for regular words is shorter than for irregular words, and the latter by testing whether response time (to respond "nonword") is longer for pseudohomophones than for other pseudowords. For ease of future discussion, we will term these differences, if obtained, the *regularity effect* and the *pseudohomophone effect,* respectively. There are other tests for indirect access to the lexicon which we shall discuss subsequently.

Unfortunately, the data on the regularity effect has not been consistent: some studies have found a regularity effect (Bauer and Stanovich 1980; Parkin 1982) and others have not (Coltheart 1978). The pseudohomophone effect, in contrast, has been obtained pretty consistently (Rubenstein, Lewis, and Rubenstein 1971; Coltheart et al. 1977), although there are some failures to find it (Dennis, Besner, and Davelaar 1985). The relevance of the pseudohomophone effect has been questioned, however, on two grounds. The first is that, while the pseudohomophone effect establishes that the rule/analogy system is involved in deciding the lexicality of nonwords, it does not establish that the system is involved in the lexical access of real words (Coltheart et al. 1977). Second, there are claims that the pseudohomophone effect may be an artifact: pseudohomophones may look more like real words than other pseudowords. The second criticism, however, can be countered because it has been shown that *deep dyslexic* patients (similar to the phonemic dyslexics discussed previously), who appear to have a grossly impaired rule/analogy system, do not show the pseudohomophone effect (Patterson and Marcel 1977).

One clear demonstration of an effect of sound-based codes on lexical decision times for words comes from an experiment by Meyer, Schvaneveldt, and Ruddy (1974). They showed that the time to decide whether TOUCH was a word was slowed down when preceded by a word such as COUCH, which induces an incorrect expectation about the pronunciation, compared to when TOUCH was preceded by an unrelated word. (If a word such as BRIBE is preceded by a rhyming word such as TRIBE, there is a small facilitation effect compared to when BRIBE is preceded by an unrelated word.)

However, even the Meyer et al. effect has been dismissed by some researchers who level a more fundamental criticism at this research: Lexical decision time may be fundamentally flawed as a measure of lexical access time. There are two fairly different versions of this argument. The first is that lexical decision time may not reflect the time for one lexical entry to reach a sufficient level of activation, but instead reflects the total excitation in the lexicon (produced by a set of lexical entries in the "neighborhood"). The second is that the lexical decision judgment may cause people to perform certain "checking" strategies, such as going through the sound code after entering the lexicon, that are specific to the task and are irrelevant to accessing the meaning of the word (Balota and Chumbley 1984, 1985; Chumbley and Balota 1984; Seidenberg et al. 1984b).

Since the lexical-decision task probably does tap processes other than lexical access, it would be nice to have some convergent validity for the Meyer et al. effect. What would appear to be the simplest way to show that sound accesses meaning would be to demonstrate the Meyer at al. effect in a categorization task (i.e., the time to decide whether a visually displayed word is a member of a semantic category such as tools or furniture). The problem with this is that categorization time depends on factors other than the time to access the word, such as how good an exemplar of the category a word is (e.g., it is easier to judge a ROBIN to be a bird than to judge a TURKEY to be a bird). These variables overpower the relatively small effect found by Meyer et al., so that while there is a hint of the biasing effect in the categorization task, it is fairly weak (McMahon 1976). Another attempt to generalize the Meyer et al. effect was by Treiman, Freyd, and Baron (1983). They used sentences such as "He made a nasty hasty remark." Their finding was that people were slower to read sentences containing two "off rhymes" than matched sentences which contained synonyms of the words. While the Treiman et al. result indicates that some sort of recoding to sound occurs during reading, it is possible that the interference effect does not occur during lexical access, but during a later, comprehension stage when the phrase is understood (see Chapter 6).

While the lexical-decision task is flawed, it appears that most of the effects found using it can be found with other tasks as well. Accordingly, it is probably worth a bit of effort to go back and try to explain the previous lexical-decision results better. Perhaps the major finding to be confronted is that the regularity effect is quite small (if it exists at all). This indicates that the direct visual route is the dominant one for accessing the meaning of words. This certainly makes sense for English because there are so many irregular words: If we relied mainly on going from the letters to sound by rules and then to meaning, lexical access would be error-prone. This raises the question of the role of the rule system in the access of a word's meaning. How can the rule (or analogy) system be involved and yet not lead to all sorts of errors? One possibility is that the direct visual route is the only one normally used, and the rule-to-sound system is brought in only when lexical access fails by the visual route. Such a model could explain why there are occasionally regularity effects: Some words in the experiment are not within the sight vocabulary of the reader, and those words are the ones to give a regularity effect. However, the model does not explain either the pseudo-homophone effect or sound-biasing effect. In the former case, it is not clear why the sound of the nonword should matter if accessing the rule system occurs only after lexical access fails. In the latter case, the sound of the previous word should be irrelevant if the direct visual route is used first.

A more convincing explanation of the data (and probably the model most widely believed) is the "horse-race" model (Coltheart 1978; Meyer and Gutschera 1975). In the horse-race model, each system (the direct visual route and the rule/analogy-to-sound route) works independently to come up with a candidate for a word. Thus, if ONE is presented, the direct visual route would access "*1*" while the rule/analogy route would access something else, perhaps "own." For regular words, both routes would access the same entry and there would be no problem. For irregular words, there is a problem for the system to decide which candidate is correct. The usual assumption is that if there is a conflict the system has to access again and "recheck," although such procedures are usually unspecified. The way proponents of the horse-race theory resolve the problem is to view competition as a race in which the lexical candidate, or horse, that is fastest wins, and postulate that the visual horse almost always wins.

In some sense, this version of the horse-race model is not too different from the direct-access model, since the direct visual route is functionally the route that produces lexical access in almost all cases. Where it differs is that the second route is actively working from the moment that the word appears rather than being activated only when lexical access fails. This difference allows the horse-race model to comfortably explain the general effects found in lexical decision. One would expect regularity effects to surface only when the direct route is slow. If we make the reasonable assumption that the direct visual system's speed in processing a word is more affected by the frequency of the word in the language than the speed of the rule system, then the horse-race model predicts that regularity effects should appear mainly for low-frequency words (which we have seen is true). The pseudohomophone effect is also easy to explain. Since both routes are working from the beginning, the pseudohomophone will activate a lexical entry through the rule system, whereas other pseudowords will not, thus leading to more errors and slower times in judging pseudohomophones as nonwords. The sound-biasing effect can be explained if we assume that the rule/analogy system can be biased by previous activation. Thus, if COUCH biases the rule system to interpret the OU in TOUCH to be pronounced /ow/, then the rule system will fail to find an entry for "touch" and thus slow lexical access relative to when such biasing is not present.

A phenomenon that argues strongly that sound-based coding is used in accessing meaning comes from the categorical-decision task. Meyer and Gutschera (1975) compared the ease of rejecting *pseudomembers* of a category to that of *nonmembers*. For example, if FRUIT is a category, PAIR is a pseudomember (i.e., a homophone of a member), and ROCK is a nonmember. They found that subjects made more errors with pseudomembers (i.e., falsely classified pseudomembers as members of the category) and were slower to respond when they were correct. Unfortunately, in the Meyer and Gutschera experiment, the pseudomembers also had more letters in common with members so that it is not clear that this result is because of visual similarity or because the pseudomembers are homophones of a category member. This has been remedied by Van Orden (1987) who controlled for visual similarity. The effect is surprisingly large: pseudomembers that differed from members by only one letter (e.g., MEET) were falsely classified as members of the category FOOD about 30 percent of the time, while nonmembers that also differed by one letter from members (e.g., MELT) were classified as members only about 5 percent of the time. Since the words were visible for 500 msec, subjects were misclassifying words a quarter of the time when they were clearly visible!

While this result clearly implicates phonological access in getting to a word's meaning, there are two possible access routes. One is the rule/analogy system to sound to lexicon route, but the other is a lexicon to sound to lexicon route (e.g., MEET activates its lexical entry by the direct visual route, which in turn activates the sound of the word that then activates "meat"). While both routes are possible, it is not at all clear why the latter route would cause so much interference, since it would seem that it should be much slower than the direct route: there are two extra steps for MEET to access the meaning of MEAT than for it to access the meaning of MEET. While the access of "meat" could be speeded up by priming from the category word FOOD, it is hard to see how access of "meat" could catch up to the access of "meet" if sound is accessed *only* after accessing the lexical entry for "meet." A follow-up experiment by Van Orden, Johnston, and Hale (1988) provides additional evidence for an indirect route to meaning: The same-sized effect is obtained when pseudohomophones are employed in a categorization task (e.g., SUTE is classified as an item of clothing as often as HAIR is classified as an animal).

The discussion of the pseudomember effect makes it clear that many of the details of the horse-race model have not been clearly worked out. One aspect, in particular, that has not been specified carefully is what happens after the first horse has won the race. Presumably, in cases where one horse wins by a large margin, the lexical-decision response is already programmed so that the second horse is irrelevant. But what about in reading for meaning? Is there interference when the second horse accesses a conflicting lexical entry, or does the winner inhibit all other lexical entries? A second aspect is that the nature of the conflict between competing horses has not been carefully worked out. How exactly does the rule/analogy horse slow down processing in the case of irregular words without producing errors?

Since most people assume that these details can be worked out, the horse-race model has been accepted as the most plausible model of lexical access. However, there is a facet of the model that should not go unnoticed. It argues that for words within our sight vocabulary, the fact that the alphabet was invented largely to capture the sound of words is virtually irrelevant. In fact, in a language like English in which there are so many irregular words, it seems to argue that the main function of the rule system is to interfere with identifying words. Since we find this aspect of the horse-race model a bit troubling, let us propose a slightly different dual-access model that seems a bit more satisfying, in that it will suggest that the involvement of the rule system aids lexical access.

In the *cooperative-access model* (Carr and Pollatsek 1985), both the direct visual and rule (or analogy) to sound routes are accessing the lexicon (as in the horse-race model). However, they are each activating a candidate set as in the Paap et al. model. Thus, when ONE is presented, the rule system activates not only "own" but also a set of words that are similar in sound such as "on," "wan," "won." (The direct route also activates a set of candidates exactly as in Paap et al.) The lexical entry that gets the most summed activation from the two systems is then identified as the word. Thus the two systems cooperate in exciting lexical entries in the visual and sound neighborhoods of the word rather than each sending forth a single lexical candidate, or horse. In the cooperative-access model, the rule system adds activation to the correct entry, although in the case of irregular words, it will add more activation to competing entries. Whether this extra activation can facilitate lexical access (on the average) depends on details of the decision process, details that have not been formulated precisely so far. Thus, we can't argue for sure that the indirect route would be functional in aiding lexical access in spite of the irregularity of English. Instead, we would like to present a process in language comprehension that indicates that such cooperative access does go on, and that a route that is more error-prone or "noisier" can in fact help a system that is less error-prone.

When we comprehend speech, there are usually two "routes": the sound of the speech and the visual information about the position of the mouth (primarily the lips). Both clearly convey information, since (a) we can comprehend speech when we don't see the speaker and (b) some deaf people can make reasonable sense out of "speech" just from reading the lips. Moreover, we have the clear impression that looking at the speaker helps in comprehension. Yet it is clear that reading the lips alone is inadequate for fully understanding speech (certain differences in the speech signal are not reflected in the external appearance of the face and mouth).

Thus it appears that the lip system must help the sound system in speech comprehension in much the way we are arguing that the analogy/rule sound system helps the direct visual system in reading. Furthermore, there is evidence that the lip information is integrated with the sound information in such a cooperative analysis. McGurk and McDonald (1976) have shown that if subjects see a videotape of a mouth saying /ga/ while they simultaneously hear /ba/ on the soundtrack, they will perceive the sound as /da/. This makes sense in terms of a cooperative computation model, since "da" is similar to both "ga" and "ba"; as a neighbor of both, "da" may get more total excitation from the two channels (sound and visual) than either "ga" or "ba."

Another point that needs to be made is that most irregular words in English are not that irregular. Most of the ones studied in the regularity-effect experiments merely have one irregular sound, usually a vowel (e.g., PINT). Even in the case of more irregular words such as ONE, while the rules would completely miss the initial /w/ sound, they would correctly predict that the final consonant sound was /n/ and would get a reasonable approximation to the vowel sound. The regularity effect might only get a clear test if the language included wildly irregular words (such as if DROON were a word and it was pronounced /step/). In fact, there appears to be a clear difference in naming times for wildly irregular words such as CHOIR and regular words (Baron and Strawson 1976; Seidenberg et al. 1984a). Thus some of the inconsistency between experiments on the regularity effect may be because some experiments used only the mildly irregular words and got negligible effects as a result. In fact, Seidenberg et al. (1984a) report large differences between what they dub "strange words" (such as CHOIR) and regular words, and smaller differences between "normal" irregular words such as PINT and regular words. They claim that the effect obtained with strange words is not due to their unusual pronunciation but to their unusual orthographic structure (many are "loan words" from other languages). Thus, they want to conclude from the same data that there is no regularity effect on high-frequency words and only a small regularity effect on low-frequency words: Strange words are slower not because they are irregular but because they look weird. Unfortunately, because there appear to be few, if any, words in English that look weird but are not irregular or vice versa, there is no easy way to resolve this problem. One possibility is to test subjects like the deep dyslexics or phonemic dyslexics who presumably do not use the sound system to access the lexicon. If Seidenberg et al. are correct, these subjects should find strange words hard to access because of their unusual orthography, whereas if access of strange words is slow for normal readers because of the irregularity of their pronunciation, the difference between strange and normal words should disappear for these subjects.

CROSS-CULTURAL STUDIES OF WORD PERCEPTION

Throughout the second half of this chapter, we have focused on two major issues. We have discussed how letters within words are processed and we have discussed the role that sound plays in word perception. We have argued that letters within words are processed in parallel, and presented a model of how letter recognition and word identification interact. We have also suggested that there are two routes to the lexicon, one that goes directly from the printed letters to the lexicon (a direct route) and one that involves initially transforming the printed letters into a sound representation and accessing the lexicon via the sound representation (an indirect route). To what extent are the conclusions that we have reached generalizable to languages other than English?

First, with respect to the issue of the importance of letter processing, we suspect that what we have said holds true for any alphabetic system. With logographic systems, the issue is something of a moot point because the printed characters represent word units. Hence, it is clear by definition that all of the characters have to be processed in such a system. With syllabaries, while we know of no direct evidence on the issue, we also suspect that the points we have made would hold true.

The second issue, the role of sound representations in accessing the lexicon, is more interesting and has been studied rather extensively (Henderson 1982, 1984; Hung and Tzeng 1981). Numerous studies have been conducted to compare (1) word perception in alphabetic systems with *shallow* orthographies (i.e., those with a close correspondence between letters and phonemes) like Serbo-Croatian (Feldman and Turvey 1983; Katz and Feldman 1983; Lukatela et al. 1980; Lukatela et al. 1978; Turvey, Feldman, and Lukatela 1984) with alphabetic systems with *deep* orthographies (i.e., those in which morphemic properties are more directly related by the writing system) like English, (2) syllabaries to English (Besner and Hildebrandt 1987; Morton and Sasanuma 1984), and (3) logographic systems to English (Tzeng, Hung, and Wang 1977). In addition, there has been some interest in comparing Hebrew (where critical information used in converting to the sound representation is not explicitly contained in the print) to English (Bentin, Bargai, and Katz 1984; Navon and Shimron 1981).

Generally, our impression is that the results of the studies mentioned above (and others) lead to the conclusion that the specific orthography may alter the extent to which a reader relies on one route or the other, but that the results are consistent with the hypothesis that cross-culturally there are two routes to the lexicon. The work done on Serbo-Croatian has led some investigators (Turvey et al. 1984) to argue that accessing the lexicon via the sound representation is not an optional strategy for readers of that language. However, there is reason to suspect that readers of that language can also access the lexicon via the direct route (Besner and Hildebrandt 1987; Seidenberg and Vidanovic 1985). The regularity of the letter-to-phoneme correspondence in a shallow orthography like Serbo-Croatian may simply lead readers to rely more heavily on the route through sound to the lexicon. Likewise, logographic systems (like the Japanese Kanji) might lead to a heavier reliance on the direct visual route than English (Morton and Sasanuma 1984). It has been suggested (Morton and Sasanuma 1984) that syllabic systems (like the Japanese Kana) have to be translated into a phonological code before lexical access is possible. However, Besner and Hildebrandt (1987) recently reported evidence consistent with the conclusion that the lexical access of words written in Kana can be achieved without reference to phonology. Finally, studies with Hebrew readers (Bentin, Bargai, and Katz 1984; Navon and Shimron 1981) show that although the direct route is very important in lexical access, the phonological route is used by these readers even though the print is more irregular than English in coding the cues used for making a translation into a phonological representation.

In summary, our argument is that while different writing systems may influence readers to rely more heavily on one route than the other, the present evidence suggests that both routes are used in all languages. Once readers have acquired the ability to decipher the written symbols, reading may be a culture-free cognitive activity (Gibson and Levin 1975; Hung and Tzeng 1981) in the sense that the writing system may have little effect on the process of reading. Thus, we believe that the points we will stress in the remainder of this book are generally true cross-culturally. Of course, differences in cultures and the structures of languages may have profound influences on how people comprehend both spoken and written discourse. Such concerns, however, are largely beyond the scope of the current book.

PROCESSING SIMPLE AND COMPLEX WORDS

Most of the literature on the identification of words that we have discussed has used short (3- to 6-letter) words. The word-superiority effect experiments (and simulations) have virtually all used 4-letter words. The regularity literature we have just discussed employs a somewhat wider range of words, but a majority are still 6 to 7 letters or fewer and have only one *morpheme* (unit of meaning). Moreover, almost all the words used were nouns with a sprinkling of verbs and adjectives. Thus, our picture of word identification is incomplete. In this section, we will explore two additional kinds of words. First, we will briefly discuss *function words* (prepositions, conjunctions, articles, and pronouns), for there is some evidence that they may be processed differently than the types of words we have discussed so far. We will then discuss what is known about the processing of complex words. Since the bulk of the research on word identification is not in these areas, our picture will remain sketchy.

Function Words

Psycholinguists often make a distinction between *function words,* which include prepositions, conjunctions, articles, and pronouns, and *content words,* which include nouns, verbs, and adjectives. While there is fairly general agreement that the two classes of words may be psychologically different, there is some uncertainty about the precise boundary between the two (e.g., most people don't know where to put adverbs). One way in which function and content words appear to be different is that function words are a *closed class;* that is, there is a relatively small number of them in the language (roughly a few hundred) and that is all. In contrast, content words are an *open class:* the number of nouns, verbs, and adjectives is not only large but not bounded, with new ones probably being invented each day. Another difference is that most content words "mean something" in a way that function words do not: A content word such as *tree* means something in isolation, but *and* means little in isolation. (However, locational prepositions, such as *above,* and pronouns seem to be about as meaningful as content words.) One possible test of "meaningfulness" would be whether an isolated word could be a meaningful utterance: One could envisage the noun *dog,* the verb *climb,* the adjective *red,* or even the abstract noun *democracy* being uttered in isolation to express something, but not the function word *of.* Most function words seem to have meaning only as joiners of content words—they are the glue that holds sentences together. Function words are also among the most frequent words in the language (*the* is the most frequent).

Much of the data suggesting that function words are special comes from the neuropsychological literature. Perhaps the most striking finding is that there are people with brain damage whose ability to read aloud and comprehend content words is virtually intact, but whose ability to read aloud and comprehend function words is markedly impaired (Coltheart, Patterson, and Marshall 1980). This pattern of deficits occurs for many of the phonemic dyslexics described earlier. It also occurs for many patients with *aphasia* (i.e., general language problems), especially for a class of patients with *Broca's aphasia*. (Patients with Broca's aphasia usually have difficulty uttering function words in spontaneous speech as well, so that their speech is "telegrammatic.") Phenomena such as these suggest that function words may be represented in a lexicon separate from content words.

One interesting experiment on the representation of function words involved patients with Broca's aphasia (Bradley, Garrett, and Zurif 1980). They found that normal subjects had no word-frequency effects with function words in a lexical decision task in contrast to the usually large word-frequency effect for content words. On the other hand, Broca's aphasics had a large word-frequency effect for both types of words. Such a result would indeed indicate a radically different storage or retrieval mechanism for function words. However, a subsequent experiment failed to replicate the Bradley, Garrett, and Zurif result. With normal subjects, Gordon and Caramazza (1982) obtained equal frequency effects on lexical decision time for open and closed class words. Thus, the exact nature of the distinction between open and closed class words is still unclear.

Complex Words

We mentioned above that there is no limit to the number of content words in a language. In fact, one of the striking aspects of human language is the generativeness of words. One way that new words are generated is to describe new places, concepts, or technological inventions. However, new words are also generated in profusion from old words. If by a "word" we mean something set off by spaces, there are languages in which new words are created every minute. For example, in German, one can either say, "the man who came over to dinner last Tuesday night" or, "the cameoverfordinnerlastTuesdaynight man." While English is not so extreme, new compound words such as *headroom* are probably being constructed each day. In fact, we are often not clear on what a word is: do you write *wire service* as one word, as two words, or do you hedge and hyphenate it?

The question we would like to raise is whether the lexical-access model proposed so far is really adequate to explain the full spectrum of words. One reason to believe that the parallel letter processing models we have considered so far may be inadequate for recognizing all words is that it may be unreasonable that all words whose meaning you know are actually stored in the lexicon. As mentioned earlier in the chapter, there are books that have tabulated the frequency of usage of English words (taken from a corpus of text such as magazine articles and books). There are many words that do not seem at all strange (e.g., ABUSIVE, CREASES, PONDER, THINNING) that have a frequency of usage of 1 part in 1 million. Even if one assumes that high school students have each read something like 4,000 pages of text a year for 10 years, and if a typical page has about 500 words on it, they have only read something like 4,000 × 10 × 500, or 20,000,000, words in their life. Thus, they have *seen* words in the 1 per million category only an *average* of 20 times in their lives. But because of statistical fluctuation, the chances are pretty good that there are many of these words in this category that they have never seen. Moreover, there are many forms of a lot of words. For the words listed above, are you confident that you have seen them in the past tense (if they are verbs) or the plural (if they are nouns)? Yet you would likely be able to recognize those words easily if you encountered them. Moreover, there are various forms of words (e.g., CHARACTER, CHAR-ACTERISTIC, CHARACTERISTICS, CHARACTERISTICALLY). It seems not unreasonable that some of these forms are not actually stored, but instead are constructed from a "base form" and some sort of rule.

Even if all words are actually stored, however, there might be good reasons to have a more complex access procedure than a single-stage parallel look-up. First of all, there might be a limit to how many letters can be accessed in parallel by the visual system. Thus, there may be some sort of sequential access for longer words, whereby they are accessed a part at a time. Since short words appear to be processed in parallel, however, the most plausible size for the units of sequential access would appear to be larger than a single letter and perhaps on the order of 4 letters or so. A second reason for some sort of sequential access is that it might aid understanding the word. That is, almost any linguistic analysis would indicate that the meaning of the word ENDED is *end* + past tense. If lexical access were in two stages, the meaning might be understood as a part of the access process rather than requiring an additional step.

The most well-developed and interesting model of sequential access has been proposed by Taft and Forster (1975) and modified subsequently (e.g., Taft 1979, 1985, 1986). In the original version, which we are still most comfortable with, the first stage of lexical access is accessing the *root morpheme*. The way the root morpheme is defined is somewhat different for the two types of polymorphemic words. *Affixed words,* the first type, have a stem and prefixes and suffixes (e.g., *END*ING, IN*CLUDE, SELECT*IVE, UN*DO*ING). For these words, the root morpheme (in italics in the examples) is simply the stem to which the prefixes and suffixes are added. The second type is *compound words,* such as HEADSTAND and TOAD-STOOL, which are made up of two essentially equal morphemes (both of which are usually words). Taft and Forster define the root morpheme of compound words to be the first morpheme. This definition goes against more linguistically motivated definitions such as Selkirk's (1982) because for most compound words in English, the second morpheme is the "root": a *headstand* is a type of stand and a *footstool* is a type of stool.

According to the Taft and Forster (1975, 1976) model, both classes of complex words are accessed by the same basic process: (a) initial access is to the root morpheme; (b) subsequently the actual word is accessed. A "file drawer" metaphor might help to explain the idea (Forster 1976). Initial access of the root morpheme allows you access to a file drawer with all the words containing the root morpheme in it. For example, in the case of ENDING, the file drawer accessed would have all words with END as the root morpheme such as ENDED, ENDING, ENDPLAY, ENDGAME. When the file drawer is accessed, search for the lexical item is restricted to these items.

While Taft and Forster's model makes the decomposition of complex words the central focus of lexical access, they do not deal with the generativeness of forming words. In fact, they assume that all the forms are stored in the file drawer rather than being constructed through rules. Our prior discussion suggests that it is likely that some complex words are constructed rather than accessed; however, there is no data on this one way or the other. Thus, we will focus (as do the researchers in the area) on whether a two-stage model of access involving decomposition is a viable theory of lexical access.

Perhaps the experiment that gives the best feeling for Taft and Forster's model is one in which subjects made lexical decisions on prefixed words. Taft (1979) coded the words for both the "surface frequency" (the frequency of the compound word itself) and for the "root morpheme frequency" (the sum of the frequency of all words containing the root morpheme). If access of complex words were merely a look-up of each word in a separate lexical entry, then one would expect the surface frequency to predict lexical decision time. In fact, Taft found that lexical decision time was affected by the frequency of the root morpheme even when the surface frequency was equated. However, Taft also got an effect of surface frequency when root-morpheme frequency was equated. Bradley (1979) carried out a similar experiment using suffixed words. For two types (words ending in -MENT and -NESS), she got only effects of root-morpheme frequency, but for the third type (ending in -ION), she got effects of neither frequency.

The explanation for Taft's result seems pretty straightforward. If the first stage of lexical decision time is accessing the root morpheme (or file drawer), then the frequency of the root morpheme should be a major determiner of lexical access time. How does surface frequency come into play in Taft and Forster's model? They view search through the file drawer as a sequential process, so that all that matters is the relative frequency of the entries in the drawer (i.e., how far down the list is the entry you are searching for). Thus, if the target word is second in the file drawer, the time to find it in the file should be the same regardless of how much less frequent it is than the first word in the file. Thus, the lower the surface frequency, the lower the word should be in the file drawer. However, how far down it is depends not only on its own frequency but on other items in the file as well. Thus, it is hard to predict how far down a word should be just from its surface frequency, except to say that it *generally* should be further down. Thus, Taft's results seem more consonant with Taft and Forster's model than Bradley's, although Bradley's results are not necessarily inconsistent with the model. (No model would easily predict why there was no frequency effect for the -ION words.)

A second line of evidence that complex words are accessed in morphemic pieces comes from priming experiments (Stanners et al. 1979). As with the priming studies described earlier in the chapter, the lexical-decision task was employed; however, the priming differed in two significant ways. First, the "prime" is not merely associatively related to the target word (like DOCTOR-NURSE), but is either the word itself or a morphemically related word. Second, the interval between the prime and target is much longer than in the associative priming studies, where the interval is usually a second or less. In most of the morphemic priming experiments, the interval between the prime and target is at least 10 or so intervening items and thus about 10 to 20 seconds. (There would likely be no priming effect over that long an interval for associated words such as DOCTOR-NURSE [Gough, Alford, and Holley-Wilcox 1981].)

Stanners et al. (1979) observed that subjects were over 100 msec faster on repeated strings than on nonrepeated strings even over these long intervals between target and prime. The key finding was that the priming effect on a word such as START was as large when it was preceded by STARTED as when it was preceded by START. If we assume that the amount of priming indexes the similarity of the access of the target to the access of the prime, then this result suggests that lexical access of STARTED involves all the processes of the lexical access of START and then some additional ones. In contrast, consistent with the model, when the stem START is used as a prime and the whole word STARTED is used as a target, there was only partial priming (Stanners et al. 1979).

The story gets more complicated, as you might expect. If a verb is less transparently related to its root, then there is only a partial priming effect. For example, SPOKEN will prime SPEAK, but only about half as much as SPEAK primes SPEAK. In addition, *derivational* affixes (affixes that change the part of speech) appear to behave differently than *inflections* (affixes that change tense or number) even when the derivation is transparent (e.g., SELECTIVE primed SELECT only about half as much as SELECT did). Thus, Stanners et al. (1979) found that the priming effect depends both on the transparency of the relationship between the complex word and its root and on the type of morphemic relation.

These experiments clearly show that morphemic decomposition is implicated in the lexical-decision task. However, as mentioned earlier, some researchers have serious misgivings about the lexical-decision task as an index of lexical access (e.g., Balota and Chumbley 1984; Seidenberg et al. 1984b): They feel that the lexical-decision task is tapping postlexical-decision processes as well. Unfortunately, it may be difficult to tap lexical access for complex words employing other tasks. For example, naming latency (i.e., the time to *begin* the pronunciation of a word) may suffer from the opposite problem as lexical decision. That is, people may begin pronouncing complex words well before they have completely accessed them. Categorization tasks tend to be difficult, since many polymorphemic words are either difficult to categorize or the categorization may depend only on the root morpheme. Perhaps the best task to employ would be to measure the time to *finish* saying the word. However, it is technically much more difficult to measure the offset of a spoken word than the onset (since it is usually more gradual), and thus this technique has not been used.

Given the above problem, can we convince ourselves that the above experiments really do say something about decomposing complex words as a stage of lexical access? First, let's consider the priming experiments. If we find that a morphemically related word such as STARTED primes START, what possible explanations are there for the phenomenon that would not involve decomposition at the point of lexical access? The first possibility is that the whole priming phenomenon is postlexical. That is, that the faster time for END when it is repeated has nothing to do with the speed of accessing the word, but instead is speeding up the decision (i.e., responding "yes" to that thing earlier makes it easier to respond "yes" now). One argument against that argument is that one gets positive priming from nonword stems such as VOLVE (which get "no" responses) to word targets such as INVOLVE (Stanners, Neiser, and Painton 1979).

A second possibility is that priming is getting at lexical access, but that the decomposition effects occur after lexical access of the prime. That is, after lexically accessing STARTED, one then decomposes it as *start* + past tense in order to understand it; the *start* that is created in this postlexical decomposition is what primes START later. While such postlexical decomposition may be part of the effect, we feel that the data argue pretty strongly that it can't be the whole effect. First, if that were all that was going on, it is hard to see why SPOKEN wouldn't prime SPEAK as strongly as STARTED primes START. Perhaps there are two effects: this postlexical morphemic priming and priming just due to letter overlap. However, there is evidence that mere letter overlap has no effect: e.g., ARSON does not prime SON at all, while DISHONEST primes HONEST (Lima 1987b). Similarly, in a tachistoscopic recognition experiment, BORING is primed by BORE but not by BORN (Murrell and Morton 1974). Thus, it appears that at least some of the priming effect is due to decomposition of the word during lexical access.

Moreover, if decomposition is postlexical, it is hard to understand why STARTED should prime START as strongly as START itself does. The fact that START and STARTED prime START equally suggests that, as Taft and Forster predict, the first stage of lexical access for END and ENDED is virtually identical. On the other hand, Taft and Forster would not predict any priming from SPOKEN to SPEAK since the root for SPOKEN is either *spoken* or *spok-* while the root for SPEAK is *speak-*. Thus, it appears either that some of the priming effect is postlexical or that the sequential access is operating in a different fashion than postulated by Taft and Forster.

Suffixes in English can be divided into two classes: inflections and derivations. Inflections are suffixes that change the tense or number of verbs or the number of nouns but preserve the part of speech. On the other hand, derivations are suffixes that change the part of speech such as -LY, -NESS, -ITY, -IVE. As mentioned earlier, in the experiments of Stanners et al., inflections whose stems appear in the target word (e.g., *STARTED*) produce full priming, but derivations whose stems appear in the target word (e.g., *SELECTIVE*) produce only partial priming. An unsolved problem is why this difference occurs. Taft and Forster have to explain such effects by postulating different orderings in the file drawer. Consider the inflected case. In the END- file drawer would be *end, ended, ending*. If we assume that *end* itself is first (because it is most frequent), then full priming from ENDED to END would occur; accessing *ended* would imply having accessed *end* since *end* is above *ended* in the file drawer. On the other hand, there may be many derivational forms such as SELECTIVE that may be at least as common as the uninflected versions (i.e., SELECTIVE may be at least as common as SELECT).

Another possible explanation for the difference is that there may be a qualitative difference in what happens when you get in the file drawer. In the case of derivations, there is a rule (admittedly with exceptions) for how you form past tense or plurals, for example, that applies to every word. In contrast, there are several ways to change verbs to adjectives (e.g., SELECT-SELECTIVE, DIFFER-DIFFERENT), which, in addition, have different meanings (e.g., the SELECTIVE noun is doing the selecting while the DIFFERENT noun is not doing the differing). Moreover, there are some verbs for which no appropriate derivation exists (e.g., PROCESS-?). This raises the possibility that inflections may be constructed by rule, whereas derivations are accessed by a specific entry in the file drawer. That is, access of all inflections entails accessing of the stem, whereas access of a derivation may not entail access of the root because they are different entries in the file drawer.

One problem for the morphemic decomposition model is how the system knows how to decompose the word. One possibility advanced by Taft (1979, 1985, 1986) is that there is an orthographic principle that defines what the first unit is rather than the first morpheme. His rule is (roughly) to take as many consonants as possible following the first vowel, and Taft dubbed this unit, which accesses the file drawer, the *BOSS* (Basic Orthographic Syllabic Structure). Much of the research on the BOSS is plagued with conflicting results, however. One piece of evidence (Taft 1979) for the BOSS is that splitting up even monomorphenic words such as LANTERN with the BOSS as the first chunk (e.g., LANT ERN) aids lexical decision times relative to splitting up the words according to phonetic syllables (i.e., LAN TERN) and to leaving them unsplit (e.g., LAN TERN). However, Lima and Pollatsek (1983) failed to replicate this effect. They found that any gap in the word was worse than if there was no gap, and furthermore found no difference between the BOSS division and the phonetic syllable division. A second paradigm devised by Lima and Pollatsek employed a priming technique, whereby the first part of a word was presented (e.g., LANT or LAN) and followed by the whole word 90 msec later. They similarly found no evidence for the BOSS (no difference between the priming effect for LANT and LAN) in monomorphemic words. Taft (1987) has recently found a difference between these conditions, however, although he used a larger interval between prime and target (250 msec). Another finding against the BOSS is that when compound words were used and the BOSS was different from the first morpheme (e.g., TEA is the first morpheme, but TEASP is the BOSS of TEASPOON), Lima and Pollatsek found that there was priming only when the morpheme was the prime. Thus, evidence for the BOSS is fairly shaky, and at present, it appears that the only safe statement we can make is that lexical access appears to involve (at least on some occasions) accessing the root morpheme.

You may have noticed that we have avoided talking about prefixes. Prefixed words present a problem, since the beginning of prefixed words is not the root. In addition, there are many "pseudoprefixed" words (e.g., REPERTOIRE) that look like prefixed words. Taft (1981) also developed a process to deal with prefixes. He hypothesized that if a word started with something that could be a prefix, the system assumed that it was in fact a prefix, stripped it off, and then located the root morpheme (e.g., RE would be stripped off REJUVENATE, and then the word looked up under the root which would be *juvenate* or some part). In the case of a pseudoprefixed word, Taft hypothesized that RE would be stripped from REPERTOIRE, the lexical entry "pertoire" searched for, and only when not located, would the lexical entry "repertoire" be searched for. He found that lexical decision times were faster for prefixed words than pseudoprefixed words; however, the difference was only about 30 msec—not plausibly the time to strip, search, and then search again. What seems more plausible is that access is going on in parallel, with Taft's decomposition route being faster than the direct route. The advantage of prefixed words over pseudoprefixed words also gives us hope for the lexical-decision task; Lima (1987a) got a similar advantage for prefixed words in a reading task, where her dependent variable was the amount of time readers fixated on the word.

A second result that argues for the dual-route theory is one obtained with suffixed and "pseudosuffixed" words. Here, there is no difference in the absolute time to make lexical decisions to the suffixed and pseudosuffixed words (e.g., SISTER vs. SENDER), but there is a route-priming effect whereby a pair of words of one class will be responded to more rapidly than a mixed pair (Manelis and Tharp 1976).

To summarize, it appears that the theory that all words are recognized through a direct look-up in the lexicon is probably too simple. At least some morphemically complex words appear to be accessed through a sequential look-up whereby the root morpheme is accessed followed by accessing the rest of the word. The data are less clear about whether there is some sort of orthographic principle that will account for how words are decomposed.

At present, this area of word processing is still quite undeveloped. One issue that has not been explored is the "grammar" of complex words (Selkirk 1982). For complex combinations such as *undeveloped*, which is both prefixed and inflected, there appear to be rules indicating how to compose the units. That is, *undeveloped* is formed by first going from *develop* to *developed* and then adding *un*. To see why this is true, consider *undevelop*. This is not a word, and if it were, it would have a different meaning than *undeveloped* (i.e., it would mean to actively undo something that was developed). This argument suggests a constructive aspect to processing complex words rather than (or in addition to) the relatively simple sequential look-up posited by Taft and Forster.

SUMMARY AND CONCLUSIONS

At the beginning of the chapter, we raised several questions about the processing of words. Some of them have turned out to have simpler answers than others. One question that was raised was whether word processing was an automatic process or whether identifying words was a major part of the mental effort that went into reading. We saw that words in isolation (at least relatively common and short words) could be identified without awareness and without intention, a seemingly automatic process. While it was far from clear that the activity involves no mental effort, the process of identifying words appears to be a relatively small part of the mental effort in reading *for the skilled reader*. We will discuss in detail the effects of context on word identification in subsequent chapters. The data from this chapter, however, allow us to make an educated guess as to what the answer will be. Since accessing the meaning of words is such an automatic and easy process when words are seen in isolation, we wouldn't expect context to speed up processing very much, if at all. We also would be surprised if identifying words in text was performed in a substantially different way than words in isolation, since it would seem wasteful to have two different machineries, each of which is so rapid and accurate.

The second conclusion is related to the first. Letters in words (at least short words) appear to be processed in parallel. To many in cognitive psychology, parallel processing is the hallmark of automatic processing. If something is done in series then it requires an attentive mechanism and therefore probably takes processing capacity.

The rest of our discussion did not yield any simple answers. In fact, the data make clear that the identification of words is a very complex process—much more than one might have supposed at the outset. A direct visual look-up, whereby the letters access a word in parallel, appears to be a necessary ingredient of fluent word identification. Otherwise, irregular words could not be recognized. However, using rules (or some equivalent analogue process) to access a word through a sound code does not seem to be necessary for accessing the meaning of a word, since irregularly spelled words can be identified easily. Moreover, certain patients who appear to be severely impaired in their ability to use rules to access sound codes are relatively normal in their ability to extract the meaning of content words. (Their fluency, however, may be impaired.)

Sound encoding appears to play some part in accessing the meaning of words in fluent reading; however, it is less clear exactly what the role is. In some views, the role is very minor: the sound system may matter only for processing a few low-frequency words (Seidenberg et al. 1984a). This conclusion is based on the small regularity effect which appears only for low-frequency words. There are data that lead to a different conclusion. First, even high-frequency words may be biased by sound codes (Meyer, Schvaneveldt, and Ruddy 1974) and words (or even pseudowords) can be misclassified as their homophones (Van Orden 1987). A major problem in deciding on the role of sound in word encoding is that irregularities in the language are usually quite minor, so that it is not clear whether one should expect a large regularity effect in the first place. There is no simple resolution to the problem. The position we have taken is that the data are consistent with a cooperative computation model, wherein entries in the lexicon are excited both by the direct visual route and by the indirect rule to sound route, with the recognized word being the entry that has accrued the most combined excitation. That is, we see the sound system as involved in most lexical access. At present, however, reasonable people can hold almost diametrically opposite views on the subject. The common ground for all positions is that direct visual access is important and that sound encoding plays some part.

There was also evidence that morphemically complex words are probably looked up in two stages, possibly with the help of morphemic rules (e.g., Taft and Forster 1975, 1976; Taft 1985). Thus word encoding appears to involve three systems—the direct visual route, a spelling-to-sound route, and a morphemic-decomposition route, i.e., a direct route and two more constructive processes. Since most of the evidence that word processing is automatic comes from the study of relatively short frequent words (i.e., those for which the direct route could predominate), it is possible that word processing is not so automatic for words whose access relies more heavily on the more constructive routes.

We should emphasize that this chapter has for the most part dealt with a relatively narrow window of word perception: We have discussed skilled readers of English reading print. However, our discussion of cross-cultural studies led us to conclude that the points we stressed were generally true for other writing systems. We have focused on English because it has been studied far more intensively than any other language. We have not discussed handwriting, since there is little data on recognition of handwriting. It is possible, however, that the perception of handwriting operates differently from print. First, since handwriting is often quite messy, sentential context may be more important in deciphering it than print. Second, since letters are not transparent visual units as in print, more constructive processes may be needed in addition to automatic letter detection.

Let us close with some comments on the relevance of the study of skilled readers to the process of learning to read. The better we understand the word-identification process in skilled readers, the better we understand what the *goal* of instruction should be. However, even a perfect understanding of the skilled reader may say little about the beginning reader. At one extreme, the adult reader may be exactly like the beginning reader, but may do everything much faster and in a much more "automated" way. At the other extreme, the beginning processes may be a crutch to get over some hurdle so that skilled reading may involve totally different processes than that of beginning reading. Thus, there may be little in the processes of skilled reading that indicates how the reader acquired those skills. We will discuss these issues in depth in chapters 9 and 10. The point we wish to leave you with is that much of the research and many of the issues in learning to read have been framed by the research on skilled reading of words that we have discussed in this chapter.

PART TWO
SKILLED READING OF TEXT

In reading text, we do much more than identify words. However, identification of words is clearly an important first step in comprehending text. As the eyes move across the printed page, presumably words are first identified and then glued together into larger structures such as phrases, sentences, and paragraphs. From these larger structures we are able to understand or comprehend the text we are reading. We are able to infer the gist of the text or infer certain relationships and store this information in memory. The central task in reading research is to understand how all this is accomplished by the reader. If we are really to understand the *process* of reading, we would like to know the details of this cognitive activity from moment to moment. For example, if a sentence such as "The man bit the dog" is read, we would like to know when and how each word was identified, when and how the reader identified the man as the actor and the dog as the recipient of the action, and when and how the reader realized that the sentence was grammatically correct but mildly absurd.

A central tenet of this book is that the record of how the eyes move during silent reading of text is by far the best way to study the *process* of reading. Other methods are useful (such as the single-word methods described in the previous chapter), but usually disturb the process of reading sufficiently so that one is never sure whether the conclusions drawn from them would generalize to normal silent reading. Since eye movements can be measured relatively unobtrusively when someone is silently reading text, they allow us to study real reading. In addition to being unobtrusive, the eye-movement record does allow us quite a bit of insight into the cognitive processes of reading (as the next several chapters will document). However, understanding the relationship of eye movements to cognitive processes in reading requires mastering some technical detail.

The plan of the next several chapters is as follows. In chapters 4 and 5, we will discuss how visual information is extracted from the printed page. Chapter 4 will present some basic facts about eye movements and discuss what information is extracted from the page on a single glance or *fixation.* Chapter 5 will then continue the discussion by examining the flow of information when the eyes move across the page during the skilled act of silent reading. More specifically, we will try to determine to what extent cognitive events control eye movements and try to relate the acquisition of the information from the printed page to the movements of the eyes. Since these two chapters focus on extraction of visual information, they naturally focus on the identification of words.

We will then move to issues beyond the indentification of words. As a bridge, we will discuss the role of inner speech in silent reading in Chapter 6. As we shall see, an important function of inner speech is in helping to integrate words into larger units. Section 3 examines how sentences are understood and how the larger mental structures that are constructed by the reader from the text influence the process of reading. Sections 2 and 3 will thus summarize our present understanding of the process of skilled reading.

CHAPTER FOUR
THE WORK OF THE EYES

When we read, we have the impression that the eyes (and mind) sweep continuously across the text except for a few places in which we encounter difficulty, and at those points, we pause to consider what we have just read or regress (go back) to reread earlier material. However, that impression is an illusion.

The two eyes move pretty much in synchrony with each other across the page (Rayner 1978a; Tinker 1958), but their progress is not continuous. The eyes come to rest for periods that are usually between 150 and 500 milliseconds (msec): These periods when the eye is close to immobile are called *fixations*. Between the fixations are periods where the eye is moving rapidly. These eye movements are called *saccades* after the French word for "jump." Saccades are *ballistic movements;* once started, they can not be altered. When we read, our eyes generally move forward about 7 to 9 character spaces with each saccade. The duration of the saccades in reading varies with the distance moved, with a typical saccade taking about 20 to 35 msec. Since, for all practical purposes, no visual information is extracted from the printed page during saccades, all visual information comes in during fixations.

The pattern of information extraction during reading is thus a bit like seeing a slide show. You see a "slide" for about a quarter of a second, there is a brief "off time," and then a new "slide" of a different view of the page appears for about a quarter of a second. This pattern of fixations and saccades is not unique to reading. The perception of any static display (such as a picture or a scene) proceeds the same way, although the pattern and timing of fixations may differ from that in reading. The only exception is when the eyes track a moving target. In that case, the eyes move relatively smoothly and useful visual information is extracted during the eye movement.

The second way in which our subjective impression is an illusion is that the eyes do not move forward as relentlessly as we think. While most saccades in reading move forward, about 10 to 15 percent move backward and are termed *regressive saccades* (or *regressions* for short). Think of regressions this way: since we make about four to five saccades in a second, we make a regression about once every two seconds. Thus, we are certainly unaware of most regressions. While some regressions reflect major confusion requiring us to go back a considerable distance in the text to straighten things out, the majority are quite short, only going back a few characters.

Another type of eye movement that is worth mentioning is the *return sweep*. This is when the eyes move from near the end of one line to near the beginning of the next. While return sweeps are right to left, they are not usually counted as regressions because they are moving the reader forward through the text. Return sweeps are actually quite complicated as they often start 5 to 7 character spaces from the end of the line and they generally go to about the third to seventh character space of the next line. While there is often an additional short right-to-left saccade after the large return sweep, the leftmost fixation is still sometimes on the second word of the line. Thus, most of the time about 80 percent of the line falls between the extreme fixations on it. (We shall explain why readers often may fail to fixate the beginning and end words of lines a bit later.) The small saccades following return sweeps are probably corrections for errors in aiming the eyes; it is difficult to execute a long saccade perfectly, since the eyes usually undershoot the target position. Since the details of such motor execution are peripheral to the concerns of most people studying reading and to our concerns here, most of the interest in eye-movement records is on what the eye does on the middle four-fifths of the line. Of course, return sweeps must be counted as well if one wants to get global measures of reading, such as the overall reading speed.

To summarize, the eyes move forward (about 7 to 9 character spaces on average) in reading, but not relentlessly so. They pause for periods of approximately 200 to 250 msec, and move backward about 10 to 15 percent of the time. In this chapter and the next, we will discuss in considerable detail much of the cognitive processing during all this activity and its relation to the ongoing pattern of eye movements. This topic is interesting in itself, as it is at the core of understanding visual cognition in reading and visual cognition more generally. In addition, understanding the details of the work of the eyes in reading is an invaluable tool for understanding the process of reading. We claim, in fact, that eye movements are by far the best tool to understand the process of normal silent reading (which undoubtedly accounts for well over 90 percent of the reading adults do). At the end of the next chapter, we will discuss alternative methods for studying reading of text (as opposed to individual words).

This chapter and the next deal with how visual information is extracted from text. The present chapter focuses on what useful information readers extract during fixations, while the next chapter focuses on how the eyes are guided through text. Necessary to understanding both topics is some basic information about eye movements in reading. These data will be far more meaningful, however, if we make them concrete by examining an example of an eye-movement record.

BASIC CHARACTERISTICS OF EYE MOVEMENTS

Figure 4.1 shows part of a page of text with a record of a reader's eye movements superimposed on the text. The average saccade length is about 8.5 characters, but the range is 1 character to 18 characters. Actually in some cases, fixations on the same letter have been combined in the record shown (the capability of doing this is contingent upon having a very accurate eye-movement recording system). The average fixation duration is 218 msec, but the range is 66 to 416 msec.

Notice that, for the most part, words are fixated only once. However, *enough* is fixated twice and *pain* and *least* are not fixated at all. Since a fixation lands on or near almost all words, it appears that a major purpose of eye movements is to bring all words close to the *fovea,* the region in the center of vision that is best for processing fine detail (see Chapter 1). However, what is causing the variability? Why are some words not fixated while others are fixated twice? Is this just miscalculation of the eye movement as in return sweeps, or does it reflect something deeper?

Similarly, why are fixation durations different? Does a long fixation time on a word indicate that the reader is taking more time processing the fixated word, or are these variations in fixation time random as well? Moreover, assuming that fixation times are not random (which indeed they are not), what fixation time do we use to index the processing time for a word? If there is a single fixation on a word, there is little choice: we simply measure the *fixation duration* on the word. However, consider the case of *brainstorm* in Figure 4.1. There are three likely candidates to measure processing time for the word. The first is the duration of the first fixation (or *first fixation duration*) which is 277 msec. (Using this measure assumes that later fixations on the word are getting at other processes, such as relating the material to earlier material, or are just mistakes of eye programming.) The second is *gaze duration,* which is the total fixation time on the word before the eye moves off (or 277 msec + 120 msec = 397 msec). (This measure assumes that the second fixation was needed to finish processing the fixated

Roadside joggers endure sweat, pain and angry drivers in the name of

	1	2		3		4			5	6	7		8
	286	221		246		277			256	233	216		188

fitness. A healthy body may seem reward enough for most people. However,

9		10	12		13		11		14	15	16			17	18		19
301		177	196		175		244		302	112	177			266	188		199

for all those who question the payoff, some recent research on physical

21		20	22	23	24			25	26		27
216		212	179	109	266			245	188		205

activity and creativity has provided some surprisingly good news. Regular

29	28		30	31		32	33		34		35		36	37
201	66		201	188		203	220		217		288		212	75

bouts of aerobic exercise may also help spark a brainstorm of creative

38		39	42	40	43		41	44		45		46		47	48
312		260	271	188	350		215	221		266		277		120	219
														50	
														179	

thinking. At least, this is the conclusion that was reached in a study that

49		51		52		53	54	57		55		56	60	59
266		213		210		216	416	200		177		113	206	220
							58							
							218							

FIGURE 4-1   An excerpt from a passage of text with fixation sequence and fixation durations indicated.

word.) The other obvious possibility is the *total viewing time*, which includes later fixations on the word that are the result of regressive saccades. In the case of *brainstorm*, the total viewing time would be 576 msec. (This measure assumes that the regression was made in order to continue processing the word in some way.)

Variation of Reading Measures

The record in Figure 4.1 is typical of adult readers. Figure 4.2 shows the distributions of individual fixation times and saccade lengths from a large corpus of data from adult readers. As can be seen in Figure 4.2, both the average saccade size and average fixation duration of our little segment (and the variability as well) are reasonably in agreement with the larger aggregation of data.

Text differences The averages and distributions in Figure 4.2 should not be regarded as numbers engraved in stone: reading measures such as

FIGURE 4-2 Frequency distribution of fixation duration (upper graph) and saccade length (lower graph) for eight college-age readers. Return sweeps of the eye have been excluded from the distribution. Short fixations following the return sweep, which are followed by corrective saccades, have also been excluded. (Reproduced with permission from Erlbaum.)

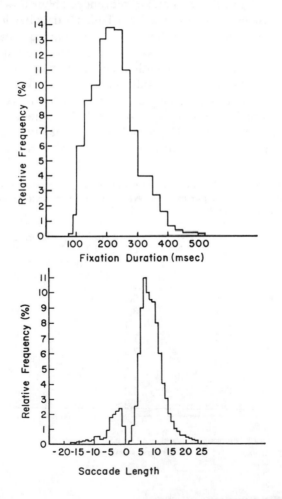

reading rate, mean fixation duration, mean saccade length, and percent of regressive fixations vary from text to text. Table 4.1 shows some of the variability for adults reading text on various topics, with apparently more difficult text requiring longer fixations, smaller saccades, more regressions, and hence a slower reading rate.

Typographic differences   Is the pattern of eye movements dependent upon typographic features, such as letter size, type of font, length of line? Tinker (1963, 1965) studied this question in some detail for English (see Morrison and Inhoff 1981 for a review of this work). His data are complex, but we believe the following brief summary captures the essence. First, the type of font made a minor difference, although all of the fonts that Tinker studied were (subjectively) relatively easy to read. There are some fonts that appear to be pathologically difficult (such as the elaborate script used in German known as "fractur"), and these may slow the reading process appreciably. However, we know of no experimental evidence of this.

Secondly, it is difficult to make inferences about how the size of the characters influences reading speed from Tinker's data because the size and the number of characters per line were confounded: there were more characters per line when the print was smaller (Morrison and Inhoff 1981). However, he also varied line length (keeping the size of the characters constant) in another study, and the differences he observed for differing size of characters appear to be explained by line-length effects. He found that there was an optimal line size of approximately 52 characters. This optimality is parsimoniously explained by a trade-off between two opposing factors. First, if the line is too long, return sweeps become increasingly difficult to

TABLE 4.1 Mean fixation duration, mean saccade length, proportion of fixations that were regressions, and words per minute (WPM) for 10 good college-age readers reading diferent types of text.

TOPIC	FIXATION DURATION[a]	SACCADE LENGTH[b]	REGRESSIONS (%)[c]	WPM
Light fiction	202	9.2	3	365
Newspaper article	209	8.3	6	321
History	222	8.3	4	313
Psychology	216	8.1	11	308
English literature	220	7.9	10	305
Economics	233	7.0	11	268
Mathematics	254	7.3	18	243
Physics	261	6.9	17	238
Biology	264	6.8	18	233
M	231	7.8	11	288

[a] In msec.
[b] In character spaces (4 character spaces = 1° of visual angle).
[c] Percentage of total fixations that were regressions.

execute and people may wind up on the wrong line. On the other hand, as we will shortly see, readers can extract information from more than one word on a line during a fixation (McConkie and Rayner 1975), but if lines are too short, readers can not take full benefit, as in the extreme case of one word per line. The optimal line length thus appears to be the best compromise between these opposing design considerations. We should remark, however, that all these effects are relatively minor, so that the fundamental conclusion to be drawn from the work on typography is that reading appears to proceed at about the same rate if the type font, size, and length of line employed are at all reasonable.

Reading distance differences In reading, the average saccade is about 7 to 9 character spaces long, or about 2 degrees of visual angle at normal reading distance. However, the value of 7 to 9 character spaces appears to be the more fundamental in that the average saccade size is 7 to 9 characters regardless of the retinal size of the text. Thus, for example, regardless of whether a given text is 36 cm or 72 cm from the eyes, the average saccade length is still about 8 characters even though 8 characters subtends twice the visual angle at 36 cm as it does at 72 cm (Morrison and Rayner 1981; O'Regan 1983). This fact suggests that the visibility of the text is relatively invariant to absolute size over an extended range of distances. (You can try this out by holding this book at varying distances and see whether varying the distance affects the ease of reading.) As a result, all the data on saccades will be expressed in *character spaces,* which appear to be the natural metric in reading, rather than degrees of visual angle.

The fact that the distance of the text (and hence the absolute size of the characters) makes little difference on saccade size is probably due to a tradeoff between two factors: when the text is nearer, the letters are bigger and easier to see; however, when the text is nearer, a given letter will be further from the center of fixation, hence harder to see (see Chapter 1). Of course, there are limits; the text will be impossible to read if a mile away or against your face. By the way, when text is moved further away it is a bit harder to read: fixation durations become slightly longer, presumably because the letters are harder to discriminate.

Orthographic differences A question related to typographic differences, but more difficult to answer, is whether the writing system influences the process of reading. All of the information we presented in this chapter so far concerning eye movements is based on data collected from readers of English. Do the characteristics of eye movements change when people read text which uses other writing systems?

Some experiments have examined the patterns of eye movements of Chinese and Japanese readers. A major problem with comparing saccade sizes in English with either of these languages is what unit of measurement to use. The previous section implied that the letter (or character space) may be the fundamental unit of measurement for English. However, there are no letters in either of these languages: the characters stand for syllables or morphemes, or both (see Chapter 2). If one measures by "characters" (i.e., a letter is a character), then eye movements of Chinese and Japanese readers tend to be much smaller than eye movements of readers of English. Chinese readers move their eyes on average about 2 characters (Shen 1927; Stern 1978). (Remember that a character is a morpheme rather than a word, so that this is less than two words.) Readers of Japanese text, which is made up of morphemic characters (Kanji) and syllabic characters (Kana) on average move their eyes 3.6 characters (Ikeda and Saida 1978). This again is less than 3.6 words, since it often takes several characters to make a word. Since the average saccade length in English is about 7 to 9 characters, or about a word and a half, it appears that the average saccade length is if anything a bit less in English than in Chinese and Japanese if one equates for number of words or morphemes.

Readers of Hebrew also have smaller saccades (about 5.5 characters) than readers of English (Pollatsek et al. 1981). Hebrew varies structurally and orthographically from English in some important ways. First, not all vowels are represented orthographically in Hebrew. In addition, many function words in Hebrew are clitic, meaning they are attached like prefixes or suffixes to content words. The effect of these differences is that Hebrew sentences normally contain fewer words and fewer letters than their English counterparts. In short, though Hebrew is basically an alphabetic system, the information is more densely packed than in English.

The average saccade lengths of Chinese, Japanese, and Hebrew readers suggest that the informational density of the text determines how far the eyes move in each saccade. This finding seems consistent with the finding that, for readers of English, as the text becomes more difficult (and hence, the informational density is greater) saccade length decreases. However, it is an open question whether the differences in informational density across languages are best thought of in terms of the density of the meaning or the amount of visual information per character (measured perhaps by the number of strokes or lines in the character). For Hebrew, the characters seem of approximately equal complexity to English, so the differences between Hebrew and English are more likely to be explained by differences in amount of meaning per character. However, the Chinese and Japanese writing systems are so different from English that it is hard to say which type of informational density is operating to produce the differences in reading. We suspect that both the visual and semantic factors are contributing.

For readers of English, difficult text also increases the average fixation duration. Fixation durations tend to be longer for readers of Japanese, Chinese, and Hebrew than for readers of English. For example, the average fixation duration for Chinese readers is around 300 msec (Shen 1927) and for Israeli readers about 265 msec (Pollatsek et al. 1981). Despite the fact that reading in these languages is slower when measured superficially (saccade lengths are shorter and fixation durations are longer), reading rates, when measured in terms of amount of meaning extracted per unit time, seem to be equivalent. In fact, when the reading rate in Hebrew is based on the number of words in the English translations of the Hebrew sentences, the average reading rate for the Hebrew- and English-speaking subjects is nearly identical (Pollatsek et al. 1981).

One final dimension of orthographies is the direction in which the characters proceed. As we pointed out in Chapter 2, there were no clear conclusions that could be drawn about the effect of the direction of print on the eye movements or the efficiency of reading. In general, the results were consistent with the hypothesis that differences in the direction of print do not matter and that all differences observed in reading speed were because the more familiar orthography is read more easily (Shen 1927; Sun, Morita, and Stark 1985). A similar conclusion follows from laboratory experiments which manipulated the direction of print.

Tinker (1955), for example, found that readers of English initially read vertically arranged English 50 percent slower than horizontally arranged text. However, with 4 weeks of practice their reading speed was only 22 percent slower than for the horizontal text. In a number of studies, Kolers (1972) has also shown that with practice readers of English can read text arranged in a right-to-left fashion fairly well. Children learning to read can also read from right to left as easily as they read left to right (Clay 1979).

Relatively short amounts of practice in the laboratory did not abolish differences in reading rate as a function of the arrangement of text (Kolers 1972). However, Kolers' studies suggest that differences between arrangements of print, if they exist, are likely to be quite small. There is some physiological reason to believe that a horizontal arrangement in any language may be better: visual acuity falls off faster in the vertical direction than in the horizontal direction. However, the evidence that no direction of text appears to be preferred over any other suggests that this physiological fact may have a negligible effect on reading.

A Few Comments about Saccades and Fixations

At the beginning of this chapter, we claimed that reading was a "slide show" in which the eyes remained glued to the spot on the page for a certain period of time (the fixation) and then moved quickly with no visual information extracted during the move (the saccade). While these claims are essentially true, they are slight oversimplifications. We will briefly discuss the complexities, so that we can set the record straight. However, for the remainder of the chapter and book, these complexities are so insignificant that we can safely use the "slide show" metaphor.

Saccades First, let us consider the assertion we made that no visual information is extracted during a saccade. You can demonstrate for yourself that little is perceived during saccadic eye movements by looking in a mirror and trying to watch your eyes move. You will not see them do so. This reduced perceptability of stimulation during saccades was discovered almost 100 years ago (Dodge 1900; Holt 1903).

Why don't we see anything during the saccade? First, the eye is moving so fast during a saccade that the image painted on the eye by a fixed stimulus would be largely a smear and thus highly unintelligible. However, we aren't aware of any smear. Thus, there must be some mechanism suppressing the largely useless information that is "painted" on the retina during the saccade. One possible mechanism is "central anesthesia": when the brain knows that the eye is making (or about to make) a saccade, it sends out a signal to the visual system to ignore (or attenuate) all input from the eyes until the saccade is over. There is in fact evidence (Matin 1974) that the thresholds for stimuli shown during a saccade (or even a bit before it begins and after it ends) are raised, with the effect much more pronounced for stimuli presented during a saccade. This threshold raising before and after the saccade is not of much importance for reading, since the letters seen in text are far above threshold. Thus, it is not clear whether these relatively small threshold effects would mean that the ability to extract information from the text would be altered significantly. (That is, it might be like the difference between reading with a 60 watt bulb and reading with a 150 watt bulb.) However, the threshold effects are more likely to be significant with the moving eye, where the contrast between the light and dark parts of the smear would be far less.

For many years, central anesthesia was accepted as the main mechanism by which information during saccades was suppressed. However, more recent experiments indicate that a different mechanism explains at least part of the suppression and perhaps all of it. It can be demonstrated that under certain (unnatural) circumstances visual input during the saccade can be perceived (Uttal and Smith 1968): when the room is totally dark prior to and after the saccade and a pattern is presented only during the saccade, a smeared image of the pattern is perceived (Campbell and Wurtz 1978). Since the blur is thus seen if no visual stimulation precedes or follows it, the implication is that the information available prior to and after the saccade during normal vision *masks* the perception of any information acquired during the saccade. This phenomenon has been related to laboratory phenomena of masking, such as those used in subliminal priming experiments (see Chapter 3).

In sum, while we can't say for sure that absolutely *no* visual information is extracted during saccades in reading, the bulk of the evidence indicates that if visual information gets in during a saccade, it is of little practical importance. Indeed, Wolverton and Zola (1983) presented a mask during each saccade as subjects read text and it was not perceived nor did it affect reading in any way.

Fixations   Our claim that the eye is immobile during a fixation is a bit of an oversimplification. As indicated in Chapter 1, very small rapid movements, called *nystagmus,* go on constantly to help the nerve cells in the retina to keep firing. However, these are so small as to be of little practical importance in studying normal reading. There are also somewhat larger movements called *microsaccades* and *drifts.* While the reasons for these movements are not completely clear, it appears that the eye occasionally drifts (i.e., makes a small and rather slow movement) because of less than perfect control of the oculomotor system by the nervous system. When this happens, there is often a small (1 character or less) microsaccade (i.e., a much more rapid small movement) to bring the eye back to where it was. Many experimenters assume that such small movements are "noise" and adopt scoring procedures in which these small movements are ignored. For example, some scoring procedures will take successive fixations that are separated by a character or less and lump them together as a single fixation. Some microsaccades may be under cognitive control as other saccades are, and thus some experimenters believe that microsaccades should be treated no differently from other saccades. Another alternative is a more sophisticated pooling procedure in which fixations are pooled if the intervening saccade is a character or less *and* at least one of the fixations is short (100 msec or less).

Most eye-movement data in reading have been adjusted using some sort of procedure that pools some fixations and ignores at least some small drifts and microsaccades. In some cases, the eye movement recording system is not sensitive enough to detect these small movements, so that such movements are automatically ignored. Others, with more sensitive equipment, decide on some sort of criterion for pooling. Since drifts and microsaccades are relatively uninteresting aspects of the eye-movement record, and since there is enough complexity in the data without worrying about them, our subsequent discussion will ignore them for the most part.

Summary

We have summarized the basic facts about eye movements during reading. The eye moves about four or five times per second and jumps an average of about 7 to 9 characters each time it moves. However, it moves back about 10 to 15 percent of the time and there is large variability in both the extent of the forward motion and the amount of time it stays in a fixation. Since virtually all the information is extracted during the fixations, the interest in fixations is on the information extracted. Since saccades exist to move the eye to another fixation, the interest in saccades is in how they help to control the flow of information extraction. In this chapter, we focus on the extraction of information during a fixation, while in the next chapter, we return to the details of the movement of the eyes and focus on the control of information flow during reading.

THE PERCEPTUAL SPAN

Since the eyes move four to five times a second during reading, it seems reasonable to assume that they move to new locations on the page because the amount of information that can be extracted from a given fixation is limited. However, some people who promote techniques for increasing reading speed claim that many of our eye movements are not necessary and that large amounts of information can be extracted from a single glance (see Chapter 12). Thus, if we are to understand which view is true—whether eye movements are a central functional part of the reading process or just a bad habit picked up from old-fashioned reading methods—we have to discover how much information from the printed page is obtained from an individual fixation during silent reading of text. As we will see, the constant movement of the eyes is not a bad habit: the region from which we can obtain useful information during each eye fixation is relatively small.

One reason that people may believe that a large amount of information can be extracted from a single fixation is that it often seems to us that we can see many words on the page at the same time. However, this is an illusion. Many of the words are seen on a fixation only in the sense that the reader knows that some wordlike object is in a given location. The brain takes the details extracted from several fixations and integrates them somehow into a perception that the detail from a wide area is seen on *each* fixation. We will discuss this integration process in the next section.

In this section, we will briefly describe various attempts to determine the size of the effective visual field (or *perceptual span*) on a fixation in reading. We will first review tachistoscopic techniques, then simple techniques based on eye movements, and conclude the section by discussing the technologically more sophisticated "moving window" technique.

Fixed-Eye Techniques

The tachistoscope, which we introduced in Chapter 1, was designed in part to determine how much useful information could be acquired during an eye fixation in reading. Psychologists hoped to measure the perceptual span by asking subjects to report all they could see when a sentence was exposed briefly, say 100 to 200 msec. Since such an exposure is brief enough to preclude the possibility of an eye movement during the presentation, the technique measures how much information can be reported from a single fixation. Thus, to some extent, the technique simulates a single fixation in reading.

An experiment by Marcel (1974) will serve to illustrate the logic of the method and its attendant problems. Marcel had subjects read a short fragment of a passage in a tachistoscope. When they reached the final word of the fragment, they read it aloud. The pronunciation of this word caused the text to disappear, and 100 msec later some more words were presented for 200 msec, just to the right of where the pronounced word had been. The subjects' task was to report as many words from the second set as possible. This second set of words was not actually text, but a sequence of words that varied in how closely they approximated normal English. When the sequence of words was essentially random, subjects were able to report just over 2 words on average (or roughly 13 character spaces), while when the sequences were close to normal English, they reported 3 or 4 words (or 18 to 26 character spaces). Since the stimuli in this last condition are most like normal text, perhaps 3 to 4 words provide a good estimate of the perceptual span in reading.

There are three potential problems with this type of research. The first is that the delay between the offset of the passage fragment and the onset of the target words is quite different from anything encountered during normal reading. The delay would be about 500 msec (about 400 msec to begin pronunciation of the last word of the first fragment plus the 100 msec experimental delay). The second problem is that the eye positions were not monitored so that the experimenter did not know where the subjects' eyes really were. The biggest problem, however, is that the experimenter has no control over the extent to which the subject is consciously guessing. In the experiment by Marcel, for example, since the subjects reported what had been seen, there was little control over the speed of the response. Thus, better performance on the sequences that closely approximated English may have been because the subject could simply guess which words were likely to follow from the constraints of the text (possibly aided by partial information obtained from the stimulus). The use of random sequences gets around the guessing problem but may disrupt the normal reading situation.

Another tachistoscopic technique that has frequently been used to make inferences about the perceptual span in reading (Feinberg 1949) involves asking a subject to fixate some point and then have him or her identify stimuli (words or letters) presented at various distances from fixation (again when no eye movement can occur). On the basis of the results from such experiments (see Figure 4.3), estimates of the perceptual span have generally been in the range of 2 or 3 words, or about 10 to 20 characters (Feinberg 1949; Woodworth 1938).

A strength of the latter method is that by the use of isolated words in the visual field, one can limit the guessing problem and get a better estimate of whether the word can be identified on the basis of the available visual information. The method has its problems, however. One was pointed out some time ago by Woodworth (1938) and later verified by Sperling (1960). As we discussed in Chapter 1, Sperling demonstrated that subjects are able to see much more than they can retain and later report. Thus, what subjects report from a brief word or letter presentation can not be taken as a complete specification of what they actually saw. Even if the verbal report coincided with what the person actually saw, there is no particular reason to believe that the estimate of the perceptual span obtained from either type of tachistoscopic presentation discussed here actually coincides with that of a fixation in reading. A second problem is that the responses are not timed.

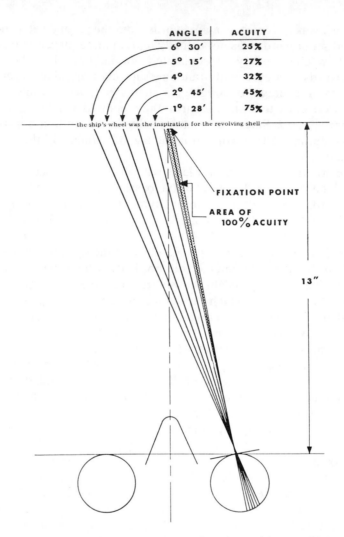

ANGLE	ACUITY
6° 30′	25%
5° 15′	27%
4°	32%
2° 45′	45%
1° 28′	75%

the ship's wheel was the inspiration for the revolving shell

FIXATION POINT

AREA OF 100% ACUITY

13″

FIGURE 4-3 Example of how perceptual span is estimated from tachistoscopic acuity data. [From Taylor 1965, reproduced with permission from the American Educational Research Association.]

Thus, one discovers whether the word can be identified on the basis of the available visual information, but not whether it can be identified as quickly as it needs to be in normal fluent reading.

Even if all the guessing problems could be removed, there might be a real difference between the perceptual span in silent reading of text and in tachistoscopic presentation of words or sentences. The perceptual span in reading could be larger either because the contextual constraint in text allows a reader to identify words with less visual information than in tachistoscopic presentations or because the requirement to hold the eye still interferes with normal perception. On the other hand, the perceptual span in reading could be smaller because the rapid sequence of fixations and the complexity of the surrounding stimulus pattern may lead to "tunnel vision" (Mackworth 1965).

Primitive "Window" Techniques

A somewhat different technique involving experimental control of what is seen on a given fixation is to present text but to limit the amount that is visible to a reader at a given moment. Poulton (1962) had subjects read aloud from text over which a mask containing a "window" was passed. Only the text in the window could be seen. Thus, the text was immobile and the window passed over it, allowing only a certain amount to be seen at once. The speed and size of the window varied systematically on different trials, and readers' eye movements were recorded. Newman (1966) and Bouma and deVoogd (1974) reversed the procedure by having the subjects' eyes fixed and having the text moving on a screen from right to left. The size of the "window" was manipulated by varying the number of letters on the screen at any moment.

These experiments have typically found that smaller windows create greater disruptions in reading than larger windows. These techniques, however, are suspect since they disrupt normal reading. The reader's natural eye movements were inhibited (in the latter case, fixation had to be maintained, while in the former, the reader had to follow the moving window); in neither situation could the reader reexamine text, as with regressions in normal reading; in addition, these particular experiments suffered because the subjects were required to read the text orally.

Natural Eye-movement Techniques

The techniques mentioned so far seem to be unsatisfactory. They involve tasks that disrupt the normal reading situation. In addition, they provide rather discrepant estimates of the size of the perceptual span with the estimated size ranging from 1 to 2 to 4 words. It would clearly be better if one could estimate the perceptual span directly from normal silent reading.

One simple technique for estimating the perceptual span from natural reading is measuring the average number of words per fixation. That is, one simply records eye movements during reading and divides the number of words read by the number of fixations used to read those words (Taylor 1965). Using such a technique, Taylor estimated the perceptual span for skilled readers to be 1.11 words. While this method is simple and unobtrusive, it is unfortunately based on the assumption that the perceptual spans do not overlap on successive fixations. In other words, it assumes that a given word or letter is never processed on more than one fixation. As we shall see, this assumption is false.

The *moving-window technique* introduced by McConkie and Rayner (1975) uses the idea of the moving-window techniques discussed before—to manipulate what is seen on a given fixation—but does so in the task of normal silent reading, where the subjects can move their eyes wherever they wish. This is accomplished by making display changes in text presented on a televisionlike screen, called a *cathode-ray tube* (CRT). This research relies upon sophisticated eye-tracking equipment being interfaced with a high-speed computer, which is also connected with the CRT. The position of the reader's eye is sampled every millisecond by the computer and changes in the text are made contingent on the location of the eye. Because this type of research has been influential for our understanding of skilled reading and has provided some clear answers concerning the size of the perceptual span, we will describe it in some detail.

In the prototypical moving-window experiment, a version of mutilated text (in which every letter from the original text is replaced by another letter) is initially displayed on the CRT. However, when the reader fixates on the text, the display is immediately modified by replacing letters, within a certain region around the fixation point, with corresponding letters from the original text. This creates an experimentally defined *window* region of normal text for the reader to see on that fixation. When the reader makes an eye movement, the text in the window area returns to this unreadable form and a new window of normal text is created at the location of the new fixation. Thus, wherever the reader looks, there is a window of normal text to read in a *background* of mutilated text. Table 4.2 shows text in four successive fixations under moving-window conditions. (Because of the sophistication of the equipment, the display changes can be made in less than 5 msec, so rapid that the reader does not see that they are taking place.)

The basic assumption in this research is that when the window becomes smaller than the reader's perceptual span, reading will be disrupted. By varying the size and location of the window region, the experimenter can determine from what area of the text the reader is actually extracting useful information. By varying the type of information in the background area, the experimenter can maintain or destroy various types of information, which may be potentially useful during reading, and can thus be

TABLE 4.2 An example of a moving window

FIXATION NUMBER	EXAMPLE	
1	Xxxxhology means persxxxxxxx xxxxxxxxx xxxx xxxx xxxxxxx. *	Xxxx xx x
2	Xxxxxxxxxx xxxxs personality diaxxxxxx xxxx xxxx xxxxxxx. *	Xxxx xx x
3	Xxxxxxxxxx xxxxx xxxxxxxxxxx xiagnosis from hanx xxxxxxx. *	Xxxx xx x
4	Xxxxxxxxxx xxxxx xxxxxxxxxxx xxxxxxxxx xxom hand writing. *	Xxxx xx x

Note: The asterisk represents the location of fixation on four successive fixations.

more analytical about the type of information that a reader is extracting from a region of the visual field.

In the original moving-window experiment, McConkie and Rayner (1975) had subjects read text when the window was 13, 17, 21, 25, 31, 37, 45, and 100 characters wide. (With a window size of 100, the entire line was almost always present.) As shown in Table 4.3, a window size of 17 meant that the reader had normal text for the letter directly fixated (in this case, *d* in *diagnosis*) and 8 character positions on either side. The subjects also read the text in the six different text mutilations shown in Table 4.3. The texts were 500-word passages and the subjects were told that they would be tested on their comprehension.

McConkie and Rayner found that reducing the size of the window had a substantial effect on reading speed—as much as 60 percent, but had no effect on readers' ability to answer questions about the text. With windows as small as 7 character positions, readers can see little more than 1 word at a time. This reduces their normal reading speed by about 60 percent, but they can still read with normal comprehension. Rayner and Bertera (1979) also found no effect on comprehension unless the window was reduced to only 1 character (in which case readers are literally reading letter by letter).

The first question that McConkie and Rayner asked was how large the window had to be for subjects to be able to read at normal speed and comprehension. The answer was 31 characters, or 15 character positions to each side of fixation. When the window size was smaller than that, the rate of reading was reduced. This finding that the perceptual span extends to something like 15 character positions from the fixation point was subsequently replicated by a number of studies (DenBuurman, Boersema, and Gerrisen 1981; Rayner and Bertera 1979; Rayner et al. 1981).

Thus, readers appear to extract some sort of useful information from about 15 characters from fixation but little beyond that. But what kind of information is it? At 31 characters wide, do readers extract the meaning of

TABLE 4.3   An example of a line of text and the various text patterns derived from it[a]

Text	Graphology means personality diagnosis from hand writing. This is a
XS	Xxxxxxxxxx xxxxx xxxxonality diagnosis xxxx xxxx xxxxxxx. Xxxx xx x
XF	XXXXXXXXXXXXXXXXXXXXXXonality diagnosisXXXXXXXXXXXXXXXXXXXXXXXXXXXXXXXX
VS	Cnojkaiazp wsorc jsnconality diagnosis tnaw kori mnlflra. Ykle le o
VF	Cnojkaiaqpawsorcajsnconality diagnosisatnawakoriamnlflrqaaaYklealeao
DS	Hbfxwysyvo tifdl xiblonality diagnosis abyt wfdn hbemedv. Awel el f
DF	Hbfxwysyvoatifdlaxiblonality diagnosisaabytawfdnahbemedvaaaAwelaelaf

[a]Note: On each line a window of size 17 is shown, assuming the reader is fixating the letter *d* in *diagnosis*.
XS = Letters replaced with *X*s—spaces preserved
XF = Letters replaced with *X*s—spaces filled.
VS = Letters replaced with similar letters—spaces preserved
VF = Letters replaced with similar letters—spaces filled.
DS = Letters replaced with dissimilar letters—spaces preserved
DF = Letters replaced with dissimilar letters—spaces filled

words, only some information about the component letters, or merely some idea of where words begin and end, which might be useful in knowing where to place the next fixation?

One way to attack the question of how far from fixation different kinds of information can be extracted is by experimentally manipulating the information that is outside the window of normal text. McConkie and Rayner (1975) investigated the perceptual span for word boundary information by comparing two kinds of altered displays outside the window. In one, all letters in words were replaced by X's but the spaces between words were preserved; in the other, the spaces were replaced by X's as well. By comparing performance in these two background conditions, one can tell how far from fixation the presence of spaces makes a difference. When the window size was 25 characters or fewer, reading was faster when spaces were present among the X's in the background than when they were not. On the other hand, when the window size was 31 or greater, there was no difference between the background conditions. Thus, it appears that out to about 15 character positions from fixation, subjects use the information of where spaces are to help guide their eye movements into that region.

McConkie and Rayner also attempted to determine how far from fixation information about the shapes of letters and words is extracted. They compared backgrounds in which the letters were visually similar (having the same pattern of ascenders and descenders) to the letters in the text with backgrounds in which the letters were visually dissimilar (shown in Table 4.3). If there is a difference between these two background conditions at a certain window size, then some information about the shapes of letters or words, or both, is being extracted beyond the end of the window. The data indicated that letter shape information was not extracted as far out as word boundary information, since there were differences between these two background conditions only for windows up to 21 character positions (10 to the left and right). It is worth noting that the "window of consciousness" for letter information is significantly smaller than that, extending little beyond the fixated word. If the fixated word is preserved and the background vaguely resembles normal text (e.g., spaces are left between the words but all letters in the background are replaced randomly), readers are rarely aware of seeing anything other than normal text (even readers who are told beforehand that it isn't normal). However, they are often aware that they are reading slowly and that something is holding them back.

Further studies have greatly increased our understanding of the perceptual span. We should point out that in many of these experiments single sentences were employed, since it is technically difficult to make display changes rapidly and not have a lot of "flicker" in the text display. Fortunately, these sentence-reading experiments have closely replicated those using passages of text, so we can be reasonably confident that the data from the sentence-reading experiments are a good approximation of what would be obtained under more natural reading conditions.

One question that was raised is whether the perceptual span is symmetric. In the original McConkie and Rayner (1975) experiment, the distance that normal text was extended was the same on both sides of fixation so that it was not possible to test whether readers extract more information from one side of fixation than the other. To test the symmetry of the perceptual span, McConkie and Rayner (1976) independently varied the left and right boundaries of the window of normal text and found that when the window extended 4 character positions to the left of fixation and 14 to the right, reading was virtually as fast as when the window extended 14 character spaces in both directions. In contrast, when the window extended 14 character spaces to the left of fixation and 4 to the right, reading was markedly impaired. Thus, for readers of English, the perceptual span is asymmetric, with information from the right of fixation being used much further out.

Rayner, Well, and Pollatsek (1980) and Rayner et al. (1982) extended the work on the size of the perceptual span. Their major finding was that the left and right boundaries of the perceptual span are somewhat differently constituted. They compared conditions in which the window was experimentally defined by the number of visible letters with those when the window was experimentally defined by the number of visible words. They found that the major determiner of the *left* boundary is the beginning of the currently fixated word. That is, when the left boundary of the window was manipulated, the speed of reading could be predicted by knowing whether the currently fixated word was visible. Beyond ensuring that the beginning of the fixated word was visible, the number of letters to the left of fixation had virtually no effect. On the other hand, the *right* boundary of the perceptual span doesn't appear to depend on word boundaries. When the window to the right of fixation was varied, the major determinant of reading speed was the number of letters visible. Given that a certain number of letters were visible, it made little difference whether whole words were preserved or whether a word was partially visible (even the fixated word). For example, the reading rate was the same when the boundary of the window was 3 letters to the right of the fixated letter as when the boundary was defined to be the end of the fixated word, in spite of the fact that in the former case, the fixated word was not entirely visible about a third of the time. The fact that reading speed did not appear to depend on whether the right boundary of the window maintains the integrity of words (see Table 4.4) suggests that readers acquire partial word information from parafoveal vision (or even from foveal vision in some conditions).

Rayner et al. (1982) reported further evidence that readers use partial word information from parafoveal vision. They asked subjects to read when (1) only the fixated word was visible and all other letters to the right of fixation were replaced by another letter; (2) the word fixated and the word to the right of fixation were visible and all other letters were replaced by another letter; or (3) the word fixated was visible and partial information about the word to the right of fixation was visible. In the third condition, either one, two, or three letters of the word to the right of fixation were

TABLE 4.4 Examples of conditions in the Rayner et al. (1982) study and reading rates associated with them (in words per minute). In the *W* conditions word integrity is preserved, while in the *L* conditions the right boundary is determined by the number of letters visible. The values in parentheses are the average number of letters visible in the *W* conditions. In all cases, the fixated letter is the second *e* in experiment.

WINDOW SIZE		SENTENCE	READING RATE
1W	(3.7)	An experiment xxx xxxxxxxxx xx xxx xxx	212 wpm
2W	(9.6)	An experiment was xxxxxxxxx xx xxx xxx	309 wpm
3W	(15.0)	An experiment was conducted xx xxx xxx	339 wpm
3L		An experimxxx xxx xxxxxxxxx xx xxx xxx	207 wpm
9L		An experiment wax xxxxxxxxx xx xxx xxx	308 wpm
15L		An experiment was condxxxxx xx xxx xxx	340 wpm

visible. When the first three letters in the word to the right of fixation were visible and the remainder of the letters were replaced by visually similar letters, reading rate was not much different from when the entire word to the right of fixation was visible. This result indicates that partial word information is utilized during reading and that an individual word may be processed on more than one fixation. These experiments, in which individual sentences were read, also indicated that letter information was obtained at least 9 characters from fixation. A similar result was obtained when subjects read longer passages (Underwood and McConkie 1985).

The moving-window technique demonstrates that information beyond 15 character positions to the right of fixation is of little use in normal reading. One possible reason for this is that the reader is busy enough processing the information that is closer to fixation, so there is little use for more information. One variation of the moving-window technique, the *moving-mask* technique, demonstrates information beyond 15 characters is of little value, even when you need to have it. The moving-mask technique is the inverse of the moving-window technique. The normal text is displayed outside the center of vision and a visual mask, moving in synchrony with the eyes, makes it impossible for the reader to obtain useful information foveally (Rayner and Bertera 1979; Rayner et al. 1981). Thus, foveal vision is completely masked (see Table 4.5), and an artificial *scotoma* of the retina—a lack of foveal vision—is created.

Rayner and Bertera (1979) found that when foveal vision (i.e., the central 7 characters around the fixation point) was masked, reading was still possible from parafoveal vision but at a rate of only 12 words per minute. When foveal vision and part of parafoveal vision (i.e., the central 11 to 17 character spaces around the fixation point) were masked, reading was almost impossible. Subjects in the experiments knew that there were words (or at least knew there were strings of letters) outside of the center of vision,

TABLE 4.5 An example of a moving mask (of 7 letters). The asterisk marks the location of fixation on three successive fixations.

```
An exXXXXXXX was conducted in the lab.
       *
An experiXXXXXXX conducted in the lab.
          *
An experimenXXXXXXXnducted in the lab.
             *
```

but could not tell what they were. They were more likely to be able to identify short function words like *the, and,* and *a,* particularly when they were at the beginning or end of the line. The errors that readers made when foveal and parafoveal vision were masked indicated that they were obtaining information about the beginning letters (and sometimes ending letters) of words in parafoveal vision, as well as letter shapes and word length information, and trying to construct coherent sentences out of the information available. For example, the sentence "The pretty bracelet attracted much attention" was read as "The priest brought much ammunition" and "The banner waved above the stone monument" as "The banker watched the snow mountain." There was no indication that the gist of the sentences was comprehended if the words were not identified.

Let us briefly recap what we know about the span of perception during reading. We know that it is limited, and the limitation on the right side appears to be chiefly due to limitations in perception. Even when foveal information is eliminated, subjects still extract little useful information about letters and words beyond about 15 character spaces. On the left side, information is extracted from a smaller area, including, at most, the word currently fixated. You may be wondering if information is obtained from the line below the one you are reading. It seems unlikely because the time lag between obtaining such information and inserting it into the flow of discourse is so long.

Before going on to explore what information is extracted from the right of fixation, let us briefly discuss what is known about the perceptual span in other orthographies. Within our writing system, moving-window experiments have been done in Dutch (DenBuurman, Boersema, and Gerrisen 1981) and French (O'Regan 1980), and the results seem to be identical to those in English.

The perceptual span in other writing systems Moving window experiments have been conducted with Japanese and Hebrew readers. Not only does the writing system affect eye movement characteristics, it also influences the size of the perceptual span. Ikeda and Saida (1978) and Osaka (1987) used the moving-window technique to study Japanese readers. (Remember, Japanese is a hybrid language consisting of morphemic characters, Kanji, and syllabic characters, Kana.) They found that the perceptual span extended about 6 characters to the right of fixation. Thus, for the Japanese writing system, the perceptual span is considerably smaller than for English if one equates a Japanese character with a letter. However, Japanese text is considerably more dense than English, leading to the observation that more information is processed per fixation. It is hard to compare across languages (since the perceptual span in English seems to be defined mainly in terms of letters), but it appears that the perceptual span is roughly two to three words in the writing systems that have been examined.

With Hebrew text, the major interest has been in the asymmetry of the perceptual span. Pollatsek et al. (1981) found that for native Israelis reading Hebrew, their perceptual span was asymmetric to the left of fixation, and that when these same subjects read English, their perceptual span was asymmetric to the right of fixation. Thus, the asymmetry of the window is not "hard-wired": asymmetry varies from language to language. Furthermore, bilingual readers can alter the area from which they extract information when they switch from language to language. The major difference between Hebrew and English, of course, is that Hebrew is read from right to left. That means that the dominant pattern of eye movements is opposite in the two languages. Thus, readers concentrate their attention on the material that is in the direction where they are about to move their eyes.

The "perceptual span" in Braille As long as we are talking about other writing systems, it might be of some interest to discuss what is known about how tactual information is "read" by the blind. The most common system for alphabetic languages is known as *Braille*. In Braille, a 3-by-2 matrix of raised "dots" represents a letter; dots thus can potentially appear in any one of six locations, and the pattern of present and absent dots defines the letter. The arrangement of the letters is from left to right with spaces between the words.

For many Braille readers, the size of the perceptual span is one letter (Bertelson, Mousty, and D'Alimonte 1985). They read with one finger (almost always the index finger) one letter at a time. Surprisingly, there appears to be no overall superiority for the right index finger; however, individual Braille readers usually show a marked superiority for either the right or left index finger (Mousty and Bertelson 1985). Braille readers also typically never skip words and maintain physical contact with the page even on "return sweeps" (although they move faster on the sweeps than when they read a line of text).

Some Braille readers use the right index finger to read and the left index finger mainly as a marker to help them find the appropriate line on the return sweep (Bertelson, Mousty, and D'Alimonte 1985). Using two fingers instead of one increases their reading speed by almost 30 percent. The most skilled Braille readers appear to use both index fingers to extract information. Some will keep their two index fingers on adjacent letters while they read the entire text. However, a more typical pattern is to move the two in synchrony on adjacent letters to the middle of a line; then continue the right index finger to the end of the line, and move the left to the beginning of the next line. The left finger starts "reading" the next line while the right is finishing the previous one (Bertelson, Mousty, and D'Alimonte, 1985). The right index finger usually rejoins the left after a word or two has been read by the left.

The perceptual span of these most skilled Braille readers thus appears to be two letters, at least some of the time, since they can read more than 30 percent faster with two fingers than with one. However, the details of what is happening are somewhat unclear. Since using the left index finger as a place marker provides appreciable benefit in itself, it is hard to know exactly how much benefit is actually a result of extracting information from both fingers simultaneously. Using this two-hand method, however, the best Braille readers can read from 100 to 140 words per minute (Bertelson, Mousty, and D'Alimonte 1985).

What Is a Reader Doing on a Fixation?

We are closing in a bit on what information the reader is extracting on a fixation. The information to the left of the fixated word in English (or to the right in Hebrew) is irrelevant because the subject is not attending to it. The moving-mask experiment and various tachistoscopic experiments suggest that information further than about 15 character spaces to the right of fixation is not used because of acuity limitations in processing text.

However, we are still not at all clear about how the information from the fixation point to the right-hand boundary of the perceptual span is used. The Rayner et al. (1982) experiment cited earlier makes it clear that more than the fixated word is processed. When the window only included the fixated word, subjects read about 200 words per minute in contrast to about 340 words per minute when there was no window. The simplest conceptual model to handle that fact would be that readers make sure to encode the fixated word on each fixation but that on some fixations they may also encode another word or two. However, the other data from Rayner et al. (1982) indicated that reality is more complex. Since readers were not particularly bothered by incomplete words—in fact, the major variable affecting reading speed was the number of letters available to the right of fixation—readers must be doing something more complex than extracting words as visual units (see also Chapter 3).

One possibility is that words are encoded only a limited distance from fixation, but that more primitive letter information is extracted further out. This conclusion emerged from a study by Rayner (1975a) which used the *boundary technique,* another variation of the moving window. In this technique, the experimenter attempts to determine what kinds of information are acquired from a particular word location in a paragraph (called the critical word location—*CWL*) when readers fixate different distances from it. This is accomplished by changing the contents of the CWL when a saccade crosses an invisible *boundary* location. The logic of the method is that if a certain aspect of the stimulus in the CWL has been encoded in the parafovea and then changed when the word is fixated, some disruption of normal reading would be expected. In particular, we might anticipate a longer-than-normal fixation after the change had been made, since the reader would have to resolve the conflict in the information obtained from the two fixations. The advantage of the boundary technique over the moving-window technique is that more precise control over parafoveal information is possible since one word is selected for manipulation. In addition, since the region of abnormal text is small, normal reading is even more closely approximated. In Rayner's experiment, the stimulus in the CWL when it was fixated (the *base word*) was always a word that fit into the text. However, the stimulus in the CWL before the boundary had been crossed was sometimes a word and sometimes a nonword (see Figure 4.4 for an example).

Rayner was able to observe a large number of instances on which the reader's eyes fixated different distances to the left of the CWL on the fixation prior to the stimulus change and then directly on the CWL after the change. It was assumed that if the reader's fixation was sufficiently far to the left of the CWL, no information would be acquired from that region. If this were the case, the reader would then fail to "notice" any of the different types of display changes. (We use the words *notice* and *detect* to mean that there is some effect on the reader's eye behavior, not that the reader is conscious of these changes; in fact, in such experiments, readers are not aware of the changes.) On the other hand, if the fixation was closer to the CWL, the reader might obtain some information, perhaps word-shape or letter information, and if the stimulus change caused a change in that kind of information, a longer fixation would result. However, if the stimulus change was a type that did not cause a change in the kind of information the reader had acquired, no change would be detected and no disruption of reading would occur.

Since some of the initially displayed stimuli in the CWL were

---

FIGURE 4-4   Boundary study: An example of the type of display change that occurred in Rayner's boundary experiment.

I.   The old captain put the chovt on the . . .
                                        1   B

II.   The old captain put the chart on the . . .
                                        B   2

Key: B—Location of the boundary which triggers a change in the display.
                                1—Location of the last fixation prior to crossing the boundary.
                                2—Location of the first fixation after crossing the boundary.

Alternatives in target location for base word *chart:*
    chart—identical word (W-Ident)
    chest—word with similar shape and letters (W-SL)
    ebovf—nonword with similar shape (N-S)
    chovt—nonword with similar shape and letters (N-SL)
    chyft—nonword with similar letters (N-L)

nonwords, this raised an interesting question: How near to the CWL did the reader's eyes have to be before the nonword letter string in the CWL affected reading? One way to investigate this was to examine fixations (grouped according to how far they were from the CWL) prior to the display change and then calculate the average fixation duration at each distance. Rayner found that the existence of a nonword in the CWL did not affect the fixation duration unless the CWL was no more than 3 letter positions to the right of the fixation point. If the CWL began 4 or more letter positions to the right of the fixation point, the "wordness" of its temporary occupant had no effect on the length of this fixation.

The duration of fixations on the CWL immediately after the display change were also examined and classified according to (1) the type of display change that had occurred and (2) the location of the previous fixation. These data are shown in Figure 4.5. Reading was unaffected by any stimulus change if the fixation prior to crossing the boundary was more than 12 character positions to the left of the CWL. When the previous fixation was 7 to 12 character spaces to the left of the CWL, the subjects did pick up information about the shape of the word (or its component letters) and information about the identity of the extreme letters of the stimulus in the CWL. If either of these changed when the boundary was crossed, the first fixation on the base word was increased. In contrast, if the initially displayed stimulus had the same word shape and the same extreme letters as the base word, very little disruption was noted. Finally, the fixation on the base word was affected by the "wordness" of the preview when the preview was as much as 6 characters away from fixation. Thus, the fixation on the base word appears to be a more sensitive measure of whether lexical information was extracted parafoveally than fixation prior to the base word.

Rayner's results were originally interpreted as evidence that word shape information is obtained from parafoveal words that the reader cannot identify. However, subsequent research (to be discussed soon) has demonstrated that when word shape effects emerge, it is really because words that begin with the same letter and share the same overall shape (as in Rayner's study) have many letter features in common. Thus, we will argue that it is letter information that is obtained beyond the region in parafoveal vision where words can be identified. Rayner's results also suggest that the meanings of words to the right of fixation are not extracted very far from the point of fixation, since the reader appears to be unaware that a nonword was present if it started further than 3 to 6 characters from it. This conclusion is reinforced by a study (McConkie and Hogaboam 1985) in which subjects were reading silently with their eye movements monitored. At certain places in the text the screen went blank and subjects were asked to report the last word that they had read. There is a guessing problem here, since the subject may be able to figure out a word not actually seen on the basis of prior context. Nonetheless, the results are consistent with Rayner's study. McConkie and Hogaboam found (see Figure 4.6) that the word readers reported most frequently was the word on which they had last fixated,

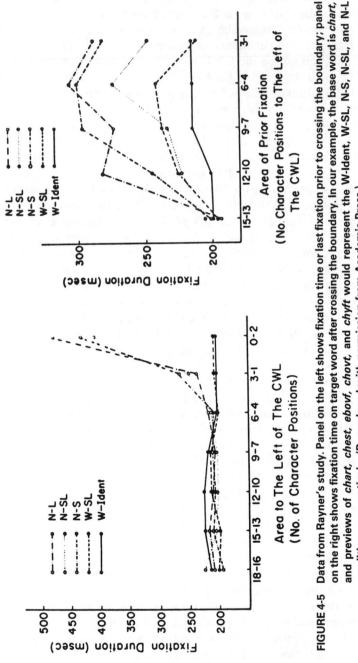

FIGURE 4-5   Data from Rayner's study. Panel on the left shows fixation time or last fixation prior to crossing the boundary; panel on the right shows fixation time on target word after crossing the boundary. In our example, the base word is *chart*, and previews of *chart, chest, ebovf, chovt,* and *chyft* would represent the W-Ident, W-SL, N-S, N-SL, and N-L conditions, respectively. (Reproduced with permission from Academic Press.)

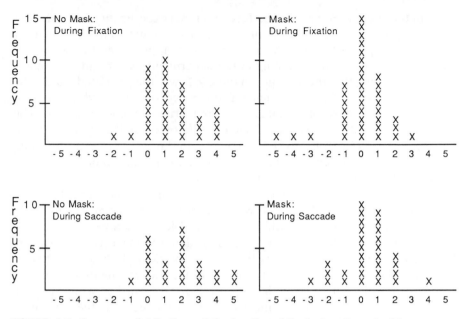

FIGURE 4-6 Fequency distributions of the location of the last read word with respect to the location of the last fixation on which text was present. 0 represents the last word fixated and 1 represents the word to its right. In the Mask conditions (right panels), a mask came on when the text went off, while in the No Mask conditions (left panels), the text just went blank. Distance is measured in word units, without regard for word length. (Reproduced with permission from North Holland Press.)

although the word to the right of fixation was sometimes reported. However, words to the left of the fixated word—or two or more to the right of the fixated word—were rarely reported.

Word skipping is another index of how far to the right of fixation words can be identified. As indicated before, the area to the left of the fixated word is ignored by the reader; if a word is skipped, it either must have been identified before it was skipped or the reader simply made a guess as to what the word was without having seen it. Since word skipping is a ubiquitous part of the eye-movement record, identification of the word to the right of fixation is reasonably common if guessing does not account for most of the skipping. At times, words can be skipped from reasonably long distances. In a later boundary experiment (see Balota, Pollatsek, and Rayner, 1985; Pollatsek, Rayner, and Balota 1986), it was found that the CWL was occasionally skipped (though less than 1 percent of the time) when the prior fixation was greater than 9 character spaces from the beginning of the CWL. Thus, it appears that the meaning of a word in the parafovea can be extracted fairly far from fixation, though this is not usually the case even with highly predictable words.

In the Balota, Pollatsek, and Rayner (1985) experiment, the base word was highly predictable from the prior sentence context. Skipping occurred much less frequently when a word other than that predicted by the context was in the CWL, so that skipping in the experiment was not merely due to readers' guessing that the stimulus in the CWL was the predicted word. This experiment differed from the original Rayner experiment, in which the base word was not highly predictable from the prior sentence context. This difference suggests that variables such as the predictability of a word can influence how far from fixation words can be encoded and meaning extracted. We will return to this issue in greater depth in Chapter 7 when we discuss processing of sentences in more detail.

To summarize, the perceptual span is limited, extending from the beginning of the currently fixated word to about 15 character spaces to the right of fixation. The area within which word identification takes place is even more limited. Readers can sometimes identify the word to the right of the fixated word (and sometimes two words, particularly when the fixated word and the next two are short words). In fact, as we mentioned earlier, readers often do not fixate either the first or last word of a line in text. Apparently, the last word of a line is often fully processed in the parafovea. It is somewhat harder to understand why the first word of a line is sometimes not fixated. One possible explanation is that the first fixation on a line is approached by a (leftward) return sweep. If a reader's perceptual span mirrors the direction of eye movements (as with the Israeli readers discussed earlier), it could be that covert attention shifts leftward on the first fixation so that the span includes the word to the left of the fixated word on those occasions.

While readers can identify words that they do not fixate, the more usual circumstance is that no word beyond the fixated word is fully identified. Since we have seen that preserving some letters in a parafoveal word aids reading, it appears that partial information about a word can be encoded on one fixation and used to aid identification of the word on the subsequent fixation. We now turn to discuss what we know about how information is integrated across fixations.

INTEGRATION OF INFORMATION ACROSS EYE MOVEMENTS

Several converging pieces of data from the last section suggested that some words are processed partially on one fixation and then finished on the succeeding fixation. Another indicant that words are processed on more than one fixation is the fact that the perceptual span is about double the average size of a saccade. (This is true in Japanese as well [Ikeda and Saida 1978].) This comparison is not completely fair, however, since the perceptual span is not an average: it is measuring the *maximum* distance that information can be extracted. However, the discrepancy between the perceptual span and the size of the average saccade reinforces the conclusion that the eye is moving to an area of text that it has processed to some extent.

Integration of information across saccades is by no means a conscious process, since we are generally not aware of our eye movements. Each eye movement changes the pattern of light on the retina, and yet we perceive a stable, coherent image of the words we are looking at. We never have the feeling of having stimulus input for a quarter of a second or so followed by a break in input due to the saccade. The research on saccadic suppression we discussed earlier explains why you don't see "junk" between the "slides." However, at present, we don't have a detailed understanding of why the gaps between fixations are not noticed. Somehow the brain is able to smooth out the discrete inputs from each eye fixation and create a feeling of a continuous coherent perceptual world.

If information about a word is obtained on two successive fixations, the first when the word is in the parafovea and the second when it is in the fovea, and if the integration process is useful in reading, the parafoveal preview of the word should facilitate later foveal processing of the word. We shall thus discuss integration of information across fixations largely in terms of such facilitation. It has been known as early as Dodge (1906) that parafoveal previews facilitate later identification. However, that facilitation, in itself, is not necessarily evidence for integration across saccades, since the word may have been fully identified in the parafovea. What is needed to document integration across saccades is to make the parafoveal preview and foveal target stimuli similar but not identical, and to determine whether there is still facilitation from the preview.

An experimental technique requiring subjects to name isolated words (originated by Rayner 1978b) has produced a lot of information about integration across fixations (Rayner, McConkie, and Ehrlich 1978; Rayner, McConkie, and Zola 1980; McClelland and O'Regan 1981; Balota and Rayner 1983). It is a miniaturization of the boundary technique. Subjects are asked to fixate on a central fixation point and when a letter string appears in parafoveal vision, they are to make an eye movement to it. During the saccade the initially displayed stimulus is replaced by a *target* word which they are to name as fast as possible. The parafoveal stimulus is thus visible for approximately 200 msec until the eye movement begins. In spite of the fact that it is visible for such an extended time, subjects are almost never aware of the identity of the parafoveal word and are rarely even aware that there has been any change! Thus they have no trouble deciding which word to name.

Figure 4.7 shows the basic pattern of results from the experiments. As seen in Figure 4.7, if the stimulus presented on fixation *n* and fixation *n+1* are identical, there is facilitation in naming the target word (compared to when a row of asterisks or unrelated letters are initially presented parafoveally). More important is the fact that facilitation occurs even if the parafoveal preview only has some letters in common with the target word.

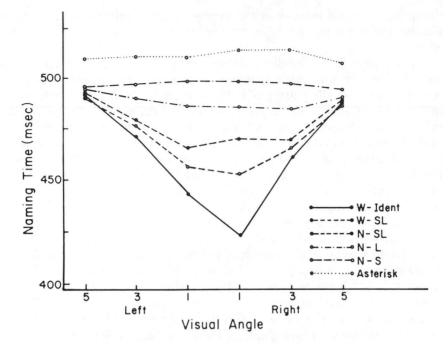

FIGURE 4-7 Mean naming times as a function of initially displayed alternative and visual angle. In our example, *chart* is the base word. The alternatives *chart*, *chest, chovt, ebovf,* and *chyft* represent the W-Ident, W-SL, N-SL, N-L, and N-S conditions, respectively. The asterisk preview was a row of asterisks. (Reproduced with permission from Plenum Press.)

As one would predict from the perceptual span experiments, the amount of facilitation depends upon how far into the parafovea the preview is. That is, there is more facilitation when the initial stimulus is 1 degree from fixation than when it is at 3 degrees and hardly any facilitation at 5 degrees (i.e., 15 character spaces) from fixation. Thus, the results indicate that only when the preview is less than 15 character spaces from fixation, can subjects use partial parafoveal information about a word to aid their recognition of that word when it is later fixated.

The fact that *chest* in the parafovea facilitates the later identification of *chart* implies that some information extracted from *chest* was useful in the later identification of *chart*. We feel that the following five potential sources of facilitation are defined so as to be exhaustive: (1) some of the *visual features* of *chest* are stored and aid later identification of *chart;* (2) some sort of *sound codes* (e.g., phonemes or syllables) activated by *chest* (perhaps the initial /ch/) aid later identification of the word *chart;* (3) some aspect of the *meaning* of *chest* has been encoded by the parafoveal view of *chart* which facilitates later identification (although that seems improbable in this particular example); (4) some of the *letters* are identified and these abstract letter identities (not the letter forms) are what are facilitating; and (5) the lexical entry of "chart" is *partially activated* by the parafoveal preview of *chest* which aids in the later identification of *chart*. The distinction we wish to draw between (1) and (4) is that the information about letters is in a visual form in (1), but a more abstract form in (4). The distinction we wish to draw between (3) and (5) is that in (3), some aspect of the word's meaning as well as its identity is activated in the parafovea. Of course, these hypotheses are not mutually exclusive, as facilitation could have more than one source. As we will see, however, the evidence points at present to a relatively simple answer: there is no evidence for any of the first three mechanisms being operative, so that, by a process of elimination, (4) or (5), or both, appear to be the sources of integration. Let us discuss the evidence against the first three sources in turn.

Is Visual Information Integrated across Eye Movements?

This alternative may seem the most plausible, since it corresponds to our intuitions that we see a single seamless world when visual information from two fixations is brought together into a single representation of the visual world (McConkie and Rayner 1976b). That is, readers may obtain gross featural information from parafoveal vision during a fixation and store it in a temporary visual buffer, which has been referred to as the *integrative visual buffer*. The visual information stored in the buffer would then be used as a base to which new information is added when the region (previously in parafoveal vision) is fixated. The alignment of the information from the two fixations would presumably be based on knowledge about how far the eyes moved and the commonality of the patterns from the two fixations. Of course, all this computation would generally be unconscious, since we are usually not aware of moving our eyes. The integrative visual buffer in reading can be thought of as being like iconic memory (see Chapter 1), except that information is preserved in the visual buffer across eye movements.

While this view of information integration is perhaps the most intuitively plausible of the alternatives, the evidence against it is quite strong. First, Rayner, McConkie, and Ehrlich (1978) showed that proper alignment was not necessary in order to obtain the results shown in Figure 4.7. (Recall that alignment or justification of two successive images in the buffer should be based on keeping track of how far the eyes moved.) They found, however, that the same pattern of results was obtained in an experiment in which the stimulus pattern rather than the subjects' eyes moved. That is, an initially presented stimulus appeared in parafoveal vision, and after a period of time approximating the sum of the saccade latency and saccadic duration (about 200 msec), the target word to be named appeared foveally and the parafoveal stimulus simultaneously disappeared. Notice that the sequence of events on the retina is the same as when the eyes move to a parafoveal stimulus: an initial stimulus impinges on the parafoveal retina followed by a stimulus in foveal vision. In one condition an eye movement intervenes between two retinal events, while in the other condition the eye movement is simulated by moving the stimulus rather than the eyes. Now, if keeping track of how far the eyes move is important for the integration process, performance should be much worse in the no eye-movement condition than in the standard eye-movement condition described earlier. Rayner, McConkie, and Ehrlich, however, found no major differences between these two conditions.

More damaging to the integrative visual buffer notion were two experiments that directly tested whether visual features could be integrated. The first demonstrated that changes in the visual form of the information had no effect if the meaning was not altered. Rayner, McConkie, and Zola (1980) found that a case change between the preview and target words (e.g., (*CASE* changed to *case*) had no effect on how long it took to name the word, even though there were still clear facilitating effects from parafoveal previews. The second tested integration of visual information in a different way. O'Regan and Levy-Schoen (1983) presented half of the letter features of a word on one fixation and the other half on the subsequent fixation. (Both stimuli were in the same spatial location.) Subjects in this condition were rarely ever able to identify the target word. In contrast, when the two halves were presented in the same spatial location one after the other in quick succession, subjects readily identified the target word. Thus, the visual information that can be integrated within a fixation can not be integrated when a saccade intervenes.

At this point, you may well be saying to yourself that all of the experiments we've described in this section do not really involve subjects in the task of reading. Perhaps, as we've pointed out before, the task used in these experiments encourages a strategy that is different from what normally happens when we read. However, it turns out to be the case that a number of experiments in which subjects are actually reading yield results consistent with the conclusions we have reached from the experiments described up to this point.

The question of whether integration is dependent upon keeping track of how far the eyes move has been tested in the reading situation as well. In these experiments (O'Regan 1981; McConkie, Zola, and Wolverton 1980), subjects were reading text, and at selected points, the entire line of text was shifted to the left or right during the saccade. In the normal state of perception, the distance that the image has moved from fixation to fixation is explained by the distance that the eye has moved. If the alignment of the visual information obtained on two successive fixations is dependent on this calculation of how far the eye has moved, then great disruption should be produced when the text is shifted. Even if it is shifted only a few characters there should be massive disruption, since the letter information in the two images will conflict in all locations. The shift was sometimes registered in the brain (if not in consciousness) because small corrective saccades sometimes occurred after the shift. These eye movements could have been because the eye landed on a position other than intended. However, shifting the text 2 or

3 character positions resulted in no conscious awareness of the shift and produced negligible effects on reading speed and comprehension.

Similarly, the issue of whether integration occurs by integrating the visual forms on two successive fixations was tested in reading text. McConkie and Zola (1979) had people read passages printed in AlTeRnAt-InG cAsE, and changed the case of every letter during certain saccades so that successive visual images would not be similar. Thus, cAsE on fixation n would appear as CaSe on fixation $n+1$ and cAsE on $n+2$. These changes were not noticed by readers and they had virtually no effect on comprehension or on reading speed. In addition, the basic finding that partial information facilitates naming of the fixated word (e.g., *chest* facilitates naming of *chart*) parallels the finding described in the previous section (Rayner et al. 1982) that silent reading was faster when the first 2 or 3 letters of the word to the right of fixation were visible than when they were altered.

In summary, all the basic findings that emerged from the parafoveal naming experiments have been corroborated in experiments involving silent reading of text. The two experimental situations thus provide convergent validity for the conclusions, combining the ecological validity of the reading situation with the more tightly controlled naming experiments in which the response is transparently tied to word identification.

Sound Codes

Let us next consider the possibility that the reader is extracting some sound-based code from the parafoveal stimulus such as the initial phonemes or the first syllable of the word. This possibility seems particularly appealing since all of the studies that we have described employing individual words required subjects to *name* the word that is present on the second fixation. Perhaps information acquired from the parafoveal word permits the subject to begin to form the speech musculature properly for saying the word. This would reduce the time needed to initiate an utterance when the target word occurs in the fovea following the eye movement.

Rayner, McConkie, and Zola (1980) assessed this possibility in two ways. First, subjects were required to make a semantic categorization ("Is it an animal?") of the target word. In such a condition, the subject does not pronounce the target word and if the facilitation is merely due to activating the beginning of the appropriate response, the facilitatory effects should disappear. Yet the experimenters found the same pattern of facilitation when semantic categorization was the task rather than naming. However, it could still be that activation of sound-based codes does not facilitate the naming response, per se, but the more basic process of identifying the word that underlies both naming and semantic classification. If so, one would expect some facilitation when the initial phoneme of the parafoveal preview was the same as the base word. However, there was no difference between when the initial phonemes of the two were the same (*casts-count*) and when they were different (*chair-count*). The argument is weakened somewhat by the finding that there was no facilitation in either case. However, the experiments demonstrate that the facilitation observed in these experiments is not due to activation of the initial phoneme.

Partial Encoding of Meaning

There are two different ways in which one might think the reader extracts partial meaning from a word. The first is that the whole word is processed, but only dimly. That is, the activation from the physical stimulation does not lead to identification of the word, but may lead to a vague idea of the meaning of the word. Perhaps a semantic feature is activated. The second way is that a specific meaningful segment of the word, a *morpheme,* is identified. We consider each of these possibilities in turn.

Semantic preprocessing   As we look around the world, we feel we have a vague idea of what things in the parafovea and periphery are. For example, if we are not directly looking at a dog, we may be aware that it is an animal, have a vague idea of its size, but may not be able to make a precise identification of it. Moreover, there is evidence in picture perception that there are possibly unconscious influences of such partial meaning on processing. For example, in picture perception, the eyes quickly move to regions judged to be informative (Mackworth and Morandi 1967; Antes 1974) or semantically anomolous (Loftus and Mackworth 1978). These phenomena suggest that something similar may be going on in reading.

However, it is important to point out that there are rather substantial differences in the stimulus pattern between text and a picture (Loftus 1983; McConkie and Rayner 1976b). With text, the pattern is rather homogenous, made up of letters and spaces, and it is likely that lateral masking of words and letters (by adjacent words and letters) is much greater in text. A single distinctive and informative feature of an object in a picture may convey meaning in a way that no single visual feature of a word does. It may well be that these distinctive features allow for rough semantic classifications of objects and guide the movement of the eye in picture perception.

Another reason that semantic preprocessing seems like an attractive explanation for parafoveal preview effects is because of the "unconscious priming" experiments described in the previous chapter (e.g., Allport 1977; Balota 1983; Marcel 1983). In these experiments, briefly presented words followed by masks are presented in the fovea. If conditions are set up right, the subject will be unable to identify the word, but the speed in identifying a semantically related word that follows will be increased. Marcel (1978) has suggested on the basis of the foveal priming studies that meaning is simultaneously available from a number of places on a page. For example, Marcel notes that if you turn the page of a book and are reading the top line, something at the bottom of the page may "catch your eye." He further argues that this is only possible if its meaning has been analyzed independently of where attention is. A key assumption in this inference is that a brief foveal presentation of a word is analogous to a word in parafoveal vision during reading.

The analogy may be misleading. While a briefly presented foveal word and a parafoveal word are both visually degraded, they are degraded in different ways: brief foveal words by their duration and by backward masking; parafoveal words by acuity and lateral masking. In reading normal text these acuity and lateral masking considerations make it difficult to identify words at increasing distances from the fixation point. The phenomenon of foveal masking is still poorly understood, but it appears that there is some sense in which the stimulus is fully identified, but something about the mask dissociates it from awareness and direct access. On the other hand, it seems implausible that partial semantic access can occur from vague information about a word, such as global shape, length, or knowing a letter or two. One possible explanation for the phenomenon that Marcel describes—something at the bottom of the page catching your eye when you turn the page—is that when you begin to move your eyes to bring them to the top of the page you may make a short fixation near the bottom of the page. Thus, this phenomenon may be explained by something similar to the foveal masking experiments rather than by semantic preprocessing in the parafovea or periphery.

In reading, there is no clear evidence supporting semantic preprocessing. One attempt to demonstrate semantic preprocessing uses a variant of the semantic priming technique described in the previous chapter. A semantically ambiguous word such as *bank* is presented in the fovea and one of two words that could disambiguate the word, *river* or *money,* are presented in the parafovea. Both words are presented briefly and the subject is tested on which meaning he or she associates with the foveal word *bank*. If subjects are at above chance in choosing the meaning suggested by the parafoveal word, then it implies that the meaning of the parafoveal word has been processed.

In fact, subjects are above chance. However, we already know that parafoveal words can be identified from our previous discussion of skipping. The key question is whether partial meaning can be processed. This has been tested (Bradshaw 1974; Inhoff 1982; Inhoff and Rayner 1980; Underwood 1980, 1981) by determining both which sense of *bank* is selected and whether the parafoveal word has been identified. If subjects can select the appropriate meaning at above chance levels, *even when the parafoveal word has not been consciously identified,* one would have evidence that semantic preprocessing has taken place. Unfortunately, the results from these experiments are not completely consistent. Some have found above chance performance and others have not. However, even in those that obtained above chance performance, it was not much above chance. In addition, the experiments that obtained above chance performance are difficult to evaluate as certain factors (such as eye location, guessing, and read out from iconic memory) were not controlled. (For a more complete discussion, see Inhoff and Rayner 1980.) In sum, there is little evidence for semantic preprocessing from these experiments.

Rayner, Balota, and Pollatsek (1986) provided a more direct test of semantic preprocessing in reading using the boundary technique described earlier. The stimulus, which appeared in the target location before the base word (*song*) was fixated, was either a visually similar nonword (*sorp*), a semantically associated word (*tune*), or a visually and semantically different control word (*door*). While the visually similar preview facilitated processing of the base word relative to the control condition (fixation time on the base word was reduced), there was no difference between the conditions employing semantically related and unrelated parafoveal previews. That is, there was no evidence for "semantic priming" in these conditions. In contrast, the pairs of related words produced the usual semantic priming effect when they were presented sequentially in the fovea.

Identification of morphemes   We appear to be down to three possibilities for integration. Either the entire lexical entry is activated, a meaningful subunit (a morpheme) is activated, or merely some of the letters are activated. Before discussing the involvement of morphemes we need to review some of the details of the parafoveal naming experiments.

Rayner, McConkie, and Zola (1980) demonstrated that significant facilitation was produced when the first 2 or 3 letters were constant across the two fixations (e.g., *chest-chart*). No facilitation was obtained when only the first letter was constant across fixations nor was there facilitation when all letters were the same except the first letter (e.g., *board-hoard*). Thus, it appears that encoding the beginning letters of the word is crucial to obtaining parafoveal facilitation. Interestingly, this was true even if the parafoveal preview was to the left of fixation and thus the beginning letters were furthest from fixation. Inhoff (1987) also found that when practiced subjects read text from right to left, a preview of the beginning 3 letters of a 6-letter word provided facilitation in reading. Of course, when reading from right to left, the beginning letters are further away from fixation so it is not just that the beginning letters of the word to the right of fixation are close to the current fixation point; there is something important about these letters. The pattern from moving-window experiments in which only the first part of word $n+1$ was exposed also indicates that the information from the first 2 or 3 letters of a word provides much of the parafoveal benefit, particularly if the remainder of the word consists of letters that are visually similar to the real letters of the word. If the remaining letters are not visually similar, readers do not read as well as when the entire word $n+1$ is present (Rayner et al. 1982; Inhoff 1988a; Lima and Inhoff 1985).

Since information from the first 2 or 3 letters of a word appears to provide much of the benefit, the logical place to look for extraction of a morpheme from a parafoveal word is at the beginning. Moreover, it also suggests that it would help to look for relatively short morphemes. Lima

(1987a) hypothesized that the beginning letters may facilitate, at least in part, because they aid in identifying the initial morpheme of a word. She tested her hypothesis using prefixed words, since most of the common prefixes have from 1 to 3 letters and because prefixes form a small set of highly familiar word–initial-letter patterns. In particular, she wanted to determine whether there was any evidence that "prefix stripping" (see Chapter 3) could begin before a word is fixated. Words with prefixes (such as *revive*) were compared with pseudoprefixed words (such as *rescue*). The stimuli were matched on number of syllables, word length, and word frequency, and a sentence frame was prepared into which either of the words would fit ("They tried to revive/rescue the . . ."). In her experiments, the boundary technique was used. Prior to the display change, the critical word location (CWL) contained the letters common to the two words plus random letters or *x*'s (*rensbl* or *rexxxx*) or simply a string of random letters or *x*'s (*kmnsbl* or *xxxxxx*). When the reader's saccade crossed the boundary, the word *revive* or *rescue* (depending upon the condition) was displayed at the CWL.

Lima found that subjects looked at the target word for less time when the initial letters of the target word were present than when they were not. She also found, as mentioned in Chapter 3, that prefixed words were fixated for a shorter amount of time than pseudoprefixed words. However, the benefit of the parafoveal preview was the same for prefixed and pseudoprefixed words. There are two possibilities for this equality. If one assumes that prefix stripping is the first step of the *only* route to identification of both kinds of words (which then has to be followed by a second access in the case of pseudoprefixed words), then prefix stripping in the parafovea is tenable: the parafoveal preview would start off the identical first stage of word identification (prefix stripping) in the two cases. However, we argued in Chapter 3 that it is more plausible to assume that access of pseudoprefixed words can go on directly, rather than having to go through the false start of prefix stripping. If this is the case, one would expect greater parafoveal benefit for prefixed words, since access of them would be aided by identifying the initial morpheme as well as the first 3 letters. Since the parafoveal benefit did not differ between prefixed and pseudoprefixed words, we have some evidence that morphemes are not extracted in the parafovea.

A second experiment employing compound words provided additional evidence against morphemic units in parafoveal information extraction. Inhoff (1988b) employed 6-letter compound words such as *cowboy*. As with Lima's experiment, he employed preview conditions in which the whole word *cowboy,* the first morpheme *cowxxx,* or no letter information xxxxxx was present in the parafovea. Inhoff employed two controls: pseudo-compound words such as *carpet,* where the first 3 letters are also a word but not a morphemic subunit, and monosyllabic words such as *priest.* He found the same preview benefit in all three cases, indicating that neither the first morpheme nor the first syllable was a significant unit in integration across saccades.

Inhoff's results appear to contradict those of Lima and Pollatsek (1983) discussed in Chapter 3. Lima and Pollatsek found that a preview of the first morpheme speeded lexical decision more than a preview of beginning letters that did not form a morpheme. However, the preview of the morpheme in the Lima and Pollatsek experiment was foveal and thus the integration was not across two fixations.

Letters vs. Words

The evidence available thus suggests that parafoveal previews help in two ways (Blanchard, Pollatsek, and Rayner 1988). First, the word in the parafovea may be fully identified (and perhaps skipped). Second, it may only be partially activated, with this partial activation speeding later identification of a word. We have reviewed rather convincing evidence that visual codes do not play any significant role in partial identification of words. The evidence also indicates that semantic preprocessing plays no role. There is no positive evidence for the involvement of sound codes, but no particularly strong tests show that it is unimportant. Furthermore, there is no evidence for the involvement of morphemes in integration across saccades.

How is information integrated across saccades? As we argued earlier, one possibility is that several letters may be identified which speeds later identification of the word. Let us briefly sketch how the process may work. Suppose the reader is fixated 7 character spaces to the left of the beginning of the word *chart* (as in Fixation I in Figure 4.4.). The reader may be able to unambiguously identify the first letter (*c*) and make some preliminary identification of the next few letters. The letters *b* and *h* share many features in common, as do the letters *c, a, e,* and *o.* After the reader has identified the *c,* it seems likely that knowledge of orthography would rule out *b* as the second letter. Similarly, the *c* can be eliminated as the third letter, though orthography or context may or may not further constrain *a* as the most likely third letter. Thus, preliminary letter identification of the letters *ch* would occur on fixation *n.* Alternatively, it may be the case that the threshold for letter identification is not reached until fixation *n+1.* In this case, preliminary letter identification for the beginning letters of a parafoveal word begins on fixation *n,* but is incomplete. Information based partly on visual features and partly on orthographic rules would begin accumulating for the beginning letters of the parafoveal word, but identification would not take place until after the eye movement.

We should like to emphasize that preliminary letter identification, as described above, involves abstract letter identities. Thus, incomplete activation of letters would have to be of the form "this letter is likely to be a *b*" rather than in the form of visual features, since changing case (and hence visual features) made no difference in the amount of facilitation. This also reinforces a point made in the chapter on word recognition. The fact that changing the case of words from fixation to fixation does not interfere with reading strongly argues that word shape is not an important cue used in recognizing words. When word shape is found to have an effect (as with some of the parafoveal priming studies) the effect is likely to be merely a byproduct of letter features. That is, when two words have the same shape, it follows that the component letters share more distinctive features.

An interesting question is whether activation of letters (primarily but not exclusively beginning letters) produces partial activation of a word. One possible model for such partial activation was given in the last chapter by the models of Paap et al. (1982) and Rumelhart and McClelland (1982). In these models, letters in letter strings not only activate the letter detectors but a neighborhood of word detectors. Thus, *chest* in the parafovea could excite a neighborhood of similar lexical entries (e.g., "chest," "chart," "chalk"), and such subthreshold activation is what produces the facilitation of the later identification of *chart*. If one made suitable assumptions that beginning letters were weighted more heavily than end letters in determining the pattern of activation, the pattern of parafoveal facilitation could be explained.

One piece of data that suggests that the facilitation is in terms of partially activated word detectors rather than fully activated letter detectors is the absence of certain kinds of errors in the parafoveal naming experiments. Some of these experiments (Rayner, McConkie and Zola 1980) were set up with pairs such as *train* in the parafovea followed by *clash* in the fovea. If the first 2 letters *tr* of the parafoveal string are fully identified on some trials and then integrated with the information from the foveal string, one might expect the subject to identify the string as *trash*. However, such errors did not occur. That is consistent with viewing facilitation as due to partial activation of a neighborhood of lexical entries. While *trash* would get reasonable excitation from the stimulus *train,* it would get little further excitation from *clash,* since the mismatch in the first letters would be weighted heavily. McConkie et al. (1982) reported similar results in a reading situation.

That is not to say that the lack of "illusory conjunctions" rules out the possibility that parafoveal facilitation can be due to letter identification. What it does rule out is a model in which some letters are fully identified in the parafovea and then those letter positions are ignored when in the fovea. There is thus no strong evidence one way or the other about whether parafoveal facilitation works through the partial activation of lexical entries or the activation of component letters. We will thus assume that both are possible.

SUMMARY

In this chapter we have discussed some basic features of eye movements. Primary among them was the fact that readers fixated a majority of words in text. The bulk of the chapter was spent in determining exactly what could be processed on a fixation. The amount of information that could be processed on a fixation was shown to be the fixated word plus some additional information to the right of it. We suggested a simple view that might explain this fact, namely that on some fixations, one word was processed, on some two, and possibly on some fixations, three words are processed. However, it appears that the story is more complicated than this, since parts of words appear to be extracted which aid identification of those words on later fixations. Thus, the task of identifying what is processed on a fixation in reading (which we will pursue in the next chapter) is not going to be simple. However, the fact that the information extracted from a fixation is limited means that there is a chance that the pattern of eye movements will be able to tell us something about the cognitive activities underlying reading. In the next chapter, we will discuss what is known about how the eyes are controlled in reading and what we can say about reading as a result.

CHAPTER FIVE
EYE-MOVEMENT CONTROL DURING READING

In the previous chapter, we discussed some basic facts about eye movements. We then examined the amount of information that was extracted
from a fixation and how this information was combined across fixations. The
two major conclusions that emerged are that the reader can process
somewhat more than the fixated word on a fixation and that some words are
processed on more than one fixation. But our picture of eye movements is
incomplete; we have said little about the time course of what is happening
from fixation to fixation during reading. When we discussed basic facts of
eye movements, we indicated, for example, that the reading rate, average
fixation duration, and average saccade length all varied with different kinds
of texts. Yet we said little about *how* the differences in the text change these
variables. That is, for more difficult text we know that reading rate slows
down, the average fixation duration increases, the average saccade size
decreases, and the number of regressions increase. However, we have not
discussed what, on a given fixation, causes the fixation to be longer, the
following saccade shorter, or a regression to be made. Similarly, we know
how much information is acquired on a fixation, but we have only touched
upon the time course of the acquisition of this information.

In this chapter, we will discuss in some detail how eye movements are
controlled in reading. We do so for two reasons. First, eye movements are

an important part of the reading process and it is important to understand all components of reading. Second, we believe that eye-movement data may be very important for making inferences about cognitive processes in reading. Indeed, in subsequent chapters we will rely heavily on eye-movement data in trying to understand various processes that occur in reading.

The issues of eye-movement control and the time course of extraction of information from the text are closely related, since the amount of cognitive control possible in reading is dependent on the speed of information extraction. We know that the average fixation in reading is about 225 milliseconds (msec). If it took only 75 msec to encode the fixated word, then there would be plenty of time to program and execute an eye movement conditional on the encoding of the word being completed. On the other hand, if it took about 225 msec to encode a word on a fixation, cognitive control of eye movements would slow down reading, assuming that programming and executing an eye movement takes appreciable time. That is, if one waited until the word were encoded to program an eye movement to move to the next word, the average fixation duration in reading would be the 225 msec encoding time plus the time it took to program and execute the eye movement to the next word (undoubtedly at least 50 msec). Thus the average fixation duration in reading would be at least 275 msec, or a lot longer than it actually is.

If the encoding time for the fixated word were 225 msec, one would need to program the eye movement in anticipation of encoding the word in order to achieve fixation durations as short as 225 msec. One possible strategy would be to program an eye movement at a fixed time after the beginning of a fixation, selecting that time so that most words would be encoded before the eye moved. If this time were judiciously selected, few regressions would be needed to go back to words that were not fully encoded, and reading could proceed with the average fixation being around 225 msec.

In other words, if words can be encoded quickly, cognitive control of eye movements makes sense. On the other hand, if words can't be encoded quickly, then it might be better to put the eyes on "automatic pilot." In either case, a procedure would be needed to interrupt the forward flow when something has not been understood, so that a regression can be made.

At this juncture, let us define a few terms that we will use in describing control of the eyes. At one extreme is the "automatic pilot" version of eye control, which we will call *global control*. By global control, we mean a model of eye control in which the eyes are programmed at the beginning of a chunk of text to move forward at a predetermined rate: on each fixation, the signal to move the eyes is made at a prespecified time after the beginning of the fixation and the saccade length is also prespecified. To account for variability in fixation times and saccade lengths, such a model would have to posit that there is random variability, both in the time to execute the eye movements and in how far the eyes actually move. Such a model would, as we mentioned, need an additional system that could interrupt and cause a regression to be made.

At the other extreme is *direct control*. Direct control means that the signal to move the eyes is the identification of the currently fixated word. It also means that the decision of where to move the eyes is based on visual information extracted from the current fixation. An intermediate position is that eye movements are under *cognitive control* (i.e., directed by information recently extracted in the text, but not necessarily by information extracted on the current fixation). In other words, direct control is the extreme case of cognitive control.

A particularly strong form of direct control is that assumed by the *immediacy hypothesis* (Just and Carpenter 1980). The immediacy hypothesis is that the eyes do not move on until all processing of the fixated word is completed. By "all processing," Just and Carpenter mean not only lexical access of the word but also its integration into the meaning of the sentence or paragraph as well. If the immediacy hypothesis were true, then examining the eye-movement record to infer cognitive processes would be easy, since fixation time on a word would index all the processing time associated with that word. At the other extreme, if global control were true, individual fixations would reveal only the rate that was preset for the passage of text, and thus little about the process of reading.

As we shall see, it appears that most eye-movement control is direct and it is possible that all eye movements in reading may be under cognitive control. That is, it appears that the movement of the eyes is largely predictable from the text currently fixated, although the relationship is more complex than Just and Carpenter hoped it was. Thus, while the eye movement record is a very valuable tool for inferring the cognitive processes of reading, it has to be interpreted very carefully. This chapter, therefore, is a guide to the use of eye movements in making inferences in reading as well as a study in the control of eye movements. We will conclude the chapter with a brief discussion of alternative methods for inferring cognitive processes in reading.

Evidence for Cognitive Control

We would have a complete account of eye movements (and probably of the process of reading) if on each fixation we could account for why the fixation duration was as long as it was and why the saccade following it moved the eyes to the particular location where they landed. Our present state of knowledge is more modest. We do know many variables that influence both the length of fixations and the direction (and size) of saccades and we can make reasonable guesses about what underlying processes are likely to modulate the behavior of the eyes. We shall begin the chapter by briefly reviewing the evidence that there is *some* cognitive control of eye movements.

We start off with such a modest agenda because, during the 1960s and early 1970s, the possibility that there was any cognitive control of eye movements was viewed with some skepticism. There were three arguments underlying this skepticism. The first was that several studies examined eye-movement records from silent reading and attempted to correlate the length of fixations and saccade sizes with certain aspects of the text (e.g., Morton 1964a). These studies failed to find any significant relationship between the eye-movement record and the text. The second was that several studies demonstrated that the length of a fixation was uncorrelated with either the length of the following saccade or the following fixation (e.g., Andriessen and deVoogd 1973). This lack of correlation suggested to some that the variability in both measures was random and hence the eyes were under global control. The third was that the time to encode a word was believed to be relatively slow (at least 200 msec) and so direct control was viewed as implausible (Bouma and deVoogd 1974). Without direct control, indirect cognitive control would be of little value. What good would be the information from a word or two back to tell you how long to fixate the current word or where to move next?

The last plausibility argument, of course, is quite weak, since the time to identify a word is likely to be considerably shorter than 200 msec (see Chapter 3). But what of the first two pieces of data? The lack of correlation between the eye-movement record and the text being read has not agreed with most subsequent reports. The earlier findings are probably due to relatively inaccurate eye recording instruments and to relatively small data sets being analyzed. The advent of more accurate eye-tracking equipment and the use of computers, which enable large amounts of data to be analyzed, have led to the discovery of interesting relationships between the text and the pattern of the eye movements (which we will discuss shortly). In contrast, the lack of correlation of fixation duration with saccade length and between successive fixation durations has been subsequently reported several times and with relatively large data sets (Rayner and McConkie 1976; McConkie and Zola 1984), so it is likely to be a fact about reading. However, it does not necessarily mean that the pattern of eye movements is random.

First, there is no strong reason to expect successive saccades to be positively correlated within a given text. While certain passages may be difficult and cause all fixations on them to be relatively long, there are also reasons to expect successive fixation durations to be negatively correlated (most notably the high probability that a long content word will be followed by a short function word and vice versa). Hence, overall, the positive and negative dependencies could very well sum to an approximately zero correlation. The independence of fixation duration from saccade length is more interesting. It raises the possibility that the decisions of *where* to move the eyes and *when* to move the eyes might be made independently (Rayner and McConkie 1976). For example, some mechanism might aim the next eye movement towards the third letter on the next word, and then a later mechanism (such as identification of the fixated word) might trigger the actual decision to move the eye. Accordingly, we will review evidence that these decisions are under separate cognitive control.

Control of saccade length There is a considerable body of data showing a close relationship between the number of letters in a word and where the reader fixates. First, Rayner and McConkie (1976) computed the probability of a fixation landing on words of different lengths and the probability of fixating on a letter within a word of a given length. They found that as word length increased, the probability of fixating the word increased. This finding is not particularly interesting, since it is consistent with global control: even a random sequence of fixations would produce more fixations on long words. However, a random sequence of eye movements would also imply that the probability of fixating on a letter would be independent of its position in a word or on the length of the word that contained it. Rayner and McConkie found that a letter in a word 4 to 7 letters long was more likely to be fixated than a letter in a shorter or longer word. As we will see, letters in short words tend to be fixated less often because short words tend to be skipped, and individual letters in long words probably tend to be fixated less often than those in middle-length words because there is more redundancy in the long words. In addition, the location of fixations in words is not random; there is a *preferred viewing location* in words between the beginning and middle letters of the word (Rayner 1979; O'Regan 1981; O'Regan et al. 1984; McConkie and Zola 1984). Moreover, the eyes tend not to land on the period or the spaces at the end of a sentence (Rayner 1975b). In addition, readers are less likely to fixate on spaces between words than on letters in words, and Abrams and Zuber (1972) found that readers did not fixate at all on blank regions of several character spaces that were inserted in the text.

The above analyses were in terms of the position of fixations. Another index of cognitive control is the length of saccades. First, the word to the right of fixation has been shown to influence the length of the saccade. The eye tends to jump further when a long word is to the right of fixation than when a shorter word is there (O'Regan 1975, 1979; Rayner 1979). In addition, the size of saccades is sensitive to manipulations in the text. Moving-window experiments have demonstrated that as window size decreases to less than 15 character spaces to the right of fixation (when the spaces between words outside of the window are filled), saccade length decreases.

The above data show that the movement of the eyes is sensitive to the length of words. Thus, the eyes appear to be guided by a computation based on the boundaries of a word (delineated by spaces). That the eyes tend to jump over blank regions indicates that such geometric computations are at least part of the story. More direct evidence for such control comes from an experiment by Morris (1987). In one condition, the only useful information to the right of the fixated word (which we term *word n*) was the spaces delimiting *word n+1* (all the letters to the right of word *n* were converted to *x*'s). In spite of the fact that word *n+1* was all *x*'s before it was fixated, the longer word *n+1* was, the longer the saccade off word *n*. Thus, word length, per se, had an effect on the size of the saccade.

There is a natural confounding of the length of a word and its frequency in the language, however; shorter words tend to be more common. Thus, some of the "word length effects" in natural reading may not be caused by word boundaries but by processing the letters in between. One clear demonstration of the effect of the letters is in studies of when words are skipped. While shorter words are skipped more than longer words, several studies have shown that words tend to be skipped if they are frequent or otherwise easier to process even when length is controlled. For example, *the* is skipped more than other 3-letter words (O'Regan 1979, 1980) and words that are predictable from the prior sentence context are also skipped more (Balota, Pollatsek, and Rayner 1985; Ehrlich and Rayner 1981). In addition, the *direction* of eye movements is under cognitive control. Readers are much more likely to make a regression when the word fixated is one indicating that the previous analysis of the sentence was invalid (Frazier and Rayner 1982; Rayner and Frazier 1987). (We mention these predictability and sentential effects now to make our case for cognitive control, but will defer discussion of them to Chapter 7.)

Control of fixation duration   We have seen that the decision of where to move is controlled both by low-level visual information, such as the position of spaces, and by higher-level variables, such as the meaning of the text. We now turn to look at the factors that control *when* we move our eyes.

Perhaps the most widely reported finding is that words infrequently used in the language require longer fixations than frequently used words (Inhoff 1984; Inhoff and Rayner 1986; Just and Carpenter 1980; Kliegl, Olson, and Davidson 1982; Rayner 1977; Rayner and Duffy 1986). Part of this difference is due to the natural confounding of word length and word frequency; infrequently used words tend to be longer than frequently used words (Kliegl, Olson, and Davidson 1982). However, even when word length is controlled, both the first fixation duration and the gaze duration on infrequent words is longer than for frequent words (Inhoff and Rayner 1986; Rayner and Duffy 1986). Second, fixation duration varies with the function of a word in a sentence. For example, the verb in a sentence receives more fixation time than do nouns (Holmes and O'Regan 1981; Rayner 1977; Wanat 1971). In addition, in sentences containing syntactic ambiguities, fixation duration increases when readers reach a ambiguous word in the sentence (Frazier and Rayner 1982). Third, fixation durations tend to be shorter on words that are predictable from the prior sentential context than on less predictable words (Ehrlich and Rayner 1981; Balota, Pollatsek, and Rayner 1985; Zola 1984). Fourth, lexically ambiguous words (words with two or more meanings like *bank*) will sometimes result in longer fixation times (Rayner and Duffy 1986). Fifth, *gaze durations* (the total time on a word before the eye leaves the word) are greatly influenced by antecedent search processes.

Antecedent search is the process of establishing an antecedent for an anaphoric noun phrase or pronoun. For example, if you're reading a passage and you encounter *the bird* in the course of reading a sentence, a search through the text representation you have built up will be initiated and you realize that *the bird* is the *robin* talked about two sentences earlier. A number of studies have shown that the distance between an anaphor and its antecedent affects gaze duration on the word; as the distance increases, gaze time increases (Ehrlich and Rayner 1983; Duffy and Rayner 1988; Schustack, Ehrlich, and Rayner 1987). Finally, fixation times vary depending upon where in the sentence or on a line the reader is looking. Gaze durations are longer at the ends of both clauses and sentences than within the clauses and sentences (Just and Carpenter 1980). These sentence and clause "wrap-up" effects probably reflect additional processing associated with understanding the sentence or clause. There are also effects on fixation duration due to the position of the word in the line of text, with the first fixation being longer and the last duration shorter than the other fixations (Rayner 1978a). This last finding makes sense in terms of what we know about parafoveal processing: the words seen on the first fixation have no benefit of parafoveal preview, and on the last fixation, there is less parafoveal information to process.

Fixation times thus appear to be sensitive to various aspects of the meaning of the text being processed. We will return in chapters 7 and 8 to use eye movements to help us understand questions about how sentential context influences the processing of words, how sentences are processed, and how higher-order structures are used in reading text. In this chapter, we will focus on how the identification of words and lower-level information, such as the location of word boundaries, are expressed in the eye-movement record. While other factors are important, word length accounts for most of the variability in gaze duration (e.g., Blanchard 1985a; Just and Carpenter 1980; Kliegl, Olson, and Davidson 1982). Thus word identification or lower-level visual factors account for most of the *forward* movement of the eyes through the page (i.e., how long the eye stays at a given point and how far it moves on), so that we can get a reasonably clear picture of eye guidance even if we ignore higher-level factors. In contrast, regressions are probably more influenced by difficulties in comprehending higher-order aspects of the text; we will defer most of our discussion of regressions to chapters 7 and 8, where sentence and text integration is discussed.

Evidence for Direct Control

It is clear from the above discussion that the cognitive processing of the text does modulate the pattern of eye movements and thus that eye movements are under some sort of cognitive control. We wish now to be more specific about delineating the sequence of operations during a fixation that leads to an eye movement being executed. First, let us consider the issue of whether there is in fact evidence for direct control. At first, it might appear that shorter fixations on a frequent word (*church*) than on a less frequent word (*mosque*) would be evidence for direct control. However, it is possible that the shorter average fixation time on *church* is due to those instances when it was fully identified in the parafovea on the prior fixation. In fact, a moment's reflection will lead you to realize that in reading normal text, one can never be certain from which fixation a given piece of visual information was extracted, so that evidence of direct control can never be gotten from a completely natural reading situation. Thus, we have to turn to techniques in which the text displayed is contingent on eye movements to find conclusive evidence for direct control.

Direct control of saccades Rayner and Pollatsek (1981) provided the first air-tight evidence for direct control of saccades. They used a variant of the moving-window technique in which the window size varied randomly from fixation to fixation. They found that the length of a saccade following a fixation increased markedly as the size of the window of normal text on that fixation increased from 9 to 17 to 33 characters. Since the variation in window size was totally unpredictable, the variation in saccade length must have been influenced by the text actually seen on that fixation. Rayner and Pollatsek (1981) also examined whether the length of the saccade following fixation n was influenced by the size of the window on fixation $n-1$. In fact, the bigger the window on fixation $n-1$, the longer the saccades following fixation n, were 1, indicating that there is delayed control of saccade length as well as direct control.

Direct control of fixation duration In order to test for direct control of fixation duration in reading, Rayner and Pollatsek (1981) presented a visual mask at the end of each saccade that effectively delayed the onset of the text. The rationale of the experiment was that if fixation duration is dependent upon information encoded on the current fixation, then delaying the onset of the text should increase fixation duration by an amount related to the text delay. To ensure that the fixation duration depended on the text delay on the current fixation, they varied the delay interval randomly from fixation to fixation. There was clear support for direct control: the fixation duration increased as the delay of text increased from fixation to fixation. (However, the delay on fixation $n-1$ had no effect on the duration of fixation n.)

A stronger test of direct control is whether the fixation duration increases by an amount equal to the text delay. If we assume that the signal to move the eyes is the identification of the fixated word, then we would expect that delaying the text by 200 msec should delay the fixation duration by 200 msec as well. The data of Rayner and Pollatsek's study are not consistent on this point. In one experiment in which the delay was constant from fixation to fixation, the fixation duration increased by the delay interval (for relatively small delay intervals). However, in the random delay experiment cited above, the fixation duration increased by a smaller amount than the delay interval. In a later experiment (Morrison 1984), both fixed and random delay conditions resulted in smaller increases in the fixation delay than the text delay. Thus it appears that the eyes do not *always* wait for the currently fixated word to be processed in order to move on.

A more striking confirmation of indirect control was the finding that when there were long delays (200 msec or more), subjects sometimes moved their eyes even before the text appeared. If you think carefully about it, these anticipatory saccades are counterproductive. That is, if the reader had fixated for 190 msec (in the 200 msec fixed delay condition) and then an eye movement occurred, text would not be presented for another 200 msec. Such eye movements thus appeared to be the result of some automatic process independent of reading. When these anticipatory saccades were removed from the data for the long fixation durations, the average increase in fixation duration was approximately equal to the text delay. This analysis suggested to Rayner and Pollatsek that fixation durations may be produced by a mixture of direct control and global control: on some fixations the signal to move the eye is some foveal processing event (such as the identification of the fixated word), while on others the fixation ends because of an anticipatory saccade (i.e., one that is programmed independently of encoding operations during reading). For shorter delay intervals, anticipatory saccades would be hard to identify, and thus the imperfect relation between text delay and fixation duration could be because those fixations are also a mixture of direct control and anticipatory saccades. A careful analysis of anticipatory saccades (Morrison 1984) indicated, however, that their length was not unrelated to the ongoing processing and that they were best thought of as being programmed on the previous fixation. Nevertheless, Rayner and Pollatsek's basic idea that fixation durations are a mixture of direct control and more indirect control may be correct.

Another interesting finding emerged from the Rayner and Pollatsek experiments. The manipulation of window size had very little effect on fixation duration and the manipulation of text delay had no effect on saccade length when anticipatory saccades were removed. This suggested, first of all, that the two decisions were made independently. It also suggested what the main contributors to those decisions were. When the smallest window size (9 character spaces or 4 spaces to the right of the fixated letter) was employed in the Rayner and Pollatsek experiments, fixation durations increased somewhat. However, there was no difference in fixation times when the larger two windows (17 and 33 character spaces) were employed. In the larger windows, the fixated word was visible most of the time, unlike in the smallest. Thus, it appears that if the fixated word is visible, there are relatively small effects of window size on fixation time (the bulk of the moving-window studies are consistent with this). Since text delay markedly affected fixation duration, it does seem as though fixation duration is mainly controlled by some event connected with encoding of the fixated word and is little affected by parafoveal information. On the other hand, since the size of the window had a clear effect on saccade length, it appears that parafoveal information has a major effect on the decision of where to move the eyes.

What Information Is Involved in Direct Control?

Let us briefly summarize what we have established. First, we argued that the movement of the eyes is sensitive to the text being read, both to low-level information such as the length of words (and the presence of spaces between words) and to higher-order variables such as the frequency of a word in the language or the predictability of a word from sentence context. Thus, the eyes are under cognitive control. Second, in the last section, we demonstrated that the movement of the eyes could be under some direct control, since very dramatic changes, such as delaying the onset of the text after the beginning of a fixation and restricting the size of the window (with a homogeneous field of x's outside the window), affected the fixation duration and saccade size, respectively. However, the latter demonstration is quite crude, since it shows that initially presenting visual "garbage" in the fovea (a homogeneous field) will delay fixation and presenting visual garbage in the parafovea will shorten saccades. We need more subtle experiments to tell us what information is actually driving the eye during reading.

Saccade length First, let us consider saccade length. Pollatsek and Rayner (1982) attempted to be more diagnostic about the role of word boundaries. In their study, the only information that was manipulated from fixation to fixation was the spaces between words (i.e., the letters in words were intact). They found that when the space between word $n+1$ and word $n+2$ was filled in, saccade length was smaller. However, they found that if the space was filled in 50 msec after the fixation began, there was no effect on saccade length or any other measure of reading. That is, filling in this space was effective only during the first 50 msec. Their conclusion was that the location of the space to the right of word $n+1$ was used to help compute where word $n+1$ was, and hence where to direct the next eye movement. An alternative possibility is that the presence of a space filler may have interfered with the identification of words $n+1$ and $n+2$. Pollatsek and Rayner attempted to minimize this possibility by employing a "noise character," which was quite visually dissimilar to letters, as a space filler in some conditions. Hence, the space filler should rarely be encoded as a letter and hence should itself rarely abet incorrect word identification. However, the space filler may have made letters near it harder to identify by lateral inhibitory mechanisms (see Chapter 1), so that we can't really be sure what the effect is on word boundaries.

A more direct test by Morris (1987) was to release the blank spaces between words in a homogeneous field (see Figure 5.1) at varying time delays. Since there were no letters to identify in the parafovea, any effect of introducing the space would have to be in providing word boundary

Full Parafoveal Mask (Control)
They help migratingxxxxxxxxxxxxxxxxxxxxxxxxx.   (beginning of fixation)
       *

They help migratingxxxxxxxxxxxxxxxxxxxxxxxxx.   (after X msec)
       *

They help migrating toadsxxxxxxxxxxxxxxxxx.   (beginning of next fixation)
            *

Releasing Both Spaces
They help migratingxxxxxxxxxxxxxxxxxxxxxxxxx.   (beginning of fixation)
       *

They help migrating xxxxx xxxxxxxxxxxxxxxx.   (after X msec)
       *

They help migrating toadsxxxxxxxxxxxxxxxxx.   (beginning of next fixation)
            *

Releasing First Space
They help migratingxxxxxxxxxxxxxxxxxxxxxxxxx.   (beginning of fixation)
       *

They help migrating xxxxxxxxxxxxxxxxxxxxxxxx.   (after X msec)
       *

They help migrating toadsxxxxxxxxxxxxxxxxx.   (beginning of next fixation)
            *

FIGURE 5-1   **Some conditions in the Morris (1987) experiment. If the space information is not released after about 50 msec, it has virtually no effect. (Asterisk indicates fixation point.)**

information. She found that the introduction of spaces produced longer saccades, and furthermore that their introduction had little effect if they occurred after 50 msec.

We know that the saccade is guided by more than word boundary information, since word $n+1$ is skipped more often when it is frequent in the language or is predictable. However, such an effect need not be direct. The first experiment documenting the direct control of letter information was by McConkie et al. (1985). Their design was similar to that of Rayner and Pollatsek in that they randomly varied window size from fixation to fixation. However, there were two differences. First, on most fixations, there was no window (the whole line of text was presented), but on those fixations on which a window was employed, the window size and location (i.e., whether the left or right boundary was farther from fixation) was varied. Second, they preserved all spaces, with all letters outside the text being replaced by random letters. They found that fixations on which there was a window produced shorter saccades, indicating that the particular letters presented on a fixation influenced the size of the saccade. Since the boundary of the window was only 4 letters to the right of the fixated letter, we can't be sure that letter information in the parafovea as well as the fovea was influencing the size of a saccade.

Thus, it appears that saccade size is under direct control of various types of information: word boundary information extracted from the parafovea early in the fixation and by letter information. It may be that letter information influences saccade size chiefly by determining how many words are identified on the fixation.

Fixation durations   The Rayner and Pollatsek (1981) data discussed previously suggested that fixation duration is controlled by identification of the fixated word. However, the increase in fixation caused by delaying the text could be caused by waiting for anything textlike to appear rather than waiting for anything as complex as the identification of the word.

The frequency of a word in the language has been commonly used as an index of word identification. That is, since word frequency influences word encoding time (see Chapter 3), if word frequency also influences fixation time, then it is assumed that the signal to move the eye (at least some of the time) is the encoding of the fixated word. To ensure that the fixated word is in fact encoded when it is fixated, however, the reader has to be denied a preview of it. Inhoff and Rayner (1986) varied the frequency of selected target words (equating the number of letters), and in one condition, subjects had no parafoveal preview. Their results were complex. When there was no preview, word frequency had no effect on the duration of the first fixation on the target word, but did have an effect on the gaze duration. That is, the speed of encoding a word (without a parafoveal preview) did not appear to influence the decision *when* to move the eye after the first fixation. However, since gaze duration primarily reflects the probability that a word is fixated twice, the speed of encoding a word appeared to affect the decision *where* to make the next fixation. The story was different when subjects had a normal preview. In that case, both first fixation and gaze duration were affected by the frequency of the fixated word.

The most parsimonious explanation of these data is that encoding of a word, if fast enough, can influence the decision of *when* the eyes move. Thus when there is a parafoveal preview to speed word identification, the frequency of the word can affect the first fixation duration. In contrast, if encoding is a little slower, it still may influence *where* the eyes go (specifically, whether the word is refixated or not). Thus, without a parafoveal preview to speed word identification, the frequency of the word can still affect the number of fixations on a word. These data suggest that part of the skill of reading is using parafoveal information to encode words rapidly enough so that the encoding of these words can efficiently program the next eye movement. We will now consider a model of how eye movements are programmed in reading.

A MODEL OF EYE-MOVEMENT CONTROL IN READING

So far, a lot of circumstantial evidence has been presented concerning how eye movements are controlled. We know that fixation times are sensitive to word frequency, to the predictability of a word in text, as well as to other indices of the comprehensibility of the word in the text. We know that saccade length is sensitive to meaningful variables such as frequency or predictability of a word (as in word-skipping), but it is also sensitive to variables such as the position of spaces and word length. It would be nice if we could continue to present data that would by logical steps lead to acceptance of a single model of eye-movement control. Unfortunately, we do not have such data, nor are we likely to have such data for some time. Instead, we will present a relatively simple model, which is consistent with much of the existing data, that can be made more complex to handle additional data. The model will therefore serve to integrate the data we have discussed with the additional data that we will introduce.

We first need to get a better conceptual organization of the timing of events on a fixation. A typical fixation is shown in Figure 5.2, with the top of the figure marking the time when the preceding saccade has ended. Meaningful visual information then strikes the retina. However, we need to consider the *eye-mind lag,* the time it takes for this information to arrive at the brain centers in which visual words are identified (see our discussion of this at the beginning of Chapter 3). There are various estimates of the eye-mind lag, which we will discuss shortly. After the visual information arrives at these brain centers, many computations are done on it, each of which may have its own time course. The boundaries of words may be computed from the positions of spaces, a computation may be done to see whether the word is orthographically legal, the lexical entry of a word is accessed, the pronunciation is accessed, the meaning is accessed, the meaning of the word is joined to the prior context in order to continue construction of the syntax and meaning of the phrase, sentence, and paragraph.

At least some of these computations could influence the decision to activate the eye-movement system. For example, when a word is identified, there may be a decision taken to direct the next fixation to the following word. This decision ("word is encoded therefore move eye to next word") may take some time (the *decision time*). When this decision is made, then presumably an eye movement to the next word is programmed. There will be some time elapsed, the *eye-movement program latency,* between when the eye-movement system is told to execute the movement and when the saccade actually starts. In addition, there will be the *saccade time,* the time that the saccade actually takes, until the next fixation is begun and the whole sequence starts again.

There are a number of additional comments that need to be made. The first is the role of the eye-mind lag. It not only delays when visual information begins to be available to the mind when the fixation begins but also prolongs the availability of visual information beyond the end of the fixation (see Figure 5.2). Thus, while the eye-mind lag causes processing of visual information in the mind to lag behind the observable events (such as the beginning of a fixation), it does not make the actual amount of time the mind has to process stimulation any shorter than the actual time it is

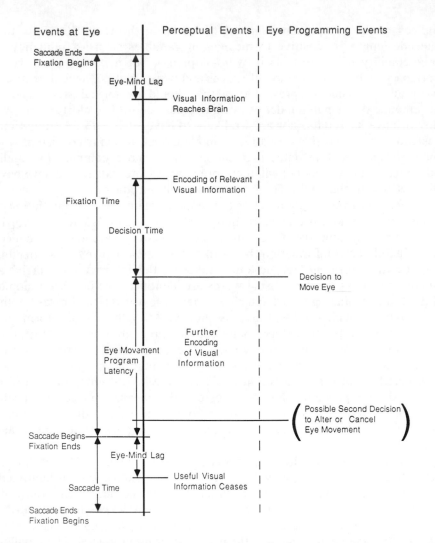

FIGURE 5-2 A simplified schema of events during a fixation relevant to eye movement control. There has been little attempt made to represent time intervals accurately by vertical distances. In addition, the eye-mind lag has been drawn to be shorter than the saccade time even though the opposite may be true. A realistic model of eye control needs to be more complex (see text). Among other things, the decision of where to move the eye is left out of the figure.

exposed. (A similar comment applies when a stimulus is masked, as discussed in Chapter 3.)

The second is that our assumption of how the eye movement is programmed needs to be elaborated. Above, we assumed that the cognitive system delivered a message ("fixate next word") and the eye-movement system could somehow calculate the geometric coordinates of the location intended and send the eyes there. For the most part, we will not concern ourselves with the details of how this is done.

The third comment is that our discussion in this section has so far assumed only direct control. We have seen, however, that on some fixations, the information that controls the saccade was extracted on prior fixations. It is also possible that on other fixations, the signal to move the eyes may merely be something like "200 msec has elapsed, so let's move the eyes." A related issue, which we will get to shortly, is when the signal to move the eyes is given. So far, we have assumed that it was during fixation n (the one terminated by the eye movement in question). We will argue shortly, however, that some of the time it is likely the eye movement that ends fixation n is programmed during fixation $n-1$. To keep Figure 5.2 reasonably simple, we have not drawn in the details of that process.

We are finally about ready to unveil our model of eye-movement control. However, we need to talk about one other unobservable event, namely a shift of attention. As we mentioned in Chapter 1, there can be internal shifts of attention independent of eye movements. We will assume that an internal attention "spotlight" moves across the page, usually in advance of the eyes. As we shall see, such an assumption will allow us to produce a relatively simple and elegant mechanism that can account for a lot of the complexity of eye movements. We will provide evidence for such a mechanism after we have presented the model. While the evidence for such an internal scanning mechanism is compelling, we admit that the evidence for the details we assume is far less so.

The basic idea of the model we will present was first articulated by McConkie (1979). He suggested that control of eye movements worked in the following manner. The internal attention spotlight moves across the page until the reader encounters "difficulty" encoding words either because the visual information is poor (due to being far from fixation or other factors) or because it is hard to understand (possibly because the word was of low frequency). At the point that difficulty is encountered, a signal to the eye-movement system is sent to move to the point of difficulty. The model is attractive because it employs a relatively simple mechanism for eye control: "a point of difficulty" is established, and the eye moves there. It also appears to predict a lot of the basic features of eye control: saccades are directed to areas that have already been processed to a certain degree; both visual and textual variables influence the size of the saccade (e.g., it accounts for skipping frequent and predictable words).

The "point of difficulty," however, is the major problem with the model. First, the model suggests that the eyes respond to difficulty with visual features similarly to difficulty with text comprehension, an assumption that is dubious. The greater problem, though, is with how and when the point of difficulty is computed. "Having difficulty" seems to be a rather complex decision to make computationally. Furthermore, *if the eye had to wait until "having difficulty" was decided upon before programming an eye movement, it would appear to make fixation durations unacceptably slow.*

These problems led Morrison (1984) to try to account for eye-movement control in a somewhat different manner. We think Morrison's account is essentially correct, and so we will present it in some detail. He preserved McConkie's notion of an attentive spotlight leading the eyes, but changed the details by which they are led. In Morrison's model, the eyes are led by successful processing rather than being drawn to where there is trouble, as in McConkie's model. Morrison postulated that words are processed one at a time by the attentive mechanism. The signal to move the attention mechanism to the next word is the successful identification of the prior word. When the attentive mechanism moves on to the next word, a signal is automatically sent out to the eye-movement system to execute a saccade to the new attended region. (The location of where the eyes are to be sent may be based on an earlier calculation of where the beginning and end of word $n+1$ are.)

A mechanism for word-skipping So far, Morrison's model seems promising. All the computations needed appear feasible (if word identification is sufficiently fast), and it can account for parafoveal preview effects since the focus of attention will arrive on word $n+1$ ahead of the eyes. So far, however, it has a fatal flaw. It predicts each word will be fixated in turn; none will be skipped and none refixated. To account for skipping (among other things), Morrison added a second key idea: that more than one eye movement can be programmed at a time. That is, each time the attention mechanism moves to a new word, a new command to move the eyes goes out *regardless of whether the previous command has been executed or not.* You can think of this situation as if the waiter (the attentive system) keeps giving the chef (the eye-movement system) new orders even though all the old orders have not been filled.

If it is to be of value, the model has to specify what happens when there is more than one "unfilled order" at the same time. This is where the model gets a bit complicated. If the lag between the first and second order is greater than about 50 to 75 msec, then both saccades are executed normally. To illustrate, let us suppose that word n is identified 125 msec after the beginning of the fixation n (followed by an attention shift) and word $n+1$ is identified 225 msec after the beginning of the same fixation (followed by a second attention shift). Let us think of the beginning of fixation n as time zero (see Figure 5.3, panel a). Thus, eye movement 1 is programmed at 125 msec and eye movement 2 is programmed at 225 msec. However, there will be a latency in executing these programs, let us say 150 msec (see Figure 5.3, panel a). Since eye movement 1 (which terminates fixation n) is executed at 275 msec, eye movement 2 (terminating fixation $n+1$) will be executed on the basis of a program initiated on fixation n.

Hence, Morrison's model can explain indirect control. It can also explain the fact that quite short fixations (100 msec or less) sometimes occur in reading. Note that fixation $n+1$ in Figure 5.3 (a) is only 100 msec.

What happens if a word is encoded really quickly and two eye

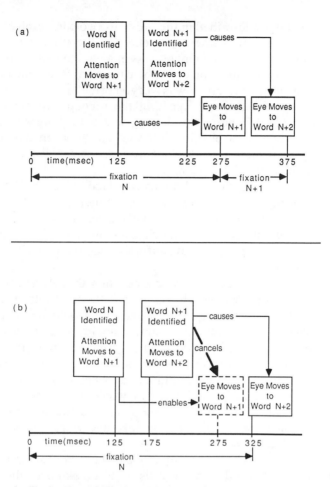

FIGURE 5-3 An illustration of Morrison's model. The top panel illustrates the situation when two eye movements are programmed on fixation *N*. Thus, fixation *N+1* is relatively short. The bottom panel illustrates the situation when a word is skipped. Since the time between the two attention shifts is very short, the eye movement program produced by the second one causes the first eye movement to be cancelled (indicated by the dashed line) and hence the eye moves directly to word *N+2*. (See text for details.)

movements are programmed with even a shorter lag between them? There is evidence from experiments with simpler stimuli that something complex happens. Becker and Jurgens (1979) had subjects maintain fixation on a cross and then asked them to move their eyes to wherever the cross moved. On some trials, the cross only moved once. However, on the trials of interest, the cross moved twice, and the subjects were supposed to move their eyes to the third location as soon as possible, omitting moving to the second location if possible. Not surprisingly, when there was a relatively long delay between the first and second moves, subjects executed an eye movement to the second location and then to the third (a model for the eye-movement pattern described in the previous two paragraphs). However, if the second movement of the cross occurred very soon after the first movement, only one eye movement was made, indicating that the eye movement to the second location could be cancelled. When the lag between the two movements of the cross was very short, the eye movement went directly to the third location (indicating the second eye movement was completely cancelled), whereas if the lag was a bit longer, a single eye movement was made to a position intermediate between the second and third locations (indicating that the first eye movement was cancelled, but influenced the location of the second).

To summarize, Becker and Jurgens provided evidence that more than one eye movement can be programmed at a time, and, furthermore, that there seems to be some mechanism that will cancel the first eye movement if the second is programmed soon enough after the first. However, in some circumstances, the first program, even if not executed, may alter the size of the second saccade.

Morrison hypothesized that the cancellation that Becker and Jurgens observed also occurs in reading. That is, if two attention shifts occur in close enough proximity, then the first eye movement would be cancelled (see Figure 5.3, panel b). Two attention shifts should occur with a short lag between them when a word is encoded quickly, presumably either because it is short, frequent in the language and/or predictable. Thus, if *the* is word $n+1$, the fixated word would be attended, and when identified, an attention shift made to *the*. It would be likely that *the* would be encoded quickly and a second attention shift made to word $n+2$ soon after the first. In that event, the eye movement to *the* would be cancelled and word $n+2$ would be the next word fixated after word *n*.

Morrison's model thus elegantly explains both how skipping of words can occur and which words are more likely to be skipped: those that are short, frequent, and predictable (i.e., those that are quickly identified). It also explains why fixations are longer when the succeeding word is skipped (Hogaboam 1983; Pollatsek, Rayner, and Balota 1986): if word $n+1$ is skipped, then the first eye movement program is cancelled and the eye has to wait until the second is executed. (Note that fixation *n* in panel b of Figure 5.3 is longer than fixation *n* in panel a.) In fact, the Morrison model is capable of accounting for much of the data that we have presented in this chapter and the last. For example, it clearly explains why fixation times are longer on a word that is longer, of lower frequency, and less predictable: the primary signal to move the eye is the encoding of the fixated word, thus the eye will move sooner the faster the word is encoded. It can also explain delayed effects on saccade length, since some saccades are programmed on fixation $n-1$.

A problem area: refixations of words As outlined above, Morrison's model does not account either for regressions or for refixations on words. Clearly, a new mechanism needs to be added to the model in order to explain regressions. Because the model postulates that a word is not fixated until the prior ones are identified, there are no incompletely identified words that need regressions to further the processing. The model does allow for two kinds of processing difficulty that are potential sources of regressions: (1) a word could be misidentified; or (2) it could be correctly identified but not yet make sense with what has been read so far. In either case, to explain regressions one must add a monitor to the model that "knows" something is wrong and interrupts the sequence of operations driven by word identification. The monitor would have, as input, higher-order processes that would know whether the current interpretation of the discourse made sense.

Refixations (fixating on the same word more than once before moving on) are a problem, even with this additional assumption, since they appear to be caused by lexical factors (at least in part). For example, as we discussed previously, Inhoff and Rayner (1986) showed that a low-frequency word was more likely to be refixated than a high-frequency word. Three types of assumptions could be added to the Morrison model that might be able to explain refixations. The first is that a subword unit, such as the morpheme, can be the unit of identification. Then attention would sometimes shift from one part of a word to another with eye movements following suit, at least some of the time. (This is not a convincing explanation of Inhoff and Rayner, however, since most of their words were monomorphemic.)

The second assumption is that not all eye movements are under cognitive control and that relatively short eye movements are sometimes programmed "automatically" (Rayner and Pollatsek 1981). Thus, when encoding times for a word are long, this "automatic" eye movement would be the first eye movement programmed and the word would be refixated unless the eye movement programmed by the attention shift came soon enough after to cancel it.

The third assumption is that some refixations may be produced by the same mechanism as regressions: namely that the cognitive system decides that something doesn't make sense and perhaps the eyes ought not to move to the next word. However, as we pointed out earlier, if such a decision is to be made early enough in the fixation to influence the saccade, it is unlikely to be due to a judgment of the form "I'm having difficulty identifying the fixated word," (which as we argued earlier should be relatively slow). On the other hand, a positive judgment that the fixated word doesn't make sense with the rest of the sentence could conceivably be made fast enough to cause refixations in this manner (see Chapter 7). In either case, it is not obvious how "whoops, something's wrong here" judgments get translated into a second fixation on a word. Intuitively, they appear to be the result of a conflict between a command to move on to the next word and a command to stop on the present word. The details of such a conflict mechanism have not been well worked out.

Some final comments on eye-movement control   The last section includes much speculation. However, we hope it indicates that Morrison's model has the potential to be patched up to be a reasonably complete account of how the eyes move (and, we hope, with not too many additional mechanisms). Let us not lose sight of the model's successes. It accounts for most of the forward movement of the eyes with only a few basic assumptions: (a) that attention moves forward word by word; (b) that eye movements go where internal attention has already moved; (c) that later eye-movement programs can cancel or alter earlier eye-movement programs; and (d) that the location of a saccade can be calculated independently of the decision to execute the saccade. With these assumptions, the model can account for the effects of word frequency and predictability on fixation durations, and word skipping and even can explain why there are occasional very short fixations. It does so without postulating any "little men in the head," but rather by joining quite simple modules. One module detects when the fixated word is identified and sends a message to the attentional and eye-movement systems. A second computes the boundaries of word $n+1$ and $n+2$ and sends these parameters to the eye-movement system to compute where to move. Much of the complexity is handled by the response cancelling and altering mechanism (Becker and Jurgens 1979) for which we have already provided substantial evidence. We have also discussed evidence indicating that word boundary information is extracted and used relatively early in the fixation as well as evidence suggesting that this calculation may be done independently of the decision of when to move.

Does attention move forward word by word?   A major assumption of the Morrison model is that there is a covert attentional system that drives eye movements. What support is there for such an assumption? We discussed evidence for covert attention in Chapter 1. Part of that evidence is physiological data (using monkeys as subjects) that show that there are brain areas implicated in covert attention in which a spatially defined region becomes activated before the beginning of the saccade and also before activation of the centers that appear to direct the saccade (Wurtz, Goldberg, and Robinson 1982). Since saccadic behavior is disrupted if these areas are damaged, the evidence points to a covert attention mechanism that precedes and directs eye movements.

The asymmetry of the perceptual span in reading supports the hypothesis that covert attention is directed to the fixated word and the words to the right (in English). We have less evidence on the second assumption: that attention moves forward word by word (or possibly morpheme by morpheme). There are two components to this assumption: (1) that letters in words are processed in parallel; and (2) that words are processed one at a time.

In Chapter 3 we discussed the evidence that the letters in short words are processed in parallel, i.e., that attention does not sweep across words letter by letter. There is additional evidence in reading that letters in words are not processed sequentially from left to right. First, Blanchard and colleagues (Blanchard 1985b, 1988; Blanchard et al. 1984) have reported a number of studies in which subjects are presented two different words on a single fixation. For example, *peaks* could be presented early in the fixation followed by a brief visual mask and then *bears* presented for the remainder of the fixation. They varied the time that *peaks* was exposed before *bears* came on. They argued that if letters were processed serially, there should be an exposure time for *peaks* so that the *p* in it would be processed but that the *r* in *bears* would be present when the internal scan came to the fourth position. If so, the subject should encode the word as *pears* on some fixations. This, in fact, never happened (see also Slowiaczek and Rayner [1987] for further evidence against a serial scan of letters).

Another attempt to rule out letter-by-letter scanning comes from a series of experiments by Inhoff et al. (1988). They presented text in which the words were normal but the order of words could go from left to right or right to left (see Figure 5.4). They reasoned that if letter-by-letter scanning operated, not only would reading be more difficult when the word order was reversed but the benefit of seeing the next word in the parafovea would be lessened as well. While they found that reading was about 30 percent slower when the order of the words was right to left, it is not strong evidence for a letter-by-letter scan. It may merely be that right-to-left saccades are more difficult to program than left-to-right saccades given the input "fixated word identified" (e.g., the calculation of *where* to move might be executed more slowly). However, they found that fixation durations decreased about equally in the two text conditions when there was a parafoveal preview of the next word in the text. The equal parafoveal benefit in the two conditions seems hard to explain if a left-to-right letter scanning mechanism were operative in normal reading. Given such a scan, when the order of the words is reversed, a large leap of attention would be needed to go from the end of the fixated word to the beginning of the parafoveal word (see Figure 5.4) that would not be needed in normal reading.

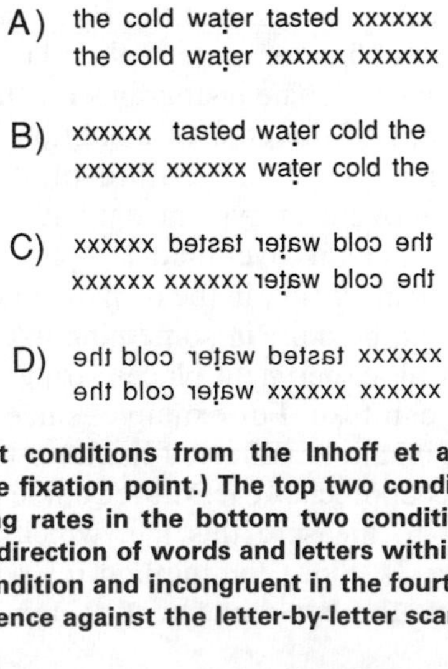

FIGURE 5-4 Sample text conditions from the Inhoff et al. (1988) study. (The dot indicates the fixation point.) The top two conditions are discussed in the text. Reading rates in the bottom two conditions were the same, even though the direction of words and letters within words was congruent in the third condition and incongruent in the fourth condition. This provides further evidence against the letter-by-letter scanning hypothesis.

The above indicates that there is every reason to believe that letters in words are processed in parallel in reading just as when words are presented in isolation (at least for short words). However, there is little evidence on whether or not attention jumps sequentially from word to word. One could make a plausibility argument in favor of it, however. Since the order of words is important in understanding the meaning of a sentence (e.g., "*Was John here?*" vs. "*John was here.*"), processing of words sequentially would help to index the order in the sentence. One type of experiment that might help to determine whether attention moved from word to word would be to delay the onset of word $n+1$ after the beginning of the fixation. If short delays made no difference in reading, it would suggest that word $n+1$ was processed only after processing of word n was complete and that attention jumps from word to word.

Are the times assumed for component processes reasonable? We have assumed that it is possible in the time of a fixation (200 to 250 msec) to encode a word, make a decision to move to the next word, and execute the program to move. This process appears to involve four sequential components: (1) the eye-mind lag; (2) the time to encode a word after it reaches the mind; (3) the time to decide to make an eye movement; and (4) the time to begin executing the eye movement (see Figure 5.2). McConkie et al. (1985) attempted to measure some of these times by examining histograms (or frequency distributions) of fixation times in a "random" window experiment. They reasoned that if the histograms differed between two window conditions, then one could infer that the eye movement system started to "notice" the difference in information at that time.

One interesting comparison in the experiment involved conditions in which the window restriction occurred only after 100 msec of the fixation. Two windows were used: the *left,* in which all text to the left of the fixated letter was replaced by other letters, and the *right,* in which all letters more than 4 letters to the right of fixation were replaced (with the spaces between words preserved in each case). The histograms for these conditions differed from each other and that of the control condition by 220 msec from the beginning of the fixation. Thus, the nature of the display change was "noticed" by the eye movement system only 120 msec after the display change. This indicates that the eye-mind lag plus an encoding operation (more complex than noticing flicker in the display) plus a decision to move or not move the eyes can all be done in something like 120 msec.

The McConkie et al. experiment places stringent upper limits on how long certain processes can take. For example, since it only takes 120 msec for a stimulus to come in and be reflected in motor behavior, it is clear that the eye-mind lag time is appreciably less. McConkie et al. discussed several physiological attempts to measure this lag, which are usually around 50 msec (also see Chapter 3). Since the method rests on measuring when an anomaly is detected by the eye-movement system, it is hard to make a precise statement from the research about how long any of the other processes in normal reading take unless one knows what kinds of encoding processes detected the anomaly (e.g., word identification, letter identification, detection of mismatch between fovea and parafovea). It is not clear, for example, how much of normal eye-movement programming time is included in the 120 msec. The alteration of the distributions may come solely from decisions to cancel the eye movement, and it may take appreciably less time to cancel an eye movement than to program one.

What is our best estimate of the time needed to identify a word on a fixation? As we mentioned in Chapter 3, a word can be clearly identified even if masked after about 60 msec. Rayner et al. (1981) showed a similar effect in reading (see also Slowiaczek and Rayner 1987). They masked the entire line of text after a fixed delay on each fixation. They found that reading was unimpaired if the mask came 100 msec after the beginning of each fixation and only slightly impaired if the mask came 50 msec after the beginning of each fixation. As indicated in Chapters 3 and 4, this time is not necessarily the time it takes to encode a word, since it may merely be the time the information is in a form such that it is impervious to visual masking. This time does seem to be a lower limit on how long word encoding takes. (Other estimates in Chapter 3 indicated that something on the order of 150 to 200 msec was an upper limit for word encoding time.)

Another way to obtain an estimate is to use the McConkie et al. method (1985) and examine the histograms of fixation times when subjects are fixating high- and low-frequency words. If one assumes that the differences are due to speed of word identification, then the point at which the histograms diverge can be taken as a measure of when the highest-frequency words are encoded. The data from Inhoff and Rayner (1986) indicate that the histograms clearly diverge at about 180 msec. Since this time includes eye-mind lag, encoding, decision time, and eye-movement programming time, it indicates that under favorable circumstances, the sum of word encoding time, the eye-mind lag, and decision and programming time takes 180 msec. Thus, the encoding time for a (high frequency) word is probably much less than 180 msec. We should stress that this conclusion is drawn from conditions in which there was a parafoveal preview, so that the "encoding time" does not include the preliminary encoding on the prior fixation. This suggests, as we argued previously, that parafoveal previews are an essential component of skilled reading, since they allow the fixated word to be encoded rapidly enough to allow a rapid "intelligent" saccade to be programmed from it.

At present, we have no particularly good way to carve up this 180 msec to estimate word encoding time and decision and eye-movement programming separately. At first, one might think that since there are short (50 to 75 msec) fixations in reading, this would be an upper limit for both decision and eye programming times. However, Morrison's model indicates that these eye movements may have been programmed on prior fixations. Experiments have been conducted (similar to Becker and Jurgens 1979) where subjects are asked to fixate in turn on a series of crosses. The usual fixation time in these experiments is in the range of 175 to 225 msec (Arnold and Tinker 1939; Rayner et al. 1983; Salthouse and Ellis 1980). Under ideal circumstances in which uncertainty about when to move is eliminated, the average latency is about 175 msec (Rayner et al. 1983). If one assumes that the subject does not need to encode anything after the first eye movement (since the crosses are continuously visible), it would appear that decision time and eye-movement programming time take the greater part of 175 msec. This appears to be much too slow in light of everything else we have discussed. Thus, it is possible that subjects in such experiments actually wait until each fixation is completed to program the next. These eye movements may also be slow because subjects are trying to aim their fixations appreciably more accurately than they do in normal reading; experiments by Findlay (1982) show that when subjects increase accuracy, the average saccade latency also increases in simple oculomotor tasks.

To summarize, direct control tells us that most of the operations listed in Figure 5.2 are quite rapid. From what we know, it is not unreasonable that a normal fixation time of 200 to 250 msec comprises about 50 msec for the stimulus to be registered in the brain, another 80 to 120 msec to encode the word, and (by subtraction) another 50 to 70 msec to decide an eye movement should be made and begin its execution. As we pointed out earlier, this rapid processing is aided by two factors: (1) the word may have been partially encoded on the prior fixation; and (2) the calculation of where to move may be done in parallel with word identification. As the above discussion indicates, however, the times for the components are little more than educated guesses. We expect that the next 10 years of eye-movement research will give us a much clearer picture of these subprocesses and how long each takes.

How Can We Use Eye Movements to Study Reading?

The data we have presented and our tentative model both show that there are quite direct links between cognitive processes (especially word identification) and the pattern of eye movements. However, the pattern is far from simple. While we know that word frequency influences the duration of a fixation, we can not say that fixation time on a word is the time to identify that word. Many of the phenomena we discussed—the presence of saccades that are programmed on prior fixations or possibly automatically, skipping of words, and processing of words on more than one fixation—make any such simple interpretation of the pattern of eye movements suspect.

Let us make the discussion more concrete by considering some of the candidates that have been put forth for measuring the time to identify a word in reading. One that has been championed by several authors is the first fixation duration on a word (Inhoff 1984; McConkie et al. 1982). For the moment, we will ignore the problems of word skipping and parafoveal previews. There is still the problem of refixations on words. Inhoff hypothesized that first fixation duration measured encoding time, whereas refixations measured "higher processes" such as text integration. While his data suggested such a clean dichotomy, later data do not. In fact, first fixation durations may be sensitive to higher-order processes (see Chapter 7), and the Inhoff and Rayner (1986) data discussed earlier indicated that whether word frequency (and presumably word identification) influences first fixation duration or number of refixations depends on whether there was a parafoveal preview. Hence, we feel that whether a variable affects first fixation duration or probability of refixations (and hence gaze duration) is likely to be a quantitative rather than a qualitative difference (Rayner and Pollatsek 1987). That is, if a cognitive operation is very fast it can affect the decision when to move, whereas if it is a little slower it may only affect the probability of refixation (we presented an explanation for this in our exposition of Morrison's model).

Thus, gaze duration would appear to be a somewhat better measure of encoding time than first fixation duration, since it is the total amount of time spent on a word before the eye moves on. (On the other hand, additional time spent fixating on a word after a regression back to it from a subsequent word probably reflects higher-order difficulty with the text and not additional time needed to identify the word.) Yet total reliance on gaze duration as the measure of word identification time is probably not satisfactory either. It assumes that all refixations are guided to spend additional processing time on the fixated word. However, eye movements are not always precisely guided. One indication of this is that the eyes land on the spaces between words about 10 percent of the time in normal reading. It is usual to assume that the word fixated on these occasions is the one following it. That is, it is assumed that an eye movement to the next word was planned but improperly executed. However, the same may be the case if a refixation is made to the last letter or two of the prior word (especially if the prior word is long). As we suggested in the model section, many refixations may be compromises between two commands: one to stay and one to move on. If so, then for those refixations, the word was identified on the first fixation, but a refixation occurred anyway.

Until we can account for refixations better, it would seem to be a prudent strategy to report both first fixation durations and some measure of refixations (gaze duration seems the simplest to comprehend) as indices of how long it takes to process the fixated word. But what about words that are not fixated? What does one do about them? One procedure (Just and Carpenter 1980) was to use gaze duration, but to count the processing time as zero on those occasions when the word was skipped. This is surely unsatisfactory, since it assumes the word took no time to process when it was skipped. Another possibility is to use a conditionalized gaze duration (Carpenter and Just 1983), which measures the average gaze duration when the word is fixated at least once. This measure probably errs in the opposite direction, since on the occasions a word is not skipped, identification is probably more time-consuming than when it is skipped.

An additional problem (the other side of the coin) is that when a word is skipped, some of the time spent fixating on the prior word is spent processing the skipped word (we presented evidence that skipping a word lengthened the prior fixation). One procedure, which seems better than any of the above, is when a word is skipped to count half of the fixation time on the prior word as processing time for the skipped word and the other half as processing time on the prior word (Blanchard 1985a; Hogaboam and McConkie 1981). The 50/50 division seems a bit ad hoc and probably inaccurate, since words are skipped presumably because they take less time to process than other words. However, we think that the general idea of apportioning the time between the two words is on the right track.

Yet another potential problem is parafoveal previews. Some of the time that is spent processing many fixated words occurs on the prior fixation. If this time is relatively constant, then parafoveal previews are not a problem, since the extra time processing word n on fixation $n-1$ would be compensated for by the extra time spent processing word $n+1$ on fixation n. On the other hand, if parafoveal previews take differing amounts of time to process, then some even more complex apportioning scheme is needed.

The final problem is what to do about higher-order processes. In all the above we have assumed that the business of reading is identifying words, and that the identification of words is the "motor" that drives the eyes forward. We have acknowledged so far two effects of higher-order processing on the eye-movement record. The first is that higher-order processes are apparently able to interrupt forward motion if higher-order trouble develops. The second is that higher-order processing may influence the time it takes to identify a word. However, we have so far tacitly assumed that the time it takes to do these higher-order processes does not affect the time it takes for the eye to move in its normal forward direction. There are two possibilities for how this could be true. (Let us assume our modified version of Morrison's model is true and the only two signals to move the eye forward are "word identified" or "x msec has elapsed.") The first is that these higher-order processes can occur in parallel with the basic eye-movement engine and hence only indirectly influence the pattern, as by affecting the time to identify a word. The second is that higher-order processes are scheduled to occur in what would otherwise be "dead-time," such as the time from when all the visual identification is completed until the visual information reaches the brain on the following fixation.

We are skeptical that higher-order processes would be completely invisible in the usual forward movement of the eyes. However, the data do suggest that the identification of words accounts for much of the variability in forward eye movements, and that the most salient impact of higher order processes on eye movements in reading is to stop or move back when there is trouble. Thus, while higher order processes may not be done *completely* in parallel with word identification or *completely* done in "holes" of time in between identifying words, one or both of these processes may explain how much of the higher order processes are carried out in reading. Chapters 7 and 8 will focus on higher order processes in reading.

One challenge to the view we are advocating comes from data that suggest readers use information in the text at any time during the fixation. The kind of experiment that suggests this is one in which the fixated word is changed from one word to another in the middle of the fixation (Blanchard, 1988; Blanchard et al. 1984). The basic finding is that people sometimes report seeing the first word, sometimes report seeing the second, and sometimes report seeing both words, with the probability of reporting either word dependent on the length of time it was exposed. Blanchard et al. (1984) argued that this phenomenon indicates that the visual information can be extracted at any point in the fixation. They go on to speculate that the process of reading is quite different from what we have suggested, and that higher order processes are driving the reading process, and when the higher order processes are ready for the next word, they "look at" the visual information to determine what it is. If this model is right, it would clearly make the interpretation of eye-movement data far more complex, since it is not at all clear how to integrate such a text-encoding process with eye-movement control.

Fortunately, the evidence for such a view is not compelling, so that one doesn't have to abandon the simpler model yet. The main problem with these experiments is that the visual changes made in the middle of a fixation may alter the normal reading process. That is, it may be that during normal reading, all the visual information is extracted in the first 50 to 100 msec after it reaches the brain. In fact, as discussed earlier, Rayner et al. (1981) showed that reading proceeded normally when the text was masked after 100 msec. However, when a display change occurs, a signal may go out to the brain that says, "Something new is out there; drop normal processing and go back and check visual input." That is, the Blanchard et al. experiments may merely show that visual information is extracted later in a fixation when there is a display change, but not necessarily during normal reading.

A problem for Blanchard et al. (1984) is to explain the Rayner et al. (1981) data. They argue, similar to our argument against their data, that it merely demonstrates that all visual information extraction *can* go on at the beginning of the fixation if you force the subject to do so, not that it necessarily *is* processed at the beginning of a fixation in normal reading. We believe that their argument is weak, however, since Rayner et al. (1981) showed not only that reading goes on in this presumably unnatural situation (where the text is masked after 50 or 100 msec on every fixation) but that it does so *with both relatively normal speed and comprehension* and without extensive practice in reading the masked text. If the subjects' normal way of extracting visual information were quite different than extracting the visual information at the beginning of each fixation, one would expect a substantial decrease in their ability to read.

From the above discussion, it should be clear that the issue of when information is extracted in a fixation is not completely settled. Hence one can not be completely comfortable that the position we have argued—a largely (but not exclusively) word-identification-driven model of eye movements—is valid. However, we feel that such an assumption is the most parsimonious given the available data and will assume it in all that follows.

OTHER METHODS OF STUDYING READING

What should emerge from our current discussion, in spite of the worries about details, is that the eye movement record is sensitive to a lot of the detail of the reading process and is capable of revealing much of the cognitive processing in normal silent reading. One of the beauties of using eye movements to study reading is that subjects just read; they don't have to do anything else. Except for the minor inconvenience of having the eyes tracked (which mainly involves keeping the head relatively still), the natural reading process is undisturbed. As such, we believe eye movements to be the method of choice in studying the process of reading and will rely on it most heavily. It should come as no surprise, however, given the technical difficulty of obtaining an accurate record of eye movements, that other methods have been used to study reading as well. This last section of the chapter will briefly outline these methods and analyze their strengths and weaknesses.

Reading Aloud

Another obvious method for studying reading "on-line" is to have people read aloud and record their vocal output (so that both its accuracy and the time course of the vocal output can be analyzed). Many experimenters have asked subjects to read a passage of text and then examined the types of reading errors that were made. In more sophisticated variations, words may be misspelled or anomalous in the passage and subjects' responses (pauses and hesitations) to such words are examined, as are the characteristics of the word the subject actually utters (Danks and Hill 1981). The main problem with this method is that it is unnatural for adults. While it is possible to read something for meaning aloud, adults rarely do so. Most of the time when someone reads aloud in the real world it is akin to a "presentation" as when someone reads poetry, or when a parent reads a story to a child. In most such cases, the reader of the text is not reading the text for the first time. It is sometimes argued that in young children reading aloud is at least as natural as reading silently, but there is very little data on this assertion.

One advantage of having subjects read aloud is that one potentially has a record of what has been processed. That is, one can see whether the reader is making mistakes and can also determine what mistakes are being made.

However, a potential problem in using the pattern of errors is that one can not be confident that the errors are errors of identification or errors of interpretation or memory. For example, when reading aloud, readers often give synonyms or paraphrases. However, it is by no means clear that they really encoded the text that way. The fact that reading aloud is only about half the speed of silent reading strongly suggests that studying reading aloud is likely to tell us at least as much about speaking as it will tell us about how meaning is extracted from print.

The problems in using the vocal record to study reading are illustrated by the work on the *eye-voice span* (Levin 1979). We suspect that the only really satisfactory way to measure the eye-voice span is by actually making a record of the eye movements and relating the eye-movement record to a record of the vocal output. When measured this way, the eye-voice span, the distance the eye is ahead of the voice, is only a couple of words on the average. But, the fact that the eye is ahead of the voice by a couple of words is problematic for the technique since the goal in studying silent reading is to discover how readers understand text on a moment-to-moment basis. That is, from what we know about the speed of lexical access, it is entirely likely that the words produced by the speech mechanism in oral reading are strongly influenced by processes occurring after the lexicon has been accessed, and thus the resulting data may say little about how the lexicon is initially contacted to arrive at the meaning of a given word. Oral reading errors have served as the basis for a view of reading in which it is believed that fluent reading is based on generating guesses or hypotheses about what the next word is (Goodman 1970; Levin and Kaplan 1970). Because the errors produced in oral reading tend to be semantically consistent with the words actually printed in the text, some workers have assumed that oral reading errors provide good evidence for this view. In reality, most oral reading errors are the result of processes occurring after the lexicon has been accessed.

The fact that the eyes are getting no further ahead of the voice than about two words is probably due to short-term memory limitations: if the eyes moved further ahead, there would be a lot of undigested material that would be likely forgotten. The eye-voice records show certain interesting features that detail this process of the eyes waiting for the voice. First, the eye-movement record often shows instances in which regressions are made so that the eyes do not get too far ahead. There are also often time-marking fixations (Levy-Schoen 1981), in which the eyes are striving again not to get too far ahead. The shorter saccades in oral reading are probably also due in part to an effort to slow down the eyes. Thus, a careful study of the eye-voice span indicates that both the eye movement pattern and the vocal record in oral reading are at best indirectly related to the acquisition of information from the printed page, at least for adults. Since the speeds of oral and silent reading are more nearly equal for beginning readers, it is possible that oral reading is a better tool for studying on-line comprehension for these readers.

Letter Cancellation, Proofreading, and Visual Search

Another type of methodology that has been used to examine moment-to-moment processes in reading involves asking subjects in an experiment to locate prespecified targets. Three types of tasks have been widely used: letter cancellation, proofreading, and visual search. In letter-cancellation tasks, subjects are asked to circle (or put a line through) every occurrence of a target letter (*e*, for example). Closely related to this task is the proofreading task in which subjects are asked to circle misspelled words. In a third variation of the visual-search task, subjects are given a target word in the passage and asked to find it. All of these tasks have provided us with important information which may be relevant for reading, but they all have a major problem associated with them. Namely, the task in all cases is really one of visual search (see Chapter 1) rather than reading for meaning, and subjects may well engage in different strategies when they search for a target than when they read to comprehend text. Indeed, a comparison of typical reading rates with the search rates obtained in each of the tasks confirms that one should be very cautious in generalizing from search tasks to reading. In normal silent reading, the average reading speed for college students is in the range of 200 to 350 words per minute. Reading speed in a letter-cancellation task is about 80 words per minute (Smith and Sterling 1982). Proofreading also tends to be slow in comparison to silent reading. On the other hand, subjects in a visual-search task in which they are to simply search for a target word tend to search at rates quite a bit faster than reading. For example, subjects in an experiment by Spragins, Lefton, and Fisher (1976) searched at rates over 150 words per minute faster than they read. Given these differences between search rate and reading rate and given the obvious differences in the goal of the subject in the tasks, it is appropriate to be cautious about generalizing results from search tasks to reading. On the other hand, it is the case that both the rate at which subjects search and the number of errors they make in search tasks are strongly affected by the characteristics of the text. Since we suspect that subjects in these tasks do use strategies that are different from reading, we will not rely heavily on them for conclusions that we will reach about reading in this book. However, these types of studies will be discussed in Chapter 12, where we discuss alternative forms of reading behaviors.

Experimentally Controlled Text Presentation

In the usual world of books, newspapers, and magazines, eye movements are used to bring new text to the center of vision. An alternative way to read is to hold your eyes still and have the words in the text march across the center of vision. Experimenters have attempted such procedures partly to understand whether fluent reading is possible without eye movements and partly in an attempt to obtain greater control over when a word in the text is actually processed.

If you tried, you could devise such a procedure by holding your eyes still and move the book in just the right way in order to bring the appropriate information into view at the right time. This would obviously be very difficult to do. Several experiments have controlled the presentation of text in just this manner: the subject looks at a screen and maintains fixation on the center while the text moves from right to left (instead of the eyes moving from left to right across the text in normal reading). With this method, comprehension is quite good when short passages are presented (Gilbert 1959; Bouma and deVoogd 1974); thus reading without eye movements is possible. This method was used chiefly to obtain measures of the perceptual span and is a bit cumbersome for studying extended reading. Thus most techniques have not attempted to have text sweep across the screen but have words appear sequentially in the middle of the screen.

A widely used technique is known as *rapid serial visual presentation* (RSVP), which was discussed in Chapter 3. In an RSVP experiment (Potter, Kroll, and Harris 1980; Juola, Ward, and McNamara 1982), you sit facing a screen in which words are presented one at a time (or perhaps as many as 3 words are presented) for exposures of 50 to 250 msec. Experiments using this technique have demonstrated that you can comprehend sentences and short passages at rates of 1,200 words per minute. In such a situation, a new word would be presented to your fixation point every 50 msec. Several measures indicate that comprehension is fairly good, particularly when the rate at which new words are presented is longer than 50 msec. In fact, if words are presented at a rate of 200 to 250 msec (about the rate at which you would move your eyes), you often read better (as measured by comprehension performance) than when you are able to make eye movements.

The RSVP experiments have suggested to some people that standard silent reading may be an outmoded technology and that a major limiting factor in silent reading is the rate at which you can move your eyes (Juola, Ward, and McNamara 1982). This conclusion must be adopted with some caution, however. Comprehension is quite good when the text is very short, but when longer text is presented using the RSVP technique, comprehension scores are not as good as when readers can make eye movements (Masson 1983).

A major problem with RSVP reading is that it is difficult to allow readers to go back and reread as in normal silent reading. (In fact none of the standard experimental procedures allow for regressions.) We have seen that readers make frequent regressions in normal silent reading. While all regressions may not be necessary, readers clearly need to look back in some circumstances, particularly if they have somehow misunderstood a segment of text, and when they are unable to do so comprehension suffers (Kennedy and Murray 1984). A second, related, factor may be fatigue. RSVP reading is subjectively very demanding. Among other things, it requires the reader's constant attention to the text. With normal text, you've probably had the experience of reading along only to find that you have understood nothing at all for the last line or two because your mind has wandered. Under such circumstances, you can easily go back and read the text your mind wandered over, but in RSVP situations you have no such luxury.

Thus, while RSVP reading is intriguing, it is not clear what its place is in the study of reading. It is possible that some new technological innovations might come along that would allow the reader to control the flow of words and regress in a natural manner so that reading could progress more rapidly than in normal silent reading and yet not produce fatigue. If it became a widely used method of reading in the culture, then it would be clearly worth studying in its own right. As it is, it is merely a laboratory phenomenon, interesting because people can apparently process connected discourse at such high speeds. It has the potential of discovering how fast certain kinds of processes can go on. However, if one is interested in understanding normal silent reading, then the status of RSVP is unclear. If RSVP is merely normal reading with "dead time" removed, then it could be a powerful tool. However, the work we have discussed in the last two chapters indicates that this assumption is unlikely; readers are processing several words in a fixation, integrating information across fixations, and programming eye movements. Hence, RSVP is likely to be qualitatively as well as quantitatively different from normal reading.

Subject-Controlled Presentation of Text

An alternative method for bringing text before the subject's eyes is to present one word at a time in the center of the screen but to let subjects control the rate manually by pushing a button each time they want a new word to appear (Aaronson and Scarborough 1976; Aaronson and Ferres 1983; Just, Carpenter, and Woolley 1982). Since the reaction time of the finger is slower than the reaction time of the eye, each word stays on the screen for an average of at least 400 msec. Thus, as with oral reading, the process of extracting meaning is being slowed down by an external process and the time course of "reading with your finger" may only indirectly be related to the acquisition of meaning. One indication is that when subjects are not given explicit instructions that they will have to recall the text after reading, they push the button at a rather steady rate with little variability across different words (Aaronson and Scarborough 1976). This contrasts with the finding we have reported that fixation durations are sensitive to various aspects of the text including the frequency of the fixated word. Also, as with RSVP reading, readers cannot make regressions to previously read material.

There are related types of experimental techniques in which each word is presented in a spatially appropriate location (as in the layout in normal text) rather than in the same spatial location. In one, the onset of a new word causes the erasure of the prior word; in another, the onset of a new word does not cause the erasure of prior words. In the former situation, once again we have the case that readers cannot regress to previously read material. Although the latter situation allows the reader to look back, when they do so is not apparent in the response times. Thus, processing time for a given word and when readers look back cannot be separated in such experiments (Rayner and Frazier 1987). However, under conditions such as those described in this paragraph, if appropriate instructions are given, variability in pushing a button to advance new words can be somewhat comparable to normal reading when eye movements can be made (Just, Carpenter, and Woolley 1982). Thus, from the point of view of the subject, reading in this kind of experiment is often quite similar to normal reading when you make eye movements; it's just that you feel you are reading slower than you normally do. In fact, Just, Carpenter, and Woolley (1982) demonstrated that reading slowed by a factor of two or three from normal reading. It is also the case that it is not possible to examine subtle differences as readily as when you have a record of the eyes' movements (Just, Carpenter, and Woolley 1982; Rayner and Frazier 1987).

The finger method presents a dilemma. If you present one word at a time, you can control both the timing of the visual material and know what visual information is being used at any moment (at least what word is processed). However, the cost of this control is that reading is slowed down in an unnatural way. If you speed up the reading process by presenting several words at a time (Mitchell and Green 1978) so that it comes close to normal reading rates, then you have lost a great deal of the control, since you are not sure which word or words are being processed at any given moment. In addition, since the use of the finger to advance text is less practiced than moving the eye (and probably even less natural even if well practiced), you are probably imposing a lot more "noise" from the motor system on the basic cognitive processes of interest than when you are studying eye movements.

As mentioned above, some of these subject-controlled methods have obtained findings similar to those obtained using eye movements. This suggests that, in the best of circumstances, what is going on may not differ too much from normal silent reading. Since these techniques are much easier to implement than a study of eye movements, the data obtained from them may be viewed as providing interesting suggestions about what is going on in normal silent reading. However, one can never be sure; if you want to know what happens in normal silent reading, the best thing to study is normal silent reading.

Word Identification Techniques

A last group of procedures that people have used to study reading of text is to have people read text, and then at some point, demand some sort of response to a given word. A whole gamut of the techniques that we discussed in Chapter 3 has been used, such as lexical decision and naming. For example, subjects read a sentence minus the last word silently. When they come to the end of what is visible, they push a button to make the last word appear and then name the last word as quickly as possible. For example, as we will discuss in Chapter 7, one might be interested in knowing whether the prior sentence context influences the time to identify the last word. The rationale for using these procedures (other than that they are easier to use than eye movements) is that they are more diagnostic than eye movements. That is, it is sometimes assumed that naming is a direct measure of some cognitive process such as word identification time, whereas one has no principled way to know what the fixation time on a word is measuring.

We are considerably skeptical about such claims for these methods. There is clearly an *a priori* difference between a measure such as naming and a measure such as fixation duration: when the subject names a word, the experimenter knows for sure that the name of the word has been encoded, whereas when the subject's eyes move, there is no guarantee that anything about the word has been processed. However, we have already seen that fixation durations are sensitive to variables such as word frequency, so we are pretty sure that the subject often does identify the word before the eyes move. Moreover, the naming time usually used is the time to the *onset* of the vocal response. There is no guarantee, in fact, that the word has been identified by the onset of the vocal response. If one used the offset of the vocal response (which is more difficult to measure), one would be sure that the word was identified, but then one would be measuring the time for the mouth to execute a complex response and hence be including complex extraneous response processes in the measure. In addition, as argued in Chapter 3, accessing the name is not the same thing as accessing the meaning, which is the process you are really interested in. (A similar argument could be made for lexical decision time or any other measure.) These worries are not merely hypothetical, since, as argued in Chapter 3, both naming and lexical decision times have been shown to be reasonably flawed indices of word identification time.

Thus, in a practical sense, it is by no means clear that naming time is any better measure of word identification time than fixation time. It may be, but that has not been conclusively demonstrated. Moreover, all of the standard cognitive tasks perturb the natural reading process by requiring the subject to do some additional task. This requirement, of course, may mean that subjects read in a very different fashion when confronted with this additional task than when they read normally.

We feel that it is likely that some additional control is probably gained when such tasks are used, but that this benefit is easily balanced by what is lost in changing the reading situation. All methods are flawed, so the best strategy is to attack a question using a combination of methods. If these methods all appear to be converging on the same answer, then one can be reasonably sure that one has discovered something of importance. An illustration of this was in our discussion of the use of parafoveal information, where the results from reading experiments and naming experiments appeared to agree on virtually all the major findings. However, at the risk of repeating ourselves, our bias in the book is that if you want to study reading, then the primary data of interest are what happens when people are actually silently reading text. The only data, given the present technology, for studying people actually reading are eye movements. The more converging data obtained from other methods, the better. But if in doubt, trust the data obtained from reading.

SUMMARY

In this chapter, we have gone to great lengths to outline a model of eye movement control. Basically, we have argued that control decisions regarding eye movements in reading are made very quickly. Indeed, we have argued that there is direct control for many fixations in reading and cognitive control for most of the rest. We outlined a simple model (but with lots of complications) that explains much of the data on eye movements in reading. The primary argument was that lexical access processes drive eye movements in reading. When lexical access occurs, attention shifts to the word to the right of fixation and a saccade follows shortly thereafter. We also argued that the information used to calculate where to look next (primarily word boundary information) is obtained very early in a fixation and that decisions about where to move the eyes and when to move are made somewhat independently, but the attentional mechanism that we described coordinates these activities.

As we indicated earlier, the primary reason that we have gone to such lengths to outline eye-movement control in reading is that we believe that eye movements in reading are more than a peripheral component of the reading processes. They can be very important in revealing important aspects of the cognitive processes that occur during reading, and you will need to understand some of the important points that we stressed in this chapter (and Chapter 4) in order to understand some of the points we will make in chapters 7 and 8. We concluded the chapter by discussing alternative techniques to eye-movement recordings that are often utilized in trying to understand reading. While all of these techniques have virtues, we prefer to rely on information obtained from eye movements. However, we clearly believe that these other techniques can provide good converging evidence concerning the reading process.

In chapters 7 and 8, we will move to issues beyond the identification of words. As a bridge to those issues, we now turn our attention to the role of inner speech in reading.

CHAPTER SIX
INNER SPEECH

When we read silently, we often experience the feeling of hearing our voice saying the words our eyes are falling on. Some readers actually move their lips at times during silent reading and there is a considerable amount of muscle activity in the speech tract as we read silently. What is the function of these activities? In the chapter on word perception we argued that access to the lexicon can proceed via a visual route or a phonological route and that phonological access of a word is not obligatory. Yet most of the time we can clearly hear our voice saying the words in the text and for most readers there is evidence of much activity. In this chapter, we will discuss these speech-related activities in terms of the possible reasons for their occurrence.

Huey (1908) argued that the inner hearing or inner pronouncing (or both) represents a crucial constituent part of comprehending text. Ever since Huey's time the role of inner speech has been controversial and there has been a considerable amount of confusion about exactly what is being investigated in studies dealing with inner speech (McCusker, Bias, and Hillinger 1981). We wish to stress at the outset that the auditory images we hear of our voice and the movements that occur in the speech tract may not necessarily be related to each other.

In this chapter, we will refer to activity in the speech tract (either muscle movement or articulatory processes) as *subvocalization,* while we will use the term *phonological coding* to refer to the mental representations of speech that can give rise to the experience of hearing sounds. We point out here that a variety of different labels have been used for what we shall call phonological coding: *speech recoding* (Kleiman 1975; Martin 1978), *phonetic recoding* (Taylor and Taylor 1983), *phonological recoding* (Coltheart et al. 1977; Wagner and Torgesen 1987), *phonemic recoding* (Baron 1973; Baron and Strawson 1976; Meyer Schvaneveldt, and Ruddy 1974), and *deep phonemic recoding* (Chomsky 1970). The different labels that have been proposed carry with them certain implicit assumptions about the nature of the internal representation. "Speech recoding" suggests an internal representation similar to that subserving covert articulation; "phonetic recoding" suggests a process of converting written words into articulatory features; and "phonemic recoding" suggests a representation based on abstract theoretical units.

We will adopt the term *phonological coding* since it is relatively neutral. Although the issues about phonological coding that these terms raise are interesting, they have not, as we shall see, been resolved because there has not been any totally satisfactory way of identifying the exact form of inner speech during reading. Psychologists interested in the role of inner speech have also not been very successful in determining how closely phonological coding and subvocalization are related. As a result, we will treat inner speech as a general phenomenon and adopt the convention of referring to both phonological coding and subvocalization as speech coding or inner speech. However, we will discuss attempts to differentiate between phonological coding and subvocalization.

One argument that is often advanced with respect to inner speech is that it is an epiphenomenon. According to this argument, inner speech is a byproduct of the way we are taught to read—we learn to read orally before we learn to read silently and inner speech during reading is merely a carryover from our initial form of reading. That is, inner speech represents a habit that persists but is of no value in silent reading and may even slow it down. While this argument is not implausible, it seems unusual that a process which is so pervasive would continue despite having little to do with understanding written text.

A direct way to demonstrate that inner speech is more than an epiphenomenon would be to show that it does play a role in comprehending written text. There are three principal techniques that have been used to study inner speech in normal readers of English: (1) measuring whether muscles in the speech tract are moving during reading, (2) determining whether a task that makes it impossible to use the speech tract for inner speech interferes with reading, and (3) determining whether sound properties of the text (such as homophony or phonemic similarity) affect reading. We will also consider different reader populations, such as deaf readers and readers of logographic languages such as Chinese. Before plunging into the data, however, we will outline several plausible hypotheses about the role of inner speech in reading; this will help to frame subsequent discussion.

INNER SPEECH AND COMPREHENSION

Some proponents of inner speech have argued that reading is little more than speech made visible. Children learning the reading process are known to sound out words and listen to themselves as they try to figure out new and unknown words. This is a prudent strategy in light of what the child brings to the process of learning to read. By the time a child begins to read, he or she is a fairly fluent user of the spoken language. It might then be argued that it is only reasonable that children should make the process of reading as similar to speech comprehension as possible in order to achieve a certain amount of cognitive economy (Gibson 1965). For older readers, it is easy to argue that this speech transformation of the printed words into auditory surrogates for comprehension does not disappear but simply becomes foreshortened and internalized. Indeed, as we shall see when we discuss electromyographic research (i.e., measurement of muscle movements), readers do subvocalize even when there is no overt behavior.

However, "speech made visible" can't be exactly the same as overt speech because we can read silently much faster than we can read aloud. If reading necessitated obtaining the identical acoustic representations as in real speech then we would read more slowly than we do. Oral reading rates are generally in the range of 150 to 200 words per minute and are a good approximation of speech rates, while silent reading rates for skilled readers are around 300 words per minute.

If inner speech is not exactly overt speech, what is it? While it is possible that inner speech is used only for occasional difficult words, it seems to be more than that. If you attend to the "voice in your head" while you read, you have the impression that the voice is saying most if not all words. It is possible, however, that your reading is slowing down to let the inner voice do this and that fewer words are said by your inner voice when you are not attending to it. Another possibility is that inner speech is in some sort of shorthand form in which certain sounds are left out or shortened (e.g., vowels) or certain words are left out, such as function words. We will return to speculations about the form of inner speech at the end of the chapter.

At this point, trying an experiment on yourself might be quite instructive in thinking about inner speech. Read the next several sentences to yourself silently, *but make sure to hear them being said in your head*. Now, at the same time, say "blah-blah-blah" out loud over and over as fast as you can. The result, which may have surprised you, is that you can easily hear the voice in your head while your mouth is fully engaged with something else. Thus, as we argued earlier, subvocalization and phonological coding are not necessarily the same thing, since they *can* go on independently.

However, they might be closely tied in actual reading, with subvocalization being the main source of phonological coding or at least making phonological coding much easier. The relationship of subvocalization and phonological coding is a major issue in this chapter. The main thing to keep in mind at this point is that there *can be* a voice in your head that says at least most of the words you read and furthermore it does not require any involvement of the speech musculature to produce it.

Now that we have some feeling for the phenomenon of inner speech, let us briefly consider what role it might play in reading. One possibility is that inner speech helps the reader access the meaning of words. The second is that it aids higher-order comprehension processes in reading. That is, after the meanings of words are accessed, there is some sort of "speech" representation of the words formed that aids in the processing of phrases, clauses, sentences, or other larger units.

The most popular theory of why inner speech aids comprehension of text is that it aids higher-order comprehension by bolstering short-term memory. As we argued in Chapter 1, short-term memory is importantly (though not exclusively) acoustic in nature. Thus, while the meanings of individual words may be accessed without needing an acoustic representation, creating an acoustic or speechlike code may be beneficial for creating a short-term representation in which words are held while other processes are done, such as working out the syntactic structure of the sentence or holding an easily accessible representation of nouns to search for the referent of a pronoun. Short-term memory may aid in such processes because it is more easily accessible than long-term memory and also because temporal order is naturally stored in a speechlike representation.

A second major issue is whether inner speech is primarily involved in aiding lexical access or postlexical comprehension processes. As we shall see, a much clearer case can be made for the role of inner speech in postlexical processes. This has led some researchers to conclude that there is no prelexical component to inner speech. Other evidence, however, indicates that this conclusion is too strong.

We now turn to the data. The first two methods that we consider attempt to measure or manipulate (or both) subvocalization so that the methods are most diagnostic on the role of subvocalization in reading. A great deal of caution, however, must be exercised when attempting to draw conclusions about inner speech from such methods.

ELECTROMYOGRAPHIC RECORDING

Electromyographic (EMG) records have been widely used to study the role of subvocalization in reading. By inserting needle electrodes inside the muscles or by placing surface electrodes on the speech organs (lips, tongue, chin, larynx, throat), it is possible to record the action potentials of the muscles during silent reading. EMGs taken during silent reading are then compared to EMGs in a condition in which subjects are asked to sit quietly without thinking about anything. (Is that possible?) Generally, EMGs are also recorded from some other part of the body, such as the forearm, where muscle activity should have no relevance for reading. In fact, normal skilled readers show little forearm activity during reading, while EMG activity in the speech tract increases markedly during reading in comparison to the baseline condition (where the subject sits quietly). In contrast, deaf readers show a considerable amount of forearm activity during reading (we shall see the reason for that later in this chapter). In a review of EMG research, McGuigan (1970) found that almost all studies reviewed found an increase in speech tract activity during language tasks (be it reading or some other form of language processing or thinking).

In addition, EMGs are clearly affected by the conditions of reading. For example, Edfeldt (1960) found that EMG activity was much greater for difficult text than for easy text and much greater for clear text than for blurred text. He also found that EMGs increased during the reading of intelligible foreign text, especially if the subject was unaccustomed to reading foreign text. Sokolov (1972) found that subjects who were translating Russian into English had considerably more speech activity when reading difficult as compared to easy translations. It is also the case that reading skill is related to EMG activity. Beginning readers show more EMG activity than skilled readers. McGuigan (1967; McGuigan and Bailey 1969) showed that the amount of EMG activity decreases as reading skill increases. Poor readers also show more EMG activity than do good readers (Edfeldt 1960).

The above data indicate that subvocalization is a normal part of natural silent reading. To our knowledge, there is little controversy about that assertion. What is less clear is whether subvocalization serves a useful purpose. Experimenters have attempted to assess the functional significance of subvocalization by determining what happens to reading when subvocalization has been eliminated. One procedure for eliminating subvocalization involves giving subjects feedback when their EMG activity exceeds a given level. This was done by buzzing a noxious noise into the subjects' ears. In one experiment (Hardyck, Petrinovich, and Ellsworth 1966) it was found that a single session of such feedback was sufficient to eliminate subvocalization (or at least evidence of it in the EMG record). There was no evidence of subvocalization when subjects were later retested. Aarons (1971) also reported that readers are responsive to feedback training and that reductions in subvocalizations last beyond the training sessions. On the other hand, McGuigan (1971) has contended that the effect of feedback training is short-lived and that subvocalizations occur again very soon after the training session. He tested subjects through feedback training and found that the level of EMG activity was the same when subjects were retested later as during the pretraining session. Thus, he argued that the effects of feedback training are short lived and transitory. We therefore see that there is uncertainty about whether such training really can eliminate subvocalization for an extended period. However, for the moment, let us assume that the procedure can be effective.

Perhaps the most frequently cited study of EMG activity is that reported by Hardyck and Petrinovich (1970). The subjects in the study were college students in a remedial English class. They were asked to read selections of easy and difficult text under three different conditions: normal, feedback, and control. In the normal condition, subjects read the text while EMG activity in the speech tract was recorded. In the feedback condition, everything was the same as the normal condition except that any increase in the amplitude of EMG activity above a predetermined relaxation level resulted in a noxious tone being sounded. Subjects were told to keep the tone off as much as possible. In the control condition, everything was the same as in the feedback condition except that the tone was triggered by an increase in the amplitude of the forearm flexor muscle over a predetermined relaxation level. Hardyck and Petrinovich found that when activity in the speech tract was decreased by way of feedback techniques, comprehension of the difficult passage suffered. In contrast, there was little comprehension loss for the easy reading selection (see Figure 6.1).

This study can be taken as evidence that comprehension (particularly of difficult text) requires subvocalization. When subvocalization was eliminated, comprehension suffered. However, the result does not necessarily

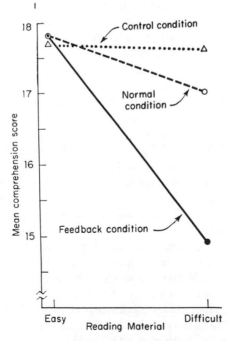

FIGURE 6-1 **Reading comprehension score as a function of experimental condition in the Hardyck and Petrinovich (1970) study. (Reproduced with permission of Academic Press and the authors.)**

indicate that subvocalization was essential for comprehension. Taylor and Taylor (1983) suggest that comprehension may have suffered simply because subjects had to pay attention to the task of learning to eliminate muscle activity in the speech tract. A related difficulty with EMG suppression techniques is that as text difficulty increases, overall muscle tone may increase and thus subjects may have to work harder to keep their EMG activity down. Another general criticism of EMG studies is that while it is clear that activity in the speech tract increases, it is not always clear that such increases are due specifically to linguistic processing. However, Locke (1971) found that EMG activity in the lips was significantly greater in passages containing a large number of bilabial consonants than in passages containing relatively few bilabial consonants. (The bilabial consonants—*b*, *v*, and *m*—require lip movement for oral pronunciation.) Garrity (1977) has provided a review of EMG research which contains further evidence that EMG activity is at least partially speech-specific.

Summary

EMG studies have provided some useful data concerning subvocalization in reading. It is clearly the case that less skilled readers exhibit more EMG activity than skilled readers and that the rate of subvocalization increases as text difficulty increases. In addition, subvocalizations appear to be related specifically to speech activity. It is less clear what happens to reading comprehension when subvocalization is eliminated. Some research suggests that it is quite easy to eliminate subvocalization, while other research suggests that it is not. However, when subvocalization is eliminated and the text is not easy to read, it appears that comprehension suffers.

It is interesting to note that studies utilizing EMG recordings have declined rather dramatically over the past 10 years. Some of the criticisms and uncertainties concerning various findings discussed above may be related to the fact that researchers are conducting fewer studies of this type. In some ways, EMG recording can be seen as a carry-over from the behaviorist tradition in experimental psychology in which higher mental processes such as thinking or comprehension are thought of as internalized speech or behavior. Accordingly, the EMG research has focused on whether covert speech is occurring during reading, and models of the reading process based on this research have been sparse in postulating cognitive processes that may be occurring during reading. A particularly thorny issue, which will be discussed more fully in the next section, is the relation of subvocalization to inner speech. (While eye movements are a similar behavioral indicator in reading, the eye-movement research reviewed in chapters 4 and 5 has concentrated heavily on inferring details of cognitive processes during reading.) We are not sure whether the lack of insight into cognitive processes lies with the EMG technique or with the orientation of EMG researchers. However, most cognitive psychologists interested in inner speech have turned to other techniques to which we also now turn.

CONCURRENT ARTICULATORY ACTIVITY

The feedback technique used in association with EMG studies represents one attempt to eliminate subvocalizations during reading. A second and more widely used technique is having the vocal tract engaged in other activity. The rationale behind the suppression experiments is very simple. If a reader's speech tract is somehow concurrently engaged during reading, he or she will not be able to subvocalize the text material. Other techniques have attempted to keep the mouth immobile. First, around the turn of the century, experiments were undertaken in which subjects placed a balloon in their mouth (with a tube for breathing), and the balloon was inflated so that they could not move their speech musculature. Analogously, subjects have been asked to bite into something and to clench their jaws so that articulation does not occur (Sokolov 1972). These methods to restrict articulation by physical means were not particularly successful, were obviously unpleasant for the subject, and thus are generally not used very much these days. Thus, we will focus on the *concurrent articulation* task as the technique to eliminate subvocalization.

The first experiment of this type was reported by Pintner (1913). Subjects in his experiment were asked to count or pronounce the syllables "la-la-la" while reading text. Obviously, if readers are forced to pronounce a well-rehearsed set of words (like a nursery rhyme) or to continuously repeat a meaningless set of sounds (like "la" or "blah") or to count aloud, they cannot engage the articulatory apparatus for the text at the same time. Thus, according to the logic of the concurrent articulation paradigm, articulatory programs could not be set in motion for the words that are being read when the subject is pronouncing words or phonemes unrelated to the text. The use of simple, well-learned material to engage the articulatory apparatus is an attempt to minimize the extent to which the articulatory suppression task demands the subject's attention and hence competes for processing resources needed in the reading process. Thus, in the ideal suppression experiment, the suppression task would *only* interfere with the speech apparatus and with no other mechanism that subserves reading. How closely this ideal has been achieved is a major issue in this research.

The focus of many of the experiments using the concurrent articulation paradigm is whether recoding to speech during reading occurs before or after the meaning of words is accessed from the lexicon (Besner, Davies, and Daniels 1981; Chmiel 1984; Martin 1978). In this section we will begin by reviewing in some detail the most influential of the concurrent articulation studies (Kleiman 1975) leading to the conclusion that postlexical processing is primarily what is being affected by concurrent articulation. We will then discuss other studies using concurrent articulation as well as some general issues concerning its use.

Suppression While Reading Words and Phrases

Kleiman's concurrent activity was *shadowing*. In the *shadowing task,* subjects listened to digits and had to repeat them aloud ("shadow them") in order to suppress subvocalization. The *primary* task (i.e., the one that subjects were supposed to attend to) was making judgments about visually presented words or sentences as quickly as possible. The judgments were indicated by manual responses and timed. The basic measure of involvement of subvocal speech was how much slower responses were in the primary task when subjects had to concurrently shadow the digits than when there was no concurrent shadowing task. Kleiman reasoned that the amount of interference due to shadowing ought to depend on the type of judgment being made. If the decision was about graphemic characteristics of words (how much words look alike), then little interference would be expected. On the other hand, if the decision was about phonemic characteristics of words (the extent to which words rhyme), then it may be quite difficult to make that decision while speaking at the same time.

In fact, Kleiman found that shadowing slowed down judgments about the visual similarity of two words only about 120 milliseconds (msec) while it slowed down judgments about rhyme approximately 370 msec. You may be wondering why shadowing had any effect on the graphemic judgment. The answer probably has to do with the fact that *any* simultaneous task is likely to have *some* deleterious effect on performance unrelated to its putative primary purpose (in this case, vocal suppression). We will return to this point later in this section.

The most important question was what happened when the decision was based on the meaning of a word. If access to the lexicon depends upon inner speech, then the meaning decision should be disrupted as much as the phonemic decision by concurrent articulation. If, on the other hand, access to meaning occurs independently of speech processing, then the judgments in the meaning task should resemble the graphemic judgment. In this latter case, the conclusion would be that speech coding in reading occurs after lexical access. In fact, Kleiman found that the amount of interference in the visual task and the meaning task was about the same (see Table 6.1). This indicates that in order to perform judgments of synonymy, it is not necessary to engage in the degree of inner speech that is necessary for the rhyme task. On the basis of these results, Kleiman argued that the meanings of individual words can be obtained without reference to inner speech.

To further test if speech recoding is used in the graphemic decision, subjects in another experiment were asked to make the same types of visual

TABLE 6.1 Major results of Kleiman's first experiment. Values in parentheses are error rates. (Adapted with permission of Academic Press and the author.)

TASK	EXAMPLE OF "YES"	EXAMPLE OF "NO"	WITHOUT SHADOWING	CHANGE WITH SHADOWING
			MSEC	
Phonemic	TICKLE PICKLE	LEMON DEMON	1,137 (8.3)	+372 (+7.7)
Graphemic	HEARD BEARD	GRACE PRICE	970 (4.5)	+125 (+0.4)
Semantic	MOURN GRIEVE	DEPART COUPLE	1,118 (4.2)	+120 (+3.8)

similarity judgments with and without shadowing. There were two types of stimuli requiring "yes" responses: phonemically similar (BLAME-FLAME) and phonemically dissimilar (HEARD-BEARD) word pairs. If subjects use speech recoding when they are not shadowing, it should facilitate the decision about phonemically similar pairs relative to dissimilar pairs. The results of the experiment indicate that shadowing hinders both types of stimuli by the same amount and support the argument that the interference observed in the visual comparison task is unrelated to speech recoding.

The pattern of results in a later experiment using sentences was quite similar to that obtained when judgments about word pairs were required. In this experiment, subjects were given a target word and, with and without shadowing, asked to read a sentence presented visually. The judgments were the same as in the word pair experiments. Thus, for example, subjects might be given the target word BURY and asked if a graphemically similar word was in the target sentence "Yesterday the grand jury adjourned. The subject then had to indicate a "yes" (as in this example) or "no" judgment with a manual response as in the previous experiments. This experiment also included a condition in which subjects had to make judgments of sentence acceptability (i.e., is it semantically acceptable?). Thus, the subject would respond "yes" to "Noisy parties disturb sleeping neighbors and "no" to the anomalous sentence "Pizzas have been eating Jerry". This condition was included in the experiment to test the notion that speech coding is used for short-term retention when a string of words has to be remembered. The acceptability judgment is likely to require working memory since the subject has to remember the subject noun of the sentence until the verb and object have been read if an accurate judgment is to be made. As can be seen in Table 6.2, Kleiman found that shadowing strongly interfered with the sentence acceptability judgment. In fact, there was even more interference than with rhyme judgment.

TABLE 6.2 Major results of Kleiman's third experiment: Values in parentheses are error rates. (Adapted with permission of Academic Press and the author.)

TASK	EXAMPLES OF STIMULI	WITHOUT SHADOWING	CHANGE WITH SHADOWING
		MSEC	
Phonemic	CREAM HE AWAKENED FROM THE DREAM (True) SOUL THE REFEREE CALLED A FOUL (False)	1,401(6.8)	312(+2.1)
Graphemic	BURY YESTERDAY THE GRAND JURY ADJOURNED (True) GATHER RUNNING FURTHER WAS TED'S MOTHER (False)	1,557(6.3)	140(+2.0)
Category	GAMES EVERYONE AT HOME PLAYED MONOPOLY (True) SPORTS HIS FAVORITE HOBBY IS CARPENTRY (False)	1,596(9.9)	78(−2.6)
Acceptability	NOISY PARTIES DISTURB SLEEPING NEIGHBORS (True) PIZZAS HAVE BEEN EATING JERRY (False)	1,431(7.3)	394(2.6)

Suppression While Reading Passages

The results of the sentence reading experiments were taken by Kleiman as evidence that inner speech comes into use for the purposes of working memory and not for lexical access. Kleiman's results have been cited widely, and there are several other studies that support and extend his general conclusion. Since his studies were done with individual words, phrases, and individual sentences, it would be interesting to know whether blocking subvocalization would also interfere similarly when people are reading connected discourse. A major problem in studying reading comprehension for extended passages, however, is that it is very difficult to test for interference in comprehension—even without any interfering task, readers forget a lot of detail. (This problem will be discussed in more detail in chapters 8 and 12.) A compromise strategy is to have people read passages about 5 to 10 sentences long and to test for memory of these materials immediately after each passage is read. The test after such a short interval should be pretty sensitive to any interference with comprehension produced by the concurrent task. While the processing of these short passages is not exactly like reading real text, it's a reasonable approximation.

The typical procedure in these experiments is to have the sentences appear one at a time on a screen at a rate preset by the experimenter and to have the reader either read silently or perform a concurrent vocal activity (e.g., counting or repeating a nonsense phrase). Thus, since reading speed is controlled, the experimenter measures whether comprehension of the passage suffers in any way from the concurrent vocal activity. In addition, Levy (1975, 1977) had subjects listen to passages while counting aloud or being silent. The listening condition represents an interesting control. At first, one might think that counting aloud would interfere more with listening. However, Levy argued that if the speech coding involved in listening does not involve an articulatory component whereas the speech coding involved in reading does (Baddeley 1979), one might observe articulatory interference only in the reading task.

Levy tested her subjects' comprehension by giving them a recognition test containing either a sentence from the test paragraph or a sentence with a slight change in wording. The changes were either lexical (in which case a synonym was substituted for one of the words in the sentence) or semantic (in which case the subject and object nouns were switched). She found that if the subject was reading, vocalization affected comprehension for both types of test sentences in which there was a change. However, no such decrease occurred during listening. In a parallel vein, Baddeley, Eldridge, and Lewis (1981) found that articulatory suppression led to a clear decrement in the subjects' ability to detect anomalous words or errors in word order.

The picture gets more complicated when we consider other studies. In a later experiment, Levy (1978) tested only for changes in meaning and found that concurrent vocal activity did not affect comprehension, and suggested that suppression may only hamper memory for literal meaning (which is contrary to her earlier results). However, in a subsequent study, Slowiaczek and Clifton (1980) demonstrated that while concurrent vocal activity did not affect memory for discrete propositions of the form "the subject verbed the object" (the ones tested in Levy [1978]), it did affect comprehension of propositions when integration of information across sentences was required. A second complication is that Levy's original finding—that there was *no* decrement due to suppression in the listening control—has not usually been replicated. However, the typical pattern in these studies (e.g., Slowiaczek and Clifton 1980) is that the decrement in performance due to suppression in the listening condition is less than that in the reading condition.

It thus appears that suppression may only affect certain kinds of comprehension tasks: those that involve literal memory for wording (which are not very interesting) or those that involve short-term memory in order for the reader to fully comprehend the meaning of several sentences.

Moreover, the effects of suppression appear to be greater for reading than listening, suggesting that the suppression is affecting the process whereby the printed text is converted to auditory form. Combined with the suppression studies using individual words (e.g., Kleiman 1975), these results suggest that inner speech has little to do with accessing the meaning of individual words but is important in later memory processes that aid the comprehension of connected discourse.

Problems with the Suppression Technique

The usual interpretation of the suppression data presented above is not an unreasonable one; however, we would be misleading you if we were to leave you with the impression that the argument for it was close to airtight. There are two major methodological criticisms of the suppression technique.

Interference is not necessarily due to suppression   One problem with the technique is that a decrement, when observed, can not necessarily be ascribed to the ability of the suppression task to use up the vocal apparatus and thus deny it to the reading process. First of all, when two tasks are performed simultaneously, some effort might be expended just for general "bookkeeping" needed to keep the two tasks distinct. Second, the suppression task itself may interfere not only with the vocal apparatus but with more general mental activity (Margolin, Griebel, and Wolford 1982). In fact, as we have seen earlier, the 100 msec decrement in the visual and semantic comparison tasks of the Kleiman experiment was explained either by bookkeeping or by general interference. It is possible to extend this argument to raise the possibility that *none* of the vocal interference effects observed in reading are really due to suppression of subvocal speech and that all are due to interference with more general mental activity.

How would such an argument go? Let's consider the Kleiman result that the rhyme judgment task is slowed by more than 300 msec. This extra interference may not necessarily be due to subvocalic suppression; it may be that the rhyming task takes more general mental activity. According to such an argument, tasks range in "difficulty" with more difficult tasks taking more general processing resources and hence interfering more with concurrent tasks.

The assumption that the rhyming task involves more general processing resources than the meaning (synonymy) task is somewhat ad hoc (although the absolute times for the rhyming task were longer than for the semantic judgment task). Is there any way to determine whether such a general interference explanation is to be preferred over the explanation that the interference effect is due to specific competition in the phonological system? One experiment (Waters, Komoda, and Arbuckle 1985) attempted to measure the general processing resources that various tasks took by assessing their interfering effects on another task (dot detection) and then subtracting those effects from the interfering effects on reading (using a technique called the *analysis of covariance*). The results, unfortunately, were somewhat mixed. Subtracting the interfering effects of the dot detection task reduced the interfering effect of the shadowing task enough that it was not statistically significant. However, the residual interference effect was still fairly large (reading was slowed about 15 percent and comprehension suffered a bit).

An additional problem with the Waters, Komoda, and Arbuckle experiment is that they chose the shadowing task as concurring activity, while the other experiments that had subjects read passages of text (e.g., Levy 1977; Slowiaczek and Clifton 1980) used a different task (either going through the numbers 1 through 10 or repeating a word or two over and over). The shadowing task, unfortunately, is probably far from ideal to study subvocal suppression. In Kleiman and in Waters, Komoda, and Arbuckle, the fastest rate of shadowing single digits is one digit per two-thirds of a second. Since normal speech is about 50 to 100 percent faster, shadowing probably does not drive the vocal apparatus as continually as one might wish. The probable reason that such relatively slow rates occur is that the task is relatively demanding of general mental resources (as the interference in the visual and semantic comparison tasks of Kleiman's experiments indicates); forcing the subject to go faster would probably cause a general breakdown in the shadowing task. A repetition task (such as going "blah-blah-blah" over and over), which was typically used in the passage comprehension studies (e.g., Levy 1975), seems a much better approximation to the ideal of tying up the vocal apparatus with a minimum use of general mental resources.

To summarize the first criticism of the suppression technique, decrements in reading, when observed, may not be due to suppression of subvocalization but to use of general mental resources. Similarly, finding a greater decrement in reading while shadowing than while performing some other concurrent task (such as finger tapping [Levy 1981]) may be because shadowing or talking is using more general mental resources rather than more speech resources. At present, only one study (Waters, Komoda, and Arbuckle 1985) has seriously tried to assess the general mental resource demands of various concurrent tasks. The results were inconclusive, but suggested that shadowing may have an effect beyond a general interference effect. No one has done a similar assessment of the repetition task. On the face of it, however, the repetition task seems to use very little general mental resources but ties up vocal resources quite effectively, and is thus a better candidate for a vocal suppression task.

The suppression task may not adequately suppress inner speech The suppression task has been also attacked from the other side. It has been argued that the absence of an interference effect does not necessarily mean that inner speech is not involved in the process of interest, such as in Kleiman's task where subjects judge the synonymy of two words. Remember, our demonstration earlier showed that phonological coding is possible while the vocal apparatus is completely tied up. Furthermore, most people's introspections are that it is not particularly difficult to hear the voice in the head while the mouth is saying something else. In other words, while such a study clearly demonstrates that *subvocalization* is not necessary for comprehension of the meaning of the two words, it may say little about whether *phonological coding* (i.e., the voice in your head) is involved.

Let's expand the argument a bit. Assume that the data are that task *X*, such as comparing the meaning of two words, is unaffected by concurrent vocalization (this is an idealization of the real data). We can safely conclude that subvocalization is not involved in task *X*, because even if the concurrent vocalization task doesn't completely suppress subvocalization (the subject might sneak it in a bit here and there), it would massively disrupt subvocalization since the mouth can do only one thing at a time. When we consider the effect of concurrent vocal activity on phonological coding (the voice in the head), we are on much less solid ground because we know that the two activities can go on at the same time (at least on a global level). While we have the intuition that the sounds coming out of the mouth must have some interfering action on the voice in the head, we do not know for sure.

For example, one possibility is that producing overt speech creates a second voice that interferes with listening to the inner voice. Studies in selective attention, however, indicate that if subjects are trying to attend to an auditory message coming from one spatial location, a second auditory message (which the subject is told to ignore) coming from a second location produces little interference in comprehending the first message (Broadbent 1958). Since the overt vocalizations appear to be coming from a different location than the inner voice, one may expect this "second voice" interference to be unimportant. What seems more plausible is that subvocalization may be needed to reinforce, extend, or perhaps adjust the inner speech being produced, so that blocking subvocalization will lead to a more impoverished form of inner speech. However, if the subject can sneak in a little subvocalization, that may be good enough to produce adequate inner speech.

This leads to a second methodological criticism of the concurrent vocalization experiments. None made a serious attempt to measure a decrement in the concurrent vocal activity caused by the reading task (possibly because of surreptitious subvocalization). This is especially a problem because there is evidence (e.g., Posner and Boies 1971) that in a dual task situation the task that is perceived as secondary is the one in which the major decrement is observed. That is, whenever the demands of the two tasks collide, the secondary one is usually the one to give. In this case, the concurrent vocal activity is almost certainly perceived as secondary, so one would expect subtle interference effects to show up in that task rather than the reading task.

Summary

To summarize, interference due to concurrent vocalization may not be a sensitive measure of inner speech because (a) one thing can be phonologically coded while another is vocalized; (b) subtle interference effects may be missed because the interference may be mainly in the vocalization task, which is not carefully measured.

We apologize for what might appear to be a lengthy methodological digression, but the concurrent task paradigm is so complex that its problems need some discussion. Our discussion indicates that few conclusions drawn from the concurrent task data are really solid. While the general interference explanation for positive effects cannot be ruled out, we feel that the data are reasonably convincing in demonstrating that both phonological coding and subvocalization are involved in short-term memory processes used in comprehending discourse. While the negative results clearly indicate that subvocalization is probably irrelevant to accessing the meanings of words, we feel less convinced that the negative results demonstrate that phonological coding is not used in accessing the meaning of words (see also Chapter 3).

A similar argument has been made by Besner, Davies, and Daniels (1981; Besner and Davelaar 1982) who distinguished between (a) "phonological recoding from print for the purpose of lexical access" and (b) "buffer storage and/or maintenance of phonologically coded information derived from print." They claim that only the latter is affected by subvocalization. They attempted to devise a task in which only (*a*) is tapped to determine whether there was an effect of concurrent articulation. For example, judgment of rhyming would take both (*a*) (phonological coding) and (*b*) (buffer storage) since the first word would have to be coded in some auditory form and then held in memory and compared with the second word. Thus, it is possible that most of the interference with the rhyming task is not due to the encoding of the auditory forms but to the storage and comparison processes. A second task devised by Besner et al. was judgment of homophony between two words. They found a markedly reduced (but still significant) interference effect, suggesting that much of the interference in the rhyming task was due to processes beyond initial encoding.

The interference effect in the homophony judgment task could still be due to (*b*), however, since the homophony judgment task involves some memory comparison (although a judgment of identity seems simpler than a judgment of rhyme). They attempted to remove all effects of (*b*) in a task where subjects were asked to judge whether nonwords sounded like real words (i.e., were pseudohomophones). It is possible that this does not require any extensive storage or comparison of sounds, as the task only requires that a single sound be accessed and used to access a nonsound code (the lexical entry). Their results were mixed. They found interference in one task in which subjects were suppressing as fast as possible, while they found no interference in a task where subjects were still going reasonably fast (about 3 digits per second) but not quite as fast as they could go.

Besner, Davies, and Daniels (1981) concluded that the latter task demonstrated that phonological encoding could go on without any interference effect. It could also be argued, however, that their latter task was not sufficiently powerful to find the effect because the subject wasn't suppressing hard enough. In addition, they (like everyone else) did not look for effects on the secondary task. However, Besner's (1987) research and arguments suggest that vocal interference tasks may produce *most* of their effects on the storage and manipulation of inner speech rather than on the initial creation of it from text. Whether concurrent vocal activity has *no* effect on creation of inner speech from written text remains to be seen.

HOMOPHONIC READING

The third paradigm used to study inner speech during reading really consists of three separate techniques that share some common characteristics. We will refer to the general paradigm as *homophonic reading,* since what is common across the three techniques is that words are used which are homophones or phonemically similar to each other. In the homophonic phrase technique, subjects are asked to judge the acceptability of phrases in which homophones (words that are spelled differently and mean different things, but sound the same, such as *meet-meat*) replace a critical word in the phrase. In the tongue-twister and phonemic similarity techniques, subjects make acceptability judgments of sentences containing a number of words that sound very similar. As we shall see, the assumptions underlying the paradigms are similar and the results across the different paradigms are also rather consistent. The relation of phonological coding to subvocalization has been explored for each of these three paradigms by having subjects engage in concurrent articulatory suppression.

Homophonic Phrases

How easy do you find it to read the following two sentences? In each, pronunciation is preserved, but the visual characteristics of the words are drastically altered.

The bouy and the none tolled hymn they had scene
and herd a pear of bear feat in the haul. (6.1)
Iff yew kann sowned owt thiss sentunns, ewe wil
komprihenned itt. (6.2)

In the first sentence (taken from LaBerge 1972) most of the words are replaced by homophones so that the sentence sounds right, but doesn't look right. In the second sentence (taken from Baddeley, Eldridge, and Lewis 1981) all of the words are misspelled (and most are nonwords), but you can still sound the words out and understand the sentence.

If reading relied totally on the use of a speech code, text that is altered but still pronounced correctly (as in these examples) should be no harder to read than unaltered text. Following this reasoning, Bower (1970) used Greek letters to symbolize English words for Greek-English bilinguals. Because the subjects in his experiments found it very difficult to read such text, he concluded that speech recoding was not used in reading. However, one can only conclude from this result that speech recoding is not the *only* route to meaning. Another diagnostic use of homophones was provided by Baron (1973). He asked subjects to judge the meaningfulness of phrases which contained either orthographically and phonetically incorrect words (such as *new I can't* or *I am kill*) or visually incorrect but phonetically correct words (such as *don't dew it* or *tie the not*). In the first case, the orthographically and phonetically incorrect words *new* and *kill* replace *no* and *ill,* and in the second case, the homophones *dew* and *not* replace *do* and *knot*. Subjects were also given meaningful phrases (*I am ill*) on half the trials. Baron's reasoning was that if speech recoding occurs, the correct sound of the homophonic errors should interfere with deciding that the sentence is not meaningful, and the homophonic errors would thus have longer reaction times for rejecting the sentence than the orthographic errors. If no recoding took place, the decision would be based on only visual features of the phrase and there would be no difference between the two conditions. Indeed, Baron found the latter pattern of results and argued that speech recoding is not necessary during reading.

It could be argued, however, that the reaction time data in Baron's experiment are not nearly as important as the error data. You see, Baron also found that readers make more errors with the homophonic phrases (*tie the not*) than the nonhomophonic phrases (*I am kill*). Thus, the error data provide support for the idea that speech recoding in reading does occur. Baron's finding of no differences in response times for rejecting phrases with homophonic and nonhomophonic words (but with more errors in the former case than in the latter) has been replicated by Doctor and Coltheart (1980) and by Banks, Oka, and Shugarman (1981). Furthermore, Treiman, Freyd, and Baron (1983), Treiman, Baron and Luk (1981), Treiman and Hirsh-Pasek (1983), and Baron et al. (1980) have all reported more errors and longer response times in rejecting phrases containing homophones than in rejecting the control nonhomophonic phrases. Thus, it now seems clear that the phrase evaluation task involves speech recoding.

Although the phrase evaluation experiment was initially designed to investigate the role of speech coding in lexical access, we don't know whether the interference effects obtained are pre- or post-lexical. That is, the sound of the homophone may only interfere when the phrase as a whole (sitting in short-term memory) is evaluated for meaning. One interpretation of the pattern of results offered is that subjects were often able to access the lexicon for the individual words (hence there would be no reaction time difference), yet the fact that postlexical speech coding occurs would lead them to make errors when they had finished reading the entire phrase.

Tongue-twisters

Another technique to examine speech coding in reading involves having subjects read sentences with tongue-twisters. Tongue-twisters contain a number of words with the same initial consonants. The well-known one, which children (and adults) try to say as fast as they can, is exemplified here.

> Peter Piper picked a peck of pickled peppers. (6.3)

It is obvious that oral reading of tongue-twisters would be slowed down by the same mechanisms that make them hard to say even when no reading is involved. That is, the parts of the speech musculature involved in articulatory programming are repeatedly involved in programming a phonetic sequence immediately after a similar sequence has been produced. What is of interest is whether the difference between tongue-twister sentences and control sentences also occurs in silent reading.

Haber and Haber (1982) gave subjects tongue-twister sentences like 6.4 and control sentences like 6.5.

> Barbara burned the brown bread badly. (6.4)
> Samuel caught the high ball neatly. (6.5)

They found that the tongue-twisters took more time than the controls and the difference between the two types of sentences was the same in both silent reading and oral reading. (Naturally, silent reading was faster than oral reading.) Ayres (1984) embedded tongue-twisters in paragraphs and obtained the same results as Haber and Haber; paragraphs with tongue-twisters took longer to read silently (and orally) than those without. The rationale in these experiments is that if articulatory programming is required in silent reading and cannot be suppressed, then the extra time to read a tongue-twister silently as compared to its control should be the same as the difference between the time needed to read tongue-twisters and control sentences orally.

The most comprehensive study involving tongue-twisters has been reported by McCutchen and Perfetti (1982). Subjects in their experiment silently read sentences and made semantic acceptability judgments. Some of the sentences were tongue-twisters, with repeated initial consonants (such as sentences 6.3 and 6.4 above), and others were matched phonetically neutral sentences (containing a mix of phonemes at the beginning of the words). Semantic acceptability judgments were longer for the tongue-twisters than the neutral sentences. In addition, concurrent vocalization with a tongue-twister phrase slowed performance. That is, when subjects had to vocalize "Pack a pair of purple pampers" while making semantic acceptability judgments, response time was slowed for both the tongue-twisters and the neutral sentences. However, McCutchen and Perfetti found that concurrent vocalization did not produce reliable specific interference when the vocalization phrase repeated the same word initial consonant (for example, bilabial /p/ as in the "Pack a pair . . ." example) as in the sentence being read.

The results of these tongue-twister studies are consistent in finding longer silent reading times for tongue-twisters than for control sentences. The interference appears to be due to the similarity of the phonetic representations automatically activated during reading. McCutchen and Perfetti argued that specific phonemes are activated during reading and that this occurs postlexically. They also argued that the lack of specific interference between concurrent vocalization and the reading task suggests that these automatically activated phonetic representations are not subvocal motor programs and that the concurrent vocalization paradigm is not an appropriate method to examine the role of inner speech in reading. This is similar to the conclusion of Besner, Davies, and Daniels (1981) discussed earlier.

Phonemic Similarity Effect

Closely related to the tongue-twister effect is the phonemic similarity effect. Baddeley and Hitch (1974) first used the phonemic similarity effect, which has a powerful effect on memory span, in a reading study. They asked subjects to make semantic acceptability judgments for sentences made up almost entirely of phonemically similar words. For example, consider sentences 6.6 and 6.7:

Crude rude Jude chewed stewed food. (6.6)
Crude rude chewed Jude stewed food. (6.7)

Sentence 6.6 is acceptable while Sentence 6.7 is anomalous. Subjects took longer to accept and reject sentences of this type than to process semantically equivalent sentences which contained words that were not phonemically similar. In a subsequent experiment, Baddeley and Lewis (1981) asked subjects to make the same types of semantic acceptability judgments while continually counting aloud. They found that articulatory suppression produced an increase in errors, but did not influence the size of the phonemic similarity effect.

In a related study, Treiman, Freyd, and Baron (1983) presented subjects with a sentence fragment and then had them perform a forced-choice sentence completion task. For example, the fragment "He made a nasty hasty" was presented with a choice of two completions, *remark* or *profusely*. Subjects were to choose the word that made a complete and meaningful sentence. Some of the fragments contained pairs of words with similar spellings but different pronunciations (as in the *nasty-hasty* pair in the example). Other pairs consisted of similar spelling and similar pronunciation (as in *never-sever*). Treiman, Freyd, and Baron (1983) found that the phonological relation between the members of a pair influenced performance: response times were longer when the pairs were spelled similarly but had different pronunciations than when the pairs were spelled and pronounced similarly. They also found an effect of phonetic coding in a sentence acceptability task: unacceptable sentences containing a critical exception word, as in Sentence 6.8, were harder to reject than those sentences containing a critical regular word, as in Sentence 6.9.

> The children plaid outdoors. (6.8)
> He wore a played shirt. (6.9)

Plaid is an exception word and *played* is a regular word (see Chapter 3).

The phonemic similarity effect studies are consistent with the idea that inner speech plays an important role in reading. In most of the studies, the data are consistent with the hypothesis that inner speech is solely a postlexical process involving holding words in working memory. However, the Treiman, Freyd, and Baron (1983) study suggests that inner speech is activated by nonlexical spelling-to-sound rules, since *plaid* would activate "played" only by such routes. This result reinforces the conclusion of Van Orden (1987) that phonetic codes are important in lexical access.

Summary

The research described in this section leads to the conclusion that inner speech is important in reading. The common thread running through the studies described here is that the *sounds* of words influence the speed and/or accuracy of silent reading. If a word that sounds the same as (or is similar to) a target word in a phrase or sentence replaces the target word, subjects have a harder time rejecting the phrase or sentence than when the target word is replaced by a word which does not sound the same. Additionally, sentences containing a number of words beginning with the same phoneme or a number of words that rhyme with each other are more difficult to read both orally and—more interestingly—silently. Researchers investigating these issues and employing these paradigms have generally attributed the effects to postlexical processing in working memory, although the Treiman, Freyd, and Baron study indicates that this conclusion is premature.

DEAF READERS

We have been pursuing the issue of how much normal silent reading relies on speech recoding for comprehension to occur. The common thread in all of the experiments that we have discussed is that researchers have tried to manipulate variables that might be related to inner speech (as, for example, by utilizing suppression studies to hinder articulatory recoding) or to find variables that might correlate with speech recoding (as in the EMG studies). A different way to pursue the issue is to investigate subjects who presumably *cannot* engage in speech recoding of a phonological type in processing text. Here, of course, we are referring to profoundly deaf individuals. As Conrad (1972) pointed out, the paradox of a "normal deaf" population is too great for the term to be meaningful. A person can be legally classified as deaf if his or her hearing does not fall within certain limits, but still have residual hearing effects. The deaf readers we are most interested in are those who have little awareness of different speech sounds. Unless they see lips moving, they do not know if someone is speaking. The subjects of most interest are also those who were either born or became profoundly deaf within the first year or so of life. Thus, they would never have used normal speech.

Can the profoundly deaf learn to read? If the answer were an emphatic no we would have some pretty good evidence that reading is only possible when speech coding is available. While most deaf children do learn to read to some extent, for the most part they do not read very well (Conrad 1972). Conrad (1972, 1977) and Treiman and Hirch-Pasek (1983) have reviewed the characteristics of profoundly deaf readers and concluded that deaf readers do not cope well with the task of reading. On average, adult deaf readers only read at about fourth or fifth grade level and only about 25 percent of the profoundly deaf would be classified as functionally literate (where literacy is defined as fourth grade reading ability). About 50 percent of the deaf with hearing loss greater than 85 decibels have virtually no reading comprehension (Conrad 1977).

That the deaf read poorly is not really surprising. First, the profoundly deaf do not learn English through the normal channels, and lacking knowledge of the sound structure of English, they do not have an opportunity to benefit from an alphabetical writing system. Second, the "spoken language" for most of the deaf people in the United States is not English but American Sign Language (ASL), which differs from English in some important ways. ASL has a lexicon of signs and borrowed words (articulated with the hands), morphemic devices for building complex words from simpler ones, and grammatical rules for combining words into sentences. These rules differ markedly from the syntax of English. Thus, these deaf subjects have an additional handicap in reading: They have to learn to read a language that differs from the one they "speak."

What is perhaps more surprising is the fact that some profoundly deaf people manage to read fairly well. Conrad (1977) estimated that by the end of their formal school training 4.5 percent of hearing-impaired students in England and Wales could read at a level commensurate with their age. Such good readers are less common among the profoundly deaf than among those with some residual hearing (Conrad 1977). Thus those who can benefit from some exposure to spoken language tend to be better readers. However, among the profoundly deaf who have virtually no exposure to spoken English, those who have deaf parents tend to read better than those who have hearing parents, presumably because the former learned ASL earlier– at about the same time that hearing people learn their native language (Treiman and Hirsh-Pasek 1983).

Investigations of profoundly deaf readers indicate that phonological coding does not occur as they read (Locke 1978; Quinn 1981; Treiman and Hirsh-Pasek 1983). Given that their language is not oral, this finding is not very surprising. Do they do any type of recoding? Treiman and Hirsh-Pasek (1983) examined 14 congenitally and profoundly deaf adults who were native signers of ASL. Fourteen hearing subjects with comparable reading levels were also tested. These subjects participated in experiments that tested for the possibility of (1) recoding into articulation, (2) recoding into fingerspelling, (3) recoding into ASL, or (4) no recoding at all. The experiments used the phrase evaluation task with homophonic words and tongue-twisters. Treiman and Hirsh-Pasek (1983) found that their deaf subjects did not have the difficulty with homophonic words that hearing subjects did, thus ruling out recoding into articulation. In addition, there was little evidence that most of their subjects recoded printed words into fingerspelling. In contrast, the subjects had considerable difficulty with sentences containing similar signs (i.e., "hand-twisters"), indicating that they did recode into signs. An interesting result was that the deaf subjects did have difficulty reading tongue-twisters, suggesting that part of the tongue-twister effect discussed previously may be due to visual similarity.

Thus, second-generation profoundly deaf readers seem to consult their native language (ASL) when reading English. Although ASL bears no direct relation to print, access to the language (possibly in an "inner" form) seems to assist reading performance. As Treiman and Hirsh-Pasek pointed out, the comprehension and memory advantages provided by one's primary language weigh heavily in the choice of a recoding system.

THE EFFECTS OF THE WRITING SYSTEM

Treiman and Hirsh-Pasek's conclusion brings us to the issue of the effects of orthography on inner speech. As we saw in Chapter 2, some nonalphabetic systems rely much less heavily on representing sound with written symbols and rarely rely upon grapheme-phoneme correspondence rules for pronunciation of words in the language. Observations such as this have frequently led to the suggestion that readers of languages that are primarily logographic (such as Chinese) go from print to meaning directly without any involvement of inner speech. There are two assumptions here that are at odds with the evidence presented earlier. First, it is assumed that the lexicon is always activated directly from the visual representation. However, we have seen in Chapter 2 that the system is not purely logographic and that the representation of some characters is (in principle) based on sound. Second, it is assumed that there is no benefit from postlexical coding of information into sound codes to aid short-term or working memory.

It is clearly the case that speech recoding occurs among Chinese readers because they make confusion errors in short-term memory for similar-sounding words and letters (Tzeng, Hung, and Wang 1977; Tzeng and Hung 1980; Yik 1978). However, some evidence suggests that speech recoding occurs to a lesser extent among readers of Chinese than among readers of English (Treiman, Baron, and Luk 1981). In addition, Kimura (1984; Kimura and Bryant 1983) found a smaller effect of concurrent articulation on Kanji then on Kana. Thus, on the basis of the available data, it appears that once logographic characters are learned, they are phonetically recoded in working memory just as English words are (Erickson, Mattingly, and Turvey 1977). However, since lexical access probably relies less heavily on the indirect route in Chinese it is possible that inner speech may be somewhat less important in Chinese than in English (Seidenberg, 1985a).

Summary of Deaf and Chinese Readers

That profoundly deaf people can read at all is sometimes taken as evidence that speech recoding in normal readers is optional (Conrad 1972). However, as we have seen, they do not read very well, and the best available evidence indicates that when reading English text deaf readers recode the printed information into their native language (ASL) for comprehension purposes. Since they have not experienced speech sounds, recoding into a phonological code is precluded from deaf readers. Instead, the information is recoded into a manual form to aid comprehension. The poor reading of deaf people is thus probably due in part to inner speech being a more efficient system of recoding than overt manual gestures.

Readers of logographic systems such as Chinese can probably access the meaning of many printed characters directly from the visual representation. However, associations between the printed word and the appropriate pronunciation are activated during reading and appear to be important in comprehending text.

THE ROLE OF INNER SPEECH IN READING

We have reviewed a large number of studies and the general conclusion to be reached from each of the paradigms used to study inner speech is that it is helpful for comprehension. Experiments that have attempted to eliminate or interfere with inner speech in some way are pretty consistent in demonstrating that when it is eliminated, comprehension usually suffers (unless the text or comprehension questions are very easy). This conclusion emerges from studies in which subvocalization is eliminated or reduced by way of feedback procedures and in which it is interfered with by concurrent articulation. Our analysis leads us to suggest that subvocalization is prevented in both of these situations, but phonological coding (hearing your voice) is not.

Studies in which subjects must silently read phrases or sentences with homophones, tongue-twisters, or a number of phonemically similar words also clearly implicate a role for inner speech in comprehension processes. That readers have about as much trouble processing such sentences when they read silently as when they read aloud is *prima facie* evidence that inner speech processes occur during reading, and that they are important components of silent reading. Additionally, the evidence we reviewed from deaf readers and Chinese readers clearly implicates the importance of inner speech in understanding written text.

For the most part, the studies which we have reviewed had as their primary objective to determine if inner speech is an epiphenomenon or if it plays an important role in reading. Exactly how inner speech facilitates reading has been considered less often. We now turn to speculations about the nature of the phonological codes that are activated and how they are utilized during reading.

What Is Inner Speech?

The most explicit proposal describing the characteristics of the phonological code activated during silent reading has been made by Perfetti and McCutchen (1982; McCutchen and Perfetti 1982). Their argument is that regardless of whether access to the lexicon is provided directly by the visual pattern of the printed word or indirectly through a rule-analogy system, a consequence of lexical access is an automatic activation of phonological features. However, they also suggest that a complete phonological representation for every word in the text does not occur because such detailed phonological activation would require too much time to be a part of efficient reading. Specifically, they suggest that phonetic specification is incomplete and biased toward the beginnings of the words. In addition, since function words (such as articles, prepositions, conjunctions) generally work as syntactic coordinators, they may not require as elaborate phonetic representations as content words.

Perfetti and McCutchen argued that an abstract phonological representation containing information about the word-initial phoneme and general phonetic shape would be very useful in reading, especially during the integration process of comprehension. Together with abbreviated semantic information activated during the initial access of the lexicon, word-initial phonetic information could provide a concise index by which to reaccess specific words if that were necessary during comprehension. Perfetti and McCutchen assumed that the codes used in the activation of the phonological representations are weighted to consonant features, rather than vowel sounds. This assumption was made for two reasons. First, consonants carry more linguistic information than vowels; consonants more specifically identify words, so they would be more helpful in securing specific lexical reference. Second, consonants do not have the acoustic duration that vowels do and so would be more compatible with the speed at which silent reading occurs. With respect to this second point, Perfetti and McCutchen also assume that the consonant code includes distinctive features of articulation.

Perfetti and McCutchen's proposals are interesting. However, there are some potential problems. First, when you listen to the voice in your head, it does not appear to be in shorthand—all the sounds appear to be there as do function words. However, it is possible that when you become conscious of inner speech, the process changes and the inner speech is less in shorthand and also slows down. The second problem is whether the shorthand form of inner speech allows it to be sufficiently comprehensible. We know from research using the RSVP paradigm that if words are presented briefly one at a time and the function words are left out, comprehension suffers (Potter, Kroll, and Harris 1980). While function words are generally syntactic coordinators, their role in reading might actually be fairly important. Thus, a phonological code should be activated for them as well. Of course, inner speech need not be the *only* memory representation that supports sentence comprehension. Part of Perfetti and McCutchen's motivation for arguing that not all words have phonological codes activated during silent reading was to account for the discrepancy in reading rate between oral and silent reading. However, it is possible that the difference between oral and silent reading rates is because a motor response for actually pronouncing each word need not occur in silent reading.

Does Inner Speech Lag Behind the Eye?

As we mentioned in Chapter 5, the voice lags behind the eyes by about two words in oral reading. (Two words would typically take about two fixations or about half a second.) While it is often emphasized that the eyes are ahead of the voice, it is important to realize that the eyes do not get very far ahead; if they do, they remain in place so as not to get any further ahead. When we consider that part of the difference between the word fixated and the word that is spoken can be attributed to the fact that the motor programs involved in speech production are relatively slow, then the lag between voice and eyes may not be as great as it seems.

What about silent reading? Does inner speech lag behind the eyes? Introspection suggests that if there is a lag, it is quite small because we seem to hear our voice pronouncing the word our eyes are looking at. But, this is all rather deceptive since all of these processes are occurring very quickly and if we try to introspect on how well our eyes and inner voice are aligned, we probably are altering the process of silent reading.

One way to study the time course of inner speech in reading is to examine fixation times on words as a function of phonetic variables. One is the number of syllables. Whereas fixation time on words can be influenced by various lexical characteristics of a word (Rayner and Duffy 1986), the number of syllables a word has (with length controlled) apparently does not influence fixation time (Crowder 1982). Previous research had demonstrated that fixation time on two-digit numbers was directly influenced by the number of syllables necessary to pronounce the word even though pronunciation was not involved in the task (Pynte 1974). The same kind of effect was also demonstrated for line drawings of objects (Noirzet and Pynte 1976). However, fixation durations on digits and line drawings are much longer than fixation durations on words. Crowder (1982) found the same kind of results with digits, but when words were used as stimuli, no effects were obtained. Crowder suggests that the reason effects were not found with words is because the phonological coding lags behind the eyes. We concur with this conclusion, but stress again that the inner voice does not lag very far behind the eyes in silent reading (less than two words).

Finally, we noted that Perfetti and McCutchen stressed acoustic durations and articulatory features as being important for the phonological code that is set up. Here, the motivation appears to be for the phonological code in silent reading to be dependent upon the speech code in general. While there is definitely a relationship between the speech code and the phonological code in silent reading, it is not clear that the latter should be totally dependent on the former. For example, we pointed out that concurrent articulation interferes with subvocalization but not necessarily phonological coding. If you are continually vocalizing "ba-ba-ba" and reading silently, you obviously cannot use the speech articulators to prompt the phonological code. This may mean that the phonological code is independent of articulatory features and acoustic durations of overt speech. It is clear that considerably more work is necessary to specify the characteristics of the phonological code in silent reading and its relationship to overt speech.

In the absence of unambiguous data and theory on the issue, our suggestion is that word identification and lexical access in silent reading result in automatic activation of a phonological code, which is not strategically controlled (see also McCutchen and Perfetti 1982; Perfetti, Bell, and Delaney 1988) and which is somewhat independent from articulation processes. The phonological code is set up very quickly for each word in the text, although there could well be a bias towards an emphasis on the word's initial phoneme. In essence, we want to suggest that the phonological code that is established for words in silent reading results in your hearing a voice saying the words your eyes are falling on. This code is identical to the kind of code that occurs when you hear yourself think. This is not to say that all thinking is based upon speech processes; purely visual thinking clearly occurs. But we want to argue that the kind of phonological coding that occurs during thinking and reading are one and the same. In this sense, we are totally comfortable with the idea of silent reading being *externally guided thinking* (Neisser 1967).

How Is the Phonological Code Used for Comprehension?

There are at least two possible ways in which phonological codes could facilitate reading other than involvement in lexical access. The first way has been mentioned earlier in the chapter and involves holding words and word order information in working memory. Because new words are processed very quickly, we would soon overload our short-term capacity if words were not chunked together in meaningful ways in working memory. Words in working memory are recoded into a phonological code and held there until meaningful units can be passed on to long-term memory. Since it is often the case that sentences have long distances between related words, having the words in a phonological code in working memory helps us to reinterpret an earlier part of a sentence in light of words that occur later in the sentence. You can always move your eyes back to the earlier part of the sentence and when the sentence is syntactically difficult readers often do (Frazier and Rayner 1982; Kennedy and Murray 1984). However, it might be more economical to use the information in working memory if it is there. Because working memory has a special capacity for temporal order information, it would readily have the information necessary for reinterpretation. Thus, one way in which phonological codes in working memory could aid comprehension is by providing access to the order in which words were read so that we can restructure and reinterpret the words in light of new information in working memory.

The second way in which phonological codes may aid comprehension is that information about prosodic structure may be available from them (Slowiaczek and Clifton 1980). It is widely recognized that spoken language has an abundance of information over and above the sounds which make up the individual words. Rhythm, intonation, and stress are all important sources of information for understanding speech. Studies in auditory language processing have shown that listeners are sensitive to prosodic structure and that they use it in sentence comprehension (see Slowiaczek and Clifton 1980). In contrast with the rich prosodic structure provided in spoken language, written language provides impoverished cues (see Chapter 2). If prosodic information is used in sentence processing, the reader must find some way to compensate for the lack of prosody in reading. Slowiaczek and Clifton argued that this is a role of phonological codes in reading. Through such codes, the reader can reorganize the written sentence into a prosodic structure. Slowiaczek and Clifton called these prosodic structures "timing trees" because they assumed they are hierarchically organized with rhythm being the basic organizing principle. According to the argument, timing trees hold language and other rhythmically organized information in working memory and provide the pattern information necessary for complex processing. Under this view, phonological codes serve to translate information into an appropriate form for language comprehension. Timing trees do not facilitate sentence comprehension simply because they last longer in working memory, but because they highlight important information.

Although Slowiaczek and Clifton's theoretical statements, like Perfetti and McCutchen's, are somewhat speculative, there is some evidence consistent with their suggestions. Kosslyn and Matt (1977) showed that the speed of silent reading of a passage was strongly influenced by the speaking rate of the person said to have written it. Prior to reading a passage, subjects in the experiment heard the voice of the supposed author of the passage. If the supposed author spoke quickly, subjects read the passage quickly; if the author spoke slowly, they read it slowly. In a series of experiments, Kosslyn and Matt convincingly argued that the effect of reading speed comes from the speaking rate of the author and not from other factors. This evidence is also consistent with introspective accounts of inner speech. When you read a letter from someone you know very well, such as your mother, you often can hear her accent, or stress, or intonation pattern (Brown 1970). Also, when you read text such as this book, you do not hear your voice in a monotone (unless perhaps you always speak in a monotone). Rather, you are aware of providing stress and intonation patterns to the words. In other words, Slowiaczek and Clifton's suggestions concerning the utilization of phonological codes to provide prosodic structure cues is consistent with our impressions of what happens when we read silently.

SUMMARY

In this chapter, we have considered the role of inner speech in reading. Evidence from a number of different types of experiments converges on the notion that inner speech serves a useful function in reading comprehension. Although the meanings of individual words can be determined without recoding written language into speech, phonological codes appear to be activated for most words we read and this phonological information is held in working memory and is used to comprehend text. Our argument has been that these phonological codes lag behind the eyes in reading. But, the inner voice in silent reading is more closely tied to eye position than is the voice in oral reading. Whereas the voice in oral reading lags behind the eyes by roughly two words, the inner voice does not lag behind nearly so much. Although inner speech consists of articulatory movements (subvocalization) and phonological codes (hearing your voice), evidence suggests that interfering with subvocalization does not necessarily interfere with the establishment of phonological codes. Finally, we considered in some detail the nature and role of phonological codes and suggested that they are primarily used to hold information about temporal order in working memory and to provide prosodic cues useful in comprehending the text.

PART THREE
UNDERSTANDING TEXT

You have probably had the experience of reading something and knowing what all the words meant, but had little idea of the meaning of what you were reading. This phenomenon indicates that understanding text is clearly more than understanding the component words; other processes are needed that take the meanings of the words, together with their order in the stream of text, to form a more global meaning.

The next two chapters are an introduction to understanding the "higher order" processes that we promised we would eventually get to in the preceding chapters. The word *introduction* in the previous sentence should be kept in mind, since the topic is vast. If our brief discussion seems interesting, there are many excellent books on psycholinguistics (Clark and Clark 1977; Carroll 1986; Foss and Hakes 1978; Garnham 1985) that cover these issues in greater depth. Given the space limitations, we will focus on comprehension *processes,* or how readers construct meaning as they read. We will only briefly touch upon the *product* of comprehension, or what is in readers' minds after they have read a passage of text. Our primary reason for deemphasizing the latter topic is that understanding the product of reading is less a topic in reading than it is a topic in understanding. That is, much of the theorizing could apply to reading, listening, watching a movie, or observing real-world events.

There are two main sections in Chapter 7. The first examines how words are processed in context. The primary issue is whether words are processed any differently when they are in text than when seen in isolation. A central theme that will run through our discussion is whether context affects the *encoding* (or lexical access) of words or only affects later stages of processing (such as tying the words into the meaning of the ongoing discourse). This discussion will serve as an introduction to later topics in two ways. First, a discussion of how higher-order processes relate to lexical access will provide an introduction to these higher-order processes. Second, it will provide a methodological introduction, enabling us to outline how researchers have attempted to distinguish between effects due to lexical access and effects due to higher-order processing such as building syntactic or semantic structures. The second half of the chapter deals with how sentences are understood, with the focus on the construction of syntactic structures, since syntax is better understood than semantics.

Chapter 8 moves on to consider how units bigger than sentences are comprehended. In the first part of the chapter, we will again look at how individual words are processed. However, in Chapter 8, the focus will be on how concepts are tied together (usually across sentences) rather than how the words themselves are identified. This will serve as an introduction to a discussion of how discourse structures are formed and retained.

CHAPTER SEVEN
WORDS AND SENTENCES

We have argued that the encoding of words is an important stage of reading, and, furthermore, that it operates pretty much the same in isolation as in context. Otherwise, a chapter on the processing of words in isolation would be an empty exercise. After Chapter 3, we gave several overviews of the process of reading text. First, we examined how the eyes move through text. The eye movement record reveals that while reading is a complex process, it is largely a word-by-word affair. The chapter on inner speech revealed an important dimension of reading: recoding to sound. One important feature of inner speech is that it probably is an indicant of the more "constructive" aspects of reading, whereby the reader is adding something to the printed record in order to help decipher its larger meaning. We now wish to step closer and look at the interaction between lexical encoding and these higher-order constructive processes in reading (since not all constructive processes are necessarily involved with inner speech).

THE EFFECTS OF CONTEXT ON WORD IDENTIFICATION

Some General Issues

In Chapter 3, we argued that higher-order processes have a relatively minor effect on word identification. First, word identification in isolation is quite fluent and automatic for skilled readers so that it doesn't need much help in the first place. Second, the time to identify words in isolation, using several measures, does not differ all that markedly from the time to read a word in text (although admittedly, in text one is doing more than identifying words). Third, in Chapter 5, we argued that variables such as word length and word frequency predicted much of the variation in readers' eye fixations. Such a result would be inconsistent with a view in which most of the processing of words was coming from "top-down" sources, such as how well the word fit into the text. (However, as we shall see later in this chapter and the next, fixation times do reflect something about higher-order processes as well.)

Such results (and others) have led some researchers (e.g., Fodor 1983) to a more radical position. They believe that there is *no* influence of higher-order processes on word recognition. Since this position has been forcefully advocated and, if true, would help to simplify an analysis of the process of reading, we will discuss the evidence pertaining to whether top-down processes have any effect on word identification. Before discussing the data, however, we would like to clarify several points.

The first is that, as we will discuss later, there are uncontroversial effects of context on the time it takes to process a word. For example, a word that is highly predictable in text will be fixated for a shorter time than one that is not predictable. Partisans of the view that higher-order processes have no influence on word identification time do not dispute these data. What they claim is that the difference in time is not due to the ease of identifying the word, but to later processes, such as the time it takes to integrate the word into the ongoing discourse structures, which are being built by the reader. In other words, a major issue in much of the literature is whether context effects are on *lexical access* or on *text integration* (the latter term is usually defined broadly enough to cover everything besides lexical access).

A second issue has arisen as to whether there is a structural reason why higher-order processes do not affect word identification. For example, Fodor and others (e.g., Forster 1979; Seidenberg 1985b) have argued that lexical access is handled by a *module* of the information processing system that can not interact in any serious way with other systems or modules. In Fodor's theorizing (which is probably the most extreme position), the only communication between the lexical identification module and the rest of the language processing system is that the lexical module sends the word that has been identified on for further processing, and if the rest of the system gets stuck (e.g., if a word is misread or mistyped), the higher-order processes can tell the lexical module to "try again" (although they could not tell the lexical module what word to look for). Fodor argued this position partially from principles he formulated about how complex systems should work.

At first it might be hard to see how one can hold to that position. For example, in doing a crossword puzzle, if several letters of a word are filled in, you can often fluently identify the correct word using the "definition" or clues provided in the puzzle, whereas you might draw a blank if none of the letters were provided. That is, the definition and partial visual information appear to interact to produce lexical access. However, proponents of a modular view would likely argue that the context effect in such cases is not top down. Instead, any effect on lexical access would be explained by invoking the mechanism of "spreading activation," used to describe the phenomenon of *priming* discussed in Chapter 3. That is, the lexical entries of related words in the definition would be activated and send automatic activation through links between them and the word being accessed, and this activation would help in access. Such a mechanism would be "intralexical" and hence not top down.

An alternative to the view that top-down processes can in principle play no part in lexical access is that they play little part in fluent silent reading because the benefits are outweighed by the costs. That is, if lexical access can go on so well without any help (as with words in isolation), there may be little benefit in speeding it up and there may be significant costs involved trying to use context in lexical access (Stanovich 1980). This argument seems particularly telling, especially if the use of context is viewed as one of conscious prediction, as in the "guessing game" models (e.g., Goodman 1967, 1970; Hochberg 1970; Levin and Kaplan 1970). In these models, conscious prediction is seen as a major factor in identifying words in text so that the visual information does not have to be fully processed. There seem to be two primary costs involved with such conscious prediction. The first is that such prediction is likely to be wrong; readers are in fact not very good at predicting the next word, even with unlimited amounts of time (Gough, Alford, and Holley-Wilcox 1981; McConkie and Rayner 1976b). Second, one would expect that such prediction would take processing resources away from the higher-order processes needed to put the words together to form syntactic and semantic structures.

Does Context Affect the Speed of Lexical Access?

This has been a major research question in cognitive psychology in the last 10 years, and the answer is still a matter of controversy. As we shall see, there is evidence for the effects of context on word identification; however, it is still unclear whether all of these effects can be ascribed to intralexical processes, such as priming, or whether an interaction between higher-order processes and lexical access needs to be invoked. A major problem in discussing the evidence is that the answer to whether context affects lexical access may depend on the situation. For example, context might have a large effect on lexical access in a situation like the crossword puzzle example where access is slow, but may not play any significant role in a fluent process, such as normal silent reading, where access is accomplished in a fraction of a second.

The first experiments attempting to demonstrate context effects in a readinglike situation (Tulving and Gold 1963; Tulving, Mandler, and Baumal 1964; Morton 1964b) were not too different from our crossword puzzle example. They had subjects read a sentence fragment such as

The skiers were buried alive by the sudden (7.1)

The subjects were then shown the target word *avalanche* very briefly in a tachistoscope. They were able to identify the target word at significantly briefer exposures when the context predicted it than when it was preceded by no context. These findings were assumed to demonstrate that context affects the identification of words. However, many researchers question whether such situations have any bearing on normal reading. The brief presentation virtually guarantees that the visual information is not fully registered and hence degraded; the identification of a word in this situation is thus likely to be the result of a slow conscious problem solving process rather than normal perceptual identification.

Accordingly, the procedure has been modified so that the target word that appears after the sentence frame is presented until the subject makes a response to it (Stanovich and West 1983). Most of these experiments have required the subjects either to *name* (Stanovich and West 1979; Becker 1985) or make a *lexical decision* on the target word (Schuberth and Eimas 1977; Fischler and Bloom 1979). While this type of procedure alters the natural reading process, the timing relations aren't too different from normal reading if the delay between the frame and the target word is relatively brief (some are as short as about 250 msec). In most of these experiments, it has been shown that a highly predictive context in fact facilitates either naming or lexical decision latency relative to a neutral condition such as the frame

The next word in the sentence will be ____ . (7.2)

(The selection of the proper neutral baseline is a major subject of controversy that we will briefly discuss later.)

Context thus appears to facilitate the processing of words in a situation in which subjects are making speeded responses to the words. There would be little controversy over that statement. Most of the controversy is over the two issues we discussed earlier: (1) Is lexical access the process that is facilitated or is the facilitation at some later stage? (2) Is the effect of context really coming from a higher-order process, such as prediction of the word in the sentence, or is it due to an intralexical process, such as spreading activation? We will defer discussion of the latter issue and concentrate for the moment on whether the speed of lexical access can be affected (in some way) by sentential context.

At present, there is considerable skepticism about lexical decision latency as being a good measure of lexical access time (Balota and

Chumbley 1984, 1985; Chumbley and Balota 1984; Forster 1979; Seidenberg et al. 1984b), since it is too susceptible to postlexical decision effects. For example, in the task described above, if a target word fits meaningfully into the context, one can decide it must be a word with no further ado. On the other hand, there seems to be little evidence that the naming task is susceptible to such postlexical effects (if the responses are rapid). Thus, if one accepts naming time as a valid measure of lexical access, the above naming studies indicate that lexical access can be affected by context in a situation approximating fluent reading.

While such studies approximate fluent reading, there are some key differences. The first, of course, is that an extraneous response (naming) is called for, and the second is that a delay is introduced between the frame and the target word. As we have argued that the best way to study fluent reading is through the use of eye movements, we will focus on how they have been employed to study context effects.

Effects of context in reading   The earliest experiment (Zola 1984; originally reported in McConkie and Zola 1981) to investigate context effects in reading employed a similar manipulation to the studies described above: the predictability of a target word was manipulated, and the average fixation time on the word and the probability of fixating on the target word were both measured. For example, a passage about the movie industry contained either the sentence

Movie theaters must have buttered popcorn to serve their
patrons. (7.3)

or the same sentence with *buttered* replaced by *adequate*. Zola found a surprisingly modest effect: fixation times were only about 15 msec shorter when the target word *popcorn* was highly predictable and subjects were no more likely to skip the target word when it was predictable than when it was not. In the studies in this section, "predictability" is usually assessed in a separate norming experiment (which precedes the main experiment) in which subjects try to guess the target word given the prior context; "highly predictable" usually means that the target word was guessed by at least 60 percent of the subjects.

In the Zola experiment, the predictable context was always established by the adjective immediately preceding the target noun (*buttered* in the example above). Ehrlich and Rayner (1981) argued that this is not typical of context in reading, and that the predictability of many words is established by a more extended lead-in. In their passages, the target words were also either highly predictable or not predictable, but the context was established earlier (see Table 7.1). Ehrlich and Rayner found that subjects skipped the target word more often when it was highly predictable than when it was not, and furthermore, that when the target was fixated, the average fixation

TABLE 7.1 Passages from the experiments of Ehrlich and Rayner (1981). Constraint refers to the predictability of the target (underlined) word in the context. The target word is underlined in the examples, but not in the experiments. In the bottom example, the low constraint condition was created by replacing *bones* with *boxes*.

HIGH CONSTRAINT (EXPERIMENT 1)

He saw the black fin slice through the water and the image of sharks' teeth came quickly to his mind. He turned quickly toward the shore and swam for his life. The coast guard had warned that someone had seen a *shark* off the north shore of the island. As usual, not everyone listened to the warning

LOW CONSTRAINT (EXPERIMENT 1)

The young couple were delighted by the special attention they were getting. The zoo keeper explained that the life span of a *shark* is much longer than those of the other animals they had talked about. The scientists decided that this man would make a great ally.

HIGH CONSTRAINT (EXPERIMENT 2)

It is often said that dead men tell no tales. But Fred was very nervous as he put his shovel into the ground where he knew the makeshift grave was. He soon uncovered the skeletal remains and cleared the dirt away. He reached down and picked up one of the *bones* and quickly threw it aside realizing that is was not what he was searching for.

---

duration was shortened about 30 to 50 msec by predictability (or more than twice as much as in Zola's experiment).

These studies thus establish that context does affect the amount of time spent on a word, although the effects are relatively modest. These results make the "guessing game" models of reading quite unlikely; if guessing were an important part of word identification, one would expect bigger effects than these in situations where the deck has been stacked to make guessing prevail. (As argued earlier, most content words are not nearly as predictable as the target words in these experiments.) However, these context effects are not necessarily due to speeded lexical access of the predictable words. It is possible that the predictable context speeds processing of the target word by allowing it to be fit into the sentence context more easily.

One way to test whether lexical access is affected is to manipulate visual aspects of the fixated word. If context interacts with visual factors, then one would have evidence that context is modulating visual processing and hence influencing lexical access. Both the Zola (1984) and Ehrlich and Rayner (1981) experiments introduced misspellings of the target word to determine whether the misspelling was detected and whether it affected processing any differently when the word was predictable from the context than when it was not. In both studies, the misspelled target word took longer to process, whether it was predictable from context or not. Unfortunately, it is hard to say more than that about the fixation-duration data, since when the target word was misspelled, it was often refixated by a regression, indicating that the misspelling had delayed effects as well as immediate effects. In addition, since the misspelling was consciously detected a reasonable percentage of the time, it is hard to know what "lexical access" means in the case of misspelled words. One result of Ehrlich and Rayner, however, suggested that context interacted with visual processing. They found that there was a smaller effect of the misspelling on skipping when the target was predictable than when it wasn't. This suggests that the predictable context allowed some shortcuts in the visual processing of the target word.

An experiment by Balota, Pollatsek, and Rayner (1985) attempted to manipulate visual information more subtly by limiting the "misspellings" to the parafovea. That is, the visual information in the target location was often different before it was fixated than when the target word was fixated. For example, in the sentence

Since the wedding was today, the baker rushed
the wedding cake (pies) to the reception. (7.4)

one of two target words was present when the target location was fixated: *cake*, which is highly predicted by the prior context, or *pies*, which is not predicted by the prior context but is an acceptable word in that context. However, prior to when a reader's eye movement crossed a boundary location in the text (in this example, the *n* in *wedding* in the second line), the string of letters presented initially in the target location (the *parafoveal preview*) could be different from the target word. The string could be identical to the target word (*cake* is a preview for *cake* or *pies* for *pies*), visually similar to the target word (*cahc* is a preview for *cake* or *picz* for *pies*), identical to the alternative word (*pies* is a preview for *cake* or vice versa), similar to the alternative word (*picz* for *cake* or *cahc* for *pies*), or visually dissimilar and semantically unrelated (*bomb* for either *cake* or *pies*).

The major results of the study are shown in Table 7.2. The skipping data are consistent with those of Ehrlich and Rayner (1981): the highly predictable word and its visually similar "misspelling" (*cahc*) were skipped more often than the unpredictable word and its "misspelling" (*picz*). The more important result was that context appeared to modulate how much the gaze duration on the target word benefited from the parafoveal preview. First, the benefit from a parafoveal preview of the predictable word (or its misspelling) was greater than that from a preview of the less predictable word (or its misspelling). That is, the gaze duration on *cake* was speeded more by a visually similar preview than the gaze duration on *pies* (see Table 7.2). Second, there was a difference between the benefit when *cake* and *cahc* were presented parafoveally and *cake* fixated, whereas there was no difference between when *pies* and *picz* were presented parafoveally and *pies*

TABLE 7.2 Fixation duration (msec) with gaze duration (msec) presented in parentheses for the 10 conditions in the Balota, Pollatsek, and Rayner (1985) study. In the high predictable condition, the target following the display change was always the predictable word (*cake* in our example), while the low predictable word (*pies*) was always the target in the remaining conditions. Apart from the Ident condition, the other conditions represent the stimulus presented in the target location prior to the display change. Ident = Identical (*cake*); VS = visually similar (*cahc*); SR = semantically related (*pies*); VD = visually different (*picz*); AN = anomolous (*bomb*).

	IDENT	VS	SR	VD	AN
High Predictable	223 (232)	218 (248)	232 (280)	236 (280)	240 (292)
Low Predictable	227 (264)	232 (263)	258 (287)	242 (277)	240 (290)

fixated (see Table 7.2). This result indicates that more letters were processed when the stimulus in the parafovea was predictable.

To summarize, several studies have demonstrated that words are fixated for shorter periods of time and skipped more often when they are predictable from the sentence context. The Balota, Pollatsek, and Rayner (1985) experiment adds two important pieces of information. First, it demonstrates that a predictable context modulates the extraction of visual information in the parafovea and thus indicates that context can affect lexical access during reading. Second, it suggests that context affects word identification in reading primarily by speeding the extraction of visual information from the *parafovea*. This makes sense, since parafoveal visual information is not as good as foveal visual information, and thus more in need of assistance from context.

What Is the Context Mechanism?

There is no definitive answer to this question. While we have been referring to the context manipulation as "predictability," the mechanism need not be prediction of the target word using higher-order processes. As we mentioned earlier, an alternative explanation offered for predictability effects is (intralexical) priming. For example in Sentence 7.4, perhaps the more efficient processing of *cake* is a result of priming from the word *wedding*, rather than from the high predictability of *cake* in that context. In fact, Stanovich and West (1983) explained their predictability effects as the sum of priming effects from the words preceding the target word.

While such an explanation is plausible, there is no conclusive evidence that priming works in that fashion. First, when a sequence of content words and pseudowords is presented and the subject is required to make a lexical decision about each stimulus, priming by a related word rapidly dissipates when a word or two intervenes between the target and the prime (Gough, Alford, and Holley-Wilcox 1981). If close contiguity of prime and target are required for priming, then it is unlikely that priming can account for most of the context effects in reading. However, the reading situation may be different from the laboratory lexical decision task in that the reader may have the priming word active in short-term memory as a result of building a meaning of the sentence, and this active short-term memory representation may do the priming (Foss 1982). Second, it is not at all clear that priming effects observed in the laboratory are necessarily due to an automatic associative mechanism. If a subject sees *doctor* as a priming stimulus, he or she may guess that the target will be *nurse* (i.e., priming itself may often be due to prediction).

We will briefly discuss attempts to distinguish between conscious predictive and automatic priming effects. Unfortunately, it is not clear that they can be used to infer very much about reading. In the reference experiment (Neely 1977) the primes were category names and the targets were category exemplars. There were three key innovations in Neely's experiment. The first was that he attempted to dissociate associative strength from conscious prediction. Certain category labels (e.g., *bird*) were followed most of the time by exemplars of another category (e.g., exemplars of *body parts*). A major question is: which exemplars were primed by *bird*, exemplars of birds or exemplars of body parts? If birds are primed, one would view the process as an automatic associative one since body parts are expected, whereas if body parts are primed, the mechanism would be seen as one of conscious prediction.

The answer to the question depends on the delay interval between prime and target (the second key innovation). At short delay intervals, automatic priming is dominant (birds are primed but not body parts), whereas at delay intervals greater than 700 msec, conscious prediction takes over (body parts are primed and priming for birds disappears). This makes sense if it takes some time to develop a conscious prediction. The third innovation was the use of *cost-benefit analysis* (Posner and Snyder 1975), which provided a converging operation that also suggests that two qualitatively different processes are occurring. The priming effect was divided into two components: *benefit,* the difference in time between a *related* prime target (*bird*) and a neutral prime (in this case a string of *x*'s); and *cost,* the difference in time between the neutral prime and an unrelated prime such as *city*. Neely found benefit but no cost for the associative priming at short intervals, but approximately equal cost and benefit for the predictive priming at longer intervals. This pattern indicates that the dichotomy suggested before is true: a conscious prediction process has significant cost associated with it (either due to predictions being wrong or to limited resources being used in the prediction process), whereas the associative process is qualitatively different (having no significant cost associated with it).

Later experiments have replicated the basic pattern of Neely's data, although some of the details have differed. For example, even situations that appear to be due to automatic priming often have *some* cost. In situations in which one expects automatic priming (usually effects at short delays), the typical pattern is that there is appreciably greater benefit than cost; whereas in situations in which one expects conscious prediction, cost is typically at least as great as benefit.

We are still a long way from reading. However, the studies discussed earlier by Stanovich and West (1979, 1983), Schuberth and Eimas (1977) and Fischler and Bloom (1979) applied cost-benefit analysis to the effects of predictive sentential context. We will concentrate on the naming studies of Stanovich and West, since they are more likely to tell us about lexical access. Stanovich and West found that at short-delay intervals predictive context produced benefit but no cost; at longer-delay intervals it produced both. It thus appears that at short intervals, in these situations, predictive context works by an automatic mechanism, but at longer intervals it works by a conscious predictive mechanism. In addition, if we accept cost-benefit analysis as a diagnostic tool of conscious versus unconscious processes, either (a) naming is a pure measure of lexical access and lexical access is affected by conscious processing or (b) naming at longer intervals is affected by postlexical processes. Stanovich and West (1983) opt for the latter interpretation.

How do we apply these findings to reading? With great care. Stanovich and West (1983), as mentioned earlier, interpreted their finding that context was used automatically in the short delay conditions as reflecting associative priming. This leap of inference is essentially based on the assumption of a dichotomy: either context works through automatic associative priming or through conscious prediction. While such an assumption has the advantage of parsimony—assume that there are only two mechanisms until there is good reason to postulate another—it may serve to blind us from the possibility that there are other mechanisms underlying context effects. Since some sort of mechanism is building up the meaning of a sentence, it seems reasonable that some sort of automatic "priming" can flow down from this meaning to the lexical entry of a word likely to be next in the sentence.

A second problem is related to the appropriate interpretation of the delay interval between the offset of the context and the onset of the target word in the naming and lexical decision experiments. It is tempting, for example, to assume that the automatic context effects at short delay intervals are like context effects in reading when the context appears immediately before the target word (as in Zola's experiment), and to assume that the conscious context effects at longer intervals are like context effects when the context is established well beforehand (as in Ehrlich and Rayner). The problem, however, is that the long delay in these experiments (which is filled with nothing) is quite different from the long delays between the context and target word in reading (which are filled with other reading activity). Thus, we think it is quite difficult to infer from these studies when the effect of context in reading would be automatic and when it would be conscious. The problem is compounded by the difficulty of imagining how to do the analogous experiment in natural silent reading. One would have to set up a neutral baseline in which the subjects are making no predictions about the word in the target position and yet devise a measure of processing so that any differences observed can be ascribed to lexical access rather than text integration. While such an experiment may be logically possible (e.g., using evoked potentials), it seems beyond our present capabilities.

Some recent experiments have established priminglike effects in reading (but without the possibility of establishing a neutral baseline to determine whether the effect is automatic or due to conscious prediction). Carroll and Slowiaczek (1986) examined the pattern of eye movements while subjects read text in which there was a pair of associatively related words in the same sentence. They observed shorter gaze durations on the second of the associatively related words only when the related words were within the same clause; the priming effects did not emerge across clause boundaries in their experiment. In contrast, Duffy and Rayner (1988) obtained priming effects over longer stretches of text. Carroll and Slowiaczek's priming effect was probably not due to either conscious or unconscious prediction, since the target word was not very predictable in many of the conditions. However, there is no firm evidence in either study that the priming effect is on lexical access rather than on a later text integration stage.

Let us attempt a summary of context effects. The evidence suggests that context does affect the speed of lexical access, although the effects are relatively modest. Moreover, context effects observed in reading are not necessarily due only to lexical access; they could be due to text integration processes as well. The fact that these effects are modulated by visual factors only argues that at least some of the effect is due to lexical access. A tidy hypothesis for such mechanisms is that they are caused by associative priming. However, there is no conclusive evidence that associative priming is indeed the mechanism by which predictability works in reading, and at present we don't even know for sure that the predictability effect in reading is an unconscious one. The facilitation of speeded naming due to predictability of the target word (e.g., Stanovich and West 1983) is similar to the facilitation of gaze durations in reading. Since the former effect is thought to be automatic (benefit with no cost), there is thus reason to believe that predictability effects in reading are also the result of unconscious mechanisms.

To this we would like to add a speculation. The experiments on reading suggest that the major effect of context on lexical access may be in the extraction of parafoveal information. First of all, the more dramatic effects of context observed are on word skipping. That is, context may help the reader skip over the next word (saving 200 msec or so), but if the reader doesn't skip, the savings are much less (about 15 to 30 msec). Moreover, since the Balota, Pollatsek, and Rayner (1985) experiment demonstrated that context was interacting with the extraction of *parafoveal* visual information, much of the savings in fixation time on a word is likely due to increased efficiency of extraction of visual information from the parafovea rather than the fovea. While context may modulate the extraction of foveal information as well, this has not been demonstrated: parafoveal and foveal information were confounded in all the other studies cited. Our analysis makes sense if one thinks that context is mainly used when the visual information is degraded in some way (a position strongly argued by Stanovich 1980). Thus, foveal information may be so good that applying context may be of little benefit. On the other hand, parafoveal information is a constant source of degraded information, whose analysis may benefit appreciably from the use of context.

How Is Lexical Ambiguity Handled in Reading?

The question of whether context affects the speed of lexical access is related to the issue of how context disambiguates the meaning of lexically ambiguous words. However, the issues are distinct. Let us consider the analogy of looking up a word in a real dictionary. In a real dictionary, finding the meaning of a word is a process that occurs *after* you come to the correct place in the dictionary. Thus, it could be that context would be irrelevant to finding the correct location, but would be helpful in deciding on the correct meaning *after* the meanings had been accessed. As in the prior section, we will see that this is a central issue. No one doubts that context affects how the reader interprets an ambiguous word; the question is whether it affects access to the lexicon or whether it merely affects later stages.

To help focus the question, let us consider two examples. First, in the sentence

The man found several insects, spiders, and other bugs in the room. (7.5)

the word *bugs* is ambiguous. In isolation, it could mean (among other things) either a small animal or a listening device. However, the prior context in the sentence makes it clear that the meaning of "small animal" is intended. Moreover, most readers are not conscious of the other meanings of *bugs* when they read the sentence.

This example suggests that perhaps only one meaning of an ambiguous word is ever accessed when it is encountered. On this view, when strong context makes clear what word is intended, the context presumably guides the reader straight to the appropriate meaning. What happens when there is no biasing context? Presumably the most "dominant" (i.e., frequently encountered) meaning of the word is accessed. If this meaning is appropriate the reader will encounter no difficulty later, but if the inappropriate meaning is accessed, the reader should encounter difficulty at the point in the sentence when it is clear that the other meaning was intended. That is, if you read the sentence

There was a bug in the room. (7.6)

you would access one of the two meanings as easily as if the word had one meaning and then encounter difficulty only if some later statement made clear that "listening device" was intended when you had originally interpreted it as "insect" (the more frequent interpretation).

In sum, if we assume that only one meaning of a lexically ambiguous word is accessed, the reader should encounter no processing difficulty with ambiguous words at the time they are encountered, but when the prior biasing context is weak or nonexistent, the reader may do a double-take later in the sentence. The data, however, indicate otherwise. In most experiments employing ambiguous words, when there is no prior biasing context, processing difficulty is usually observed on or shortly after the ambiguous word—well before later material would clarify the meaning. In contrast, there is little or no processing difficulty observed when the prior context strongly biases the interpretation of the ambiguous word.

The seminal experiments on lexical ambiguity were actually done with people listening to sentences with ambiguous words (Foss and Jenkins 1973; Swinney and Hakes 1976). Processing difficulty was measured by the time taken to identify a phoneme in a word right after the target word. Unfortunately, the phoneme monitoring task has several potential artifacts, or problems, so there is still some dispute as to the validity of these results (Mehler, Sequi, and Carey 1978; Newman and Dell 1978). However, the same pattern was found in reading by Rayner and Duffy (1986, 1987; Duffy, Morris and Rayner 1988). In a sentence such as

He put the (straw, wheat) in the barn for the cows.   (7.7)

when there was no prior disambiguating context, gaze durations were longer on the ambiguous word *straw* (which has two equally likely interpretations) than on the unambiguous control word *wheat*. In contrast, when there was a strong prior unambiguous context, there was no difference between the times to fixate the ambiguous and unambiguous words.

These results suggest that our original analysis is wrong. One possible explanation is that ambiguity is handled in two different ways. If there is a strong unambiguous prior context, only one of the meanings is accessed, but if there is no prior context, both meanings are accessed and are held in short-term memory until the text disambiguates the meaning (assuming that the disambiguation is important for understanding the meaning of the material). According to such a model, there would be several reasons to expect lexical ambiguity to have a disruptive effect on processing when there is no prior biasing context: accessing two meanings could take more processing capacity than accessing one meaning; holding two meanings in short-term memory could use processing capacity; or choosing between the two meanings could take time/or use processing capacity. On the other hand, such a model would predict that lexical ambiguity would produce little or no disruptive influence on processing when the ambiguous word is preceded by strong unambiguous context, since only one of the meanings would need to be processed. If such an explanation is valid, prior context modulates how meaning is extracted from the lexicon and would hence be evidence against modularity.

As you might expect, these data are known by the modularity theorists, and they also have an explanation for them. According to the modular view, both meanings are accessed regardless of prior context, but since lexical access is viewed as an automatic process, accessing two meanings should take no more processing capacity than accessing a single meaning. When there is no prior biasing context, both meanings would be put into short-term memory and disruption would be observed, either from capacity used to hold the items in short-term memory or from selecting between them (as in the other account above). The more difficult case to explain is when prior context disambiguates the word. How does a modular view account for no awareness of the other meaning and no disruption in reading when there is a strong disambiguating context? It posits that both words are accessed and that context very quickly selects one meaning. This selection is rapid enough so there is no awareness of the unintended meaning and must be efficient enough to produce no disruption of reading. That is, in Sentence 7.5, both the "insect" and "listening device" meanings of *bugs* are accessed, but the "listening device" meaning is very quickly inhibited by the prior context.

At this point, you may deem this latter explanation as being quite farfetched. Why bother to postulate the access of the meaning "listening device" when its access is not open to consciousness and hence unobservable? The answer is that an ingenious experiment has made such a process observable. A minor problem is that the experiment and most of the subsequent research has involved *listening* rather than reading; however, the research that exists on reading suggests that the processes are quite similar in the two cases.

How can one detect the access of a meaning that one is not conscious of? Answer: through the miracle of priming. Swinney (1979) presented subjects with spoken passages containing sentences such as Sentence 7.5 above. *Immediately after the target word was presented* (aurally), the subject saw a single word on a screen and made a lexical decision response to it. The key comparisons were among the lexical decision times to *ant* (related to the contextually determined animal meaning of *bugs*), *spy* (related to the other meaning of *bugs*), and *sew* (a word unrelated to either meaning of *bugs*). (Needless to say, he equated factors such as the length and frequency of the three words in English.) The key question, of course, is whether the lexical decision to *spy* is any faster than to an unrelated word such as *sew*. If it is, then the listening device meaning of *bugs* was accessed. In fact, Swinney found that *bugs* primed *ant* and *spy* equally, suggesting that both meanings of an ambiguous word are accessed, *even when the prior context strongly disambiguates the meaning of the word*. He also found that the priming effect on *spy* disappeared when the lexical decision task was delayed by about 200 msec, indicating that context quickly inhibited the "wrong" meaning of *bugs*.

Other experiments have replicated the basic result (Onifer and Swinney 1981; Seidenberg et al. 1982; Tanenhaus, Leiman, and Seidenberg 1979) and extended it by demonstrating that both meanings of an ambiguous word are accessed (using priming as the indicator of access), even when one of the meanings is highly dominant such as *boxer*. However, in these cases, the less dominant meaning (type of dog) was no longer active after about 200 msec, even when the prior context did not disambiguate the word. Thus, it appears that rapid inhibition of one of the meanings is produced not only by prior sentence context but also by a more dominant meaning of a lexical item inhibiting a weaker one. It is at present not established how strong the dominance relation has to be to produce this rapid inhibition.

Even though these experiments are not about reading, we have discussed them in some detail because they have been very influential in shaping how psycholinguists view the relation of lexical access to higher-order processes. In fact, these experiments were instrumental in shaping the view of lexical access as a module independent of higher-order processes. While the basic result has held up, we should briefly discuss a few problems. The first is that there are some situations in which prior context did appear to eliminate or reduce the priming effect of the "wrong" meaning. In these cases, there was always a highly related word several words prior to the target word (Seidenberg et al. 1982). This pattern of results was, in fact, what led people to advocate a qualitative difference between associative priming (as being intralexical) and other context effects (as being between the lexicon and a different mental module). In any case, there is evidence that in some situations, context appears to have an effect on whether one or both meanings of the ambiguous word are accessed.

A second problem is whether the paradigm really does get at whether both meanings are accessed in normal listening. Since the listening task is interrupted by the lexical decision task, the ·interruption may cause the "wrong" meaning to be accessed, whereas it might not in the normal listening situation. More specifically, it has been argued that the target stimulus *spy* might send backward associations to *bugs* that might help facilitate the lexical decision (Glucksberg, Kreuz, and Rho 1986). At present, this issue is unresolved, although the balance of evidence appears to be against the backward association view (Burgess, Seidenberg, and Tanenhaus 1988).

How do the results of listening studies on ambiguity relate to reading? First, in a reading analogue of the Swinney experiment (using the RSVP task), Kintsch and Mross (1985) obtained results similar to those in listening—priming of both meanings of the ambiguous word—indicating that lexical access is modular in reading as well. In addition, lexical ambiguity appears to disrupt reading in pretty much the same places as in listening. *Moreover, in listening, access of both meanings of an ambiguous word has been found (with the priming task) in the same places where no disruption has been found with phoneme monitoring.* This strengthens the view that that disruption effects due to lexical ambiguity, when observed, are most likely due to postlexical selection processes rather than to greater difficulty in accessing the multiple meanings of ambiguous words.

In sum, it appears that a modular view of lexical ambiguity is the most parsimonious one in listening: both meanings of an ambiguous word are accessed and only then does selection among the meanings occur. One issue that is currently unresolved in the listening studies is whether *all* meanings of an ambiguous word are accessed, no matter how infrequent the meanings are. Even when there was a meaning that was dominant, the less dominant meaning was not all that rare (usually given by at least 10 percent of the subjects when the word was seen or heard in isolation). It seems unlikely that extremely unusual meanings would also be accessed automatically; we need evidence, however, since intuitions in this area may be unreliable.

The above discussion indicates that disruptions caused by lexical ambiguity in reading and listening are due to post-lexical processes. We now turn to eye movement studies of lexical ambiguity in reading (Carpenter and Daneman 1981; Duffy, Morris, and Rayner 1988) to see whether a coherent interpretation of disruption effects is consistent with modularity theory. In particular, Duffy, Morris and Rayner (1988) investigated how the prior context and the dominance of the more probable meaning of an ambiguous word modulated the processing of an ambiguous word. At the beginning of this section, we presented the data for the words where both meanings were (approximately) equally dominant: with strongly biasing prior context, there was no disruption, but when there was no biasing context, there was both a longer gaze duration on the ambiguous word (than on the unambiguous control) and there was disruption later in the sentence as well. There was a different pattern of results when one of the meanings of an ambiguous word was much more dominant (e.g., *boxer,* where the ''fighter'' meaning is much more likely than the ''breed of dog'' meaning). When there was no prior biasing context, fixation times on the ambiguous words were no longer than on the unambiguous controls, whereas when the prior context strongly indicated the less dominant meaning, fixation times on the ambiguous words were longer than on the controls.

Can we explain this pattern of results with the modular theory? We have already explained the data with equally biased words in some detail. Now let us try the other data. When there was no biasing context, the ambiguous word took no longer to process than the (unambiguous) control word. This fits in with the listening data that indicate that both meanings are accessed, but if one is much more dominant it quickly inhibits the other. As with strong disambiguating context, this inhibition appears to be automatic, causing no disruption in reading. On the other hand, when the prior context indicated the less dominant meaning, gaze durations on the ambiguous target word were longer than on the control word. This indicates that the two processes (dominance and prior context) are fighting each other in some way, making the selection process harder and causing disruption. One possibility is that both meanings are brought into short-term memory, but because the two selection factors are approximately balanced, the selection process takes time and short-term memory is taxed. Another possibility is that the dominant meaning sometimes actually inhibits the contextually appropriate meaning; when the dominant meaning doesn't make sense, a second access of the lexical item is required to find the correct meaning.

There is some suggestive evidence in support of the modularity hypothesis in these data. When lexical ambiguity caused disruption on the target word (in the cases where there was no prior context and equal dominance or prior context and unequal dominance pitted against each other), these effects "spilled over" to increase fixation times on the following word. We think it is unlikely that effects on the fixation duration on word $n+1$ reflect lexical access of word n. Since at least part of the disruption effect is likely to be due to postlexical processes, it is perhaps parsimonious to assume all of it is until there is definitive evidence to the contrary.

Duffy, Morris, and Rayner (1988) also looked for disruptive effects later in the sentence (in their experiments, context was usually consistent with the less dominant interpretation of the ambiguous words). There was little such disruption when *prior* context biased the word, indicating that subjects had indeed chosen the meaning consistent with the prior context. When only the *subsequent* context disambiguated the meaning, there was quite a bit of disruption later in the sentence when one of the meanings was highly dominant (and thus inconsistent with the context). The latter finding is consistent with the above claim that a highly dominant meaning quickly inhibits the less dominant meaning: thus the subject has to recompute later in the sentence when that dominant meaning is found to be wrong. There was also some (though less) disruption later in the sentence even when the two meanings were approximately equally dominant. One possible explanation is that the more dominant meaning inhibits the less dominant meaning some of the time, even when they are approximately equally dominant. (Since "dominance" is a group property—"equal dominance" means that about half the subjects chose one meaning out of context and half chose the other—it is possible that for some subjects, some of the meanings of "equally dominant" words were highly dominant.)

Let us try to summarize what we have said about the effects of context on lexical access. As we have just argued, a modular view for how context affects lexical ambiguity in listening is fairly compelling and is consistent with the data on reading. On this view, both meanings of a lexically ambiguous word are automatically accessed and then one is quickly inhibited, either by the much more dominant meaning or by a prior biasing context. If neither of these mechanisms inhibits multiple meanings, then both presumably are consciously processed and put into short-term memory to await disambiguation. The exception appears to be that in certain contexts one word primes one meaning of a later word; in that case, there is evidence that only the primed meaning is accessed.

In sum, it appears, as we claimed at the outset, that word identification is a relatively autonomous process. Whether it is as completely autonomous as a modular view would have it is a hotly debated topic at present. In the arena of lexical ambiguity, the data in support of modularity appear stronger; the only demonstrated effect of "context" on lexical access occurs when there is a strongly associated word several words before the target word. In the experiments on speed of lexical access, it was shown that a highly predictable context affects the speed of lexical access, probably chiefly by modulating the efficiency of parafoveal information extraction. While it is plausible that predictable contexts often contain words strongly related to the target, there is at present no evidence that intralexical priming is the sole causal agent for the context effects observed in reading. In fact, intralexical priming is an implausible explanation of the skipping of predictable function words in text (O'Regan 1980), since they are not lexical associates of the proceding words.

If the modular hypothesis is true, the only way lexical access differs for words in text from words in isolation is that words in text are sometimes primed by related words in the text. Even if it is false, the effects of context on word identification (whether due to lexical or postlexical processes) are usually pretty modest. It takes a very predictable context to have a major effect on skipping, and when words are fixated, even very predictable context appears to influence fixation times by at most 30 to 50 msec. Thus, we feel quite comfortable in the basically bottom up view of reading that we are presenting to you. That is, the reader first identifies each word in turn (perhaps somewhat modified by prior context) and then puts these lexical entries together to form higher-order structures such as phrases, clauses, sentences, and propositions. We now turn to discuss how these high-order structures are formed.

UNDERSTANDING SENTENCES

The remainder of this chapter will focus on the sentence. Sentences are obviously important units in reading (or listening), roughly corresponding to "idea units." They are universally marked in alphabetic writing systems and are starting to be marked even in writing systems like Chinese. The special character of the sentence is perhaps best illustrated by the notion of grammaticality: that is, that there are definite "rules" for sentence construction which allow one to decide that a sentence is not a legal utterance. Thus, the string of words

Feature language a lives our daily of pervasive is. (7.8)

is not acceptable as an utterance. We can not decide whether it is true or false, or even whether it is nonsensical. This contrasts with sentences such as

Curious green ideas sleep furiously.   (7.9)

which, while apparently nonsensical, might be an acceptable description of a nightmare, and with

'Twas brillig and the slithy toves did gyre and gimbol in the
wabe.   (7.10)

(from the famous Jabberwocky by Lewis Carroll) which uses nonsense for much of its vocabulary, but is clearly in an acceptable grammatical form. As we will see in the next chapter, there are more—and less—coherent sequences of sentences in discourse, but there appear to be no absolutes that would make a higher-order unit, such as a paragraph, "ungrammatical." Thus, the sentence appears to be a special unit that is worth our time understanding in some detail.

Sentences can be understood on many levels. For example, consider the sentence:

Could you give John the book?   (7.11)

On one level you could understand its syntax. That is, one could identify *you* as the subject, *could give* as the verb, *book* as the object, and understand that the sentence is the question form of

You could give John the book.   (7.12)

You would also be able to determine subunits of the sentence such as phrases, and be able to identify the structure of the sentence. As "Jabberwocky" illustrates, it is even possible to understand the structure of a sentence that does not convey meaning.

A second level is understanding the literal meaning of the sentence. That would involve identifying the function of various concepts: *you* as the "agent" of the action *give* and *John* as the "recipient" of that action and *book* as the "theme" of that action. While at first, these terms might seem to be the same as in the syntactic analysis, there are differences. For example, in the passive sentence

The girl was kissed by John.   (7.13)

girl is both the subject and the recipient of the action, and *John* is the agent. The problem goes beyond active and passive sentences, since in the pair of sentences

John is easy to please. (7.14a)

John is eager to please. (7.14b)

John is the person being pleased in 7.14a but the "pleaser" in 7.14b. Understanding the functions of the component words is only the first step in understanding a sentence. Understanding the full meaning of a sentence involves an additional step of putting the components together in order to to decide, for example, whether the question (as in Sentence 7.11) is answerable or not and whether a declarative sentence (Sentence 7.12) is true or not.

A third level of sentence understanding is deducing what the speaker or writer intended to convey. Perhaps the most natural interpretation of Sentence 7.11 is that the question is really a polite form of a command indicating that the speaker wants you to give the book to John. However, there are other possible interpretations: if the *you* is a child and the book very heavy, it might be a genuine question about the subject's ability to convey the book to John; or the book might be very expensive, and so raise the question of the subject being able to afford it as a gift.

It will be useful in our subsequent discussion if we talk about these three levels of analysis: the syntactic structure of the sentence, the literal meaning of the sentence, and the interpretation of the sentence. Not all psycholinguists would agree that all three levels are psychologically real. For example, some (see Riesbeck and Schank 1978; Schank 1972) argue that you can go from the text directly to the intended meaning without needing a separate syntactic analysis or a stage where a literal meaning is computed. However, we feel that an adequate discussion of sentence understanding involves discussing all three levels.

In this chapter, we will focus on the first two levels. The third more naturally falls in the next chapter, where we discuss the understanding of discourse more generally. In the next section, we will briefly discuss some proposals about what it might mean to understand at these first two levels.

Syntax

Linguists influenced by Chomsky's work have (until recently) focused most of their efforts on understanding syntax. Perhaps the major reason was that because syntax appears to follow tight rules, it was more amenable to study. In fact, *phrase structure grammar,* proposed by Chomsky in his book *Syntactic Structures* (1957), has been the point of reference for virtually all theories of syntax since then. There are two important aspects to phrase structure grammars. The first is a tree structure (see Figure 7.1) which is intended to represent the syntactic structure of the sentence. A tree structure is most easily interpreted going from the top node *S,* which represents the sentence. Going down, one encounters various nodes such as *NP* (noun phrase) and *VP* (verb phrase), which represent structural units in the sentence. An important feature of the structure indicated by the tree is that some units are "further down" than others, so that, for example, the subject *NP* is just under the sentence node, while the object *NP* is "below" the *VP* and is thus in a more subordinate position to *S*. The structure goes down to the constituents of the phrases until one reaches individual words (or sometimes morphemes) at the bottom. Assuming the theory to be correct, the tree structure provides part of the description of the grammatical function of the words and phrases of a sentence.

The second feature of the system is that a small number of rules (called *phrase structure rules*) determine which structures are grammatical. That is, when one gets to a node such as *NP*, there are only a certain number of permissible sequences of linguistic entities into which an *NP* can get written at the next lower level (e.g., *NP* can be rewritten as Det + Adj + Noun). Note that in many languages such as English both the order and contiguity of the constituents is important, and that Det + Adj + Noun indicates that those constituents have to appear next to each other in that particular sequence. This set of rules constitutes an important part of the *grammar* for the language. The hope for a grammar is that it will (1) only be able to generate grammatical sentences and (2) be able to generate all possible grammatical sentences. The initially proposed phrase structure grammars almost satisfied the first criterion and in fact could generate a wide variety of sentences, such as in Figure 7.1, where the rule VP $\rightarrow$ V + sentence allows us to embed a whole sentence within another sentence, giving us sentences (if the rule is applied several times) that are quite complex.

However, as Chomsky (1957, 1965) argued, these phrase structure grammars do not satisfy criterion (2) and are thus not an adequate explanation of English syntax (or that of any language so far studied). Even relatively simple sentences, such as

Can you open the door?   (7.15)

were not adequately explained by phrase structure grammars, since the verb and subject are in the wrong order. Much of the work in linguistics in the last 20 years has dealt with alternative proposals by Chomsky and others to handle the complexities of word order changes and also complexities in which items that appear to be in the same phrase are not near each other in the sentence. Chomsky's original proposal, called *transformational grammar,* has been largely abandoned, and there are several competing current linguistic theories that attempt to deal with these complexities. For the most part these theories are beyond the scope of our discussion. However, most current linguistic theories use phrase structure grammars as their core (although the phrase structure rules are expanded); this allows them to generate all possible sentences, but the rules are loose enough that they generate nonsentences as well. Accordingly, many have "selectional restriction rules" to filter out nonsentences. Thus, it seems appropriate to think of phrase structures as a reasonable metaphor to represent the basic information in the reader's head when the syntax of a sentence has been comprehended.

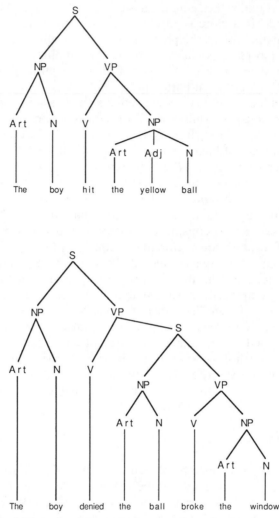

FIGURE 7-1 (Top) Example of how phrase structure rules can be used to generate a simple declarative sentence. (Bottom) Example of how phrase structure rules can be used to generate a more complex sentence. (The analysis given here is a bit simpler than that proposed by most current linguistic theories.)

A few caveats are in order here. The first is that neither linguists nor we are claiming that readers are necessarily aware of having such a structure in their head, but merely that they behave as if they had such a structure. The second is that linguists are not claiming that the rules of syntax are necessarily what is held up in school to be "good grammar." Instead, they are merely claiming that speakers and writers (and listeners and readers) operate with a fixed set of rules that allow them to utter or interpret language. For example, a dialect such as "Black English" is constrained by a grammar, but it differs from the grammar of "Standard English." Similarly, young children's language at varying ages might be explained by grammars different from adult grammar. The third is that even the best speakers and writers are occasionally ungrammatical; however, this is viewed as a minor defect in *performance* (i.e., a slip in execution) rather than as a statement about the basic linguistic *competence,* since the speaker or writer would recognize the mistake if the utterance were "played back."

A central problem that confronts someone interested in reading is how on earth the reader goes about constructing the appropriate syntactic structure from a given sequence of words coming into the eyes. People have sometimes misinterpreted the tree diagrams presented above as theories about how sentences are processed, where output (speaking and writing) involves starting at the top and going down and input (listening and reading) involves working your way back up. A bit of thought should reveal, however, that the diagrams are nonsensical if interpreted as a "flow of information." The structures are merely claims about what is in your head after having understood the syntax, but say nothing about the process by which it is acquired. Thus, even if phrase structure grammars were the correct theory of English syntax, we would still be faced with the formidable task of trying to understand how trees are constructed (i.e., how sentences are *parsed*). Parsing will be a major topic later in the chapter.

Semantics

Semantics means "meaning." In this chapter, we will concentrate on the literal meaning of a sentence, or roughly that meaning that allows you to decide if a sentence is true or false, rather than on a deeper or metaphorical meaning or on the cosmic significance of the sentence. For example, some studies on semantics of sentences involve subjects reading sentences and looking at pictures and deciding whether a sentence such as

The boy hit the ball. (7.16)

is a true description of a previously seen picture. The definition of "literal" is not particularly satisfactory for questions or for conditional or hypothetical utterances, so that forming rigorous definitions to distinguish literal meaning from other types of meaning remains a problem for people trying to define "the meaning of a sentence."

There have been many attempts to characterize the kind of structure one might have in the head when one has understood the meaning of a sentence. One that has been influential in psycholinguistic research is a *propositional* representation. In one form (Kintsch 1974), each meaning relation is represented by a proposition. Thus, sentence 7.16 would be represented by the proposition (*hit, boy, ball*). The proposition notation indicates that the concepts "boy" and "ball" are related, assigns the meaning of "hit" to the relation, and presumably indicates that the first argument is the hitter and the second the hitee. In Kintsch's system, the sentence

John hits the red ball. (7.17)

would be represented by two propositions, (*hits, John, ball*) and (*red, ball*). Saying that a sentence is represented by a series of propositions isn't too interesting. Where the system derives some power is through linking up nodes that propositions have in common (in this case, "ball"). This leads to the representation of the "meaning" of text in Kintsch's model being represented as an interconnected structure of propositions. (We will discuss Kintsch's work more fully in Chapter 8.)

A similar kind of system was developed by Rumelhart, Lindsay, and Norman (1972) which was modeled after a system of grammar called *case grammar* (Fillmore 1968). In their system, verbs are central and other major nodes are concepts, such as "agent," "recipient," and "instrument," related to the verbs. As in Kintsch's model, the nodes interconnect to relate various ideas being expressed in the text. (Anderson and Bower [1973] proposed a similar model which is also widely cited.)

We will defer further discussion of semantics until later. Our motivation for briefly mentioning these models at this point was to suggest some possibilities as to what it might mean to represent the meaning of a sentence (or a larger unit of discourse). As we will see in the next chapter, there is a lot of controversy about whether these propositional models are on the right track. Some researchers have suggested that visual imagery is necessary for a complete representation and others have argued for a more neutral representation (e.g., *mental models,* Johnson-Laird 1983) that is neither propositional nor imaginal. In any case, we face the same problem as with syntax: if one of these models is a good approximation to how meaning is represented, how does the structure actually get built? Most of these models in fact have little to say about how these structures are constructed, since their focus is on how these structures are amalgamated to represent larger units of discourse.

A Few Key Issues

One issue that will keep coming up is the relation between syntactic and semantic processing. As mentioned earlier, the "Jabberwocky" example indicates that syntactic analysis can be done even without comprehending the meaning of most words. On the other hand ungrammatical utterances such as "*Me eat now*" can be comprehended, suggesting that some sort of meaning can be apprehended in the absence of a syntactic analysis. These examples suggest that semantic analysis and syntactic analyses *can* go on independently of each other. A major question is whether they *do* in normal fluent reading.

There are essentially three positions that can be taken. The first is that the processes are sequential: syntactic analysis is done first followed by semantic analysis (although we don't think anyone really believes that a whole sentence is syntactically analyzed before any semantic analysis begins). The second is independent parallel processors: syntactic and semantic analyses are done by relatively independent systems working in concert on the incoming text in no strictly defined order. The third is that syntax and semantics are not distinct levels, but just part of the same analysis. We believe that the evidence is quite strong that at least certain aspects of syntactic and semantic analysis are done independently. We are less sure about the sequencing of syntax and semantics. However, since the sequential model is conceptually the simplest, we think that an instructive way to discuss the literature is to entertain the hypothesis that syntactic analysis is the first step in the understanding of sentences and then determine whether there are data that compel one to abandon that hypothesis. Thus, we will first discuss how readers compute the syntax of sentences.

SYNTACTIC PROCESSING

Any theory of syntactic processing would assume that the syntactic classes of individual words are identified (though probably not consciously) as a first step in arriving at an overall syntactic structure of the sentence. For example, in order to assign the subject, verb, and object in each clause (a major part of syntactic processing), one must know the syntactic function of each word in the clause. That is, you must know which words are nouns or pronouns, and thus could serve as subjects or objects, and you must know which words are verbs. Moreover, you must know the transitivity properties of the verb (i.e., whether it requires, allows, or does not allow a direct object) to determine whether to search for a direct object in the clause or to determine that "John went the door" is ungrammatical.

Surprisingly, the question of how syntactic information is extracted from words has not been a major area of research. That is not to say that the question of how syntactic information of individual words is accessed is unstudied. For example, psycholinguists have investigated the syntactic complexity of verbs. That is, some verbs, such as *reported,* are viewed as more complex than others, such as *discussed,* because they can serve a wider variety of syntactic functions. For example, one can say "Jim reported the event" and "Jim discussed the event"; but while one can say "Jim reported that the event. . . ," one cannot say "Jim discussed that the event. . . ." It was hypothesized that syntactically more complex verbs would be more difficult to process because more possible syntactic interpretations would have to be brought forward in the sentence. Unfortunately, studies on this issue have not been able to show processing time differences as a function of complexity (Cutler 1983; Foss and Hakes 1978; Rayner and Duffy 1986).

Since psycholinguists have not had much success with studying the access of the syntactic properties of words, most of the work has assumed that these properties are accessed somehow and has concentrated on what is done with them in terms of creating a syntactic structure. In fact, early psycholinguistic research focused almost exclusively on establishing the psychological reality of such syntactic structures, usually by establishing the psychological reality of the units (such as phrases and clauses). For example, subjects were asked to read a sentence and to indicate (in a number of ways) where they would put "breaks" in it. For the most part, such experiments showed that naive subjects' intuitions about what constituted units in a sentence were fairly similar to those of linguists (see Levelt [1978] for an excellent review of this research).

A somewhat more exotic method (known as the "click localization") was used in listening (Fodor and Bever 1965; Garrett, Bever, and Fodor 1966; Bever, Lackner, and Kirk 1969). Subjects listened to a sentence in one ear while they heard a click in the other. The major finding of these experiments was that when subjects were asked to indicate when the click occurred, they tended to report that the click occurred during a break between clauses even when it occurred elsewhere. While some of the conclusions of the click studies are controversial, the studies do indicate that there may be something special about clauses. Incidentally, in reading there is also evidence that some extra processing occurs at the ends of clauses and sentences (Just and Carpenter 1980).

However, the question of whether syntactic units are real for ordinary readers or listeners as well as for linguists isn't really a very interesting one, since units such as phrases and clauses must be real at *some* level. The major question of interest in syntactic processing is: If such units or structures are real, how are they used in understanding language? The question has two parts: (1) How are they used in reading (or listening), that is, in encoding the material in the first place? (2) How are they used in guiding memory or in later use of the material? We will focus almost exclusively on the first part, the on-line creation and use of syntactic structures, since the latter part is not really about reading but about memory.

Syntactic ambiguity   If syntactic structures are to be built up word by word, the system that is building them has a major problem. As words are encountered, one finds more than one way to parse them. In extreme cases, such as

They are flying planes. (7.18)

the sentence is ambiguous even at the end. (*Flying* could either be an adjective modifying *planes* or part of the verb.) Many sentences are syntactically ambiguous even though one isn't aware of the ambiguity. For example, in

John drove down the street in the car. (7.19)

semantics seems to rule out the syntactic possibility that the street is in the car. These ambiguous sentences are just the tip of the iceberg, however, since the syntactic function of the beginning words in many sentences is often quite ambiguous until more of the sentence has been read.

In spite of this ambiguity, people make few mistakes in parsing sentences. There would be three simple ways to build a parsing machine to avoid mistakes. The first would be for it to construct *all* logically possible alternative syntactic structures as it went along (analogous to retrieving all meanings of an ambiguous word) and then to eliminate the ones ruled out by each new word that came along. The second would be to entertain one possible structure, and then if that didn't work, go back to the beginning and try again (through the set of all possible structures) until one was found that was appropriate for the set of words. The third would be to hold the information in some sort of short-term memory buffer until there was enough evidence to rule out all but one structure, and then to do the syntactic processing.

The problem with the first way is that it endangers taxing limited resources, since many structures are possible at the beginning of a typical sentence. The problem with the second is that unless a clever strategy is used for trying out structures, one will have to go back to the beginning of a sentence many times before arriving at a correct interpretation (an even more serious problem when attempting to parse speech). The problem with the third is that it really begs the question: How does the system in fact know that enough syntactic information is present so that it is syntactically unambiguous without having tried at least tentative constructions of syntax?

Thus it appears that there is a dilemma. If you entertain all possible interpretations, your mind will be overwhelmed; if you just choose one, you are in danger of coming up with the wrong interpretation part way through the sentence and then having to recompute the structure; if you hold back, you don't know when to begin computing a structure. One solution to the problem is go with the first way and invoke meaning rather than structure. That is, semantics will bail you out and quickly rule out many interpretations. We will discuss the interaction of syntactics and semantics later, but for the moment, we will argue that this solution is at best a partial one. First, from the standpoint of plausibility, in many cases it seems irrelevant. For example, in Sentence 7.19 above, you would have had little strain in processing the beginning of the sentence even though there were many possible structures and there was no semantic cue to help you out. Second, as we shall see, much of the available research suggests that semantics does not enter into the earliest stages of building a syntactic structure.

It seems implausible that we build all possible syntactic structures (even subconsciously) since that would involve too great a mental strain; there must be some sort of strategy for constructing at most a few structures. There have been several proposals by linguists and psycholinguists for such strategies. The earliest, which we shall refer to as the *clausal model* (Bever 1970; Fodor, Bever, and Garrett 1974), involved simple pragmatic heuristics, such as "take a noun-verb-noun sequence as actor-action-object," and "take the first clause to be the main clause unless there is a subordinating conjuction." The rules that the clausal model used to explain parsing processes are clearly not fully adequate (e.g., the first would misconstrue passive sentences). While it is logically possible that an expanded set of such rules would do a reasonable job, such a hodgepodge of rules seems like an unsatisfactory theory of parsing. It would seem better if there were some basic principles guiding the parsing. Several such parsing theories have appeared in recent years (Kimball 1973; Frazier 1979; Frazier and Fodor 1978; Frazier and Rayner 1982; Marcus 1980). At present, none could be considered a definitive theory of parsing, although they all are big improvements over the clausal model. We will now describe one particular theory of parsing, the *garden-path* model of sentence processing (Frazier and Rayner 1982). We would like to point out that there are alternative theories of how people parse sentences. For example, Ford, Bresnan, and Kaplan (1983) have proposed a model in which parsing is based on lexical properties of verbs and other words that take "arguments" rather than by phrase structure rules (as is the case in Frazier and Rayner's garden-path model). Because of space limitations we will not discuss alternative approaches, but will focus on the garden-path model both because it seems quite promising and because it has led to some interesting experiments on reading.

The fundamental idea of the Frazier and Rayner garden-path model is that a string of words in a sentence is assigned an initial syntactic analysis on the basis of purely structural information. Thus, readers incorporate each new word into a phrase structure representation of a sentence following two general principles called *minimal attachment* and *late closure*. According to the minimal attachment principle, readers attach incoming material into the phrase marker being constructed using the fewest nodes consistent with the well-formed rules of the language under analysis. For example, minimal attachment predicts that in sentences 7.20 and 7.21 the phrase *the answer* will initially be taken as the direct object of the verb *knew*, even though this leads to a revision of this analysis in Sentence 7.21 where *the answer* is in fact the subject of a new clause. The reason, according to the application of the minimal attachment principle, is that the analysis of Sentence 7.21 includes an additional node (the *S* node in Figure 7.2) to the one in Sentence 7.20.

| The girl knew the answer by heart. | (7.20) |
| The girl knew the answer was wrong. | (7.21) |

The late closure principle is that if grammatically permissible, the reader attaches new items to the phrase or clause currently being processed. Late closure favors attachment to preceding items over attachment to subsequent items, allowing Sentence 7.22 to be parsed correctly, but causing Sentence 7.23 to be initially parsed incorrectly (see Figure 7.3).

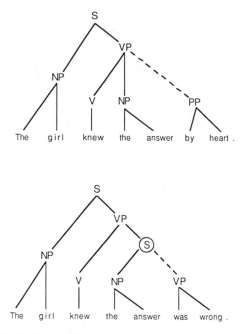

FIGURE 7-2 Syntactic structures for sentences 7.20 and 7.21.

Since Jay always jogs a mile this seems like a short distance
to him.   (7.22)
Since Jay always jogs a mile seems like a short distance
to him.   (7.23)

Each of these strategies can be viewed as a consequence of a general tendency of the syntactic processor to adopt the first available syntactic analysis of an input (Frazier 1985, 1987). This tendency is determined by time pressures and by restrictions on short-term memory capacity. Minimal attachment, for example, follows from the fact that a nonminimal attachment analysis of an input always requires the accessing of more rules than the minimal attachment analysis (Frazier and Fodor 1978). Therefore, assuming that it takes more time to access more rules and that the processor operates under time pressure, the minimal attachment analysis of an input will always be chosen. The late closure analysis of an input may be attributed to the fact that attaching an input item to material just received demands less memory search than retrieving material that occurred earlier, and structuring the input material with material following it would entail delaying analysis until the subsequent material had been received and analyzed.

Frazier and Rayner (1982) presented experimental evidence in support of the strategies outlined above. Readers' eye movements were recorded as they read sentences like 7.20 to 7.23. If you think about it, it seems that

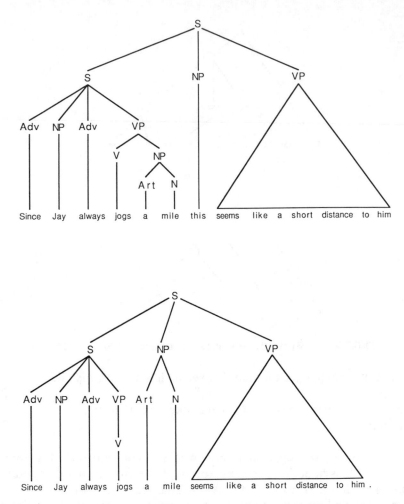

FIGURE 7-3 Syntactic structures for sentences 7.22 and 7.23. Triangles denote phrases whose analysis is not given in the figure.

Sentence 7.23 is more difficult to process than Sentence 7.22. But why? As we indicated above, according to Frazier and Rayner the answer is the principle of late closure. In the case of these sentences, the *key region* is the phrase *a mile* and the word following it. According to the principle of late closure, when *jogs* is encountered, a verb phrase is being constructed which could take an object. When *a mile* is encountered, there is no reason to close the phrase, so that *mile* is incorporated into the phrase as the direct object of *jogs*. In Sentence 7.22, this is the correct interpretation, so the reader proceeds without difficulty. In Sentence 7.23, since *a mile* is in fact the subject of the next clause, the reader needs to recompute the syntactic structure at *seems,* the point when the object interpretation of *a mile* is untenable, and thus there is processing difficulty.

Frazier and Rayner (1982) tested the late closure principle by looking at the pattern of eye fixations during reading. The key question is what happens at the point of disambiguation (*this* in Sentence 7.22 and *seems* in Sentence 7.23). If the reader is constructing both possible syntactic interpretations up to that point, then one might expect fixations in the sentence to get progressively longer as more short-term memory capacity is taken. More crucially, one would expect that there will be a slow-down in processing *for either sentence* when the point of disambiguation is reached, as the reader then has the information to select the appropriate syntactic structure. On the other hand, the late closure principle predicts that there should be a difference in what happens in the two sentences: large disruption in Sentence 7.23 at the point of disambiguation and no disruption in Sentence 7.22.

In fact, there was little disruption in Sentence 7.22, but there was severe disruption in Sentence 7.23 as soon as the reader fixated the disambiguating region (*seems*). The disruption in Sentence 7.23 was indexed by long fixation times on either the disambiguating word or the succeeding one, or regressions from those words, or both (see also Kennedy and Murray [1984] for similar results). The regressions were usually either directed to the ambiguous region or to the beginning of the sentence. These data make it clear that the syntactic structure of the sentence is being computed quite quickly. If the fixation time on *seems* or the direction of the saccade off it is affected, it means that the classification of *seems* as a verb and the detection of the mismatch of that with the syntactic structure previously constructed is all computed in less than about 250 msec. Even if the disruption is not until the next fixation, it still means that the syntactic computations are done well within a half a second or so.

Frazier and Rayner tested the second parsing principle (*minimal attachment*) and also found that it predicted similar parsing difficulties. To refresh your memory, the principle is that when a new word is being attached to a sentence, it will be attached in such a way as to create the fewest nodes. Consider again sentences 7.20 and 7.21. Interpreting *the answer* as the direct object of the verb requires fewer nodes to be postulated than interpreting it as the subject of the sentential complement (see Figure 7.2). Hence, according to the minimal attachment principle, Sentence 7.21 (in which *the answer* turns out to be part of a sentential complement) should take longer to process than Sentence 7.20 (in which *the answer* is the direct object) and the complexity of Sentence 7.21 should be associated with the need to revise the structure assigned to *the answer* once the following words are encountered. Frazier and Rayner provided confirming evidence for this prediction as they found that readers had difficulty with Sentence 7.21 when they reached the point of disambiguation. Their experiments thus suggest that readers do in fact carry forth only one global interpretation of a sentence, and that the interpretation must be recomputed in some cases.

Some people have criticized this type of study because the stimuli are, to some extent, "unnatural." (This is a recurrent potential problem in psycholinguistics when one creates experimentally controlled text.) In particular, it has been claimed that Sentence 7.23 is unnatural because it should be written with a comma after *jogs*. On some level, however, that is the point of the study: a comma is often used in such sentences because without it the reader is likely to misparse it because of his or her standard parsing routines. However, grammar does not require a comma in sentences such as 7.23; such sentences commonly appear in natural discourse. (One of the authors encountered, and misparsed, many such sentences when reading Tolkien's *The Lord of the Rings* to his daughter.)

Similarly, inserting "overt complementizers" in sentences containing temporary structural ambiguities (e.g., inserting *that* after *knew* in 7.21), removes the problems that readers often have when such grammatical markers are absent (Ferreira and Clifton 1986; Mitchell and Holmes 1985; Rayner and Frazier 1987). However, sentences without overt complementizers are both grammatical and common in natural discourse.

To summarize, the work on syntactic ambiguity indicates that syntactic ambiguity is dealt with in a different way from lexical ambiguity. Whereas more than one meaning of an ambiguous word appears to be accessed and the correct meaning chosen from among them (although extremely rapidly in some cases), the processing system does not have the same luxury in the case of syntactic ambiguity. It appears that only one syntactic structure is constructed, and if that isn't appropriate, then the system needs to recompute a new syntactic structure. The distinction makes sense, since it is likely that meanings of words are items that are ever-present in memory and can be "looked up" at little or no cost, whereas syntactic structures need to be constructed, and such construction demands scarce processing resources and is not likely to proliferate. Since only one parse appears to be done at a time, the parsing system needs efficient strategies to come up with the correct parse a reasonable percentage of the time and to recover gracefully when it misparses.

The contrast of lexical ambiguity with deeper syntactic ambiguity raises the question of how the reader deals with ambiguity produced by the syntactic ambiguity of the words themselves. For example, the sentences

I know that the desert trains young people to be especially
tough. (7.24)
I know that the desert trains are especially tough on young
people. (7.25)

are ambiguous up through the word *trains*. There is ambiguity because *desert trains* could either be a noun and a verb or an adjective and a noun. (However, the following word—an adjective or a verb—disambiguates the syntactic assignment.) How does the parsing system deal with this? There seem to be three possible hypotheses: (1) a single structure is somehow decided upon (perhaps using the more likely category of the words); (2) both structures are computed and then one is eliminated when the disambiguating information comes; and (3) the parser waits until the disambiguating information comes before incorporating the ambiguous words into the structure.

These three possibilities were tested by Frazier and Rayner (1987) using sentences like 7.24 and 7.25 and control sentences (Sentences 7.26 and 7.27) in which prior information (the word *this* or *these*) disambiguated the syntactic categories of *desert* and *trains*.

I know that this desert trains young people to be especially
tough. (7.26)
I know that these desert trains are especially tough on young
people. (7.27)

One analysis compared these disambiguated versions to the prior versions where disambiguation was only possible later in the sentence (usually at the word following the second syntactically ambiguous word: *young* or *are* in the above examples). The major finding was that readers spent less time on the key words (e.g., *desert trains*) when there was no prior disambiguating context than when there was. In addition, when there was no prior disambiguating context they spent more time on the rest of the sentence than when there was. This pattern of data rules out the hypothesis that multiple syntactic structures are computed when there is ambiguity, since that hypothesis would predict that readers should spend more time on *desert trains* when prior context leaves their syntactic assignment ambiguous since multiple structures would have to be constructed at that point.

The other two hypotheses are consistent with the obtained pattern of data, however. Let's first consider the delay hypothesis, since the prediction is simpler. Reading time on *desert trains* should be longer when the prior context disambiguates the syntactic categories of the words because the reader then computes the syntactic structure (and this takes some time), whereas when the prior context does not disambiguate, the reader delays computing the syntactic structure. In contrast, reading time should be longer for the rest of the sentence when the prior context does not disambiguate things because the reader has delayed the syntactic computation until then. The immediate assignment of one syntactic structure makes a similar prediction, however. We will assume that (in the ambiguous case) the immediate assignment is made to the structure which is more available (and hence easier to make). Thus, on average, processing *desert trains* will take less time in the ambiguous case than the unambiguous case because the disambiguating information might force the reader to make the less preferred syntactic analysis. Moreover, reading times for the rest of the sentence should be longer in the ambiguous case since the wrong analysis would be made half the time and some recomputation would be needed, as in Frazier and Rayner's earlier study (1982) discussed above.

The hypotheses can be distinguished by comparing the preferred version with the nonpreferred version. (Preference was assessed by asking other subjects to complete the sentences given only the ambiguous beginning). Frazier and Rayner (1987) demonstrated that there was little difference between the times to process the preferred version of the ambiguous string (in the example, interpreting *desert* as a noun) and the nonpreferred version. Thus, the likelihood that a word is in one syntactic class or another does not appear to force an immediate assignment of the syntactic class of that word. In addition, the same pattern of data was observed in sentences such as

Some of us weren't aware that the church pardons very few
people.   (7.28)
Some of us weren't aware that the church pardons are difficult to obtain.   (7.29)

where the key words *church pardons* had the same thematic roles in the two versions. Thus, the reader appears to be holding back the interpretation of the sentence because of syntactic rather than semantic ambiguity.

These results are different from the earlier Frazier and Rayner (1982) findings on minimal attachment and late closure, where the reader doesn't hold back but instead computes a single syntactic structure immediately. The two cases differ, however, in that the ambiguity has two different causes. In the Frazier and Rayner (1987) studies, it is because of ambiguity in the syntactic category of the assignment of the lexical items themselves, while in the Frazier and Rayner (1982) studies it is because of ambiguities in the syntactic structure that must be constructed. Frazier and Rayner (1987) argued that the difference between these situations accounts for the different pattern of results. Apparently, in circumstances where developing an analysis of an input involves active computation of a representation (necessary in the case of syntax, since the indefinite number of syntactic structures of a language cannot be prestored), the language processor adopts the first analysis available. When multiple analyses of an input are precomputed (or stored in memory), the language processor may consider various alternatives and quickly select one interpretation (as in the case of lexical ambiguity) or delay making an interpretation in hope of quickly getting relevant information (as in the case of syntactic category ambiguity as studied by Frazier and Rayner). In any case, the results support our earlier statement about the distinction between access of information from the lexicon and creating syntactic structures: multiple meanings or syntactic categories appear to be accessed for individual words at little or no cost, whereas only one syntactic structure appears to be constructed at a time (even at the expense of delaying the construction of a structure).

SEMANTICS

The question of how semantic information is put together to construct the overall meaning of the sentence is clearly an important one. Unfortunately, we know little about how it is done. One reason we know more about syntactic processing is that we have some clearer idea of what the units are (phrases, clauses) and also have some agreement about how parsing would go on. In contrast, the meaning of a sentence is a more nebulous affair, and as we have seen previously, there is far less agreement about how the meaning should be represented. For example, should the meaning of "The dog bit the boy." be represented by a proposition, a pictorial image, something else, or all of the above? In addition, the question of how the meaning of a sentence is constructed seems virtually open-ended. In addition to figuring out agent-action-recipient relations (which should be relatively easy given the appropriate parse), virtually all areas of logic must be dealt with—including quantifiers (e.g., "some," "many," "most"), negation, conditionals—as well as general world knowledge.

Whether the analysis in the above paragraph is correct or not, there is much less to be said about how meanings of words are put together (probably with the help of syntactic analysis) to form "the meaning of a sentence." We will briefly review two questions to give a feeling for how questions about semantics have been attacked and the difficulties attendant with trying to ask questions about semantics.

Semantic Features

One intriguing idea about semantics is that word meanings may not be unitary but bundles of "semantic features." For example, *giraffe* would presumably be represented by features such as "animal," "long-necked," "browsing," and "spotted." The theoretical idea has been particularly well worked out in the area of verbs; some theories have even claimed that all verbs can be built up out of 10 or so semantic features (e.g., Schank 1975).

An important reason for postulating semantic features is as part of a theory of understanding a sentence in which the semantic features of individual words are put together to form the meaning of a sentence. A major problem that could be attacked by such a theory (Katz and Fodor 1963) is the resolution of semantic ambiguity. For example, in a sentence like

$$\text{The orchestra played at the colorful ball.} \tag{7.30}$$

the word *orchestra* serves to determine the appropriate meaning of *ball*.

One test of the semantic feature idea is to see whether the *complexity* (i.e., number of semantic features) of a verb influences the fixation time on that word or the immediately following words. For example, a causative verb such as *killed* is viewed as more complex than the noncausative verb *died* because *killed* means "caused to die", and the morphologically negative verb *dislike* more complex (because it means "not like") than the positive verb *like*. When Rayner and Duffy (1986) looked at whether fixation times were longer on complex verbs than on simpler verbs, they found that they were not.

This mostly negative finding with respect to verb complexity is not necessarily damaging to the semantic feature hypothesis. If all the semantic features are accessed in parallel at the point of lexical access (as multiple meanings appear to be), then there is no particular reason to expect that fixation durations need to be longer on more complex verbs. Thus, the semantic feature hypothesis appears to need a better test than the above.

On the other hand, there appears to be a very interesting phenomenon that argues strongly for the semantic feature hypothesis. Consider the following sentence:

How many animals of each kind did Moses take on the Ark?   (7.31)

Many people read the sentence unaware that it is anomalous (Erickson and Mattson 1981). It is not merely that the word *Moses* is not read, since if *Jerry* or *Newton* were substituted for it, the anomaly would probably be apparent. What appears to be happening in the example is that as the meaning of the sentence is built up, semantic features are used from each new word. However, if the word shares enough semantic features with the correct word, its meaning may be (incorrectly) integrated with the emerging meaning of the sentence.

Unfortunately, the phenomenon still has the status of a demonstration, since the examples cover a few similar cases involving proper names. It appears to us, though, that a fuller exploration of this type of "illusion" could provide important evidence on how the meaning of a word is actually used in constructing the meaning of a sentence.

Verification

As mentioned earlier, one definition of having understood "the meaning of a sentence" is to be able to decide whether it is true or false. In fact, many experiments have been done on this general theme. We will mention two varieties. The first is the "sentence-picture" verification experiment. Typically, the subject sees a picture of a red circle, followed by sentences such as "The circle is red." (*True Positive*); "The circle is not red." (*False Negative*); "The circle is green." (*False Positive*); or "The circle is not green." (*True Negative*). The subjects are asked to judge the truth or falsity of the sentence as quickly as possible. The focus in these experiments is to understand how negation is handled.

The data typically show that negative sentences take longer to verify than positive sentences, with "true negatives" being the hardest. A model to explain the data (Trabasso, Rollins, and Shaughnessy 1971; Chase and Clark

1972) proposes that a picture (e.g., a red circle) is encoded as Affirmative(circle,red), whereas the four sentences above would be encoded as Affirmative(circle,red), Negative(circle,red), Affirmative(circle,green), and Negative(circle,green), respectively. The two propositions are then compared, looking for matches and mismatches in either the argument within the parentheses or the affirmation or negation. The subject presumably answers "true" given that both parts match or both parts mismatch and answers "false" given only one match. If one assumes that mismatches take longer to compute than matches, the general data pattern can be predicted.

While these experiments are interesting in determining how logical relations are handled, there is considerable controversy over whether they say much about how such relations are computed in reading. In addition, while the overall framework of the above analysis seems reasonable, the details of the representation often have to change from experiment to experiment depending on the details (e.g., whether the picture comes before or after the sentence). In fact, such experiments may be more relevant for telling us something about how propositions are put together in text or discourse. At the risk of jumping ahead of ourselves, let us briefly mention one interesting point.

Clearly, people are rarely put in the situation of reading in order to verify pictures. However, the fact that true negatives are so hard (Wason 1965) may tell us something interesting. Some people have suggested that the usual purpose of negation is to contradict something the speaker or writer thinks the listener or reader believes to be true. That is, if you see the sentence

Saturn is not the biggest planet. (7.32)

you would suppose that the writer thought that you believed that Saturn was the biggest planet. In terms of the above experiment, most negative statements are like the "false negatives" since they directly disprove what is presupposed (the picture is the presupposition). Thus, 7.32 would be harder to understand if you know that Jupiter is the biggest planet (since the sentence would be like a true negative) than if you believe Saturn is (since the sentence would then be a like a false negative).

In sum, the sentence-picture verification experiments have suggested plausible propositional formats in which negation in sentences is encoded and plausible ways in which such formats are used to compare these sentences to nonlinguistic stimuli. However, they say little about how these propositional formats are constructed, or whether they are dependent on the context in which they appear.

The second type of verification experiment has focused on retrieval of information from long-term memory. For example, subjects are asked to judge the truth and falsity of sentences such as "All dogs are animals." "Some dogs are animals." "Some women are writers." "Some dogs are stones." (Meyer 1970). As with the sentence-picture verification experiments, the subject is asked to respond as quickly as possible and his or her response is timed. This area, like the sentence-picture verification literature, is voluminous, so we can at best scratch the surface.

While the details of the data are not consistent across experiments, certain patterns have emerged. Most important is that true statements are usually easier if the two concepts are semantically related, while false judgments are usually easiest if the two concepts are very dissimilar. The former is explainable in terms of a "priming" mechanism (Collins and Loftus 1975); however, the latter is not. A more comprehensive explanation is that there may be a two-stage mechanism in these judgments (especially for those of the form "all X are Y"). If the two concepts are very similar, then the subject judges "true"; if they are very dissimilar, the subject judges "false"; but if they are intermediate in similarity, the subject needs to go to a second stage where the relationship is judged more carefully (Meyer 1970; Smith, Shoben, and Rips 1974). The model makes sense because the subject is under time pressure. The first stage can be thought of as a crude judgment: "featural overlap" between the two concepts (Smith, Shoben, and Rips 1974) that can be computed very quickly, but will only be approximately true (e.g., it is false that "All lions are tigers."). The second stage is a slower stage in which the actual logic of the statement is decided by a more conscious and effortful process.

The general form of the model is interesting in that it suggests that certain types of information may be retrieved from long-term memory much more rapidly than others. More generally, the data from these experiments have provided some interesting suggestions about how semantic information is retrieved from long-term memory. However, it is not clear how much they say about how such information is actually retrieved in reading. A major problem is that the pattern of data appears to be quite dependent on the particular types of questions asked. For example, if there are many statements of the form

All tigers are lions. (7.33)

"false" responses are fast and accurate (Glass and Holyoak 1975), contrary to the two-stage model. That is, it appears that there are many strategies that subjects have in these experiments for making these judgments, and the particular ones used may depend on the types of questions used in the experiment.

In addition, since the focus has been the retrieval of information from long-term memory, much of the "reading" is short-cut. In a typical experiment, the subject will see nothing but statements of the form "All X are Y.", so that they are unlikely to be actually reading *All* or *are* for most of the experiment. Thus, while the experiments may tell us about how the information about X and Y is retrieved and compared, it is not likely to tell us much about how the quantification *all* is encoded or related to the two nouns in actual reading.

In sum, verification experiments have looked at how the truth of certain simple sentences is computed. To get useable data, however, certain artificial constraints have been placed on these sentences: either they are all in a standard format and/or they relate to a narrow set of real-world concepts (as in the sentence-picture experiments). This has caused the focus to shift from (a) studying how semantic structures are constructed from incoming text to (b) attempting to discover how the structures that have been constructed are used in the particular response-time task in the experiment. This shift in focus has the obvious consequence of leaving us in the dark about how semantic structures are built. In addition, since much use of the information in such experiments is "strategic" (i.e., task-dependent), not much has emerged in the way of general statements about the form of the semantic representation. While we have hinted that a feature representation is possible (e.g., Smith, Shoben, and Rips 1974) there are many other proposals (e.g., Meyer 1970; Glass and Holyoak 1975). Perhaps the answer is that there are myriad semantic structures that can be built, and the structure that is built is highly dependent on the situation. We hope not, or at least that there are general principles governing how semantic structures are built; otherwise, studying semantic processes in reading will be quite difficult.

SYNTAX AND SEMANTICS

As we remarked earlier in the chapter, a major topic of interest in psycholinguistics has been the relationship between syntax and semantics. The focus on syntax in psycholinguistics in the 1960s and 1970s was based on an assumption (sometimes explicit) that syntactic processing could be understood without having to invoke computations about the meaning of the phrase, clause, or sentence. That is to say, it was assumed that either syntactic processing was prior to semantic processing or at least that the processes went on more or less independently.

Let us make clear what we mean here by "semantic processing," since people arguing against the above hypothesis have, in our opinion, misinterpreted it. They have taken the above position to be claiming that no processing of meaning is done before the syntax is computed. The evidence on lexical ambiguity (among other things) makes clear that the meaning of individual words is accessed immediately, and thus that processing of meaning at the lexical level does not wait for syntax. However, the two key questions are (1) Does the presumably effortful operation of constructing larger meanings need to wait for at least some syntactic processing to be completed? and (2) Does meaning (either pragmatic information or contextual information) influence syntactic processing, and if so, how? Since we know fairly little about how "higher-order" meaning is constructed, we have little to say about the first question. However, there has been some very interesting work on the second, which indicates, somewhat surprisingly, that neither pragmatic information nor contextual information has much influence on the early stages of syntactic processing.

There are two sets of experiments which lead to this somewhat surprising conclusion: one set by Rayner, Carlson, and Frazier (1983) and another set by Ferreira and Clifton (1986). Rayner et al. investigated the contribution of syntactic, semantic, and pragmatic information in sentence comprehension. In their first experiment, they asked subjects to read sentences like the following:

The florist sent the flowers was very pleased with herself. (7.34)

The performer sent the flowers was very pleased with herself. (7.35)

The performer who was sent the flowers was very pleased with herself. (7.36)

The performer sent the flowers and was very pleased with herself. (7.37)

Given the choice of reading the string *the florist sent the flowers* in 7.34 as a simple active clause (meaning "the florist sent flowers to someone") or as a type of relative (called a *reduced relative*) clause (meaning "the florist who was sent the flowers"), people tend to prefer the simple active structure. Most sentences that start out this way do turn out to be simple active structures. But if the reader interprets the sentence as a simple active sentence, there is an inconsistency when the word *was* is encountered. Thus, some type of reanalysis of the sentence is required. To determine whether semantic factors influence the syntactic interpretation of the sentence, sentences like 7.35 were included in which the person or thing mentioned at the beginning of the sentence was more likely to be the recipient or object of the action. For example, in 7.35 performers are more likely to have flowers sent to them than to send flowers to others. Rayner et al.'s study thus examined whether this real-world knowledge about performers would induce readers to assign different semantic roles to nouns like *performers,* and whether this semantic assignment would affect the syntactic analysis. Would readers be more likely to assign the reduced relative structure to 7.35 than 7.34?

Rayner et al. examined readers' eye movements and, by measuring how long they paused and how much they slowed down their reading, determined how surprised they were when they reached the disambiguating words (*was very*). They distinguished (as did Frazier and Rayner 1982) *second pass reading time* from *first pass reading time*. Second pass reading time is the sum of fixation durations on a critical region of the sentence that are preceded by a regression from another region of the sentence. The major finding was that readers paused an equal amount of time in the disambiguating region on their first pass in sentences like 7.34 and 7.35 and they also regressed to the beginning of the sentence equally often in the two sentence types. In comparison, when they read sentences like 7.36 or 7.37, readers paused for less time on the words *was very,* since these sentences are not structurally ambiguous.

By distinguishing between first pass and total reading times as well as examining how well readers were able to answer questions about the sentences, Rayner, Carlson, and Frazier (1983) were able to conclude that readers initially pursue just one syntactic analysis of a sentence, but that they arrive at the semantically and pragmatically plausible interpretation of a sentence, even when that interpretation is not sturcturally preferred. In order to explain the pattern of results, Rayner, Carlson and Frazier (1983) proposed the existence of a *thematic processor* that operates in parallel with a syntactic processor. The thematic processor evaluates the plausibility of the "thematic frames" associated with "the head of a phrase" and selects the sematically and pragmatically most plausible one.

In a second study, Rayner, Carlson and Frazier (1983) examined the relationship between the syntactic and thematic processors. Specifically, they studied how the thematic processor could guide or change syntactic analyses. Consider the following pair of sentences:

> The spy saw the cop with the binoculars but the cop didn't
> see him. (7.38)
> The spy saw the cop with the revolver but the cop didn't
> see him. (7.39)

Sentence 7.38 is ambiguous with respect to the person holding the binoculars, while 7.39 leaves little doubt that the cop had the revolver. The minimal attachment strategy described earlier suggests that the instrumental reading of *with the binoculars* (putting them in the hands of the spy) should be preferred. Of course, if this is true, the syntactic parser should also initially prefer the instrumental reading of 7.39 (making *the revolver* a viewing instrument even though this reading is quite bizarre). Rayner, Carlson and Frazier found that reading times were significantly shorter for sentences like 7.38 (where the pragmatically more plausible analysis coincided with the analysis preferred on structural grounds) than for sentences like 7.39 (where the pragmatically preferred analysis conflicted with the structurally preferred analysis). While the ultimate interpretation of the sentence reached by readers was consistent with pragmatic considerations of real world plausibility, the eye movement data indicated that a conflict between pragmatic and structural preferences leads to longer reading times and some need for reanalysis.

A third experiment by Ferreira and Clifton (1986) is also relevant here. They had subjects read sentences such as

> The defendant examined by the lawyer turned out to be
> unreliable. (7.40)
> The evidence examined by the lawyer turned out to be
> unreliable. (7.41)

In 7.40 when the phrase *by the lawyer* is encountered, a recomputation must take place. That is, minimal attachment predicts that *examined* will be interpreted as the verb of the main clause because this is the simplest structure. However, it appears that in 7.41, which is structurally the same as 7.40, semantics should help out in disambiguating the sentence. Thus, it seems as if 7.41 should be easier to process than 7.40, since *evidence* is inanimate and extremely unlikely to examine anything. Surprisingly, Ferreira and Clifton (1986) found very little difference between sentences like 7.40 and 7.41 on first pass reading times.

These experiments reported by Rayner, Carlson, and Frazier (1983) and Ferreira and Clifton (1986) thus suggest that the initial syntactic parsing of a sentence goes on relatively independently of the meaning of the sentence. Further evidence for this conclusion comes from a second experiment reported by Ferreira and Clifton (1986). Consider the similar pair of sentences

Sam loaded the boxes on the cart before lunch. (7.42)

Sam loaded the boxes on the cart onto the van. (7.43)

The minimal attachment principle suggests that when the phrase *on the cart* is read, it is simpler to attach it as a locative prepositional phrase, indicating where the boxes were loaded, rather than to make it part of the object *boxes on the cart,* indicating which boxes Sam loaded (see Figure 7.4). Thus, the minimal attachment principle predicts that 7.42 should be easy to process and 7.43 more difficult, because the wrong syntactic structure would be created and a recomputation would be needed when the reader arrived at the point of disambiguation *(onto his van).* As we discussed above, Frazier and Rayner (1982; see also Rayner and Frazier 1987) found that readers in fact had difficulty with sentences like 7.43 when they reached the point of disambiguation.

In the second experiment by Ferreira and Clifton (1986), semantic plausibility was determined by the prior context. For example, in 7.43 above, the plausibility of the non-minimal attachment interpretation (see Table 7.3) was increased by prior context sentences, which distinguished the boxes on the cart from other boxes in the room. They found that the prior context did not influence the first pass reading times, but had a marked effect on how well people could answer questions about the target sentence.

Thus, the work of Rayner, Carlson and Frazier (1983) and Ferreira and Clifton (1986) leads to a relatively simple, and perhaps counterintuitive, answer about the place of meaning in arriving at a correct parsing of a sentence, namely that parsing initially appears to be the unique job of a syntactic processing "module," and only when there is some type of trouble detected does the semantic system come into the picture. The result seems counterintuitive because in some cases (e.g., the evidence vs. defendant sentences above), the one seems much easier to process than the other. However, we should remind you that the reanalysis stage, though delayed,

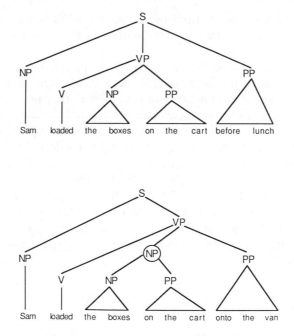

FIGURE 7-4 Syntactic structure for sentences 7.42 and 7.43. Triangles denote phrases whose analysis is not given in the figure. The circled NP in the lower panel is the extra node in the lower structure. (Ferreira and Clifton 1986, with permission of Academic Press and the authors.)

may not be delayed all that much. That is, even if about four or five fixations intervene between initially encountering the words and arriving at the correct syntactic interpretation, it would only be about a second of elapsed time. Thus, you might only be dimly aware of any processing difficulty (remember, readers are unaware of many regressions).

We certainly don't mean to suggest that these experiments conclusively demonstrate that, in all cases, the initial syntactic processing of a sentence is uninfluenced by meaning. There are certainly counter-proposals (Crain and Steedman 1985; McClelland, 1987) in which it has been suggested that meaning and context do influence initial syntactic parsing. Rayner, Carlson, and Frazier's analysis of these minimal attachment sentences may only apply to cases in which the prepositional phrases are "tightly linked" to the verb (e.g., are "case arguments" of the verb). In cases where the

TABLE 7.3 Biasing context for Sentence 7.43

Sam worked at a factory warehouse. His job was to make sure that boxes of merchandise were ready to be delivered. Sam had to fill up a van so it could go out. He had a pile of boxes on a cart and another pile on the floor. He knew some guys from another department needed the cart. *Sam loaded the boxes on the cart onto the van.* Then he was free to take a much needed break.

---

prepositional phrases specify time and location (and thus are not required by the verb), semantics appears to enter earlier in the analysis (Taraban and McClelland 1988).

The evidence, however, is pretty clear in the particular cases we discussed that the parsing strategies first yield their normal analysis, regardless of meaning or context, and then some other processes intervene to create a more cognitively acceptable analysis. Moreover, the examples chosen seem to be cases in which one would have expected meaning or context to play a major part (as we tried to argue earlier). An interesting and complex question that these experiments raise is exactly how semantics does help to sort out the syntax eventually. The most reasonable explanation is, as we mentioned above, that there is a thematic processor that works in parallel with the syntactic parser. The basic argument from the Rayner et al. (1983) study is that reanalysis of a string of words (following an initial parse based on structural preferences) can be started very quickly on the basis of semantic information.

CONCLUSIONS

In this chapter, we have tried to introduce you to how psycholinguists have tried to investigate how words are formed into sentences. We first looked at the question of how higher-order processes affect the identification of words. This issue is important, partly because we are tacitly assuming that these higher-order structures are built up word by word as the reader goes through the text. If these higher-order processes significantly modulate the basic process by which words are identified, then (1) the data in Chapter 3 are largely irrelevant and (2) reading will be almost impossible to study if everything depends on everything else.

In fact, there is little conclusive evidence that higher-order processing has any effect on the identification of words. The selection of the appropriate meaning of a lexically ambiguous word appears to occur only after lexical access of all (or at least most) meanings have been accessed. An exception to the previous statement on lexical ambiguity is that a prior related word may cause only one meaning of an ambiguous word to be accessed. Thus the only context effects on accessing multiple meanings of an ambiguous word appear to be due to intralexical priming. The evidence concerning the effect of context on the speed of lexical access is less clear. When a word is highly predictable from the prior context, the extraction of visual information, and hence lexical access, is speeded a bit; the effect of predictability appears particularly strong in the extraction of parafoveal information, where the visual information is poorer. It is possible that all of the effects of context are due to intralexical priming; however, we are skeptical, especially in the case of skipping predictable function words.

We then discussed a theory of how a reader parses a sentence to arrive at an appropriate syntactic structure. A major problem for parsing is to deal with syntactic ambiguity; virtually all sentences are temporarily ambiguous at some point. The evidence on syntactic ambiguity indicates that it is handled differently from lexical ambiguity: it appears that only one syntactic structure is computed, and if this structure is incorrect, a new structure must be built. Such a parser could work efficiently: if it usually made the correct parse, but was able to recompute gracefully when the original parse turned out to be incorrect.

Some proposals for how the meanings of sentences are understood were then discussed. Two heavily studied situations are the handling of negation in sentence-picture verification and the handling of logical relationships. From both types of situations, certain regularities emerged. The experiments on negation indicated that negation took extra time to process, and that judgment times could be predicted by the numbers of mismatches between the semantic representation of the picture and the semantic representation of the sentence. The experiments on logical relations between semantic categories indicated that subjects may first be able to access a crude measure of how related two concepts are before accessing a full relation between the concepts. However, neither paradigm tells us very much about how semantic structures are constructed during reading. Moreover, it may be that the semantic structure that is constructed depends heavily on the particular verification task. Thus, it is not clear how much we can generalize from such tasks to reading, in which the reader usually presupposes the truth of statements rather than verifying them. In this regard, we briefly discussed the possible relation of the negation experiments to processing of text.

We concluded by discussing the relationship of meaning to syntactic processing and argued that, at present, the evidence indicates that plausible meaning appears to affect parsing only (if at all) when the sentence is misparsed and needs to be reanalyzed. There is not much to be said about the converse issue. While it would seem that certain syntactic operations must be done before serious construction of meaning is computed (e.g., assignment of subject-verb-object relationships), little is known about whether syntactic construction is prior to semantic construction or just separate from it.

We would like to conclude on a note of cautious optimism. While our present knowledge of how sentences are read is meager, the basic outline is in place. The information flow appears to be primarily bottom up, going from words to syntactic structures to semantic structures. In addition, a significant number of interesting psycholinguistic theories are appearing that give reasonable accounts of how various parts of sentence understanding are carried out. Moreover, a variety of interesting paradigms have been developed to get at important issues. In particular, we feel that eye movements are a valuable index of syntactic and semantic processing. Our prediction is that substantial progress will be made in sentence understanding in the next 10 years. If this book is revised, this may be the chapter that will need the most substantial revision.

CHAPTER EIGHT
REPRESENTATION OF DISCOURSE

In the last chapter the focus was on how words are put together to form sentences. Presumably the product of this understanding is something we might term "the meaning of the sentence." We now move ahead to the question of how sentences (or their components) are put together to form "the meaning of the text" that is being read.

Most discussions of this topic emphasize that the meaning of the text is more than the sum of the meaning of the individual sentences. First, consider the following pair of sentences.

John went into the jewelry store. Mary enjoyed the present. (8.1)

The sentences are clear, but the reader has to "fill in" the information that John bought a present and gave it to Mary to make the ideas connect. This kind of filling in is common in normal discourse.

Second, consider the following passage (Bransford and Johnson 1972):

The procedure is actually quite simple. First you arrange things into different groups. Of course, one pile may be sufficient depending on how much there is to do. If you have to go somewhere else due to lack of facilities, that is the next step, otherwise you are pretty well set. It is important not to overdo things.

That is, it is better to do too few things rather than too many. In the short run this may not seem important but complications can easily arise. A mistake can be expensive as well. At first the whole procedure will seem complicated. Soon, however, it will become just another facet of life. It is difficult to forsee any end to the necessity for this task in the immediate future, but then one can never tell. After the procedure is completed one arranges the materials in groups again. Then they can be put into their appropriate places. Eventually they will be used once more and the whole cycle will have to be repeated. However, this is part of life.   (8.2)

While one understands the meaning of each sentence (in some sense), the passage as a whole is meaningless. On the other hand, if one knows it is describing "doing your laundry," it becomes meaningful. This indicates that comprehension is more than just understanding the literal relations between objects and the temporal sequence of events, and that some sort of broader pragmatic real-world knowledge must be used, which includes plans and intentions and causation. Similar types of knowledge are needed, of course, to fill in the information in example 8.1.

There is little controversy about what has been said so far. Where the arguments start is on the relation between this higher order meaning (such as what doing laundry is all about) and the smaller-scale information such as knowing that object X is on top of object Y and event A occurred before event B. In other words, everyone agrees that real-world knowledge has to actively intervene in reading in order for comprehension to take place; the question is how.

One position is that the higher-order information drives the whole system. A currently popular view is that there are long-term memory representations that are variously called *schemas, scripts,* or *frames* and that all information is understood in terms of filling information into those schemas. In the laundry example, if the passage were titled "Laundry," the title would activate your laundry schema, which would contain a scenario of having dirty laundry, putting it in bags or baskets, putting it in the washer, adding soap, etc.; all the information in the text would be understood in terms of fitting it into that memory structure. A central problem for schema theory is where the reader gets the schema to guide his or her comprehension. Often, it is not announced by a title or opening sentence. Moreover, when the text is not describing a stereotyped experience such as doing laundry, the reader is unlikely to have a prestored schema. (We will discuss schema theory in detail in the second half of the chapter.)

A second position (one with which we are more sympathetic) is that there may be more "local" structures built up largely through using syntax, the literal meaning of words, and general heuristics of discourse. These local structures would then periodically get amalgamated into the more global or schematic meaning of the passage. A currently popular theory of discourse processing by Kintsch and van Dijk (1978) uses the terms *microstructure* and *macrostructure* for the local and global levels of representation, respectively. We will adopt their terms, although our use may be somewhat different from theirs.

We feel that, at present, a complete theory of how the meaning of discourse is represented is far beyond our grasp. The meaning of even so short and artificial example as "Laundry" would probably include visual images of laundry, some model about how clothes go from dirty to clean, feelings about doing laundry, knowledge about how laundry relates to the rest of life, and so forth. Moreover, "the meaning" of most prose would include some representation of the style, the position of the author on the subject, and many other factors. In fact, most theories of discourse representation concentrate on one aspect of how meaning is represented and ignore the others. Thus, we believe that a more atheoretic treatment is justified.

The research on discourse can be divided into two major areas. The first focuses on how meaning is constructed as the reader moves along in the text. As our examples indicated, such construction implies that inferences (large and small) must be made in order to understand the text. Research in the area concentrates on asking *when* inferences are made and *what kinds of information* are important in making these inferences. The second focuses on understanding the structure of the mental representation that has been built up as a result of reading. Researchers seeking to discover the structure of completed mental representations usually have inferred the structure from the reader's memory of discourse.

We will discuss the construction of meaning first. The common thread in this research is that meaning is constructed by connecting the sentence being read to the memory representation of the prior text and by the knowledge that the reader brings to the situation. A formalization of this idea is called the *given-new contract* (Clark and Haviland 1977; Haviland and Clark 1974). According to Clark and Haviland, there is a "contract" between speaker and listener or between writer and reader that each new unit of discourse (presumably a sentence) is conveying something new (or else why bother saying anything?). In order for the new idea to make any sense, however, it must tie in with what has been going on. Therefore, according to the given-new contract, virtually all sentences have a "given" part that makes reference to some prior part of the discourse (although perhaps not explicitly) and a "new" part, which is the sentence's additional contribution to the reader's knowledge.

Clark and Haviland proposed that this given-new contract lies at the heart of understanding each sentence's relation to the ongoing discourse. Using the given-new contract as a framework, they further proposed a general strategy for connecting a sentence to the prior discourse. It has three components: (1) finding out which part of the sentence is the "given" and which is the "new"; (2) finding what the "given" refers to; and (3) attaching the "new" to that place in the discourse structure.

Much of the work on the given-new contract has focused on the first component. Clark and Clark (1977) claim that there are linguistic conventions that allow a reader to determine, just from reading a sentence, which part is given and which is new. For example, they cite several types of conventions that indicate given versus new information. One is passive versus active sentences, so that in 8.3a

The boy hit the ball. (8.3a)
The ball was hit by the boy. (8.3b)

the boy is assumed to be the given information and the ball is the new information, while in 8.3b the opposite is true. One test for which information is given and which is new is to think of the sentences as answers to questions. In this case, 8.3a is the more natural way to answer "What did the boy hit?" while 8.3b is the more natural way to answer "Who hit the ball?".

The above example suggests that word order may play a part, and that the material in the beginning of the sentence tends to be the given information. However, there are other ways of indicating given versus new. For example, in

It was the boy who was hitting the ball. (8.3c)

the boy is now the new information. Moreover, in speech, stress can change the listener's interpretation, so that in *The BOY hit the ball.* if *The BOY* is stressed, it is probably the new information.

Many of the experiments on this topic ask the reader (or listener) to indicate which is the given or new information. Most of the research has focused on demonstrating that readers usually identify the given or new information as the theory would predict. Thus, there has been little work on how these judgments are made on-line. Another kind of demonstration of the given-new contract involves presenting a short passage that appears to violate the given-new contract, such as

The preacher had made meticulous plans. (8.4a)
It was the preacher who shot the old man. (8.4b)

and showing that readers have difficulty in processing the second sentence.

The bulk of the research we are about to discuss, however, assumes that the given-new contract conventions are observed. Even when the conventions are not violated (as they are in 8.4), the reader is still often faced with the decision of whether a concept refers back to prior material or whether it is new. In addition, when a decision is made that some segment of text is given (i.e., refers to the prior discourse), the reader is faced with deciding which prior material is being referred to. The central question in the next section is how and when these decisions are made.

We will begin by discussing the simplest kind of connection, *anaphora*—the identification of a noun or pronoun with a previously mentioned noun or noun phrase. In discussing both this process and more complex inferences, it will be useful to distinguish between several types of knowledge that might be drawn upon. The first is what we will call the literal meaning of a sentence. That would include the literal meanings of words as well as meanings that could be inferred from the structure of the sentence, such as identification of the agent, recipient of the action, and relationships among things (such as relations among concepts or actions in time and space). A second source would be grammatical rules that govern, for example, the use of *a* or *the* in bridging concepts from different sentences. A third would be general "rules of discourse" that are tacit contracts between the writer and reader about what is an easy way to express something. One example would be not using a pronoun to refer to someone who hasn't been mentioned for several pages. These "rules" would not be as strict as grammatical rules because one is unlikely to specify what gap between pronoun and noun distinguishes acceptable from unacceptable usage. Rather, these rules are likely to be "rules of thumb" based on factors such as short-term memory limitations, notions of what types of ideas are generally expressed in print, and perhaps cultural norms. Lastly, there is specific real-world knowledge (*pragmatics*), such as the knowledge that gifts are bought in stores, that allows you to connect the sentences in 8.1.

It is conceivable that all of these forms of knowledge are used in drawing inferences, and some models of reading assume that they are (Rumelhart 1975). However, some forms of knowledge may be more accessible or easier to apply, so that, given the time pressures of reading, some may be rarely used, or used only as a back-up if all else fails. We will attempt to summarize our current knowledge about how such inferences are drawn.

As we discuss various studies, it will become apparent that none of the available techniques used to study inferences are free of criticism. The major issue is when inferences are made. In the technique that is most widely employed, the relationship between the prior text and a target sentence is varied, and the inferential processing is assumed to be reflected in the time to read the target sentence (Graesser 1981; O'Brien, Duffy, and Myers 1986). This technique, however, can only diagnose the locus of inferential processing in certain circumstances. While the other techniques used have their own flaws, the results of a number of studies (using diverse techniques) dealing with several types of inferences are consistent in the conclusions reached. We will begin by discussing anaphor and then move to other types of inferences. The types of inferences that we will discuss are not exhaustive, but are representative of the inferences a person is called upon to make when reading text.

MAKING CONNECTIONS: THE BUILDING BLOCK OF COHERENT DISCOURSE

Anaphora

Text would not make sense if each new sentence discussed concepts unrelated to those in prior sentences. While one doesn't need to repeat words in order for the reader to be able to form a connection (see Example 8.1), words are frequently repeated across sentences to help form connections; if a word is not literally repeated, synonyms or pronouns are used instead. While *anaphora,* the process of referring to a prior concept, is an inferential procedure, one may forget that an inference is required since it seems so simple. In all cases when a word is an anaphor, the reader has to decide *which* previous concept is being referenced, and in most cases, decide *whether* a previous concept is indeed being referenced.

Pronouns The task of finding the antecedent for a pronoun is probably the simplest anaphoric task for the reader. In all cases, the pronoun refers to some noun in the discourse, so the reader's task is merely to figure out *which* noun. There are a few cases in which the antecedent appears after the pronoun, such as

Because he was late, Jim started speeding. (8.5)

These cases appear to be somewhat special, however, and the antecedent appears soon afterwards in the same sentence. In our discussion, we will ignore these cases (partly because we are focusing on how sentences are tied together) and assume that the reader's task is deciding which previously cited noun is the antecedent of a pronoun.

How does the reader make this assignment? Grammatical rules come into play. For example, gender obviously determines pronoun assignment: *he* could not refer to a previously mentioned woman. However, pronoun assignment does not always preserve the number of the noun as in "Every week the teacher gives her best pupil *a prize.* She buys *them* in the supermarket." While there are no other strict rules of grammar governing pronominal reference, there are some conventional rules of thumb. One is parallelism of form, so that in the pair of sentences

John lent Jim his car. He also lent him his TV. (8.6)

it is clear that *he* is John and *him* is Jim. However, the rule isn't absolute. In "John lent his car to Bill because he . . . ," *he* could refer to either, as made clear in the following sentences, which are acceptable and readily understandable.

John lent his car to Bill because he needed it. (8.7a)
John lent his car to Bill because he was generous. (8.7b)

Another factor that helps to determine pronoun assignment is the "implicit causality" of the verb in the prior clause. For example, consider

Mary won the money from Helen, because she . . . (8.8a)
Mary punished Helen, because she . . . (8.8b)

In (8.8a), *she* probably refers to *Mary* and in (8.8b), *she* probably refers to *Helen*. These two factors appear to be a little bit "looser" than gender or number assignment in that violation of them would yield sentences that would be strange but not ungrammatical. Caramazza et al. (1977) have shown that people reliably use these discourse cues in reading.

Other factors may also affect assignment of the antecedent to the pronoun. One that has received considerable attention is the distance between the pronoun and the antecedent. In normal text, it is very rare for a pronoun to be separated from its antecedent by more than a few sentences. This suggests that when a pronoun is encountered and the antecedent is not in some sort of short-term memory, the antecedent may be difficult or impossible to find. In fact, Clark and Sengul (1979) found that as the distance between the pronoun and prior antecedent increased, the reading time of the sentence containing the pronoun increased. Since the test sentence (containing the pronoun) is held constant in the comparison, the increase in processing time must be due to greater difficulty in integrating the test sentence with the prior sentences, and is likely a result of greater difficulty in connecting the pronoun to the antecedent when the distance between them is greater.

We will discuss the "distance effect" first, since it has been used to ask a key question about pronoun assignment. Does the reader make the assignment on the fixation on which the pronoun is encoded or later? The second issue that will come up is whether the "distance effect" is really due to a surface variable, such as the number of words (or elapsed time) between the pronoun and its antecedent, or to a deeper structural aspect of the text. As we shall see, the physical distance, itself, is probably irrelevant.

Ehrlich and Rayner (1983) varied the distance between pronoun and antecedent, and attempted to measure the time course of the effect by examining the pattern of eye movements on the sentence that contained the pronoun. There were three levels of distance: *near,* when the noun was the word immediately before the pronoun; *intermediate,* where about a line of text intervened; and *far,* where at least three lines of text intervened. A central purpose of the experiment was to test the *immediacy hypothesis* of Just and Carpenter (1980, see Chapter 5), which states that *all* linguistic operations, such as finding the antecedent of a pronoun, are completed before the eyes move on to the next word. A major problem in this research is identifying the fixation on which the pronoun is encoded, since it is usually fixated much less than half the time. Since the perceptual span extends to the right of the fixated word but not to the left of it (see Chapter 4), Ehrlich and Rayner assumed that if the pronoun was not fixated, then it was encoded on the fixation to the left of the pronoun. That is, the "encoding" fixation for a pronoun was either on the pronoun itself or on the prior word.

There were two major findings. First, the fixation time on the "encoding" fixation was significantly longer (about 20 msec) than the previous one (in all distance conditions), suggesting that the reader was immediately starting to search for the antecedent in all conditions. However, in the immediate and near conditions, the two fixations following the encoding fixation returned to normal length, but those two fixations in the far condition got even longer. Ehrlich and Rayner concluded that the process of searching for the antecedent begins immediately, but in the case of the far condition, the search often continues for another fixation or two.

We should hasten to point out that the first conclusion is only suggestive. The longer fixation time on the encoding fixation may not be due to searching for the anaphoric antecedent, but rather to lexical access taking longer on that fixation. Since different text was seen on the encoding fixation than on the other fixations in the sentence, a comparison of absolute fixation times is not definitive. On the other hand, the difference between the far condition and the other two conditions on the two fixations following the encoding fixation rules strongly against the immediacy hypothesis, if we assume that the distance effect (i.e., the difference in processing time on the target sentence as a function of the distance of the antecedent) is due to differences in time to look up the antecedent. Since at least part of this difference occurs on fixations downstream from the encoding fixation, at least some of the look up process is not immediate.

To summarize, the Ehrlich and Rayner experiment shows that there is at least some delayed effect of distance and thus that the immediacy hypothesis is too simple, but it does not conclusively demonstrate that there is any immediate effect, since the longer "encoding" fixation could be due to factors other than anaphoric reference. Similar findings of delayed distance effects have been reported by Carroll and Slowiaczek (1987), strengthening the case against the immediacy hypothesis.

The distance effect itself appears not to be a universal phenomenon, however. Some experiments by Blanchard (1987) and Carroll and Slowiaczek (1987) failed to find any distance effect (either delayed or not). This led Clifton and Ferreira (1987) to hypothesize that the distance effect may not be a distance effect after all. They noted that distance effects were observed in experiments only when the antecedent noun was no longer the "topic of the discourse" in the far condition and hypothesized that the distance effects (when observed) were due to deeper processing considerations, such as whether the antecedent noun had been kept in some sort of active memory.

Clifton and Ferreira tested this hypothesis using a phrase reading task, in which the reader saw a passage a phrase at a time and pushed a button to get the next phrase to appear. Reading time for a phrase was measured by the time between two button pushes. An example of one of their passages is as follows

> Weddings can be / very emotional experiences for everyone involved. / The cigar smoking caterer / was obviously / on the verge / of tears, / and the others / were pretty upset too. / In fact, / the organist, / who was an old maid, / looked across the room / and sighed. / <u>She was</u> / <u>still looking for</u> / <u>a husband.</u>   (8.9a)

(The slashes indicate the boundaries between phrases.) Of primary interest was the reading time for the underlined target sentence containing the pronoun *she*. In this example, *the organist* is the topic of the sentence prior to the target sentence and thus, according to this explanation, quite available as the antecedent for the *she* in the last sentence. On the other hand, if the middle two sentences are replaced by

> The cigar smoking caterer / was obviously / on the verge of tears, / having just noticed that /the organist, / who was an old maid, / was holding hands / with someone else.   (8.9b)

the organist is no longer the topic of the sentence prior to the target sentence, and thus would be much harder to find as the antecedent of *she*. Clifton and Ferreira also varied how far back in the passage the antecedent *organist* was, and found that distance, per se, had no effect on reading time for the target sentence. In contrast, there was a large effect on reading time for the target sentence, depending on whether the organist was still the topic of discourse. As with the reading experiments measuring eye movements, they found that a large portion of the effect was delayed (i.e., after the phrase containing the pronoun).

To summarize, the research on the distance effect has two major findings. First, the assignment of the antecedent of a pronoun is not always done immediately. Second, it appears that the difficulty of finding the antecedent is only affected by distance indirectly; distance reflects (imperfectly) other deeper factors such as whether the antecedent is still the topic of discourse (Anderson, Garrod, and Sanford 1983; Clifton and Ferreira 1987; Garrod and Sanford 1982, 1985).

The work on the distance effect thus shows that the availability of the noun in memory influences the speed of anaphor assignment. There are other types of discriminative cues that influence the speed of making the anaphor assignment. Vonk (1984) examined two: the gender of the noun and the implicit causality of the verb. Her sentences were similar to the "verb causality" sentences (8.7 and 8.8), except that there were also versions in which gender disambiguated the assignment such as

> Mary won the money from John, because she . . .   (8.10a)
> Mary won the money from Jane, because she . . .   (8.10b)
> John punished Mary, because she . . .   (8.10c)
> Jane punished Mary, because she . . .   (8.10d)

In the experiment, subjects read individual sentences like these (except that they were complete sentences) and immediately afterward named the antecedent as quickly as possible. Eye movements on the sentences were also recorded.

Vonk found that subjects named the correct antecedent virtually all the time, even in sentences like 8.10b and 8.10d, when the gender of the pronoun didn't disambiguate the assignment. Thus, the implicit causality of the verb indeed has powerful effects on pronoun assignment. A very interesting finding emerged from the pattern of fixation times. Vonk distinguished between "first pass times" and "second pass times" (i.e., fixations before and after a regression was made [see Chapter 7]). The first pass times indicated that fixations on the pronoun were longer in 8.10a and 8.10c when the gender information made the antecedent of the pronoun unambiguous (i.e., when the gender of the two names was different) than when it didn't in 8.10b and 8.10d. In contrast, first pass fixation times on the verb phrase following the pronoun, as well as second pass fixation times on the entire sentence, were longer when gender did not disambiguate the antecedent of the pronoun.

Vonk's results are consistent with the following simple hypothesis. Readers assign the antecedent of the pronoun as soon as it is fixated when gender cues determine the antecedent (thereby lengthening that fixation); whereas the assignment is delayed when readers rely on implicit causality (lengthening fixations downstream). While things might not be quite that simple, the data compel us to conclude that the act of pronoun assignment is more immediate when gender is the cue than when the implicit causality of the verb is the cue.

The bulk of the data thus indicate that the process of assigning the antecedent of a pronoun is often delayed beyond the fixation on which the pronoun is encoded. This makes sense: if the pronoun is placed in short-term memory when lexical access is complete, there is no reason to keep looking at it. As long as lexical access is reasonably autonomous from higher-order processes (as we have argued in prior chapters), the reader should be able to identify subsequent words while looking up the antecedent of the pronoun. However, when gender cues are used, the lengthened fixation time on the pronoun itself indicates that look-up processes *can* have immediate effects on eye-movement behavior.

In summary, pronominal reference is governed not only by linguistic rules but by a looser set of discourse guidelines, which are based on the type of verb, parallelism of form, and whether the noun is still the topic of discourse. Most of the experiments show that at least some of the process of assigning the antecedent is done on fixations after the one on which the pronoun is encoded and slows down processing on these later fixations. However, Vonk's work suggests that, in the case of using gender cues, much of the assignment may be done on the fixation on which the pronoun is encoded. It is not clear whether that difference is due to a qualitative difference in the way gender information is used or merely because the gender information can be used more quickly.

Let us close this section with a few comments. The first is, as Vonk argues, that semantic information is used quite quickly. Since fixations are longer on the pronoun when the two names have different genders, the gender information must be processed and accessed at the time the pronoun is fixated. Since the pronoun in examples 8.10 is only two words after the second name, this information is registered in at most two fixations, or at most about half a second. The second comment is that the Vonk technique, while interesting, may overstate the immediacy of processing. Since the stimuli were single sentences and the central task was to make the pronoun assignment, readers may have done so more quickly than they would have in ordinary silent reading. The third is that we have not said why processing is slowed on later fixations because of anaphoric search. The simplest possibility is that the process that is creating the discourse structure eventually needs to have the assignment made in order to continue and it stops lexical access until the antecedent is located.

Noun or Concept Repetition

When a noun is encountered in discourse, the reader does not generally know if it has an antecedent. The literal repetition of nouns or noun phrases often helps to indicate that there is an anaphoric relationship. For example, in the passage

> Zak hopped into a waiting car and sped around the corner. The old car lost a wheel and smashed into the building. (8.11a)

car in the second sentences is the same car as in the first. However, literal repetition of a noun in successive sentences is not necessarily an anaphoric reference. In

> Zak hopped into a waiting car and sped around the corner. He swerved to avoid the parked car and smashed into the building. (8.11b)

the car in the two sentences is different.

There are clearly grammatical rules that help the reader decide if a concept has an antecedent in the text. The most common is the use of the definite article *the* or the indefinite article *a* or *an*. For example, in the first passage, if the second sentence started out with "An old car," the car in the second sentence could not be the same as in the first. However, the choice of an article in the second passage is not so simple. While referring to "a parked car" would be unambiguous and perhaps a bit clearer, the second passage is certainly acceptable. Thus, while the indefinite article almost certainly indicates a new concept, the definite article does not always refer to an old one. Indeed, there are many situations where the definite article is naturally used for new concepts.

> Mary looked for shallots in her local grocery store. Eventually she found them in the biggest supermarket in town. (8.12)

Here, *a* would be unacceptable before *biggest*.

In the "Zak" examples (taken from Yekovich and Walker 1978), the process by which one sorts out whether the car in the second sentence is the same as in the first is by no means simple. To figure out that "the parked car" is different from the first car calls for the pragmatic knowledge that when Zak is swerving, he is still probably driving the first car (since no other has been mentioned and therefore the car being hit must be a different car). For example, in the sentences

> Zak hopped into a waiting car and sped around the corner. He screeched to a stop at the curb and leaped out. Jumping into a truck, he swerved to avoid the parked car and smashed into a building.   (8.13)

"the parked car" in the third sentence is probably the same as in the first.

The point of the above discussion is to illustrate that the task of determining whether an object mentioned in a sentence has an antecedent is not always dictated by grammatical rules. The above examples make clear that specific pragmatic knowledge may be needed (at least in some cases). However, there may be general discourse "rules of thumb" that guide the decision.

Yekovich and Walker (1978) investigated whether direct repetition of the word or the article enhanced the ability of the reader to make an anaphoric reference. Subjects read "passages" of two sentences such as

> The accused youth sobbed quietly and asked for (the/an) attorney.
> The attorney examined the statement of the arresting officer.   (8.14)

The technique they used (adapted from Haviland and Clark 1974) was to present the sentences sequentially. A fixed time was allowed for reading the first sentence, but the second sentence was exposed until the subject indicated (by pushing a button) that it had been comprehended. The critical dependent variable was the comprehension time of the second sentence. Yekovich and Walker found that subjects took significantly longer reading the second sentence when the first sentence referred to "an attorney" rather than "the attorney." However, if the pair of sentences was instead

> The contented mother rocked slowly and hummed (the/a) tune. The tune soothed the temper of the fussy newborn.   (8.15)

it took no longer to read the second when "a tune" was in the first sentence than when "the tune" was.

Thus, the effect here is not due to the mere repetition of the word *the*, since the effect depended on the verb. "Hummed" and the other verbs like it are *directive;* they presuppose that a particular object is being acted on—a particular tune is being hummed or a particular rock is thrown. In contrast, "wanting an attorney" does not presuppose a particular attorney is wanted.

Thus, if the verb presupposes that a particular exemplar is intended in the first sentence, repetition of *the* does not facilitate the connection.

A later experiment (Schustack, Ehrlich, and Rayner 1987) studied anaphora by manipulating the distance between the antecedent and the *target* noun (e.g., floor). (In the near condition the antecedent floor was in the sentence prior to the target floor, while in the far condition one sentence intervened between the two.) When subjects read the passages, gaze durations on the target word were about 20 msec shorter when floor appeared in the previous sentence than when it appeared one sentence further back. (Subjects also skipped the target word more when the antecedent was closer.)

To diagnose the locus of processing underlying the distance effect, they ran another experiment in which the same passages were used, but the measure was different: subjects had to name the target word aloud. This was a word-by-word reading task (subjects pushed a button to get the next word), and when the target word appeared, there were asterisks next to it, indicating that it was the word to be named. If one assumes that naming does not tap discourse integration processes (see the discussion in Chapter 7), it should be possible to determine whether the distance effect is tapping lexical access or the difficulty of making an inference. In fact, distance had no effect on the time to name the target word, indicating that distance did not affect lexical access but instead affected discourse processing. That is, more distant prior mention of floor didn't appear to affect the time to retrieve the word, but did affect the time to integrate it into the structure of the text.

Schustack, Ehrlich and Rayner (1987) also varied the predictability of the target word by using either specific or general verbs immediately prior to the second mention of the target (e.g., "swept the floor" versus "cleaned the floor"). In contrast to distance, predictability had equal effects on gaze duration and naming time, indicating that predictability was affecting lexical access time (perhaps through intralexical priming). In addition, the effects of predictability and distance were additive. As mentioned in Chapter 1, Sternberg's "additive factors" logic suggests that if two effects are additive, they are influencing different stages of processing. These data thus provide converging evidence that distance is in fact affecting discourse integration stages (such as the ability to make anaphoric connections).

Two qualifications are needed. First, the experiment only allows us to conclude that the distance of the prior mention influences discourse integration; prior mention itself may affect lexical access as well. To conclude that prior mention, per se, had no effect on lexical access, one would have to compare naming times when there was no prior mention with when there was prior mention. In fact, there is reason to believe that prior mention should have some priming ability at the distances involved in the experiment (Stanners et al, 1979). Second, as with pronoun work, the distance effect may not be due to distance. In the distant conditions, the target word was no longer the focus, but in the near conditions it was.

Another technique used for studying anaphora is to vary the degree of association between a noun and its antecedent. Garrod and Sanford (1977) employed sentences like

> A (robin/goose) would sometimes wander into the house. The *bird* was attracted by the larder. (8.16)

and measured the reading time for each sentence. They found that the reader in fact took longer to read the second sentence when the concept in the first sentence (*goose*) was more distantly related to *bird*.

Garrod and Sanford also investigated the case where there is no anaphoric relation (such as the "Zak" example 8.11). They contrasted sentences like

> A (bus/tank) came roaring round the corner. (8.17)
> A pedestrian was nearly killed by the *vehicle*. (a)
> It nearly smashed some *vehicles*. (b)
> It nearly hit a horse-drawn *vehicle*. (c)

If (a) is the second sentence, *vehicle* refers to *bus* or *tank,* while if (b) or (c) is the second sentence, it doesn't. They found a relatedness effect (*bus* versus *truck*) of almost 100 msec in (a), a reduced relatedness effect of 50 msec in (b), and virtually no relatedness effect in (c). They used (c) to argue that the relatedness effect was in fact tapping anaphoric reference rather than semantic priming: if the effect was coming from better priming of *vehicle* by *bus* than *tank,* then one should obtain a relatedness effect in all three conditions.

The key question they attempted to answer is whether readers search through memory for an antecedent even when there is none. They used the relatedness effect as an indicator of whether readers were going back to "tank" or "bus." The data from conditions (b) and (c) suggest that there is no simple answer to the question. Condition (c) indicates that when the surrounding context (*horse-drawn*) makes it clear that *vehicle* is something new, no search is made, but when the context is less constraining as in (b), search is made some of the time, resulting in a reduced relatedness effect.

Thus, the Garrod and Sanford (1977; Sanford and Garrod 1981) experiments indicate that the decision to search for an anaphoric antecedent is influenced by something about the surrounding context. However, the data do not make clear what is involved in the decision to either initiate search or not initiate search. One possibility is that the decision to initiate search is provoked by an automatic mechanism similar to priming: some sort of spreading activation between one node in the lexicon (e.g., "bus") and another (e.g., "vehicle") signals the reader that a related concept has been read recently. It then may be that an "editing" mechanism at a higher level will cancel the search quickly if it becomes clear that *bus* can not be the antecedent of *horse-drawn vehicle*.

Let us summarize the points we have made about anaphora. First, while there are grammatical rules that regulate how anaphoric connections are made, the decision about whether there is an antecedent (in the case of nouns) and the decision about what the antecedent is (in the case of both nouns and pronouns) usually can not be made solely on the basis of such rules. Much of the decision about which prior noun (if any) is the antecedent is governed either by general heuristics (such as parallelism of form) or specific pragmatic knowledge. Second, it is firmly established that at least some of the process of making the anaphoric link is delayed past the fixation on which the pronoun is encountered. While Vonk's experiment shows that at least some of the linkage is done on the encoding fixation when gender is the selection cue, it is yet to be determined in other cases whether any of the anaphoric linkage is done on the encoding fixation. Finally, it appears that the difficulty of making an anaphoric linkage is influenced by complex features of ongoing processing rather than simple features such as the number of words between the target noun or pronoun and its antecedent. Two variables that have been documented are whether the antecedent is still the topic of discourse and the semantic relatedness between the target and the antecedent. We will return later to discuss experiments that probe the processes by which anaphoric antecedents are searched if they are not immediately available.

Inference

So far we have discussed the simplest kind of connection (anaphora), in which a word refers back to a single word. However, as indicated in our first example (8.1), it is common for text to demand of the reader that an inference be made. We touched on this question at the beginning of the chapter with our example of a pair of sentences in which the reader has to "fill in" some information. The classic experiments of Haviland and Clark (1974) demonstrated that with a pair of sentences such as

> Last Christmas Emily went to a lot of parties.
> This Christmas she got very drunk again. (8.18a)

as compared to

> Last Christmas Emily became absolutely smashed.
> This Christmas she got very drunk again. (8.18b)

the second sentence takes longer to read when the reader has to draw an inference (as in the former pair). This example indicates that at least some of the inference needed to bridge the gap must be made while reading the second sentence; if the reader made all of the inferences during the first sentence, then there would be no reason that the second sentence would take longer in the first pair.

Much of the research on inference has been concerned with the issue of *when* the reader constructs an inference. The conclusion that will emerge is that readers are cautious: in general they appear to wait until they have to make an inference before doing so. We should note that there are many kinds of inferences that a reader might make when reading text; however, due to space limitations, we will concentrate on only three types of inference: *instrumental, elaborative,* and *causal.*

Instrumental inference An opportunity for making an instrumental inference is presented by the sentence "The man swept the floor."; if one infers that a broom had been used for sweeping, then one has made an instrumental inference. The conclusion drawn from the early work on instrumental inference was that such inferences were in fact routinely drawn. Unfortunately, the conclusion was premature since the memory technique employed is seriously flawed (Alba and Hasher 1983; McKoon and Ratcliff 1981, 1986; Singer 1979).

In the typical experiment (e.g., Anderson and Ortony 1975; Paris and Lindauer 1976), the subject is asked to read a passage which might contain a sentence such as "The container held the apples." or "He was stirring the soup." At the end of the passage, the subject is given a cue word such as *basket* (for the first example) and asked to recall the sentence containing the idea. The basic finding is that subjects are quicker to recall the sentence given *basket* than given *bottle* (another type of container). The difference is ascribed to the subjects making the inference that the container is a basket at the time of reading the sentence. However, another interpretation is that the effect is due to differential ability to find "container" in memory at the time of recall.

Singer (1980) attempted to distinguish between the two hypotheses by varying the "forward" and "backward" associative strengths between the cue and the target. For example, in the sentence with "stirring soup," the forward association to the cue *spoon* is strong, while the reverse association is weak; on the other hand, the forward association from "stirring soup" to *ladle* is weak while the association from *ladle* to "stirring soup" is strong. If an instrumental inference was producing the differences in cued recall, one would expect that the strength of the forward association (from "stirring soup" to the instrument) should predict the efficacy of the cue. Instead, he found that the backward associations (from the instrumental cues to "stirring soup") predicted the ease of recall, indicating that the cued recall task was mainly tapping search processes at the time of recall.

As a result of the difficulties with the memory technique, Singer (1979) studied instrumental inference using the same reading time technique mentioned several times earlier. Subjects read pairs of sentences such as

The boy cleared the snow with a shovel. The shovel was heavy.

(8.19a)

The boy cleared the snow from the stairs. The shovel was
heavy.   (8.19b)

and the reading time for the second sentence was recorded. In fact, reading
time for the second sentence was longer in 8.19b than in 8.19a, indicating
that integrating *shovel* with the prior sentence was more difficult when it
was not explicitly mentioned. Singer reasoned that if readers had inferred
"shovel" while reading the first sentence of 8.19b, then there should have
been no difference.

Unfortunately, this is not a particularly sensitive technique for detecting whether instrumental inferences are ever made upon encountering the
first sentence. The observed difference in reading times could be due to
readers making inferences only some of the time or even making inferences
all the time, but not creating as strong a representation in memory as if the
word was present. A second set of experiments (Dosher and Corbett 1982)
probed for instrumental inference using the "Stroop task" (see Chapter 3).
In these experiments, subjects read sentences like the first sentence of 8.19b.
Immediately afterward, a probe word appeared that was either a semantic
associate of "shovel" or an unrelated word. The probe word was written in
colored ink and the subjects' task was to name the color as rapidly as
possible.

The logic of this technique is a bit like that of priming. It has been
shown that the time to name the color of a probe word is slowed down if a
semantic associate of the word has immediately preceded the target word
(presumably because the name of the probe word is then more available to
interfere with the color name). However, Corbett and Dosher found in
several experiments that when a semantic associate of "shovel" was used as
the probe word, there was no effect on the color naming time. Thus, it
appeared that the concept "shovel" was in no way activated by reading such
a sentence. In addition, they asked subjects to recall the sentences later, and
found that they rarely recalled the instrument as being present in the
sentence when it was not.

Their only positive evidence for subjects making instrumental inferences came from an experiment in which subjects were instructed to make
instrumental inferences. In that case, naming time for the color was affected
by use of a semantic associate of "shovel" as the probe. (Strangely, they
observed facilitation rather than inhibition.) Corbett and Dosher's results
thus indicate that subjects *can* make instrumental inferences but do not
normally choose to do so.

Elaborative inferences   Another type of simple inference that readers might make is to infer a general concept from a specific concept or vice
versa. For example, when *robin* is encountered, does the reader actively
infer that it is a bird? Or conversely, if a general category label such as *bird* is
encountered, does the reader elaborate and attempt to make an
inference as to what type of bird it is? Garrod and Sanford (1977) presented

evidence that suggested that readers automatically make inferences from instances to more general categories but not vice versa. There were four different versions of the pair used in 8.16

> A (robin/goose) would sometimes wander into the house. The *bird*
> was attracted by the larder. (8.20a)
> A *bird* would sometimes wander into the house. The (robin/goose)
> was attracted by the larder. (8.20b)

They found that the second sentence in 8.20a was read much more quickly, indicating that a specific concept in memory is found as the antecedent of a general concept more easily than the converse. Garrod and Sanford pointed out that using the general concept as the antecedent of a specific one (as in 8.20b) is very rare in natural discourse, indicating that there almost may be a qualitative difference between what is going on in 8.20a and 8.20b. They suggested that the cause of the difference is that a memory representation of "bird" is activated by the mention of either *robin* or *goose,* enabling a direct anaphoric link between that active "bird" memory representation and *bird* in 8.20a. However, this is not the only possible explanation. It could be that specific instances are just easier to find in short-term memory than general category labels. What seems clear from their example, however, is that in most cases it is unlikely that readers elaborate specific instances of a general concept (that is, when readers see *bird,* they are unlikely to think of a specific bird).

The work discussed so far suggests that readers usually do not draw *elaborative inferences* (i.e., inferences that enhance or embellish the text). The only case in which there is any suggestion of an inference being drawn is that when readers encounter *robin,* they draw the inference that it is a bird. This seems like a minimal elaborative inference, since it is almost logically necessary to know a robin is a bird in order to understand what *robin* means in the sentence. An elaborative inference that is a bit more complex is inferring a specific instance from a general category label within a fairly constraining context. For example, in the passage

> All the mugger wanted was to steal the woman's money. But when
> she screamed, he stabbed her with his *weapon* in an attempt to quiet
> her. He looked to see if anyone had seen him. He threw the *knife*
> into the bushes, took her money, and ran away. (8.21a)

the inference that the weapon was a knife from "he stabbed her with his weapon" is not a logical inference like knowing that a robin is a bird: the weapon could be an icepick, spear, or any other sharp instrument. However, if you were quizzed before the last sentence as to what you thought the weapon was, you would probably respond "knife."

O'Brien et al. (1988) employed passages such as these to determine whether readers were in fact making such inferences before they got to the sentence containing *knife*. The technique was basically the same as in many of the studies above; reading time on the last sentence was measured and compared with reading time on a passage in which *knife* had been explicitly mentioned previously (e.g., *weapon* was replaced with *knife*). They found that the last sentence took no longer to read when "knife" was implicit than when it had been explicitly mentioned. It thus appears that "knife" has been inferred when *weapon* is used in the second sentence: otherwise it should be more difficult to establish the antecedent for "the knife" in the last sentence.

In contrast, when the second sentence did not strongly suggest "knife,"

> But when she screamed, he assaulted her with his (knife/weapon) in an attempt to quiet her. (8.21b)

the last sentence in 8.21a took longer to read when "knife" was not explicitly mentioned earlier. Thus, it appears that readers do not always draw such elaborative inferences when the context is unclear. O'Brien et al. found that the difference in reading time for the last sentence was due mainly to a longer gaze duration on *knife* when it had not been explicitly mentioned in the second sentence. This finding indicates that the longer reading time for the last sentence when *knife* was not present earlier was in fact due to greater difficulty in finding the antecedent for it. It also demonstrates that the process of searching for the antecedent is *begun* immediately.

Causal inference. A somewhat more complex inference that a reader might draw is a *causal inference*. For example, when reading a passage like

> John was eating in the dining car of a train. The waiter brought him a bowl of soup. Suddenly the train screeched to a halt. The soup spilled in John's lap. (8.22a)

readers undoubtedly make a causal link between the sudden halting of the train and the soup spilling. Before they get to the last sentence, do readers infer that the soup will spill in John's lap? This type of inference is not logical: it might not spill if the bowl isn't very full and it would only spill in his lap if he were sitting down. Yet, the event of the soup spilling seems probable, and furthermore, the narrative seems to be pointing in that direction.

Duffy (1986) distinguished three possibilities of how such a causal link might be drawn. The first is *backward inference:* the reader waits until getting to the soup-spilling sentence before searching back in the text for the cause or explanation of the event. The second is *specific expectation:* the reader generates a specific expectation or prediction from the first three sentences that the soup is going to spill, which is confirmed by the fourth sentence. The third is *focusing,* in which certain aspects of the text advertise themselves as likely to be followed up, so that when something comes up that has no transparent precedent, these focused items in memory are assumed to be the appropriate places to find the rationale for what follows. One might view the focus model as the reader using mental "highlighter" on some sentences in memory.

In one experiment, Duffy presented subjects with passages like the one above. For example in 8.22a, they read the first three sentences and then were shown the fourth sentence and asked to judge if it was a good continuation of the passage. The control passage had a different third sentence

The train began to slow down entering a station. (8.22b)

which makes the causal link less likely but still possible. Unsurprisingly, readers took less time in judging that the fourth sentence was an appropriate continuation in the first ("screeching to a halt") version of the passage, indicating that they were making a causal inference at some point. What was of greater interest was that when the fourth sentence was not a good continuation, such as,

That night the whole forest burned down. (8.22c)

readers were quicker to judge that it was not a good continuation in 8.22a. This appears to rule out the backward inference model. If readers made such causal inferences merely searching back from the last sentence, then the time to judge that 8.22c was not a good continuation should have been the same, since there was nothing about fires in either version of the passage.

Instead, the difference indicates that readers are doing something active to the text that is shaping how they will process the next sentence they encounter. But are they actually generating a specific prediction of what is coming up next? Duffy assessed this by using a probe memory test. Subjects read passages like the "soup" passage, and then after either the "screeched to a halt" or "slow down" sentence, they got a single probe word (*soup*) and judged whether it had been in the passage or not. The idea is that if the "screeched to a stop" sentence generated a specific prediction of soup spilling, "soup" should have been more available and hence easier to judge that it had been in the passage. In fact, there was no difference between the two conditions, indicating that such an inference was not made.

Duffy's data thus suggest that the process of causal inference in reading is complex. It is neither sitting back and waiting until you don't understand why something is true and then searching, nor is it making best guesses about what is going to happen as you go along. Instead, it appears to be a process of highlighting information that you are likely to need later for future linkage. What indicates to the reader that the "screeching train" sentence should be highlighted? In this case, it seems to be important because the topic apparently has been changed from the meal to the train, even though there has been no closure on the eating episode. Thus, the reader seems to be warned that the "screeching train" will somehow be important.

To summarize, the reader appears to be quite cautious about making inferences (Corbett and Dosher 1978; Duffy 1986; McKoon and Ratcliff 1986; Singer 1979; Singer and Ferreira 1983). Even such "obvious" elaborative inferences as instrumental inferences do not appear to be made most of the time. Instead, readers appear to make inferences only when they have to: that is, when they have to decide how the current text ties in with what has come before. Why are readers so cautious? One possibility is that reading is demanding enough of processing resources even without elaborative inferences; there are words to be encoded, sentences to be parsed, and anaphoric antecedents to be searched. A second possibility is that the costs of being wrong outweigh the benefits of being right. Many inferences that seem "obvious" when you know the answer are not in fact so obvious: the weapon didn't have to be a knife; the sentence didn't have to be about soup spilling (it could have been about an accident or about robbers closing in on the train). It seems likely that most real text is constructed so that there are very few sentences that merely confirm inferences that the reader has already made. Rather, as the "given-new" contract suggests, each sentence adds a new idea that the reader must tie in with what has gone on before.

Given the "minimal effort" view in the above paragraph, why does the reader bother to highlight certain passages? The answer may be that it is a good compromise between doing nothing and having to generate specific hypotheses. It may take little effort, and the hypothesis that something is likely to be used later on will be right much more often than a specific hypothesis about how it will be used. Clearly, much research is needed on what causes something to be "focused" (i.e., targeted for future use) and how backward search processes are influenced by what is focused. The Duffy experiment indicates that causal inferences make use of such focusing, and our earlier discussion of anaphora involving pronouns suggests that such focusing may be responsible for "distance effects" there as well. Thus, focusing may be an important component of a wide range of processes linking the "given" part of a sentence to its appropriate antecedent.

The O'Brien et al. (1988) experiment indicates that elaborative inferences are drawn *some* of the time. When their passages were constructed to "hit the reader over the head" with the plausibility of the inference, elaborative inferences were drawn. However, in their other passages (where the inferences were still reasonably plausible), the data indicated that readers were not making elaborative inferences.

Reinstatement and Memory Search

Our discussion so far has concentrated on the issues of: (a) the cues that are used by the reader to make an anaphoric or inferential connection;

(b) the immediacy with which the connection is made; and (c) the extent to which inferences are drawn by the reader before they need to be. In this section, we will concentrate on how such connections are made. In order to make the processes involved during the connection more transparent, the research has dealt with how connections are made when reinstatement of the earlier material is necessary.

Reinstatement means that the prior material was not in short-term memory so that a presumably effortful and/or time-consuming operation is necessary to reactivate or reinstate it into short-term memory. Clearly, at our present state of knowledge, we never know for sure if a certain word or phrase is in short-term memory. Studies of reinstatement have generally tried to ensure that material needs reinstatement by (a) making sure it is at least several sentences back; (b) making sure it is no longer the current topic of discourse; and/or (c) using a theory of discourse processing to predict whether the material is in short-term memory.

The process of reinstatement was touched on when we discussed the "distance effect" with pronouns or repeated nouns. There, it appeared that the reader took more time to read a target word or phrase if the anaphor was no longer part of the topic of discourse. A particularly striking example of topic change causing reinstatement is provided in a series of experiments by Lesgold, Roth, and Curtis (1979). They presented (for example) a narrative involving a woman driving some children to a picnic and seeing smoke coming from the forest. In some versions, there was a topic change—an incident about a bee flying around in the car—followed by a target sentence that was about the forest being on fire. Lesgold, Roth, and Curtis found that reading times on the target sentence were substantially longer when the target sentence was preceded by the irrelevant passage, indicating that subjects were taking substantial time searching memory for the antecedent statements suggesting a fire. Similar results indicating that reinstatement of old material takes time were also found by Cirilo (1981), Cirilo and Foss (1980) and Miller and Kintsch (1980).

The process of reinstatement raises several questions. First, exactly what is reinstated? Is it merely the word or concept that is specifically referred to in the target sentence or is it something larger, such as the clause or "idea" that contains the concept? Second, how does the reader search through inactive memory to find the material to reinstate? Third, how long does the reinstatement last? Is the material just reinstated long enough to make the link or is it held longer? Since there may not be general answers to the above questions (as different anaphorical relations may be handled differently), the experimental results we discuss should be viewed only as suggestive. The experiments have an interest beyond the specific conclusions, however, since they involve creative methods for getting at the more general questions.

Dell, McKoon, and Ratcliff (1983) attempted to probe the details of reinstatement using a priming paradigm. Subjects were asked to read short passages such as 8.23. (A new word appeared every 250 msec.) In addition, subjects were told that at times the text would disappear and a single word would be presented, which they were to name as fast as possible. Of major interest was when the word to be named appeared early in the paragraph and was reinstated later.

> A *burglar* surveyed the garage set back from the street. Several milk bottles were piled at the curb. The banker and her husband were away on vacation. The$_1$ criminal$_2$ slipped$_3$ away$_4$ from the$_5$ streetlamp.$_6$ (8.23)

In the passage above, for example, the anaphoric relation of interest was between the critical word *burglar* in the first sentence and the word *criminal* in the fourth sentence. The idea is that if "burglar" is reinstated by *criminal,* then the naming time for *burglar* should be faster than if it was not reinstated. To provide a control, some subjects saw the passage with an alternative fourth sentence: "A cat slipped away from the streetlamp." To measure the time course of reinstatement, the probe *burglar* would be presented at any of the points in the last sentence indicated by the numbers 1 through 6; faster naming time at one of the points for *burglar* in the "criminal" version than in the "cat" version would be taken as evidence that the concept "burglar" had been reactivated by that point.

Dell, McKoon, and Ratcliff found evidence for reactivation of "burglar" at positions 2 and 3, indicating it was reinstated quite soon after seeing *criminal.* Of equal interest were the naming times to the "companion" word *garage,* which was in the clause containing *burglar* in the first sentence. If naming times to *garage* are also lowered after seeing *criminal* in the last sentence, that would be evidence that more than the concept "burglar" is reinstated. In fact, Dell, McKoon and Ratcliff found faster naming time at positions 2 and 3 for *garage* in the "criminal" version, indicating that a larger unit such as a clause had been reinstated. However, they found that the priming effect for *garage* went away at positions 5 and 6, whereas the priming effect for *burglar* did not. Hence, it appears that the larger idea is only reinstated briefly and the more specific concept "burglar" is reinstated for a longer period of time.

The inclusion of the *garage* probe also rules out an alternative explanation of the data. A priori, faster naming times to *burglar* could have been due to lexical priming between "criminal" and "burglar." However, the faster naming times to *garage* can not be due to any lexical priming from "criminal." While it is possible that "garage" is reinstated but not "burglar," it seems quite implausible. Thus, the faster naming times to *burglar* and *garage* are almost certainly both due to reinstatement of a unit of text that includes them both.

O'Brien (1987) and O'Brien and Myers (1985) also investigated the nature of the search process during reinstatement. O'Brien (1987) employed passages in which a sentence near the end could reinstate either an early or late target concept. [As with Dell, McKoon, and Ratcliff the target was a specific concept (e.g., "major") that was reinstated by a superordinate (e.g., "officer").] O'Brien took great care to ensure that neither the early nor the late target concept would be in short-term memory prior to reinstatement: even the late target sentence was several sentences back from the point of reinstatement; neither target was related to the focus of the discourse; and an analysis using the model of Kintsch and van Dijk (see the next section) also indicated that neither would be in short-term memory. To illustrate, one passage was about a newsman arrested by the military of a foreign country, and the *early target* concept was "major" and the *late target* concept was "banker." (In the passage, a major arrests the newsman and a banker shares the cell with him.) There were two possible target sentences at the end of the passage. Both involved a conversation between the newsman (after he was released) and the American ambassador: in one, the ambassador asked the newsman to remember the rank of the arresting officer and in the other to remember the profession of his cellmate.

O'Brien found that the time to read the target sentence was substantially longer when it reinstated the early concept, presumably because the search for the earlier concept took longer. This suggests that search goes backwards through the reader's memory for the text. However, he found that the rated importance of the clause containing the antecedent also influenced reading time. Thus, it appears that the search is not strictly based on recency but may start with more important units of the text and work downward. Further evidence for backward search came from a probe task. When subjects were asked to *verify* short sentences after reading the paragraph (i.e., judge that the meaning of the sentence was contained in the paragraph), subjects were faster to verify the sentence containing *major* when it was reinstated by the last sentence. However, verification times for the sentence before the one containing *major* were unaffected. It thus appears that search does not continue past the target sentence.

O'Brien and Myers (1985) also investigated the effect of reinstatement on memory for the text. They employed the passages used by Ehrlich and Rayner (1981) described in Chapter 7. In these passages, one of two words appeared in a critical position. One of the words was highly predictable from the context and one was not (similar to the example in Table 7.1). For example, a passage might be about a long dry summer and forest rangers, and the key word was either *fires* or *fines*. O'Brien and Myers felt that one reason that reading time for the sentence containing *fines* was longer than for the sentence containing *fires* was that the reader would need to search through the memory of the prior text for some antecedent of *fines*, whereas the antecedent for the predictable word *fires* would be in short-term memory and no search would be needed. They also reasoned that the reactivation of the earlier text during the reinstatement process and the additional connections needed to tie it into the current material should enhance the memory of both the target sentence and the material preceding it.

O'Brien and Myers first looked at reading times to get evidence that subjects were indeed expending more effort when the target word was not predictable. Note that a longer reading time on the unpredictable target word itself is most plausibly explained by longer lexical access time (see Chapter 7). Lexical access time, however, would not plausibly "spill over" to the remaining part of the sentence on the subsequent line. In fact, reading times on the line subsequent to the target word were longer when it was *fines* instead of *fires,* indicating that subjects were doing something extra in the former case. As predicted, they found enhanced memory for both the target sentence and prior sentences (but not for material subsequent to the target sentence) in the *fines* paragraph, indicating that the subject was actively searching backward through the text to find a connection for the unpredictable word, *fines.* In their study, however, there is no single place in the prior text where there is an unambiguous antecedent for the unpredictable word, so that the reader could have connected *fines* to a number of places in the prior text or may not have made any connection at all. Thus, the data leave open the question of whether the enhanced memory for the prior text is due to the search process itself or to making a successful connection.

To summarize, the work on reinstatement indicates that the reinstatement process starts relatively quickly. It also indicates that readers initiate some sort of search process—through their memory representation of the text—that primarily goes from more recent items and works backwards. The search process appears to enhance memory for both the material that initiates the search and the material that is found. (The evidence is ambiguous on whether memory material that is merely searched through is also enhanced.) Lastly, it appears that more than just a single concept is reinstated, although it appears that continuing activation for "companion" material is relatively short lived. We should reiterate that these conclusions are extremely tentative. First, a limited number of reinstatement situations have been studied: a general concept referring back to a specific exemplar, and in the case of O'Brien and Myers, the anphoric situation is fairly vague. Second, the passages used were paragraphs; the strategies that readers employ might change when they read larger segments of discourse.

Before going on to models of discourse processing, we wish to close with a few comments about anaphora and inference. The major thrust of the "given-new contract" is that the reader is continually seeking to connect the text currently being read with what has gone on before. Most of the research we have reviewed has covered some component of how this linkage is accomplished. [A major component of the Kintsch and van Dijk (1978) model presented in the next section is to explicate more formally how the linkage takes place.] While such linkage is a normal state of reading, some parts of text do not refer to anything that has previously occurred. Usually the writer provides a cue for the reader that there is a major change of topic, such as, "Meanwhile, back at the ranch. . . ." or "And now for something really different. . . ." It would appear that a major purpose of such statements is to inform the reader to turn off the search process and to begin building a new discourse structure. [See Ausubel (1960) and Rothkopf (1970) for a fuller discussion of "advanced organizers."]

Another device, which relates to the given-new contract, is the use of phrases like "To summarize . . . " or "In other words . . . ". Here the reader is being told that something is not new or is merely a summary. It is our impression that when such cues are missing, readers often have difficulty in reading text. Why is that the case, since there is no difficulty connecting the new material to the old? It would seem that part of the given-new contract must be that (unless explicitly stated to the contrary) each new sentence is supposed to add something new.

If our argument is valid, it suggests that a second major goal of the reader is to locate and analyze the "new" thing being said, unless instructed to the contrary by a literary device such as in the prior paragraph. Presumably if nothing is new, some sort of "error signal" occurs which produces disruption. This analysis suggests that segments of discourse are continually being monitored for subsegments of "newness." If so, there are interesting questions that could be asked about such a process. One would be about the unit of discourse that is expected to contain a subsegment that is new; is it a sentence or something longer or shorter? Another would be about the reader's criteria for "newness." We doubt that the judgment of newness depends on superficial criteria; good style usually dictates that a summary or restatement phrase the idea in a different way. If so, then a relatively "deep" level of meaning is being continually updated by the reader and used to check for "newness." As far as we know, this has not been a topic of research in reading, but we expect that it could be an interesting one if developed.

DISCOURSE STRUCTURES

So far, we have discussed the processes by which the reader attempts to connect each sentence and concept with what has come before. But why is the reader continually doing this? Presumably, the goal of reading is to extract some sort of coherent structural "meaning" from the text that is related to prior experience and prior mental structures.

Perhaps the most influential theory of how the process of text comprehension takes place is that of Kintsch and van Dijk (1978). A brief presentation of it at this point will be helpful for several reasons. First, in overall outline, it represents a good guess as to how readers process text. Second, a presentation of it will illustrate, given our present level of knowledge, how vague and incomplete such a theory must be. Third, the model has helped to shape some of the more interesting research on discourse processing. After discussing the Kintsch and van Dijk model and research related to it, we will discuss some criticisms of the model and alternative models.

The Kintsch and van Dijk model has been the focus of a great deal of research on discourse processing. This is because it is probably the only model that combines a broad framework with enough specificity to be able to make nonobvious predictions. Its major shortcoming—it oversimplifies many aspects of discourse processing—is in some ways a strength in the present context. That is, it will allow us to give you both a sense of what a "bare-bones" model of discourse processing would look like and what would be needed for a more complete model. It also makes contact with both the processes and products of reading and thus serves as a bridge between the two. In a later version of the theory (van Dijk and Kintsch 1983), there are attempts to remove some of these oversimplifications. The later version is less satisfactory, unfortunately, because it substitutes vagueness for oversimplification, and has had less impact on the field than the earlier version, which we are about to discuss.

Kintsch and van Dijk's Model

As we mentioned at the beginning of the chapter, an important distinction in the model is between *microstructure* and *macrostructure*. Microstructure represents a level of discourse in which elements called "propositions" are put together into a connected structure. This structure is a relatively superficial representation of the text. The macrostructure is the "gist" of the text. It is an edited version of the microstructure tied into "schemas" from long-term memory. It is supposed to be a deeper representation of the text.

The basic two units of analysis in the model are the *argument* and the *proposition* (see Table 8.1). An argument, in essence, is the representation of the meaning of an individual word; practically, synonomous words could be (and usually are) represented by the same argument in the Kintsch and van Dijk representation. A proposition is a unit of meaning roughly corresponding to a phrase or clause. A proposition is a set of arguments joined together with a special argument, a *predicate* (listed first), as the focus. Some propositions represent actions with a verb as the predicate: for example (TEACH, SPEAKER, STUDENT) represents the idea that the speaker is teaching student(s). Other propositions represent adjective noun combinations (VIOLENT, ENCOUNTER) and (ALL, STUDENT). Others represent ideas in phrases such as (OF REALITY, VOICE), others conjoin concepts such as (AND, STUDENT, SPEAKER), and others express location and time (TIME: IN, ENCOUNTER, SUMMER) or (LOCATION: AT, CAL STATE LOS ANGELES). In all cases, the notation not only conveys that the concepts go together but contains some of the meaning. In (TEACH, SPEAKER, STUDENT), for example, TEACH is understood to be the verb, the second argument, SPEAKER, the agent, etc. (See Table 8.1 for examples of propositions.)

As you can see in Table 8.1, a single sentence is usually broken down into several propositions. However, propositions can be defined recursively so that a proposition can have other propositions as arguments. For example, in the proposition (COMPLAIN, STUDENT, 19), *19* stands for the proposition (HARASS, POLICE, STUDENT). Thus, by this recursive

TABLE 8.1 A paragraph and the propositions extracted from it. Lines indicate sentence boundaries. Propositions are numbered for ease of reference and a number in a propositional argument refers to the proposition with that number. (The same numbers appear in Figure 8.1.) Adapted from Kintsch and Van Dijk (1978) with permission from the American Psychological Associaton and the authors.

A series of violent, bloody encounters between police and Black Panther Party members punctuated the early summer days of 1969. Soon after, a group of Black students I teach at California State College, Los Angeles, who were members of the Panther Party, began to complain of continuous harassment by law enforcement officers. Among their many grievances, they complained about receiving so many traffic citations that some were in danger of losing their driving privileges. During one lengthy discussion, we realized that all of them drove automobiles with Panther Party signs glued to their bumpers. This is a report of a study that I undertook to assess the seriousness of their charges and to determine whether we were hearing the voice of paranoia or reality.

PROPOSITION NUMBER	PROPOSITION
1	(SERIES, ENCOUNTER)
2	(VIOLENT, ENCOUNTER)
3	(BLOODY, ENCOUNTER)
4	(BETWEEN, ENCOUNTER, POLICE, BLACK PANTHER)
5	(TIME: IN, ENCOUNTER, SUMMER)
6	(EARLY, SUMMER)
7	(TIME: IN, SUMMER, 1969)
8	(SOON, 9)
9	(AFTER, 4, 16)
10	(GROUP, STUDENT)
11	(BLACK, STUDENT)
12	(TEACH, SPEAKER, STUDENT)
13	(LOCATION: AT, 12, CAL STATE COLLEGE)
14	(LOCATION: AT, CAL STATE COLLEGE, LOS ANGELES)
15	(IS A, STUDENT, BLACK PANTHER)
16	(BEGIN, 17)
17	(COMPLAIN, STUDENT, 19)
18	(CONTINUOUS, 19)
19	(HARASS, POLICE, STUDENT)
20	(AMONG, COMPLAINT)
21	(MANY, COMPLAINT)
22	(COMPLAIN, STUDENT, 23)
23	(RECEIVE, STUDENT, TICKET)
24	(MANY, TICKET)
25	(CAUSE, 23, 27)
26	(SOME, STUDENT)
27	(IN DANGER OF, 26, 28)
28	(LOSE, 26, LICENSE)
29	(DURING, DISCUSSION, 32)
30	(LENGTHY, DISCUSSION)

(continued)

TABLE 8.1 *(Continued)*

PROPOSITION NUMBER	PROPOSITION
31	(AND, STUDENT, SPEAKER)
32	(REALIZE, 31, 34)
33	(ALL, STUDENT)
34	(DRIVE, 33, AUTO)
35	(HAVE, AUTO, SIGN)
36	(BLACK PANTHER, SIGN)
37	(GLUED, SIGN, BUMPER)
38	(REPORT, SPEAKER, STUDY)
39	(DO, SPEAKER, STUDY)
40	(PURPOSE, STUDY, 41)
41	(ASSESS, STUDY, 42, 43)
42	(TRUE, 17)
43	(HEAR, 31, 44)
44	(OR, 45, 46)
45	(OF REALITY, VOICE)
46	(OF PARANOIA, VOICE)

definition, a proposition can stand for a fairly complex thought. As you can see in Table 8.1, many propositions are of this recursive type.

Several comments are in order at this point. The first is that the microstructure is not the list of propositions in Table 8.1, but a structure built out of them. In fact, as we will see presently, much of the theory is about the creation of these structures. The second is that the model says little about how the processor forms these propositions. It relegates lexical access, syntax, and most of the nitty-gritty details that we discussed earlier in the book to "earlier processing"; it merely assumes that propositions are formed—somehow. The third is that while Kintsch and van Dijk have proposed a methodology to aid an experimenter to construct a set of propositions from a corpus of text, the analysis of prose into propositions is quite complex and far from objective. It should also be pointed out that bridging inferences are added, if needed, to the set of propositions actually in the text (e.g., that the present in Sentence 8.1 was bought from the jewelry store). Again, the process by which this is done is left largely unspecified.

A primary goal of the Kintsch and van Dijk model is to explain coherence of text. In the model, coherence is achieved both in the microstructure and the macrostructure by overlap of arguments in propositions. We will focus on the microstructure. According to Kintsch and van Dijk, the reader is continually attempting to link propositions that share a common argument; in the usual representation, this is signified by a line drawn between the numbers representing two propositions (see Figure 8.1). Here again, much of the detail of the actual processing that leads to linking "common" arguments is assumed but not specified. For example, the

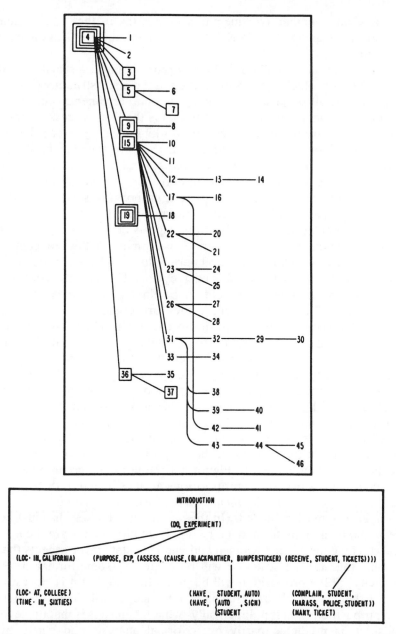

FIGURE 8-1 (Top) The complete "coherence graph" representing the microstructure of the "Bumperstickers" paragraph of Table 8.1. The numbers represent propositions and the number of squares around a proposition indicate the number of cycles it was held in STM for processing. (Bottom) The macrostructure for the Bumperstickers passage. The basic schema is a "scientific report" schema, and the important propositions from the microstructure are incorporated into it. [Reproduced from Kintsch and Van Dijk (1978), with permission from the American Psychological Association and the authors.]

decision about whether two mentions of *car* (as in the "Zak" example earlier in the chapter) are referring to the same argument is assumed to be made somehow.

The end product of all this linking of propositions is a structure called a *coherence graph* which is a representation of the microstructure (see Figure 8.1). However, all propositions sharing common arguments are not necessarily linked. A major feature of the model is that the process of linking is limited by the capacity of short-term or working memory. According to the model, propositions can be linked only if they are together in short-term memory (STM). This STM assumption has several consequences. First, the actual coherence graph formed by the reader will be shaped by STM limitations. Second, the amount of time a proposition stays in STM is an important determinant of how well it is remembered.

Indeed, one of the best-worked-out aspects of the model is the general process by which the coherence graph is formed. A key concept is the processing *cycle,* which is a temporal period during which a particular set of propositions is linked. At the end of each cycle, STM is emptied except for a few key propositions that are kept to be linked to the next set. In the "bumpersticker" example above, cycles are coincident with sentences (which are between 7 and 12 propositions each). However, Kintsch and van Dijk are not strongly committed to the sentence as the invariable unit of the cycle. Another central idea in the theory is the concept of *level.* The coherence graph is thus not merely a bunch of propositions linked to each other because some are at higher levels (the more "important" propositions) than others (see Figure 8.1). The level that a proposition is on is also an important factor in determining how well it is remembered.

To get some feel for how this aspect of the model works, let's work through a cycle. In the first cycle, the propositions are linked together into the coherence graph shown in Figure 8.1. How is this graph determined? One requirement is that all the propositions must be linked. If they are not all linked, either there is *reinstatement* of a proposition from long-term memory or an *inference* must be added. (In this case, since the text has just begun, there would be no long-term memory representation.) How are the levels of the hierarchy determined? Kintsch and van Dijk state three aspects that will determine this: (1) the structure will be guided by some formal criteria of "simplicity"; (2) a proposition will be put at the "top" if it is closest to the title; (3) the "schema" or (pragmatic knowledge) will help to determine which proposition is on top. Practically, what that means is that the level of a proposition is predicted partly by a formal analysis and partly by the experimenter's intuition of what is important.

At the end of cycle 1, four propositions are selected to remain in STM and the propositions of the second sentence are brought in, and a new part of the coherence graph is formed and added to what was constructed in cycle 1. (The assumption of four for the size of the set held over is relatively arbitrary.) After the coherence graph is constructed to incorporate Sentence

2, four of those propositions are kept and the propositions from Sentence 3 are brought into STM, and so on. There is a specific assumption being made about the propositions being kept in STM. Called the *leading-edge* strategy, this assumption has as its criteria keeping propositions because they are "high-level," because they are recent, or both (see Figure 8.1). This strategy implies that, on average, higher-level propositions are in short-term memory longer than lower-level propositions.

Thus, the microstructure is built up as a single interrelated structure a cycle at a time. At the same time that all of the above is going on, the macrostructure (gist) is also being built. The macrostructure is assumed to be built by attaching "important" aspects of the microstructure to a preexisting "schema." In this case, the "schema" is like a scientific report in that it has a prearranged format (Introduction, Method, Results, Discussion) together with subheadings and expectations about what functions will be served by each of these sections (see Figure 8.1). The schema is "filled in" with selected propositions drawn from the microstructure. One goes from the microstructure to the macrostructure by deleting "unimportant" propositions, adding generalizations of propositions, and adding inferences. Readers thus are assumed to store both the microstructure and macrostructure when reading, and memory of the text is assumed to depend on both the microstructure and macrostructure. Of course, retrieval of propositions from either source is assumed to be fallible.

The above is a brief sketch of the Kintsch and van Dijk model. Let us try to summarize its basic features before moving on. First, the reader is assumed to break down the text into units called propositions. Second, the process of understanding is assumed to have, as a major component, the linking of these propositions into a coherence graph, which forms the microstructure. Third, a second component of synthesis is the formation of a second structure, the macrostructure, which consists of prior pragmatic knowledge called a "schema" combined with an edited and shortened version of the microstructure.

While the model provides an admirably detailed account of how discourse might be processed, there is a lot missing. As mentioned earlier, the model says little about the details of how propositions are formed. In addition, while it focuses on the construction of the coherence graph, there are crucial details missing, such as how inferences are formed, how propositions are reinstated, and exactly how the whole process goes on in real time. Moreover, the model (or any propositional network) is, at best, an incomplete representation of how "meaning" is understood (a problem that is acknowledged by Kintsch and van Dijk and which we will discuss later).

Much of the early experimental work inspired by the model focused on the "levels effect": namely that higher-level propositions are remembered better than lower-level propositions. According to the model, higher-level propositions would be better remembered because they are held in short-term memory longer (as discussed above) and they are more likely to be incorporated into the macrostructure. In fact, the levels effect has been demonstrated many times (e.g., Kintsch and Keenan 1973; Kintsch et al. 1975; Meyer 1975).

A second focus of the earlier work was to demonstrate the reality of propositions. In particular, it was shown that reading time was predicted by the number of propositions in a sentence or paragraph (Kintsch and Keenan 1973). That is, even with the number of words held constant, the reading time for a passage with more propositions was greater than for a passage with fewer propositions.

While both of these demonstrations are of interest in establishing the model, neither seem like compelling evidence in favor of it. As mentioned earlier, the analysis of levels has a large intuitive component, so that a demonstration of a levels effect on memory may largely be due to the experimenter's intuitions about the importance of various propositions rather than to any intrinsic feature of the model. The demonstration that reading time can be predicted by the number of propositions is stronger evidence in favor of the model. However, there may be other measures of "denseness" of the text that would make similar predictions.

A particularly interesting test of the Kintsch and van Dijk model was conducted by McKoon and Ratcliff (1980). Since this study is interesting methodologically as well, we will describe it in some detail. They used a variation of the priming technique to get at the structure of discourse memory. In one experiment, subjects saw "paragraphs" like the following:

(1) The businessman gestured to a waiter.
(2) The waiter brought coffee.
(3) The coffee stained the napkins.
(4) The napkins protected the tablecloth.
(5) The businessman flourished documents.
(6) The documents explained a contract.
(7) The contract satisfied the client.   (8.24)

A propositional analysis of this paragraph is presented in Figure 8.2. Notice that Proposition 2 and Proposition 5 are closer in the microstructure than are Proposition 4 is to Proposition 7, even though the pairs of propositions are equally far apart in the surface representation of the text. Thus, the arguments, "waiter" and "documents" are closer in the microstructure than are the arguments "napkins" and "client" (even though the two pairs of words are equally far in the surface text). McKoon and Ratcliff tested for closeness using a recognition memory procedure. After reading the paragraph, subjects saw a series of *probe* words, which they were to judge as having been present in the paragraph or not. (Their responses were timed.) Of primary interest was the effect of one probe word (the *prime*) on the response time to the following probe word (the *target*). The logic is that if responding to one probe word speeds up responding to a second probe word, then the words are "closely linked" in some memory structure, just as the

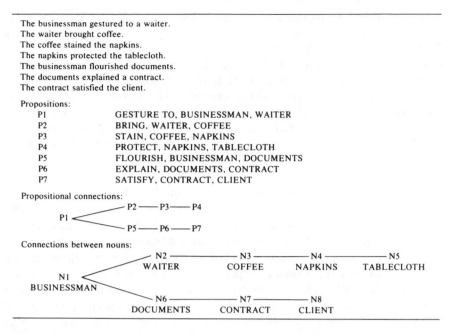

The businessman gestured to a waiter.
The waiter brought coffee.
The coffee stained the napkins.
The napkins protected the tablecloth.
The businessman flourished documents.
The documents explained a contract.
The contract satisfied the client.

Propositions:

P1	GESTURE TO, BUSINESSMAN, WAITER
P2	BRING, WAITER, COFFEE
P3	STAIN, COFFEE, NAPKINS
P4	PROTECT, NAPKINS, TABLECLOTH
P5	FLOURISH, BUSINESSMAN, DOCUMENTS
P6	EXPLAIN, DOCUMENTS, CONTRACT
P7	SATISFY, CONTRACT, CLIENT

Propositional connections:

P1 — P2 —— P3 —— P4
P1 — P5 —— P6 —— P7

Connections between nouns:

N2 —————— N3 —————— N4 —————— N5
WAITER   COFFEE   NAPKINS   TABLECLOTH

N1
BUSINESSMAN

N6 —————— N7 —————— N8
DOCUMENTS   CONTRACT   CLIENT

FIGURE 8-2 A paragraph from McKoon and Ratcliff (1980) together with the propositional analysis and propositional structure. (Reproduced with permission from Academic Press and the authors.)

phenomenon of *cat* priming *dog* in a lexical decision task argues that "cat" and "dog" are closely linked in some sort of memory structure. McKoon and Ratcliff found that *waiter* primed *documents* more than *napkins* primed *client* indicating that "waiter" and "documents" were more closely linked in memory than "napkins" and "client" (as predicted by the Kintsch and van Dijk model).

A problem with the above experiment is that the text was not very natural. Accordingly, McKoon and Ratcliff used more natural paragraphs such as the following:

> Early French settlements in North America were strung so thinly along the major waterways that land ownership was a problem. The Frenchmen were fur traders, and, by necessity, the fur traders were nomads. Towns were few, forts and trading posts were many. Little wonder that the successful fur trader learned to live, act, and think like an Indian. Circulation among the Indians was vital to the economic survival of the traders.   (8.25)

The probe task in the second experiment was also more meaningful, in that subjects were given sentences such as *The fur traders were nomads.* and asked to respond whether the idea was stated in the paragraph. (The probes essentially tested for memory of propositions.) Again, McKoon and Ratcliff looked at the effect of one probe on the next, and contrasted the priming effects of propositions that were near in the surface representation but far in the propositional structure with those that were near in the propositional structure but far in the surface. They found, for example, that *Circulation among the Indians was vital.*, which was near *The fur traders were nomads.* in the propositional structure but far in the surface, primed *The fur traders were nomads.* more than *Land ownership was not a problem.*, which was near *The fur traders were nomads.* in the surface but far in the propositional structure.

A summary of Kintsch and van Dijk's model   Let us try to summarize some of the main features of the Kintsch and van Dijk model, the evidence for it, and some of the problems with it. The first feature is that the reader's memory consists of propositions joined together. Both experiments showing that reading time is a function of the number of propositions and the McKoon and Ratcliff priming experiment offer some evidence for the psychological reality of the proposition and of the microstructure. The proposition is also an important aspect of recall experiments; Kintsch and van Dijk argue that it is the natural unit to score memory for prose. We will return to the memory issues later. We should also reiterate that the model makes no attempt to indicate how (or even exactly when) discourse is broken down into propositions.

The second feature is the notion of coherence, achieved by connecting propositions with common concepts. Such a mechanism is clearly implied by the work on anaphora discussed prior to the introduction of the Kintsch and van Dijk model. The cycling process provides some detail on how structures are built up and there is evidence to support some of the details, such as the "leading edge" strategy (e.g., Fletcher 1981); however, much of the detail is omitted. The work on reinstatement we discussed in the previous section is one attempt to put more flesh on the "bare bones" of the model.

The third feature is the notion of levels. Kintsch and van Dijk's work impressively documents that "level" is an important concept. What is less clear, unfortunately, is whether the concept of level flows naturally from the architecture of the model or whether level is largely an ad hoc concept imposed from above by the macrostructure (and is largely determined by the experimenter's intuition about what is important). We will return to issues relating to "importance" later as well.

The fourth feature is the distinction between micro- and macro-structure, which is the distinction between a relatively literal memory and "gist." While Kintsch and van Dijk don't identify microstructures with short-term memory and macrostructures with long-term memory, the model does carry with it the suggestion that "gist" will be remembered better than the details of the microstructure. We will shortly discuss research that looks at memory for various aspects of the text.

The two major criticisms of the Kintsch and van Dijk model are (1) that too many of the details of processes that they mention are not well worked out; and (2) that coherence and the understanding of discourse entails more than just tying propositions together with links, and hence that other structures are going to be needed besides networks of propositions. Much of the work on discourse memory has revolved around the adequacy of argument overlap more specifically and a network representation more generally as a way to talk about understanding. Before embarking on that, let us briefly discuss research that touches on the "gist" versus literal memory distinction made in Kintsch and van Dijk.

"Meaning" versus "Detail"—Two Kinds of Memories?

Most people would agree that memory for the gist of a text is much better than memory for the detail. There are two ways in which Kintsch and van Dijk's model accounts for that. First, propositions that are important are both rehearsed more in short-term memory and more likely to be copied over into the macrostructure. Second, much of the detail of text (e.g., the exact choice of words, the details of the syntax) does not make it into the propositional structure. This suggests that there are two levels of "detail." First, the detail of text that is not represented by propositions (such as most aspects of the syntactic structure) may be lost completely once it has left short-term memory. Second, "unimportant" propositions are incorporated into the microstructure (and hence are part of a long-term memory representation), but are far less retrieveable than "important" propositions which are incorporated into the macrostructure. We now turn to research that attempts to determine whether there are details of text that are in fact lost quickly, and if so, how they are to be characterized.

In a seminal experiment by Sachs (1967), subjects listened to passages of text. The text was interrupted at times for a recognition memory test in which the subject was to judge whether the test sentence had appeared in the text. It was made clear to subjects that they were supposed to respond "no" when a sentence expressed the same meaning as one they had read but had a different wording. Sachs' major finding was that recognition memory was at about chance levels for certain kinds of wording changes even when memory was tested less than a minute after the material was encountered. For example, if subjects heard a passage containing the sentence

He sent a letter about it to Galileo, the great Italian scientist. (8.26a)

they were as likely to respond "yes" to the following sentence

He sent Galileo, the great Italian scientist, a letter about it. (8.26b)

as to the one they actually heard. In addition, their ability to detect changes from active to passive voice (or vice versa) and changes in wording (i.e., substitution of a synonym) was little better than chance level. In contrast, a meaning change (e.g., reversal of subject and object) was recognized about 90 percent of the time.

Sachs' results were widely interpreted as showing that the surface form of the syntax (see Chapter 7) was not retained as part of the memory representation. However, even deeper aspects of the syntax appear to be lost. For example, Johnson-Laird and Stevenson (1970) showed that less than a minute after presentation, subjects were unable to determine which of the following sentences they had heard.

John liked the painting and he bought it from the duchess.
John liked the painting and the duchess sold it to him.
The painting pleased John and he bought it from the duchess.
The painting pleased John and the duchess sold it to him.   (8.27)

In 8.27, not only are the surface structures of the four sentences different, but John is the agent of the first two sentences and the recipient in the latter two sentences. What seems to be common is something just at about the propositional level (i.e., the liking relation between John and the painting and the transaction between John and the duchess).

Garnham (1981) also showed that some of the details of propositions are lost. For example, he used a passage about a party that started with

By the window was a man with a martini.   (8.28a)

The passage later contained one of the following sentences:

The man with the martini waved to the hostess.
The man by the window waved to the hostess.   (8.28b)

Subjects were unable to discriminate which of the two they had seen. While this latter example seems, at first glance, compatible with Kintsch and van Dijk's notion of inserting one proposition as an argument in another proposition, we are not sure that it really is. In Kintsch and van Dijk's representation, concepts are the arguments in the propositions. But "the man with the martini" and "the man by the window" are not the same concept—they just happen to refer to the same person in this sentence. Thus if these memory experiments bear on the type of structure one wants for representing discourse, it appears that the propositional representation needed is somewhat further removed from the surface representation than in Kintsch and van Dijk's representation.

We should warn you that the above experiments had subjects listen to passages rather than reading them. In fact, the results look somewhat different for reading. Sachs (1974) found appreciably better memory for surface details (especially passive-active differences) when subjects read passages rather than listened to them, even though the same materials were used in the reading and listening tasks. While there may be a deep reason for the differences between reading and listening, we think there may a simple (and basically uninteresting) reason for them. Other studies (e.g., Johnson-Laird and Stevenson 1970) have shown, unsurprisingly, that when subjects are warned in advance about the type of memory test, they will remember detail appreciably better than if they are not warned. In Sachs' experiments, subjects hear or read many passages and receive many tests. They are thus suitably warned and may spend time memorizing detail that they would not normally do. However, memory for detail in her reading condition was appreciably better than in her listening condition even though subjects are equally aware of the memory tests. A (admittedly ad hoc) reason for the difference is that reading is a self-paced task while listening is not. Thus, while readers can slow down when they want to memorize detail, listeners do not have the luxury of slowing down the tape recording at the moment they wish to do so.

The key question is what detail subjects retain in natural situations, since they may be employing special strategies in psychology experiments. An optimal experiment would be to test subjects only once in a situation in which they were merely trying to understand the text. Such an experiment was conducted by Wanner (1974). The "text" his subjects heard was instructions to them as subjects in a psychology experiment. Thus, they should have been listening naturally but carefully. He interrupted them a few seconds after hearing the key sentence and tested whether they heard "mark carefully" or "carefully mark." They were at chance level.

The research discussed above indicates that much of the syntactic and lexical detail of text is lost rapidly, especially when the text is presented aurally. In reading, however, the detail is sometimes retained fairly well. The better memory observed in reading is due either to an important difference between reading and listening or to memorization strategies that are unique to the laboratory experiments. If the listening data are a more appropriate indicator of what memory for discourse would be like under more natural situations, then it appears that, in general outline, the propositional representation of Kintsch and van Dijk is on the right track about the level of detail that has any kind of permanence in memory.

Such a picture must be an oversimplification, however, since we know that we remember some detail when reading or listening, even if we are not trying to memorize the material. Keenan, MacWhinney, and Mayhew (1977) conducted a naturalistic memory experiment (on listening, unfortunately) that demonstrated that certain details are remembered days afterwards. The material that subjects were asked to remember was taken from a seminar discussion in which they had all participated (and which the experimenters unobtrusively tape recorded). Subjects were asked a day or two later to discriminate certain written sentences that had been said in the discussion from paraphrases of them. Keenan et al. found that subjects could make quite good discriminations when the exact wording had communicative importance (e.g., when a witty way of phrasing something was being used to help excuse something the speaker had done wrong). Similar details of phrasing were much less well remembered when they didn't have communicative importance.

Several important controls were run in the experiment. First, subjects who knew the speakers (but weren't present at the discussion) were at chance level discriminating which sentences were actually spoken in the discussion and which were paraphrases. Therefore the subjects in the main experiment were making their discrimination not on the basis of what the speakers were likely to say but on how they actually said it in the context of the discussion. Second, naive subjects who heard the sentences out of context showed no difference in their ability to detect the wording of important and unimportant sentences. Therefore the communicative importance of a sentence was not a function of the sentence per se but of the context in which it was uttered.

The Keenan, MacWhinney, and Mayhew experiment indicates that there are certain aspects of communication, such as the tone, and certain richness of detail (if "important" in some intuitive sense) that are not easily represented in a propositional network such as Kintsch and van Dijk. (We expect that similar findings would obtain in reading as well.) A propositional model such as Kintsch and van Dijk would have to posit that the reader adds the detail or tone as an added "mental note" proposition, similar to the process by which an inference proposition is added. Unless some guidelines are provided for how such detail is added, such a propositional explanation seems quite unsatisfactory.

We should emphasize that the Keenan, MacWhinney, and Mayhew experiment tested memory for detail over the period of days rather than minutes. Thus, while some detail is lost in less than a minute, other detail is remembered for days. There may be a level of detail, however, that is remembered after a minute or so, but not after several hours or days. Kintsch (1974) approached this issue by determining whether subjects would treat inferential statements that were made in the text any differently from those inferences that were implicit. If they did respond to explicit and implicit inferences differently, then one would have evidence that a relatively literal form of the text was present in the subject's head at the time of testing. Kintsch employed a *verification* task, in which subjects had to determine whether a given proposition was consistent with the text or not. For example, such a proposition might be *A discarded cigarette started a fire*. In the explicit version, the paragraph that subjects read contained the sentences

A carelessly discarded cigarette started a fire. The fire destroyed
many acres of virgin forest.   (8.29a)

while the implicit version read

A burning cigarette was carelessly discarded. The fire destroyed
many acres of virgin forest.   (8.29b)

Kintsch found that the time to verify the explicity stated proposition was appreciably faster than the implicitly stated one for an immediate test, while there was little difference between the two when the test was delayed 15 minutes.

This result suggests that a certain level of detail is used in retrieving information right after a sentence has been read but is not present (or unavailable) even 15 minutes later. This kind of finding (see also Baggett 1975) helped to suggest the microstructure-macrostructure distinction in the Kintsch and van Dijk model. In terms of the model, the natural explanation is as follows. First, the inferential proposition (which is important) is assumed to be copied into the macrostructure whether it is present in the text or not. Second, for the immediate test, the subject verifies the proposition using both the microstructure and the macrostructure, and the verification is faster when the proposition is explicit because it is better represented in the microstructure. For the delayed test, both microstructure and macrostructure are still present in memory; however, propositions in the microstructure are much less available than those in the macrostructure, so that virtually all memory comes from the macrostructure and hence there is no difference in the speed of retrieval.

To summarize, details of the syntax and wording tend to be lost quite quickly (well within 30 seconds), suggesting that text is quickly recast into something like a propositional representation, where meaning is represented independently of its form of presentation. It then appears that another level of detail tends to be relatively unavailable after 15 minutes or so. This is indicated by the Kintsch experiment, where subjects appear to treat explicit and implicit propositions equally at this delay [see also Bransford and Franks (1971), Dooling and Lachman (1971)]. However, you should be careful to not oversimplify these results and conclude that detail is completely lost. First, while the memory for detail is poor in many experiments, it is above chance level (e.g., Sachs 1974) even in the listening condition. Second, the Keenan, MacWhinney, and Mayhew experiment indicates that "detail" of a kind that is not easily accounted for by some sort of propositional representation is well remembered if it is an important part of the communicative tone or statement. In addition, we should point out that detail of even a more surface form is remembered in reading. Readers can often remember where on a page they read something (Christie and Just 1976; Rothkopf 1971; Zechmeister and McKillip 1972) and sometimes make regressions back to the place where an anaphoric antecedent was on the page, indicating that its location was remembered (Carpenter and Just 1977; Ehrlich 1983).

Macrostructures

While some detail appears to be completely lost, it is clear that memory for text is in general not all or none. That is, a lot of material in the text is contained in memory, but some of it is a lot less available. In addition, propositions in text are not independent of one another in that some statements tend to be remembered only when others are. These facts (and others) are driving forces behind the idea that there are "discourse structures" that underlie readers' memory of text. In this section, we will give a brief overview of such models of discourse structure.

Kintsch and van Dijk's (1978) theory of macrostructure is only one out of many similar theories that have gone under the general heading of "schema" theories. [In fact, they changed many of the details of the macrostructure in the later version of their theory, van Dijk and Kintsch (1983).] The fundamental claim of "schema" theories is that there is a prestored "schema" which determines how all the information in the text is understood and stored in memory. For example, in the "Laundry" passage at the beginning of the chapter, the assumption of schema theorists is that you understand the passage (given the title "Laundry") because the title allows you to retrieve a schema from your real-world knowledge for doing laundry. You then tie the information in the passage into the retrieved schema.

One of the reasons that schema theories attracted interest was that they appeared at a time when psycholinguistics had pretty much ignored the role of real-world knowledge in understanding discourse. A major thrust of these theories was to demonstrate that many of the inferences of the kind we discussed in the first part of the chapter are not possible from the literal meaning of the sentences, but instead are contingent on real-world knowledge such as what it is actually like to do laundry or why men go to jewelers.

Most schema theories agree, in outline, how schemas are used by the reader. An example used widely, the "restaurant schema," will help to illustrate the point (Bower, Black, and Turner 1979; Schank and Abelson 1977). A restaurant schema, retrieved from memory, is essentially a structured sequence of events in a meal. Both a schema and certain *default values* for what happens are retrieved. The default values are presumably the sequence of actions that occur in your "normal" restaurant experience; clearly, these default values could be different for different people. The information of the story is then incorporated into the schema so that if the first sentence is about entering the restaurant and the second sentence is about ordering food, the schema would fill in the missing steps, such as waiting to be seated, sitting down, getting menus, and so forth. New information would be added to the schema only to the extent that it added to the schema or was different from the default values. For example, if there was a statement that the restaurant had no menus, it would be added to the schema, but a statement that the restaurant had menus would probably not be added because a restaurant having menus is probably the default value.

Such an account seems, in outline, a plausible explanation of how one would understand a description in a text of a scene in a restaurant. The problem that many people have with schema theories, however, is whether they progress beyond the level of description in the last paragraph to say anything really interesting about how people process discourse. There are three primary questions about schema theories that we will use to organize the discussion of them. First, if the theory is stated in terms of a concrete model, is it a plausible and interesting representation of how real-world knowledge is stored and/or used? Second, even if the details of the model are questionable, does it point to important units of discourse or important variables for evaluating comprehension or memory? Third, even if the details are vague, does schema theory say anything interesting about how prior knowledge guides processing and/or memory of text? (For an excellent discussion and critique of schema theories, see Alba and Hasher 1983.)

Schema Representations

The notion of schema has been invoked at many levels of specificity. At the vague extreme, "schema" has been used as a synonym for real-world knowledge, and at the other extreme, formal models of schema structure have been proposed. Most schema theories (inspired by work in artificial intelligence) have cast schemas as structures of propositions (as in Kintsch and van Dijk), partly because such structures are compatible with certain widely used programming languages like LISP. To a large extent, these formalisms look something like those of Kintsch and van Dijk. That is, they are usually a connected hierarchical network. Such a formalism expresses certain ideas: the structure indicates an idea of closeness as reflected by the number of links between two concepts or propositions; some idea of units (analogous to phrases or clauses in a syntactic structure) as reflected by nodes in the hierarchy; some idea of importance, with more important things on top of the hierarchy; and some idea of sequencing or order, governed either by rules or by knowledge.

A major problem with schemas is the vagueness of the "size." Is a schema doing your laundry? putting the coin in the washing machine? a day in your life? a week in your life? While one could possibly counter that criticism by saying that schemas are nested (i.e., there are little schemas that are in bigger schemas), there is little in the way of current theorizing that usefully indicates what "grain" of schema is activated and used at a particular moment. In practice, schemas have usually been invoked at two levels: first, the "episode" or "script" (as in the laundry or restaurant example); and second, at the level of a schema for a whole story or discourse. One example of the latter was the "Scientific Report" schema that was invoked by Kintsch and van Dijk to organize the macrostructure of the "Bumperstickers" passage (Figure 8.1); such a schema involved an Introduction, Method, Results, and Discussion sections, together with subsections of each. We will discuss a second example shortly.

A second major problem with schema theories is that they imply (at either the episode or story level) that real-world knowledge is invoked in handy prepackaged units (a "lexicon" of generic experiences). While such generic experiences are plausible for understanding uninteresting segments of a narrative, such as the background for an episode in a restaurant, to the best of our knowledge, there is no convincing demonstration that they handle situations of greater interest. The other theoretical option would be to make schemas less generic and to have the "lexicon" include an "eating out with your girlfriend and her parents on June 12, 1985" schema. Such an option would of course drastically increase the number of schemas in memory. Since schema theories were originally proposed to deal with the problem of rapidly accessing relevant knowledge from the vastness of long-term memory, most schema theorists have opted for relatively small numbers of schemas with individual ones being stereotyped generic experiences.

We will briefly discuss schema theory at the two levels that it has been invoked, the episode level and the story level. Most research involving schemas at the episode level has not been particularly concerned with the details of the formalisms in representing schemas. Instead, they have concentrated on demonstrating the impact of such schemas on the memory of a text passage. Two of the major claims are that: (1) information that cannot be fit into a schema is lost and (2) information is only encoded in terms of schemas, so that an episode will be remembered only in terms of the general schema and in those details that change "default values" (as discussed in the restaurant example above). In other words, researchers advocating these views have essentially argued that there is no functional structure like Kintsch and van Dijk's microstructure and that all memory is in terms of something like a macrostructure.

These extreme claims, in general, have not been supported by the data (see Alba and Hasher 1983). For example, if sentences are presented in random order rather than in a coherent text format, subjects show recall well above chance (e.g., Thorndyke 1977). Memory for such material that cannot be fit into any schemas is worse than that for coherent text, but the extreme claims by schema theorists that it is lost appear to be false. One could counter and say that readers are using some sort of schema even when they try to remember random sequences of text. While it is undoubtedly true that readers are trying to make some sort of sense out of these sentences, it seems unlikely that they can use schemas, as the term is usually used (i.e., fairly large packages of real-world knowledge).

Similarly, readers have difficulty discriminating statements that represent "default values" of a schema that were actually in the passage from those that were not stated. However, while people's ability to make such discriminations is usually poor, it is generally above chance level, even when such tests are made an hour later. To illustrate this research, let us consider an experiment by Graesser, Gordon, and Sawyer (1979).

Instead of doing a formal analysis, Graesser, Gordon, and Sawyer constructed episodes and obtained ratings from some subjects as to how "typical" actions in the episodes were of the schema (i.e., typical actions would be "default values"). They tested subjects for their memory an hour after reading the passages and made attempts to prevent subjects from thinking about the passages in the interval. A recognition memory test was employed: subjects saw sentences and were asked to judge whether they had actually been in the passage or not. They found that subjects' ability to discriminate atypical statements that had actually been in the passages from those that hadn't was quite good, while subjects' ability to discriminate typical statements that had been in the passage from those that hadn't was poorer. However, subjects' ability to discriminate sentences they had seen from those they hadn't was at chance level only for a special set of "extremely typical" sentences. Graesser, Gordon, and Sawyer took these results to support the schema view of text comprehension. However, it should be emphasized that subjects are able to discriminate most typical statements at above chance level in this and other similar experiments.

While such experiments demonstrate that subjects' memories tend to be guided by schemas (or some aspect of prior real-world knowledge), they don't argue convincingly that all memory is encoded into the schema framework. Most of these results can be explained at least as well in terms of a dual storage mechanism (e.g., Kintsch and van Dijk 1978), in which a more-or-less literal version is stored together with some memory of the gist. At the time of a memory test, subjects presumably would say that a sentence had been seen either if it was literally represented (in the microstructure) or if it was a plausible inference from the gist. The poorer discrimination for highly typical items would be explained by positing that such information would be present in the elaborated schema or macrostructure as a "default value," regardless of whether it was in the text or not.

We should point out an apparent paradox of this aspect of schema theories. On the one hand, they make the prediction that if something doesn't fit well into a schema, it is less well remembered (the "laundry" example). On the other hand, they make the prediction that things that fit more poorly into a schema are remembered better than things that are too typical. Presumably, the resolution to this paradox is that certain items fit so poorly that they cannot be incorporated at all, while other items fit well enough to be incorporated into the schema but are atypical enough to be memorable. However, there are very few guidelines at present for indicating when typicality will help memory and when it will hurt. This is a problem for schema-theory-inspired research in other areas, such as picture perception, where similar experiments demonstrate opposite predictions from schema theory (e.g., Antes and Penland 1981; Friedman 1979).

The experiments dealing with larger-scale schemas have had a somewhat different focus. For the most part, they have not made strong claims about schemas being the sole form of memory representation, but instead have tended to use specific theoretical schemas as frameworks for evaluating subjects' processing and memory of text. To give you the flavor for this type of research, we will briefly discuss an attempt at outlining a larger-scale schema, known as a "story grammar."

"Story grammars" As the name implies, a *story grammar* is an attempt to construct a set of rules that can generate a structure for any story. This notion was introduced by Rumelhart (1975) and applied in more detail

by others (e.g., Thorndyke 1977; Mandler and Johnson 1977). We will consider Thorndyke's experiment in some detail. As can be seen in Figure 8.3, the basic structure of a story is determined by a set of rules. At the highest level, the story is divided into a sequence of subsections: SETTING, THEME, PLOT, RESOLUTION. There are rules characterizing how the other units are organized. Basically, the two main ideas are that (1) stories have units that involve subgoals of some actor who attempts to reach these goals, and (2) these *attempts* have *episodes* within them that allow episodes and attempts to be nested within others, resulting in a hierarchical structure (see Figure 8.3).

Thorndyke had two stories that he analyzed using the story grammar formalism. (One is presented in Table 8.2.) His major manipulation was to create more or less coherent versions of the stories. For the most part, this was done by manipulating the THEME; it was either in its normal place, at the end of the story, or it was omitted. In addition, he created versions of the story in which sentences were in random order. (The theme of the story is indicated in Figure 8.3) The subjects' task was to read the story and to remember as much of it as possible. As in most of the studies in this section, subjects were told not to worry about the exact wording, but to reproduce the sequence and meaning of the text as well as possible. In addition, each sentence was removed after the subject had read it to control the order in which material was read.

Unsurprisingly, subjects remembered the propositions in the normal passages better than in the variants and those in the random versions least well of all. Of greater interest was the following. First, while the version in

TABLE 8.2 "Circle Island" story from Thorndyke (1977). With permission of Academic Press and the author.

(1) Circle Island is located in the middle of the Atlantic Ocean, (2) north of Ronald Island. (3) The main occupations on the island are farming and ranching. (4) Circle Island has good soil, (5) but few rivers and (6) hence a shortage of water. (7) The island is run democratically. (8) All issues are decided by a majority vote of the islanders. (9) The governing body is a senate, (10) whose job is to carry out the will of the majority. (11) Recently, an island scientist discovered a cheap method (12) of converting salt water into fresh water. (13) As a result, the island farmers wanted (14) to build a canal across the island, (15) so that they could use water from the canal (16) to cultivate the island's central region. (17) Therefore, the farmers formed a procanal association (18) and persuaded a few senators (19) to join. (20) The procanal association brought the construction idea to a vote. (21) All the islanders voted. (22) The majority voted in favor of construction. (23) The senate, however, decided that (24) the farmers' proposed canal was ecologically unsound. (25) The senators agreed (26) to build a smaller canal (27) that was 2 feet wide and 1 foot deep. (28) After starting construction on the smaller canal, (29) the islanders discovered that (30) no water would flow into it. (31) Thus the project was abandoned. (32) The farmers were angry (33) because of the failure of the canal project. (34) Civil war appeared inevitable.

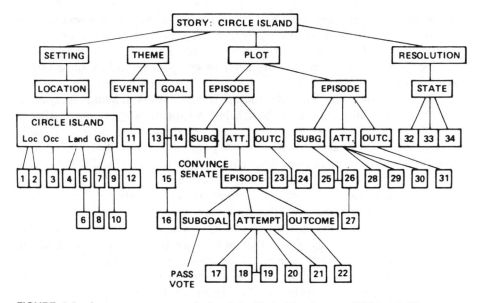

FIGURE 8-3 A story grammar analysis of the Circle Island story of Table 8.2 (Thorndyke 1977). The numbers in the boxes refer to the clause numbers in the story. (Reproduced with permission of Academic Press and the author.)

which the theme came last was remembered less well than the normal story, it was remembered better than if the theme was omitted; thus, while having the theme to organize the episodes was good, the episodes could be organized after the fact to some extent. Second, Thorndyke analyzed recall as a function of level in the hierarchy. He found that level had no effect in the random sequences and a large effect in the more meaningful sequences; thus, the memorability of a sentence was not due to the sentence itself but to its function in the discourse being read.

Other research using this basic framework has focused on the validity of the episode and the hierarchical nature of the organization. For example, Black and Bower (1979) demonstrated that episodes tended to be recalled as units, and Meyer and McConkie (1973) showed that lower-level episodes were not recalled if the episode "above" in the hierarchy was not recalled. Another demonstration of the reality of episodes is that reading time for sentences at the ends of episodes tends to be long, indicating that subjects are putting together the sequence of events in the episode (Haberlandt, Berian, and Sandson 1980). However, subjects in the Haberlandt, Berian, and Sandson experiment were told in advance that they were going to have to remember the details of the stories. While this doesn't detract from the reality of episodes as processing units, it does leave open the question of whether long reading times at the ends of episodes would be observed in more natural reading situations.

Such phenomena indicate that this story-level schema analysis is capturing something important about what is happening in the processing of text. The controversy in this area is about whether the theory is really adding anything of value to what a naive person would predict. First, let us consider the formalism of story grammars. While it can be used to outline, in a general sense, many simple stories, the sequences of events given are by no means universal, and hence the formalism is not really a grammar. As a result, it is not really clear whether story grammars say anything more than that a story has a background, a series of episodes, and a conclusion, and the sequence is logical in the sense that actors are trying to achieve goals in some sort of way. Second, as already discussed in connection with Kintsch and van Dijk, the construction of a hierarchy by the experimenter in these structures often rests on his or her intuition rather than on a formal structural analysis of the passages.

To state our criticism in a somewhat different way: we suspect that if a naive person were asked to provide an outline of a story, it would look quite a bit like that produced by the story grammar. This criticism does not indicate that story grammars are invalid; in fact, if a story grammar analysis were wildly at odds with intuition, it would probably be wrong. However, it does indicate that much of the formalism may just be a restatement of intuition. It is the lack of convincing evidence that the formalisms of story grammars (or schema theories more generally) are going beyond intuitively obvious predictions that is the major weakness of the area.

Summary of schema theory   Schemas have been primarily used to explain how material is remembered. While there have been some interesting attempts (Sharkey and Mitchell 1985; Sharkey and Sharkey 1987) to examine the effects of schemas on moment-to-moment processing in reading, most of the research inspired by them in fact demonstrates that real-world knowledge succeeds in shaping subjects' memory for the text being read. However, it is less clear whether anything particularly novel is being said about how subjects process text. Much of the research demonstrates that memory for text is quite a bit better if the material makes sense than if it doesn't. For many of those demonstrations, the formalism is not very crucial to determining whether the discourse makes sense or not. Secondly, schema theory points to certain units in the text (e.g., episodes). The identification of such units is important; at the present state of research, however, it is not clear that the analysis has proceded beyond what one would naively expect. Third, the "default value" idea of episodic schema suggests that certain information may be more poorly stored in memory because it is redundant. Most research indicates, however, that the memory representation is not only in terms of a prestored schema that is elaborated on by the text, but that some sort of more literal form of the text (such as Kintsch and van Dijk's microstructure) is also used.

Alternatives to Schemas

The research discussed above has used the idea of a schema mainly as a heuristic device to investigate memory, and with the exception of story grammars, little of the research has taken the formalism very seriously. As indicated earlier, schemas are propositions connected in some sort of network. The network represents notions of nested units (analogous to phrases in sentences), notions of importance, and notions of sequence. While there have been some claims that such a propositional representation is quite neutral and can in principle represent any kind of memory or knowledge, there are counterclaims that these networks either cannot, or do not easily, represent important aspects of meaning.

We will discuss two lines of research that have pointed out shortcomings in the way typical networks handle knowledge. Both indicate that important aspects of meaning have been ignored in the typical representations. The first line of research can perhaps be handled by a minor restructing of the models. The second, however, argues for an overhaul of how meaning is conceptualized.

The role of causality   Clearly, an important ingredient of whether text is coherent is whether the sequence of ideas makes some sort of sense. However, schemas, as usually constituted, do not do a particularly good job of explaining whether text does in fact make sense. In a model such as Kintsch and van Dijk, the microstructure is knitted together as long as the propositions contained within have sufficient overlap of arguments. Thus, a completely meaningless series of statements that all referred to the same "dog" would have a coherent microstructure. Second, in such a model, the propositions would have to fit into some sort of prearranged "schema" in order for a macrostructure to be constructed. Thus, given such a model, it is not clear that a sequence that did not make any temporal or causal sense would be handled any differently than one which did as long as they both had sufficient concept overlap and neither fit a preexisting schema. In fact, research has indicated that sequences that are linked causally are remembered better and read more quickly than those that are not (Black and Bern 1981; Fletcher 1986; Haberlandt and Bingham 1978; Myers, Shinjo, and Duffy 1987).

Trabasso and his colleagues (e.g., Trabasso and Sperry 1985; Trabasso and van den Broek 1985) have mounted an ambitious attempt to model the role of causality in discourse comprehension. In essence, the model is extremely simple. Each proposition is rated as to whether it is *causally related* to each other proposition. The criterion is that proposition A is a cause of B if (in the context of the narrative) B could not have happened if A did not happen. Consider, for example, the beginning of a narrative analyzed in detail by Trabasso and Sperry (1985).

> A father and his son / were taking their donkey to town / to sell him / at the marketplace. / They had not gone a great distance, / when they met a group of pretty maidens / who were returning from the town. / . . . / The donkey, not liking to be tied / kicked so ferociously / that he broke the rope / tumbled off the pole into the water / and scrambled away into the thicket. (8.30)

Some of the causal connections are of the obvious physical kind, such as "kicked so ferociously" being a cause of "that he broke the rope." Others are less obvious. For example, "to sell him" is a putative cause of "were taking their donkey to town" because while selling is not necessary to take a donkey to town, in the context of the narrative, they presumably wouldn't have taken the donkey to town if they weren't going to sell him. In addition, "They had not gone a great distance" is analyzed as a cause of "they met a group of pretty maidens," since they presumably would not have met the maidens if they hadn't left home.

The second step in the analysis is to connect all the causal connections into a connected graph of such connections. The graph is simplified so that if A causes B, B causes C, A causes C, only the connections between A and B and between B and C are indicated, and the connection between A and C would be inferred from the existence of the other two. The networks obtained were analyzed in several ways, but of primary importance are the number of causal connections that a given proposition is attached to, and whether they are part of a *causal chain*. A causal chain is a chain of causal connections that starts at the beginning of an episode (with the introduction of the main actors) and ends with the meeting of the goals (or failure to meet the goals) of the actors. While the analysis thus presumes some elements of "story grammars" to help set up the causal chain and some degree of judgment, the procedure of determining causal links and creating the structure seems fairly objective and easy to apply.

A major goal of the research was to demonstrate that these causal structures could predict the rated importance of a statement. In fact, both the number of connections and whether or not a proposition was in a causal chain were found by Trabasso and Sperry (1985) to be important determiners of rated importance. They also predicted both immediate and delayed recall as well (Trabasso and van den Broek 1985). Moreover, a causal analysis also predicts the time subjects take to retrieve information; the length of the causal chain from the beginning of the narrative predicts the time subjects take to answer factual questions about the narrative (O'Brien and Myers 1987).

A major reason why this research is important is that it suggests a relatively simple (and hence tractable) model for how readers can *construct* a discourse structure rather than having to fill in the details of a "prefab" schema. However, Trabasso's causal model appears to represent a promising beginning rather than a well-worked-out theory. First, there is nothing in the current version that says anything about the process of making causal connections. As with much of the theorizing on discourse processing, readers are assumed to make connections and build structures, but little is said about how or when it is done. Second, there is little said about exactly how the causal structure is related to other structures. For example, in the analysis of Trabasso and van den Broek (1985), variables derived from story-grammar analyses were shown to affect recall in addition to those of the causal analysis. However, little is said about how the two would coexist in a single structural model. Third, as it now exists, the concept of "causal connection" seems too broad. In the example, physical causal connections, such as kicking causing the rope to break, are mixed in with motivational ones, such as bringing the donkey to town in order to sell it, and with mere temporal or enabling ones, such as walking and happening to meet some girls. It seems unlikely that an adequate model of discourse processing can really treat these various causal connections as being the same thing. For example, prior research (Black and Bern, 1981) showed that "real" causal connections were much more powerful than mere temporal ones such as the walk causing the meeting of the girls. While Trabasso and Sperry acknowledge different types of causal connections, at present, they make no use of these differences.

To summarize, the process of finding causal connections is undoubtedly an important component of understanding text. The work of Trabasso and his colleagues seems like an interesting first step in developing a model of tractable complexity in dealing with causality.

"Mental models" The term *mental models* was coined by Johnson-Laird (1983) to refer to a kind of model for representing "meaning." A major thrust of Johnson-Laird's research has been to underscore the inadequacies of the standard propositional representations in understanding how meaning is represented in the brain. While some of his specific proposals are interesting and instructive, the general term *mental model* is about as vague and unenlightening as the term *schema*.

Johnson-Laird (1983) and others (e.g., Dresher and Hornstein 1976; Fodor 1978) have strongly criticized the standard way in which computer-science-inspired models (usually expressed as propositional networks) represent "meaning." In these models, the meaning of a larger conceptual unit is represented by a series of interconnections between abstract conceptual nodes. These interconnections might also be labeled and have some meaning as well. Thus, a sentence such as "John threw the ball to Mary." would be represented by some sort of interconnections which would establish that "John," "threw," "Mary," were all related, and furthermore would have represented that "John" is the "agent," "threw" is the "action," "Mary" the "recipient." Furthermore, there would presumably be interconnections between these abstract nodes representing the concepts to their sensory representations, so that one could go from this abstract representation to "look up" what the nodes "John," "threw," "action," "agent," and so forth actually mean in the real world. However, the important point is that these representations do not provide for any meaningful way to put together these real-world meanings (such as what John looks like or is capable of doing and what throwing looks like and means) to understand the meaning of the whole sentence. Johnson-Laird's major thrust is to give a plausible account, for some situations at least, of a type of representation that would allow one to put together component meanings in order to understand a larger meaning.

One case a bit removed from most normal discourse processing is understanding of logical syllogisms. For example, if you encountered the two statements

All dogs are canines. All canines are animals. (8.31a)

you would be able to infer that all dogs are animals even if you didn't know that beforehand. Johnson-Laird proposes that people understand such syllogisms, not by going through formal logical procedures but by making schematic examples that represent the assertions. For example, you might represent "All dogs are canines." as follows

dog = canine
dog = canine
dog = canine
    (canine)
    (canine) (8.31b)

with the parenthetical notation indicating that there may or may not be other canines besides dogs. There is nothing magic about those being five items in the list; the basic idea is that the proposition is represented schematically by a small number of canines that are dogs and a small number of canines that may or may not be dogs to stand in for the potentially large number that could be in either category. Johnson-Laird posits that you represent the second statement in a similar manner. He then provides rules by which the representations of the two are combined to give you

dog = canine = animal
dog = canine = animal
dog = canine = animal
    (canine)=(animal)
    (canine)=(animal)
        (animal) (8.31c)

which is a representation from which you can read off the conclusion that all dogs are animals.

While this particular syllogism may seem so obvious that it doesn't require all this fuss, Johnson-Laird demonstrates that his representation explains not only how people can draw the appropriate conclusion easily in this case but also why people have difficulties in making syllogistic conclusions in other cases. For example, can you conclude that 8:32a is true from knowing 8.32b to be true?

Some of the chemists are not artists. (8.32a)
None of the artists are beekeepers. Some of the chemists are
beekeepers. (8.32b)

Johnson-Laird's explanation for the difficulty in solving such syllogisms is that they require people to form and examine many different mental models that could represent the possible ways that the two component mental models constructed from 8.32b can be combined. Depending on how patient you are, the requirement to try out these mental models will result in either a long time to reach a conclusion and/or an error in reasoning. (By the way, 8.32a does follow from 8.32b.)

Clearly, syllogisms such as these seem artificial compared to a lot of reasoning that goes on in natural discourse. However, syllogistic reasoning is a part of understanding discourse and the standard propositional representation seems incapable of giving a good account of how it is understood and misunderstood.

A second situation that Johnson-Laird applies mental models to is spatial reasoning. For example, given a set of statements such as

The spoon is to the left of the plate.
The plate is to the right of the knife.
The fork is in front of the spoon.
The cup is in front of the knife. (8.33)

the average person can construct a model of the items so that they can tell whether a picture is consistent with the information or not. However, Johnson-Laird shows that there are some descriptions that are harder to encode because there are greater numbers of possible mental models consistent with them. Again, his formalism seems to capture how people understand the meaning of the statements.

While this example also seems a bit artificial, similar reasoning must also be involved when the reader constructs a representation of a setting that a novelist is describing, such as a room in which an important action takes place. Often, the description of the subsequent action presupposes that the reader has constructed a reasonable model of the room or whatever setting has been described. (Johnson-Laird gives an example from Sherlock Holmes.)

As these examples indicate, Johnson-Laird is still reasonably far away from applying mental models in any systematic way to constructing discourse structures. (He does have reasonable accounts of some general phenomena, such as some aspects of anaphora.) We suspect that the problem may be that no specific kind of structure will be adequate for understanding various types of knowledge. Instead, certain types of mental models will be needed for spatial reasoning, others for logical reasoning, others for understanding the interrelations of physical forces, others for understanding interpersonal interactions, and so forth. We think that Johnson-Laird's work is on the right track in showing the inadequacy of a propositional structure for representing meaning. In fact, several schema theorists (e.g., van Dijk & Kintsch 1983) appear to agree and have attempted to incorporate "mental models" into their theories.

A recent study that cleverly illustrates the use of mental models in a more natural reading situation is by Glenberg, Meyer, and Lindem (1987). They gave subjects passages of the following form

> John was preparing for a marathon in August. After doing a few warm-up exercises, he (took off/put on) his sweatshirt and went jogging. He jogged halfway around the lake without too much difficulty. Further along the route, however, his muscles began to ache. (8.34)

On key trials, subjects would be probed after reading the paragraph on whether the word *sweatshirt* had been in it. They found that subjects took longer to respond "yes" in a version of the paragraph where John took off his sweatshirt than in a version where he put it on. They argued that such a result can only be explained if the reader is constructing a mental model of John with his sweatshirt on in the latter case which remains in the "foreground" of the paragraph because John does (even though the sweatshirt itself is never mentioned or alluded to again).

At present, the focus of the mental model approach has been on demonstrating the inadequacy of conventional propositional network models. In that spirit, we hope that these examples illustrate that propositional structures are unlikely to represent much of what anyone would want to call the "meaning" of the text. The problem with a mental model approach is that it is dangerously open-ended: a different mental model may be needed for each situation and there may be a large number of types of mental models. If so, there may be little of interest that can be said about mental models in general. Instead, we suspect that the most fruitful way to study meaning may be as Johnson-Laird has done: take a limited situation but make a serious attempt to model its meaning. When enough such situations are well understood, then something approaching a general theory might be fruitfully attempted.

"Readability"

As you are no doubt now aware, most of the theories of discourse focus on one aspect of text in which the theorist is interested such as causality and discourse coherence in terms of amount of argument overlap and the like. You may think that such an approach is misguided. Instead, why not do the following? First, think of all the aspects of text that can plausibly affect reading difficulty, starting with lexical variables such as the frequency of the words in the language, the length of the words, moving through syntactic variables measuring complexity of sentences (such as the length of sentences, number of phrases in a sentence, number of clauses in a sentence), and then moving to more semantic variables, such as the number of propositions and the complexity of the causal structure. Then take all of these measures and see how well the combination can predict how difficult readers find the text.

Presumably, if you can come up with objective measures for each of the above predictor variables, and some combination of those variables in fact do a pretty good job of predicting how difficult readers find the text, then it would appear there is some sense in which you can say that you understand discourse processing. In addition, if you can find out which variables are doing most of the prediction, you can understand which text variables are really important in understanding discourse. Moreover, one would have a method for predicting difficulty of text that should have implications for helping to design educational curricula and other practical applications.

There is, in fact, a reasonably large and fairly old literature on the topic (for reviews, see Chall 1958; Kintsch and Vipond 1979). Most of the impetus was practical; people were trying to use objective techniques for measuring the relative difficulty of different texts for educational purposes. More recently, as correlational methods have gotten more sophisticated, the emphasis has been more on trying to understand which variables are the most important. While this enterprise is of some value, we think the conclusions that can be drawn are limited, and we doubt that much new can be learned beyond what is already known.

As we have indicated, the method is basically correlational. Typically, a set of passages are taken from various texts (let's say there are 50 such passages), and various objective indices, such as average word length, average word frequency, average sentence length, average number of phrases per sentence, are computed for each of the paragraphs. A group of subjects is asked to read the passages, and then some measure of reading difficulty (usually the average reading speed in words per minute) is computed for each passage. Finally, the reading times for the 50 passages are correlated with each of the objective indices, and the pattern of correlations is analyzed by a technique known as *multiple regression* in order to achieve enlightenment.

One problem with the technique may already be apparent: why use reading speed as a measure of how much difficulty the reader is having? Presumably a measure of the reader's comprehension of the passage is needed as well. This leads to a very thorny issue: how does one measure comprehension? As you are probably aware from taking reading comprehension tests of varous kinds, most "reading comprehension questions" tap many things besides your comprehension of the text. For example, many of the multiple-choice type of questions that ask about the gist can often be answered on the basis of prior knowledge and very minimal understanding of what the passage is about. On the other hand, as we have seen earlier in the chapter, asking the subject to recall the passage is not a very satisfactory method, since readers forget a lot of the detail even under the best of circumstances. Moreover, testing the readers for recognition of detail, such as dates or names of minor characters, does not seem to be testing for what one would want to call comprehension.

In other words, if one wants to measure comprehension, it can't be done in a vacuum; one needs a theory of what comprehension is (Kintsch and Vipond 1979). Perhaps the solution is to use several measures of comprehension, each tapping a different facet of comprehension. For example, one could measure how many essential points of the story or passage are remembered, how much of the causal structure is remembered, the number of propositions that are recalled, how much lexical detail is remembered, and so forth. The problem then is that most of the reason for the enterprise is lost, since the goal we started with was to determine which variables are important for some global measure of readability. As a result, recent experiments (e.g., Kintsch and Vipond 1979) have measured readability using both reading speed and comprehension in terms of a memory test, in which memory has typically been measured in terms of something like number of "idea units" or propositions (inspired by theories such as Kintsch and van Dijk). However, much of the earlier research merely used reading speed as the measure of text difficulty.

Even if one had the perfect behavioral measure of reading difficulty, there are still major problems in drawing any firm conclusions from the method. The basic one is that the method is correlational. As you undoubtedly know, it is difficult to draw causal inferences from correlational data. We will illustrate the problem by reviewing some of the findings. Many different educational researchers have come up with readability formulas, with about 50 or more now current (Kintsch and Vipond 1979). Most are general purpose, but some are intended to apply only to specialized areas such as chemistry texts. A major aspect of all of these measures is that simple "low level" variables (especially the average word length and the number of words per sentence) are important components of the formulas, since they are highly predictive of how difficult the text is. (Usually, the average length of a word is the most predictive.) What can one infer from that? Unfortunately, very little.

First, let us take the average length of a word. As we indicated in Chapter 3, the average length of a word is highly correlated (negatively) with its frequency in the language. Thus, one can't be sure whether the relation one is observing is because of physical factors (such as longer words take longer to process because they have more visual information) or because longer words are less frequent and thus harder to locate in the lexicon (see Chapter 3). There is no way to understand from correlational data which aspect is truly operative, or whether both are. (In contrast, as discussed in Chapter 5, one can experimentally control one variable and vary the other to get some idea whether each of the variables operating separately has some effect.) The problem is worse when considered in the context of prose passages, since texts with longer words will also tend to have longer and more complex sentences and express more complex ideas. While multiple correlation techniques allow you to understand something about whether a variable has any effect when the effect of another is taken into account, it does not really allow you to conclude very much.

One reason why the "low level" variables tend to do much of the predicting is that they are probably more reliable indices of the underlying psychological constructs that they are supposed to be measuring than are the higher-order variables. Word length is a reliable measure of the amount of visual information needed to be extracted from the word and also, since it is highly correlated with word frequency, a reliable measure of lexical-access time. In contrast, a complexity measure derived from Kintsch and van Dijk's and/or Trabasso's analysis of structure is probably at best capturing only a part of what one would want to call "semantic complexity."

Another way to view the problem with the correlational method is to think about readability measures as a guide to the writer. Let's say that we know that text with shorter words and shorter sentences tends to be more readable than text with longer words and longer sentences. Does it follow that if we have a text with long words and long sentences, we should go about rewriting it so as to make both word and sentence length shorter? Perhaps to some extent. If we have statements like "eschew obfuscation" or run-on sentences, it might be a good idea to change them. However, the underlying ideas in "difficult text" are often inherently complex. Thus, longer sentences and more complex sentence structures are probably needed to explain these ideas, and they will take longer to read than simpler sentences expressing simpler ideas. Using simpler sentences will probably either make the text incomprehensible (if one is still trying to express the same ideas) or simplify it to the extent that many of the original ideas are removed.

To summarize, readability formulas are of some value in allowing an educator to predict how difficult a group of subjects will find a given text. However, the correlational data from which they are obtained are not of much help in understanding discourse processing. While having better and more theoretically inspired indices of higher-level processes will help somewhat, we are skeptical that this approach to text comprehension will lead very far. A recent development along the same lines has been to predict moment-to-moment processing using the same techniques. For example, if the gaze duration on a word (see Chapter 4) is the variable one is trying to predict, then one would use such indices as word length, sentence length, and position in the sentence to predict the gaze time. In other words, the word rather than the passage of text is the unit of analysis. While using smaller units allows one to be more diagnostic, the problems of the above discussion still obtain. For example, word length still predicts a large percent of the variability (Just and Carpenter 1980; Kliegl, Olson, and Davidson 1982). In addition, such an analysis assumes the *immediacy hypothesis* (i.e., that the time spent on a word reflects all the processing done on that word and that word only). As we discussed in chapters 4 and 5, strong versions of the immediacy hypothesis are false and may not be even a particularly good approximation, especially when discourse variables are involved (see the discussion of the "distance effect" on anaphora earlier in this chapter).

SUMMARY

This chapter is likely to be the most controversial in the book, since there are widely diverging views on the merits of current work on discourse processing. At one extreme, some people view the extraction of higher-order meaning as the question of central interest in reading and view all other questions as technical details. In general, our experience is that most students unacquainted with research on reading hold a view close to that. At the other extreme are people who look at measures such as readability and conclude that higher-order variables are of lesser importance and that most of the reading process can be understood by understanding how people access words and put them into simple syntactic and semantic structures. In addition to predicting readability differences in texts, measures of word retrieval, such as naming times for words, predict differences in reading ability between individuals (e.g., Perfetti and Hogaboam 1975).

People who believe that understanding how discourse is structured and how meaning is extracted are *the* questions to be asked in reading will probably find this chapter too brief and the tone of many of our comments too negative. Our position on discourse processing research is not that the issues aren't important; they are. However, we are not convinced that the tools that we have at present are adequate for getting at many of these issues.

Let us make an analogy that we believe is not terribly unfair. Whether there is intelligent life elsewhere in the universe is clearly an interesting and important question. In fact, there has been a considerable amount of research and theorizing, by people like Carl Sagan, devoted to the issue. However, at our present level of knowledge, it is probably largely a waste of time, since we have virtually no data about other solar systems and little idea of what the possible conditions for life forms are (as exemplified by the surprise about the recent discovery of life forms that exist at high temperatures around the thermal fissures in the ocean floors). It may not be totally valueless to construct theoretical models of other solar systems from plausible assumptions about how suns are born (again, largely based on speculation). However, we feel that time might be better spent on other issues until the technology improves (e.g., pictures of other solar systems may be obtained with the space telescope, if it ever goes up) so that there is some data worth theorizing about.

In the case of discourse processing, we are not sure whether the problem with the present research is current technology, current theorizing, or whether the problems are just too complex ever to be handled satisfactorily. In any event, our feeling is that, for the most part, the research isn't getting anywhere. In the first place, the typical theory about how discourse is processed usually only deals with one or two aspects of the problem. Unfortunately, the brain system, which handles these high-order aspects of discourse for the reader, may not be sufficiently modularized in order for one to get away with this approach. Second, even if there were an adequate theory, it is not clear how one would devise tests of it. On the one hand, one could use natural text and use a correlational approach (as discussed in the previous section). We think such an approach is basically unsatisfactory. On the other hand, one can attempt to manipulate text so as to vary one aspect (such as the causal structure) and leave everything else the same. This is extremely difficult to do and still have your experimental materials resembling text that people would read in the real world. Third, the tools being used to get at understanding are fairly crude. Much of the research on discourse structure uses memory as the primary variable. While memory taps what has been comprehended in text, the relationship between memory and comprehension is far from simple.

As our tone probably indicates, we have a more positive feeling about the material in the first half of the chapter. In general, we feel that "big issues" often have to be "snuck up" on. The global question of how discourse is represented may be too big for us now or in the forseeable future, but the questions of how anaphoric links are constructed, how someone finds the "given" and the "new" in a sentence seem tractable, and furthermore promise to provide data that will help in eventually formulating how discourse is represented.

An eventual understanding of reading will clearly require, as an important component, an understanding of how discourse is represented and how this representation is constructed. However, we feel that our understanding of discourse representation has progressed little beyond that of the man or woman in the street, and we are not optimistic that there are any breakthroughs lurking around the corner. We hope we are wrong.

PART FOUR
BEGINNING READING AND READING DISABILITY

Up to this point, we have focused on the skilled reader and on the kind of processing activities that he or she engages in during reading. However, we do not become skilled readers by accident. The task of learning to read involves a great deal of effort, both for children and for illiterate adults trying to learn to read. In the process of becoming a skilled reader, the cognitive activities involved may be considerably different at different levels of skill, particularly in the recognition and identification of words. What may be a relatively automatic and effortless process for adults may be a plodding, time-consuming and effortful process for young children. A key question is whether the reading process in children is just a slower version of what goes on in adults or is qualitatively different.

Chapter 9 will focus on learning to read and the cognitive and perceptual prerequisites that seem to be important for beginning readers. In this chapter we will discuss the alphabetic principle that we mentioned in Chapter 2 and the important role it plays in learning to read in our culture. We will also discuss "early readers" (children who learn to read without any formal instruction) and the concept of "reading readiness." We will conclude Chapter 9 by describing the methods typically used by teachers to help children learn to read.

Chapter 10 deals with the development of the skill of reading. In this chapter, we will discuss stages of reading development and then move to a review of the kinds of cues used by beginning readers in identifying and recognizing words. Much of the remainder of the chapter deals with issues that we have discussed in Part 2 (in relation to skilled reading), and we will discuss how various aspects of the reading process (word recognition, inner speech, the use of contextual information, eye movements, and comprehension processes) are affected by the development of the skill of reading.

You will notice when you read chapters 9 and 10 that we say virtually nothing about emotional and motivational factors involved in learning to read. That is not because such factors are unimportant. It is clear that children need to have the appropriate motivation to want to learn to read; if they do not, they will have difficulty learning. If they have negative emotional responses to school and the process of learning to read, their academic achievement will suffer. But this book is primarily interested in reading from a cognitive perspective, and to cover the emotional and social issues adequately would probably require an additional volume.

In Chapter 11, we turn our attention to individuals who have trouble learning to read. Most of the chapter deals with *developmental dyslexia* (difficulty in learning to read in the absence of obvious neurological, emotional, or motivational handicaps). However, in the chapter we will also discuss two other groups, "poor readers" and those with *acquired dyslexia.* "Poor readers" are discussed chiefly to emphasize that developmental dyslexics are not merely normal readers who happen to be a bit slower than average. Acquired dyslexics (individuals who could once read fluently but have lost the ability due to some sort of brain damage) are of interest both for insights they give about the components of normal reading and as a source for hypotheses about the problems of developmental dyslexics.

In sum, the focus in this section is not on the skilled reader but on "nonstandard" readers: children learning to read, and people who do not read well.

CHAPTER NINE
LEARNING TO READ

Children learning to read are faced with a very difficult task. For skilled readers, many of the component processes involved in reading occur fairly automatically and effortlessly, yet for the beginning reader they may be plodding, time-consuming activities. In this chapter, we examine a number of characteristics of learning to read, focusing on the skills or component processes that the child must acquire. While we will touch on cross-cultural issues, the focus of the chapter will be on learning to read English.

Much of the research literature dealing with learning to read has centered on the issue of which type of instructional method is best for effectively teaching children to read. Indeed, there are volumes and volumes filled with investigations of this issue. The major instructional methods that have typically been contrasted are some form of a *whole word* approach versus a *phonics* approach. In whole word instruction (sometimes called the *look-say* method), children are taught a *sight vocabulary* of 10 to 20 words (words presented on flash cards that they learn by rote). Subsequent words are also learned as wholes, although not necessarily out of context. In contrast, phonics approaches, while often beginning with a small sight vocabulary, stress the relationship between the grapheme (printed letter) and phoneme (sound representation). Unfortunately, as we pointed out in Chapter 2, the correspondence between the phoneme and grapheme is complex and critics of this approach have often argued that this lack of perfect correspondence causes confusion for beginning readers.

In a major review of the research on this issue, Chall (1967) found that there were many conflicting studies in the literature, but that the majority seemed to favor a phonics approach. However, her review also indicates that the teacher may be as important as the specific type of instruction used. It is somewhat disheartening to survey the vast number of studies that have been conducted on the issue of the most appropriate instructional method for teaching reading and to see the large amount of conflicting evidence that emerges. Much of the problem has to do with the research designs used in these studies, in which children in classroom A are taught by a whole word approach and those in classroom B are taught phonics. In such designs, certain critical factors (such as the specific teacher) are often confounded with the type of instruction given. Later studies have used more sophisticated experimental designs, but a fair amount of controversy still persists.

An even bigger problem than weaknesses in the experimental designs is the fact that the entire issue is emotion-laden for those who have vested interests in teaching children to read. Beginning reading instruction is a big business with various publishing companies interested in convincing school districts that their particular program is the best on the market. Many individual educational researchers interested in the issue of learning to read have also participated in the development of various curricula. As a result, professional conferences dealing with beginning reading instruction are sometimes filled with emotional sessions in which purported researchers often sound more like evangelists than scientists. Unfortunately, intuitions often seem to carry more weight than any compelling evidence for or against a given position.

Given these problems, is there much hope of making meaningful statements about how children learn to read and how to best instruct them? We believe that there is hope, but we base our optimism as much on the results of laboratory studies in which the component skills of reading are investigated as on the results of large-scale instructional studies. A major problem with large-scale classroom studies is that the results are seldom analytic either with respect to the particular reading skills mastered or the aspects of the teaching method that are particularly beneficial. In contrast, laboratory studies have the potential to be analytic about the important processes involved in learning to read. Critics of the approach we advocate will argue that laboratory studies are remote from the actual classroom situation in which the mechanics of learning to read are acquired. However, for the most part, the laboratory studies are not at variance with either the classroom studies or with common sense.

In this chapter, we will begin by discussing the demands of an alphabetic system. We will then discuss issues of reading readiness and prerequisites to reading. Finally, we will discuss the various types of methods used to teach children to read.

THE ALPHABETIC PRINCIPLE

As we pointed out in Chapter 2, the critical difference between writing systems is how the writing system codes the units of the language. At one extreme is a writing system that directly codes meaning. At the other extreme is the alphabetic system which operates on the principle that a written symbol is associated with a phoneme. The existence of logographic writing systems demonstrates that learning to read can take place by association of a symbol with meaning. However, it is at some cost that such learning takes place. While the Chinese writing system is not purely logographic (see Chapter 2), readers of Chinese must learn a large number of characters. A vocabulary of 5,000 to 7,000 characters may be typical of literate Chinese adults, but children master only about 3,500 characters by learning 500 to 600 characters per year during each of the first 6 years in school (Leong 1973). Chinese children spend a considerable amount of time at home working on Chinese characters. In contrast, American children appear to spend appreciably less time and effort in mastering an equivalent number of words.

The alphabetic system has a clear advantage over logographic writing systems, since it requires fewer than three to four thousand associations to be learned. The alphabetic system gains this economy of learning by creating correspondences between units of writing and units of speech; it takes advantage of the fact that speech is already associated with meaning in the language. The various alphabets of the world, despite differences in the appearance of the letters making up the script, are all consistent with the same principle that written symbols are associated with phonemes. However, most alphabetic characters are not merely symbols for individual phonemes (see Chapter 2). Most languages represent the relation between letters and phonemes in more complex ways (e.g., the silent *e* in English). Some alphabets reflect their syllable origins more clearly than others by not having letters for most vowels (such as in Hebrew and Arabic). Many, like English, also use the alphabet to represent morphology at the expense of phonology.

In spite of this complexity, the basic principle that letters represent phonemes is the same across all alphabetic systems and this principle is the key to a *productive writing system* (Perfetti 1985). A productive writing system is one that produces an indefinitely large number of words and morphemes from a small set of reusable symbols (or letters). While this productive value of alphabetic systems results in a great deal of economy in learning to read them, it also can result in confusion for beginning readers. There are two reasons for confusion and difficulty in learning the system: the abstract nature of the phoneme (especially consonants) and the fact that alphabets do not code each of their vowels with a unique symbol. Let's consider each of these obstacles for children learning to read.

The first obstacle is that young children often have an imperfect idea of what phonemes are. This is because phonemes are abstractions rather than natural physical segments of speech (Liberman, et al. 1967). However, this is less of a problem for vowels since they last long enough to be heard and they are less dependent upon context than consonants. The /ae/ (pronounced "aah") sound in *bat* is about the same as in *laugh* and in each word the sound can be clearly heard and isolated. Thus a teacher can point to the *a* in *bat* and say /ae/ and the child can hear it because it does not depend much on the sound that precedes or follows it. This is not true with consonants, especially stop consonants. The phoneme /d/, for example, is an abstraction since both its perception and production are highly dependent on vowels that precede and follow it. First, the /d/ in *dime* is quite different acoustically from the /d/ in *dome* or the /d/ in *lid*. Second, you can't say /d/ by itself. When a teacher tries to explain that the word *dime* begins with the phoneme /d/, there will be a problem because she will produce /d/ plus a bit of the following vowel because some vocalization is necessary. If she adds the vowel sound /ay/ (pronounced "eye"), it will be correct for *dime* but not for *dome*. If she tries to omit the vowel (which is impossible to do), she will probably produce /duh/, and the resulting sound will not be a component of either *dime* or *dome*.

What all of this means is that it will be very difficult for children learning to read to isolate and discover phonemes such as /t/, /d/, /p/, and /b/. Thus, it follows that applying the alphabetic principle (the idea that a written symbol is associated with a phoneme) will be especially difficult because it depends on associating the abstract phoneme /d/ (or any other consonant) with a specific grapheme, in this case the letter *d*. Associating two elements will be especially difficult for the child if he or she only understands one of them, knowing the letter *d* but not being sure about the abstract phoneme.

The second obstacle for children learning to read, the fact that alphabets do not code each of their vowels with a unique symbol, is much greater in some alphabetic languages than others. Part of the reason for the complexity is that alphabetic languages are economical. For example, American English has more than a dozen vowel sounds but only five standard vowel letters. That means that *a, e, i, o,* and *u* have to do double and triple duty, even with some help from *y* and *w* (*y* and *w* both can change vowel sounds as in *saw* and *say; y* can also substitute for *i*). For example, *cat, car,* and *cake* each use the letter *a* for a different vowel phoneme. Most of these differences are not arbitrary, since the regularity of pronunciation, which is the major advantage of a productive alphabet, is largely present: the pronunciation of *a* in *cake* is determined by the presence of a final *e* and the pronunciation of *a* in *car* is determined by the presence of the *r* and the absence of a final *e*. It is therefore not accurate, as some have argued, to say that English spelling is chaotic. While the mapping of vowels to letters is less complex in languages such as Spanish and Italian, which have fewer vowel sounds in the spoken language, there are few orthographies in which each vowel letter represents a unique vowel sound.

In addition to the economy versus complexity tradeoff, which we have just described, there is also a tradeoff of explicitness and morphological transparency. This tradeoff is between the explicitness of the writing system in representing the phonemes of the language and the transparency of the writing system in representing the morphology of the language. A fully explicit system, for example, could associate the grapheme *a* only with /ae/ (as in *fat*) and invent some other symbol for /e/ (as in *fate*). Unfortunately, this would obscure important morphological facts that are reflected in English. For example, the use of *a* to represent two different phonemes in *nature* and *natural* may be confusing as a guide to pronunciation but serves to remind the reader of their noun-adjective relation, and is typical of English morphological spelling (see Chapter 2).

In summary, there are problems in understanding the alphabetic principle. As we've argued, there are two major problems: phonemes are perceptual abstractions, and alphabets sacrifice phoneme explicitness for symbol economy or morphological transparency, thereby complicating the orthography. Inasmuch as English orthography sacrifices explicitness for both symbol economy and morphological transparency, there have been some attempts to alter it for the purpose of teaching children to read.

The *initial teaching alphabet (i.t.a.)* proposed by Pitman (Pitman and St. John 1969) is the best known. The i.t.a. contains 44 letters, one for each English phoneme, including 16 vowels. Twenty-four of them are identical to those in the traditional alphabet (eliminating *q* and *x*) and 20 of them are new. Some of the new ones are ligatured (connected by a loop to each other). The i.t.a. has no uppercase letters, and sentences begin with larger versions of the lowercase letters. In an attempt to retain some economy, Pitman used a number of digraphic symbols. For example, *oi* symbolizes the vowel in *toy* and *ie* symbolizes the vowel in *kite*. An advantage of the digraphs is that they retain one of the letters of the regular alphabet, which the child will eventually have to use. The main point of spelling reform writing systems like the i.t.a. is that words are spelled like they sound. Thus, we have *enuf, woz, laf,* and *sed* for *enough, was, laugh,* and *said.* In addition, however, there are a number of words that result from the digraphs and ligatured graphemes that look somewhat unusual (see Table 9.1).

There have been a number of studies that have tried to assess the effectiveness of the i.t.a. in teaching children to read. There seems to be good agreement that, on average, children using the i.t.a. learn to read better for the first two years of school than those who learn to read using standard English orthography. This suggests that a simpler and more explicit orthography may be easier in learning to read. The practical significance of i.t.a. is less clear, however, because of the problem of transferring to standard English orthography; no matter how effective the i.t.a. might be in aiding children as they initially learn to read, they will still have to transfer to the regular alphabet. The studies are inconclusive on this latter point, but it appears that when children who have learned i.t.a. have to transfer to the

TABLE 9.1 The Initial Teaching Alphabet (From Downing 1965). With permission of the author.

TABLE 1

THE INITIAL TEACHING ALPHABET

Number	Character	Name	Example	Traditional spelling
1	æ	ae	ræt	rate
2	b	bee	bıg	big
3	c	kee	cat	cat
4	d	dee	dog	dog
5	ɛɛ	ee	mɛɛt	meet
6	f	ef	fill	fill
7	g	gae	gun	gun
8	h	hae	hat	hat
9	ie	ie	tie	tie
10	j	jae	jelly	jelly
11	k	kae	kit	kit
12	l	el	lamp	lamp
13	m	em	man	man
14	n	en	net	net
15	œ	oe	tœ	toe
16	p	pee	pıg	pig
17	r	rae	run	run
18	s	ess	sad	sad
19	t	tee	tap	tap
20	ue	ue	due	due
21	v	vee	van	van
22	w	wae	will	will
23	y	i-ae	yell	yell
24	z	zed or zee	fizz	fizz
25	ʂ	zess	houses	houses
26	wh	whae	when	when
27	ꜯh	chae	ꜯhick	chick
28	ꝑh	ith	ꝑhaut	thought
29	ſh	thee	ſhe	the
30	ʃh	ish	ʃhip	ship
31	ʒ	zhee	meʒuer	measure
32	ŋ	ing	siŋ	sing
33	ɑ	ah	fɑr	far
34	au	au	autum	autumn
35	a	at	appl	apple
36	e	et	egg	egg
37	i	it	dip	dip
38	o	ot	hot	hot
39	u	ut	ugly	ugly
40	ω	oot	bωk	book
41	ꞷ	oo	mꞷn	moon
42	ou	ow	bou	bough
43	oi	oi	toi	toy

standard alphabet, they read no better than children who are initially taught with the standard alphabet.

Another attempt to deal with the difficulty of learning an alphabetic language has been the use of a syllabary. Syllabaries use an intermediate speech level between the printed symbol and the word level. However, a syllabary does not have the intrinsic problem of phoneme abstractness that the alphabet does. A syllable is a real acoustic unit whose duration can be measured and which is relatively invariant in different contexts. These facts, along with the fact that syllabaries remain the basis for some writing systems (such as Japanese Hiragana), led Gleitman and Rozin (1973, 1977; Rozin and Gleitman 1977) to attempt to teach children to read by using a syllabary.

Children with severe reading problems were in fact able to read the rebus-based syllabary that they devised (Rozin, Poritsky, and Sotsky 1971). A rebus is a picture that suggests its name, and this name is often used in magazines designed for young children just beginning the reading process. As can be seen in Figure 9.1, a picture of a can is first used as a symbol for the word *can* and then for the syllable /can/ (as in *candy*). Gleitman and Rozin did not, like Pitman, intend the syllabary as a substitute for an alphabet because a syllabary system would be impractical in English with its thousands of syllables. The point of their demonstration was that early instruction with a syllabary can introduce the child to the concept that the print encountered in reading corresponds to speech rather than meaning. However, there was no evidence that the syllabary facilitated the reading of normal English.

An overwhelming value of a productive coding system (either a syllabary or an alphabet) is that once it has been mastered, it allows the reader to read words never before seen. Only a writing system that has a mediating speech level between written symbols and language meanings can

FIGURE 9-1 Example of syllabary writing (Gleitman and Rozin 1973). The title is "Candy for Andy." (With permission of the International Reading Association and the authors.)

do this. While a syllabary may be easier to master than an alphabetic language at early stages, a syllabary for English is probably unworkable (as argued above). The work with i.t.a. suggests that a more explicit and less efficient alphabet may also be easier to master. However, it seems unlikely that the current English orthography will be replaced in the foreseeable future. Therefore, the rest of this chapter concentrates on the process of learning to read English, such as it is. (While it is not perfect, it is productive and efficient.) As we shall see, understanding the complex relationship between the printed symbols and phonemes represents the major step in acquiring the skill of reading.

EARLY READERS AND "READING READINESS"

When a child begins reading, he or she has already had at least 3 or 4 years of language experience. Children generally begin to talk between 12 and 18 months of age, with girls usually more precocious than boys. By the time they are 5 years old they have an extensive vocabulary. Although syntactic and semantic development of language processes is not complete, they are fairly proficient language users, and though not as skilled as adults, they communicate quite effectively.

In the United States, formal instruction in reading begins during the first grade. However, kindergarten usually involves some preliminary reading instruction called *reading readiness training,* which includes learning the names of the 26 letters of the alphabet. In addition, parents and television programs like "Sesame Street" and "Electric Company" have exposed many preschool children to print, different letters of the alphabet, grapheme-phoneme (letter-sound) relationships, and blending principles even before they get to kindergarten.

Everyone would agree that learning to read involves developing and applying many skills (e.g., learning to move the eyes left to right, learning letter forms, learning what phonemes are). We will discuss these skills in the next section. What is more controversial is whether learning these skills (or at least some key subset of them) depends on the child reaching some basic stage of cognitive development. A common view, held by many developmental psychologists interested in reading, has been that children must reach the so-called *concrete operations* stage of cognitive development before they can learn to read successfully. This stage of cognitive development is one in a series of stages proposed by Jean Piaget (1952). The notion of concrete operations is best exemplified in terms of one of the famous conservation experiments, in this case the conservation of number. The experimental task comes in two phases. In the first phase the child is shown two identical quantities lined up next to each other which appear to be identical. Perhaps two rows of coins are lined up with six coins in each row and with the coins (in both rows) equally spaced. The child is then asked if the number of coins in the two rows is the same, and even the child who has not attained the concrete operations stage usually judges them to be equal. The experimenter then changes the appearance of one of the rows, either by spreading the coins out or by bunching them up. Now the two rows, though equal in number of coins, are unequal in length. Once again the child is asked to compare them. This time the child in the pre-concrete stage often judges them to be unequal and usually says that the longer row is also the more numerous. Children up to the age of about seven make this type of error quite regularly, while older ones generally answer correctly (Piaget 1952).

Piaget's conclusion, and the generally accepted one, is that the concept of *invariance* (the idea that things remain the same despite being in different forms) develops as children get older. Younger children, he claimed, believe that lengthening a row makes it more numerous and shortening less so, while older children understand that quantities do not change unless something is added or taken away. Many developmental psychologists have concluded that the concept of invariance, which is characteristic of the concrete operations stage of cognitive development, is a prerequisite for reading.

There are two possible conclusions that one could draw from such a statement. The first is that developmental stages progress by a biological clock (though different for each child) and that any instruction in reading is fruitless if the child has not reached the appropriate developmental level. The usual estimate (given this view) of the age at which concrete operations begin (for the large majority of children) is 7. If so, it is hard to understand why reading instruction is successful in countries in which it begins at age 5 (e.g., England). The second possible conclusion is that there is a best instructional procedure (which may be unrelated to reading) to develop the general concept of invariance. There are, however, few principled arguments about what this best training procedure would be. In fact, it is not at all clear that the concept of invariance is developed in an all-or-none manner. Children who fail in one version of Piaget's conservation task often succeed in other versions that seem to make exactly the same demands on their understanding of the invariance principle (see Bryant and Bradley 1985). This suggests that if invariance needs to be learned to master reading then the best procedure would be to teach invariance in the reading context (Goswami 1986).

One line of evidence that has been put forward for the relevance of a Piagetian stage analysis to reading is that there is a correlation between initial reading performance and one or another of the various measures of mastery of concrete operations, such as conservation (Murray 1978). A second is that there is some evidence (to be discussed shortly) to suggest that older children given initial reading instruction at the same time as younger children will benefit more from it and show better performance than the younger children. (The assumption made here is that the older children were more likely to have been in the concrete operations stage than the younger ones.) Let us consider each of these lines of evidence in turn.

First, the finding of a correlation between mastery of concrete operations and reading performance does not necessarily imply that mastery of conservation (or invariance) enables reading; perhaps mastery of reading helps mastery of conservation or perhaps there is some common cause helping the two. Moreover, the correlation between the two variables is not as strong as it should be if invariance were absolutely necessary for reading to begin. This is exemplified by investigations of *early readers*.

While most children in the United States learn to read during the first year of school, when they are about 6 or 7, a small percentage (less than 1 percent) of children know how to read when they enter school. In such cases, parents are often involved in teaching their children to read, but some children actually learn by themselves with only a little help from their parents. Some learn to read from watching television, particularly by associating the printed message in commercials with the spoken word (Torrey 1969). Investigations of these early readers do not reveal anything remarkably different between them and other children (Durkin 1966; Briggs and Elkind 1973; Clark 1976). While their average IQ score is higher on average than the rest of the population, with median IQ scores of 121 and 133 in two studies (Durkin 1966), the range of their IQ scores (between 82 and 170) indicates that many children who are early readers do not have unusually high IQs. Early readers come from varied racial and socioeconomic backgrounds. Parents and teachers tend to portray them as having good memory, concentration, curiosity; and persistence. Interviews with parents of early readers have suggested that mothers of early readers have higher educational levels than mothers of nonreaders and that fathers of early readers read to them more often than do fathers of nonreaders (Briggs and Elkind 1973).

Briggs and Elkind gave a large battery of perceptual, motor, cognitive, and personality tests to early readers and nonreaders matched on age, sex, IQ, race, and socioeconomic status. For the most part, the differences between early readers and nonreaders were small. Early readers did better than nonreaders on some Piagetian conservation tasks. Briggs and Elkind interpreted the results as providing support for the hypothesis that learning to read presupposes certain logical abilities that allow children to group the complex encoding and decoding rules which link graphemes and phonemes in English. However, the differences between the groups on the concrete operations task were relatively small and it was certainly not the case that all early readers had mastered the conservation tasks and all the control subjects had not. Thus it is hard to argue for a qualitative difference between the early readers and the control nonreaders.

The second line of evidence for the relevance of concrete operations to reading is that older children appear to master reading somewhat more easily than younger children. Feitelson, Tehori, and Levinberg-Green (1982) studied the reading performance of kibbutz children who were all taught to read at the same time. Children in the group ranged in age from 5 years to over 7 years when they received their first formal instruction in reading. Feitelson, Tehori, and Levinberg-Green found that at every point that they tested the children, the older children did better than the younger ones. They concluded that when reading instruction is attempted before the child reaches the concrete operations stage, many difficulties occur. However, there are other differences between 5 and 7 year olds besides their cognitive capabilities. Seven year olds are more likely to follow instructions and probably have a longer attention span. Indeed, our own observations of our children as they were learning to read indicates that they struggled initially with the task, but at some point everything seemed to click. Perhaps the older children can deal with the frustrations of the task better in order to master the skill.

While older children may be more ready to read than younger children (for cognitive or other reasons), the data indicate that younger children are ready to read as well. The age at which children receive their first formal reading instruction varies considerably from country to country. In Great Britain, for example, reading instruction generally begins around 5 years of age and in Denmark and Sweden it generally begins around 7 years of age. In France and Japan, formal instruction begins at the age of 6. In all these countries, literacy is close to 100 percent, so we can assume that the instruction is reasonably successful.

Within educational circles in the United States, it has often been argued that before children can learn to read they need to achieve a state termed *reading readiness*. (Exactly what "reading readiness" consists of is very vague.) Consistent with the above cultural data, achieving reading readiness is often thought to depend on proper training rather than biological determination. In practice, children entering school are often given reading readiness training with various types of visual perception and auditory discriminations. Can reading readiness training accelerate the development of the appropriate cognitive strategies needed for reading? The question is hard to answer because "reading readiness training" is a term that covers almost any activity that goes on in kindergarten. In the past, it might not have been unusual to find children spending much of the school year "getting ready to read" by performing a number of physical exercises assumed to be related to reading. Some of them are pretty distantly related to reading, such as learning to walk on a balance beam. While training on general skills will probably produce some benefit on reading, a large number of educators now believe that such a scattered approach is not efficient. Indeed, the idea now appears to be that if the goal is for children to learn a particular skill (like reading), it is more efficient to teach it directly than to expect it to transfer from other learning (Singer and Balow 1981). Various types of training may help with the growth of children's cognitive development, as well as skills related to reading; direct instruction in reading, however, is probably more beneficial to reading.

PREREQUISITES TO READING

As children approach the reading task, they are forced to use or learn skills that have not previously been of particular importance. While children learn to speak quite fluently without receiving formal instruction, reading involves formal instruction for the vast majority of children. Before children will be successful in learning to read, they must be able to learn rules efficiently (either taught explicitly or deduced by inference) concerning the relationship between printed symbols and semantic referents. In order to become proficient in reading, it is evident that children not only must learn rules that apply to the perception and comprehension of words, they must also learn or adapt some very specific skills. Here, we will briefly discuss some skills that appear to be crucial to the development of efficient reading: recognizing letters, discriminating left from right, gaining cognitive control of eye movements, becoming conscious of the word as a unit, and developing linguistic (or phonological) awareness.

Letter Recognition

Despite the fact that some methods of reading instruction emphasize the perception of whole words, proponents of all methods of instruction recognize that it is essential for the child to be able to recognize the 26 letters of the alphabet. Comprehending that the squiggles on the page correspond to letters represents a major step toward becoming successful in recognizing words.

Durrell (1958) found that children who learned to read successfully in the first year of instruction had acquired a large amount of letter knowledge prior to entry into school, though there were large individual differences. He found that early skill in letter knowledge was a good predictor of early progress in reading during the first year of instruction. Numerous other studies have demonstrated that knowledge of letter names in kindergarten or at the beginning of first grade was the best predictor of early reading achievement (e.g., Bond and Dykstra 1967; Stevenson et al. 1976). However, early ability to name letters was not related to continued success in reading in the second and third grade (Stevenson et al. 1976). Thus, letter recognition appears to be necessary for progress in early reading, but children who know the letters earlier apparently will not necessarily become the best readers when they are in the middle grades of elementary school.

Exactly what is involved in learning to recognize letters? The consensus would appear to be that letter recognition involves discriminating the distinguishing features of letters. In learning to recognize letters, it is very common for children to confuse letters that look alike—*b* and *d* are often confused, as are *p* and *q*. Presumably this is because these pairs of letters differ only on a single feature. Numerous studies, mostly with adults as subjects (but some examining children's letter recognition errors), have been undertaken to infer the visual features of letters from the patterns of errors made when individual letters are presented. In adults, the research tends to be conducted under highly controlled experimental situations in which a letter may be exposed very briefly (say 50 milliseconds) and the subject must identify it. In children, the research tends to be less well controlled from some perspectives, but the data are generally obtained in relatively natural situations. On the basis of these types of studies, various lists of distinguishing features have been compiled for both upper and lower case letters. Table 9.2 presents one example.

In learning to recognize letters, children must be able to determine the features that differentiate one letter from another. Nodine and his colleagues, using eye movement patterns to reveal what features are attended to, compared pre-readers and children just beginning to read with older children (Nodine and Evans 1969; Nodine and Lang 1971; Nodine and Simmons 1974; Nodine and Steuerle 1973). (Very large letters were used in order for the experimenters to be able to determine which feature was fixated.) Children in these experiments were asked to make same-different judgments about pairs of letters, letterlike symbols, or letter strings, while their eye movements were recorded. When children were shown nonword pairs, for example, containing middle letters of either high visual confusability (*ZPRN*) or low visual confusability (*EROI*), several differences between third grade readers and pre-reading kindergarten children were found. First, older children looked more frequently at those parts of the nonwords relevant for making an accurate decision. Second, older children were more proficient at processing distinctive feature information. The younger children shifted their fixation back and forth between the stimuli more than the older children and did not look as frequently at that part of a letter which distinguished it from a similar letter (e.g., *G* and *C*). Finally, the visual scanning strategies of the older children were more planned and deliberate than those of the younger children. We shall return to this last finding in the section on eye movement control.

While the same-different task is different from reading, Nodine's research suggests that, for the child beginning the reading process, letter recognition involves being able to identify the distinguishing features of letters. When this skill is acquired, same-different judgments of visually similar letters (*C* and *G, b* and *d*) are made quite easily. Before this skill is acquired, the discrimination is quite difficult.

Directional Orientation

Children often have trouble discriminating letters that are mirror images of each other (*b* and *d*). Many researchers have suggested that this problem is an instantiation of a general problem children have with spatial orientations. Young children beginning the reading process sometimes may not know the difference between the general concepts of "left" and "right." Since words are printed from left to right in English, directional skills are not only necessary for discriminating letters but important for being able to read text. As children begin reading, they often have problems keeping their place on the page. Beginning reading books are often printed in large letters and with only a few words on each page (the remainder of the page being occupied

TABLE 9.2 Distinctive features (based on Gibson 1969) for capital letters of the alphabet. Each letter is described by a series of "yes" or "no" statements (yes = +; no = blank) about a limited number of visual properties. With permission of Prentice-Hall.

FEATURES	A	E	F	H	I	L	T	K	M	N	V	W	X	Y	Z	B	C	D	G	J	O	P	R	Q	S	U
Straight																										
Horizontal	+	+	+	+			+								+				+							
Vertical		+	+	+	+	+	+	+	+	+						+		+				+	+			+
Diagonal	+							+	+	+	+	+	+	+	+								+	+		
Diagonal								+	+	+	+	+	+	+	+								+	+		
Curve																										
Closed																+		+			+	+	+	+		
Open vertically																				+						+
Open horizontally																	+		+							
Intersection	+	+	+	+			+	+					+			+						+	+	+		
Redundancy																										
Cyclic change		+						+	+			+				+	+				+				+	
Symmetry	+	+	+	+	+		+	+	+		+	+	+	+		+	+	+			+					+
Discontinuity																										
Vertical	+			+				+	+	+				+								+				
Horizontal		+	+			+	+								+											

338

with pictures) to help children discriminate the letters as well as to help keep their place. It is not uncommon to find children using their fingers to keep their place as they read.

Clay (1979) discussed a number of factors associated with difficulties children have with directional behavior. She argued that prior to entry into school, children's movements have not been constrained with respect to direction. Upon beginning school, the child has to learn to relate the body, the two eyes, and two hands to a page of print which has directional constraints. The child must learn that the page is made up of lines (which have direction), made up of words (which have direction), and made up of letters (which have a fixed orientation and consist of strokes, lines, features, and angles). Clay also reviewed various types of instructions that can be given to children to facilitate directional learning. She proposed that any child who has been in instruction for 6 months and is still confused about direction needs special attention.

It is clear that acquiring directional skills is important in learning to read (Clay 1970). Indeed, there is some evidence that learning to read, and the directional skills associated with it, have strong carry-over effects to nonverbal tasks. For example, Elkind and Weiss (1967) found that beginning readers reported a series of pictures, which were arranged along the sides of a triangle, from left to right instead of as a sequence around the triangle. They suggested that the act of learning to read dominated the perceptual exploration of all two-dimensional material during the acquisition of directional behavior. Indeed, many adults also tend to scan pictures in a left-to-right direction, no doubt a carry-over from the reading process, though left-to-right processing of pictorial material is not as rigid in adults as it is in children.

At this point, it is important to remind you that there is nothing sacred about left-to-right scanning in reading (see Chapter 2). It is just that English is printed from left to right and the child must adapt to this convention. Israeli children read from right to left and they acquire the skill of reading about as easily as those learning to read English.

Eye Movement Control

Quite closely related to directional behavior is eye movement control. Prior to beginning reading, children have rarely had to focus their attention so precisely upon a specified region of a stimulus array. For example, children tend not to make a large number of eye movements when looking at television. And, prior to reading, a series of saccades in any particular direction is not called for. There is some indication that pre-reading children have difficulty controlling their eye movements because they have a hard time holding fixation on a target (Kowler and Martins 1982), and saccadic latency in simple oculomotor tasks is longer in younger children than in older children (Cohen and Ross 1977; Groll and Ross 1982).

We pointed out when discussing Nodine's research that the scanning strategies of the older children were more planned and deliberate than those of pre-readers (see also Vurpoillot 1968). All of the experiments suggest that as children's cognitive processes develop to deal with progressively more complex stimuli, their eye movement patterns change as their scanning strategies become more systematic and as they develop efficient strategies for dealing with the given task. Eye movements thus provide valuable evidence concerning the cognitive strategies employed. Indeed, as we shall see in Chapter 10, eye movement patterns during reading show a steady progression, so that as reading skill progresses the number of fixations decreases, saccade length increases, fixation duration decreases, and the number of regressions decreases. These changes in eye movement behavior in reading correspond to other changes that are taking place as children become more proficient in the task of reading.

Reading thus involves children becoming more adept at controlling their eye movements, focusing on specific words, and moving in a left-to-right direction. As a result, training is sometimes given to children to improve their eye movement patterns during reading. For some children, gross oculomotor problems may present a source of difficulty in reading and oculomotor training might be beneficial for them. However, this is only a small percentage of all children. For most children, changes in eye movement patterns appear to follow from their increased skill in reading proficiency (see Chapter 10). For children beginning the reading process, the main challenges are focusing attention on the relevant part of the word or text and processing information more effectively during eye fixations.

Word Consciousness

It is sometimes assumed that words are natural units and that young children beginning the reading process (who speak quite fluently) are aware of the separate words they are combining and recombining in their speech. However, as Ehri (1979) pointed out, more careful consideration of children's experiences with words and the relationships between words and meanings raises some doubts about the plausibility of this assumption. Young children typically experience most words in the context of other words, and their attention is centered on the meanings conveyed by these spoken combinations, not on their linguistic structure. Moreover, there are no consistent auditory signals segmenting speech into word units. Thus, in normal spoken discourse, words as components are neither salient nor clearly marked.

There is substantial evidence to indicate that children beginning the reading process are not conscious of separate words. For example, pre-reading children who are asked either to tap or to point to different symbols as each word is said do not perform very well (Huttenlocher 1964; Holden and MacGinitie 1972; Ehri 1975, 1976). In the Holden and MacGinitie study, kindergarten children were given the task of pointing to a poker chip as they uttered each word in sentences containing several words. They found that children were sometimes able to break the sentences apart, though they did not do so very often. Words with greater lexical meaning were sometimes isolated accurately, but function words were frequently combined with adjacent units. Whether function words were isolated or combined with other words seemed to be primarily dependent upon the rhythmic pattern imposed on the sentence by the child. Holden and MacGinitie pointed out that the use of printing conventions as a standard for correct segmentation is somewhat arbitrary and that beginning readers may have trouble segmenting sentences correctly because their notion of word units and boundaries is discrepant from conventional boundaries. However, on the basis of their data, it is questionable whether beginning readers can be regarded as possessing a definitive notion of word units at all. Indeed, beginning readers appear to lack a clear notion of words as units and, when forced to distinguish units in a sentence segmentation task, respond on the basis of the most salient cues in the sound track (Ehri 1975). Some words get marked correctly by accident because stress and pause location happen to isolate them.

Studies using printed material in which children had to mark word boundaries in sentences or to place space markers between words also reveal a lack of word consciousness in beginning readers (Holden and MacGinitie 1972; Meltzer and Herse 1969; Mickish 1974). This is not at all surprising since we would not expect children who cannot read printed words (and have no decoding skills) to be aware of word boundaries. Since the spaces between words are so perceptually salient, the concept of word boundaries should evolve quite naturally as children learn to read.

Finally, Pick et al (1978) showed 3- to 8-year-old children letter strings varying in length, and asked them to judge if each string was a word. (Many of the strings were words.) Pre-readers had a tendency to say a string was a word irrespective of whether or not it was, particularly if the string was more than one letter. They generally indicated that one-letter strings were not words. Table 9.3 shows the responses to different types of letter strings by the different groups of subjects. Between nursery school and kindergarten, there were decreases in the acceptability of nonword items that were judged to be words. Thus, it appears that by kindergarten most children acquire some knowledge about a variety of characteristics of printed words even though they do not yet know how to read. They know that letters have a correct orientation, perhaps a result of the fact that they spend a great deal of time in kindergarten learning about single letters. They also learn something about the combinations of letters of which words are composed (that, for example, words are not composed of all consonants or all vowels).

Linguistic and Phonological Awareness

Linguistic awareness is a knowledge of linguistic structure that is at least partly accessible to awareness (Liberman et al. 1980; Mattingly 1972;

TABLE 9.3 Percent of children responding that stimulus was a word (Pick et al, 1978). With permission of the society for Research in Child Development.

	SINGLE-LETTER WORDS	SINGLE-LETTER NONWORDS	LONG WORDS	LONG NONWORDS	5-LETTER WORDS	UNFAMILIAR WORDS	FAMILIAR INITIALS
3–4 years	48	54	85	87	81	80	77
5 years	14	6	88	75	86	81	75
Kindergartners	26	29	59	53	66	66	59
Grade 1	62	16	50	34	63	35	41
Grades 2, 3	58	23	58	8	82	22	29

	MEANINGFUL NONWORDS	PRONOUNCEABLE CLUSTERS: NONWORDS	CONSONANT CLUSTERS	VOWEL CLUSTERS	MISORIENTED LETTERS (COULD BE WORDS)	MISORIENTED LETTERS (COULD NOT BE WORDS)
3–4 years	85	83	80	80	73	72
5 years	87	80	83	71	61	56
Kindergartners	59	62	59	51	38	35
Grade 1	51	30	23	17	35	30
Grades 2, 3	29	18	5	4	20	2

Rozin and Gleitman 1977). Every level of language has its own structure: phonological, morphological, and syntactic. Writing introduces another structure, namely, orthographic structure. In each case, an aspect of reading depends on knowledge of linguistic structure a particular.

We should point out that linguistic awareness or knowledge does not depend on its being verbalized. Rather, it has to be implicitly available to a child in his or her encounters with everyday language. You probably do not consciously know the rules of grammar that make a given string of words grammatical or ungrammatical, yet you can with fairly good accuracy distinguish a grammatical from an ungrammatical string of words. Likewise, children may not necessarily have to be able to verbalize the relationship that exists between the graphemes and the phonemes to be able to have an awareness of the alphabetic principle. However, learning to read requires that some kinds of linguistic structure be brought to at least a partly explicit level of knowledge. If the teacher says that the first sound of *apple* is "ahh" (/ae/), the beginning reader must mentally operate on something that corresponds to the word *apple* and something that corresponds to the phoneme /ae/. A beginning reader who has some knowledge that words are independent linguistic objects and that they consist of meaningless speech sounds is a better bet for learning to read than a child who does not.

Of all the things we have discussed as being important prerequisites for reading, one aspect of linguistic awareness—*phonological awareness* (or the awareness of the relationship between a printed word and the sound representation for that word)—is probably the most important. Children will undoubtedly have difficulties reading if they have spatial orientation problems that lead them to attempt to read text from right to left, if they continually get confused about which direction to move their eyes or if they cannot discriminate visually similar letters. Indeed, as we shall see in Chapter 11 when we discuss reading disabilities, some children do have spatial orientation problems and experience reading problems. However, the percentage is relatively small. It is far more common for children to exhibit some type of language problem that hinders their reading development. But we're getting ahead of ourselves a bit. Let's get back to the issue at hand, that of linguistic awareness.

As we pointed out in an earlier section of this chapter, the discovery and application of the alphabetic principle is not easy for beginning readers. In addition, a large number of recent studies (Backman 1983; Bradley and Bryant 1978; Bruce 1964; Calfee, Chapman, and Venezky 1972; Calfee, Lindamood, and Lindamood 1973; Fox and Routh 1975, 1976, 1984; Helfgott 1976; Juel, Griffith, and Gough 1986; Liberman 1973; Lundberg, Olofsson, and Wall 1980; Torneus 1984; Zifcak 1981) all make it clear that discovering the alphabetic principle is the key to successfully learning to read. Concerning this discovery, Ehri (1979) has stated, "If the light were not so gradual in dawning, the relationship between speech and print might count as one of the most remarkable discoveries of childhood." Central to learning the alphabetic principle is developing phonological awareness.

There are several tasks that have been employed to measure phonological awareness. One, *segmenting,* is to ask a child to divide a spoken word into its component phonemes and do something with the components (e.g., say them individually, count them, or rearrange them). Other examples of tasks that get at phonological awareness include *blending* (e.g., combining a /n/ sound and an /o/ sound to produce /no/) and the ability to detect rhyme and alliteration (successive words beginning with the same sound). Many observers of children's initial reading problems have noted that beginning readers in fact have problems with segmenting, blending, rhyme, and alliteration (Calfee, Chapman, and Venezky 1972; Savin 1972). It is also known that older readers are better at phonological awareness tasks than beginning readers (Golinkoff 1978). There has been some debate, however, about the appropriate interpretation of this latter finding. Is it that phonological awareness assists in reading development, or is it that learning to read improves children's awareness of words as sequences of sounds?

In the remainder of this section, we will not review all of the studies that have dealt with the importance of phonological awareness. We will instead discuss only a few key studies and focus on the chicken-egg issue of whether phonological development aids reading or vice versa. It is impressive that virtually all of the studies that have been conducted dealing with phonological awareness yield consistent results despite the fact that different tasks have been used.

Stanovich, Cunningham, and Cramer (1984) administered 10 different phonological awareness tasks to a group of children whose reading ability was assessed one year later. The tasks used were representative of those used in most other studies. The extraneous cognitive requirements inherent in the tasks varied widely, although they all measured phonological awareness in some way. Performance on those tasks which involved a rhyming response did not correlate with subsequent reading progress. However, the other tasks did and when combined were very strong predictors of subsequent reading progress. Impressively, the relative predictive accuracy of the phonological awareness tasks was equal to or better than more global measures of cognitive skills, such as an intelligence test or a reading readiness test. Thus, the various measures of phonological awareness that have been used seem to be measuring something important to reading.

Let's consider a few further studies that demonstrate the importance of phonological awareness for the development of the reading skill. Rozin, Bressman, and Taft (1974) demonstrated a striking relationship between a rather low level of phonological awareness and reading development. They held up two cards, one containing (for example) the word *mow* and the other *motorcycle.* Both words were pronounced carefully and the children were asked to point to the card containing the appropriate word. If children understand that *motorcycle* has a longer pronunciation (with more phonetic segments) than *mow,* they should be able to easily choose the correct card. Rozin, Bressman, and Taft found that pre-readers were little better than chance on the task and that there was a transition between guessing at pre-kindergarten age and doing fairly well after the first grade. This corresponds to the period during which reading instruction is initiated. They also found that elaborate training procedures and systematic explanation failed to produce gains in children who could not do the task. However, this latter finding is somewhat inconsistent with a large number of more recent training studies that have demonstrated that phonological skills can effectively be taught to pre-readers (Content et al. 1982, 1986; Bradley and Bryant 1983; Lean and Arbuckle 1984; Lewkowicz 1980; Treiman and Baron 1983; Williams 1980).

In a number of studies, Liberman and her colleagues (Liberman et al. 1977) have shown that children who are good at segmenting are also good at reading. Fox and Routh (1976) found that children who were proficient at segmenting a syllable into phonemes benefited from training in blending more than children who were not. In a study which examined segmenting ability and teaching method, it was found that children taught by a phonics method were better at segmenting than children taught by whole word methods (Alegria, Pignot, and Morais 1982). This finding is presumably because phonics methods draw more attention to the sounds of language than do whole word methods. Baron and Treiman (1980) also found that segmenting ability was better when children were taught to read with the use of rules (phonics method) than with whole word instruction.

In a very influential study, Morais et al. (1979) compared the segmenting ability of ex-illiterate adults in Portugal with other adults who had never learned to read. Those who could not read possessed some capacity for phonemic segmentation, but were not nearly as good as those who could read. This finding has been taken as evidence that learning to read (and write) makes one more aware of the sound and formal properties of language. A number of researchers have thus concluded that segmenting ability is strongly influenced by learning to read and that reading leads to segmenting ability, and not vice versa (see Ehri 1983).

Indeed, a study by Read et al. (1986) demonstrated that it is learning to read an alphabetic system that allows phonological awareness to develop. They compared two groups of Chinese readers in a segmental analysis task: those who could read an alphabetic system for representing Chinese and those who could read only the logographic script. The nonalphabetic readers, while fluent in reading the usual logographic writing, did very poorly on the segmental analysis task. The mean scores of the nonalphabetic and alphabetic literates in the Read et al. study were strikingly similar to those of the Portuguese illiterates and ex-illiterates, respectively, in the Morais, Alegria, and Content (1987) study. Apparently, Chinese nonalphabetic literates (who had been reading fluently for 40 years) share with Portuguese illiterates the inability to analyze speech at the segmental level.

In a similar vein, Mann (1986) observed that the development of segmental skills is delayed in Japanese beginning readers—who learn to read Kana—compared to American children.

The above studies demonstrate that phonological awareness does not develop spontaneously, but that its development is closely related to learning to read. The unanswered question, of course, is whether developing phonological awareness is a necessary skill for learning to read. Bradley and Bryant (1983) assessed the phonological awareness of 4- and 5-year-old children who could not yet read. The children were orally presented three or four words each containing three letters. All but one of the words had the same initial, middle, or final sound. The child's task was to identify the "odd man out." For example, if presented with *cot, pot, lot,* and *hat,* the child should choose *hat* as the odd one. If presented with *win, sit, fin,* and *pin,* the correct choice is *sit.* Bradley and Bryant found that performance in the task *before any reading had begun* was a good predictor of how well the child would read 3 or 4 years later.

In addition, Bradley and Bryant examined the effects of phonological awareness training on learning to read. A group of children with poor phonological awareness skills were trained in 40 sessions over a 2-year period to select which of a set of pictures of common objects had the same beginning, middle, or final sounds. (The training involved no experience with printed words or letters.) At the end of the study, these children were reading better than a group given no training. Another group of children were trained to classify pictures into categories (such as "farm animal"). In contrast, training for this group had no effect on their reading. A final group was taught to classify by sounds and then taught which letters represented the sounds. These children fared the best of all the groups in reading at the end of the training.

Bradley and Bryant's study and others like it (Maclean, Bryant, and Bradley 1987; Olofsson and Lundberg 1983) are important because they provides clear evidence that making young children aware of the sounds of their language in nonreading tasks will also help them learn to read. However, the data we reviewed earlier (Morais et al. 1979; Read et al. 1986; Mann 1986) make it clear that learning to read an alphabetic language develops phonological awareness (see also Bertleson et al. 1985). The reciprocal relationship is apparent from a recent longitudinal study by Perfetti et al. (1987). They concluded that the ability to blend phonemes plays a causal role in the acquisition of reading, while the acquisition of reading plays a causal role in the development of the awareness that words can be segmented into phonemes (see also Wagner and Torgesen 1987). More specific tests of such ideas will undoubtedly reveal more about the relationship between learning to read and phonological awareness. In general, though, it is clear that phonological awareness and the development of reading skill (for alphabetic writing systems) go hand in hand.

Summary of Early Reading and Prerequisites to Reading

What conclusions can we reach about early reading instruction, reading readiness, and prerequisites to reading? We have noted that a small percentage of children learn to read in the absence of formal instruction. However, there appears to be nothing qualitatively different about them than other children. For most children, learning to read involves formal instruction, and across different cultures the age at which formal instruction begins varies by as much as 2 years. These cultural variations in the beginning of formal reading instruction fly in the face of a biologically programmed version of reading readiness. If we take such an idea of reading readiness seriously (i.e., the idea that all children must have reached a certain stage of cognitive development before they can be taught to read), then we should expect more reading problems in cultures that begin reading instruction early than in those that begin later. That is, it is difficult to believe that all children in England would have reached the ideal state of "readiness" or be more advanced cognitively than children from other cultures. Yet, the rate of reading problems in England is similar to that in the United States. These variations suggest that cultural expectations are an important determiner of when children begin to read.

There must be developmental limits, however, as to what age children can be profitably taught reading. Evidence suggests that the effort put into teaching children to read at very early ages has few long-term benefits because the late starters often catch up with the early achievers once they begin reading instruction (Coltheart 1979). Conversely, we reviewed evidence that indicated that delaying the onset of reading instruction to around the age of seven has no serious side effects; when children between the ages of 5 and 7 from the same culture are given beginning instruction at the same time, the older children do better (Feitelson, Tehori, and Levinberg-Green 1982). We are left then with an intriguing puzzle concerning the most appropriate point at which to start formal reading instruction, but it does appear that direct instruction in reading is more beneficial than spending time on reading readiness exercises, which may or may not be directly related to reading.

We also considered some prerequisites to reading. Before children can learn to read they have to know the letters of the alphabet and to master the orientational skills associated with reading in the direction of the print. However, we also saw that while knowledge of the letter names in kindergarten is the best predictor of reading in the beginning year of instruction, by the second and third year of reading the advantage initially associated with knowing the letters has all but dissipated.

What emerges most clearly from the research we have reviewed in these two sections is that phonological awareness is intimately related to progress in learning to read. Children who do well on phonological awareness tests prior to the onset of reading do well in mastering reading and the difference persists throughout the early school grades. Although some studies found that training on segmenting skills did not improve performance (Rozin, Bressman, and Taft 1974), other studies have provided clear evidence that training can facilitate performance in segmentation abilities (Bradley and Bryant 1983; Content et al 1982; Lewkowicz 1980; Treiman and Baron 1983; Williams 1980) and reading performance in general (Bradley and Bryant 1983). Although many different types of phonological awareness tasks have been used, it has been established that most of the tasks are measuring much the same thing (Stanovich, Cunningham, and Cramer 1984). Thus, studies of phonological awareness indicate that it is central to understanding children's development of the reading skill. The research findings concerning reading instruction also indicate that knowledge of the relationship between the printed symbol and the sound pattern of the language is very important in learning to read. We now turn to that topic, discussing first the characteristics of different instructional methods.

METHODS OF TEACHING READING

At the beginning of this chapter, we noted that the two primary methods used to teach children to read are whole word (or look-say) instruction and phonics instruction. In this section, we describe the major aspects of each method as well as the "language experience" approach to teaching reading. Then we will discuss our observations of what teachers actually do in classrooms in which children are taught to read. We conclude the section with a discussion of some recent studies that have attempted to assess the relative merits of different instructional methods for teaching children the skill of reading.

Prior to beginning our discussion of different instructional methods, it is important to point out that there are a large number of reading programs commercially available. Because these programs can be expensive, all the schools within a given district will often use the same program since bulk buying is generally cheaper. These reading programs consist of workbooks (sometimes called *primers)* for children as well as instructor's manuals. While these reading programs generally adhere to one particular type of method for teaching reading, within the individual classroom teachers have a fair amount of flexibility in what they actually do.

Whole Word Instruction

If you have been in a foreign country or listened to someone talking in a foreign language, you are aware that the stream of speech seems almost continuous. This illustrates that spoken language is an almost continuous stream of sound with hardly any gaps of silence separating the individual words. If you were a young child trying to break the sounds of your own language into individual words, you would find it quite difficult, as we pointed out when we discussed word consciousness. When children begin to read, they gradually discover that word units exist and are represented by clusters of symbols separated by spaces. The general rationale behind whole word methods of reading instruction is that the child does not recognize that the letters represent sound units, so the entire pattern of letters is taught wholistically as representing a particular word. Typically, the child is shown a flash card with a word on it and the teacher will pronounce the word and ask the child to say it as well. Generally, the teacher starts with a small set of words and gradually expands the set.

Another major rationale behind using the whole word approach is that many words in English are irregular in spelling. Such words, it is argued, must be learned partly or wholly in terms of their visual appearance. Another major argument in favor of the whole word method is that it promotes reading for meaning at a very early stage of reading development. When a child has developed a small sight vocabulary, this vocabulary can be deployed in various combinations to construct meaningful sentences. Gradually, new words are introduced in such a manner that the context clarifies their meaning. The pronunciation of the word is given by the teacher, who indicates, whenever possible, a similarity in spelling between the word to be read and a word already in the sight vocabulary. After an initial sight vocabulary is established, many teachers start to emphasize that the letter symbols represent sounds. Each phoneme is dealt with in turn until the child is able to make fairly automatic letter-to-sound conversions.

Phonics Instruction

In its purest form, the phonics approach starts with a limited set of letters which can be built into many different kinds of words. Gradually more letters are added and then the children are given consonant blends. As some words keep recurring, the child also develops a sight vocabulary during these early stages. The individual letters are taught by the sounds they make and then children are induced to blend the sounds of novel letter combinations.

The important point about a phonics approach is that it teaches an analytic approach to words, one that is designed to exploit the alphabetic principle. The major criticisms of the phonics approach are that it is very boring for the child and that it obscures the function of reading (i.e., extracting meaning from print). Constant practice at producing phonemes and blending them together into a word is a drill that children find almost deadly. These problems have resulted in a general shift to include phonics instruction with meaning emphasis programs. We will now discuss the so-called meaning emphasis programs and then discuss some differences between reading programs with a code emphasis (phonics) and those with a meaning emphasis.

Meaning Emphasis Instruction

A method of instruction that is sometimes thought of as being halfway between the phonics and whole word methods is the so-called linguistic method (Bloomfield and Barnhart 1961). This method involves the child encountering a limited set of words similar in spelling construction that are combined to form sentences ("A fat cat ran after a bad rat."). The linguist Bloomfield was an advocate of this method, which was incorporated in a set of reading primers. The method is similar to the whole word approach except that a phonics type of decoding is also encouraged by the teacher (an example of such a program is shown in Figure 9.2).

In general, meaning emphasis programs stress language experiences of the child. Thus the child dictates short stories to a teacher or aide and is taught to read the words that he or she has dictated. Instruction in learning individual words usually emphasizes whole words, though some phonics drill may be incorporated into the program at later stages.

A somewhat more radical approach to the teaching of reading and a justification for meaning emphasis approaches has come from the work of Frank Smith and Kenneth Goodman. Their views can be referred to more directly in Goodman (1967, 1970), Smith (1971, 1973), and Smith and Goodman (1971). They have referred to their method of teaching reading as the "psycholinguistic method," yet it is worth noting that the term

I see Pug.
I see Pug run.
See Pug run, Ted.
See Pug go.

Ride, Ted, ride!
Go, Pug, go!

FIGURE 9-2 A page from a linguistic-based program. (With permission of The Economy Company.)

"psycholinguistic" as they use it bears little relationship to what most psychologists think of with respect to that term (see Perfetti, 1985).

As we have pointed out in earlier chapters, Goodman views the reading process as a "psycholinguistic guessing game" in which the reader tries to figure out meanings. There are thought to be three types of cues in this guessing game: *graphophonic, syntactic,* and *semantic* (Goodman 1970). The graphonic cues represent rather general knowledge of spelling-sound relations; the syntactic cues are the reader's knowledge of syntactic patterns and the markers that cue these patterns (such as function words and inflectional suffixes); and the semantic system is everything else (such as the reader's knowledge of word meanings and knowledge of the topic). Tongue in cheek, Perfetti (1985) suggested that if pragmatics had the currency in the 1960s as it has these days, there would no doubt have been a fourth cueing system. The "psycholinguistic" approach to reading is one that emphasizes the reader's use of all relevant information in an attempt to get at the meaning of the text. As Perfetti also noted, it is an interactive model, but without specific suggestions as to how things interact.

The major failing of this approach to teaching reading is that it does not recognize that one of the proposed cueing systems is more central or important to the process of learning to read than are the others. Children who have mastered the alphabetic principle and learned the code have knowledge that enables them to read no matter how much the semantic, syntactic, and pragmatic cues conspire against them. As we argued in Chapter 7, most content words in print are not very predictable, so in most places in text, context cannot substitute for the ability to identify a word.

Since the instructional implications of Smith and Goodman's approach are not very clear, many of the "psycholinguistic methods" used by teachers in schools are not necessarily what Smith and Goodman had in mind. Smith and Goodman (1971) renounced "psycholinguistic instruction" and suggested that their ideas have been misused. The only important instructional principle that can be gleaned from their ideas is that phonics shouldn't be taught. The essence of their ideas seems to be that learning to read, like learning to speak, is a natural act, and the child teaches him or herself how to do it. This view is in marked contrast to the more common one that learning to read is not a natural act (Gough and Hillinger 1980) which generally requires some assistance from teachers in making explicit the alphabetic principle. Overall, the psycholinguistic approach to teaching reading is short on specifics. It seems compatible with any meaning emphasis approach. However, it may be more accurate to say that it is incompatible with any approach that includes code instruction as a significant part of teaching.

While we have been rather critical of the Goodman-Smith view, we do note that their views have helped produce a growing trend to make reading instruction more meaningful. In some sense, they may also have a point when emphasizing that what the child does (rather than what the teacher does) is of utmost importance in learning to read. As Crowder (1982) pointed out, it is the highest vanity for instructors to suppose that learning is caused directly by what they do. Learning to read is mainly caused by what the learner does and the instructors' role is to make it a bit easier.

Comparing Teaching Methods

The teaching of reading has a long history of debate and contention. Although the argument has taken on many different forms, the critical issue is whether or not decoding (phonics) should be taught directly or indirectly and whether it should be taught early or late. The major alternative to the phonics approach has been the whole word method. In fact, the whole word method was the predominant method of teaching reading in the United States until quite recently. Today, meaning emphasis programs are widely used. However, there has also been a growing awareness of the importance of phonics instruction that makes explicit the alphabetic principle.

Currently, the two primary types of programs are often referred to as *meaning emphasis* and *code emphasis*. The meaning emphasis programs rely mainly on stories (called *basals)* and building up a sight vocabulary Figure 9.3 shows an example of a basal reader based on the whole word method. Within the meaning emphasis programs there has been a general shift toward including phonics instruction, but the programs devote much less time to teaching decoding skills. In contrast, while there is some attention to making materials meaningful and interesting in the code based programs, there is a much greater emphasis on phonics. While there are thus points of overlap between the methods, clear differences do emerge when they are analyzed.

Sally Works

Sally said, "Oh my!

Work, work, work!

Dick and Jane work.

Mother and Father work.

Who will play with me?"

FIGURE 9-3 A page from a whole-word program. (With permission of Scott Foresman.)

One contrast is in the choice of vocabulary. In a study comparing the content of basal readers with code-based programs, Willows, Borwick, and Hayvren (1981) found major differences in the first 50 words introduced by the two types of programs. The code emphasis programs introduced words that were more orthographically regular and that included a more restricted set of grapheme-phoneme correspondences. On the other hand, the basal readers had a less selective set of words; there were more irregular words and less controlled grapheme-phoneme correspondences.

Beck (1981) analyzed four basal programs and four code programs to determine the extent to which they in fact taught grapheme-phoneme correspondences in the first grade. In the basal programs, the stories read during the first third of the year contained virtually no words for which all the grapheme-phoneme correspondence were taught. Even by year's end, the basal programs had taught correspondences sufficient to decode only about half of the words appearing in the stories. With the code programs, she found that 79 percent to 100 percent (depending upon the exact program) of the words were decodable on the basis of taught correspondences. Beck concluded that the basal readers make it more difficult than the code programs for beginning readers to recognize that words encountered in reading can be decoded on the basis of the relationship between the letters and their associated sounds (i.e., the alphabetic principle).

These differences between the materials are a reflection of the basic principles of the code and basal programs, respectively. The goal of code programs is to teach grapheme-phoneme correspondences. The goal of the basal readers is to introduce words familiar to the child from oral language experience. Since many high frequency words are irregular, this sometimes results in lessons in the basal readers that contain words of higher frequency but greater irregularity (Beck, 1981; Willows, Borwick, and Hayvren 1981). Thus, whatever gains basal readers achieve in word familiarity are likely to be offset by losses in encoding ability.

Appeals to research evidence have sometimes been made as support for a given method of teaching reading (Williams 1979). For example, the experiments of Cattell (1886) and Reicher (1969) have been cited as support for the whole word method. However, these experiments have only a tenuous connection to how reading instruction should proceed, since they deal with skilled readers rather than beginning readers and since they do not really imply that words are processed as visual patterns (see Chapter 3). Instead, it appears that a general orientation to teaching and learning, rather than a careful reading of research results, has been the main motivation for meaning emphasis approaches. Intuitions of many in the field of teaching reading have led to an emphasis on meaning approaches and making text experiences as meaningful as possible. Indeed, some advocates of meaning approaches to teaching reading have even argued against the use of basal readers because the same workbooks are given to all children. Instead, they advocate individualized instruction in which all children would read different books—those that are of interest to them.

The advocacy of meaning approaches has led to initial reading instruction programs that are much more entertaining than the time-honored ABC method that was used for hundreds of years. The ABC method is a most basic type of phonics approach in which children are taught the letters' names, then simple syllables, then words. The child would spell the syllable and then pronounce it: "double-you-ay-ell-ell-wall." Later, more and more syllables and words are mixed in, usually with the same spelling requirement prior to pronunciation. The *New England Primer, Webster's Spelling Books,* and *McGuffey's Readers* were the major sources of reading programs from the 1700s until the 1900s. Pictures were introduced into these programs, but for the most part the emphasis was on phonics drill. While there is little evidence indicating how successful the ABC method was in teaching reading, we must assume that there was some dissatisfaction with it, since there were changes made in the late ninetenth century.

While there can be no doubt that meaningful experiences with text and meaning-based approaches are more interesting to children than drills on phonics, one inescapable conclusion cannot be overlooked: successful reading requires some awareness and mastery of the alphabetic principle. While most children will discover this principle for themselves when it is not explicity taught, teaching methods that make the principle explicit should make the task easier for children approaching the task of learning to read. In fact, teaching methods that focus on making the alphabetic principle explicit appear to be at least as beneficial as those that focus on making reading meaningful. (We will discuss the evidence shortly.) However, empirical research is generally irrelevant to real-world decisions about how publishers design reading programs and which reading program is adopted by a school district. Willows, Borwick, and Hayvren (1981) concluded from their content analysis of widely used programs that publishers' decisions about various features of their programs are largely based upon intuitions, arbitrary decisions, and marketing considerations (e.g., price). We assume that the decisions of school districts are made on a similar basis.

What actually goes on in a classroom? To this point, we have been discussing the different types of methods used to teach children to read as if the reading program adopted determines what actually goes on in the classroom. However, good teachers are eclectic in their approach to teaching children to read and only loosely base their instruction on the reading program. They know almost by instinct, but also from experience, that phonics is important and that children must discover the alphabetic principle, but they also recognize that when learning is made meaningful and exciting, children learn much more. Our own observations of a number of classrooms (as well as interviews with teachers in the United States and England) suggest that irrespective of the particular reading program employed in a given school district, good teachers use a combination of methods to teach beginning readers. However, there do appear to be school districts in which the teachers are required to rigidly follow one method or the other. With this exception, the major difference between different ways that a child are instructed in initial reading is best thought of in terms of the relative amount of time or emphasis that is given to phonics training.

In spite of the variability in what happens in individual classrooms, the following account is probably representative. When children enter school, the teacher spends a great deal of time reading to them. Stories are often read to the children in order to encourage further language development and to cultivate a desire on the part of the child to want to discover what is within a book. This is further encouraged by showing attractive pictures illustrating the story. There is generally also training given to help the child learn letter names. Oftentimes, training in learning different letters involves the use of various mnemonics in which different characters (or actors) are used to help remember the different letter names. Figure 9.4 shows an example of such letter mnemonics. Training is also given in left-right discriminations and perhaps some visual discriminations.

Initially written words are introduced sometimes by starting with the

FIGURE 9-4 Examples of letter mnemonics (Ehri, Deffner, and Wilce 1984). (With permission of the American Psychological Association and the authors.)

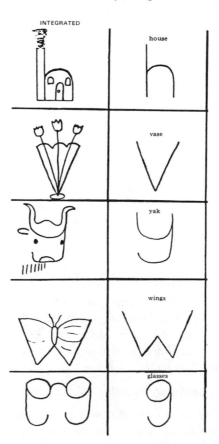

name of the child written on his or her exercise book. Many teachers use the strategy of providing exercise books and having the child dictate to them at first. The child may draw something and then is asked to provide a story about the object he or she has drawn. In such a way, labels are provided for all sorts of objects in the child's environment. Ten to 20 words will then be introduced to the child and the child learns them by sight. This is typically referred to as the child's initial *sight vocabulary*. Some time during this stage, the first reading primer or reading workbook is introduced by the teacher.

As we mentioned earlier, the teacher usually has a large number of reading programs to choose from (although some school districts enforce their methods by restricting the materials available to the teacher). The programs do vary rather widely in the extent to which their initial emphasis is upon a phonics or a whole word approach. Our impression is that teachers using phonics based programs try to make the process as meaningful as possible by supplementing the program with language based experiences. Those using programs that have a primary emphasis on a meaning based approach will strive to make certain that the alphabetic principle is taught to the children. Evidence that most teachers are quite eclectic in their teaching of initial reading comes from that fact that most adults do not know how they were taught to read. Learning of the alphabetic principle, either from the reading workbooks or from the teacher, involves drill in grapheme-phoneme correspondence rules and blending; children are also taught other important components of the alphabetic principle such as how digraphs such as *th* work. While this is going on, language experiences are still emphasized as children shift over from the teacher's writing in their exercise book to their writing in it themselves.

The major point in this section is that most children receive some instruction in whole word methods and some instruction in phonics. Phonics instruction is generally preceded by the child's learning 10 or 20 words in a sight vocabulary. Whole word instruction is often based on the assumption that children will discover the grapheme-phoneme relationships for themselves, or failing this, the teacher will provide such instruction. Thus, the major distinction between instructional methods differ is one of relative emphasis.

Finally, we should note that most teachers we know would stress that the home environment often plays a major role in how well children in their classrooms adapt to the task of learning to read. Children from homes where the importance of books and knowledge are valued will generally be more motivated to learn to read and see its inherent value. Many educators stress that the amount of time children are read to at home is a good predictor of how easily they will adapt to the task.

Research on Beginning Reading Instruction

At the beginning of this chapter, we noted that a great many studies have been conducted to determine the best way to teach initial reading.

However, as we noted earlier, many of the results are contradictory. Our intuition is that many of the conflicting results are due to two factors: many teachers are quite eclectic in their approach, and independent of the particular method of teaching used, most children figure out important principles for themselves. Thus, many children taught in a primarily meaning based program will figure out for themselves the alphabetic principle. These two factors would tend to cancel out any effects of specific instructional methods in many classrooms. There may well be some teachers who stick rigidly and righteously to the only program used in their school or school district. Thus, it may be possible to find some children who have been taught almost exclusively by one method or the other. But as we have argued a number of times in this chapter, such teachers are more the exception than the rule.

Despite some conflicting results, when individual studies are considered there is a still a consistent theme running through various summaries of research comparing code based (phonics) instruction with meaning based instruction (Chall, 1967, 1979; Williams, 1979). For example, Chall (1967) concluded that code emphasis programs produced better performance in word recognition and spelling and did not diminish interest in reading (ostensibly one of the disadvantages of code based programs). Williams (1979) concluded that the measurable advantages of code based programs for reading achievement were small and confined to word recognition and spelling, primarily during the first two years of school. However, she also concluded that there was no measurable advantage of meaning based approaches even in measures of comprehension. Thus, there seems to be no way of getting around the conclusion that code emphasis programs do not hurt comprehension and provide at least some help for word recognition.

A number of recent comparative longitudinal studies have also reached similar conclusions. Evans and Carr (1985) evaluated two programs in 20 first grade classrooms. Half of these were traditional "teacher-directed" classes in which instruction used basal readers with phonics drills and applications. The other half of the classes were taught in less traditional "student-centered" classrooms in which teacher instruction constituted only 35 percent of the day's activity. In the latter, reading was taught primarily by an individualized language-experience method in which students produced their own workbook of stories and banks of words to be recognized.

Evans and Carr (1985) characterized these two groups as "decoding oriented" and "language oriented." Despite some differences in emphasis of how teaching should be conducted, the two groups did not differ in the amount of time spent on reading tasks. The two groups were also matched on relevant socioeconomic variables, and they were virtually identical on measures of intelligence and language maturity. The clear result, however, was that the decoding group scored higher on year-end reading achievement tests, including comprehension tests. Additionaly, the language-experience group did not show any higher achievement in oral language measures based on a storytelling task. Perfetti (1985) has also summarized some of the results of the Pittsburgh Longitudinal Study (see Lesgold & Curtis 1981; Lesgold and Resnick 1982) which also show quite clearly that instruction that emphasizes the alphabetic principle does not produce "word callers" who are insensitive to contextual meaning.

Summary of Methods of Teaching Reading

In this section, we have reviewed the major instructional methods used to teach children to read. Research on the relative effectiveness is sometimes quite confusing as there are many conflicting results. Our explanation of the contradictory results, aside from the possiblitity of poor research designs, is that most teachers are eclectic in their approach to teaching reading and many children, particularly bright ones, will discover the alphabetic principle even if it is not explicitly taught to them. While there are some contradictory results concerning the effectiveness of different instructional approaches, the weight of the evidence indicates that code emphasis instruction is more effective in teaching young children to read. Presumably the reason for this is that phonics approaches make the alphabetic principle explicit.

SUMMARY

In this chapter we have discussed the basic cognitive and perceptual prerequisites to learning to read. We have also discussed early readers (children who learn to read without formal instruction), and the evidence suggests that such children are not dramatically different from other children who learn to read in a schoolroom with a teacher providing assistance in learning the process. The concept of reading readiness was discussed, and we argued that direct practice on reading-related activities was probably more beneficial than practice on various types of nonreading activities thought to be related to reading. Of the various prerequisites to reading that we discussed, we argued that phonological awareness was the most important. In large part, the development of phonological awareness indicates that children have some appreciation of the alphabetic principle. Understanding the alphabetic principle—that written symbols are associated with specific phonemes—represents the major hurdle for children learning to read. We also discussed various methods of teaching reading and concluded that code emphasis instruction (phonics) is effective in teaching beginning readers because it makes explicit the alphabetic principle. However, it is clearly the case that meaning approaches are valuable, since they make the task of reading (and uncovering the alphabetic principle) more interesting to children. We also argued that good teachers are eclectic and tend to combine the positive aspects of different methods of teaching reading.

CHAPTER TEN
STAGES OF READING DEVELOPMENT

Nothing is as central to the field of child development as the notion of stages. With respect to motor, cognitive, language, perceptual, and moral development, highly influential theories have been proposed in which children are seen as developing towards maturity by passing through a series of stages. While it might be quite easy to accept the idea of a natural sequence of stages that children pass through in learning to walk or talk, there is no really compelling reason to expect the same to be true of learning to read. After all, reading is a product of cultural evolution rather than a biologically evolved skill like walking or talking; it depends on cultural transmission for its continued existence.

Nevertheless, some investigators of the processes involved in learning to read have proposed a series of stages that children go through to become proficient readers (Chall 1983; Ehri and Wilce 1987; Gough and Hillinger 1980; Marsh et al. 1981; Mason 1980). In this section, we will discuss the stages of reading development proposed by Marsh et al. (1981). The four proposed stages are (1) linguistic guessing, (2) discrimination net guessing, (3) sequential decoding, and (4) hierarchical decoding (see Table 10.1). We view these "stages" as increasingly complex strategies that children attempt as their cognitive skills increase rather than as a biologically driven sequence that all children go through. Moreover, it is unreasonable to think that all

TABLE 10.1 Stages of Reading Development

Stage	Description
Linguistic guessing	Glance and guess
Discrimination net guessing	Sophisticated guessing
Sequential decoding	Learns simple grapheme-phoneme correspondences
Hierarchical decoding	Skilled reading

children would progress sequentially through the stages. Let's consider each of the stages proposed by Marsh et al. in turn.

Linguistic Guessing

The young child in the first stage of reading is seen as approaching the task of word recognition with a strategy of simple rote association (Gough and Hillinger 1980). This rote association is between a previously unanalyzed visual stimulus (the printed word) and an unanalyzed oral response. The child is said to select one aspect of the stimulus (such as the first letter or some other arbitrary characteristic of the word) and to associate it with an oral response. This initial strategy would be encouraged by a whole word approach in which an unanalyzed word is the required response. When presented with an unfamiliar word out of context, the child is often unable to respond. If, however, the same word is presented in a sentence or story, the child in this stage will often guess at the word using prior context as a guide. Thus the strategy is to substitute a syntactically and semantically appropriate word for the unknown word. The stage is not static, however, since the child is gradually establishing a set of visual letter and word recognition units.

Discrimination Net Guessing

In the second stage, the child typically responds to an unknown isolated word on the basis of its shared graphemic cues with a known word. Whereas in the linguistic guessing stage the child is usually limited to using only the first letter, in the discrimination net guessing stage, additional cues such as word shape, word length, and final letter are added to the repertoire. The term *discrimination net,* borrowed from computer science, means that the child processes graphemic cues only to the extent they are necessary to discriminate one printed word from another.

Evidence consistent with the characteristics of the first two stages can be gleaned from observational studies of beginning readers' oral reading errors in classroom settings (Biemiller 1970; Cohen 1974; Weber 1970). These studies, however, suggested that an additional stage may have to be added to the first two of Marsh et al. Biemiller (1970) studied beginning readers who were taught by a whole word method and proposed three stages. In Stage 1, only context guided the child's wild guesses. In Stage 2, children preferred to make no response rather than make a wild guess, while in Step 3, they used both graphic and contextual constraints so that their response was consistent with both partial graphemic cues and with the sentence context. In the latter stage, the errors that children made were consistent with the print (so that *bay* might be read as *boy*). This was in marked contrast to Stage 1, where the error generally did not bear a relationship to the printed word or perhaps bore only a slight resemblance to the print (reading *brother* when the word was *boy*). Cohen (1974) examined the oral reading errors of beginning readers taught by a phonics method. The three stages observed were no response, nonsense errors, and word substitutions. Thus both studies observed a "no response" stage in addition to the two stages of Marsh et al., but in a different position in the sequence. The difference may be because the children in the two studies were taught by different teaching methods.

An important point to note about the difference between the linguistic guessing stage and the discrimination net stage is that while the errors that are made in the former stage are often consistent with the context, they are usually not based at all on the misread word (though they may sometimes have a letter in common). As Ellis (1984) pointed out, when a beginning reader reads "the boy went to the moon in a rocket" as "the boy went to the moon in a spaceship," it is not necessarily because the child has extracted some semantic information from the word *rocket*. Indeed, if *cauliflower* is substituted for *rocket* the child might just as easily say *spaceship*. Words that are not known are simply guessed on the basis of the context. In contrast, in the discrimination net stage, the errors are often a result of an attempt at analysis of the target word, since the error is often consistent with many of the graphic cues.

Sequential Decoding

The third stage is characterized by the use of combination rules which allow the child to decode novel words. As exposure to printed words increases, the child is taught (or sees for himself or herself) that many letters or letter groups are pronounced the same way in different words and that it is possible to work out what a new word is by sounding it out. The child begins to have an appreciation for the alphabetic principle.

Marsh et al. suggested that two factors underlie the shift from the strategies of Stages 1 and 2 to the more analytic strategies of Stage 3. They suggested that the major environmental factor is the increase in the number of words that children are exposed to. If the number of words they are exposed to is limited, a rote learning or discrimination net strategy is satisfactory. In many basal reading programs only a few words are taught, and these are chosen to be graphemically dissimilar to each other. However as the set of words in the printed material increases, memory load increases and a rote learning strategy has diminishing returns, as does the use of a discrimination net strategy, since exposure to more and more words invariably means that more of them will be graphically similar to each other. The second factor identified by Marsh et al. as underlying the shift from Stage 2 to Stage 3 is the increase in cognitive processing capacity as the child becomes more cognitively mature. Thus, children in Stage 3 are able to process the order of a series of letters and to coordinate this series with a series of sounds. The sounding out process in sequential decoding is said to work in a simple left-to-right manner, only using simple invariant relations between individual letters and sounds.

The shift from Stage 2 to Stage 3 is also clear from observational studies reported by Cohen (1974) and Barr (1974). Both studies found that by the end of the first grade, children produced nonword errors and errors not in their print vocabulary; however, they found that method of instruction made a difference. In Barr's study, for example, all children started out using a rote strategy as indexed by their substitution errors in reading words that they did not know. However, all children in the phonics group switched to a decoding strategy by the end of the first grade, while only some of the children in the look-say group did.

Hierarchical Decoding

The decoding skills of the Stage 3 reader are fairly basic, but as the child gains even more experience his or her decoding skills become more sophisticated. In Stage 4, rules become context-sensitive so that, for example, the grapheme c is pronounced /ess/ before i, but /kay/ before o, and vowels are lengthened by a final e. It is during this stage that the child begins to use *analogy* as an alternative device for decoding. As we saw in Chapter 3, adult skilled readers use analogies to pronounce nonwords (and words that they do not know). When children reach Stage 4, they presumably have entered the highest stage in the acquisition of literacy and, in essence, process words and text in the same way as adults. They may continue to improve on the efficiency and scope of their reading skill, but the nature of the total system does not undergo any further qualitative changes.

Summary of Stages of Reading

As we noted at the beginning of this section, the four different stages that Marsh et al. identified may not necessarily be characteristic of every child. Yet, they do provide a fairly reasonable description of many children's reading progress. Results of experimental studies, to which we turn next, also seem quite consistent with the hypothesized stages, and so we have adopted the stage notion as a working hypothesis of how children develop reading skill.

Another study consistent with the idea that children pass through a series of stages in their reading development is a longitudinal study reported by Mason (1980). She distinguished three stages of printed word learning. Stage 1 children were described as context-dependent learners who process words mainly by attending to visually distinctive cues. They could read words in a typical context (such as stop signs or milk cartons) but not in isolation. They could learn to identify 3 or 4 printed words on a 10-word list, but they could not read these words when the case of the letters was altered, and they forgot most of what they had learned after a 15-minute delay. Stage 2 children were visual recognition learners. In contrast to context-dependent learners, they could read a few words out of context and they had mastered letter names. They often preserved initial consonants when they misread words (e.g., *key* for *kit*). They were able to learn and remember words on the 10-item list better than context-dependent learners and could even recognize some of the words when letter cases were altered. Stage 3 children were letter-sound analyzers who had mastered grapheme-phoneme correspondence rules. They could use this knowledge to decode unfamiliar printed words accurately and could read multisyllabic words. In addition, they had no difficulty learning words on the 10-item list and could read them almost perfectly even when letter cases were changed and after a 15-minute delay. Thus, Mason's Stages 1 and 2 seem quite consistent with those of Marsh et al. and her stages 3 seems to subsume both Stage 3 and 4 of Marsh et al.

All the stage models we have presented agree that children initially approach reading by using a strategy of rote association when given their first few sight words. When presented with a word they do not know out of context, they will be unable to respond. However, if that same word is presented in the context of a sentence or short story, they will respond with a semantically and syntactically appropriate word. They do not really do any analysis of the word, but rather guess at it on the basis of the prior context. This is the linguistic guessing stage. As children are exposed to more and more print, when they encounter a word they do not know, they will sometimes prefer to make no response or say "I don't know that word" rather than make a wild guess. But soon their responses to unknown words can be characterized as being consistent with both the graphemic cues and the context. In this discrimination net stage, errors are a result of an attempted analysis of the target word and are generally consistent with the graphic characteristics of the unknown word. Perhaps the major breakthrough in reading occurs when the child realizes (either from explicit instruction or from deducing the principle) that many letter or letter groups are pronounced the same way in different words and that it is possible to determine what a new word is by sounding it out. This third stage is referred to as sequential decoding since the process generally operates in a simple left-to-right manner. The term "decoding" is appropriate because the child in this stage can only deal effectively with invariant relations in the form of a simple code between letters and sounds. The final stage, hierarchical decoding, represents the point between the ages of 8 and 10 when the child has more or less acquired the basic skill of an accomplished reader. Decoding skills are much more sophisticated than in Stage 3 and the child can use analogies in determining what new and unknown words are.

IDENTIFICATION CUES

In the last section, we drew upon the results of observational studies to help characterize the different stages of reading development. While such studies are extremely valuable, there are also serious limitations associated with them. For one thing, they depend completely on error analyses and do not tell us anything about what strategy children are using when they read words correctly. In fact, children read many words correctly even in the earliest stages of reading. Though the correct response may sometimes be due to guessing, much of the time it is not. Thus, while error analyses tell us quite a lot about what strategies are used when words are not known, it is only by inference that we can gather what happens when words are read correctly.

Second, the naturalistic studies that we have cited have been largely confined to the first year of formal reading instruction. While there are many studies that have examined oral reading errors for older children, we tend to view them with some suspicion. The reason for this is that after the child moves into Stage 3 and, particularly, Stage 4 and is able to read text reasonably well, the eye-voice span comes into play. For beginning readers, the eye is not ahead of the voice as they struggle with each word. But, by the end of the first grade and the beginning of the second grade, the eye is ahead of the voice. Characteristics of the timing or discrepancy between the eyes and the voice make it highly likely that the oral response is a product of the lexicon (because the word has already been processed by the eyes and is likely in short-term memory) rather than the means of accessing the lexicon. Thus the errors made by children who have entered Stages 3 and 4 could well be memory rather than encoding errors. As a result, we prefer data from experimental studies to those of oral reading errors when characterizing the cues children use to identify words.

In this section we turn our attention to laboratory experiments in which children with different levels of reading ability (in terms of the number of years that they have received formal instruction in reading) are tested on controlled tasks dealing with reading "words." (Many employ pseudo-words; but from the child's perspective, they could be words not in his or her vocabulary.) We will discuss the role of three types of specific cues in word identification: graphemic, orthographic, and grapheme-phoneme correspondence cues. Following a discussion of each, we will discuss research dealing with the unit of processing in beginning readers.

Visual and Graphemic Cues

We have seen that children often substitute a word in text with a word bearing some visual or graphemic relationship to the printed word. Their errors provide some clue to what cues are actually being used. However, with more controlled tasks, it may be possible to be more diagnostic about what aspect or aspects of the word they are using. Before we discuss this research, let's make a distinction between visual and graphemic information. By *visual* information, we mean gross aspects of words that are independent of identifying letters; the two most frequently cited are word length and word shape. By *graphemic* information, we mean information specific to the letters making up a word, such as distinctive features of letters and specific letters (like the beginning letters).

Visual cues   The length of a printed word is a simple visual cue that even the youngest readers can try to apply to identifying a word. While it is simple, we have seen (in Chapter 9) the pre-readers do not use it as a cue in discriminating between words of grossly different lengths. Children are likely to be able to make this discrimination in very early stages of reading. However, since word length is not a very useful cue in identifying words— far too many words share the same length—there has not been much interest in studying how sensitivity to this cue develops and whether it plays *any* role in word identification.

There has been more interest in *word shape* (Groff 1975), since some researchers believe that word shape information is important in children's word identification (Haber and Haber 1981). Usually, word shape is defined by the pattern of ascenders and descenders in a word (printed in lowercase letters). Thus, *shape* would have the same word shape as *clogs*. Since word shape has usually been investigated in conjunction with graphemic cues, we will discuss them together below.

Graphemic cues   As we mentioned before, children often focus on the initial letter of words. Most teachers are aware of it and many experimental studies have documented it. For example, Marchbanks and Levin (1965) and Williams, Blumberg, and Williams (1970) found that the first letter is the primary cue used in word identification by beginning readers. The task used in these studies was delayed matching-to-sample test in which children were shown a nonword such as *cug*. They were then shown a response card with four alternatives on it and asked to point to the one "most like" the stimulus. Each of the alternatives was similar to the stimulus in a particular way. One alternative (*che*) had the same first letter, the second (*tuk*) had the same second letter, the third (*ilg*) had the same third letter, and the fourth (*arp*) had the same overall word shape. Thus the alternative selected should reveal the most salient cue used by the child in word identification. Marchbanks and Levin found that the first letter was the most important cue and the last letter was the second most important for both kindergarten children and first grade children, while shape was the least used cue.

Williams, Blumberg, and Williams replicated these findings for first grade children. The kindergarten children in their study, however, showed no consistent selections. They also used adults as subjects and found that these proficient readers used complex strategies, including visual and aural matching as well as shape, as a basis for choice. Both studies concluded that specific letters, and not the overall shape of the words, form the basis of recognitiion for the child beginning the reading process. An additional study found that even the small use of word shape declined with age (Fisher and Price 1970).

As an alternative to the word shape hypothesis, Gibson (1971) suggested that children perceive words by detecting their distinctive features. She further suggested that with increasing age and schooling there is a change in feature analysis and extraction in that older children are able to extract higher order features. Rayner (1976) and Rayner and Hagelberg (1975) used the delayed matching-to-sample task described above in an attempt to diagnose the use of distinctive features. In the experiments, children were initially shown a stimulus such as *cug* and then asked to point to the response alternative most like the stimulus. Three of the six response alternatives (*cwq, oug,* and *owg*) preserved many of the distinctive features of the letters of the stimulus in the correct spatial location while three others (*cqn, jun,* and *jqg*) did not. Notice that two of the alternatives maintained each letter in its correct serial position (for example, the *c* in the first position is preserved in *cwq* and *cqn*).

Rayner and Hagelberg found that children at the beginning of kindergarten (without formal reading instruction) did not have a consistent pattern of responses, whereas first grade children relied very heavily on the first letter. In a subsequent experiment, Rayner (1976) tested children from kindergarten through sixth grade. Kindergarten children tested toward the end of the school year (rather than near the beginning, as in the Rayner and Hagelberg study) chose alternatives with the same beginning letter (e.g., chose either *cwg* or *cqn*) 48 percent of the time whereas first graders chose on the basis of the first letter 60 percent of the time. Both these groups chose alternatives that preserved the feature information of the second and third letters only 55 percent of the time (chance being 50 percent). Two clear developmental trends emerged from the data. First, there was a tendency for children to choose the response alternative with the same first letter as the stimulus up until the second grade, followed by a leveling off between second and fourth grade, and finally a decreasing tendency to rely on the first letter thereafter. The second major trend was an increasing tendency to choose response alternatives that preserved the letter feature information (so that either *cwq, ouq,* or *owq* was more likely to be chosen than *cqn, jun,* or *jqg*).

Research by Ehri (1980; Ehri and Wilce 1979) demonstrates that beginning readers use information about the first two letters. They were taught to read several pseudowords (such as *wheople* or *weeple*), and knowledge about the orthography of these words was tested by having them spell the words after training in reading. Although many errors in spelling occurred, the children definitely tended to retain the cues necessary for discriminating the words (as in the discrimination net stage). Every misspelling by children who were taught to read the nonword *wheople* began with *wh*, while every misspelling of *weeple* began with *we*. In addition, Reitsma (1983a, 1983b) found that young readers start early to produce a memory for word-specific letter patterns. Moreover, this memory for particular words was accurate enough for them to notice an alteration of only a single grapheme (even though the sound pattern was unaltered).

Let's summarize what these experiments tell us with respect to the use of graphemic cues. Beginning readers clearly use the initial letter as an important—and often the only—cue to word identification. As children progress, they use more of the visual information in the word. In some of the studies above, the information being used could either be interpreted as word shape information or letter feature information. In the studies, there is no way to distinguish them. However, it seems to us more parsimonious to think of the relevant variable as letter feature information. First of all, when word shape is pitted against letter information (Marchbanks and Levin 1965; Feitelson and Razel 1984), word shape is hardly ever used. Since the external configuration is not a good differentiator of words and thus not a good cue for word identification, it seems unlikely that children would attempt to use it except at very beginning stages. Instead, it would appear that as children progress beyond using the first letter, they extract progressively more of the graphemic information.

Orthographic Cues

As children become more proficient in identifying words, it is also evident that they become more sensitive to orthographic rules. Rosinski and Wheeler (1972) had children in grades one, three, and five point out the member of a pair of words that was the most like a word. The stimuli consisted of a pseudoword consistent with English spelling rules and a letter string that was not consistent with orthographic rules. The beginning readers were very close to chance in their judgment accuracy, whereas the older children were well above chance (69 percent to 80 percent correct) in picking a pseudoword over a letter string.

Studies in which children are asked to search for a target letter in strings of words, pseudowords, and letter strings (Juola et al. 1978; McCaughey et al. 1980) have also demonstrated that children are sensitive to orthographic cues. Kindergarten children, first, second, and fourth graders, as well as adult subjects, participated in the experiments. The search time for the kindergarten and first grade children did not differ between pseudowords and letter strings, indicating that they were unable to use orthographic structure to facilitate their search. The second and fourth graders were, however, influenced by orthographic structure and they searched faster through pseudowords than letter strings.

The above studies do not indicate, however, whether orthographic information is actually used in identifying words. One task that gets closer to that question is the delayed matching-to-sample task. Doehring (1976) employed a matching-to-sample task in which subjects were required to indicate which of three alternative items was identical to a sample item. Using three letter items, he showed that subjects were faster on pseudowords than orthographically irregular letter strings from the second through the eleventh grade (considering every grade between). Snowling and Frith (1981) also found that texts in which orthographic cues were altered were difficult for children to read.

In addition, numerous studies have been conducted using brief exposures to determine the extent to which orthographic cues are viable in recognizing words by children beginning the reading process. Although there is some variability across the studies [see Barron (1981a) for an excellent review], the results generally suggest that, sometime between the second and fourth grade, children are able to use some of the gross characteristics of orthographic structure in recognizing words. The usual test for whether orthographic structure is being used is to compare the identification of an orthographically regular string of letters (*dorch*) with an orthographically irregular string (*ohrdc*). Children in first grade may be able to use orthographic structure on a limited scale, but they often perform around the chance level in tasks in which they must discriminate between strings containing orthographic or nonorthographic information. Unfortunately, since orthographically legal strings are usually compared to grossly illegal ones, it is hard to tell from these studies exactly what kinds of orthographic knowledge are being acquired at different ages.

Grapheme-phoneme correspondence cues   While children clearly learn to use graphemic and orthographic cues as reading skill develops, neither cue in and of itself will enable the child to identify new words. In fact, one could easily argue that what appears to be the use of orthographic structure and more attention to all of the letters in a word (rather than just focusing all attention on the first letter) is little more than a byproduct of the fact that the child is effectively learning to read words. That is, as reading skill increases and word knowledge increases, children will be bound to produce results in experiments so as to suggest that these cues are important in their word identification. However, graphemic and orthographic knowledge is not sufficient to enable a child to read new words. In order to do that, the child must master either grapheme-phoneme correspondence rules or be able to make analogies from known words. (As we discussed in Chapter 3, "rules" and "analogies" are hard concepts to differentiate; accordingly, we will use the terms fairly interchangeably.)

The results of some important training studies suggest that knowledge of grapheme-phoneme rules is critical when it comes to reading new words. Bishop (1964) trained college students to make vocal responses to novel visual stimuli. One group learned to make phoneme responses to individual Arabic letters while the other group learned to make word responses to strings of Arabic letters. In each case there was a regular one-to-one correspondence between the grapheme and the pronunciation; in the case of the single characters, the correspondence was between the letter and the phoneme; while in the case of the words, the correspondence was between the word and the pronunciation of the word. Each of these training situations mimics the major methods used to teach children to read. In the case in which there is a grapheme-phoneme correspondence, a phonics approach is mimicked, while in the alternative case, a whole word approach is mimicked. Following the preliminary training (which took a few more trials to criterion on average for the letter group), both groups of subjects were required to read a new set of words constructed from the original characters. It was found that the subjects who had been taught the grapheme-phoneme correspondence rules could read many more "new" words than those trained with a whole word procedure. Some subjects in the latter group were able to successfully read the new words, but it appeared that they had discerned for themselves the correspondence that existed between the letters and the sound pattern.

Jeffrey and Samuels (1967) carried out a similar study using kindergarten children and a set of specially constructed letters (see Figure 10.1). As in Bishop's study, the results showed that the number of new words that could be pronounced correctly was much greater for the children who had learned the sounds of the individual letters than for those whose training required them to learn whole words. Both groups of children went on to learn the intended pronunciation of the new words, but the word group needed twice as many trials as the letter group before they knew all of the words.

The results of these studies suggest that detailed training on specific grapheme-phoneme correspondences may be the best way of equipping children to handle new words when they are encountered. Are children applying these rules to processing words that they have already seen? Backman et al. (1984) tested 7 and 8 year olds on their ability to pronounce regular and irregular words. Backman et al. found that the children were more accurate in reading high frequency regular words than in reading high frequency irregular words and tended to regularize the irregular words. This result indicates that these children were tending to use spelling-to-sound rules to name these words. (However, since they were 75 percent accurate in naming the irregular words, they were not merely relying on the rules.) In contrast, older children (9 and 17 year olds) were equally accurate in reading

FIGURE 10-1 Examples of stimuli used in the Jeffrey and Samuels (1967) study. (With permission of Academic Press and the authors.)

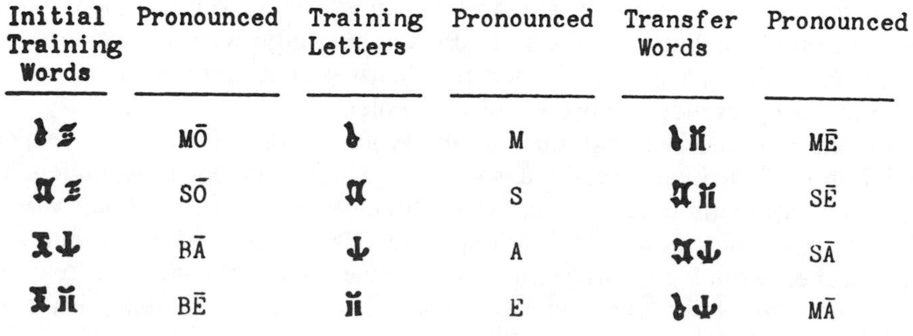

Initial Training Words	Pronounced	Training Letters	Pronounced	Transfer Words	Pronounced
❢ ⅀	MŌ	❢	M	❢ ⅀	MĒ
⅀ ⅀	SŌ	⅀	S	⅀ ⅀	SĒ
⅄ ⬇	BĀ	⬇	A	⅄ ⬇	SĀ
⅄ ⅀	BĒ	⅀	E	❢ ⬇	MĀ

aloud regular and irregular words, showing a decreased reliance on spelling-to-sound rules. A number of studies (Pick et al. 1978; Snowling 1980; Waters, Seidenberg, and Bruck 1984) have similarly found that around fourth or fifth grade, children show essentially the same pattern of responses as adults in tasks in which grapheme-phoneme correspondence rules can be applied.

Evidence that even younger children are able to use rules or analogies comes from research by Goswami (1986). She showed young children a word which they could not read (like *beak*), pronounced it, and then asked them to read other words. Some of these shared the same spelling patterns and had a sound in common with the original word (*bean, peak*), while others did not. She found that beginning readers were able to work out the analogical relationship for themselves. Some 5-year-old children on the verge of reading (the study was done in England) could even make analogies between the ends of words.

Goswami's results are important because they not only show that children can use analogies to read words they do not know, but because her results show quite clearly that children are capable of using analogies at earlier stages in their reading development than many accounts of reading development would suggest (such as the model we described by Marsh et al. 1981). Further evidence consistent with the idea that children can use analogies early in learning to read comes from a study reported by Pick et al. (1978). Pick et al. taught nonreading kindergarten children to read 12 words. After mastering the 12 words, 18 transfer words were presented. The 18 transfer words were composed of the same medial vowels and the same initial and final consonants as the training words. There were three types of transfer words, and they varied in terms of whether they shared an initial consonant-vowel combination, a final vowel-consonant combination, or no combination with the training words. Pick et al. found that beginning readers were much more likely to be able to read words that shared an initial consonant-vowel combination with the training words. Note that the children probably could read the words through analogy with words that they did know. Pick et al. found that beginning readers could use shared information most effectively at the beginnings of words, since, as we pointed out earlier, that is where they focus much of their attention.

Baron (1979) found that children use large unit analogies (like generalizing from *peak* to *beak* in Goswami's study). However, he also found evidence that smaller units (as in the Pick et al. study) were used as well as large ones. One piece of evidence for this was that chidren made errors ignoring the presence or absence of final (silent) *e*.

Baron suggested that the variability found in the extent to which children rely on word-specific associations versus analogies depended, in part, on the method of reading instruction. Whole word methods would clearly lead to the use of word-specific associations whereas phonics approaches would encourage the use of rules and analogies for reading nonwords. However, as Baron pointed out, it is also possible that quite apart from the method of instruction there are individual differences in the extent to which children beginning the reading process rely on word-specific associations versus analogies in establishing words in the lexicon (Treiman 1984; Treiman and Baron 1983). One thing that is clear from the research of Baron (1979) and Goswami (1986) is that the use of analogies is an effective strategy that can be taught to children to provide them with a larger repertoire of strategies for dealing with learning new words. Perhaps the best conclusion that can be reached from the research on the use of word-specific associations versus analogies is that children can use both mechanisms for reading words, particularly when the use of analogies is taught to them.

Which cues are the most important?   We have seen that graphemic, orthographic, and grapheme-phoneme correspondence cues are used by children in learning to read. Generally by fifth grade, children's responses are very much like those of adult skilled readers in various studies investigating the different types of cues that we have been discussing. Consistent with the observational studies that we described earlier, children at the earliest stages of learning to read rely heavily on graphemic cues. As reading skill increases, rule-based cues become more important as children learn to pay attention to the entire word (including all of the letter features), its orthographic structure, and grapheme-phoneme correspondence rules. Most of the studies we have discussed to this point examined the role of a particular type of cue independent of the others. We will now turn to some recent studies that have attempted to assess the relative importance of the various cues.

As we have seen, the beginning letter is a potent cue for word identification for beginning readers. Children beginning the reading process often erroneously produce a word that begins with the same letter as a target word (often totally ignoring other factors, such as word length). Is this because the first letter is graphically distinct or because of phonetic factors? As reading begins, children learn to focus their attention from left to right. This fact, together with the fact that beginning and end letters suffer less lateral masking than medial letters, could make the beginning letter visually distinct from other letters. However, Ehri and Wilce (1985) have argued that the importance of the beginning letter is really due to phonetic rather than visual factors.

Ehri and Wilce divided kindergartners into three groups based on their ability to read words: "pre-readers" (no words read), "novices" (a few words read), and "veterans" (several words read). They were then taught to read two kinds of words: simplified phonetic spellings whose letters corresponded to sounds (such as *JRF* for *giraffe*) and visual spellings whose letters bore no sound correspondence but were more distinct visually (see Table 10.2). Pre-readers learned to read visual spellings more easily than phonetic spellings, while novices and veterans learned to read the phonetic spellings more easily. These results suggest that when children move into reading, they rapidly shift from using graphemic or visual cues to directly

TABLE 10.2 Phonetic and visual spellings in the Ehri and Wilee (1985) study. With permission of the International Reading Association

Nouns	Phonetic Spelling	Visual Spellings
GIRAFFE SET		
knee	NE	FO
giraffe	JRF	WBC
balloon	BLUN	XGST
turtle	TRDL	YMP
mask	MSK	UHE
scissors	SZRS	QDJK
ELEPHANT SET		
arm	RM	FO
diaper	DIPR	XGST
elephant	LFT	WBC
comb	KOM	UHE
pencil	PNSL	QDJK
chicken	HKN	YMLP

accessing words using phonetic cues as mediators. Interestingly, tests of subjects' memory for the spellings of the target words revealed that initial letters were more salient than final letters but that the initial letters were more salient in the phonetic spellings than in the visual spellings. This was true even among subjects who had learned the visual spellings to criterion. In addition, initial letter salience was evident only among beginning readers who could use phonetic cues effectively to learn words. Ehri and Wilce thus concluded that the salience of the initial letter in word learning is a result of phonetic recoding and is not due to any type of visual distinctiveness of the initial letters of words.

A study by Beverly and Perfetti (1983) used a word similarity task to examine whether children learning to read are more sensitive to the visual and graphemic cues of printed words or to the phonemic information. Second grade children's judgments of word similarity were compared to those of older children and adults. The subjects were allowed to judge the similarity of a pair of words according to whatever criteria they chose to use. The visual, graphemic, and phonemic similarity of the pairs was systematically varied. For example, *new* and *sew* are identical in length and similar in word shape (visual cues) and share constituent letters (graphemic cues), but are different phonemically. *Sew* and *show* on the other hand are not similar in length and shape, but they have some graphemic similarity and very high phonemic similarity.

Given that the pair could vary in the similarity of visual, graphemic, and phonemic cues, what kinds of cues would be used to judge overall similarity? For second graders, shared visual cues (word length), shared letters, and shared phonemes all contributed to perceived similarity, with shared letters receiving the most weight. In fact, shared letters, independent of shared phonemes, were the most important cue for all age groups, including adults. This finding is consistent with those reported by Rayner (1976), which we described in detail earlier. The weight given to shared phonemes depended on age and reading skill. While second graders and less skilled fourth graders did not use phonemic similarity at all, adults and good fourth and sixth graders used shared phonemes as an important cue. Second grade subjects were quite unlikely to use vowel similarity as a cue. The results of this study suggest that beginning readers are more tuned to the way a word "looks" than the way it "sounds."

In a similar study, Pick et al. (1978) asked children in first, third, and fifth grade to judge the similarity of two pairs of words that were identical either at their beginnings or ends. The youngest children based more of their judgments on the beginnings of words than the older children did. Children who knew how to read at least moderately well based more of their judgments of similarity on the ends of words. However, words with visually identical ends were judged similar much more frequently when they rhymed than when they didn't.

Finally, consider a study by Rayner (1988) in which children participated in a delayed matching-to-sample task. In one condition, they were asked to choose the response alternative that was "most like" the target word. In a second condition, they were asked to choose the response alternative that "sounded most like" the target word. In a third condition, they chose the alternative that "looked most like" the target word. On the basis of the response alternatives that were chosen, Rayner was able to assess the extent to which the choice was made on the basis of phonemic, visual, graphemic, or orthographic cues.

Pre-readers and beginning readers (who could read about 20 percent of the words on a graded word list they were given) responded on the basis of word shape and the beginning letter when asked to choose the alternative most like the target. For them, "most like" clearly meant the alternative that looked most like the target. Even when they were instructed to respond on the basis of the alternative that sounded most like the target, they continued to respond on the basis of visual and graphemic similarity. Intermediate readers (8-year-old children who could read about 90 percent of the word list) also tended to equate the instruction to choose the alternative "most like" the target with the word looking like the target. However, word shape was not at all a salient cue for them, while orthographic cues were. They tended to choose alternatives that conformed to English spelling rules. When instructed to choose the alternative that sounded most like the target, they were able to do so quite well. But few of them spontaneously chose an alternative which sounded like the target when given the instruction (in the first task) to choose the one most like the target. In contrast to this, advanced readers (10-year-old children who could read all of the words on the word list) spontaneously tended to choose the response alternative which sounded most like the target when simply told to choose the alternative most like the target. When instructed to choose the alternative that looked most like the target, these advanced readers were also able to do this quite easily.

From Rayner's study we can see that young beginning readers are not very flexible in their strategies. They tended to rely on visual and graphemic cues in making judgments about words (even though they had phonics instruction as part of their curriculum). They either knew the words on the reading list or did not and were not very good at guessing words they did not know. In contrast, children with at least two years of reading experience were very sensitive to orthographic structure. In a lexical decision task, they could easily say "yes" to words and "no" to orthographically illegal (and unpronounceable) nonwords, but they had a very difficult time rejecting pseudowords (i.e., orthographically legal and pronounceable nonwords). They tended to respond "yes" very often to pseudowords as if they believed that if a letter string is pronounceable it must be a word. That they had strategies for using grapheme-phoneme correspondence rules in analyzing words is evident from the fact that when instructed to choose the alternative sounding most like the target they could do so fairly well. Advanced readers' primary strategy for analyzing words clearly also involved the use of grapheme-phoneme correspondence rules. However, they were more flexible than younger readers in using alternative strategies in the various tasks.

In summary, most of the results we discussed in this section are consistent with the stages of development that we discussed earlier in this chapter and with many of the observational studies upon which the stages are based. The results of these studies indicate that children move from almost total reliance on visual and graphemic cues to more flexible strategies. Sensitivity to orthographic cues appears to evolve quite early (around the second grade). By fourth grade, children have developed the use of grapheme-phoneme correspondence rules so that their performance is much like skilled readers'. They are also quite flexible in the use of a number of strategies for analyzing words and are sensitive to orthographic and graphemic cues, as well as phonemic cues. They are also able to use analogies in reading words they do not know. Second grade readers appear to have analytic strategies (such as the use of analogy and phonemic cues) available to them, but they are not as flexible in using them as are the 10 year olds.

The one inconsistency in the studies we've reviewed is that only Ehri and Wilce's study suggests that beginning readers rely on phonetic cues. There are two possible reasons for the discrepancy. One is that the other studies used judgmental tasks; perhaps children can use phonetic cues to access words before they are able to use them in conscious decisions about words. The second is that the phonetic cues Ehri and Wilce studied may have been much simpler; the phonetic cue may merely have been a conversion of the first letter to a phoneme, while the other studies tapped much more complex coding (e.g., the sounds of differently spelled words that rhymed).

Units of processing   The evidence described so far in this chapter indicates that as children's reading skills improve, they move from focusing on single letters to paying attention to the entire word. Such a shift implies that they are using larger units for processing as they become more proficient readers. As we saw in Chapter 3, one major focus of research on word recognition has been to determine what the unit of processing is and there has been a great deal of speculation to the effect that the development of word recognition is characterized as involving increasingly larger units (Gibson 1971; LaBerge and Samuels 1974). As we shall see later in this chapter when we discuss eye movements, beginning readers sometimes average two or three fixations per word, also suggesting that they use units smaller than the word for processing.

Samuels, LaBerge, and Bremer (1978) asked second, fourth, and sixth grade children, as well as adults, to make semantic category decisions (animal or nonanimal) about words which varied in length (three to six letters). They obtained a developmental change: response time did not increase at all as word length increased for the adult subjects, while response time increased markedly as word length increased for the second graders. Response time for fourth and sixth graders also increased with increasing word length, but not nearly as much as for the second graders. These results suggest either that children move from processing words letter by letter to processing words as wholes as reading skill increases, or that as reading skill increases children are able to process letters in parallel.

In order to evaluate developmental changes in units of processing, Drewnowski (1978) used a letter detection task in which subjects were required to detect every instance of the letter *t* by circling it in prose passages, scrambled passages, and lists of words. Children in grades one to five and adults participated in the study. Drewnowski found that all subjects, except first grade children, made more errors in circling the letter *t* in the word *the* in prose passages than in circling the letter *t* in a control word such as *thy* (see also Mohan 1978; Cunningham et al. 1988). Thus, only the children who were reading at first grade level appeared to rely on letter-by-letter processing when they could use higher units. Fourth and fifth grade children and adults made more errors when the *the*s were in normal prose than when they were in scrambled prose. In contrast, the second and third graders made equal numbers of errors in the two conditions. Thus the second and third grade children appeared to be processing the text at the level of individual words in the task.

Barron (1981a) reviewed a large number of other studies attempting to assess the size of the unit of processing in children beginning the reading process. His review points out that there are some inconsistent results in the literature, particularly as a function of the nature of the task used to assess the unit of processing. For example, Friedrich, Schadler, and Juola (1979) had second and fourth grade children search for a target that could be either a word, a member of a category, a syllable, or a letter. They found that both groups of children could search fastest for a word, followed by category members, syllables, and then letters. These results suggest a problem for the hypothesis of a progression from lower to higher order units in development, as even the younger subjects apparently could use words as units before they could use syllables. Barron concluded that the available evidence suggested that children develop the ability to attend to several units of processing (such as spelling patterns, syllables, some morphemes) about the same time (between grades two and four) and that this ability coincides with the development of the use of orthographic structure.

Summary of Stages of Reading Development

Let's try to summarize what we know about beginning reading. A large number of studies are fairly consistent in yielding similar patterns of results as children become more mature in the skill of reading. At the beginning of reading, children may know a few words as a result of rote associations (Gough and Hillinger 1980). When children are presented words that they do not know in isolation, if they try to generate a response, it will most often be a wild guess. When presented with a word in context that they do not know, the child will most often guess a word using the prior text as a guide for the guess. With more experience with print, beginning readers come to focus on shared graphemic features of unknown words and words that they do know. Errors that they make on words in isolation and in context share similar graphic features with words that they know. Particularly salient is the initial letter. At first, the initial letter is salient because of its visual distinctiveness, but at some point children begin to grasp in some small measure the orthographic regularity of the alphabetic principle. Thus children (either by being explicitly taught the relationship or by discerning it for themselves) realize that many letters are pronounced the same way in different words and that it is possible to determine what a new word is by sounding it out. Finally, as the child gains even more experience with print, decoding skills become even more sophisticated and the child learns to use analogies or rules as an alternative device for decoding. It does appear, though, that the child has the capability of using analogies some time before they are used frequently (Goswami 1986). Perhaps one goal of instruction should be to help young readers develop such strategies more rapidly.

As the child progresses through the various stages in becoming proficient at reading, there is also a progression toward using grapheme-phoneme correspondence rules for learning new words. The progression towards using grapheme-phoneme correspondence rules accompanies a development from focusing on a single characteristic of printed words (the initial letter or perhaps some distinctive letter) to attending to all of the letters in the word. While the importance of decoding processes using grapheme-phoneme correspondence rules cannot be overemphasized, it is important to note that the use of such rules will not automatically guarantee success in reading every new word because there is not a one-to-one relationship between graphemes and phonemes. However, most words are regular in the sense that their pronunciation follows from more complex rules. On the other hand, many common words (like *was*) are irregular in their pronunciation. For many of these words, though, if the child uses the rules to derive the pronunciation, they may arrive at a close enough approximation to the actual pronunciation to correctly identify the word. In addition, some irregular words have "close neighbors" or other words spelled like they are, yet pronounced irregularly. For example, once a child knows the word *laugh* and is presented the infrequent word *draught,* he or she may respond /draft/ by analogy to *laugh.* Prior to the development of analogy strategies, children would respond /drawt/, which is more in keeping with grapheme-phoneme correspondence rules. A few irregular words are exceptions in that there are no other words spelled and pronounced as they are. In this case, the child must learn word-specific associations between the printed word and its pronunciation.

In essence, then, the ability to use higher-order rules and analogies to read new words represents the highest level of reading skill. It is difficult to associate specific ages to the various stages that a child goes through because children will advance to a stage at different paces. On top of this is the fact that reading instruction varies as a function of culture. However, for alphabetic writing systems, children must develop to the highest level if they are to become competent readers. For most children, the highest stage is reached between the ages of 8 and 10. One may improve on the efficiency and scope of one's reading skill after reaching this stage, but the total system does not undergo any more qualitative changes.

ACCESSING WORD MEANINGS

So far in this chapter, we have focused primarily on how children are able to read (or produce the name of) new words. This clearly represents the most difficult aspect of reading and the ability to do so means that the major breakthrough in reading has occurred (some refer to it as "breaking the code"). However, most of the words children read are not new words at all, but words they already know. When they already know a word (i.e., it is in their *print lexicon*), how do they access the meaning of that word? It appears for the youngest beginning readers the print lexicon is almost totally the result of word-specific associations in which the child associates some particular aspect of the word with its meaning and subsequently recognizes it on that basis. However, as reading skill increases, it is evident that the print lexicon comes to contain not only information about how the word looks but about letter patterns and the sound of the word, as well as the meaning (Ehri 1983). Given the importance of phonological processes in learning to read that we documented in Chapter 9, one might be tempted to conclude that as children become proficient in reading, they primarily access the print lexicon through phonology: that is, they obtain the meaning of the word by converting the word to its sound representation and then accessing the meaning by way of the sound representation. However, as we argued in Chapter 3, skilled readers often access their print lexicon with only minimal involvement of sound codes. It would be natural to conclude, therefore, that there is a developmental trend whereby sound codes become increasingly less important in accessing the lexicon.

The Developmental Shift Hypothesis

Much of the research on children's access to word meanings has been concerned with the above issue: whether or not there is a developmental shift from relying exclusively on phonological information for accessing the lexicon to using both phonological information and direct visual access (Barron 1981a, 1986). There have been several studies designed to test this hypothesis. Rader (1975) asked children in second, fourth, and sixth grade, as well as adults, to decide if pairs of orally or visually presented words rhymed (such as *buy* and *pie*) or belonged to the same semantic category (such as *dog* and *cat*), and measured their response times. She predicted that if phonological access drops out with increasing age then the categorization task should initially be slower than the rhyming task, but that the difference should decrease as children got older. In addition, she predicted that such a pattern would be unique to judgments about written (as opposed to spoken) words. Her logic was as follows. First, the use of phonological information is obligatory with auditory presentations; hence the difference between the rhyme task and the category task (which was slower than the rhyme task) can be used as a baseline to evaluate the relative speeds of extracting rhyme and category information from sound codes. Second, since the use of phonological information is obligatory in the rhyming task but not in the category task with visual presentation (as the rhyming pairs did not share corresponding spelling patterns), a smaller rhyme-category difference with visual than with auditory presentation would indicate that phonological information was not being used in the category condition. Contrary to the developmental shift hypothesis, Rader found that the rhyme category difference was smaller with visual than auditory presentations for all age groups. For the second graders, the effect was confined to the "yes" responses, but the general pattern of results suggests that even second grade children do not require phonological access to the lexicon.

Barron and Baron (1977) took a slightly different approach to testing the developmental shift hypothesis. They asked children in first, second, fourth, and eighth grade to decide if picture-word pairs rhymed (the picture of a horn paired with the word *corn*) or went together in meaning (the picture of a shoe paired with the word *sock*). To determine if phonological mediation was involved in accessing word meanings, subjects were required to say the word *double* aloud at the same time they made the rhyme and meaning decisions. As we saw in Chapter 6, the rationale of the concurrent articulation task is that it ties up the subjects' auditory and articulatory mechanisms and interferes with the rhyme and meaning decisions to the extent that the decisions involved the use of these mechanisms. Barron and Baron's rationale was that if the youngest children are relying more heavily on phonological information than the older children, the concurrent vocalization task should interfere more with both types of decision. Although subjects in all five grades made more errors on the rhyming task when they were concurrently vocalizing, concurrent articulation did not have any effect on the meaning task at any grade level, including grade one. These results are consistent with Rader's and do not support the developmental shift hypothesis.

A third study by Condry, McMahon-Rideout, and Levy (1979) also examined the developmental shift hypothesis. They presented second and fifth grade children, as well as adults, with a target word and two "choice words." The subjects' task was to decide which of the choice words was similar to the target word in a specific way: graphically, phonologically, or semantically. The incorrect choices were varied systematically so that, for example, if the target word was *plate* and the correct choice word was *dish* in the semantic condition, subjects might have a distractor (such as *wait*) that rhymed with the target (*plate*) on some trials and a distractor that didn't rhyme on other trials. Condry, McMahon-Rideout, and Levy hypothesized that if children shift from using phonological coding to using both direct visual access and phonological coding, then rhyming distractors in the semantic task should have a decreasing influence on children's performance as they got older and more experienced with print. In fact, this hypothesis was not confirmed; rather, the influence of rhyming distractors tended to increase rather than decrease as children grew older.

While Rader (1975), Barron and Baron (1977), and Condry, McMahon-Rideout, and Levy (1979) all used slightly different tasks, their results are similar in that they are all inconsistent with the developmental shift hypothesis, in which children are assumed to shift from accessing the lexicon strictly by phonology to accessing the lexicon both by phonological codes and by direct visual codes. Instead, the results suggest that phonological coding is not necessary for accessing word meanings from first grade through adulthood (Barron 1981a, 1986). In essence then, the developmental shift hypothesis in which children are seen as moving from phonological codes to access the lexicon to both phonological and direct visual routes must be turned on its head; the progression appears to be from accessing the lexicon without phonology to the ability to use phonology as well as direct visual access.

There are several sources of information consistent with this progression. First, as we saw in the prior section on word identification cues, children rely on visual or graphemic cues early in reading, moving to phonological cues later in the development of the reading skill. Second, children often enter reading instruction knowing the meanings of a small group of printed words, yet having only rudimentary knowledge of how to

read words aloud except by associating whole words with their corresponding pronunciations, or by using a limited set of large unit analogies (Baron
1979). Third, as we have also seen, learning to read words is often very
difficult and time consuming, and children who have trouble acquiring
reading skill seem to be deficient in their use of print-to-sound translation
procedures (Barron 1981b; Bradley and Bryant 1978; Perfetti and Hogaboam 1975) and may be particularly reliant on visual cues when identifying
words.

It should be pointed out that there are some inconsistencies in the
research in this area. Some studies (see Backman et al. 1984; Reitsma 1984)
have found evidence to suggest that younger readers rely more heavily on
phonological information in word decoding than older children do. Such a
finding is consistent with the developmental shift hypothesis, but inconsistent with many of the other studies we have reviewed in this section. Jorm
and Share (1983) have a reasonable hypothesis to explain this discrepancy.
They point out that all of the studies which failed to support the developmental shift hypothesis used a restricted range of words (generally content
words which were high in frequency and concreteness). Thus, these studies
clearly indicate that with words of this type, beginning readers can and do
use the visual route to the lexicon. However, as Jorm and Share pointed out,
this does not necessarily imply that less frequent and abstract words are
processed in the same way; with such words phonological coding may often
be the first stage before visual access becomes possible. With increasing age,
the size of the lexicon for which such phonological coding is unnecessary
should increase dramatically. Backman et al.'s (1984) data support the Jorm
and Share hypothesis. Backman et al. found that beginning readers rapidly
learn to recognize high frequency words from visual input alone, while at the
same time they are expanding and consolidating their knowledge of spelling-
sound correspondences. However, they also found that beginning readers have difficulty reading homographic spelling patterns (*-ave, -own*)
which have different pronunciations in different words (*have-wave, town-
mown*) and in such cases did rely on phonological information in word
decoding.

Picture-Word Interference

Recently, a number of studies have used a variation of the standard
Stroop task that we described in Chapter 3 to investigate the access of word
meanings by beginning readers. In the picture-word interference task,
introduced by Rosinski, Golinkoff, and Kukish (1975), subjects are required
to name a line drawing of a picture as rapidly as possible. Printed inside the
picture is a word or letter string which may or may not be related to the
picture. Subjects are faster naming the picture when the appropriate label is
printed on the picture (the word *apple* inside a picture of an apple) than when
the picture is presented alone (Ehri 1976; Posnansky and Rayner 1977). If

FIGURE 10-2 Examples of stimuli in the picture-word interference task. The top row contains examples of incongruous words and pictures; the bottom row contains congruous examples.

the label printed inside the picture names another object, there is interference in naming the picture.

Of greatest interest for our present purposes is the reliable finding that when the picture and label printed on the picture are semantically incongruous (the word *house* printed on the picture of an apple), there is greater interference than when the label is a nonword (like *dorch*). This finding has been obtained with beginning readers as well as older children and has been interpreted as indicating that the interference is semantically based and that word meaning access is not phonologically based even for beginning readers (Golinkoff and Rosinski 1976; Rosinski, Golinkoff, and Kukish 1975). If it were phonologically based, the argument is that there should be as much interference from a pronounceable nonword as from a word.

There is a problem with this line of argument. Because children have had less experience reading nonwords than words, the phonological and articulatory codes of nonwords would be less available than for words and hence may be less likely to interfere with the articulatory response for the picture label. However, Ehri (1977) showed that highly familiar function words produce no more interference than nonsense words for third and sixth graders, whereas adjectives and nouns produced more interference. These results were obtained even though the function words could be read aloud as rapidly as the nouns and adjectives. More importantly, Rosinski (1977) demonstrated that, for second, fourth, and sixth graders (and adults, as well), word labels belonging to the same semantic category as the picture produced more interference than word labels that did not belong to the same semantic category. These results suggest that the picture-word interference effect involves semantic information and does not occur solely because of competing verbal responses.

In subsequent research, Guttentag and Haith (1978) found that although beginning readers tested near the end of the first grade showed more interference on semantically related than on unrelated picture-word pairs, they did not show any more interference on pictures printed with easy to pronounce nonwords (*lart*) than with unpronounceable nonwords (*lbch*). In contrast, more pronounceable nonwords produced more interference than less pronounceable nonwords for third graders and adults. These results are consistent with a visual to visual-phonological developmental shift because they suggest that beginning readers can access the lexicon without being able to effectively use phonological information. However, it should be noted that the less pronounceable nonwords in the experiment were also less consistent with orthographic constraints than were the pronounceable nonwords.

Finally, Posnansky and Rayner (1977) found that even beginning readers were able to use the phonological characteristics of print in their studies. For example, subjects were faster naming the picture when the label had the same sound (*leef* or *lefe* on a picture of a leaf) than when it did not (*loef* or *lofe*). However, subjects were also faster when the label preserved most of the graphemic characteristics of the picture name (*leef*) than when it did not (*lefe*). The important point about the experiments was that there was no interaction with age, so that the beginning readers showed essentially the same pattern as did the older children and adults in the experiments. Posnansky and Rayner's results suggest that beginning readers may be able to use both visual and phonological information in accessing word meanings.

Summary

Research on the development of word meaning access provides very little support for the hypothesis that there is a developmental shift from reliance on phonological codes to the use of both phonological and visual codes. There is some evidence consistent with just the opposite hypothesis, namely that development proceeds from almost total reliance upon graphemic information to the use of both phonological and visual codes. However, the most plausible hypothesis may be that beginning as well as skilled readers can use both graphemic and phonological information to access word meanings. Beginning readers may, however, be more reliant on graphemic information when reading familiar words, since they have not yet received a great deal of instruction in (or have not yet figured out) analytic print-to-sound translation strategies. Once they learn how to translate print into sound rapidly and accurately, they are able to use phonological processing in accessing the meaning of words, particularly unfamiliar words.

INNER SPEECH

As we discussed in Chapter 6, inner speech serves the function of aiding comprehension processes. To what extent does it aid beginning readers' comprehension of text? This isn't an easy area to evaluate because children learn to read orally before they read silently. Indeed, children are not encouraged to read silently until the middle to end of first grade. Thus, it shouldn't be at all that surprising that activity (as measured by EMG) in the speech tract of beginning readers is significantly larger than activity for older children (Edfeldt, 1960; McGuigan, Keller, & Stanton, 1964). Perhaps much of the activity during initial silent reading is merely a carry-over from their oral reading.

It is probable that activity in the speech tract (subvocalization) is of less importance to comprehension processes than phonological coding. Most of the research on speech processes associated with reading has focused on issues such as phonological awareness and its role in learning to read or on phoneme-grapheme correspondence rules as cues to word identification. A number of studies have dealt with the role of phonological recoding in accessing the meaning of words. As we have seen, there is not a great deal of evidence consistent with the developmental shift hypothesis, in which children move from initial reliance on phonological coding to both phonological coding and direct visual access to the lexicon. Studies of this type are generally meant to deal with the role of prelexical phonology. In this section, we are interested in postlexical phonology—the extent to which phonological recoding aids in comprehension.

A number of studies by Liberman and Shankweiler and their colleagues (Brady, Shankweiler, and Mann 1983; Katz, Shankweiler, and Liberman 1981; Liberman et al. 1977; Mann, Liberman, and Shankweiler 1980; Mark et al. 1977; Shankweiler et al. 1979) and others (Byrne and Shea 1979) demonstrated the importance of speech-related processes for childrens' ability to read effectively (though see Hall et al. 1983 for contradictory data). The primary way of diagnosing whether phonological recoding is used by the subject is to determine whether it is harder to process acoustically confusable material than control material (see Chapter 6). Liberman and Shankweiler found that the use of speech codes in working memory distinguished good second grade readers from poor second grade readers. This, however may only be true of early stages. Olson et al. (1984). showed that the relationship holds for second grade readers but not for older readers. Liberman and Shankweiler originally argued that recoding printed material into a speech code in working memory was critically important in efficient reading and that good and poor readers could be distinguished by their recoding ability. But since they obtained the same results when stimuli were presented to the eye and the ear, it is hard to argue that differences in recoding are related specifically to reading ability. Nevertheless, the results of these studies support the idea that inner speech is important for children's comprehension of discourse.

In the above research, it was generally assumed that the function of phonological coding of print is to bolster the short-term memory representation. An alternative hypothesis (Beggs and Howarth 1985) is that the development of inner speech accompanies a strategy of reading aloud "with expression" and that it is a manifestation of the need to prestructure oral utterances (see also Slowiaczek and Clifton 1980). Beggs and Howarth's hypothesis, consistent with the results of Clay and Imlach (1971) is that good 7-year-old readers read with expression while less skilled beginning readers were still at a word-by-word level. Beggs and Howarth's data are also supportive of their hypothesis. They found that reading comprehension for beginning readers improved when certain prosodic features were indicated in the text (i.e., stressed words were printed in boldface). However, subjects in Beggs and Howarth's study read the text aloud, and for the demonstration to be really convincing, children would have to read the text silently.

The concurrent vocalization technique has not been used in situations when children are reading meaningful text. As we pointed out in Chapter 6, such studies have been one primary source of information bolstering our knowledge of the role of phonological recoding in skilled reading. A phrase-evaluation study reported by Doctor and Coltheart (1980) is one of the few developmental studies that obtained evidence relevant to the issue of postlexical phonological recoding and reading comprehension. In Doctor and Coltheart's study, children were given sentences of the following types:

1. I have the time. (Meaningful sentences containing no homophones.)
2. I have no time. (Meaningful sentences containing homophones.)
3. I have know time. (Meaningless all-word sentences that sound correct.)
4. I have blue time. (Meaningless all-word sentences that sound wrong.)
5. I have noe time. (Meaningless sentences containing nonwords that sound correct.)
6. I have bloo time. (Meaningless sentences containing nonwords that sound wrong.)

Young children made more errors with nonsense sentences which sounded correct (5) than with those that sounded wrong (6). On the surface, this finding indicates the use of prelexical phonological coding, since nonwords like *noe* do not have lexical entries. However, it was also found that the children were more likely to be fooled by sentences where both prelexical phonological coding and postlexical phonological recoding are possible (3) than by sentences where only prelexical phonological coding is possible (5). Furthermore, the effect declined with age. Finally, a recent study by Coltheart et al. (1986) using Doctor and Coltheart's stimuli (but different subjects) and further analyses came to the conclusion that the phonological effects in the earlier study were due to postlexical processing and that the development of nonlexical grapheme-phoneme conversion codes lags behind direct visual access. It therefore seems that children do rely on postlexical phonological recoding to aid comprehension processes.

THE USE OF CONTEXT

We have seen earlier in this chapter from observational studies that the errors beginning readers make are often consistent with the context. A number of experimental studies have examined developmental changes in children's use of contextual information as they become more proficient readers.

Reviewing the literature on the role of context in word recognition, Stanovich (1980) concluded that less skilled readers compensate for slower or poorer word identification skills by relying more on context to facilitate ongoing word identification than better readers do. West and Stanovich (1978) required third graders, fifth graders, and adults to name words presented either in isolation or after incomplete sentence contexts. The children were faster naming words shown in context than those shown in isolation, but the adults showed no difference. Perfetti, Goldman, and Hogaboam (1979) found that skilled 8- to 10-year-old readers made less use of sentence context in facilitating word naming than did children of the same age who were not as proficient in reading. This result suggests that even by the age of 8 or 10, children's word identification processes are becoming so efficient that immature reliance on contextual information is already disappearing.

Other studies have attempted to manipulate the speed of lexical access to determine whether faster lexical access time is a plausible explanation for the decreasing context effect with increasing age. For example, Stanovich, West, and Freeman (1981) asked second grade children to read words preceded by either a congruous, incongruous, or neutral context. Each child was given practice recognizing one-half of the words in isolation. The effect of context on naming time decreased for the practiced words and increased with word difficulty (as measured by word length and word frequency). Thus practice with words made the children look like adults. In another study, Schwantes (1981) asked third grade children and college students to make lexical decisions about words that were either visually degraded or undegraded. These decisions were made either with or without congruous sentence context. In the undegraded condition the standard result was obtained: contextual facilitation was greater for third graders than for the skilled readers. However, when word identification was slowed by degrading the target words, the context effect was as large for the skilled readers as for the third graders. That is, degraded words made adult's use of context look like children's.

Ehrlich (1981) asked children in second, fourth, and sixth grade to read passages of text aloud in which certain target words were replaced by other words. (The children were instructed to read the text exactly as it was printed.) The replacement words were either visually similar to the target (*house-horse*) or differed in overall word shape (*shark-sharp*) and were anomalous in the text. Ehrlich measured the probability that the replacement word was read as the target word and also measured the hesitations and pauses that children made before uttering the replacement word. She found that beginning readers were much more likely to misread the replacement word as the target word than the older children. Likewise, the beginning readers were much less likely to hesitate or pause prior to reading the replacement word than older children. Again, these results indicate that beginning readers are more reliant on context to read words than older readers.

Summary of Inner Speech and the Use of Context

The small amount of research that has been done on inner speech suggests that as children have more experience reading, they become more proficient in using phonological coding as an aid for comprehension. Given that we have argued that skilled readers use inner speech to aid their comprehension, particularly of difficult text, it is likely that children do so as well. The role of inner speech in children's reading is an area that needs considerably more research carried out before we will be able to completely understand the issue.

The research that has been done on the use of contextual information is much more definitive and consistent with observational studies; as children gain more experience reading and word recognition processes become more automatic, their reliance on context decreases.

EYE MOVEMENTS AND THE PERCEPTUAL SPAN

As we noted in Chapter 4, beginning readers make more and longer fixations, shorter saccades, and more regressions than skilled readers. Beginning readers' average fixation duration is around 350 milliseconds, their average saccade length is 2 to 5 characters, and about 25 percent of their eye movements are regressions. As children become more proficient in the skill of reading, their eye movement patterns show systematic changes: they make shorter fixations, longer (and fewer) saccades, and fewer regressions (Buswell 1922; Rayner 1978a; Taylor 1965). Table 10.3 shows some summary statistics taken from Buswell and Taylor. Buswell (1922) observed that by fifth grade, most of the indices of eye movements in reading have stabilized. The one aspect of eye movements that continues to change until the end of high school is the number of regressive eye movements.

Why do eye movement characteristics change as greater skill is acquired in reading? Noting that the length of the saccade increases with reading skill, many researchers have suggested that children beginning the reading process have smaller perceptual spans than their more skilled counterparts. A generally accepted explanation for this phenomenon is that children beginning to read are focusing all of their attention on the fixated word and they are inefficient in the use of parafoveal and peripheral

TABLE 10.3 Developmental Characteristics of Eye Movements During Reading (Rayner, 1978a). Adapted with permission of the American Psychological Association.

CHARACTERISTIC	GRADE LEVEL												
	1	2	3	4	5	6	7	8	9	10	11	12	COLLEGE
Fixations per 100 words	224	174	155	139	129	120	114	109	105	101	96	94	90
Regressions per 100 words	52	40	35	31	28	25	23	21	20	19	18	17	15
Span of recognition[a](words)	.45	.57	.65	.72	.78	.83	.88	.92	.95	.99	1.04	1.06	1.11
Fixation duration (msec)	330	300	280	270	270	270	270	270	270	260	260	250	240
Words per minute	80	115	138	158	173	185	195	204	214	224	237	250	280
Fixations per line of print	15.5	10.7	8.9	7.3	6.9	7.3	6.8	[b]	7.2	5.8	5.5	6.4	5.9
Fixation duration (msec)	432	364	316	268	252	236	240		244	248	224	248	252
Regressions per line	4.0	2.3	1.8	1.4	1.3	1.6	1.5		1.0	.7	.7	.7	0.5

Note. The upper set of means is taken from S. E. Taylor (1965), and the lower set from Buswell (1922).
[a] Computed by dividing the number of words in a passage by the number of fixations in the passage.
[b] Data not reported.

information and hence have a smaller perceptual span than skilled readers (Fisher 1979).

The technique most commonly used to assess the perceptual span in beginning readers simply involves dividing the number of words on a line by the number of fixations on the line. By such a method, Taylor (1965) argued that the perceptual span for second grade children was 0.57 words, for fourth grade children was 0.72 words, and for sixth grade children 0.83 words. College students, by this measure, had a perceptual span of 1.11 words. A second technique used to infer that beginning readers have a smaller perceptual span than skilled readers has utilized tachistoscopic presentations of words and letters in eccentric vision (Fisher and Lefton 1976). We discussed both of these techniques in Chapter 4 and indicated that there were several problems with each. The primary problem with the first technique is that it wrongly assumes that there is no overlap of information from fixation to fixation and the primary problem with the second technique is that it is very likely that normal reading and tachistoscopic report vary enough to induce different strategies.

A third technique used to infer that children have smaller perceptual spans than skilled readers involves having subjects read mutilated text in which the spaces between words have been filled in with various types of letters or characters (Fisher and Montanary 1977; Hochberg 1970; Spragins, Lefton, and Fisher 1976). (Since we didn't discuss this technique in Chapter 4, we will discuss it in some detail here.) These researchers found that the absence of word boundary cues interfered markedly with reading fluency in older children (fifth and sixth graders) and concluded that the more skilled readers were at a disadvantage with the mutilated text because they had developed more efficient skills through the use of extrafoveal vision and the mutilated word boundary cues interfered with their strategy; younger children, in contrast, were assumed to be bound to foveal processing and therefore it did not matter to them that the word boundary information was missing.

There are two difficulties with this research. First, as Fisher and Montanary (1977) found, beginning readers do show some disruption from the mutilated text. Second, with this technique it is impossible to determine if the slowdown in reading should be attributed to difficulties related to processing information in eccentric vision or to difficulties associated with foveal word identification processes. Pollatsek and Rayner (1982) demonstrated that much of the difficulty in reading such text is a result of filling in the space to the right of the fixated word and hence that much of the mutilation effect is likely due to disruption of identification of the fixated word rather than to disruption of parafoveal information extraction.

The three techniques described above are consistent in indicating that beginning readers have a smaller perceptual span than skilled readers; however, the prior discussion indicates that there are problems associated with each of them. More recently, Rayner (1986a) used the moving window technique that we described in Chapter 4 to investigate the size of the perceptual span of children at the beginning of the second, fourth, and sixth grade. Rayner found that beginning readers do have a slightly smaller perceptual span than skilled readers; the span of beginning readers extends about 11 character spaces to the right of fixation in comparison to about 15 character spaces for skilled readers (see Chapter 4). Thus the span is bigger than half the size of the span of skilled readers, which was the estimate from the technique used by Taylor (1965). Rayner also found that beginning readers, like skilled readers, use word length information for determining where to look next, and that the perceptual span for beginning readers (again like skilled readers) is asymmetric to the right of fixation. Apparently, one year of reading allows beginning readers to direct much of their attention to the right of fixation.

While the perceptual span of beginning readers was only slightly smaller than that of skilled readers in Rayner's study, a window of only 5 characters (2 to the left and 2 to the right of fixation) reduced beginning readers to 62 percent of their normal reading rate (in comparison to 40 percent and 44 percent for fourth and sixth graders, and 34 percent for adult skilled readers). It thus appears that the beginning readers' smaller perceptual span is due to the fact that they devote more of their attention to foveal word processing during a fixation than do skilled readers. Indeed, when fourth grade children were given difficult text to read, the size of their perceptual span decreased to that of beginning readers.

In summary, the perceptual span of beginning readers is slightly smaller than that of skilled readers (Rayner, 1986a). However, neither the smaller perceptual span nor eye movements per se account for beginning readers' slower reading rate, since we have seen that children have significantly more trouble decoding individual words even when they are in isolation. It is possible that poorer control of eye movements is one cause of beginning readers' slow reading. However, it is likely that eye movements merely reflect the fact that central cognitive processes are slower in beginning readers than in older children and that many of the component processes in reading have not yet become automatic (LaBerge and Samuels 1974), and that longer fixation durations, more fixations (resulting in shorter saccades), and more regressions are a result of the greater effort needed for encoding and word recognition processes on the part of beginning readers.

COMPREHENSION PROCESSES

We shall not have a great deal to say about the comprehension processes of children learning to read. We have suggested on a number of occasions in this chapter that by fifth grade, children are very much like adult skilled readers. We suspect that this point is also true of comprehension processes. This is not to say that fifth grade children comprehend text as well as skilled readers. Certainly, if you give them difficult text to read (text that has many unfamiliar words and which is about an unfamiliar topic), they may not comprehend very much of the text. Our point is that while adults may have more knowledge to bring to bear upon the reading task, and even more strategies for comprehension, the way knowledge and strategies are brought to bear is quite similar for fifth graders and adults (Keenan and Brown 1984; Bock and Brewer 1985).

Children younger than those in the fifth grade do have problems comprehending text. Indeed, one can easily make the case that the younger the child, the more difficulties there may be in comprehension. But this general statement is quite independent of the modality of the discourse. Younger children have more difficulties comprehending spoken stories or stories on television than do older children. Reasons for this are fairly obvious: younger children do not have as much general knowledge of the world. Also, they are not as apt to infer motivational processes in characters in stories or infer why writers are presenting certain types of information as part of the plot development. By school age, most children have an adequate implicit knowledge of narrative forms (Stein and Glenn 1979), but the richness of that knowledge continues to progress as they become more proficient in reading. Young children also often have difficulties in comprehending because they take everything quite literally; metaphors and idioms often go right over their heads. Speakers of foreign languages also have problems understanding metaphors and idioms, but they also know when they did not understand something and often try to infer the nonliteral interpretation. Beginning readers often get hung up on the literal meaning and do not know why they cannot understand the story, or they are often oblivious to the fact that they do not understand. This brings us to another point about beginning readers: they are not very good at monitoring their own comprehension processes.

A vast literature (Baker and Brown 1984; Brown 1980; Markman 1979, 1981; Golinkoff 1976; Ryan 1982; Myers and Paris 1978) on how well beginning readers are able to monitor their own comprehension processes has revealed that they have deficits in comprehension strategies: they are not very cognizant of the extent to which they are understanding text. Some studies (Palinscar and Brown 1984; Paris and Jacobs 1984; Paris, Cross, and Lipson 1984) have demonstrated that instruction in teaching comprehension monitoring is quite beneficial, so it would seem that beginning readers do have the capability to monitor how well they are reading. Apparently, however, beginning readers typically do not do so unless specifically instructed. Why might this be?

We have argued above that children's comprehension difficulties are not peculiar to reading. However, when children are reading, comprehension may suffer from something that is very important to the reading process, namely decoding (or word identification processes). Baker and Brown (1984) argued that most younger readers have little awareness that they must attempt to make sense of the text; rather they focus on reading as a decoding process and not as a meaning gathering process. Omanson (1985) and Perfetti (1985) have argued that lexical processes are heavily involved in comprehension processes: if there are a lot of "hard" or unfamiliar words in the text, children do not understand very well (Marks, Doctorow, and Wittrock 1974; Wittrock, Marks, and Doctorow 1975). If children are given vocabulary instruction, comprehension of texts that contain the instructed words improves significantly (Beck, Perfetti, and McKeown 1982; Kameenui, Carnine, and Freschi 1982; McKeown et al. 1983; Omanson et al. 1984). Thus, it would seem that instruction both on vocabulary development and on the use of effective comprehension monitoring strategies can be beneficial for childrens' comprehension processes.

Merely training a child to say words quickly will not necessarily result in improved comprehension (Fleisher, Jenkins, and Pany 1979). However, practice at actual reading may strengthen both decoding processes and comprehension; Samuels (1979) reported that children with difficulty in reading benefited from systematic re-reading of meaningful passages of text. Apparently, re-reading text raises the readers' fluency and maintains comprehension.

In summary, let us try to be clear about what we have said about comprehension processes in beginning readers. We have argued that some of the difficulty is not peculiar to reading: beginning readers do not have as much world knowledge as more skilled readers do. Furthermore, beginning readers do not have efficient comprehension monitoring strategies. We would, therefore, fully expect that on tests of comprehension the principle would hold that younger children would not comprehend as much as older children (Keenan and Brown 1984; Williams, Taylor, and DeCani 1984). We have also suggested that a major obstacle for comprehension that is peculiar to reading is that younger children do not know as many words as older children and this lack of vocabulary knowledge hinders comprehension. Thus, instruction aimed at improving children's comprehension strategies will aid understanding, but instruction on vocabulary development and decoding processes will also foster comprehension.

SUMMARY

In this chapter, we initially discussed four stages of reading. We argued that the four stages of reading (linguistic guessing, discrimination net guessing, sequential decoding, and hierarchical decoding) should not be thought of as a biological sequence that all children go through. Rather, we suggested that they should be viewed as increasingly complex strategies that children attempt in reading words as both their cognitive skills and reading experience increase. We then discussed a number of component aspects of reading skill and found that by fifth grade, children's reading performance is much like skilled readers across a wide range of variables that have been investigated. We do not wish to argue that fifth grade children are just like skilled readers. Because they do not have as much general world knowledge and they do not have as extensive a vocabulary as skilled readers do, they cannot comprehend everything that an adult skilled reader can. Also, some processes involved in reading may not be as automatic in fifth grade children as they are in skilled readers. The point is that while there may well be some differences between fifth grade children and skilled readers, the basic processes that are crucial for effective reading have become pretty automatic and the basic strategies involved in comprehension of text have emerged. Thus, differences that exist between fifth grade children and skilled readers are primarily quantitative and not qualitative.

CHAPTER ELEVEN
DYSLEXIA

In the preceding chapters, we discussed the process of learning to read. As we pointed out there, despite some variation in teaching methods and cultural approaches to teaching reading, most children do learn to read quite well. However, some children do not do particularly well in reading and, more seriously, some grow to adulthood without obtaining fluency in reading. As we shall see in a moment, part of the problem can be traced to general cognitive abilities since there is a strong correlation between reading achievement and a child's score on an intelligence test. This isn't the whole story, however, since there are some people who, despite average or above average scores on intelligence tests, do not read well (or at all, in some cases). But we're getting ahead of ourselves a bit. We will begin this chapter by discussing the relative frequency of reading problems. We will then discuss in order: *poor reading, acquired dyslexia,* and *developmental dyslexia*. The term *dyslexia* is used to describe individuals with normal to high intelligence who have severe reading problems. In the case of *acquired dyslexia,* the disability is due to some type of known brain damage, while in *developmental dyslexia* there is no identified brain damage.

From our point of view, developmental dyslexia is the most interesting type of reading problem because the factors underlying its etiology have proved to be very elusive. Much more headway has been made in understanding poor reading and acquired dyslexia than in understanding developmental dyslexia. Our primary focus in this chapter will be on developmental dyslexia and we will discuss other types of reading disabilities as contrasts to developmental dyslexia. Cognitive psychologists are only one of many types of researchers interested in reading disabilities. Educators, neurologists, pediatricians, epidemiologists, statisticians, behavioral geneticists, educational psychologists, neuropsychologists, and developmental psychologists are all keenly interested in various types of reading problems. In discussing reading problems, it is necessary to be somewhat interdisciplinary in focus so we will borrow from related fields as necessary, but we will rely most heavily on the work of cognitive psychologists. Cognitive psychologists have been very influential in analyses of poor reading and acquired dyslexia, but not quite as successful in dealing with developmental dyslexia. But then, no other discipline has been very successful either.

RELATIVE FREQUENCY OF READING DIFFICULTIES

To some degree, the notion of "reading difficulties" is a statistical phenomenon. We usually define how well a child is progressing in reading by how well he or she does on various standardized tests of reading skill that are routinely administered in elementary school. The important thing to realize about these tests is that they are based on the statistical principle of random error. That is, the tests have been given to a large number of people and the questions involve different levels of difficulty. One aspect of random error is that roughly half of the people who take the test will score above average and the other half will score below average. Figure 11.1 shows the results of a hypothetical reading test given to a large sample of sixth grades. Let's say that the test is given to 1,000 sixth graders in the middle of the school year and the average reading level obtained is 12 years and 6 months (150 months). The standard deviation of the test scores is 12 months. This represents how much variability there is in the different test scores that our sixth graders obtain. Since random error is usually assumed to follow the normal (or "bell-shaped") distribution, 68 percent of the children taking the test will score between 138 months and 162 months on the test. Those scoring around 138 months on the test are 1 year behind in reading and those scoring 162 are reading a year ahead of their grade level. By looking at

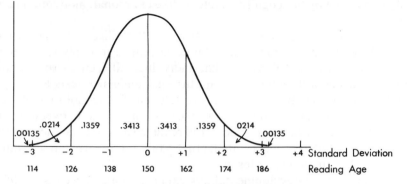

FIGURE 11-1   **A hypothetical frequency distribution of reading scores. Values within different regions represent the percentage of students falling between the two scores (roughly 34 percent fall between 150 and 162).**

Figure 11.1, you can see that 2.3 percent of the sample score 2 years or more below the average. Those who score between 1 and 2 years below their expected reading level will be referred to as *poor readers*. Those scoring 2 or more years below their expected reading level will be referred to as *dyslexic readers*.

Now the problem is not quite as simple as suggested above because if we take general cognitive abilities into account, then issues of categorization become more complex. That is, estimates of children's general cognitive abilities are also based upon the results of standardized tests based upon the normal distribution. IQ scores are normally distributed around a mean of 100 with standard deviations of 15 to 20 (depending upon the particular test used). Because there is a very high correlation between reading achievement scores and IQ scores, most of those reading well below the mean are probably doing so because of "low intelligence." Thus, for those with an IQ score of 80, we would expect them to be reading well below their grade level. We will refer to children who have reading problems that are related to intelligence as being *backward readers*. In contrast, we will refer to children whose IQ scores fall in the normal range but who read between one or two grade levels below normal, as *poor readers*. Sometimes children who are not reading well because of emotional, motivational, or social reasons are also classified as backward readers or sometimes poor readers. An additional problem in interpretation is that IQ scores as well as reading scores can be unduly influenced by noncognitive factors (like emotional, motivational, and social factors).

We should note that we are using the term "intelligence" as shorthand to avoid awkward circumlocutions. We do not mean to imply that "intelligence" is a unitary attribute or that individual differences in cognitive abilities are necessarily innate or that current intelligence tests are tapping the full range of cognitive skills that are relevant for school or real-world situations. The main distinction we wish to make is between mental functions that are *relatively* specific to the reading situation and the cognitive functions that underlie most intellectual ability and are tapped (albeit imperfectly) by "intelligence tests."

The category of developmental dyslexia is important because it differs from the other categories on the basis of statistical, etiological, and educational grounds. The statistical argument for dyslexia rests on the difference between general backwardness and a specific disability with respect to reading. A child of 10 with a "mental age" (determined from an IQ test) of 8 and a "reading age" (determined from a reading achievement test) of 8 is at a reading level consistent with his or her measured intellectual abilities. Yet, the child is *backward* because the reading level is behind the chronological age. On the other hand, a child of 10 with a mental age of 11 and a reading age of 8 is more than 2 years retarded in reading and would generally be categorized as a developmental dyslexic. As we said above, developmental dyslexics are generally defined as being 2 years behind in reading and (importantly) their disability is not due to intelligence, motivation, social, or emotional problems. Further, their reading problems are not the result of known brain damage. We have just given the standard definition for developmental dyslexia. It has often been criticized because it is a "definition by exclusion." That is, by definition we can say what developmental dyslexia is not, but we don't know as much about what it is, despite wide-scale research efforts of late. The exclusionary definition is all we have for the moment, so we will adopt it here as well.

Basically, we are arguing that developmental dyslexia is the most interesting of all of the types of reading disability because we cannot pinpoint its causes. With backward readers, we can attribute their reading problems to a general lack of intelligence. That is, if we argue that there are individual differences in cognitive ability, some people will be below average. With acquired dyslexia we can pinpoint the brain damage and document selective impairments in reading due to this damage. But, with developmental dyslexia, otherwise normal individuals have a problem more or less specifically with reading. This latter notion is also a bit fuzzy because it seems unlikely that someone who cannot read well will not, as a result, also experience some difficulty with other academic subjects.

In addition, the requirement that the child must be reading two grade levels below expectation creates a problem for identifying very young readers who may be susceptible to severe reading problems, since, by definition, a child in first or second grade cannot be reading two grade levels below where they should be. In contrast, it seems like a relatively simple and straightforward matter to identify children who should be classified as developmental dyslexics from third or fourth grade on: we're looking for children with average intelligence (and no obvious reason for why they should not read well) who are two or more levels below their grade level in reading. However, in the literature it turns out that it is not that easy for researchers to agree if a given sample of disabled readers is dyslexic or not. An even bigger problem is identifying the relative frequency of developmental dyslexics in the population. The reason for this has to do with a couple of statistical problems. The first has to do with the standard error of measurement. We will not go into great detail about this problem. What is important to understand is that standardized tests have a built-in error factor in the way they are constructed so that for any given child the "true" reading or intelligence score may not be that which is given by the test.

A more serious problem is the phenomenon of *regression to the mean*. This is a phenomenon that occurs when the correlation between two given variables is less than unity. While reading achievement and intelligence are correlated, the correlation is not close to 1.0 (usually about 0.7). Regression to the mean says that if a child scores poorly on one variable, he or she will tend to score somewhat higher on the other variable (though still usually below average). Regression to the mean works the other way at the top end of the distribution, so that children with very high IQs will tend to have reading scores that are closer to the mean (but still usually above average). In other words, just because a child has a low IQ, we shouldn't expect him or her to be as poor a reader since factors other than intelligence influence reading (as indexed by the fact that the correlation is significantly below 1.0).

Regression to the mean thus raises a conceptual problem for the definition of developmental dyslexia. The idea behind the exclusionary definition is that you don't want to include someone as a dyslexic if the poor reading can be "explained" by a low IQ. One way around this problem is to use a multiple regression technique where equations can be used to predict a child's expected reading age based both on intelligence scores (the mental age) and chronological age. Thus, the discrepancy between reading level and predicted reading level is a key notion for the concept of developmental dyslexia.

Various studies reported by Rutter, Tizard, and Whitmore (1970); Yule (1973); Berger, Yule, and Rutter (1975); and Yule et al. (1974) have used multiple regression equations to predict a child's expected reading age from his or her chronological age and intelligence. These researchers examined the distribution of children with developmental dyslexia, specifically those who were two standard deviations below their predicted reading age. If reading ability closely followed the normal curve that we discussed earlier, about 2.3 percent of all children should have had scores two standard deviations below the mean. In fact, between 3.5 percent and 6 percent of the children fell two or more standard deviations below the norm, which produced a "hump" on the bottom end of the curve. The higher incidence of children at the bottom end of the distribution than would be expected if the poorer readers were simply the bottom end of a normal distribution suggested that the dyslexics represented a different population. More recently, the existence of this "hump" has been shown to be an artifact of a "ceiling effect" in the reading test used by Rutter and Yule (Rodgers 1983; Share et al. 1987; Van der Wissel and Zegers 1985), leading many in the field of developmental dyslexia to suggest that there is no qualitative difference between dyslexics and other readers. Even though the hump is probably not real, other data suggest that dyslexics are indeed different from backward readers (Hulme 1987). In their original work, Rutter and Yule compared developmental dyslexics and backward readers, and Table 11.1 presents a summary of their findings.

The two groups differed on intelligence as should be expected because it was part of the selection procedure. However, as can be seen in Table 11.1 there was a higher percentage of boys in the developmental dyslexia group. The backward readers had developmental delays in many areas such as walking, fine and gross motor movements, motor impersistence (difficulty in sustaining a motor act initiated by a verbal command), copying, and so on. There was also a general overall delay in speech and language in this group. In contrast, the dyslexic children seemed to be retarded only in speech and language.

In addition, the dyslexics and the backward readers tended to be different in educational terms due to the differential prognosis of developmental dyslexia and general reading backwardness (Yule 1973). The finding in a follow-up study was that even though the dyslexics and backward readers were initially equated on reading level, 4 years later the dyslexics were 6 months behind the backward readers in reading level. In other words, the less intelligent children made greater progress in reading over the 4-year period. It is also interesting to note that the dyslexic children were better at math than the backward readers. These results all reinforce the idea that the dyslexics have some kind of specific handicap.

How frequent is developmental dyslexia then? The figure of 3.5 percent to 6 percent that we cited earlier represents a very substantial number of children. Other estimates have ranged as high as 15 percent (Satz, Rardin, and Ross 1971; Satz et al. 1978). However, most of these estimates are likely to include some children whose reading levels were less than 2 years below the expected reading level and are not strictly defined as being dyslexic. In any case, even if 5 percent of the children were categorized as dyslexic (a rather liberal estimate, in our opinion), we are talking about a large number of children.

TABLE 11.1 Factors in backward and dyslexic readers (Adapted from Thomson 1984 with permission of Arnold Press.)

Backward readers	Dyslexics
Mean IQ 80	Mean IQ 102
General developmental delays/abnormalities	Speech and language delays/abnormalities
54% boys	76% boys
Better prognosis	Very poor prognosis
Overt neurological features	Fewer overt neurological features
Frequent organic dysfunctions (e.g., 11% cerebral palsy)	No organic dysfunctions
Motor and praxic difficulties more common	Motor and praxic difficulties less common
Higher incidence large families	Lower incidence of large families
Higher incidence of low status or disadvantaged homes	Lower incidence of disadvantaged or low status homes

Before we move on to discuss different types of reading problems, we would like to make a few comments about the term *developmental dyslexia*. The word *dyslexia* implies that the child does not acquire *reading* (and generally spelling and writing) very easily and the word *developmental* implies that the problem is in the initial learning. The term also suggests that dyslexia is a cognitive language disorder of development. Incidentally, the literal meaning of the word *dyslexia* means "difficulty with reading." Sometimes the problem is not simply reading, but includes spelling, writing, and other aspects of language, though it is clearly the case that some dyslexic readers do not have spelling problems (see Frith 1980). In fact the problem for many dyslexics may well be one of language, as we shall see. Since this book is about reading, however, we will focus on the issue of reading and not say much about spelling and writing. Other terms are often used to describe the same syndrome (e.g., *strephosymbolia, acute dyslexia, specific reading retardation, specific reading disability, specific dyslexia, specific learning disorders*), but we will stick to the term *developmental dyslexia* here to avoid confusion.

One problem with the term "dyslexia" is that many parents and teachers think of it as a medical term, and as a result believe that the child can never learn to read, write, and spell and that the prognosis is hopeless. We suspect that dyslexic children can be taught to be more effective in reading. However, it may be accurate to assume that the prognosis is not as good for a dyslexic child as for one who is simply a poor reader (with adequate intelligence). The other problem with the term is that parents and teachers sometimes think of dyslexia as a disease. We've heard many parents say "My child has dyslexia" just as if they were saying "My child has the measles." While dyslexia may be due to some type of abnormality in the brain or in the way the brain processes informaiton, it is not a disease. It would be more appropriate to say "My child is dyslexic," just as we would say "My child is a diabetic." Perhaps, we're splitting hairs here, but we want to make a point. It is also interesting to note that whereas at one time dyslexia was treated by many as a social disease, in some respects it has become downright fashionable to be abe to proclaim "I have dyslexia." More recently, it has sometimes become a rationalization for children not doing as well in school as they should.

In summary, it may seem to you that developmental dyslexia is a rather fuzzy concept. In fact, many people deny the existence of a group of readers who have a special problem, arguing instead that reading problems can be best thought of as a continuum with some children simply not reading as well as others (see Bryant and Bradley 1985 for discussions of this issue). Our own casual observation is that researchers who work primarily with young children may be inclined to think of the issue of reading disability as one of a continuum, while those who work with older disabled readers tend to believe that there is a definite group of disabled readers that we can call dyslexic. Those who work exclusively with young children may not have observed many severely disabled readers.

As we shall discuss in a later section of this chapter, our own experiences with some very bright adults who could not read have convinced us of the reality of the concept of dyslexia. Thus our own bias is to believe that there is a distinct group of readers who should be categorized as dyslexic. However, we would make two points of clarification. First, we suspect that many children are categorized as dyslexic (both for research purposes and for educational practice) who should not be. The concept of developmental dyslexia should be reserved for the most severely disabled readers. Second, as we shall argue, the disabled readers, who we will call dyslexic, do not all have the same symptoms and underlying causes of their problem. Far too many cognitive psychologists interested in reading disabilities have blithely accepted the notion of a single cause of reading problems and much of the research has been focused on finding that cause.

Dyslexia is a very controversial issue, as you have probably discerned by now. Before we can really meaningfully discuss developmental dyslexia, it is necessary to place it in the context of other types of reading problems. We now turn to a discussion of poor reading.

POOR READERS

Let's start out by clarifying the distinction between poor readers, backward readers, and dyslexic readers. *Poor readers,* sometimes referred to as "less-skilled readers" in the literature, are those who are reading between one and two standard deviations below grade level. In terms of the distribution shown in Figure 11.1 about 13 percent of the population will be between 1 and 2 years behind in reading level. Since the correlation between reading scores and IQ scores is pretty high, a large fraction of this 13 percent is accounted for in terms of the low intelligence, and thus are *backward readers* by our previous definition. Of more interest are those whose IQ scores are such that they should be reading better than they are. They have been the topic of frequent investigations by cognitive psychologists and we shall now turn to that research.

Poor readers have been examined extensively by cognitive psychologists in studies in which they are matched on chronological age and IQ scores to children who are reading at grade level or above. Experimenters have studied good and poor readers in numerous tasks devised by cognitive psychologists to study normal word recognition and reading processes. In comparison to good readers, poor readers are not as sensitive to orthographic structure (Mason 1975; Massaro & Taylor 1980; Katz 1977), take longer to name words (Curtis 1980; Perfetti and Hogaboam 1975; Hogaboam & Perfetti, 1978; Perfetti, Finger, and Hogaboam 1978), are not as effective in using the speech code for processing linguistic stimuli (Shankweiler et al. 1979), do not do as well on tasks tapping phonemic awareness (Bryant and Bradley 1985; Golinkoff 1976), are more reliant on context (Perfetti, Finger, and Hogaboam 1978; Perfetti and Roth 1981), do not use syntactic structure as effectively (Weinstein and Rabinovitch 1971), are not as efficient in the use of working memory (Kail et al. 1977; Kail and Marshall 1978), do not have as good verbatim recall of text (Perfetti and Goldman 1976; Goldman et al. 1980), have shorter memory spans (Farnham-Diggory and Gregg 1975; Torgesen and Goldman 1977), and so on. Indeed, the trick seems to be to find something that poor readers (matched on IQ) are as good at as good readers. We shall not review all of the research done on poor readers; an excellent summary of the work is found in Perfetti (1985).

Poor readers do more poorly than good readers on virtually any task we give them. The critical issue is why. One reason for the differences may have to do with inadequate matching of intelligence. Although researchers interested in differences between good and poor readers generally try to match children in terms of IQ scores, it is difficult because of problems relating to regression to the mean. It appears that most studies are not successful in this endeavor (Wolford and Fowler 1984; Crowder 1984). Thus, many of the differences that we have mentioned above (and others) may be due to the fact that the poor readers are not as bright as the good readers.

When IQ differences are controlled, it appears that good and poor readers differ primarily on the basis of short-term memory for linguistic information (Byrne and Shea 1979; Katz, Shankweiler, and Liberman 1981; Liberman et al. 1982; Mann 1984; Mann, Liberman, and Shankweiler 1980; Perfetti and Goldman 1976; Shankweiler et al. 1979; Wolford and Fowler 1984) and on the ability to code information phonetically in short-term memory (Brady, Shankweiler, and Mann 1983; Mann and Liberman 1984; Mann, Shankweiler, and Smith 1985; Mark et al. 1977). As we saw in the previous chapter, phonological awareness is an important aspect of learning to read, and it appears that poor readers are not as sophisticated in processing linguistic information as are good readers.

Thus, when differences due to IQ are accounted for, it still appears that there are subtle differences in language processing capabilities that distinguish good readers from poor readers. Of critical importance here is the extent to which instruction geared to this problem can facilitate poor readers' processing of linguistic stimuli. A longitudinal study by Bradley and Bryant (1983) suggests that appropriate instruction can help remedy the deficiency. Excellent discussions of the issues that we have cursorily touched on here are provided by Crowder (1984), Mann (1984), and Perfetti (1985).

Another factor that may be critically important is that poor readers may be suffering from some type of *developmental lag*. While the concept of a developmental lag has frequently been applied to the problem of dyslexia (see Satz, Rardin, and Ross 1971), it now appears that the concept can more appropriately be used with respect to poor readers (Beech and Harding 1984; Curtis 1980; Stanovich, Nathan, and Vala-Rossi 1986). For example, Stanovich et al. (1986) administered a number of tasks assessing listening vocabulary, phonological awareness, general name retrieval ability, decoding skill, word recognition speed, and the ability to use context to speed word recognition. Good third grade readers and poor fifth grade readers were matched on overall reading level, and it was found that the profiles of these two groups on the various tests were quite similar. Other results showing that poor readers (of an older chronological age) were very similar to younger good readers have been reported by Curtis (1980) and Mindell (1978). In comparison, studies of dyslexic children have produced a confusing pattern of results regarding the applicability of the developmental lag notion, particularly in the area of phonological abilities (compare Backman et al. 1984; Beech and Harding 1984; Bisanz, Das, and Mancini 1984; Snowling 1980, 1981). Stanovich et al. (1986) provided some very compelling arguments concerning why the notion of a developmental lag is much more appropriate for poor readers than for dyslexic readers, and we concur completely with their assessment.

In essence then, we have argued that poor readers' problems can stem either from their lower "intelligence" level, from poorer short-term memory codes for linguistic material, and/or from a developmental lag associated with the fact that they have not matured with respect to various reading subskills. While increases in age will magnify the difference in reading performance between those who read adequately and developmental dyslexics, the story is likely to be different for at least some poor readers. A case can be made (Stanovich 1986) that early failure in school will retard later learning. However, many poor readers master reading, and thus as they grow older, discrepancies between their reading performance and those of good readers in elementary school may become less apparent.

We now turn to our discussion of dyslexia. We will first discuss acquired dyslexia, however, since it is better understood and will serve as a tool for helping us to understand developmental dyslexia.

ACQUIRED DYSLEXIA

We pointed out in Chapter 1 that the cerebral cortex of the brain is divided into two functionally separate halves. The left hemisphere (in most people) is responsible for language processing. Left-hemisphere injuries, resulting from stroke or serious assault due to gunshot wounds, car accidents, or other injuries, often result in language problems. Disorders of speech comprehension or production occurring as a result of brain damage are known as *aphasias*. There are several recognized varieties of aphasia depending upon the precise nature of the language problem (Lenneberg 1965; Kertesz 1979). Aphasic patients often experience reading difficulties as part of their more general language impairment. Sometimes, however, reading problems are the predominant (or only) symptom. We will focus on the latter case and talk about such patients as suffering from acquired dyslexia.

In acquired dyslexia, the approximate locus and severity of the brain damage is known. However, the exact location and nature of the brain injury is often not clear. This is one reason why only rather general statements can usually be made about the disability from knowing the exact location of the injury. Another problem with making statements relating functional disorders to the location of the damage is that many mental functions do not appear to be sharply localized. (There also appear to be individual differences between patients where functions are localized.)

The general approach that cognitive psychologists have taken is to ask how the component processes involved in normal reading might be organized so that they would exhibit the types of word reading error patterns that emerge from acquired dyslexia. This work has been very influential with respect to certain views of the reading process and has suggested that there are two main word reading routes (Marshall and Newcombe 1973; Shallice and Warrington 1980): a phonological encoding route, using grapheme-phoneme correspondence rules, and a direct route. We have already briefly discussed some of this work in Chapter 3 in conjunction with work on normal readers. (The latter work also suggests that there are two routes to the lexicon.)

While the work that has been done to elucidate aspects of normal reading by studying acquired dyslexics has been very influential, we feel that a certain amount of caution is necessary. That is, acquired dyslexics do have very serious problems with reading. By necessity, since comprehension of connected discourse is either impossible or quite difficult for most of these patients, the research has focused on single word reading. Some see this as a virtue of the research while others see it as somewhat problematical; as we have pointed out before, reading involves more than just stringing together the meanings of individual words. Our major concern about generalizing from work on acquired dyslexia to normal reading is that it involves a certain amount of faith that the processes involved in normal reading can be accurately inferred on the basis of rather global injuries to the brain. The processes and strategies adopted by acquired dyslexics to cope with the task of reading a word may be quite different than those used by normal readers.

Our intention here is not to debate the relative merits of studying brain damaged individuals versus studying normal readers. Our primary interest in the phenomenon of acquired dyslexia in this chapter is how the research can enlighten us with respect to the problem of developmental dyslexia. In this respect, the work on acquired dyslexia has been most impressive in terms of the categorization systems that have emerged to classify the different types of reading errors that occur. We must point out that there is a considerable amount of variation in the terminology used in categorizing the errors that acquired dyslexics make in reading individual words. While the categorization schemes sometimes seem a bit arbitrary and idiosyncratic, a certain amount of consistency seems to be emerging.

The three major acquired dyslexic syndromes that have emerged are called *deep* (or *phonemic*), *phonological,* and *surface* dyslexia. Actually, there are a number of other syndromes that have been described and we shall discuss some of them shortly. However, deep, phonological, and surface dyslexia have been the most intensively investigated. Briefly, deep and phonological dyslexics have great difficulty in using the phonological route in reading. They appear to use the direct route from letters (graphemes) to meaning, and therefore require a semantic representation of the word before obtaining a phonological representation of it. They cannot read pseudowords and they are unable to read words they do not understand, since no semantic representation is available for the word (in the same way that no semantic representation is available for a nonword). Deep dyslexics also characteristically make semantic errors (or *semantic paralexias,* as they are sometimes called). Thus when shown the word *kitten* they may respond "cat." Additionally, deep dyslexics are affected by the imageability or concreteness of the word. Other symptoms include visual errors (where the error response is visually similar to the word shown), morphological errors (suffix or prefix adding), and a greater facility with content words than function words. Phonological dyslexics, while similar to deep dyslexics in some ways, do not make semantic errors and are not sensitive to the imageability or concreteness dimensions of stimuli. Visual errors are made, but much less frequently than in deep dyslexics.

In contrast to deep and phonological dyslexics, surface dyslexics rely on the phonological route to reading words. For them, a semantic representation is not always forthcoming; it is quite possible for a word not to be understood even though it is pronounced correctly. They are not sensitive to the semantic dimensions of words, but being sensitive to factors such as word length and regularity of spelling, they are affected by the graphemic representation. Also, in contrast to deep and phonological dyslexics, surface dyslexics can read pseudowords (in some cases almost as well as words). We will now consider in a bit more detail each of these syndromes as well as a few other types of acquired dyslexia.

TYPES OF ACQUIRED DYSLEXIA

In this section, we will not discuss all the types of acquired dyslexia that have been reported in the literature. Rather, we will focus on those that are most relevant for our later discussion of developmental dyslexia. Table 11.2 gives an overview of the symptoms of the different types we will discuss. We begin by discussing the three major syndromes.

Surface Dyslexia

Much of the interest in the acquired dyslexics stems from a seminal paper by Marshall and Newcombe (1973) in which surface dyslexia was described along with deep dyslexia and visual dyslexia (both to be described shortly). We mentioned above that surface dyslexics rely almost exclusively on the phonological route. They appear not to recognize words as wholes, but resort to a strategy of sounding out the word. A person reading in this

TABLE 11.2 Varieties of Acquired Dyslexia (adapted from Ellis 1984). Adapted with permission of Erlbaum.

Surface dyslexia
Patient appears to read by phonic mediation. Some whole-word reading retained, but patient may misinterpret homophones showing that final access to the semantic system is via the auditory word recognition system. For many words the patient attempts to assemble a pronunciation with a consequent liability to "phonic" errors; other errors appear to be visual approximations similar to the errors of visual dyslexics. Regular words are read more successfully than irregular words. Principal deficits appear to be disconnection of visual word recognition system from the semantic system together with unavailability either of some visual word recognition units or some connections between those units and the corresponding phonemic word production units.

Deep dyslexia
A complex syndrome whose central, defining symptom is the occurrence of semantic errors in single-word reading. Other symptoms include visual, visual-then-semantic and derivational errors, difficulty reading abstract words and function words, and an almost total inability to read nonwords.

Phonological dyslexia
Patient is able to read many familiar words aloud with understanding, though may have some problems with function words and inflected words. No effects of regularity, imageability, or length. Virtually unable to read unfamiliar words or nonwords aloud suggesting impairment of grapheme-phoneme conversion and/or phonemic assembly.

Visual dyslexia
Patient makes frequent visually based errors in word recognition despite sometimes being able to name all the component letters of the target word. Deficit possibly due to "slippage" within the visual word recognition system.

Attentional dyslexia
Patient makes frequent visual segmentation errors when shown groups of words. Difficulty naming letters in strings but not letters in isolation.

Word-form dyslexia
Patient appears to name each letter of a word either aloud or subvocally before identifying the word; therefore reading time increases with the number of letters in the word. Reading is mediated via the patient's intact spelling system.

Direct dyslexia
Occurs in some patients having "presenile dementia." Intact word naming (and apparently nonword naming) despite a lack of any indication that the patient understands the words being read. Arguably reading aloud is sustained by intact connections between visual word recognition units and phonemic word productions units despite disintegration of semantic system.

---

way should be more likely to arrive at the correct pronunciation when the word shown is a regular word than when it is an irregular word. Indeed, surface dyslexics are more successful in reading regular words than irregular words. For example, Shallice and Warrington (1980) found that their patient read 36 out of 39 regular words correctly, but only 25 out of 39 irregular words correctly.

Surface dyslexia has been intensively studied (Patterson, Marshall, and Coltheart 1985) and some interesting patterns have emerged. The errors made by surface dyslexics often look like unsuccessful attempts to apply grapheme-phoneme correspondence rules. Sometimes the errors are non-words, for example reading *island* as *izland* or *sugar* as *sudger;* and sometimes the errors are other words, for example, reading *disease* as *decease* or *guest* as *just.* In both cases, the errors can be described as *phonic approximations,* in which the pronunciation is based on treating the target word as if it were an alphabetically transparent one. Marshall and New-combe (1973) explained these regularizations as being due to the unsuccessful application of grapheme-phoneme correspondence rules, but Marcel (1980) and Henderson (1982) have argued that they can be accounted for as well or better by the use of inappropriate analogies.

Regardless of which mechanism best explains phonic approximations, there is little doubt that the meaning surface dyslexics ascribe to a word follows from the pronunciation they give to it. For example, a well-known error reported by Marshall and Newcombe involved the patient misreading *listen* as *liston* (pronouncing the *t* which should be silent) and adding, " . . . the famous boxer" (referring to Sonny Liston, the former boxing champion). On another occasion, the same patient read *begin* as *beggin* and said, "That's collecting money."

While many of the errors that surface dyslexics make can be traced to reliance on the phonological route to the lexicon, they sometimes make what can be described as visual errors (such as misreading *precise* as *precious* and *foreign* as *forgiven*). Holmes (1973) characterized this type of error as being more hastily produced than the more common, laboriously produced errors that bear some phonological similarity to the target word. We should also point out that surface dyslexics are able to read many irregular words correctly. If the phonological route were all that was available, surface dyslexics presumably should always mispronounce irregular words. The fact that they do not suggests that the problem is complex and that lexical information stored prior to brain damage does play a role in reading words. However, surface dyslexics make many errors and most of them are phonologically similar to the target word.

Deep Dyslexia

There has been a great deal of attention paid to the deep dyslexia syndrome (Coltheart, Patterson, and Marshall 1980). Deep dyslexics find words that have concrete, highly imageable referents easier to read than abstract words. They also find new words (those they did not know before their injury) and nonsense words virtually impossible to read. Deep dyslexics make several different types of reading errors (while also reading some words correctly). First, and most strikingly, they make semantic errors in which, for example, *ape* is read as *monkey* or *forest* is read as *trees.* Second, they make visual errors such as reading *signal* as *single.* Third, they appear to make errors that are a combination of a visual error followed by a semantic error such as *sympathy* read as *orchestra* (via *symphony*). Fourth, they make derivational errors such as reading *builder* as *building.* Finally, they make function word substitutions such as reading *his* as *in* or *quite* as *perhaps*. Although function words are some of the most common in the language, they apparently create difficulties for deep dyslexics. The errors that are made generally involve substituting another apparently random function word.

Although patients with symptoms like those of deep dyslexia had been reported previously, the first full description was provided by Marshall and Newcombe (1966). Marshall and Newcombe suggested that deep dyslexics have lost the capacity for grapheme-phoneme conversion. They argued that the direct route to the lexicon may be inherently prone to substituting incorrect pronunciations that are similar in meaning to the target word. Semantic errors in normal readers presumably do not occur because of the simultaneous activation of the phonological route.

The alternative to that proposed by Marshall and Newcombe is that the semantic component of the lexicon may be impaired in deep dyslexics in some way (Ellis 1984). Indeed, Ellis (1984) has argued that such a proposal may be necessary to explain why deep dyslexics find abstract words difficult to read. It has been shown that deep dyslexics can sort abstract words and nonwords into separate piles fairly accurately (Patterson 1979), indicating that their inability to access the names of abstract words is due to something more subtle than failure to contact the lexicon. It is also possible that problems with function words may arise because they are too abstract, though Morton and Patterson (1980) have linked the problem of reading function words with the occurrence of derivational errors and suggested that certain grammatical processes are impaired. Friedman and Perlman (1983) reported that their deep dyslexic patient made semantic errors when naming objects as well as naming words, supporting Shallice and Warrington's (1980) contention that word retrieval problems may be the cause of semantic errors in some deep dyslexics.

Once again, we see than an explanation of this syndrome becomes rather complex. In fact the explanation becomes even more complex when we consider the suggestion (Coltheart 1980b; Patterson and Besner 1984; Saffran et al. 1980) that in deep dyslexic patients the left hemisphere reading processes have been completely destroyed and the remaining word identification abilities are largely those of the right hemisphere (abilities which are dormant or supplementary in normal readers). We shall not attempt to adjudicate between rival theories concerning the cause of the reading errors made by deep dyslexics. The main characteristic to keep in mind is that deep dyslexics make many semantic errors when reading target words.

Phonological Dyslexia

In phonological dyslexia, the major deficit is in reading pseudowords. As Ellis (1984) has pointed out, it is unlikely that phonological dyslexia would have been detected if researchers were not on the look out for it, which probably explains why it has only been reported in recent years

(Beauvois and Derouesne 1979; Shallice and Warrington 1980; Patterson 1982; Funnell 1983).

Phonological dyslexics can read most familiar, real words with ease, but are very poor at reading aloud even simple pseudowords such as *pib* or *cug*. This characteristic has generally been taken as evidence for a substantial loss of the capacity for grapheme-phoneme conversions, despite the fact that they can read (and understand) familiar words. Their symptoms further suggest that they primarily use the direct route to the lexicon (which does not rely on letter-to-sound conversions) which remains relatively intact. The phonological dyslexic reported by Patterson (1982) sometimes misread function words and made a large number of derivational errors. Neither of these problems, however, was present in the phonological dyslexic reported by Funnell (1983). The major distinction between deep dyslexia and phonological dyslexia is that semantic paralexias do not occur in phonological dyslexia.

Visual Dyslexia

Case studies of acquired dyslexics have demonstrated that the type of visual error made varies from patient to patient, presumably because different parts of the direct visual route to word recognition are impaired. We have already seen that surface dyslexics make some visual errors in reading words. Other patients show as their primary characteristic errors that are visually related to the target word. Shallice and Warrington (1977) described a patient who made many *visual segmentation errors* (reporting *glade* when shown *glove* and *spade*), even when given unlimited time to view the target words. They called this syndrome *attentional dyslexia*.

Marshall and Newcombe (1973; Newcombe and Marshall 1981) described a slightly different form of visual dyslexia. Their patient misread *cap* as *cob, met* as *meat,* and *rib* as *ride.* All of these errors might be considered as some type of impairment of visual analysis if it were not for the fact that the patient could correctly name all of the letters yet misread the word. Visual dyslexics show a marked tendency to what Coltheart (1981) called *approximate visual access,* or a tendency to accept as sufficient a less than perfect overlap between the word and the response given. Errors of approximate visual access occur in other forms of acquired dyslexia and in children beginning the reading process, as we have seen.

Word-form Dyslexia

This syndrome is sometimes also referred to as letter-by-letter reading (Patterson and Kay 1982). In this type of acquired dyslexia, the patient appears to name each letter of a word either aloud or subvocally before identifying the word. Thus, word naming time increases with the number of letters in the word. According to Shallice and Warrington (1980) word naming is mediated via the patient's intact spelling system.

Direct Dyslexia

This syndrome is often referred to as nonsemantic reading. The patient has intact word naming (and apparently pseudoword naming) without any indication that he or she is understanding the words that are being read (Schwartz, Marin, and Saffran 1979; Schwartz, Saffran, and Marin 1980; Shallice, Warrington, and McCarthy 1983). While both routes to the lexicon may be intact, the semantic component of lexicon is apparently severely damaged.

Summary of Acquired Dyslexia

Our primary source of information on acquired dyslexia is case studies. That is, neuropsychologists, upon finding a brain-damaged patient with reading difficulties, have generally done rather thorough investigations of an individual patient's ability to perform various language-related tasks. For acquired dyslexics, the focus has been on their ability to read words and nonwords. Over the past few years, a number of cases have been documented and categorized as to the nature of their disability, primarily in terms of the types of reading errors they make (though sometimes also on the basis of the locus of the brain damage).

Although many different types of acquired dyslexia have been described, this does not mean that every patient that has been identified falls neatly into one or another of the recognized categories. Indeed, patients often show *mixed* symptoms, and the cases described in the literature tend to be the relatively small proportion of *pure* cases. Even so, there are individual differences between patients grouped together as deep dyslexics or surface dyslexics. Nevertheless, the fact that pure cases exist establishes the existence of different types of acquired dyslexia. This point will be important when we move to our discussion of developmental dyslexia. Finally, we note again that work on acquired dyslexia has been very influential in shaping current views of how word recognition processes work. The existence of so many forms of acquired dyslexia with separate symptoms provides strong support for the notion that the cognitive abilities of normal readers are made possible by the activity of separate components or modules, which remain separate and dissociable despite a considerable amount of concerted and orchestrated activity (Ellis 1984).

DEVELOPMENTAL DYSLEXIA

As we argued earlier, developmental dyslexia is the most controversial, most elusive, and least understood reading problem. We will begin this section by reviewing the concept of developmental dyslexia. We then will turn to a discussion of whether the disability is due to a unitary cause. (In our opinion, the major obstacle to an adequate understanding of developmental dyslexia has been the tacit assumption of researchers that there is a single underlying cause to the problem.) We will then compare acquired and developmental dyslexia to ascertain the extent to which such comparisons can enlighten us with respect to the latter phenomenon. Finally, we will discuss the concept of subtypes of developmental dyslexia.

If you were to ask your neighbors what a dyslexic reader is, they might well respond by saying that it was someone who could not read because they saw words and letters backwards. In reality, there's little evidence to support such a notion, but many myths and ill-conceived notions about developmental dyslexia exist. With respect to confusing the direction or orientation of words and letters, dyslexic readers do not make such mistakes any more frequently than beginning readers (Liberman, et al., 1971; Lyle, 1979; Lyle & Goyen, 1968). As we shall see, some developmental dyslexics may manifest visual-spatial problems, but many do not. To give some idea of the varieties of developmental dyslexia, we begin by reporting three case studies of adults who have severe reading problems. As such, all could be categorized as developmental dyslexics, since none of them suffers from any known brain damage.

The Concept of Developmental Dyslexia

Case studies   Consider three cases of adults who read very poorly, but who are very intelligent individuals. Let's call them Tom, Dave, and Jane, describing them simply in the chronological order that we met them. More details about these case studies can be found in Pirozzolo and Rayner (1978) and Rayner (1985).

When we met Tom, he was 22 years old and a very proficient computer programmer. Although he was a whiz at programming, his reading ability was very limited. He often did not respond to notes left for him because he could not read the words. Messages that were left had to be printed in large letters. Even though his father was a professor at a well-known university, Tom dropped out of school at the beginning of high school. His academic career was undistinguished and what progress he made in school was done by listening carefully. Eventually, he found the whole routine rather depressing and left. Yet he was fully conversant with world and local events because he watched the news on television. Casual conversations with him would not lead anyone to suspect that he had a major disability. As we have already pointed out, he was an extremely facile computer programmer. He seemed to have no problems with mathematical concepts nor with the type of logic necessary for programming. At one point, we were successful in getting him to read and monitored his eye movements. When presented with text that was too difficult for his reading ability, he fixated on almost every letter and at the end could not report the sentence that had been presented.

Dave is actually representative of four or five individuals whom we have seen. When we met him, he too was 22 years old. He owned his own auto repair shop and was doing quite well in his chosen vocation. He came to see us because his girl friend was a student in one of our courses. After a lecture on dyslexia, she came forward and indicated that her boyfriend could not read very well and she thought perhaps he was dyslexic. His reading was quite a bit better than Tom's, but yet he read no better than fifth grade level. In spite of that, he graduated from high school with an average between B and C. He claimed to have developed very sophisticated listening strategies during school. He was further helped by sympathetic friends, who shared their class notes with him and read the assigned readings to him. Tests of his IQ showed him to be normal, and any casual conversation with him would lead to the conclusion that he was a very well-informed and friendly individual. When he was presented text that was at his reading level, his eye movement patterns were very much like a fifth grader. When presented text more in line with his chronological age, his eye movement patterns became fairly chaotic and looked very much like those of a child presented with text that was above his or her reading level.

Jane, too, is representative of a couple of such readers whom we have seen. Jane's problem is a bit more obvious than is the case with either Tom or Dave. Jane was referred to the Developmental Disabilities Clinic at the medical center of a well-known university. She was attending a small state university nearby and was referred after she consistently demonstrated problems with spatial orientation tasks. For example, although she was in training to be a physical education instructor in high school, she continually reversed the position of players on a volleyball test. She had a difficult time remembering her left and her right. When you shoot a lay-up with a basketball, if you shoot with your right hand you are supposed to jump off your left foot. Yet she could never remember which was her left or right hand or her left or right foot. Though she had been on her campus for three years, and in some sense knew that the psychology building was to the left as she came from her dorm, she often had difficulties finding the building and often had friends walk with her to classes. Another striking characteristic of Jane was that she did mirror writing. She is left-handed and when writing twists her hand around. Moreover, when you are sitting across from her, her script is written perfectly normally from your perspective but is a mirror reversal from her own perspective (see Figure 11.2).

Jane's intelligence is quite high as measured by standardized tests. Her reading performance of text in its normal orientation is around fifth grade level. Yet, surprisingly, if the text is rotated to be upside down, her reading skill improves markedly. She reported that in school she often turned the book upside down to read, but diligent teachers continually told her that one cannot read with the book upside down. She was quite emotional about this and did not like to read upside down (she seemed to feel there was some stigma associated with it), but admitted that at times she did so under pressure. When she did so, she felt rather guilty, a carryover from her teachers' correcting her positioning of the text. When we graph readers's eye movements, normal readers move steadily from left to right, as shown in Figure 11.3. In contrast, when reading text in its normal orientation, Jane showed a tendency, when she reached the end of one line, to drop her eyes

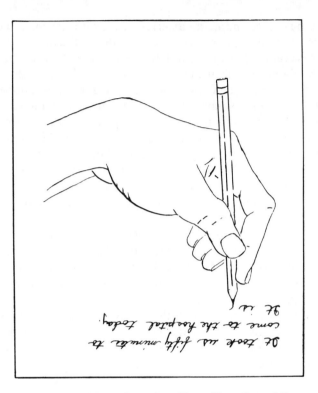

FIGURE 11-2 Jane's handwriting orientation. [From Pirozollo and Rayner (1978), with permission of Academic Press.]

FIGURE 11-3 Examples of staircase and reverse staircase patterns during reading. The upper portion of the figure shows a typical staircase pattern in which the saccades proceed primarily left to right across the line followed by a return sweep movement to the next line. The lower portion shows examples of the reverse staircase pattern (marked by arrows) in which there are clusters of right-to-left saccades. [Reproduced from Rayner (1985) with permission from Erlbaum.]

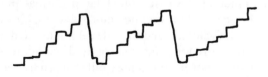

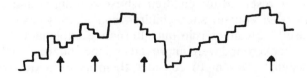

down to the next line and make a series of right-to-left movements, rather than make a return sweep, as normal readers do, to the beginning of the next line. After several of these right-to-left movements, Jane would then move to near the beginning of the line and start a series of left-to-right movements. In general, there was a tendency for her to make large numbers of these right-to-left movements, sometimes at the end of the line and sometimes not. These right-to-left movements, being opposite to the normal staircase pattern characteristic of normal readers, are referred to as a *reverse staircase pattern* and have been documented by others (Zangwill & Blakemore, 1972; Pavlidis, 1981). Interestingly, when the text was turned upside down, the reverse staircase pattern disappeared and her eye movements looked quite normal (apart from the fact that they progressed from right to left across the line).

Unlike Jane, testing of the other two dyslexic readers revealed only some rather subtle differences, which probably could not explain their reading problems (see also Crowder 1982). Yet, they clearly have reading problems. How can we account for their problems? We shall return to this issue at the end of this chapter. For now let's review again the criteria for classification of developmental dyslexia. (We should warn you that the concept of developmental dyslexia has sometimes been opposed, and the notion of subtypes of developmental dyslexia has certainly not achieved universal acceptance.)

Definition of dyslexia The definition of developmental dyslexia proffered by the World Federation of Neurology is similar to the one given at the beginning of the chapter.

> [Dyslexia is] a disorder manifested by difficulty in learning to read despite conventional instruction, adequate intelligence, and sociocultural opportunity. It is dependent upon fundamental cognitive disabilities which are frequently of constitutional origin. (Critchley 1975.)

Let's review a couple of points in this definition that we mentioned earlier. First, developmental dyslexics must have normal intelligence. In practice, this generally means that a child must have an IQ score of 90 or higher to be considered dyslexic. Second, developmental dyslexics must have experienced adequate reading instruction and adequate sociocultural opportunities. Obviously, a normal child may fail to learn to read because he or she has not received adequate instructional help. Likewise, a normally intelligent child could be handicapped because of a deprived environment. However, we would not want to call these children dyslexic because the term *dyslexia* is reserved for children whose reading is unexpectedly and distinctly poor. Of course, such children *could* be dyslexic, but in these particular cases we cannot rule out alternative explanations. Only if the schooling and background were improved and the children still failed to read effectively would we want to consider them as dyslexic. Note that the requirements set down by the World Federation of Neurology generally mean that children diagnosed as dyslexic tend to be bright children from middle class (or better) homes and attending good schools. In reality, there is no reason to suppose that developmental dyslexia is a middle- or upper-class phenomenon. However, psychologists and reading specialists feel most confident that poor reading in children from such backgrounds is not the result of other more obvious causes of reading failure.

Although the definition of dyslexia offered by the World Federation of Neurology claims that the problem is "frequently of constitutional origin," in practice the defining criteria are psychological and social. Thus, the frequency of developmental dyslexia is an issue that has to be approached with a certain amount of caution. As we've seen, to qualify as dyslexic a child must have an IQ of a certain level, home and school environment must pass minimum requirements, and the level of reading proficiency must be below what is expected given the age and IQ of the child. Let's forget for a moment the issue of home and school standards and focus on the issue of IQ versus the level of reading proficiency. We have said that the usual criteria for calling a child dyslexic is that his or her IQ must be 90 or better with a reading age 2 years below the chronological age. As we've seen, a survey of the school population using these criteria would uncover a certain percentage of children who would qualify as dyslexic, perhaps 5 percent of the population. However, if we required an IQ of 110 or above, we would then reduce the percentage of dyslexic children. On the other hand, if we loosened the criteria with respect to the level of proficiency so that the reading age need only be 18 months below the chronological age, we would then increase the percentage of dyslexic children.

It has probably occurred to you that if the percentage of dyslexic children in the population can be raised or lowered so easily, almost by whim, then the very notion of dyslexic may be dubious. If it cannot be diagnosed precisely, how valuable is the concept? Although dyslexia is not a disease, the term is useful in psychology and medicine. Consider for a moment the concept of obesity. A person is called obese if his or her weight substantially exceeds that of a normal person of the same height and sex. A great deal of medical and psychological research has been done on obesity and a great deal of progress has been made in understanding its causes. However, the dividing line between normality and obesity is entirely arbitrary and, just like dyslexia, one can raise or lower the percentage of people who are classified as obese simply by altering the criteria. Understanding this fact does not invalidate the concept of obesity any more than it invalidates the concept of dyslexia (Ellis 1984).

Unitary Explanations of Developmental Dyslexia

We know that developmental dyslexia is more prevalent among males than females, among left-handers than right-handers, and that it tends to run in families, leading some to suggest that dyslexia is due to genetic factors. However, the evidence is really quite mixed on the extent to which genetic factors are related to dyslexia (see Thomson 1984 for a review). In addition, psychologists interested in dyslexia have tended to assume that there is a single underlying cause. To review all of the research on developmental dyslexia would be a monumental task, beyond the scope of this book. One would find a great deal of contradictory evidence and patterns of results that are complex and difficult to unravel. The interested reader is referred to books by Vellutino (1979) and Thomson (1984) for comprehensive reviews of the dyslexia research.

Because the unitary approach has been taken historically, we will review some examples and discuss some of the contradictory data that have emerged. As to why there is so much contradictory research, our own view is that (1) often children who do not really qualify as being dyslexic are included in the dyslexic sample; and (2) the unitary approach is inappropriate. With respect to the first point, it appears that many studies have included in the dyslexic sample children who really should be categorized as backward or poor readers. Thus, at times, researchers have not taken great care in selecting dyslexic readers. Lately, there has been considerable controversy not only about this issue but also about the appropriate control group to compare to dyslexic readers on various performance measures. The issue is whether the appropriate control group for dyslexic readers should be one matched on chronological age or on reading age (Backman, Mamen, and Ferguson 1985; Bryant and Goswami 1986). In other words, should developmental dyslexics be compared to children of the same age group or children who are at the same reading level? An issue like this cannot be resolved here, but perhaps the wisest strategy would be for researchers to include both types of control groups in their studies dealing with dyslexic readers.

With respect to the second problem, researchers interested in dyslexia have often assumed that all dyslexics are alike and proceeded to conduct their research based on that premise. There is no doubt that a majority of developmental dyslexic readers have some type of language processing problem (Vellutino 1979). But, as we shall see, it seems likely that there may be more than one language processing deficit underlying developmental dyslexia (as there was in acquired dyslexia). We shall return to this issue later, but the point that we want to stress here is that a great deal of the research on developmental dyslexia has been inappropriately motivated by the desire to uncover *the underlying cause of dyslexia*. This approach has led to studies in which the tasks are selectively chosen so that the deficits that dyslexics show are likely to fit in with the particular theoretical biases of the experimenter. The result has been that there is a great deal of contradictory evidence concerning developmental dyslexia, and much of the literature has revolved around debates concerning the extent to which factor A or factor B better accounts for reading problems. Such research motivated by the unitary explanation approach has not been very fruitful.

We will consider three different types of unitary explanations that have been proposed and intensively investigated. We will consider first the idea that dyslexia is due to faulty eye movements. Then we will discuss research dealing with the possibility that it is due to a perceptual disorder. Finally, we will consider arguments suggesting that developmental dyslexia is due to a deficiency in left-hemisphere processing. In discussing these different explanations, we will move from explanations relying primarily on peripheral components of the reading act (eye movements) to more central components (deficit in brain function).

Faulty eye movements Developmental dyslexics' eye movement patterns differ from those of normal readers in that dyslexics make many more fixations per line and have longer fixation durations, shorter saccades, and a higher frequency of regressions than normal readers (Rayner 1978a). To what extent do the eye movements, per se, represent the cause of reading problems? Individuals with oculomotor disorders, such as saccade intrusions (Ciuffreda, Kenyon, and Stark 1983) or congenital jerk nystagmus, have accompanying difficulties with reading. Are eye movements likewise a contributing causative factor in developmental dyslexia? Obviously, if a person has difficulty controlling the eye movements that are so necessary for reading to proceed smoothly, then learning to read presents enormous difficulties.

It can easily be demonstrated that during reading the eye movements of dyslexic readers are different from those of normal readers. However, the real issue is whether these erratic eye movements are the cause of dyslexia or a consequence of the failure to learn to read. If you think about it, it should be obvious that if you tried to read Hebrew or Japanese (assuming that you cannot read either of these languages), your eye movement pattern would be pretty erratic (i.e., different from skilled readers of those languages). In a summary of eye movement research published some time ago, Tinker (1958) argued quite strongly that eye movements were not a cause of reading problems, but rather were a reflection of other underlying problems. Most authors reviewing the evidence on eye movements and reading problems since then have tended to agree with Tinker's conclusions. The issue, assumed by Tinker to have been settled, was dramatically brought back into the spotlight by some recent work reported by Pavlidis (1981, 1985). Pavlidis presented data that, he suggested, indicated a central malfunction in dyslexics, namely a sequential disorder and/or oculomotor malfunction.

Pavlidis appropriately noted that any study of developmental dyslexia, based on reading experiments alone, would be open to the criticism that dyslexics' eye movement patterns during reading differ from normal readers' because dyslexics do not read well. He reasoned that if the cause of dyslexia is constitutional (e.g., due to a sequential disability or oculomotor malfunction), one would expect that it should manifest itself not only in reading but also in other tasks in which sequencing and eye movements are important. Thus, Pavlidis asked his dyslexic subjects to fixate continuously on a fixation target that jumped from left to right or right to left across a screen. He reported that when the target moved from left to right, dyslexic subjects showed significantly more right to left saccades than did normal readers.

Pavlidis' results are consistent with a number of case studies of dyslexics (see Rayner 1985) in demonstrating erratic eye movements in dyslexic readers. Indeed, Pavlidis's results are consistent with the eye movement characteristics of one of the dyslexic readers (Jane) that we described earlier. Many dyslexic readers have a tendency to move their eyes from right to left during reading. Zangwill and Blakemore (1972) character-ized this as an "irrespressible tendency" to move the eyes from right to left. Pavlidis reported that his dyslexic subjects, when reading text, showed the characteristic *reverse staircase pattern,* in which there are clusters of right-to-left saccades. Hence, he concluded that erratic eye movements (moving from right to left when the task calls for movements from left to right) and the reverse staircase pattern are characteristic of dyslexic readers. Pavlidis (1983) also tested backward readers, for whom IQ or other factors can be used to account for their poor reading performance; the backward readers did not differ from the normal readers in the task where they had to follow the movement of the target.

Pavlidis' results are potentially interesting from a practical standpoint: if eye movements are a cause of dyslexia, the disability could be diagnosed by means of a simple oculomotor test, and perhaps dyslexics could be helped by training programs designed to improve reading by focusing on eye movements. However, a number of attempts to replicate Pavlidis' findings have failed (Black et al. 1984; Brown et al. 1983; Olson, Kliegl, and Davidson 1983; Stanley, Smith, and Howell 1983). In fact, in all of the other studies, there was no indication that the dyslexic readers differed from the normal readers in the frequency of right-to-left saccades in Pavlidis' task. Stanley, Smith, and Howell (1983) pointed out that they also failed to find differences between their dyslexic and normal readers' eye movement patterns in a visual search task. When asked to read text, however, the two groups differed markedly. Adler-Grinberg and Stark (1978) and Eskenazi and Diamond (1983) reported similar findings. Pavlidis (1981) also observed that dyslexic children were less able to maintain fixation than normal readers. However, Eskenazi and Diamond found that as many normal children as dyslexics had difficulty in maintaining fixation.

What can we conclude about the relationship between eye movement control and developmental dyslexia? While some dyslexic readers show erratic eye movement patterns in nonreading tasks, it is clearly the case that most do not. However, even for those who show faulty eye movement patterns in reading and nonreading tasks, the eye movements are probably reflecting more serious underlying problems and, in and of themselves, are not the cause of the reading problem (see Rayner 1983, 1985). We shall return to this point later.

Before leaving this section on the contribution of eye movements to reading difficulties, let's consider another recent suggestion by Stein and Fowler (1982, 1984) concerning the potential role of eye movements in developmental dyslexia. Stein and Fowler reported that a large proportion of the dyslexic children that they have studied have problems associated with vergence eye movements (small movements that keep both eyes pointing at the center of attention) and the development of oculomotor eye dominance. The problem when reading, which the development of ocular motor dominance of one eye helps to solve, is that of defining visual direction when the eye position signals disagree. For normal readers, the two eyes move conjugately, meaning that they move at about the same time and move the same distance. However, Stein and Fowler have argued that the development of conjugate eye movements in dyslexic children has not occurred. Thus, the two eyes are pointed in slightly different directions leading to impaired perception. In normal readers, moving the two eyes from a far object to a near object will lead to the two eyes being aimed in slightly different directions, but the eyes quickly converge upon the point fixated by the dominant eye.

In testing the dyslexic children referred to them, Stein and Fowler found that a high percentage demonstrated unstable vergence control. In subsequent testing, half of these visual dyslexics were given plano spectacles (i.e., window glass), in which the left eye was occluded, to wear for 6 months when reading and writing. The other half were treated in exactly the same way except the plano spectacles they wore were not occluded. They reported that 51 percent of the children who started with poor vergence control gained control after 6 months of occlusion compared with 24 percent who gained control wearing plain spectacles. The reading of the children who gained control during the 6 months of occlusion improved by almost an additional 6 months relative to their age; those who did not receive occlusion regressed by 0.4 months. Stein and Fowler (1984) concluded that monocular occlusion may assist one-sixth of dyslexic children to develop reliable vergence control, and thereby may help them to learn the read.

Stein and Fowler's results are interesting and suggest that many dyslexic readers do have visual perception problems. As noted earlier, most current theories about the etiology of developmental dyslexia favor a language problem rather than a perceptual problem. However, Stein and Fowler's results are consistent with the central point that we wish to argue, namely, that there is more than one reason or underlying cause of developmental dyslexia. Most of Stein and Fowler's subjects were referred to a vision clinic. Thus in their sample the odds are increased that dyslexic subjects will manifest visual perception problems. However, the existence of even a small percentage of dyslexics with a visual deficit is consistent with the idea that a basic language deficit cannot account for all of the reading problems manifest in developmental dyslexia.

Perceptual disorder Suppose that the eyes moved quite normally, but that dyslexic readers were impaired in their ability to extract visual information from the printed page, analyze the patterns, and retain those patterns (that is, the forms of letters and words) for future reference. Then clearly dyslexic readers would have a very difficult time learning to read. From time to time it has been proposed that developmental dyslexia is caused by some sort of general perceptual deficit, the details of which vary from theory to theory. A great deal of evidence, summarized by Vellutino (1979), has led to the conclusion that this proposal is incorrect. For example, Mason and Katz (1976) required normal and dyslexic children to search for a target shape in a set of unfamiliar shapes and found no difference in the search rate for the two groups. Similarly, Ellis and Miles (1978) found no difference in the speed with which normal and dyslexic children could judge whether or not pairs of letters were the same or different.

Failures to find differences between normal and dyslexic children on tasks such as those just described have led many to conclude that developmental dyslexia is not a simple perceptual disorder. Certainly there are perceptual tasks in which dyslexics fare worse than normal children. However, if these tasks involve the use of alphabetic materials then we must again ask the question of whether the poorer performance is a consequence or a cause of the difficulty with print. While the majority of researchers interested in developmental dyslexia would appear to agree with Vellutino's assessment that a perceptual deficit is not at the heart of developmental dyslexia, a number of recent studies have provided support for the notion that at least some developmental dyslexics do have a perceptual problem. Unfortunately, there are some conflicting results in the literature. This fact is quite clear from a number of studies which have focused on the initial stages of visual information processing in normal and dyslexic readers.

Studies of the initial stages of visual information processing in dyslexia have relied upon two major techniques: backward masking and temporal integration of sequential displays. Backward masking occurs when the perception of a temporally leading test stimulus is impaired by a trailing masking stimulus displayed in close spatial proximity. The temporal separation between the onset of the test stimulus and the onset of the masking stimulus is known as the stimulus-onset-asynchrony (or SOA). Performance in backward masking studies is widely regarded as an index of the rate of visual information processing; the assumption is that the impairment in performance is the result of insufficient time to process the test stimulus before the arrival of the mask. Comparisons of performance under conditions of backward masking seem to indicate that dyslexic children require longer SOAs than normal children to escape the effects of the mask (DiLollo, Hanson, and McIntyre 1983; Lovegrove and Brown 1978; O'Neill and Stanley 1976; Stanley and Hall 1973). Thus, these studies suggest slower rates of visual information processing in dyslexic children. However, this finding is not without exception; other studies have found no significant difference between the two groups (Arnett and DiLollo 1979) and some have actually reported results consistent with *faster* processing rates in dyslexics (Fisher and Frankfurter 1977; Stanley 1976).

Just as backward masking is thought to provide an index of the rate of initial visual information processing, temporal integration of successive visual displays is said to provide an index of the duration of visible persistence. The term *visual persistence* refers to the lingering visibility of an image for a short period after the termination of a brief visual stimulus. Recall that in Chapter 1, we talked about iconic memory as representing the initial stage of visual information processing. There are technical reasons for distinguishing between iconic memory and visible persistence (Coltheart 1980a), but they are well beyond the discussion at hand. Two methods have been widely used to study differences between normal and dyslexic readers. The primary method used to assess visible persistence involves presenting a given stimulus twice in rapid succession, with a blank interval (called the inter-stimulus interval, or ISI) of variable duration inserted between the two displays. The ISI is then adjusted to a critical duration at which the observer can just distinguish the double flash from a single uninterrupted display. The second method involves presenting two (or more) different stimuli displayed in rapid succession separated by a variable ISI. At long ISIs the sequential stimuli are seen as separate configurations (such as a vertical line followed by a horizontal line), but at short ISIs the display sequence is integrated into a single percept (a cross).

Several studies comparing normal and dyslexic readers have reported a longer duration of visible persistence in dyslexic children (DiLollo, Hanson, and McIntyre 1983; Lovegrove, Billing, and Slaghuis 1978; Lovegrove and Brown 1978; O'Neill and Stanley 1976; Stanley 1975; Stanley and Hall 1973). Similar studies, however, have reported no differences between the two groups (Arnett and DiLollo 1979; Howell, Smith, and Stanley 1981; Stanley and Molloy 1975). A further study (Morrison, Giordani, and Nagy 1977), which employed a delayed-probe technique, also reported no differences between dyslexic and normal children for ISIs up to 300 milliseconds.

Although attempts have been made to explain these contrasting results (see DiLollo, Hanson, and McIntyre 1983), the picture is very murky. Other research dealing with perceptual deficits that lead to differences between normal and dyslexic children in the perception of auditory sequences (Bakker 1972; Godfrey et al. 1981; Tallal 1980) is likewise controversial. But one cannot doubt that some dyslexic children do have perceptual disorders that impair reading performance (DiLollo, Hanson, and McIntyre 1983; Lovegrove, et al. 1980; Slaghuis and Lovegrove 1985). Of late, the argument seems to be that *some* dyslexic readers have perceptual disorders (see DiLollo, Hanson, and McIntyre 1983; Slaghuis and Lovegrove 1985), rather than that dyslexia is due to a unitary perceptual problem.

Before leaving this section, we should like to note that it has also often been argued that developmental dyslexia is due to a short term memory disorder. Dyslexic readers often do poorly on memory span tests which measure, for example, the number of digits that can be repeated correctly after a single hearing (Rugel 1974). Does this mean that dyslexia is caused by a short term memory problem? It may be that the problem is really a verbal deficit (Baddeley, Thomson, and Buchanan 1975). Although many dyslexics perform worse on short term memory tasks than normal readers, not all dyslexic readers do badly (Torgesen and Houck 1980).

Left-hemisphere deficit It is often argued that developmental dyslexia is due to underdevelopment of the left hemisphere of the brain. In virtually all right-handed people and about half of the left-handed people, language is specialized in the left hemisphere while spatial processing is specialized in the right hemisphere. Information coming into the right side of the body is transmitted more quickly to the opposite side of the brain. Information in the right visual field also goes to the left hemisphere more quickly than it goes to the right hemisphere. The information may get to the right hemisphere via direct connections (which are slower than to the left) or by crossing the corpus callosum (which connects the two hemispheres). One rather influential theory of developmental dyslexia offered by the neurologist Orton (1928) proposed that *mixed dominance* between the two hemispheres was the locus of the problem. As we pointed out previously, dyslexia is more prevalent in left-handers than in right-handers (in terms of proportions). This observation has also led to the speculation that problems associated with the relationship between learning to write and specific brain functions are causal factors in developmental dyslexia. For example, in right-handers, the hand for writing would be controlled by the language (left) hemisphere, making learning to write relatively easy. If left-handers had language specialized in the left-hemisphere (as some do, though many have it specialized in the right hemisphere), there would be a mismatch between the writing hand and the language center in the brain. This mismatch, it has been argued, would lead to language problems that would manifest themselves in reading and writing.

A great deal of research on the relationship between hemispheric specialization and developmental dyslexia has yielded conflicting results. In normal readers, it is typically found that there is a right visual field superiority for processing words and letters and a left visual field superiority for processing nonverbal stimuli, such as faces and pictorial information (Pirozzolo and Rayner 1977). Remember that a right visual field superiority implies left hemisphere processing and a left visual field superiority implies right hemisphere processing. Studies by McKeever and Huling (1970) and McKeever and VanDeventer (1975) found a right visual field superiority for word recognition by disabled readers. Olson (1973), however, was unable to find a right visual field superiority for verbal stimuli in dyslexic readers. Marcel, Katz, and Smith (1974; Marcel and Rajan 1975) found a reduced right field superiority in their dyslexic readers and argued that this represented a linguistic superiority of the disabled readers' right hemisphere rather than a left hemisphere dysfunction. In direct contrast to these results, Yeni-Komshian, Isenberg, and Goldberg (1975) reported that disabled readers have increased right visual field superiorities. Studies examining developmental dyslexia via presentation of auditory stimuli to the left or right ear (and analogously to the right and left hemispheres) have likewise produced contradictory results. The causal relationship between dyslexia and hemispheric specialization that has been developed to explain the inconsistent pattern of results has also differed dramatically. In essence, there are suggestions to the effect that developmental dyslexics have underdeveloped left hemispheres, underdeveloped right hemispheres, and overdeveloped right hemispheres (in comparison to normal readers). Clearly, once again we have conflicting and contradictory results and explanations.

The problem with unitary explanations Why is there so much contradictory data with respect to developmental dyslexia? As we have said, we suspect that in many cases children who are merely poor readers are often included in the dyslexic sample. There is an even more serious problem, which we also alluded to earlier. The unitary explanation approach is inappropriate. With respect to this point, the problem with the approach is that researchers have (1) assumed all developmental dyslexics are alike in their symptoms and difficulties; (2) assumed that since developmental dyslexia is a unitary syndrome, it must have a single cause; and (3) developed a theory to explain the one and only cause of dyslexia. Our argument is that the contradictory evidence that exists invalidates such an approach. Furthermore, there is increasing evidence consistent with the idea that developmental dyslexia, like acquired dyslexia, consists of different subtypes. We shall now turn to evidence consistent with that notion. First, we will discuss recent attempts to link acquired dyslexia and developmental dyslexia. Then we will discuss independently motivated investigations supporting the concept of different subtypes.

COMPARING ACQUIRED AND DEVELOPMENTAL DYSLEXIA

If it is the case that there are different reasons or underlying causes of developmental dyslexia, then we ought to be able to document different characteristics of dyslexics suspected of having different problems. As we have pointed out, acquired dyslexics show symptomatic differences that enable researchers to categorize them according to the types of errors they make when they attempt to read isolated words. Do word reading errors of developmental dyslexics lead to the possibility of categorizing them according to symptomatic errors? Let's begin by considering some recent proposals aimed at determining if there are systematic similarities between developmental dyslexia and various types of acquired dyslexia.

Similarities to Acquired Surface Dyslexia?

Holmes (1973, 1978) was the first to argue for a similarity between developmental dyslexia and acquired surface dyslexia. As we pointed out earlier in this chapter, surface dyslexics predominantly read phonically and generally arrive at the meaning of a word on the basis of its sound properties. Often the phonetic form of the word from which its sound is generated is achieved by breaking the written form into single letters or letter groups to which analogies or correspondence rules are applied. Thus, phonic errors such as regularizing *bread* to *breed* occur as do errors such as reading *bike* as *bick*. In this latter case, the reader has failed to lengthen the vowel in a word that ends in *e*. Precisely these same sorts of reading errors were made by the developmental dyslexic subjects (four boys between the ages of 9 and 13) studied by Holmes.

In addition to Holmes' dyslexic boys, Coltheart et al. (1983) have recently reported a developmental surface dyslexic girl (called C.D.). C.D. was of normal intelligence (verbal IQ 105, performance IQ 101) with normal speech production and comprehension. She showed no marked deficit in short term memory capacity and had no history or evidence of any form of neurological abnormality. Yet when tested at the age of 15 and despite adequate educational opportunity, her reading age was 4 or 5 years behind, and the reading errors she made were very much like those made by surface dyslexics. When asked to define a word before saying it, her definition always matched her subsequent pronunciation. At the same time, it is clear that her problems were not due to a perceptual deficit, since she could name all of the letters in a word she had just misread. For example, shown *check* C.D. responded, "part of your face . . . cheek . . . C.H.E.C.K." This define-then-pronounce task revealed another aspect of her dyslexia that a simple reading aloud task would most certainly have failed to show. Shown *pane* she said, "something which hurts . . . pain . . . P.A.N.E." Shown *bowled* she said, "fierce, big . . . bold . . . B.O.W.L.E.D." It is very interesting that Newcombe and Marshall (1981) described an acquired surface dyslexic patient who made exactly the same sorts of homophone confusion errors. Finally, like acquired surface dyslexics, C.D. was much more successful at reading regular words aloud than irregular words.

The fact that C.D.'s reading skill is at least 4 years below what would normally be expected of her clearly justifies labeling her as dyslexic. Yet, as we saw in Chapter 10, children learning to read show an advantage for regular words over irregular words and they also make errors that are very much like those made by C.D. In fact, C.D.'s performance was indistinguishable from the reading age controls included in the study by Coltheart et al. (1983; see also Bryant and Impey 1986). It is hard to determine exactly what this implies, but it is at least possible that in some types of developmental dyslexics there is a developmental lag in the normal process of learning to read.

Similarities to Acquired Deep Dyslexia?

Jorm (1979) was the first to point out what he considered to be important similarities between developmental dyslexia and acquired deep dyslexia. One of Jorm's points was that both developmental dyslexics and deep dyslexics have trouble when it comes to reading nonwords like *bint* aloud. Work by Snowling (1980, 1981) and Seymour and Porpodas (1980) has demonstrated that developmental dyslexics are slower and less accurate at reading pseudowords than normal children with the same reading age. However, Baddeley et al. (1982) pointed out that developmental dyslexics are not totally incapable of reading psuedowords in the same way that acquired deep dyslexics are. Jorm also showed that developmental dyslexics, like deep dyslexics, are better at reading imageable words aloud than abstract words. However, once again, Baddeley et al. showed that this superiority for imageable words extended to normal children. They argued that abstract words may tend to be learned later than imageable words and that the age of acquisition may be the reason for the "imageability effect" in both normal children and developmental dyslexics.

Jorm's comparison of developmental dyslexia to acquired dyslexia has resulted in a certain amount of controversy (Baddeley et al. 1982; Ellis 1979; Snowling 1983). The primary issue seems to be the extent to which semantic errors occur when words are read by developmental dyslexics. Since, we know that both skilled readers and beginning readers (particularly the latter) will make semantically related errors when reading connected text aloud, the real issue is whether developmental dyslexics make semantic confusions when reading isolated words as do deep dyslexics.

Recently, Johnston (1983) described an 18-year-old girl (C.R.) whose reading age was only 6 years and 2 months. Johnston categorized C.R. as a developmental deep dyslexic. Let's examine C.R. more closely. She was better at reading imageable nouns than abstract nouns and was extremely poor at reading nonwords. The types of errors that she made are particularly interesting. Over the course of several sessions, C.R. was given 382 words to read aloud. She was able to read 78 words correctly and unable to give any type of response to 219 words. Of the errors that C.R. made, 50 were categorized as visual errors by Johnston's criterion of at least half of the letters in the error being present in the stimulus word (e.g., reading *cigar* as *sugar* and *cost* as *cot*). C.R. also made derivational errors and function word substitutions. All of these types of errors occur in acquired deep dyslexia, but none is unique to that syndrome. Most crucial are the five semantic errors which C.R. made (*office* read as *occupation, chair* as *table, table* as *chair, down* as *up,* and *seven* as *eight*). It is the case that if you have never seen a particular word before and are forced to guess at what it is, the probability of your guess bearing a fortuitous semantic relationship to the unknown word is surprisingly high (Ellis 1984; Ellis and Marshall 1978). However, for C.R.'s semantic errors to be attributable to chance, one would expect quite a number of her errors to be neither visually nor semantically similar to the target word (Ellis 1984). In fact, only 15 of her errors were neither visually nor semantically related to the target. Additionally, she also made one visual-then-semantic error (*sleep* read as *lamb,* presumably via *sheep*). As Ellis (1984) pointed out, such errors had hitherto only been observed in acquired deep dyslexics.

C.R. may be a genuine developmental deep dyslexic, but there are two small problems. First, one would ideally like to see cases with a higher incidence of semantic errors in reading single words. Second, C.R. suffered from a head injury when young and it is not at all certain that there was no brain damage. More recently, Siegel (1985) has reported data on six children who made semantic errors for words presented in isolation. Five of the six children showed higher performance IQ than verbal IQ scores. (The performance IQ score largely taps spatial abilities.) They were unable to read sentences, but could read some words in isolation. They also could not read nonwords. Siegel pointed out that there was no known neurological impairment in any of the children and argued that a small subset of developmental dyslexics show error patterns when reading single words like that of acquired deep dyslexics. There are two slight problems with Siegel's developmental deep dyslexics. First, their IQ scores tended to be somewhat low (average verbal score was equal to 85 and the average performance score was equal to 97). Second, they also appeared to be almost as retarded in mathematics as in reading. Nevertheless, both Siegel and Johnston have been able to demonstrate error patterns in some children with reading difficulties that are very reminiscent of acquired deep dyslexics.

Similarities to Acquired Phonological Dyslexia?

Recently, Temple and Marshall (1983) produced the first detailed description of a developmental phonological dyslexic. Seymour and Mac-Gregor (1984) have also described a subject (L.T.) with a phonological impairment associated with the pattern of performance similar to that of acquired phonological dyslexics (see also Campbell and Butterworth 1985; Temple 1985). Here, we will focus on H.M., the subject described by Temple and Marshall. As we pointed out earlier in this chapter, acquired phonological dyslexics rely to a large extent on direct visual word recognition; they read irregular words as well as they read regular words, but are very poor at pronouncing pseudowords and unfamiliar words. Phonological dyslexics are prone to both visual and derivational errors, but they do not make semantic errors when reading single words aloud.

H.M. was 17 years old when tested by Temple and Marshall, and she showed exactly the same pattern of abilities and disabilities as acquired phonological dyslexics. Her IQ, memory span, and command of the spoken language was quite normal, but her reading age was only 10 or 11 years. She was as good at reading irregular words as regular words, though she made both visual and derivational errors. Her reading of pseudowords and unfamiliar words was very poor. When presented with 10 very simple trigrams, she read 4 incorrectly (*bix* as *back*, *gok* as *joke*, *hib* as *hip*, and *nup* as *nap*). These errors illustrate her tendency to use an approximate visual access strategy and to read pseudowords as real words.

Similarities to Other Types of Acquired Dyslexia?

In addition to the case studies that we have described, in which researchers have attempted to make links between the three most common types of acquired dyslexia and developmental dyslexia, a number of other recent reports have dealt with the possible similarity of certain developmental dyslexics to other types of acquired dyslexia. Space limitations preclude the possibility of discussing any of these in detail. Hence, we will just mention that there have been attempts to link developmental dyslexia to acquired visual dyslexia (Seymour and MacGregor 1984) and word form dyslexia (Prior and McCorriston 1983; Seymour and MacGregor 1984). Additionally, Seymour and MacGregor (1984) described a case of morphemic dyslexia.

From the case studies we have described in this section, we hope it is clear that developmental dyslexic subjects differ considerably in the patterns of errors they make when reading words. The intent of most of this research has been to make apparent possible relationships between acquired and developmental dyslexia. What can we conclude from this research? We now turn to that important question.

Similarities of Acquired and Developmental Dyslexia

So far in this section, we have described the characteristics of errors made when reading isolated words by some developmental dyslexics that are quite similar to errors made by acquired dyslexics. It has been argued by those researchers who have presented these case studies that C.D. is a case of developmental surface dyslexia, C.R. is a case of developmental deep dyslexia, and H.M. is a case of developmental phonological dyslexia. Assuming for the moment that each of these examples is truly a case of developmental dyslexia that is analogous to acquired dyslexia, and given that a number of cases have now been described for each of the three major types, exactly what can they tell us about developmental dyslexia?

Holmes (1978) suggested that in developmental dyslexia we are seeing a *retardation* in the normal process of learning to read. Thus, C.D. may have become stuck at the level of reading ability typical of a normal child in Stage 3 (sequential decoding stage) of reading development. Children in this stage resemble acquired surface dyslexics in the advantage they show for regular over irregular words, and in the sorts of errors they make. Likewise, it could be argued (see Ellis 1984; Bryant and Impey 1986) that there is a similarity between young children in Stages 1 and 2 (linguistic guessing and discrimination net guessing), acquired phonological dyslexia, and developmental phonological dyslexia. Thus, H.M. may be stuck at an early stage in the normal process of learning to read.

Because the work on the similarities between acquired and developmental dyslexia is so new, it is difficult to know exactly what "retardation" means. Two possibilities are that there is either a developmental lag in the normal process of learning to read or a fixation on an early stage of reading development. The concept of a developmental lag has been proposed from time to time by various researchers. For example, Mindell (1978) showed that dyslexic children looked very much like reading age controls (in terms of the patterns of errors made) on orientation errors they made for letter (confusing *b* and *d*) and word (*tap* for *pat*) stimuli and that age-matched controls performed significantly better (see also Bryant and Impey 1986). The concept here is that developmental dyslexics are simply developmentally delayed in progressing to higher level skills important to reading. However, as we pointed out earlier in this chapter, there is now some indication that a developmental lag concept can better explain the performance of poor readers than of dyslexics (Stanovich, Nathan, and Vala-Rossi 1986). The alternative possibility seems to be much more serious in that it implies that rather than simply being delayed in reading development, the dyslexic is stuck at a level of reading skill characteristic of beginning readers. Unfortunately, the work contrasting acquired and developmental dyslexia is so recent that we do not yet have any firm answers to this and many other questions.

We feel that comparing acquired and developmental dyslexia is a step in the right direction for researchers to take, because such an approach highlights the fact that there are many reasons for dyslexia and moves us away from the unitary approaches, which have proved to be so unsuccessful. However, there is also a critical danger with such an approach. It is that one must be very careful when comparing adult brain damaged individuals with children with reading problems. With brain damaged patients there is a known site of brain impairment, while with children with reading problems there is not. There are also a number of methodological problems involved in comparing such subjects (see Snowling 1983). But the major problem is that an uncritical adoption of the assumption that developmental dyslexics fall into the same categories that acquired dyslexics do can hinder an accurate description of developmental dyslexia syndromes.

TYPES OF DEVELOPMENTAL DYSLEXIA

In addition to the recent attempts to compare acquired and developmental dyslexia, a number of researchers have been interested in specifying the extent to which developmental dyslexics differ. Here, the primary approach

TABLE 11.3 Subtypes of Developmental Dyslexia [adapted from Thomson (1984) with permission of Arnold Press].

	VISUAL-SPATIAL	LANGUAGE	ARTICULATORY
Boder (1971)	9% dyseidetic	63% dysphonetic	
	├────────────┤	├──────────────────────────────┤	
	22% mixed dyseidetic- dysphonetic		
	├──┤		
Mattis, French, and Rapin (1975)	16% (5%) visual-spatial difficulties	38% (63%) language disorder	37% (10%) articulatory and graphomotor difficulties
	├────────────┤	├────────────────────┤	
percentages in parentheses reflect the Mattis 1978 results with younger dyslexics		├──┤	
Denckla (1977)		articulatory and graphomotor difficulties 12% ├──┤	
	4% visual-perceptual disorder	54% language disorder ├──────────────────────┤	
	├────────────────────────┤	dysphonetic sequencing difficulties 13% ├──────────────────────────────────────┤	
		verbal memorization disorder 10% ├──┤	

has been to delineate different subgroups of developmental dyslexics. We will review some of the more influential attempts.

Boder (1971, 1973) examined the reading and spelling performance of 107 dyslexic children and identified two patterns of performance among these children. One group of dyslexics (called *dysphonetic* dyslexics) exhibited weaknesses in auditory skills and read words as wholes rather than decoding them into phonetic units. Spelling errors were typified by the misapplication of phoneme-to-grapheme rules. These children were described by Boder as possessing a limited sight vocabulary of words which they are able to recognize visually; they were, however, very poor at phonic decoding. Because these children attempt to bypass phonology whenever possible, they also make reading errors that involve semantic substitutions (though the errors were for words in text rather than in isolation). Boder's second group of dyslexics (called *dyseidetic* dyslexics) exhibited weaknesses in the ability to discriminate and analyze the visual gestalts of words. Although phonetic abilities are presumably intact in these children, reading suffers from the laborious process of sounding out even the most familiar combination of letters. Spelling errors frequently involve letter and word reversals and confusions. In contrast to dysphonetic dyslexics, dyseidetic dyslexics appear to spell everything phonetically because of the inability to revisualize the correct word. A third group of dyslexics was also identified by Boder: a mixed dyseidetic-dysphonetic group. It is unclear as to whether this group represents a single dyslexic syndrome, but obviously such disability would result in even more serious reading problems than either of the more pure categorizations.

Somewhat similar to Boder's classification is that of Mitterer's (1982) division of dyslexic readers into *whole-word* and *recoding* types. Of the 27 subjects that he studied, 10 relied predominantly on whole-word recognition by sight and an additional 10 relied predominantly on phonic mediation. These two groups differed in their performance on a number of tasks though they were indistinguishable on overall IQ scores (and even IQ subtests scores) and standardized reading test performance. The recoders read substantially more regular than irregular words correctly (as they should, since they used phonic mediation). Whole-word dyslexics, in contrast, showed no such difference: if a word was in their sight vocabulary they could read it (whether it was regular or irregular): but if it was not in their sight vocabulary, they could not read it. Recoders' errors on words were predominantly phonic and included a substantial portion of pseudowords. In contrast, the errors of the whole-word dyslexics were predominantly visual and included very few pseudowords. Similarly, recoders gave regular pronunciations to pseudowords and read very few of them as real words whereas whole-word dyslexics tended not to give the expected regular pronunciations to pseudowords and instead read many as real words. Results quite similar to those reported by Mitterer have recently been reported by Treiman and Hirsh-Pasek (1985).

Other classifications of subgroups of dyslexic readers based on clinical neuropsychological evaluations of dyslexic children and adults (see Mattis, French, and Rapin 1975; Pirozzolo 1979) have revealed one large group of dyslexic readers with a severe language disability which is manifest in the inability to carry out rapid verbal tasks (Denckla and Rudel 1976), anomia (Mattis, French and Rapin 1975), and agrammatism (Pirozzolo 1979). While such dyslexic readers are sometimes referred to as *auditory-linguistic* dyslexics, we shall refer to them as *language deficit* dyslexics. The second group of dyslexic readers have been shown to have weaknesses in visual perception (Mattis, French and Rapin 1975) or spatial and oculomotor functions (Pirozzolo and Rayner 1978). Finger agnosia, directional disorientation, and atypical handwriting orientations have also been observed in children with this form of dyslexia, which we shall refer to as *visual-spatial* dyslexia.

One large group of developmental dyslexics is characterized by a naming problem. This has been typically assessed by having the children name line drawings of common objects or colors (Denckla and Rudel 1976). While they can name them correctly, they are typically about 50% slower than normal children in doing so. Further examination of these subjects indicates that they can semantically categorize these drawings normally, so that the problem appears to be accessing the phonological system from visual input (Murphy, Pollatsek, and Well 1988). In spite of their difficulties with accessing phonological codes, they appear to rely on the grapheme-phoneme route to the lexicon at least as often as good readers, since they show a large difference in naming regular and irregular words and have difficulty determining that *pseudohomophones* (such as *braik*) are not words. Thus, one might be tempted to classify these subjects as surface dyslexics. Whether this naming problem is characteristic of all surface developmental dyslexics remains to be seen.

We could continue on with this discussion of types of developmental dyslexia as other subtypes have been proposed (see Denckla 1977; Doehring and Hoshko 1977; Lovett 1987). We hope the point has become clear, however, that developmental dyslexia probably has many underlying causes. Thus, few of the researchers arguing for a given underlying cause of developmental dyslexia are likely to be wrong. That is, there probably are developmental dyslexics with a perceptual disorder (as argued for example by Lovegrove and his colleagues), or an eye movement disorder (as argued by Pavlidis and by Stein and Fowler), or a short term memory disorder. But, the point is that a perceptual disorder, or eye movement disorder, or short term memory disorder is not the only cause of reading problems. It appears to us, however, that the majority of developmental dyslexics do have some sort of language deficit (Vellutino 1979). Note that even among developmental dyslexics with a language deficit, the reason for the type of deficit varies.

While most evidence points to the prevalence of language deficits, it is hard to quantify that statement because of selection factors. For example, if a given researcher has a reputation for doing work on eye movements, for instance, then clinicians in the area will tend to refer individuals with reading problems to him or her. Exactly this sort of thing has happened to us. In contrast, researchers who have a reputation for dealing with language problems will tend to be sent dyslexics with language problems. Thus, each will get a different impression of the prevalance of the different subgroups of dyslexia.

If, as we have been arguing, developmental dyslexia can have a number of underlying causes, then it ought to be possible to differentiate dyslexic readers into different groups and observe differences in performance depending upon the hypothesized nature of the deficit. Indeed, some attempts to do this have already taken place (Mitterer 1982; Pirozzolo 1979; Treiman and Hirsh-Pasek 1985; Lovett 1987). Dyslexic readers can be categorized in advance on the basis of their performance on some important measure (Mitterer 1982) or on the basis of a discrepancy between subtests of an overall IQ test. For example, Pirozzolo (1979) was interested in a number of performance measures and categorized developmental dyslexics as language deficit or visual-spatial dyslexics on the basis of IQ subtest discrepancies; language deficit dyslexics had a higher performance than verbal IQ score, while visual-spatial dyslexics had a higher verbal than performance IQ score. Such procedures may not be infallible, but they do provide a systematic manner in which to go about categorizing dyslexic readers in advance of measuring performance differences of some type.

Other case studies. Earlier in this chapter we described two dyslexic readers called Dave and Jane. We also described rather briefly some of the characteristics of their eye movement patterns when reading. Let's consider these patterns in a bit more detail. Our purpose in doing so is that an examination of their eye movement patterns confirms what we have been arguing, namely that there are different underlying reasons for developmental dyslexia.

Dave and Jane had normal IQ scores with Dave having a verbal score of 97 and a performance score of 114, and Jane having a verbal score of 104 and a performance score of 98. Table 11.4 shows representative values for differences in key eye movement measures for a normal reader (PP) and Dave and Jane. As seen, when reading text at comparable levels, there are major differences between the normal reader and the two dyslexic readers. The pattern of eye movements also differs. Table 11.5 shows two lines of text read by PP and by Dave and Jane. PP has an average fixation duration of 220 milliseconds, average saccade length equals 8.4 characters (forward saccade length equals 9 character spaces, regressive saccade length equals 3 character spaces), and 17 percent of the eye movements are regressions. About 72 percent of the words receive a fixation. In contrast, for the two developmental dyslexics about 90 percent of the words receive a fixation. Dave has an average fixation duration of 310 milliseconds, average saccade length is 5.5 character spaces (with no difference between forward and regressive saccades), and about 35% of the saccades are regressions. Jane has an average fixation duration of 335 milliseconds, an average forward saccade length of 7 character spaces and an average regressive saccade length of 8.5 character spaces, and about 30 percent of the eye movements

TABLE 11.4 Average Eye Movement Measures for Normal and Dyslexic Readers

	NORMAL	DYSLEXIC
Average fixation duration	200-250 msec	300-350 msec
Average saccade length	8-9 characters	3-6 characters
Frequency of regressions	10-20%	30-40%

	PP[1]	DAVE	JANE
Average fixation duration	220 msec	310 msec	335 msec
Average saccade length (forward)	9 characters	5.5 characters	7 characters
Average saccade length (regression)	3 characters	5.5 characters	8.5 characters
Frequency of regression	17%	35%	30%

[1] PP = normal reader.

As society has become progressively more complex, psychology has

1	2	3	4		5	7		8	9
234	310	188	216		242	188		177	159
						6			
						144			

A

assumed an increasingly important role in solving human problems.

11		12	13	15 14		16		18
244		317	229	269 196		277		202
10						17		
206						144		

As society has become progressively more complex, psychology has

1	3	2	5		6	7	8	9	10	15	12		13	14
311	277	115	412		198	403	266	295	311	193	317		600	312
		4								11	18			
		222								277	206			
											19			
											415			

B

assumed an increasingly important role in solving human problems.

16		21		22	24		25	26	27		28	31	32
369		302		244	310		383	119	487		413	277	366
17		20		23			29				33		
415		177		288			200				361		
							30						
							117						

As society has become progressively more complex, psychology has

1		2	3	6	7	5	9		11	10	13
282		476	322	197	472	483	177		290	268	276
4					8		12				14
177					257		476				399

C

assumed an increasingly important role in solving human problems.

19		21	22	23		18	25	26		16		15
167		320	297	302		336	256	325		259		391
20				24				17		27		28
428				399				323		446		281

are regressions. Both dyslexic sybjects make many more fixations than the normal reader and, of course, comprehension is markedly poorer in the two dyslexics.

What is interesting is a comparison of the pattern of the two dyslexic readers. Dave can be characterized as having a language processing deficit. Fixations are quite long, there are many regressions, and when difficulty is encountered, he resorts to the strategy of attempting to use the context to disambiguate the text. If that fails, every letter may be fixated in an attempt to decode the word. Subjects with language processing deficits like Dave tend to make short forward saccades; their regressions also tend to be short, often shorter than the forward saccades. Figure 11.4 shows the eye movement pattern for each of the three readers. The normal reader shows a typical "staircase pattern" in which the eye moves mainly from left to right. By contrast, Dave shows what can be called a "partial staircase pattern" in which the movements are from left to right, with numerous regressions over material already traversed. In examining the pattern for Jane, we can identify a "reverse staircase pattern," in which there are clusters of right-to-left saccades. Also, the amplitude of right-to-left saccades exceeds that of left-to-right saccades. Thus, an examination of the pattern of eye movements reveals different characteristics for Jane than for Dave. Jane can be characterized as having a visual-spatial processing deficit.

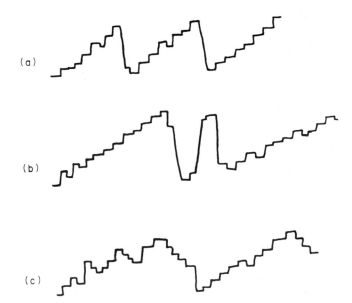

(a)

(b)

(c)

FIGURE 11-4 Eye movement patterns from three different readers. The top pattern is for reader PP, the middle pattern is for Dave, and the bottom pattern is for Jane. [Reproduced from Rayner (1986b), with permission from Wiley.]

SUMMARY

In this chapter we have discussed reading disability. We concentrated on developmental dyslexia, but also discussed poor readers and acquired dyslexia. Our focus was on developmental dyslexia because it is the least understood of the various types of reading disabilities and because we think it is the most interesting. Our primary argument has been that there is not a single underlying cause of developmental dyslexia, but that there are many reasons why a person may have difficulty acquiring literacy. Although it is not well understood at the present time, it is reasonable to think of developmental dyslexia as consisting of various subtypes. As researchers learn more about the various types of developmental dyslexia, we will not only learn more about the nature of the deficiencies that lead to reading problems, but also about reading in general.

PART FIVE
TOWARD A MODEL OF READING

As we told you in Chapter 1, this book has taken the careful reading of text as the standard or prototypical form of reading. However, it is obvious that you can engage in various forms of reading in which your cognitive processes may be different from when you carefully read a textbook or newspaper article. When you read light fiction you often read much faster than when you read a textbook. Sometimes you skim a newspaper article to get some relevant information but ignore other aspects of it. We could try to categorize how various forms of nonstandard reading differ from the norm, but we have chosen not to do this since there is not much research on the topic. Instead, what we will do in the beginning of Chapter 12 is focus on speedreading and proofreading as examples of nonstandard reading.

Throughout this book, we have implicitly suggested that most skilled readers are alike in their cognitive processing activities during reading. However, it is possible that there are major individual differences between skilled readers. Research in cognitive psychology typically involves setting up an experiment (like those discussed throughout the book) in which a group of subjects is asked to perform a task that is thought to be relevant to reading. The primary data that are then examined are group averages on some measure or measures. While various types of statistical tests applied to these data ensure that the group averages are indicative of what most subjects in the experiment are doing, the possibility remains that there are individual differences in the cognitive activities relevant to reading. Our own impression is that while there are some obvious individual differences in how people use information in recognizing words and in their strategies in various tasks (particularly comprehension strategies), for the most part readers do similar things. Research on this issue will be discussed at the end of Chapter 12.

The final chapter of the book, Chapter 13, will present a model of the reading process. To create an appropriate context for our model, we will briefly describe some other models of the reading process that have been widely cited. Our model should not be thought of as revealed truth about reading. Rather, the model is intended as a vehicle for achieving the primary goal of Chapter 13: integrating and summarizing the material of the prior chapters.

CHAPTER TWELVE
SPEEDREADING, PROOFREADING, AND INDIVIDUAL DIFFERENCES

Throughout most of the rest of this book, we have been discussing reading as the careful processing of written material. As we said in Chapter 1, we have approached reading in terms of someone carefully reading a textbook, a newspaper article, or a novel in which you must read carefully in order to pay attention to the plot. However, it is clearly the case that we can read in different ways under certain conditions. For example, when you read a novel which is not particularly intellectually stimulating, but which has a certain amount of entertainment value (or "escapism") associated with it, you may be aware of reading much faster than usual. If you think carefully about it, your introspections may suggest that you are skipping over large sections of the text. You probably do this because many parts of such novels are either totally predictable or very redundant. We would classify your reading behavior in such a situation as a mixture of reading (where you are carefully processing the text) and *skimming*. By skimming, we mean the type of reading activity in which you skim over the text without really deeply comprehending it. In this chapter, we shall review alternatives to the type of careful reading that we have been discussing in the rest of this book. In particular, we will begin the chapter by discussing speedreading, followed by a discussion of research on proofreading. Along the way, we will discuss the concept of skimming on a number of occasions. We will conclude the chapter by discussing individual differences in reading.

Individual differences are important to consider because of the possibility that different readers are doing different things or using different processing strategies. If this were the case, then it would seem unlikely that any single model of reading would be able to capture the essence of these individual differences. From a great deal of research on memory processes, cognitive psychologists know that while there are similar memory structures, different individuals use different strategies in trying to store information in these structures. It is possible that people read in vastly different ways? As we shall see, the available evidence indicates that there are individual differences in reading rate and comprehension processes. However, it appears that speed of encoding written material and the size of working memory can effectively account for these differences and that most readers are doing pretty much the same thing when they read. But, we're getting ahead of ourselves a bit. Let's first consider speedreading.

SPEEDREADING

Perhaps nothing related to reading is as controversial as the topic of speedreading. As we saw when we discussed the process of learning to read, there is a great deal of emotion and evangelicalism associated with that topic. However, with the topic of learning to read there are primarily professional educators involved in the nature of the debates, and there can be little doubt that such individuals do have the interests of children uppermost in their hearts (though some of them may be misguided). With the topic of speedreading, the fickle finger of profit-making is involved and various types of advertisements are used to encourage the unsuspecting public to accept the claims of speedreading proponents. It is quite likely that somewhere in your community there is some type of profit-making organization advertising speedreading.

Let's examine the claims of speedreading proponents and then consider these claims in light of the research evidence that is available. We begin by noting that there is not very much in the way of good research on the topic of speedreading per se. By this we mean that much of the research that has been done on speedreading is flawed either because appropriate control groups were not run (to compare speedreaders with normal readers, for example) or because appropriate controls were not taken to accurately access comprehension or speed of reading. The good research that is available tends to cast serious doubt on the claims of speedreading proponents.

Speedreading proponents claim that you should be able to increase your reading speed from 200 to 350 words per minute (the normal range for college students) to 2,000 words per minute or even faster. There have been speedreaders who purport to have rates in excess of 10,000 words per minute. Central to the claim of speedreading proponents is the idea that the brain is rather lazy and only effectively processes a small proportion of what it is capable of doing. In particular, speedreading proponents argue that reading speed can be increased by taking in more information per eye fixation and by eliminating inner speech, which is seen as a drag on reading speed. By processing more per fixation, the brain is presumably forced to operate closer to maximal capacity, and supposedly there will be no loss of comprehension. In order to process more per fixation, speedreaders are often taught to move a finger rapidly across a line. The eyes are supposed to keep up with the finger so that the speed of visual processing is increased. Eventually, the finger is used as a pointer as it zigzags down the page with the reader taking in large chunks of information. The central claim of speedreading proponents is thus that reading speed can be dramatically increased without any loss of comprehension.

According to speedreading proponents, readers can take in a large number of words on each fixation. From Chapter 1, where we discussed the problems associated with acuity, you will recall that the evidence indicates that the ability to resolve the details of letters presented parafoveally and peripherally with respect to the fixation point is severely limited. Thus, we make eye movements every 250 milliseconds (on average) to bring a given region of text into foveal vision. If you recall the research we described in Chapter 4 dealing with the size of the perceptual span, you will remember that the results clearly document that the area from which a college student (at average reading speeds) obtains useful information is relatively small. In experiments using the moving window technique (McConkie and Rayner 1975; Rayner and Bertera 1979; Rayner, Well and Pollatsek 1980; Rayner 1984; DenBuurman, Boersema and Gerrisen 1981; Underwood and McConkie 1985) it has been found that readers are not influenced by erroneous material lying more than 4 letter spaces to the left of fixation or more than 15 letter spaces to the right of fixation.

While the moving window experiments are compelling evidence against the idea that readers can obtain information from an entire line of text in a single fixation, it could be argued that the experiments cannot be generalized to speedreaders. Perhaps speedreaders do something very different from normal readers on each fixation. Indeed, some data on the eye movements of speedreaders have been obtained (Llewellyn-Thomas 1962; McLaughlin 1969) and they suggest that speedreaders are doing something very different. In these studies, the mean fixation duration was normal or slightly above normal, and both readers who were studied moved their eyes down the middle of the left-hand page and then up the middle of the right-hand page, skipped a number of lines per saccade, and only fixated once on each line on which they fixated. Notice that this peculiar pattern of eye fixations actually results in the reader processing half of the material in the opposite sequence that the author intended. That is, when the speed-reader moves up the right-hand page, he or she is processing the textual information in a different order than the author intended to convey it. McLaughlin concluded that speedreading has only limited usefulness be-cause of confused and sometimes fabricated recall. However, he suggested that it is possible and employed peripheral vision and parallel processing as explanatory mechanisms. Given what is known about peripheral vision and parallel processing, however, his arguments are not very compelling.

In contrast to Llewellyn-Thomas and McLaughlin, Taylor (1962) recorded the eye movements of graduates of a speedreading course and reported very little indication of a vertical line of progression. Those subjects who showed the greatest tendency to move down the center of the page had the poorest scores on a true-false test, scoring no better than chance. Taylor (1965) and Walton (1957) concluded that eye movement patterns of speedreaders closely resemble the eye movement patterns produced during skimming of text.

Perhaps the most complete study of the eye movement characteristics of speedreaders was carried out by Just, Carpenter, and Masson (1982; see also Just and Carpenter 1987). In their study, the eye fixations of speedreaders (reading at rates around 600 to 700 words per minute) and normal readers (reading around 250 wpm) were compared. In addition, normal readers were asked to skim the text (producing "reading" rates around 600 to 700 wpm). When subjects were tested after reading, the speedreaders did as well as the normal readers (when reading at their normal speed and not skimming) on general comprehension questions or questions about the gist of the passage. On the other hand, when tested about details of the text, speedreaders could not answer questions if they had not fixated on the region where the answer was located. Normal readers, whose fixations were much denser than the speedreaders, were able to answer the detail questions relatively well. When normal readers were asked to skim the text, both their eye movement patterns and comprehension measures were similar to those of speedreaders.

In general, the results of research investigating the characteristics of speedreaders' eye movements is consistent with the idea that they are skimming the text and not really reading it in the sense of reading each word. Apparently, they are doing a lot of filling in on the basis of what they already know about the topic being read or what they can surmise from those portions of the text they have actually read.

Although we have never tested speedreaders using the moving window paradigm, it is our observation that fast readers (reading rates around 400 to 500 wpm) may not be better in the use of peripheral vision than are slower readers (reading rates around 200 wpm). For example, in the type of study in which a mask moved in synchrony with the eyes (Rayner and Bertera 1979), it was the fast readers who were most disturbed by this situation, not the slower readers. If fast readers are fast because they can use parafoveal and peripheral vision more effectively than slow readers, we would expect them to do better than slow readers when foveal vision is masked, since they should be able to read more effectively from nonfoveal vision. But, in fact, they were more disrupted than the slower readers. Likewise, when faster readers are compared to slower readers in the moving window type of experiment discussed in Chapter 4, fast readers do not have a larger region of effective vision than slower readers (see Underwood and Zola 1986).

It is certainly the case that fast readers have fewer fixations per line than slow readers (Rayner 1978a) and they seem to skip over short words more frequently than slow readers do. But, to reiterate, what evidence we do have is not necessarily consistent with the notion that fast readers can use eccentric vision more effectively than slow readers. Such a conclusion seems also to be consistent with the finding that attempts to train readers to use peripheral vision effectively have not been successful and the comprehension assessments have been equivocal (Brim 1968; Sailor and Ball 1975).

Let's turn now to the second major claim of speedreading proponents. As we suggested earlier, advocates of speedreading also claim that reading speed can be dramatically increased by eliminating inner speech. As we pointed out in Chapter 6, we all hear an inner voice pronouncing the words that our eyes are traversing as we read. As we indicated in that chapter, it is not at all clear what the relationship is between the voice we hear and activity in the speech tract and/or auditory images. Speedreading proponents are generally not very clear about what they have in mind when they suggest that we should eliminate inner speech. Their idea seems to be that we should be able to read in a purely visual mode and that an involvement of speech processes will slow us down. In essence, the argument seems to be that inner speech is a carryover (or habit) from the fact that we are taught to read orally before we read silently.

Just as the research evidence on eye movements and speedreading does not seem to be consistent with the speedreading position, the evidence on elimination of inner speech and reading comprehension does not seem consistent with the position. We will not review the evidence on inner speech again (see Chapter 6); however, the general finding is that if the text is anything but rather simple prose, then an attempt to eliminate inner speech results in marked impairments in comprehension. In principle, while purely visual reading might be possible, the bulk of the evidence indicates that inner speech plays a critical role in comprehending most written discourse.

Why do so many people believe speedreading is effective? The reason is that it is portrayed as increasing speed without decreasing comprehension. However, a major problem is assessing comprehension. Let's consider some anecdotal accounts about speedreading. First, consider some observations from a psychologist who enrolled in a speedreading program and then described his experiences (Carver, 1971, 1972). Prior to beginning their instruction, students in speedreading programs are typically given a test (called a *pre-test*), which measures both their reading speed and their comprehension. At the end of their training program, they are given another test measuring these same two components (called a *post-test*). One observation concerning these two types of tests is that the material read on the pre-test is often harder than that on the post-test. In addition, trainees are sometimes tested repeatedly on the same material, so it is inevitable that their performance will improve with training.

More serious is another problem related to the manner in which performance is assessed. A new student in a speed reading course is typically asked for his or her speed of reading. This is generally measured in a straightforward way and turns out to be in the range of 200 to 350 wpm. After the course, what is usually measured is the *Reading Efficiency Index* (which we'll call the *RE Index*). The RE Index is based on the argument that rapid reading rates should be qualified by the percentage of the material that the reader is able to comprehend. Students in the program thus have their comprehension measured with a post-test and the reading rate is multiplied by a percent score on the comprehension test. Thus, if a reader had a reading rate of 5,000 wpm and scored 60 percent on the comprehension test, his or her RE Index would be 3,000 wpm. Unfortunately, we seldom know how well a person would score on the comprehension test if he or she had not read the passage before taking the test. If a multiple-choice test with four questions is used, chance performance would be 25 percent and thus a person who "read" 5,000 wpm and understood absolutely nothing would get a score of 1,250 wpm. Should a score of 60 percent be multiplied by a very rapid reading rate (such as 5,000 wpm) to yield an RE Index of 3,000 wpm? It doesn't seem quite fair.

Using this line of reasoning, Carver reanalyzed a study (Liddle 1965) that is widely cited by speedreading proponents as support for speedreading. In Liddle's study, graduates of a speedreading program were compared to readers who had signed up for the program but had not yet taken the course. This is in fact a good control group, because people who elect to take speedreading courses could conceivably be different in some important dimensions from other people. Both groups of subjects were tested for both speed and comprehension on reading selections using both fictional and nonfictional material. The reading rates were between 300 and 1,300 wpm faster for the graduates than for the control group. However, there was actually a significant decline in comprehension for the graduates on the fictional test material (an outcome that is not emphasized in the commercial publicity). Instead, much has been made of the fact that the comprehension scores were not reliably different from each other in the tests of the nonfictional material; the speedreaders scored 68 percent correct and the control group scored 72 percent correct.

Carver administered the same comprehension test to a group of subjects who had never read the passage. These people obtained a score of 57 percent correct. Common sense and guessing apparently allowed subjects who had never read the material to score only a bit below those who had read the material. If we take this new control group's score (57 percent) as the zero point against which to evaluate the results of Liddle's study, a different conclusion emerges. The control subjects who read the passages scored 15 percentage points above the chance level and the speed readers scored only 11 percentage points above it. From this perspective, the speed reading course can be said to have caused a decline in comprehension of 4/15 (or 27 percent). While the difference is quite small, it does qualify the conclusion that there was no comprehension loss for the nonfictional material (and we already know that the comprehension loss caused by speedreading was statistically significant for the fictional material). More generally, Carver's observations raise serious questions about the methods by which reading efficiency is measured. The RE Index, particularly in the context of speed reading, is a dubious measure that may only be limited by the rate at which people can turn pages of text (Crowder 1982).

Our second anecdotal account is from Crowder and is based on a case history from the *Journal of Reading*. The incident deals with a performance contract between a speedreading firm and a school district. The contract called for a dramatic increase in the reading skills for the entire seventh grade of the school district in return for a fee of $110,000. The terms of the contract specified that of the 2,501 children in the seventh grades of the district, 75 percent or more would quintuple their reading speeds (or better) and at the same time these same children would gain at least 10 percent in comprehension scores. In order to accomplish this, the students were each to spend 24 hours in classroom instruction and 22 hours outside of class practicing what they learned in the reading class.

Reading performance for the entire seventh grade class is shown in Table 12.1. The first column shows performance on a vocabulary test. As you can see, there was an increase in this measure, but we would anticipate that children of this age would show an increase on this measure anyway. The second column shows a large increase in reading speed; in fact, there was a quadrupling in the post-test over the pre-test. The measure shown is an actual words per minute measure and does not involve the RE Index. The third column of the table shows that overall comprehension scores were low (about 33 percent correct), and that there was little difference between the pre-test and the post-test.

How do these performance measures square with the contract? Of all of the seventh graders in the district, 259 students both quintupled their reading speed and increased their comprehension scores by 10 percent. Thus, only about 13 percent of the children involved met the objectives set

TABLE 12.1 Results of Speed Reading Program. (Adapted from Crowder (1982) with permission of Oxford Press.)

	PERFORMANCE MEASURE		
Test	Vocabulary	Words per minute	Comprehension*
Pre-	21.5	155	5.2
Post-	24.4	657	4.9

* Maximum possible = 15.0

out by the contract. At face value, these data are certainly problematical for the speedreading firm. But the problem is even worse than it appears. For one thing, the standardized test used to obtain these results has an accompanying leaflet stating that the reading rate results are not useful unless comprehension rates are 75 percent or better. As we can see in Table 12.1, the obtained scores were more like 33 percent, and so the reading speed measures are not really interpretable. Furthermore, as we discussed above, we have no idea how well people would do on the comprehension test if they never read the passages. Would such a control group be able to score 33% correct?

An even more serious problem is that the measurement procedure was changed from the pre-test to the post-test. (We mentioned this general problem earlier.) The reading rates were supposed to be measured on a 3-minute sample of reading and this was done on the pre-test. However, the speedreading firm argued for a shorter reading period on the post-test because the full passages used in the test contained only 1,000 words. Thus, anyone reading faster than 333 wpm would finish before 3 minutes was up and therefore his or her true reading rate would be indeterminate. Of course, one way to solve this problem would be to have a clock in the reading room and have students write down the time that they finished reading. Such a procedure would probably involve lots of monitors to ensure that students actually finished when they said they did. The speedreading firm proposed instead to sample reading for 30 seconds on the post-test and then double the obtained figure to get an estimate of wpm. The school district agreed to this proposal, but it was probably a mistake to do so.

Years and years of research on tests and measurement has told us that a short test of anything is less likely to be reliable than a longer test. Some time later, 440 of the seventh graders who had participated in this program were asked to read, and estimated reading rates were obtained based on either a 30-second sample of reading or a 3-minute sample. The short reading test gave a mean rate of 780 wpm while the long test gave a mean rate of 205 wpm (with all tests taken from the same materials). This result certainly makes the results shown in Table 12.1 dubious. There may have been other questionable activities and abuses involved in this particular example, but you probably have the point. The school district settled for an award of $99,000 rather than the contracted $110,000; the rate of return for the speedreading firm would have been about $2,500 for each $75 invested (Crowder 1982).

You may want to argue that the examples we have provided represent isolated dishonest business marketing tactics and that such isolated cases or malicious business ethics should not discredit the true value of the product being sold. We would not want to argue that all speedreading firms are dishonest in their approach. Our point is that as consumers we should be aware of what can and cannot be accomplished in speedreading programs. Unfortunately, the average person does not have the specialized knowledge needed to evaluate the types of claims made by many speedreading programs.

Our own impressions concerning speedreading programs are that such programs can improve reading speed. However, it is not necessary to pay exorbitant fees to increase your reading speed. By simply practicing reading faster, you can learn to increase your reading speed dramatically (Glock 1949; Tinker 1958). Reading speeds of 600 wpm may be obtainable with reasonably good comprehension (provided that the reading material is fairly undemanding; when the text is difficult, it is necessary to read more slowly to comprehend effectively, as we have already seen). While we have been very negative about speedreading programs, they probably do provide training that has a very specific value. Skimming, after all, is a very important skill in our society. In careers that depend on the written word, there is simply too much information to be assimilated thoroughly, and we are constantly forced to select what we look at. Those unable to skim material would find they spent their entire day reading.

In the 1960s there was a lot of publicity (often from speedreading firms) about high government officials (including President John F. Kennedy) who were purported to be speedreaders. It was argued that such officials could pick up a copy of the *Washington Post* or the *New York Times* and read the front section from beginning to end in a few minutes. Lest we be too gullible and believe that these officials were actually reading, consider the knowledge and information that such an official would bring to the task. Before looking at the newspaper, the government official is probably briefed daily about important world events. Indeed, he or she may well be involved in establishing policy matters and would have first-hand knowledge about many of the events reported in the front section of the newspaper. In contrast, the average person would come to such a situation with very few facts at his or her disposal and would probably have to read fairly carefully in order to completely understand any given article. On the other hand, suppose that you watched the Chicago Bears' victory over the New England Patriots in the 1986 Super Bowl. Having watched the game firsthand, you could read the *Times* report of the game fairly quickly and a week later, when *Sports Illustrated* ran its story on the game, you could quickly skim the article looking for some information which you did not previously have (such as an interview with a player or coach that occurred 3 days after the game). While this particular example is related to sports, we all have pockets of specialized knowledge (the stock market, music, movies, experimental psychology, politics). There is written information in all areas that is prepared for the general reader. For those areas where you already have specialized knowledge or where you already know most of the facts (as in our Super Bowl example) you can skim over the material quite easily.

Conversations we have had with graduates of speedreading courses also lead us to believe that what is effectively being taught is a method for skimming. Most graduates of such courses point out that their reading speed increased as a result of taking the course and most of them acknowledge that they learned to skim effectively. However, with respect to the more extreme claims of speedreading programs (namely, that the program really teaches people to *read,* not skim, at very fast rates), graduates are somewhat divided. Some insist that the program does not work or that they cannot read at fast rates, and a few say that they could read at astronomical rates but they stopped doing it. According to these people, speedreading was like "gobbling down mashed potatoes," and they had to stop because reading lost its appeal. Finally, there do appear to be a small percentage of the graduates of speedreading courses who insist that they can do it and they appear to be rather aggressive in asserting it.

This is probably a good place to bring up one final anecdote about speedreading. One of the authors of this book was once interviewed (along with a number of other psychologists who had done research on the process of reading) by the *Washington Post* for an article on speedreading. Many of the points that have been brought out in this section were brought out by the psychologists interviewed. At the end of the interview (after all of the points about eye movements and acuity had been discussed), this author and a couple of other psychologists were asked, "Is speedreading really possible?" This author's response was rather cautious and was something like the following: "I have not directly done research on speedreaders, but based on all of the research that I and others have done on eye movements in reading and from what is known about the visual system and acuity, I can't imagine that reading rates of over 600 words per minute are really possible." The article appeared in the *Post* and many other newspapers around the country. A number of letters were received from irate speedreaders around the country, including one who wrote, "Just because you can't imagine something, doesn't mean that it can't happen. Quit living in an ivory tower and learn the joys and ecstasy of speedreading."

Those letters are securely locked away in a file cabinet, yet we continue to maintain that the kinds of reading rates advertised by speedreading programs are not possible. Speed readers appear to be intelligent individuals who already know a great deal about the topic they are reading and are able to successfully skim the material at rapid rates and accept the lowered comprehension that accompanies skimming (Carver 1985). The research by Just, Carpenter, and Masson (1982) clearly showed that speed readers' comprehension of detailed information was severely limited, and Homa (1983) showed that overall comprehension, aside from gist, was very poor in speed readers.

Perhaps at this point it is appropriate to end this discussion of speedreading with Woody Allen's classic line: "I took a speedreading course and read *War and Peace* in two minutes. It's about Russia."

Summary

Although the topic of speedreading receives a great deal of publicity and interest, the available evidence suggests that "speedreaders" are skimming the material and not really reading. Successful speedreaders appear to be intelligent individuals who already know a great deal about the topic they are reading. When so-called speedreaders are tested on comprehension, they often do quite well on questions dealing with the gist of the passage, but they cannot answer questions dealing with details unless their eyes fixated in the region where the information to answer the question was located. Also, as we have seen previously, comprehension of difficult material requires the capability of recoding the visual information into subvocal speech. Thus, speed readers can skim easy material much more readily than they can skim difficult material.

PROOFREADING AND VISUAL SEARCH

While there has been very little good research on speedreading, there has been a great deal of good research on the process of proofreading. Research on proofreading typically involves appropriate experimental controls and well-designed studies. Thus, psychologists who are experienced in issues concerning experimental design would not have the same uneasy feelings as they do about speedreading research. However, from our point of view, there is a problem with research on proofreading; many researchers who study proofreading presume that the results of their studies will inform us about the process of normal reading. While it is possible that results of research on proofreading have important implications for reading, the two tasks are quite different.

When you read a passage of text, your primary goal is to comprehend the passage. When you proofread a passage you are generally looking for typographical errors, misspellings, and omitted words, and as a result, comprehension is not the goal. Sometimes proofreading is very much like a visual search task (indeed, in many experimental instantiations of proofreading, subjects are asked to search for the presence of certain target letters), and other times it is very much like skimming. While we do not doubt that at times comprehension processes get in the way of proofreading (so that you inadvertently start paying more attention to the meaning of what you are proofreading than the task at hand), we are suspicious about the extent to which results of experiments on proofreading can inform us about reading.

Let's make an analogy here. You have probably had the experience of reading some material, and after some time realizing that you have been daydreaming and understood nothing of what you have "read." Your eyes kept moving over the text and you may have even been conscious of a few of the words in the text. In fact, you may have gone through a whole page in "daydream mode" and not comprehended much of the passage at all. Would we want to entertain the possibility that "reading" under such circumstances could inform us about the process of normal reading? Perhaps we might learn something, but the odds are that the results of such research (if we could experimentally induce people to read in "daydream mode" in the first place) would not be very informative. With these caveats in mind, let's review some of the research on proofreading and the general conclusions that can be reached from the research.

Widespread interest in proofreading originated with some experiments reported by Corcoran (1966, 1967). We should point out that the task Corcoran and most later researchers favored, while similar to proofreading (i.e., detection of misspellings and other mistakes), was really a slightly different task: visual search. He asked subjects to go through a passage and mark all instances of the letter *e*. What he found was that subjects missed *silent e's* nearly four times as often as pronounced *e's*. In a second experiment, he used a real proofreading task: subjects were asked to mark as quickly as possible places in text where letters were missing. He found that an absent silent *e* went unnoticed significantly more often than an absent pronounced *e*. Corcoran originally interpreted his findings as evidence of the importance of acoustic coding in a visual task like reading (see Conrad 1972). However, subsequent research has suggested that while acoustic codes may play some part in the "proofreader's error," they are not the primary source of the problem (see Smith and Groat 1971).

Try counting the number of occurrences of the letter *f* in Table 8.2. When presented with short passages such as this, subjects tend to overlook the *f's* in the word *of*. Indeed, if subjects are originally asked to count the number of times that the word *of* occurs, they come up short there also. There is now a rather substantial literature (see Haber and Schindler 1981; Healy 1976, 1980, 1981; Healy and Drewnowski 1983; Drewnowski and Healy 1977, 1980) showing that proofreaders tend to miss letters in short function words like *of, the,* and *and*. That the effect has something to do with reading is clear from the finding that errors on such words occur much more frequently when the function word is embedded in coherent text than when it occurs in scrambled text or in word lists (Schindler 1977). Thus, it appears that with coherent text, it may be difficult for proofreaders to turn off their reading habits which are so deeply ingrained.

On the basis of this type of research, there has been a great deal of theorizing about perceptual units in reading. But, again, our impression is that task differences make generalizations from proofreading to normal reading somewhat dubious. If experiments force readers to fixate on every function word (as in Schindler's word list arrangement); the proofreader's error decreases markedly. We know that in reading, short function words are often not fixated (see Chapter 5) and the fact that subjects miss target letters in such words is probably highly related to where they fixate. Proofreading errors of this type can thus be explained in terms of a model such as that of Paap et al. (1982), which we discussed in Chapter 3, without having to postulate special perceptual units for short, common function words. Presumably it takes less perceptual evidence to fire off the lexical entry of a predictable function word. Thus the appropriate letter detectors would be less activated when a function word is read than when a content word is read (especially if the word was not fixated). If target letters are identified on the basis of the activation of both letter detectors and word detectors, one would predict poorer identification of letter targets in function words.

Most subsequent research in the area used the visual search task. The metaphor that reading is "visual search for meaning" goes too far: reading is more of a construction of meaning than a search for a prestored meaning (see Chapter 7 and 8). However, studies comparing visual search and reading have revealed some interesting findings. For example, Spragins, Lefton, and Fisher (1976) asked subjects to search through text for a target word and compared eye movement characteristics to when these same subjects read text. Table 12.2 shows the differences in primary eye movement characteristics and search (or reading) rate in the two different conditions. Notice that search rate was considerably faster than reading rate. Subjects achieved the faster rate in the search condition primarily by moving their eyes a greater distance with each saccade than in reading. In essence, subjects' performance in the search task appears to be quite similar to that of subjects who are skimming text, as we described in the previous section. As in situations in which reading and skimming are compared (see Just, Carpenter, and Masson 1982), the data from Spragins et al. suggest that more information is being processed per fixation in the search task than in reading. However, it is not clear that more visual information is really processed per fixation in the search task (Rayner and Fisher 1987). First, as we argued earlier, the perceptual span in reading is appreciably larger than the average size of a saccade; thus it is hazardous to use the size of the size of the saccade to infer the amount of visual information extracted. In addition, at least some of the difference in the speed of the tasks is due to discourse comprehension processes; it seems quite likely that if a surprise comprehension test were given, subjects in the reading condition would do considerably better than those in the search condition.

Another point that should be stressed is that the speed of search varies widely from task to task. For example, the more visually similar the target is to the distractors (i.e., nontarget letters) the slower the search and the shorter the saccades (Rayner and Fisher 1987). In addition to being influenced by changes in the materials, the rate at which subjects are able to process information in visual search tasks depends a great deal upon exactly what they are asked to do. When subjects are asked to count all occurrences of given targets, their "reading" rate may be as slow as 50 to 80 words per

TABLE 12.2 A Comparison of Reading and Search for a Target Word. (From Spragins, Lefton, and Fisher 1976)

	WPM	WORDS PER FIXATION	SACCADE LENGTH	FIXATION DURATION
Reading	256	1.2	5.6	234
Search	435	2.2	10.1	244

minute (wpm). When they are asked to search for a given target word, their rate may be as fast as 400 to 500 wpm.

As we pointed out in the prior section, the speed of "reading" also depends on the exact task. When people skim text their "reading" rates range between 500 and 1,000 wpm, whereas in normal reading, reading rates for college age students typically range between 200 and 350 wpm. Some people might want to argue that results from these different tasks are generalizable to one another. However, our inclination would be to argue that each involves different strategies and processes on the part of the subject. Thus, we might well have a model of proofreading for misspellings that differs from a model of proofreading (or searching) for a target word. And both types of models would be different from a model of reading, in which the goal is to comprehend the text.

FLEXIBILITY IN READING

We have been discussing tasks that are ostensibly related to reading yet still differ in critical ways from reading. We have argued that these differences may induce strategies that require quite different cognitive operations than those of normal reading. To what extent are we able to vary our strategies within the task of reading itself? Do we read in different ways depending upon our purpose? We suggested at the outset of this chapter that we do. In fact, it has long been recognized that people have some flexiblilty in the way they read a passage. In addition, it is generally accepted that the ability to be flexible in reading is a characteristic of better, more mature readers. Walker (1938) found that skilled readers are more adaptive to the nature of the material than less skilled readers, in that the skilled readers' eye movement patterns are more responsive to their comprehension of the material.

A number of studies have been aimed at assessing the degree to which readers demonstrate flexibility in reading. One measure that has often been used to assess such flexibility is reading rate. The efficient reader is thought to be one who will modify his or her reading rate according to the difficulty of the material being read, the familiarity of the material, or the purpose of reading (whether seeking to gain only an overview of the passage or to understand and remember factual details from the passage). Studies that have investigated the effects of these variables, however, have found surprisingly small changes in reading rate. Although most of the studies have found some changes in reading rate resulting from the manipulations of passage difficulty or of instructions to the readers, this change has usually been quite small (Carillo and Sheldon 1952; Rankin 1970).

Aside from being directed to vary their reading rate, readers are also advised to focus on the acquisition of different types of information from passages, depending upon their purposes in reading them (Tinker 1965). That readers are able to do this is nicely demonstrated in studies by Anderson and Pichert (1978) and Pichert and Anderson (1977). In these studies, subjects were asked to read stories from two different perspectives. Thus, a story was read about two boys playing hooky from school who go to one of the boy's homes, because his mother was never there on Thursday. The story describes quite a bit about the house which they are playing in. For example, since the house is quite old it has some defects, such as a leaky roof, a damp and dusty basement, and so on. On the other hand, because the family is quite wealthy, they have a lot of valuable possessions, such as ten-speed bikes, a color TV set, a rare coin collection, and so on. Half of the subjects in the experiment were asked to read the passage from the perspective of a homebuyer and half from the perspective of a burglar. Clearly, a leaky roof is important to a homebuyer but unimportant to a burglar. The reverse is true of a color TV set or rare coin collection. Anderson and Pichert found that what readers could remember from the passage was influenced by the perspective they had been asked to take.

In an experiment designed to investigate the flexibility of reading strategies, McConkie, Rayner, and Wilson (1973) asked groups of readers to read a series of passages. Each group only had to answer one type of question after each passage. For example, some subjects were consistently given questions testing numerical facts presented in the passage, some were consistently given recognition questions, and others were given questions that tested higher order understanding of the passage. After a number of passages, subjects were given all three types of questions in a surprise test.

McConkie, Rayner, and Wilson found that readers were able to adopt different strategies as reflected by their reading rate and by the types of question they could answer. They found that when readers were given a certain type of question consistently after each passage, they were able to increase reading speed and still answer that type of question quite well. But, on the surprise test the subjects had a difficult time answering questions of the type different from those they had been experiencing. However, subjects who were given questions that encouraged them to read more slowly and carefully were better able to answer questions that were different from those they had been receiving.

We can see then that skilled readers are able to be quite flexible in their approach to reading. What readers can remember from text appears to be a sensitive indicator of their purpose in reading. Variations in reading rate across different strategies are not quite as obvious, however, which may imply that (within a broad range) when the reader is trying to comprehend some aspect of the text, reading rate will not vary too much. However, again, when the purpose is to read for very specific types of information or to skim the material, reading rate increases rather dramatically over that when more general comprehension processes are involved.

INDIVIDUAL DIFFERENCES

As we saw in Chapter 11, the question of what differentiates a good reader from a poor reader is an important one and one to which considerable attention has been paid. In this section, however, we will not devote much space to that question. An excellent book by Perfetti (1985) goes into great detail about differences between good and poor readers. Essentially, much of the literature suggests that differences in "intelligence" and in short term memory can account for much of the difference between good and poor readers. All other things being equal (which they probably never are), someone with an IQ score of 120 will be a better reader than someone with an IQ score of 90. IQ scores and various measures of reading ability are known to be highly correlated, and undoubtedly intelligence can account for much of the difference between people who might be classified as good and poor readers. Perfetti's (and others) analyses lead to the striking conclusion that when IQ differences are taken into account, differences in short term memory processing can account for much of the difference between good and poor readers.

Our primary concern in this section will be to examine the extent to which there are differences among readers who we would generally consider to be good readers. In essence, throughout this book, we have been discussing reading as if the processes and strategies involved were very much the same for all people. Is it possible that readers are doing somewhat different things and still coming out with the same product, namely, comprehension of the text?

Let's begin this discussion at the most basic level. We know that during reading, eye movements are very important in the sense that they serve as the means by which readers are able to acquire new information from the text. We also know, as we pointed out in Chapter 4, that there are differences in the eye movement characteristics of good readers. If you look at Table 12.3, it is obvious that some people read fast because they make fewer fixations than readers who are not quite so fast, while others may read a bit faster by making shorter fixations. In fact, while reading rate can be increased by making either fewer fixations or shorter fixations (or both), most of the increase is generally due to making fewer fixations. In light of the individual differences that are evident in Table 12.3 and on the basis of data collected in his lab, Rothkopf (1978; Rothkopf and Billington 1979) has suggested that individual differences in eye movement patterns are extremely important. Rothkopf has reported what appear to be marked differences in readers in both their eye movement patterns and their responses to changes in reading task demands, and has warned that eye movement patterns of different individuals may not be sufficiently alike to warrant a single theoretical model of reading processes. On the other hand, on the basis of a large-scale examination of individual differences in eye movement patterns as subjects read easy and difficult text under six different experimental conditions, Fisher (1983) concluded that the extent of individual differences in reading styles is not sufficient to challenge the validity of a general model of reading behavior. Fisher found that most individual differences in terms of eye movement behavior are found at the level of main effects and do not interact with task demands. In other words, there are

TABLE 12.3 Mean Fixation Duration, Mean Saccade Length, Proportion of Fixations That Were Regressions, and Words per Minute (WPM) for 10 Good College-Age Readers. [From Rayner (1978a) with permission of the American Psychological Association.]

SUBJECT	FIXATION DURATION[a]	SACCADE LENGTH[b]	REGRESSIONS (%)[c]	WPM
KB	195	9.0	6	378
JC	227	7.6	12	251
AK	190	8.6	11	348
TP	196	9.5	15	382
TT	255	7.7	19	244
GT	206	7.9	4	335
GB	205	8.5	6	347
BB	247	6.7	1	257
LC	193	8.3	20	314
JJ	241	7.2	14	230
Mean	215.5	8.1	10.8	308

Note. For these subjects there was a correlation between mean fixation duration and mean saccade length of .81; that is, the faster readers had shorter mean fixation durations and longer mean saccade lengths. Thus, the WPM score correlates about .89 with both mean fixation duration ($-.89$) and mean saccade length.

[a] In msec.
[b] In character spaces (4 character spaces = 1° of visual angle).
[c] Percentage to total fixation that were regressions.

differences between readers, but these differences remain when the task is changed from reading to search, for example.

Our contention is that although there are clearly individual differences in eye movement characteristics and patterns among good readers, in terms of eye movements most good readers are pretty much doing the same thing. For the most part, this observation derives from the large number of studies we have done using the moving window paradigm. In those studies, the effect of a restricted window affects all readers in pretty much the same way. That is, when small windows are presented, readers decrease saccade length (and make more fixations) and increase fixation duration in contrast to when larger windows are presented. Thus, while there are indeed individual differences in eye movement characteristics, our sense is that they are not particularly important in explaining reading performance. In large part, this is because of the anatomy of the eye in which the distinction between foveal, parafoveal, and peripheral regions of text holds for all readers.

In an attempt to determine what differentiates a good fast reader from a good slower reader, Jackson and McClelland (1975) tested subjects on a number of information processing tasks. Table 12.4 and Figure 12.1 show some of the primary results from the experiment. Let's run through the different tasks that were used. First, however, note that the mean reading speed (words per minute) for the average readers was 260 wpm and the mean reading speed for the fast readers was 586 wpm.

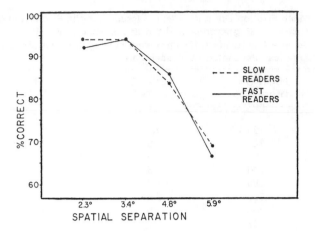

FIGURE 12-1 Percentage of letters correctly reported in letter separation task for each spatial separation. Means for fast readers and slow readers are plotted separately. [From Jackson and McClelland (1975), with permission of Academic Press and the authors.]

In the free report task, five-word sentences, such as "Dan fixed the flat tire," were presented for 200 milliseconds. All the sentences contained short words, as in the example. Subjects were asked to fixate on a target point and then the sentence was presented symmetrically around the fixation point. After each exposure, subjects wrote down as much of the sentence as they could. They were instructed to write down any letters they saw, whenever they recognized letters without identifying the whole word. The number of letters reported and the number of words reported are in the columns labeled *Free letters* and *Report words,* respectively. The column labeled *Sentences* presents the percentage of time that subjects were able to report all five words from the sentence. In a single letter threshold task, capital letters were presented starting at 20 milliseconds and subjects were asked to report the letter. If the subject could not report the letter, the duration of the exposure was increased incrementally until the subject could report it. The column labeled *Threshold* presents the average exposure duration of the final 20 trials.

In the unrelated letter task, eight randomly chosen letters (all consonants) were presented for 200 milliseconds. After each exposure, subjects wrote down eight letters in any order, guessing if necessary. The results of this task are shown in the column labeled *Unrelated letters*. In the forced choice test, subjects were shown a sentence, such as "Kevin fired a new worker," for 200 milliseconds and then asked to indicate if the word *fired* or *hired* was present in the sentence. In all of the tasks in which stimuli were presented for 200 milliseconds, the exposure of the stimuli was preceded and followed by a mask consisting of overlapping O's and X's. In the final task, the letter separation task, two letters were presented at different distances to the left and right of fixation for 200 milliseconds and subjects had to write down the letters. The results of this task are shown in Figure 12.1.

TABLE 12.4 Individual Subject Result[a] [From Jackson and McClelland (1975) with permission of Academic Press and the authors.]

SUBJECT	SPEED	COMPREHENSION	EFFECTIVE READING SPEED	FREE LETTERS	REPORT WORDS	SENTENCES	THRESHOLD	OVERALL SPAN	UNRELATED LETTERS	FORCED CHOICE
JC	206	70	144	43	37	0	64.5	79	53	57
MS	242	85	206	86	83	40	54.0	94	47	82
MW	257	80	206	65	63	15	49.0	81	52	65
PS	299	70	210	41	36	0	50.5	77	50	68
EM	268	80	215	62	61	20	44.0	88	57	76
JS	286	90	260	66	66	20	54.5	88	59	79
Mean	260	79	207	61	58	16	52.7	85	53	71
MT	451	80	361	82	74	25	46.5	88	71	79
CG	525	80	420	78	70	15	50.5	73	63	75
SH	615	70	430	90	88	50	50.2	81	66	79
GS	528	90	475	93	89	45	57.0	88	66	79
FM	542	90	487	87	83	40	42.0	85	61	81
BG	855	90	769	93	87	50	49.5	92	57	83
Mean	586	83	490	87	82	39	49.3	85	64	79

[a] All numbers are percentage correct except Speed and Effective reading speed (words per minute) and Threshold (milliseconds).

Jackson and McClelland found that there were no differences between the average and slow readers in what they termed the *sensory tasks*. That is, on the single letter threshold task, thresholds for the two groups did not differ. Also, on the letter separation task, there was likewise no difference between the two groups. On all other tasks, however, there was a difference in favor of the fast readers. Jackson and McClelland concluded that breadth of field from which the reader can utilize visual information was approximately the same for the fast-reader group and the average-reader group. What apparently distinguishes the two groups is that faster readers are able to encode more of the contents of each fixation, whether or not higher order linguistic structure is present. The results of the study also suggested that differences in reading speed are not due to the reader's ability to infer or fill in missing information.

Jackson and McClelland's analysis that differences in reading speed were not due to basic sensory skills is consistent with what we have been arguing in this section. More recently, a large number of studies (Carr 1981; Graesser, Hoffman, and Clark, 1980; Jackson and McClelland 1979; Jackson 1980; Daneman and Carpenter 1980, 1983; Masson and Miller 1983; Frederiksen 1982; Palmer et al. 1985; Baddeley et al. 1985) have been undertaken to examine how relatively good readers may differ from each other in component skills related to reading. The primary approach taken by these different investigators has been to present subjects with a large battery of tests (as did Jackson and McClelland) and then to determine how the different tasks (and differences on these tasks) correlate with some measure of reading performance.

Rather than reviewing all of the types of tasks that have been used and the general outcome of each study, we will present the important points to be gleaned from this research. The tasks that have been used in these studies include tests of sensory functions, verbal and quantitative reasoning skills, memory span, listening comprehension, visual letter matching, lexical decision, naming, picture-sentence verification, semantic categorization, and so on. Among the important results that have emerged from this research are the following. First, reading performance on these various information processing tasks correlates rather well when words are used as stimuli but not so well when letters are used (Palmer et al. 1985). Second, reading speed and comprehension have different correlations with the information processing measures (Palmer et al. 1985; Jackson and McClelland 1979). This finding basically suggests that factors that affect reading speed may differ somewhat from those factors that affect comprehension processes. Third, much of the variability in reading speed appears to be due to the speed with which subjects can access memory codes for meaningful material as in word identification (Jackson and McClelland 1979; Jackson 1980). Fourth, much of the variability in comprehension processes appears to be related to working memory differences between fast and average readers (Baddeley et al. 1985; Daneman and Carpenter 1980, 1983; Masson and Miller 1983). For example, the research suggests that readers with small working memories devote so many resources to the decoding aspects of reading that they have less capacity for retaining earlier verbatim wording in working memory. Finally, while reading speed is only moderately correlated with listening comprehension, reading comprehension ability is apparently indistinguishable from listening comprehension ability (Palmer et al. 1985; Jackson and McClelland 1979).

In essence, the evidence from these studies dealing with individual differences suggests that good readers do not differ at the basic sensory or perceptual level in terms of what they perceive in a fixation [see Underwood and Zola (1986) for evidence showing that the perceptual span does not differ for good and poor readers]. Rather, the speed with which material can be encoded and accessed in memory appears to play a part in determining reading speed, and the size of working memory appears to play a role in determining comprehension processes. As such, these data do not imply that fast and average readers (all of whom we would want to categorize as relatively good readers) are doing vastly different things. Readers may use sophisticated strategies that help them remember things that they have read, and some may be more adept than others in using these strategies. When we examine individual differences in terms of on-line and immediate processing of text, it appears that almost all good readers are doing essentially the same thing; some may do it a bit slower (hence their reading speed will be slower) and some may not have as good working memory abilities (hence their comprehension will not be quite as good) as others. Yet, the bottom line is that there are many more similarities than differences and hence it is justifiable to try to construct a general model of the reading process. In the next, and final, chapter, we will discuss models of reading in an attempt to bring together the conclusions we have reached throughout the book.

SUMMARY

In this chapter, we discussed alternative types of "reading" such as speedreading, skimming, and proofreading. We also discussed individual differences in reading. With respect to speedreading, we concluded that people who read at very fast rates are primarily skimming the text, picking up the gist of what they are reading, as well as a few details. However, they are not able to get all of the detail from the text that normal readers do, and they are more willing than normal readers to accept the lowered comprehension that accompanies skimming.

In proofreading, the usual task is to look for spelling or grammatical mistakes, and to ensure that each sentence makes sense. However, most of the research on proofreading has used a visual search variant of the task in which subjects search for all instances of a given target letter or target word. We argued that the link between these types of tasks and reading is quite tenuous. The work on skimming and proofreading (as well as research in which readers are instructed to read for different purposes) does demonstrate that skilled readers are quite flexible in the range of reading, or readinglike, behaviors they can employ; they can modulate the "reading" speed as a function of their task or goal. Also, what they can comprehend from the passage will be influenced by the reading task or their goal; subjects reading for a specific type of information may not be able to remember much of what was unrelated to that which they were trying to acquire.

In the final section of the chapter, we reviewed research dealing with individual differences. There are clear individual differences in reading speed; some people read more slowly than others, and the slower readers make shorter saccades (or more fixations) and/or have longer fixations. However, in terms of basic perceptual processes, the data suggest that skilled readers are all doing pretty much the same thing. Readers undoubtedly use sophisticated strategies to help them remember what they have read, but the basic way in which information is initially encoded and processed is quite similar for all skilled readers. Thus we suspect that it is reasonable to attempt to specify a single general model of the process of reading that will be appropriate for virtually all skilled readers.

CHAPTER THIRTEEN
MODELS OF READING

Our goal in this final chapter is to pull some of the threads together and to summarize some of the things that we know about reading. Thoughout the book, we have concentrated on presenting you with what is really known about reading. In many cases, however, the data were incomplete or equivocal and so we summarized the best available evidence. When it was necessary, we provided some theoretical interpretation, and our interpretations have been guided by an implicit general theory of the reading process. However, in summarizing, we believe that it is useful to make this theory of reading more explicit. In order to place our theory in some context, we will briefly present examples of *top-down, bottom-up,* and *interactive* models of reading that have been proposed by others before presenting our model of reading.

TOP-DOWN MODELS

The primary characteristic of top-down models is that the "top" of the information-processing system, the part that is constructing the meaning of the passage, controls the information flow at all levels. We indicated in Chapter 1 that a major motivation for top-down models is a belief that the reader needs to overcome various bottlenecks in the processing system by using general world knowledge and contextual information from the passage being read to make hypotheses about what will come next during reading. The reader is generally seen as engaging in a cycle which involves the generation of an initial hypothesis of what will be read next, confirmation of the hypothesis by minimially sampling the visual information on the printed page, and then the generation of a new hypothesis about the next material to be encountered. One difficulty with this class of models is that their proponents have never been very explicit about what kinds of hypotheses are being entertained. But there are other problems as well.

The best-known top-down models of the reading process are those proposed by Goodman (1970) and Smith (1971). (While Goodman's model can also be viewed as an interactive model, it is virtually a top-down model because there is so little constraints on the interactions and because bottom-up processing plays such a minor role.) Figure 13.1 shows a flow-chart of the reading process according to Goodman. It is important to point out that the model was initially developed on the basis of Goodman's experience with beginning readers. As we saw in Chapter 10, children learning to read often engage in guessing behavior. However, our analysis (and that of many others as well) suggests that the highest level of reading skill (acquired around fourth or fifth grade) *does not* involve guessing behavior (or an over-reliance on contextual information) but rather quick and efficient analyses of the printed words (see Stanovich 1980). While Goodman's model was originally developed to account for how children learn to read, he considers it a model of skilled reading as well. Goodman concedes that there are differences between beginning and more skilled readers; however, he claims that the process is basically the same for both, involving a "selective, tentative anticipatory process" (i.e., hypothesizing what will come next), which is a central feature of the model.

As with all models of the reading process that we will consider, the processing sequence in Goodman's model begins with an eye fixation on new material. Notice that there are programs in long-term memory that are assumed to regulate word encoding. After the reader selects *graphic cues* from the field of vision, he or she uses this information to help formulate a *perceptual image* of part of the text. The selection of visual information is guided by a number of factors including the reader's strategies, cognitive style, and prior knowledge. The primary guide to the selection of visual information, however, is the contextual constraint imposed by the material previously analyzed (though how this contextual information guides selection of visual features is not very clear). The resulting perceptual image contains both what the reader sees and what he or she expected to see.

The next stage of the process is somewhat obscure. The reader searches his or her memory for related syntactic, semantic, and phonological cues and uses them to enrich the perceptual image. It is not clear to us how these types of cues can be related to a perceptual image unless the image is first identified as a sequence of letters or a word (e.g., how does

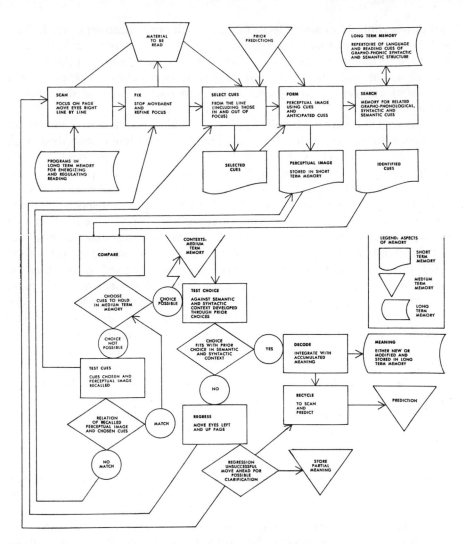

FIGURE 13-1 The Goodman (1970) model of reading. [Reproduced with permission of the National Council of Teachers of English and the author.]

knowing to expect a noun aid in identifying visual features?). This appears to be a problem since identification of the word occurs at a later stage (according to the model).

At this point in the sequence, the reader tries to make a tentative choice consistent with the graphic cues. (Although it is not made explicit in the model, the tentative choice is apparently a guess about the identity of one of the words in the text.) If the reader is successful in guessing the word, the resulting choice is held in something that Goodman refers to as *medium-term memory*. If the reader is not successful, he or she looks back to the earlier text. Once this choice has been made, it is tested against the prior context for grammatical and syntactic acceptability. If it fits in with the earlier material, its meaning is assimilated with prior meaning from the text and the results are stored in long-term memory. At this point, a hypothesis about the forthcoming text is made and the cycle is repeated. If the word is not consistent with the prior context, the reader makes a regressive eye movement and repeats the earlier operations until a suitable sequence of words is found.

As we have implied at various places in earlier chapters, this model has several weaknesses and shortcomings. The major problem is that, despite all of the boxes and arrows shown in Figure 13.1, it does not really specify much about the reading process. For example, it does not specify how the various nonvisual sources of information are drawn upon and used to modulate the formation of the perceptual image. Nor does it specify how the system deals with graphic cues that are repeated in successive fixations. At the word recognition level, the model lists some of the sources of information which might be used to make a tentative choice about the identity of the word, but it does not specify how this information is used to facilitate the choice and it does not indicate if some types of information are more important than other types. Similarly, processes beyond the level of word recognition are likewise very vague. Before checking that the identified word is compatible with prior context, it is necessary for the reader to parse and interpret the part of the sentence analyzed to date. However, the model makes no provisions for procedures of this kind nor does it give any hint as to how these procedures might work, nor does the model really explain how the meaning that is currently analyzed is assimilated with prior meaning.

This lack of precision is undoubtedly due, in part, to how little we know about how "higher-order" processes work (see chapters 7 and 8) and is a feature shared by all the models we discuss, including our own. However, this lack of precision is a particular problem for a model that relies so heavily on top-down mechanisms to explain the reading process. Thus, it is difficult to determine exactly what Goodman's model claims about the process of reading. However, as Mitchell (1982) pointed out, despite the overall lack of precision and clarity, the model is very clear on one point: reading is a predictive process. According to the model, the reader samples the print just enough to confirm his or her guess of what's coming and prior context strongly influences the earliest stages of processing, such as the selection of graphic cues, the formation of the perceptual image, and the initial identification of words. The evidence that we have presented throughout this book provides little support for these claims.

Bottom-Up Models

As we pointed out in Chapter 1, bottom-up models generally argue that processing is very fast and that information flows through the processing system in a series of stages. The basic idea is that visual information is initially sampled from the printed page and the information is transformed through a series of stages with little (if any) influence from general world knowledge, contextual information, or higher order processing strategies.

Models proposed by Massaro (1975), LaBerge and Samuels (1974), and by Mackworth (1972) are often cited as bottom-up models of the reading process. However, neither the Massaro model nor the LaBerge and Samuels model are comprehensive models of the reading process and the Mackworth model has not really attracted much attention. (In addition, the Massaro model really has significant interactive aspects.) The most comprehensive bottom-up model of reading (and the one that has been the most influential) was proposed by Gough (1972). In the first stage (see Figure 13.2), visual information around the fixation point is entered into iconic memory where it remains available until the reader makes another fixation. The information in the iconic buffer is used as raw material for the purpose of identifying the letters in the word. This recognition process operates serially (from left to right) across the display so that processing is letter by letter. During the course of this process, the device responsible for letter recognition (the Scanner) consults pattern recognition routines stored in long-term memory. The string of letters from the words in the center of vision are placed in a Character Register and immediately operated on by a mechanism (the Decoder) which maps characters onto a string of systematic phonemes, which are hypothetical entities that are systematically related to speech but are capable of being set up much more rapidly than speech itself. The Decoder makes use of a Code Book of grapheme-phoneme correspondence rules and the end products of the process are stored temporarily in a form analogous to a tape recording (inner speech).

The phonemic representation, supplemented by reference to the Lexicon, is used to identify the fixated words, and they are held in Primary Memory (short-term memory) until the sentence can be parsed and placed in a more permanent storage called TPWSGWTAU ("the place where sentences go when they are understood"). The comprehension device makes use of syntactic and semantic rules in the course of understanding the sentence. Gough called this device "Merlin" to emphasize that it had magical properties (or at least that the properties were difficult to specify). The remainder of the model was designed to account for oral reading and consists of stages involved in producing the vocal response in oral reading. Gough's model, like Goodman's, has several weaknesses. Unlike Goodman, however, Gough has recognized many of these limitations [see Gough, (1985) and Gough and Cosky (1977)] and acknowledged where he was wrong on certain key points (Gough 1985).

What are the limitations of the original model? First, as in Goodman's model, there is no provision for dealing with letters that are processed on more than one fixation. As Mitchell (1982) pointed out, duplication of this kind would cause great confusion to the processing system if the model were interpreted literally. However, Gough was correct in his assessment of the size of the perceptual span (note that the model was proposed before

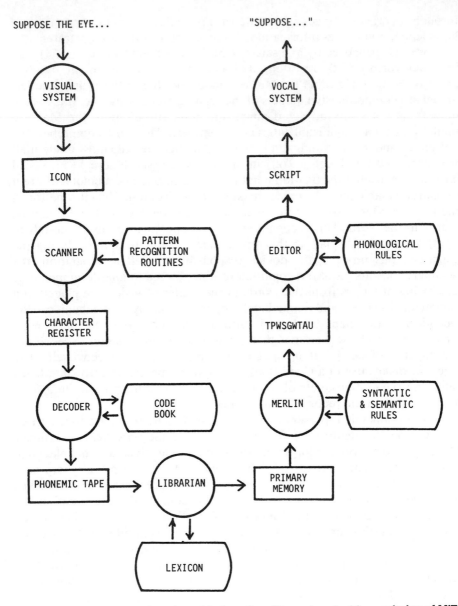

FIGURE 13-2 **The Gough (1972) model of reading. [Reproduced with permission of MIT Press.]**

the moving window experiments were conducted). Second, again like Goodman, the model says little about how eye movements are controlled in reading. Gough did suggest that difficulties in parsing might cause fixations to be prolonged or might lead to regressions being made (or both), but these proposals are not represented in the flow diagram of the model. The model does not consider the possibility that eye movements might be influenced by other aspects of processing, and it says nothing about how normal forward saccades are guided. Third, the model does not really deal with how higher-order comprehension processes (such as integrating sentences and propositions together) take place, and the role of inference is unclear. Finally, the model has often been criticized because of the lack of flexibility that is attributed to the reader. The reader has no choice of operations or strategies to use in different reading tasks and has little freedom to vary the sequence of operations in any way (Mitchell 1982).

In addition to the weaknesses mentioned above, subsequent research has indicated that several aspects of the original model were incorrect. For example, it is clear that the phonemic route to the lexicon is not the only one that is available to the reader. It is likewise clear that the individual letters of a word are not processed in a serial left-to-right fashion.

Despite these difficulties, Gough deserves a great deal of credit for stimulating a lot of research on reading. The major virtue of the model was that it made very clear predictions, predictions that could be tested—and have been. Much of the research stimulated by the model, ironically, has served to highlight the weaknesses of the model. But unlike top-down models of reading like those of Goodman (1970) and Smith (1971), which are so vague as to be untestable, Gough was very clear in stating what he thought was happening during reading. As a result, we have learned much more about reading from this model than from the top-down models. Finally, we would also like to note that Gough presented his model when the top-down models of the reading process were very much in vogue and argued that context plays a rather minor role in lexical access long before it became at all fashionable to do so.

Interactive Models

Interactive models have a great deal of currency at the moment in cognitive psychology. In interactive models, readers are usually assumed to be drawing upon both top-down and bottom-up information before eventually settling upon an interpretation of the text. Perhaps the most frequently cited examples of interactive models of reading are those of Rumelhart (1977) and McClelland (1986). Figure 13.3 shows Rumelhart's model. We shall not describe it in much detail because in our opinion it is not a comprehensive model of the reading process (which Rumelhart acknowledged). While the model gives a reasonable account of how context and the reader's expectations can influence the reading process, it says nothing about the basis on which various kinds of hypotheses are generated nor does

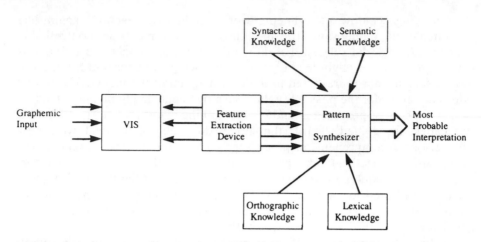

FIGURE 13-3 The Rumelhart (1977) interactive model of reading. [Reprinted by permission of Lawrence Erlbaum Associates.]

it specify the relative importance of the contribution of the various knowledge sources (syntactic, semantic, orthographic, and lexical) depicted in Figure 13.3. Moreover, the model says nothing about the control of eye movements, the phonological route in word recognition, backup strategies used in word recognition, or comprehension issues beyond the level of the sentence. However, Rumelhart's primary goal was to provide a framework for the development of models that are alternatives to the serial flow-chart models (like those of Gough, Mackworth, and Massaro) and that place more emphasis on highly interactive parallel processing mechanisms. The more recent McClelland model builds on the Rumelhart model and does include a mechanism to partially account for eye movements and how information is integrated across fixations, but it is still not a comprehensive model of the reading process.

A comprehensive model of the reading process that is primarily interactive in flavor has been presented by Just and Carpenter (1980). Figure 13.4 shows a diagram of this model. As in the Goodman and Gough models, the processing sequence begins during an eye fixation. The Get Next Input stage is quite short and follows from a decision to move the eyes to a new location if all necessary processing has been completed. Just and Carpenter suggested that this decision is made when a list of conditions has been fulfilled. A general condition is that the meaning of the word must be accessed, while a more specific condition might be that the word is transferred to working memory. When all of the processing associated with the fixated word is completed, the Get Next Input stages moves the eyes

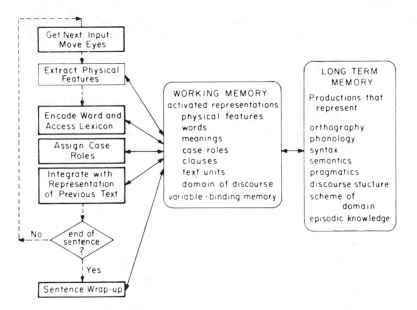

FIGURE 13-4 The Just and Carpenter (1980) model of reading. (Solid lines denote data-flow paths, and dashed lines indicate canonical flow of control.) (Reprinted with permission of the American Psychological Association and the authors.)

forward one or two words and processing of the next fixated word begins (initially involving the extraction of physical features).

In the Encode Word and Access Lexicon stages, the word is perceptually encoded and the underlying concept is activated. The concept serves as a "pointer" to locate a more precise meaning representation. Assign Case Roles (or determining the syntactic function of words) is the first of the processes that determine relationships among words. This stage of processing includes a clausal segmentation procedure, since case assignments are made within clauses.

Another important component of the model is the integration process, since clauses and sentences must be related to each other by the reader to capture the coherence of the text. There are two major places where integration can occur. First, when each word is encountered, an attempt is made to relate it to previous information. The second is a running clause interpretation, which is updated as each word of the clause is read. Readers use two basic strategies to integrate old and new information. First, readers can check to see if new information is related to information already in working memory (this might entail trying to relate new information to a topic already active in working memory). A second strategy, which takes longer than the first, is to search for explicitly marked old information (as in a relative clause). It is during this stage that errors of interpretation are encountered and corrections are attempted. Readers do not, however, usually have to go back to the beginning of the sentence to reinterpret it. Rather, they use heuristics that allow them to detect the error more efficiently.

In the Sentence Wrap-up stage, the reader attempts to resolve any inconsistencies within the sentence and to search for referents that have not been assigned. Since the ends of sentences indicate that one thought has ended and another is to begin, the reader knows that this is an appropriate place to attempt integration. However, readers may also do some wrap-up at the ends of clauses or at the ends of units larger than a sentence.

Perhaps the most important aspect of the Just and Carpenter model is the concept of a "production system." A *production system* is a formalism in which procedural knowledge is embodied in a set of *condition-action* rules. (The production systems are presumably stored in long-term memory.) The *condition* part specifies what elements should be present in (or absent from) working memory to enable an *action*. For example, one parsing production specifies that if an article (*the, an,* or *a*) has been encoded (condition), a slot for a noun phrase should be established (action). According to Just and Carpenter, productions are executed in *recognize-act cycles.* On each cycle, the contents of working memory are assessed and all productions whose conditions are satisfied are executed concurrently, thereby modifying the contents of working memory. Then the new contents of working memory are assessed and another cycle occurs, and so on. A central aspect of the model is that a production executes as soon as working memory contains sufficient information to enable it (rather than holding information in working memory until an executive decides what to do with it). This assumption is what leads to the "immediacy hypothesis," discussed in Chapter 5. Another important point about the Just and Carpenter model is that several productions may fire at the same time, meaning that several computations may occur concurrently.

Not everyone would agree that the Just and Carpenter model is truly an interactive model, since the basic information flow appears to be basically bottom-up unless errors of processing are detected. However, top-down processes do influence bottom-up ones, and the model allows for any stage to be influenced by any stage executed earlier or simultaneously. This point, together with the idea that several productions can fire at the same time, plus the fact that there are lots of interactions—between the processing stages (on the left of Figure 13.4) and working memory and between working memory and long-term memory—leads us to categorize it as an interactive model.

While the Just and Carpenter model has several virtues and is able to explain many phenomena of reading (see Just and Carpenter 1987), it also has some weaknesses. It is somewhat ironic that much of the criticism of the model has come from eye movement researchers (Fisher and Shebilske 1984; Hogaboam and McConkie 1981; Kliegl, Olson, and Davidson 1983;

Slowiaczek 1983), since much of the model is based on how long readers look at words serving different functions in text (i.e., gaze duration data). One criticism is that the model does not give sufficient attention to how eye movements are controlled or to parafoveal processing of words. Related to that is the criticism that the 50 msec estimate of the duration of the Get Next Input stage (i.e., the eye movement latency) may be too short (see Chapter 5). In addition, there is evidence that higher-order processing spills over from one fixation to the next (thus violating the immediacy assumption). Many of these criticisms have been dealt with by Just and Carpenter (see Carpenter and Just 1983; Just and Carpenter 1986; Thibadeau, Just and Carpenter 1982) in subsequent updates of the original model.

The major criticism of current interactive models is that it is not clear what they predict in advance about various types of processes during reading. That is, they can account for all sorts of data (and many of the models involve various types of computer simulations that can mimic human performance), but the extent to which they can provide a clear prediction of the outcome of an experiment is very uncertain (in contrast to bottom-up models, which often provide clear predictions). To a certain extent, this criticism is unfair because it may well be that many of the complex processes that occur during reading will be impenetrable to psychological experimentation. But the traditional tests of a model in experimental psychology have always been how well the model can predict behavior (as well as explain it), how much research it generates. While interactive models are very good at explaining behavior, it is yet an open question as to how well they will predict and how much research they will generate.

Our Model of Reading

We have been quite critical in our evaluation of models of the reading process. Before presenting our model, let us clarify a few points. First, many of the criticisms directed at the other models can be directed at ours (especially our vagueness about higher-order processes). The model we will present reflects out theoretical biases and how we interpret the majority of the evidence on the reading process. Second, we are not particularly tied to this model as THE TRUTH ABOUT READING. Instead, we see the model as a (temporary) working model or convenient way of summarizing the evidence that we place the most credence in. Thus, we view the model as part of the process of understanding reading and the criticism we just discussed in connection with interactive models is valid for our model; it summarizes our way of viewing reading rather than making explicit predictions. As we continue to learn more about the reading process, we will refine the model (as will proponents of other models) until we (and they) hone in on one that accurately captures all of the facts about reading. When that happens, we will have understood reading. However, given the complexity of the reading process, it would probably take an entire book to describe such a model.

As we indicated in Chapter 1, our model is primarily a bottom-up model, but top-down processes do interact with the bottom-up processes. All of the models that we have considered have their strengths and weaknesses as we have indicated. We suspect that making the relationship between eye movements and other processing explicit is a strength of our model. What we will present here is a sketch, and thus we could be easily criticized for the lack of detail in the model. In our defense, many of the details can be found in other chapters and thus the model is, in some sense, distributed through the book. However, like all models, ours will be somewhat vague about the role of higher-order processes. In essence, we see the model as a way of determining which aspects of reading we are secure of in our understanding, as well as identifying those aspects of the reading process where our understanding is weak.

The various components that are shown in Figure 13.5 represent different aspects of the reading process. Notice that *saccade* and *eye fixation* are circles to mark them as observable behaviors which can be distinguished from processing activities (represented as boxes) or from memory structures (working memory and long-term memory). Working memory involves three components or modules: (1) a module that holds inner speech; (2) a syntactic parser; and (3) a thematic processing module. Long-term memory has three components of interest: (1) the lexicon; (2) real-world knowledge, of which (3) the text representation (which is the product of what has been read) is a part. We should note that the components of working memory and of long-term memory which are included in Figure 13.5 do not exhaust the subcomponents of each structure; they merely represent those components that are most important for reading.

As in the other models we have considered, the processing sequence begins during an eye fixation with the initial encoding of the printed words. The initial encoding process can be thought of as two separate processes occurring in parallel, *foveal word processing* and *parafoveal processing*. The former process is concerned with processing the letters (in parallel) in the word that the eyes are fixated on. Parafoveal processing involves extracting visual information to the right of fixation: word and letter information, and word length information that is used in determining where to look next. The size of the perceptual span, or region of effective processing, is determined by these processing activities and (as we described in Chapter 4) this region extends from the beginning of the currently fixated word to about 15 character spaces to the right of fixation.

Turning our attention to the fixated word, *lexical access* takes place. While lexical access occurs subsequent to the initial registration of visual information, it may occur very rapidly, especially if it is aided by a parafoveal preview of the letter information from the prior fixation. Lexical access can proceed via one of two routes, a direct route from the printed letters (indicated by the digit *1* in Figure 13.5) or an indirect route involving the application of rules and/or analogies to create an auditory code (indicated by the digits *2* and *3* in Figure 13.5). As we indicated in chapters 3 and

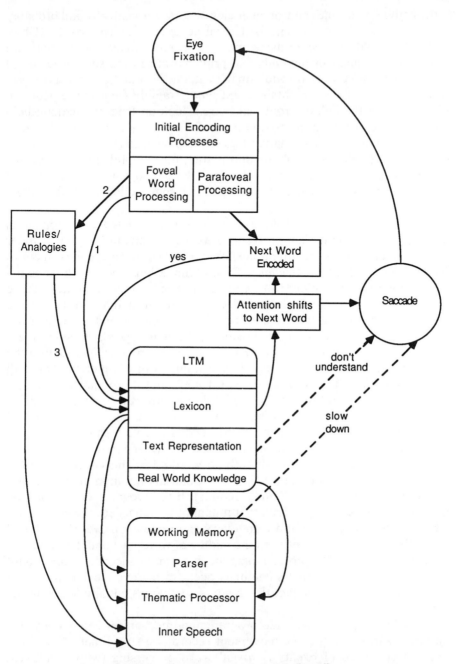

FIGURE 13-5 Our current model of reading.

6, the activation of rules and/or analogies occurs automatically and probably serves as a subsidiary system for lexical access of familiar words. (Obviously, it would be the primary means for recognizing words that are relatively infrequent or unfamiliar in print but are in the spoken lexicon.) The meaning of the word (in addition to syntactic information such as its part of speech) is presumably obtained extremely rapidly from the lexicon. In addition, both the indirect route and direct look-up from the lexicon help activate an acoustic representation (as well as activity in the speech tract), which we characterized in Chapter 6 as *inner speech*. Inner speech is used as a system for temporarily holding information for comprehension processes because it holds a sequential and relatively literal record of the recently read information in working memory (possibly with some added intonations from speech).

When lexical access of the fixated word is completed, attention shifts to the next word to the right of fixation. As we outlined in Chapter 5, under normal circumstances the attention shift is followed by an eye movement to the next word in the text. Because of acuity limitations, most of the time the word to the right of fixation (word $n+1$) cannot be identified and the saccade brings the fovea to the preferred viewing location in that word. But the letters at the beginning of word $n+1$ have been processed and identified in an abstract code and this prior processing of the word speeds its subsequent identification. However, word $n+1$ will sometimes be identified before the next saccade can take place (as we also outlined in Chapter 5). This will produce another attention shift (to word $n+2$) and a program for another saccade being set up (for word $n+2$) while the program for the saccade to word $n+1$ was still being programmed. Under these circumstances, parallel programming of saccades occurs. If the second attention shift occurs early enough in the current fixation, the program for a saccade to word $n+1$ can be aborted and the eye will move directly to word $n+2$. This cancelling of the first saccade is not without cost, however, and the duration of the fixation will be increased (by about 30 milliseconds). If the program for the saccade to word $n+1$ is far enough along that it cannot be cancelled, the reader will either fixate on word $n+1$ and with a very short latency move to word $n+2$ or will fixate somewhere between the middle of word $n+1$ and the middle of word $n+2$. This parallel programming mechanism for saccades can account for very short fixations that sometimes occur in the eye movement record during reading and for the fact that readers sometimes initially fixate on the end of a word.

While the parallel saccade programming mechanism can account for important aspects of the eye movement record, we stress that most of the time the sequence of events is foveal word processing (with parafoveal processing occurring in parallel), lexical access, attention shift to the next word, saccade to the next word, and the cycle starts again (with the preview benefit useful in speeding the initial foveal processing).

When lexical access is completed, not only does attention shift to the next word, but the meaning of the currently fixated word is integrated into an ongoing text representation which is being built in working memory. If for some reason the word is difficult to integrate into this microstructure, the eye may remain in the current fixation. Thus both lexical access (if the word is infrequent, the eye will remain on it) and text integration processes can influence how long a reader looks at a word. Often, when the word is difficult to access or integrate, the reader will make a second fixation on the word. (Occasionally, even more than two fixations are made on a word.) When these kinds of processing difficulties occur, the normal processing cycle (with respect to the relationship between lexical access and eye movements) is also disrupted.

Turning now to the higher-level components of the model, working memory is conceptualized as having various subcomponents that are used in comprehending text. The inner speech mechanism is part of working memory and it serves to hold an ordered and relatively literal record of what has been read. Thus readers experiencing difficulty comprehending can either consult the inner speech representation or simply look back in the text. The other two major subcomponents of working memory operate on the output from the lexicon to structure a syntactic representation (the parser) and to provide an ongoing semantic representation (the thematic processor).

The parsing device parses strings of words into their appropriate syntactic constituents. It uses parsing strategies such as *minimal attachment* and *late closure,* which we described in Chapter 7. The parser receives input from the lexicon about the syntactic class of each word as it is read, and, on the basis of this information, constructs a syntactic representation. In general, the parser constructs only one syntactic representation of a sentence and does so quite quickly after lexical access. However, when the word itself is syntactically ambiguous (e.g., the word can be either a noun or a verb) and the parse of the sentence up to that point allows either interpretation, it appears that construction of the parse is delayed until disambiguating syntactic information is processed.

While the parsing device parses strings of words into syntactic constituents, the thematic processor monitors the semantic content of the text by examining alternative thematic interpretations and selecting the semantically and pragmatically most plausible one. The thematic processor has available to it real-world pragmatic information as well as information that came earlier in the text. As we suggested in Chapter 7, the thematic processor operates somewhat independently from the parser in that it operates on output from the parser and can order the parser to recompute, but it does not have the ability to share its information to help the parser do its job. Thus the parser will sometimes be "garden-pathed" because it computes only the structurally preferred analysis of a sentence and ignores pragmatic and contextual information. When the thematic processor detects that the syntactic parsing is inconsistent with either pragmatic or with prior contextual information, a signal is sent to the ongoing eye movement control system to relinquish control. This results in the reader either making a number of fixations in the same region of the text or making a regression. The detection of an anomaly by the thematic processor also results in the parser engaging in reanalysis. Sometimes the reader will look back to the point of ambiguity; other times, as the parser consults information currently in working memory, the reanalysis takes place without the eyes moving back. In either case, reanalysis is usually selective and does not necessitate back-tracking through the text, since the reader knows the point at which he or she went wrong.

At this point, exactly what happens gets quite obscure. We have said something about what happens when there is an inconsistency between the output of the parser and the output of the thematic processor. What happens when the output is consistent (which is most of the time)? What is in working memory would be the meaning (or meanings) of individual words, together with a syntactic parse of the sentence (or sentence fragment, if the reader has not finished the sentence) and an acoustic representation from inner speech (which may be trailing behind the other processes a bit). We have little idea of when or how this all gets converted to "meaning." There are somewhat conflicting hints about when meaning is constructed. Prior context appears to disambiguate the meanings of ambiguous words in less than half a second, so one might assume that construction of meaning in working memory is reasonably on-line and does not usually wait for the end of a clause or sentence. However, these rapid effects of context may be a result of excitation and inhibition within the lexicon (related to priming) and not the result of "higher-order" processes operating on working memory (see Chapter 7). On the other hand, effects of meaning on syntactic interpretation seem to be often delayed (the effects mainly being seen on "second-pass" times), so that the construction of meaning appears to wait for at least some syntactic units to be constructed (see Chapter 7). Our best guess is that the construction of meaning is not likely to be immediate most of the time, since it may need to have the results of the syntactic parse before certain kinds of decisions are made.

As you can see, we are getting into deeper and deeper water. We haven't really said what construction of meaning is. Does it involve some sort of analysis into component propositions (or other units of meaning) as Kintsch and van Dijk postulate? Does it involve some sort of active linking operation to create a microstructure? Where and when do editing routines come into play (if they do so at all) in order to create the gist, causal structure, and so forth? Presumably some aspects of this comprehension process often control how long words or propositions stay in working memory (as with the "leading edge strategy" of Kintsch and van Dijk) and how they get tied into preexisting mental structures. Whether the primary thrust of all this activity is at the low level of linking propositions with common arguments, at the higher level of creating a causal structure, creating a mental model, or fitting current material into a schema is still quite uncertain. The work on anaphor and inference suggests that some of the work of construction is done by highlighting certain aspects of text that appear likely to be followed up on (as with causal inference). However, most of the work appears to be done either at the point at which the inference absolutely has to be made or at the point an anaphoric link has to be created in order for the text to remain coherent. Here again, the suggestion is that the inference is not made immediately but at some time within the phrase or clause (see Chapter 8).

When these inferences are not successfully made, the signal of "don't understand" is sent to the eye movement system; then either a regression is executed, or the eye may hold in place while working memory is interrogated in order to come up with an alternate interpretation. The latter process may also involve searching long-term memory, as when reinstatement of an earlier proposition is necessary (see Chapter 8). Syntactic misparsing seems to be able to send information to the eye movement system within a quarter of a second (see Chapter 7); it seems reasonable to assume that semantic problems can be communicated about as quickly to the eye movement system. Whether the comprehension process also slows down the eye when its computations are correct but running too far behind lexical access is an open question. Such a mechanism would, however, seem likely in beginning readers.

To summarize, the situation is pretty murky after we leave the lexicon. Processing is probably quite interactive (although syntactic processing is very likely prior to most of the semantic construction) and reasonably on-line (although most of the semantic processing probably lags behind the eye by at least one fixation). Unfortunately, it is premature to draw any more definite conclusions than that about how semantic processing works or what it constructs.

How are readers likely to differ? First, let us consider variation among the population that would be considered "skilled readers." We think there is likely to be little difference among skilled readers in the way the early processing is done, although there is evidence that there are differences in the speed of lexical access and the relative weight placed on the direct and indirect routes (Baron and Strawson 1976). In addition, there is little evidence that skilled readers differ in the size of their perceptual spans. In contrast, there are undoubtedly marked differences among skilled readers in both their overall knowledge and in their comprehension strategies. Similarly, an individual reader will differ similarly from text to text, depending on his or her knowledge of the "world" which the text is describing. While it has been clearly demonstrated that what a person knows about a topic will influence their comprehension (Chiesi, Spilich, and Voss 1979), it is less clear whether readers also differ markedly in their strategies of parsing text.

How does the reading process change for skilled readers when they skim as opposed to read carefully? There is little hard information on this. We assume that lexical access is pretty much the same in the two conditions, but the details of higher-order processing must differ considerably. While it is often assumed that readers fill in a lot of the details when they skim, Just, Carpenter, and Masson's (1982) data suggest that much of the detail is just lost. The exact nature of the filling-in process in skimming is not clear. For example, do readers attempt to fill in everything on the basis of accessing key content words, or do they read small areas carefully and then skip over relatively large areas of text until they stop to "graze" at another important area? We suspect that the latter mechanism is more prevalent.

Is the basic mechanism of reading different for children? The evidence indicates by the time children reach the fifth grade (and probably well before that), they are reading just about like adults. By the fourth grade and as long as they are reading easy text, their perceptual span appears to be the same as adults. It appears (see chapters 9 and 10) that the process of lexical access develops over time, involving the need for more careful visual analysis of the stimulus as well as phonological awareness to fully involve the indirect route. The fact that developing this route seems to be so closely involved with developing the skill of reading suggests to us that the indirect route is quite important even in skilled reading (contrary to some current beliefs). Of course, children will differ markedly from adults in terms of the amount of knowledge they have or in terms of their comprehension strategies (e.g., they are often oblivious to the characters' motivations in stories).

Do people with reading difficulties differ qualitatively from normal readers? Most of the research has involved people with lexical access problems, so we can't say very much about differences in "higher-order" processes. Presumably children who, by having low IQs, are excluded from the category "dyslexia" have less real-world knowledge, less accessible real-world knowledge, poorer comprehension strategies, or some combination of the three. For the adult *acquired dyslexic* readers, much of the interest has been focused on readers who have either a damaged "direct" or "indirect" route to the lexicon, although there are of course other categories of acquired dyslexia as well. Whether *developmental dyslexics* can be similarly categorized is an open question. Some exhibit symptoms similar to *surface dyslexics* (i.e., those who use only the indirect route), but we doubt that the acquired dyslexia syndromes will provide more than a rough guide for the problems in developmental dyslexia. While much of developmental dyslexia does appear to relate to difficulty in accessing sound codes, there are other linguistic and nonlinguistic problems as well.

FINAL THOUGHTS

We would like to end with a final note about models and theoretical development. In this book, we have provided you with an overview of important subcomponents of the reading process. While we acknowledge the importance of putting all of the information together to have an overall model of the reading process, it is also our suspicion that the greatest advances in understanding reading will come through researchers working on each subcomponent process. In other words, we suspect that great breakthroughs in understanding reading will not come from a group of researchers proposing an overall model of the reading process that explains everything about reading. Rather, as we understand each of the component processes in reading better, we will be able to put them together to understand the "big picture." Certainly, the past 20 years of research on reading attests to the fact that cognitive psychology is a cumulative science and that each small step we make in understanding some aspect of reading puts us one step closer to solving the fascinating puzzle of how the mind works during reading.

REFERENCES

AARONS, L. 1971. Subvocalization: Aural and EMG feedback in reading. *Perceptual and Motor Skills, 33,* 271–306.

AARONSON, D., and FERRES, S. 1984. The word-by-word reading paradigm: An experimental and theoretical approach. In D. Kieras and M. Just (eds.), *New methods in reading comprehension research.* Hillsdale, NJ: Erlbaum.

AARONSON, D., and SCARBOROUGH, H. S. 1976. Performance theories for sentence coding: Some quantitative evidence. *Journal of Experimental Psychology: Human Perception and Performance, 2,* 56–70.

ABRAMS, S. G., and ZUBER, B. L. 1972. Some temporal characteristics of information processing during reading. *Reading Research Quarterly, 8,* 40–51.

ADAMS, M. J. 1979. Models of word recognition. *Cognitive Psychology, 11,* 133–176.

ADLER-GRINBERG, D., and STARK, L. 1978. Eye movements, scan paths and dyslexia. *American Journal of Optometry and Physiological Optics, 55,* 557–570.

ALBA, J. W., and HASHER, L. 1983. Is memory schematic? *Psychological Bulletin, 93,* 203–231.

ALBERT, M. 1975. Cerebral dominance and reading habits. *Nature, 256,* 403–404.

ALEGRIA, J., PIGNOT, E., and MORAIS, J. 1982. Phonetic analysis of speech and memory codes in beginning readers. *Memory & Cognition, 10,* 451–456.

ALLETON, V. 1970. L'Ecriture Chinoise. *Que Sais-je?, 1374,* Paris: Presses Universitaries de France.

ALLPORT, D. A. 1977. On knowing the meaning of words we are unable to report: The effects of visual masking. In S. Dornic (ed.), *Attention and performance VI.* Hillsdale, NJ: Erlbaum.

ANDERSON, A., GARROD, S., and SANFORD, A. J. 1983. The accessibility of pronominal antecedents as a function of episode shifts in narrative text. *Quarterly Journal of Experimental Psychology, 35A,* 427–440.

ANDERSON, J. R., and BOWER, G. H. 1973. *Human associative memory*. Washington, DC: Winston.

ANDERSON, R. C., and ORTONY, A. 1975. On putting apples in bottles: A problem of polysemy. *Cognitive Psychology, 7,* 167–180.

ANDERSON, R. C., and PICHERT, J. W. 1978. Recall of previously unrecallable information following a shift in perspective. *Journal of Verbal Learning and Verbal Behavior, 17,* 1–12.

ANDRIESSEN, J. J., and DEVOOGD, A. H. 1973. Analysis of eye movement patterns in silent reading. *IPO Annual Progress Report, 8,* 29–35.

ANTES, J. R. 1974. The time course of picture viewing. *Journal of Experimental Psychology, 103,* 62–70.

ANTES, J. R., and PENLAND, J. G. 1981. Picture context effects on eye movement patterns. In D. F. Fisher, R. A. Monty, and J. W. Senders (eds.), *Eye movements: Cognition and visual perception*. Hillsdale, NJ: Erlbaum.

ARNETT, J. L. and DILOLLO, V. 1979. Visual information processing in relation to age and to reading ability. *Journal of Experimental Child Psychology, 27,* 143–152.

ARNOLD, D., and TINKER, M. A. 1939. The fixation pause of the eyes. *Journal of Experimental Psychology, 25,* 271–280.

AUSUBEL, D. P. 1960. The use of advance organizers in the learning and retention of meaningful verbal material. *Journal of Educational Psychology, 51,* 266–274.

AYRES, T. J. 1984. Silent reading time for tongue-twister paragraphs. *American Journal of Psychology, 97,* 605–609.

BACKMAN, J. E. 1983. Psycholinguistic skills and reading acquisition: A look at early readers. *Reading Research Quarterly, 18,* 466–479.

BACKMAN, J. E., BRUCK, M., HEBERT, M., and SEIDENBERG, M. S. 1984. Acquisition and use of spelling and sound correspondences in reading. *Journal of Experimental Child Psychology, 38,* 114–133.

BACKMAN, J. E., MAMEN, M., and FERGUSON, H. B. 1984. Reading level design: Conceptual and methodological issues in reading research. *Psychological Bulletin, 96,* 560–568.

BADDELEY, A. D. 1979. Working memory and reading. In P. A. Kolers, M. E. Wrolstad, and H. Bouma (eds.), *Processing of visible language* (Vol. 1). New York: Plenum.

BADDELEY, A. D., ELDRIDGE, M., and LEWIS, V. J. 1981. The role of subvocalization in reading. *Quarterly Journal of Experimental Psychology, 33A,* 439–454.

BADDELEY, A. D., ELLIS, N. C., MILES, T. R., and LEWIS, V. J. 1982. Developmental and acquired dyslexia: A comparison. *Cognition, 11,* 185–199.

BADDELEY, A. D., and HITCH, G. 1974. Working memory. In G. Bower (ed.), *The psychology of learning and motivation* (Vol. 8). New York: Academic Press.

BADDELEY, A. D., and LEWIS, V. 1981. Inner active processes in reading: The inner voice, the inner ear, and the inner eye. In A. M. Lesgold and C. A. Perfetti (eds.), *Interactive processes in reading*. Hillsdale, NJ: Erlbaum.

BADDELEY, A. D., LOGIE, R., NIMMO-SMITH, I., and BRERETON, N. 1985. Components of fluent reading. *Journal of Memory and Language, 24,* 119–131.

BADDELEY, A. D., THOMSON, N., and BUCHANAN, M. 1975. Word length and the structure of short-term-memory. *Journal of Verbal Learning and Verbal Behavior, 14,* 538–548.

BAGGETT, P. 1975. Memory for explicit and implicit information in picture stories. *Journal of Verbal Learning and Verbal Behavior, 14,* 538–548.

BAKER, L., and BROWN, A. L. 1984. Metacognitive skills and reading. In Pearson, P. D., Barr, R., Kamil, M. L. and Mosenthal, P. (eds.), *Handbook of reading research*. New York: Longman.

BAKKER, D. J. 1972. *Temporal order in disturbed reading: Developmental and neuropsychological aspects in normal and reading-retarded children*. Rotterdam: Rotterdam University Press.

BALOTA, D. A. 1983. Automatic semantic activation and episodic memory encoding. *Journal of Verbal Learning and Verbal Behavior, 22,* 88–104.

BALOTA, D. A., and CHUMBLEY, J. I. 1984. Are lexical decisions a good measure of lexical access? The role of word frequency in the neglected decision stage. *Journal of Experimental Psychology: Human Perception and Performance, 10,* 340–357.

BALOTA, D. A., and CHUMBLEY, J. I. 1985. The locus of word-frequency effects in the pronunciation task: Lexical access and/or production? *Journal of Memory and Language, 24,* 89–106.

BALOTA, D. A., POLLATSEK, A., and RAYNER, K. 1985. The interaction of contextual constraints and parafoveal visual information in reading. *Cognitive Psychology, 17,* 364–390.

BALOTA, D. A., and RAYNER, K. 1983. Parafoveal visual information and semantic contextual constraints. *Journal of Experimental Psychology: Human Perception and Performance, 8,* 726–738.

BANKS, W. P., OKA, E., and SHUGARMAN, S. 1981. Recoding of printed words to internalize speech: Does recoding come before lexical access? In O. J. L. Tzeng and H. Singer (eds.), *Perception of print.* Hillsdale, NJ: Erlbaum.

BARON, J. 1973. Phonemic stage not necessary for reading. *Quarterly Journal of Experimental Psychology, 25,* 241–246.

BARON, J. 1979. Orthographic and word specific mechanisms in children's reading of words. *Child Development, 50,* 60–72.

BARON, J., and STRAWSON, C. 1976. Use of orthograhic and word-specific knowledge in reading words aloud. *Journal of Experimental Psychology: Human Perception and Performance, 2,* 386–393.

BARON, J., and THURSTON, I. 1973. An analysis of the word superiority effect. *Cognitive Psychology, 4,* 207–228.

BARON, J., and TREIMAN, R. 1980. Use of orthography in reading and learning to read. In J. F. Kavanagh and R. L. Venezky (eds.), *Orthography, reading, and dyslexia.* Baltimore: University Park Press.

BARON, J., TREIMAN, R., FREYD, J., and KELLMAN, P. 1980. Spelling and reading by rules. In U. Frith (ed.), *Cognitive processes in spelling.* London: Academic Press.

BARR, R. 1974. The effect of instruction on pupil's reading strategies. *Reading Research Quarterly, 10,* 555–582.

BARRON, R. W. 1981a. The development of visual word recognition: A review. In G. E. MacKinnon and T. G. Waller (eds.), *Reading research: Advances in theory and practice* (Vol. 3). New York: Academic Press.

BARRON, R. W. 1981b. Reading skill and reading strategies. In A. M. Lesgold and C. A. Perfetti (eds.), *Interactive processes in reading.* Hillsdale, NJ: Erlbaum.

BARRON, R. W. 1986. Word recognition in early reading: A review of the direct and indirect access hypothesis. *Cognition, 24,* 93–119.

BARRON, R. W., and BARON, J. 1977. How children get meaning from printed words. *Child Development, 48,* 587–594.

BAUER, D., and STANOVICH, K. E. 1980. Lexical access and the spelling-to-sound regularity effect. *Memory & Cognition, 8,* 424–432.

BEAUVOIS, M. F., and DEROUESNE, J. 1979. Phonological alexia: Three dissociations. *Journal of Neurology, Neurosurgery and Psychiatry, 42,* 1115–1124.

BECK, I. L. 1981. Reading problems and instructional practices. In G. E. MacKinnon and T. G. Waller (eds.), *Reading research: Advances in theory and practice.* New York: Academic Press.

BECK, I. L., PERFETTI, C. A., and MCKEOWN, M. G. 1982. Effects of long term vocabulary instruction on lexical access and reading comprehension. *Journal of Educational Psychology, 74,* 506–521.

BECKER, C. A. 1985. What do we really know about semantic context effects during reading? In D. Besner, T. G. Waller, and G. E. MacKinnon (eds.), *Reading research: Advances in theory and practice* (Vol. 5). New York: Academic Press.

BECKER, W., and JURGENS, R. 1979. An analysis of the saccadic system by means of double-step stimuli. *Vision Research, 19,* 967–983.

BEECH, J. R., and HARDING, L. M. 1984. Phonemic processing and the poor reader from a developmental lag viewpoint. *Reading Research Quarterly, 19,* 357–366.

BEGGS, W. D. A., and HOWARTH, P. N. 1985. Inner speech as a learned skill. *Journal of Experimental Child Psychology, 39,* 396–411.

BENTIN, S., BARGAI, N., and KATZ, L. K. 1984. Orthographic and phonemic coding for lexical access: Evidence from Hebrew. *Journal of Experimental Psychology: Learning, Memory, and Cognition, 10,* 353–368.

BERGER, M., YULE, W., and RUTTER, M. 1975. Attainment and adjustment in two geographical areas. 2: The prevalence of specific reading retardation. *British Journal of Educational Psychology, 126,* 510–519.

BERTELSON, P., MORAIS, J., ALEGRIA, J., and CONTENT, A. 1985. Phonetic analysis capacity and learning to read. *Nature, 313,* 73–74.

BERTELSON, P., MOUSTY, P., and D'ALIMONTE, G. 1985. A study of Braille reading: Patterns of hand activity in one-handed and two-handed reading. *Quarterly Journal of Experimental Psychology, 37A,* 235–256.

BESNER, D. 1987. Phonology, lexical access in reading, and articulatory supression: A critical review. *Quarterly Journal of Experimental Psychology, 39A,* 467–478.

BESNER, D., COLTHEART, M., and DAVELAAR, E. 1984. Basic processes in reading: Computation of abstract letter identities. *Canadian Journal of Psychology, 38,* 126–134.

BESNER, D., and DAVELAAR, E. 1982. Basic processes in reading: Two phonological codes. *Canadian Journal of Psychology, 36,* 701–711.

BESNER, D., DAVIES, J., and DANIELS, S. 1981. Reading for meaning: The effects of concurrent articulation. *Quarterly Journal of Experimental Psychology, 33A,* 415–437.

BESNER, D., and HILDEBRANDT, N. 1987. Orthographic and phonological codes in the oral reading of Japanese Kana. *Journal of Experimental Psychology: Learning, Memory, and Cognition, 13,* 335–343.

BEVER, T. G. 1970. The cognitive basis for linguistic structure. In J. R. Hayes (ed.), *Cognitive development of language.* New York: Wiley.

BEVER, T. G., LACKNER, J., and KIRK, R. 1969. The underlying structures of sentences are the primary units of immediate speech processing. *Perception & Psychophysics, 5,* 225–234.

BEVERLY, S. E., and PERFETTI, C. A. 1983. *Skill differences in phonological representation and development of orthographic knowledge.* Paper presented at the Biennial Meeting of the Society of Research in Child Development, Detroit, MI.

BIEMILLER, A. 1970. The development of the use of graphic and contextual information as children learn to read. *Reading Research Quarterly, 6,* 75–96.

BISANZ, G. L., DAS, J. P., and MANCINI, G. 1984. Children's memory for phonemically confusable and nonconfusable letters: Changes with age and reading ability. *Child Development, 55,* 1556–1569.

BISHOP, C. H. 1964. Transfer effects of word and letter training in reading. *Journal of Verbal Learning and Verbal Behavior, 3,* 215–221.

BLACK, J. B., and BERN, H. 1981. Causal coherence and memory for events in narratives. *Journal of Verbal Learning and Verbal Behavior, 20,* 276–288.

BLACK, J. B., and BOWER, G. H. 1979. Episodes as chunks in narrative memory. *Journal of Verbal Learning and Verbal Behavior, 18,* 309–318.

BLACK, J. L., COLLINS, D. W. K., DEROACH, J. N., and ZUBRICK, S. 1984. A detailed study of sequential saccadic eye movements for normal and poor reading children. *Perceptual and Motor Skills, 59,* 423–434.

BLANCHARD, H. E. 1985a. A comparison of some processing time measures based on eye movements. *Acta Psychologica, 58,* 1–15.

BLANCHARD, H. E. 1985b. Investigations of information utilization during fixations in reading. *Proceedings of the 7th Annual Cognitive Science Meeting,* San Diego, CA.

BLANCHARD, H. E. 1987. Pronoun processing during fixations: Effects on the time course of information utilization. *Bulletin of the Psychonomic Society, 25,* 171–174.

BLANCHARD, H. E. 1988. The pattern of utilization of visual information during fixations in reading. *Perception & Psychophysics.* In press.

BLANCHARD, H. E., MCCONKIE, G. W., ZOLA, D., and WOLVERTON, G. S. 1984. Time course of visual information utilization during fixations in reading. *Journal of Experimental Psychology: Human Perception & Performance, 10,* 75–89.

BLANCHARD, H. E., POLLATSEK, A., and RAYNER, K. 1988. *The acquisition of parafoveal word information in reading.* Paper presented at the annual meeting of the Midwestern Psychological Association, Chicago.

BLOOMFIELD, L., and BARNHART, C. L. 1961. *Let's read: A linguistic approach.* Detroit, MI: Wayne State University Press.

BOCK, J. K., and BREWER, W. F. 1985. Discourse structure and mental models. In T. H. Carr (ed.), *The development of reading skills.* San Francisco: Jossey-Bass.

BODER, E. 1971. Developmental dyslexia: A diagnostic screening procedure based on three characteristic patterns of reading and spelling. In B. Bateman (ed.), *Learning disorders* (Vol 4). Seattle: Special Child Publications.

BODER, E. 1973. Developmental dyslexia: A diagnostic based on three atypical reading-spelling patterns. *Developmental Medicine and Child Neurology, 15*, 663–687.

BOND, G. L. and DYKSTRA, R. 1967. The cooperative research program in first-grade reading instruction. *Reading Research Quarterly, 2*, 5–142.

BOUMA, H., and DE VOOGD, A. H. 1974. On the control of eye saccades in reading. *Vision Research, 14*, 273–284.

BOWER, T. G. R. 1970. Reading by eye. In H. Levin and J. P. Williams (eds.), *Basic studies on reading*. New York: Basic Books.

BOWER, G. H., BLACK, J. B., and TURNER, T. J. 1979. Scripts in memory for text. *Cognitive Psychology, 11*, 177–220.

BRADLEY, D. 1979. Lexical representations of derivational relations. In M. Aranoff and M. Kean (eds.), *Juncture*. Cambridge, MA: MIT Press.

BRADLEY, D., GARRETT, M., and ZURIF, E. 1980. Syntactic deficits in Broca's aphasia. In D. Caplan (ed.), *Biological studies of mental processes*. Cambridge, MA: MIT Press.

BRADLEY, L., and BRYANT, P. E. 1978. Difficulties in auditory organization as a possible cause of reading backwardness. *Nature, 271*, 746–747.

BRADLEY, L., and BRYANT, P. E. 1983. Categorizing sounds and learning to read—A causal connection. *Nature, 301*, 419–421.

BRADSHAW, J. L. 1974. Peripherally presented and unreported words may bias the meaning of a centrally fixated homograph. *Journal of Experimental Psychology, 103*, 1200–1202.

BRADY, S., SHANKWEILER, D., and MANN, V. 1983. Speech perception and memory coding in relation to reading ability. *Journal of Experimental Child Psychology, 35*, 345–367.

BRANSFORD, J. D., and FRANKS, J. J. 1971. The abstraction of linguistic ideas. *Cognitive Psychology, 3*, 331–350.

BRANSFORD, J. D., and JOHNSON, M. K. 1972. Contextual prerequisites for understanding: Some investigations of comprehension and recall. *Journal of Verbal Learning and Verbal Behavior, 11*, 717–726.

BRIGGS, C., and ELKIND, D. 1973. Cognitive development in early readers. *Developmental Psychology, 9*, 279–280.

BRIM, B. J. 1968. Impact of a reading improvement program. *Journal of Educational Research, 62*, 177–182.

BROADBENT, D. E. 1958. *Perception and communication*. London: Pergamon.

BROADBENT, D. E. 1984. The maltese cross: A new simplistic model for memory. *Behavioral and Brain Sciences, 7*, 55–94.

BROOKS, L. 1977. Visual pattern in fluent word identification. In A. S. Reber and D. L. Scarborough (eds.), *Toward a psychology of reading*. Hillsdale, NJ: Erlbaum.

BROWN, A. L. 1980. Metacognitive development and reading. In R. J. Spiro, B. C. Bruce, and W. F. Brewer (eds.), *Theoretical issues in reading comprehension*. Hillsdale, NJ: Erlbaum.

BROWN, B., Haegerstrom-Portnoy, G., Adams, A. J., Yingling, C. D., Galin, D., Herron, J., and Marcus, M. 1983. Predictive eye movements do not discriminate between dyslexic and normal children. *Neuropsychologia, 21*, 121–128.

BROWN, R. 1970. Psychology and reading. In H. Levin and J. P. Williams (eds.), *Basic studies on reading*. New York: Basic Books.

BRUCE, D. J. 1964. The analysis of word sounds by young children. *British Journal of Educational Psychology, 34*, 158–170.

BRYANT, P. E., and BRADLEY, L. 1985. *Children's reading difficulties*. Oxford: Blackwell.

BRYANT, P. E., and GOSWAMI, U. 1986. Strengths and weaknesses of the reading level design: A comment on Backman, Mamen, and Ferguson. *Psychological Bulletin, 100*, 101–103.

BRYANT, P. E., and IMPEY, L. 1986. The similarities between normal readers and developmental and acquired dyslexics. *Cognition, 24*, 121–137.

BURGESS, C., SEIDENBERG, M. S., and TANENHAUS, M. K. 1988. Nonword interference and lexical ambiguity resolution. *Journal of Experimental Psychology: Learning, Memory, & Cognition*. In press.

BUSWELL, G. T. 1922. *Fundamental reading habits: A study of their development*. Chicago: Chicago University Press.

BYRNE, B., and SHEA, P. 1979. Semantic and phonetic memory codes in beginning readers. *Memory & Cognition, 7*, 333–338.

CALFEE, R. C., CHAPMAN, R., and VENEZKY, R. 1972. How a child needs to think to learn to read. In L. W. Gregg (ed.), *Cognition in learning and memory.* New York: Wiley.

CALFEE, R. C., LINDAMOOD, P., and LINDAMOOD, C. 1973. Acoustic-phonetic skills and reading: Kindergarten through twelfth grade. *Journal of Educational Psychology, 64,* 293–298.

CAMPBELL, F. W. and WURTZ, R. H. 1978. Saccadic omission: Why we do not see a grey-out during a saccadic eye movement. *Vision Research, 18,* 1297–1303.

CAMPBELL, R., and BUTTERWORTH, B. 1985. Phonological dyslexia and dysgraphia in a highly literate subject: A developmental case with associated deficits of phonemic processing and awareness. *Quarterly Journal of Experimental Psychology, 37A,* 435–475.

CARAMAZZA, A., GROBER, E. H., GARVEY. C., and YATES, J. 1977. Comprehension of anaphoric pronouns. *Journal of Verbal Learning and Verbal Behavior, 16,* 601–609.

CARILLO, L. W., and SHELDON, W. D. 1952. The flexibility of the reading rate. *Journal of Educational Psychology, 43,* 299–305.

CARPENTER, P. A., and DANEMAN, M. 1981. Lexical retrieval and error recovery in reading: A model based on eye fixations. *Journal of Verbal Learning and Verbal Behavior, 20,* 137–160.

CARPENTER, P. A., and JUST, M. A. 1977. Reading comprehension as eyes see it. In M. A. Just and P. A. Carpenter (eds), *Cognitive processes in comprehension.* Hillsdale, NJ: Erlbaum.

CARPENTER, P. A., and JUST, M. A. 1983. What your eyes do while your mind is reading. In K. Rayner (ed.), *Eye movements in reading: Perceptual and language processes.* New York: Academic Press.

CARR, T. H. 1981. Building theories of reading ability: On the relation between individual differences in cognitive skills and reading comprehension. *Cognition, 9,* 73–114.

CARR, T. H. 1982. What's in a model: Reading theory and reading instruction. In M. H. Singer (ed.), *Competent reader, disabled reader: Research and application.* Hillsdale, NJ: Erlbaum.

CARR, T. H., DAVIDSON, B. J., and HAWKINS, H. L. 1978. Perceptual flexibility in word recognition: Strategies affect orthographic computation but not lexical access. *Journal of Experimental Psychology: Human Perception and Performance, 4,* 674–690.

CARR, T. H., MCCAULEY, C., SPERBER, R. D., and PARMELEE, C. M. 1982. Words, pictures, and priming: On semantic activation, conscious identification, and the automaticity of information processing. *Journal of Experimental Psychology: Human Perception and Performance, 8,* 757–777.

CARR, T. H., and POLLATSEK, A. 1985. Recognizing printed words: A look at current models. In D. Besner, T. G. Waller, and G. E. MacKinnon (eds.), *Reading research: Advances in theory and practice (Vol. 5).* Orlando, FL: Academic Press.

CARROLL, D. W. 1986. *Psychology of language.* Monterey, CA: Brooks/Cole Publishing.

CARROLL, P., and SLOWIACZEK, M. L. 1986. Constraints on semantic priming in reading: A fixation time analysis. *Memory & Cognition, 14,* 509–522.

CARROLL, P., and SLOWIACZEK, M. L. 1987. Modes and modules: Multiple pathways to the language processor. In J. Garfield (ed.), *Modularity in knowledge represention and natural language processing.* Cambridge, MA: MIT Press.

CARVER, R. P. 1971. *Sense and nonsense in speed reading.* Silver Spring, MD: Revrac.

CARVER, R. P. 1972. Speed readers don't read; they skim. *Psychology Today,* 22–30.

CARVER, R. P. 1985. How good are some of the world's best readers? *Reading Research Quarterly, 4,* 389–419.

CATTELL, J. M. 1886. The time it takes to see and name objects. *Mind, 11,* 63–65.

CHALL, J. 1958. *Readability: An appraisal of research and application.* Columbus: Ohio State University.

CHALL, J. 1967. *Learning to read: The great debate.* New York: McGraw-Hill.

CHALL, J. 1979. The great debate: Ten years later, with a modest proposal for reading stages. In L. B. Resnick and P. A. Weaver (eds.), *Theory and practice of early reading* (Vol. 1). Hillsdale, NJ: Erlbaum.

CHALL, J. 1983. *Stages of reading development.* New York: McGraw-Hill.

CHASE, W. G., and CLARK, H. H. 1972. Mental operations in the comparison of sentences and pictures. In L. W. Gregg (ed.), *Cognition in learning and memory.* New York: Wiley.

CHEESMAN, J., and MERIKLE, P. M. 1984. Priming with and without awareness. *Perception & Psychophysics, 36,* 387–395.

CHIESI, H. L., SPILICH, G. J., and VOSS, J. F. 1979. Acquisition of domain-related information in relation to high and low domain knowledge. *Journal of Verbal Learning and Verbal Behavior, 18,* 257–274.

CHMIEL, N. 1984. Phonological recoding for reading: The effect of concurrent articulation in a Stroop task. *British Journal of Psychology, 75,* 213–220.

CHOMSKY, N. 1957. *Syntactic structures.* The Hague, Netherlands: Mouton.

CHOMSKY, N. 1959. A review of *Verbal Behavior* by B. F. Skinner, *Language, 35,* 26–58.

CHOMSKY, N. 1965. *Aspects of the theory of syntax.* The Hague, Netherlands: Mouton.

CHOMSKY, N. 1970. Phonology and reading. In H. Levin and J. P. Williams (eds.), *Basic studies on reading.* New York: Basic Books.

CHOMSKY, N., and HALLE, M. 1968. *The sound pattern of English.* New York: Harper and Row.

CHRISTIE, J., and JUST, M. A. 1976. Remembering the location and content of sentences in a prose passage. *Journal of Educational Psychology, 68,* 702–710.

CHUMBLEY, J. I., and BALOTA, D. A. 1984. A word's meaning affects the decision in lexical decision. *Memory & Cognition, 12,* 590–606.

CIRILO, R. 1981. Referential coherence and text structure in story comprehension. *Journal of Verbal Learning and Verbal Behavior, 20,* 358–376.

CIRILO, R., and FOSS, D. 1980. Text structure and reading time for sentences. *Journal of Verbal Learning and Verbal Behavior, 19,* 96–108.

CIUFFREDA, K. J., KENYON, R. W., and STARK, L. 1983. Saccadic intrusions contributing to reading disability: A case report. *American Journal of Optometry and Physiological Optics, 60,* 242–249.

CLARK, H. H., and CLARK, E. V. 1977. *Psychology and language.* New York: Harcourt Brace Jovanovich.

CLARK, H. H., and HAVILAND, S. E. 1977. Comprehension and the given-new contract. In R. O. Freedle (ed.), *Discourse production and comprehension.* Norwood: Ablex.

CLARK, H. H., and SENGUL, C. J. 1979. In search of referents for nouns and pronouns. *Memory & Cognition, 7,* 35–41.

CLARK, M. 1976. *Young fluent readers.* London: Heinemann Educational Books.

CLAY, M. M. 1970. An increasing effect of disorientation on the discrimination of print: A developmental study. *Journal of Experimental Child Psychology, 9,* 297–306.

CLAY, M. M. 1971. *Reading: The patterning of complex behaviour.* Auckland, New Zealand: Heinemann Educational Books.

CLAY M. M., and IMLACH, R. H. 1971. Juncture, pitch and stress as reading behavior variables. *Journal of Verbal Learning and Verbal Behavior, 10,* 133–139.

CLIFTON, C., and FERREIRA, F. 1987. Discourse structure and anaphora: Some experimental results. In M. Coltheart (ed.), *Attention and Performance 12.* London: Erlbaum.

COHEN, A. S. 1974. Oral reading errors of first grade children taught by a code emphasis approach. *Reading Research Quarterly, 10,* 616–650.

COHEN, M. E., and ROSS, L. E. 1977. Saccade latency in children and adults: Effects of warning interval and target eccentricity. *Journal of Experimental Child Psychology, 23,* 539–549.

COLLINS, A., and LOFTUS, E. 1975. A spreading-activation theory of semantic processing. *Psychological Review, 82,* 407–428.

COLTHEART, M. 1978. Lexical access in simple reading tasks. In G. Underwood (ed.), *Strategies of information processing.* London: Academic Press.

COLTHEART, M. 1979. When can children learn to read-And when should they be taught? In T. G. Waller and G. E. MacKinnon (eds.), *Reading research: Advances in theory and practice* (Vol. I). New York: Academic Press.

COLTHEART, M. 1980a. Iconic memory and visual persistence. *Perception & Psychophysics, 27,* 183–228.

COLTHEART, M. 1980b. Reading, phonological recoding and deep dyslexia. In M. Coltheart, K. Patterson, and J. C. Marshall (eds.), *Deep dyslexia.* London: Routledge & Kegan Paul.

COLTHEART, M. 1981. Disorders of reading and their implications for models of normal reading. *Visible Language, 15,* 245–286.

COLTHEART, M., DAVELAAR, E., JONASSON, J. T., and BESNER, D. 1977. Access to the internal lexicon. In S. Dornic (ed.), *Attention and Performance VI*. London: Academic Press.

COLTHEART, M., and FREEMAN, R. 1974. Case alternation impairs word recognition. *Bulletin of the Psychonomic Society, 3*, 102–104.

COLTHEART, M., MASTERSON, J., BYNG, S., PRIOR, M., and RIDDOCH, J. 1983. Surface dyslexia *Quarterly Journal of Experimental Psychology, 35A*, 469–495.

COLTHEART, M., PATTERSON, K., and MARSHALL, J. C. 1980. *Deep dyslexia*. London: Routledge & Kegan Paul.

COLTHEART, V., LAXON, V. J., KEATING, G. C., and POOL, M. M. 1986. Direct access and phonological encoding processes in children's reading: Effect of word characteristics. *British Journal of Educational Psychology, 56*, 255–270.

CONDRY, S. M., MCMAHON-RIDEOUT, M., and LEVY, A. A. 1979. A developmental investigation of selective attention to graphic, phonetic, and semantic information in words. *Perception & Psychophysics, 25*, 88–94.

CONRAD, R. 1972. Speech and reading. In J. F. Kavanagh and I. Mattingly (eds.), *Language by ear and by eye*. Cambridge, MA: MIT Press.

CONRAD, R. 1977 The reading ability of deaf school-leavers. *British Journal of Educational Psychology, 47*, 138–148.

CONTENT, A., KOLINSKY, R., MORAIS, J., and BERTELSON, P. 1986. Phonetic segmentation in prereaders: Effect of corrective information. *Journal of Experimental Child Psychology, 42*, 49–72.

CONTENT, A., MORAIS, J., ALEGRIA, J., BERTELSON, P. 1982. Accelerating the development of phonetic segmentation skills in kindergartners. *Cahiers de Psychologie Cognitive, 2*, 259–269.

CORCORAN, D. W. J. 1966. An acoustic factor in letter cancellation. *Nature, 210*, 658.

CORCORAN, D. W. J. 1967. Acoustic factor in proofreading. *Nature, 214*, 851–852.

COWAN, N. 1984. On short and long auditory stores. *Psychological Bulletin, 96*, 341–370.

CRAIK, F. I. M., and LOCKHART, R. S. 1972. Levels of processing: A framework for memory research. *Journal of Verbal Learning and Verbal Behavior, 11*, 671–684.

CRAIN, S., and STEEDMAN, M. 1985. On not being led up the garden path: The use of context by the psychological parser. In D. Dowty, L. Karttunen, and A. Zwicky (eds.), *Natural language processing: Psychological, computational, and theoretical perspectives*. Cambridge: Cambridge University Press.

CRITCHLEY, M. 1975. Developmental dyslexia: Its history, nature, and prospects. In D. D. Duane and M. B. Rawson (eds.), *Reading, perception, and language: Papers from the world congress on dylexia*. Baltimore, MD: York Press.

CROWDER, R. G. 1982. *The psychology of reading: An introduction*. New York: Oxford University Press.

CROWDER, R. G. 1984. Is it just reading? *Developmental Review, 4*, 48–61.

CUNNINGHAM, T. J., Healy, A. F., Kanengiser, N., Chizzik, L., and Willits, R. L. 1988. Investigating the boundaries of reading units across ages and reading levels. *Journal of Experimental Child Psychology, 45*, 175–208.

CURTIS, M. E. 1980. Development of components of reading skill. *Journal of Educational Psychology, 72*, 656–669.

CUTLER, A. 1983. Lexical complexity and sentence processing. In G. B. Flores d'Arcais and R. J. Jarvella (eds.), *The process of language understanding*. New York: Wiley.

DANEMAN, M., and CARPENTER, P. A. 1980. Individual differences in working memory and reading. *Journal of Verbal Learning and Verbal Behavior, 19*, 450–466.

DANEMAN, M., and CARPENTER, P. A. 1983. Individual differences in integrating information between and within sentences. *Journal of Experimental Psychology: Learning, Memory, and Cognition, 9*, 561–584.

DANKS, J. H., and HILL, G. O. 1981. An interactive analysis of oral reading. In A. M. Lesgold and C. A. Perfetti (eds.), *Interactive processes in reading*. Hillsdale, NJ: Erlbaum.

DELL, G. S., MCKOON, G., and RATCLIFF, R. 1983. The activation of antecedent information during the processing of anaphoric reference in reading. *Journal of Verbal Learning and Verbal Behavior, 22*, 121–132.

DENBUURMAN, R., BOERSEMA, T., and GERRISEN, J. F. 1981. Eye movements and the perceptual span in reading. *Reading Research Quarterly, 16*, 227–235.

DENCKLA, M. B. 1977. Minimal brain dysfunction and dyslexia. In M. E. Blaw, I. Rapin, and M. Kinsbourne (eds.), *Child Neurology*, New York: Spectrum.

DENCKLA, M. B., and RUDEL, R. 1976a. Naming of pictured objects by dyslexics and other learning disabled children. *Brain and Language, 3,* 1–15.

DENCKLA, M. B., and RUDEL, R. 1976b. Rapid "automatized" naming (RAN): Dylexia differentiated from other learning disabilities. *Neuropsychologia, 14,* 471–479.

DENNIS, I., BESNER, D., and DAVELAAR, E. 1985. Phonology in visual word recognition: Their is more two this than meats the I. In D. Besner, T. G. Waller, and G. E. MacKinnon (eds.), *Reading research: Advances in theory and practice (Vol. 5).* New York: Academic Press.

DILOLLO, V., HANSON, D., and MCINTYRE, J. S. 1983. Initial stages of visual information processing in dyslexia. *Journal of Experimental Psychology: Human Perception and Performance, 9,* 923–935.

DIRINGER, D. 1962. *Writing.* London: Thames & Hudson.

DOCTOR, E. A., and COLTHEART, M. 1980. Children's use of phonological encoding when reading for meaning. *Memory & Cognition, 8,* 195–209.

DODGE, R. 1900. Visual perception during eye movement. *Psychological Review, 7,* 454–465.

DODGE, R. 1906. Recent studies in the correlation of eye movement and visual perception. *Psychological Bulletin, 13,* 85–92.

DOEHRING, D. G. 1976. Acquisition of rapid reading responses. *Monographs of the society for research in child development, 41,* No. 165.

DOEHRING, D. G., and HOSHKO, I. M. 1977. Classification of reading problems by the Q-technique of factor analysis. *Cortex, 13,* 281–294.

DOOLING, D. J., and LACHMAN, R. 1971. Effects of comprehension on retention of prose. *Journal of Experimental Psychology, 88,* 216–222.

DOSHER, B. A., and CORBETT, A. T. 1982. Instrument inferences and verb schemata. *Memory & Cognition, 10,* 531–539.

DOWNING, J. 1965. *The initial teaching alphabet reading experiment.* Chicago: Scott Foresman.

DOWNING, J., and LEONG, C. K. 1982. *Psychology of reading.* New York: Macmillan.

DRESHER, B. E., and HORNSTEIN, N. 1976. On some supposed contributions of artificial intelligence to the scientific study of language. *Cognition, 4,* 321–398.

DREWNOWSKI, A. 1978. Detection errors on the word *the:* Evidence for the acquisition of reading levels. *Memory & Cognition, 6,* 403–409.

DREWNOWSKI, A., and HEALY, A. F. 1977. Detection errors on *the* and *and:* Evidence for reading units larger than the word. *Memory & Cognition, 5,* 636–647.

DREWNOWSKI, A., and HEALY, A. F. 1980. Missing *-ing* in reading: Letter detection errors in word endings. *Journal of Verbal Learning and Verbal Behavior, 19,* 247–262.

DUFFY, S. A. 1986. Role of expectations in sentence integration. *Journal of Experimental Psychology: Learning, Memory, and Cognition, 12,* 208–219.

DUFFY, S. A., and RAYNER, K. 1988. Eye movements and antecedent search: The effect of antecedent typicality and distance. Manuscript submitted for publication.

DUFFY, S. A., MORRIS, R. K., and RAYNER, K. 1988. Lexical ambiguity and fixation times in reading. *Journal of Memory and Language, 27,* 429–446.

DURKIN, D. 1966. *Children who read early.* New York: Teachers College, Columbia University.

DURRELL, D. D. 1958. First grade reading success study: A summary. *Journal of Education, 140,* 2–6.

DYER, F. N. 1973. The Stroop phenomenon and its use in the study of perceptual, cognitive and response processes. *Memory & Cognition, 1,* 106–120.

EDFELDT, A. W. 1960. *Silent speech and silent reading.* Chicago: University of Chicago Press.

EGETH, H., JONIDES, J., and WALL, S. 1972. Parallel processing of multi-element displays. *Cognitive Psychology, 3,* 674–698.

EHRI, L. C. 1975. Word consciousness in readers and prereaders. *Journal of Educational Psychology, 67,* 204–212.

EHRI, L. C. 1976. Do words really interfere in naming pictures? *Child Development, 47,* 502–505.

EHRI, L. C. 1977. Do adjectives and functors interfere as much as nouns in naming pictures? *Child Development, 48,* 697–701.

EHRI, L. C. 1979. Linguistic insight: Threshold of reading acquisition. In T. G. Waller and G. E. MacKinnon (eds.) *Reading research: Advances in theory and practice* (Vol. 1). New York: Academic Press.

EHRI, L. C. 1980. The role of orthography in printed word learning. In J. G. Kavanagh and R. L. Venezky (eds.) *Orthography, reading, and dyslexia.* Baltimore: University Park Press.

EHRI, L. C. 1983. Influence of orthography on phonological and lexical awareness in beginning readers. In J. Downing and R. Valtin (eds.) *Language awareness and learning to read.* New York: Springer-Verlag.

EHRI, L. C., DEFFNER, N. D., and WILCE, L. S. 1984. Pictorial mnemonics for phonics. *Journal of Educational Psychology, 76,* 880–893.

EHRI, L. C., and WILCE, L. S. 1979. The mnemonic value of orthography among beginning readers. *Journal of Educational Psychology, 71,* 26–40.

EHRI, L. C., and WILCE, L. S. 1985. Movement into reading: Is the first stage of printed word learning visual or phonetic? *Reading Research Quarterly, 20,* 163–179.

EHRI, L. C., and WILCE, L. S. 1987a. Cipher versus cue reading: An experiment in decoding acquisition. *Journal of Educational Psychology, 79,* 3–13.

EHRI, L. C., and WILCE, L. S. 1987b. Does learning to spell help beginning readers learn to read words? *Reading Research Quarterly, 22,* 47–65.

EHRLICH, K. 1983. Eye movements in pronoun assignment: A study of sentence integration. In K. Rayner (ed.), *Eye movements in reading: Perceptual and language processes.* New York: Academic Press.

EHRLICH, K., and RAYNER, K. 1983. Pronoun assignment and semantic integration during reading: Eye movements and immediacy of processing. *Journal of Verbal Learning and Verbal Behavior, 22,* 75–87.

EHRLICH, S. F. 1981. Children's word recognition in prose context. *Visible Language, 15,* 219–244.

EHRLICH, S. F., and RAYNER, K. 1981. Contextual effects on word perception and eye movements during reading. *Journal of Verbal Learning and Verbal Behavior, 20,* 641–655.

ELKIND, D., and WEISS, J. 1967. Studies in perceptual development, III: Perceptual exploration. *Child Development, 38,* 553–561.

ELLIS, A. W. 1979. Developmental and acquired dyslexia: Some observations on Jorm. *Cognition, 7,* 413–420.

ELLIS, A. W. 1984. *Reading, writing and dyslexia: A cognitive analysis.* London: Erlbaum.

ELLIS, A. W., and MARSHALL, J. C. 1978. Semantic errors or statistical flukes: A note on Allport's "On knowing the meaning of words we are unable to report." *Quarterly Journal of Experimental Psychology, 30,* 569–575.

ELLIS, N. C., and MILES, T. R. 1978. Visual information processing in dyslexic children. In M. M. Gruneberg, R. N. Sykes, and P. E. Morris (eds.) *Practical aspects of memory.* London: Academic Press.

ERDMANN, B., and DODGE, R. 1898. *Psychologische Untersuchungen uber das Lesen.* Halle, Germany: M. Niemeyer.

ERICKSON, D., MATTINGLY, I. G., and TURVEY, M. T. 1977. Phonetic activity in reading: An experiment with Kanji. *Language and Speech, 20,* 384–403.

ERICKSON, T. D., and MATTSON, M. E. 1981. From words to meaning: A semantic illusion. *Journal of Verbal Learning and Verbal Behavior, 20,* 540–551.

ESKENAZI, B., and DIAMOND, S. P. 1983. Visual exploration of nonverbal material by dyslexic children. *Cortex, 19,* 353–370.

EVANS, M. A., and CARR, T. H. 1985. Cognitive abilities, conditions of learning, and the early development of reading skill. *Reading Research Quarterly, 20,* 327–350.

EVETT, L. J., and HUMPHREYS, G. W. 1981. The use of abstract graphemic information in lexical access. *Quarterly Journal of Experimental Psychology, 33A,* 325–350.

FARNHAM-DIGGORY, S., and GREGG, L. W. 1975. Short term memory function in young readers. *Journal of Experimental Child Psychology, 19,* 279–298.

FEINBERG, R. 1949. A study of some aspects of peripheral visual acuity. *American Journal of Optometry and Archives of the American Annals of Optometry, 26,* 49–56, 105–119.

FEITELSON, D., and RAZEL, M. 1984. Word superiority and word shape effects in beginning readers. *International Journal of Behavioral Development, 7,* 359–370.

FEITELSON, D., TEHORI, B. Z., and LEVINBERG-GREEN, D. 1982. How effective is early instruction in reading? Experimental evidence. *Merrill-Palmer Quarterly, 28,* 485–494.

FELDMAN, L. B., and TURVEY, M. T. 1983. Word recognition in Serbo-Croatian is phonologically analytic. *Journal of Experimental Psychology: Human Perception & Performance, 9,* 288–298.

FERREIRA, F., and CLIFTON C. 1986. The independence of syntactic processing. *Journal of Memory and Language, 25,* 75–87.

FILLMORE, C. J. 1968. The case for case. In E. Bach and R. T. Harms (eds.) *Universals in linquistic theory.* New York: Holt, Rinehart and Winston.

FINDLAY, J. M. 1982. Global visual processing for saccadic eye movements. *Vision Research, 22,* 1033–1045.

FISCHLER, I., and BLOOM, P. 1979. Automatic and attentional processes in the effects of sentence context on word recognition. *Journal of Verbal Learning and Verbal Behavior, 18,* 1–20.

FISHER, D. F. 1979. Dysfunctions in reading disability: There's more than meets the eye. In L. B. Resnick and P. A. Weaver (eds.), *Theory and practice of early reading* (Vol. 1). Hillsdale, NJ: Erlbaum.

FISHER, D. F., and FRANKFURTER, A. 1977. Normal and disabled readers can locate and identify letters: Where's the perceptual deficit? *Journal of Reading Behavior, 9,* 31–43.

FISHER, D. F., and LEFTON, L. A. 1976. Peripheral information extraction: A developmental examination of reading process. *Journal of Experimental Child Psychology, 21,* 77–93.

FISHER, D. F., and MONTANARY, S. P. 1977. Spatial and contextual factors in beginning reading: Evidence for PSG-CSG complements to developing automacity? *Memory & Cognition, 5,* 247–251.

FISHER, D. F., and SHEBILSKE, W. L. 1984. There is more that meets the eye than the eyemind assumption. In R. Groner, G. W. McConkie, and C. Menz (eds.), *Eye movements and human information processing.* Amsterdam: North Holland.

FISHER, D. G. 1983. An experimental study of eye movements during reading. Unpublished manuscript. Murray Hill, NJ: Bell Laboratories.

FISHER, V. L., and PRICE, J. H. 1970. Cues to word similarity used by children and adults: Supplementary report. *Perceptual and Motor Skills, 31,* 849–850.

FLEISHER, L. S., JENKINS, J. R., and PANY, D. 1979. Effects on poor readers' comprehension of training in rapid decoding. *Reading Research Quarterly, 15,* 30–48.

FLETCHER, C. R. 1981. Short-term memory processes in text comprehension. *Journal of Verbal Learning and Verbal Behavior, 20,* 564–574.

FLETCHER, C. R. 1986. Strategies for the allocation of short-term memory during comprehension. *Journal of Memory and Language, 25,* 43–58.

FODOR, J. A. 1978. Tom Swift and his procedural grandmother. *Cognition, 6,* 229–248.

FODOR, J. A. 1983. *Modularity of mind.* Cambridge, MA: MIT Press.

FODOR, J. A., and BEVER, T. G. 1965. The psychological reality of linguistic segments. *Journal of Verbal Learning and Verbal Behavior, 4,* 414–420.

FODOR, J. A., BEVER, T. G., and GARRETT, M. F. 1974. *The psychology of language.* New York: McGraw-Hill.

FORD, M., BRESNAN, J., and KAPLAN, R. 1983. A competence-based theory of syntactic closure. In J. Bresnan (ed.), *The mental representation of grammatical relations.* Cambridge, MA: MIT Press.

FORSTER, K. I. 1970. Visual perception of rapidly presented word sequences of varying complexity. *Perception & Psychophysics, 8,* 215–221.

FORSTER, K. I. 1976. Accessing the mental lexicon. In R. J. Wales and E. C. T. Walker (eds.), *New approaches to language mechanisms.* Amsterdam: North-Holland.

FORSTER, K. I. 1979. Levels of processing and the structure of the language processor. In W. E. Cooper and E. Walker (eds.), *Sentence processing: Psycholinquistic studies presented to Merrill Garrett.* Hillsdale, NJ: Erlbaum.

FOSS, D. J. 1982. A discourse on semantic priming. *Cognitive Psychology, 14,* 590–607.

FOSS, D. J., and HAKES, D. T. 1978. *Psycholinquistics: An introduction to the psychology of language.* Englewood Cliffs, NJ: Prentice-Hall.

FOSS, D. J., and JENKINS, C. M. 1973. Some effects of context on the comprehension of ambiguous sentences. *Journal of Verbal Learning and Verbal Behavior, 12,* 577–589.

FOWLER, C., WOLFORD, G., SLADE, R., and TASSINARY, L. 1981. Lexical access with and without awareness. *Journal of Experimental Psychology: General, 110,* 341–362.

FOX, B., and ROUTH, D. K. 1975. Analyzing spoken language into words, syllables, and phonemes: A developmental study. *Journal of Psycholinguistic Research, 4,* 331–342.

FOX, B., and ROUTH, D. K. 1976. Phonetic analysis and synthesis as word attack skills. *Journal of Educational Psychology, 68,* 70–74.

FOX, B., and ROUTH, D. K. 1984. Phonemic analysis and synthesis as word attack skills: Revisited. *Journal of Educational Psychology, 76,* 1059–1064.

FRANCIS, W. N., and KUCERA, H. 1982. *Frequency analysis of English usage: Lexicon and grammar.* Boston: Houghton Mifflin.

FRAZIER, L. 1979. *On comprehending sentences: Syntactic parsing strategies.* Bloomington, IN: Indiana University Linguistics Club.

FRAZIER, L. 1985. Syntactic complexity. In D. Dowty, L. Karttunen, and A. Zwicky (eds.), *Natural language parsing.* Cambridge: Cambridge University Press.

FRAZIER, L. 1987. Sentence processing: A tutorial review. In M. Coltheart (ed.), *Attention and Performance XII.* Hillsdale, NJ: Erlbaum.

FRAZIER, L., and FODOR, J. D. 1978. The sausage machine: A new two-stage parsing model. *Cognition, 6,* 291–326.

FRAZIER, L., and RAYNER, K. 1982. Making and correcting errors during sentence comprehension: Eye movements in the analysis of structurally ambiguous sentences. *Cognitive Psychology, 14,* 178–210.

FRAZIER, L., and RAYNER, K. 1987. Resolution of syntactic category ambiguities: Eye movements in parsing lexically ambiguous sentences. *Journal of Memory and Language, 26,* 505–526.

FREDERIKSEN, J. R. 1982. A componential model of reading skills and their interrelations. In R. J. Sternberg (ed.), *Advances in the psychology of human intelligence.* Hillsdale, NJ: Erlbaum.

FRIEDMAN, A. 1979. Framing pictures: The role of knowledge in automatized encoding and memory for gist. *Journal of Experimental Psychology: General, 108,* 316–355.

FRIEDMAN, R. B., and PERLMAN, M. B. 1982. On the underlying causes of semantic paralexias in a patient with deep dyslexia. *Neuropsychologia, 20,* 559–568.

FRIEDRICH, F. J., SCHADLER, M., and JUOLA, J. F. 1979. Developmental changes in units of processing reading. *Journal of Experimental Child Psychology, 28,* 344–358.

FRITH, U. 1980. *Cognitive processes in spelling.* London: Academic Press.

FUNNELL, G. 1983. Phonological processes in reading: New evidence from acquired dyslexia. *British Journal of Psychology, 74,* 159–180.

GARNHAM, A. 1981. Anaphoric reference to instances, instantiated and non-instantiated categories: A reading-time study. *British Journal of Psychology, 72,* 377–384.

GARNHAM, A. 1985. *Psycholinguistics.* London: Methuen.

GARRETT, M. F., BEVER, T. G., and FODOR, J. A. 1966. The active use of grammar in speech perception. *Perception & Psychophysics, 1,* 30–32.

GARRITY, L. I. 1977. Electromyography: A review of the current status of subvocal speech research. *Memory & Cognition, 5,* 615–622.

GARROD, S., and SANFORD, A. J. 1977. Interpreting anaphoric relations: The integration of semantic information while reading. *Journal of Verbal Learning and Verbal Behavior, 16,* 77–90.

GARROD, S., and SANFORD, A. J. 1982. The mental representation of discourse in a focused memory system: Implications for the interpretation of anaphoric noun-phrases. *Journal of Semantics, 1,* 21–41.

GARROD, S., and SANFORD, A. J. 1985. On the real-time character of interpretation during reading. *Language and Cognitive Processes, 1,* 43–59.

GELB, I. J. 1963. *A study of writing.* 2nd ed. Chicago: University of Chicago Press.

GIBSON, E. J. 1965. Learning to read. *Science, 148,* 1066–1072.

GIBSON, E. J. 1969. *Principles of perceptual learning and development.* New York: Appleton-Century-Crofts.

GIBSON, E. J. 1971. Perceptual learning and the theory of word perception. *Cognitive Psychology, 2,* 351–368.

GIBSON, E. J., and LEVIN, H. 1975. *The psychology of reading.* Cambridge, MA: MIT Press.

GILBERT, L. C. 1959. Speed of processing visual stimuli and its relation to reading. *Journal of Educational Psychology, 55,* 8–14.

GLASS, A. L., and HOLYOAK, K. J. 1975. Alternative conceptions of semantic memory, *Cognition, 3,* 313–339.

GLEITMAN, L. R., and ROZIN, P. 1973. Teaching by use of a syllabary. *Reading Research Quarterly, 8,* 447–483.

GLEITMAN, L. R., and ROZIN, P. 1977. The structure and acquisition of reading I: Relations between orthographies and the structure of language. In A. S. Reber and D. L. Scarborough (eds.), *Toward a psychology of reading*. Hillsdale, NJ: Erlbaum.

GLENBERG, A. M., MEYER, M., and LINDEM, K. 1987. Mental models contribute to foregrounding during text comprehension. *Journal of Memory and Language, 26,* 69–83.

GLOCK, M. D. 1949. The effect upon eye-movements and reading rate at the college level of three methods of training. *Journal of Educational Psychology, 40,* 93–106.

GLUCKSBERG, S., KREUZ, R. J., and RHO, S. H. 1986. Context can constrain lexical access: Implications for models of language comprehension. *Journal of Experimental Psychology: Learning, Memory, and Cognition, 12,* 323–335.

GLUSHKO, R. J. 1979. The organization and activation of orthographic knowledge in reading aloud. *Journal of Experimental Psychology: Human Perception and Performance, 5,* 674–691.

GLUSHKO, R. J. 1981. Principles for pronouncing print: The psychology of phonography. In A. M. Lesgold and C. A. Perfetti (eds.), *Interactive processes in reading*. Hillsdale, NJ: Erlbaum.

GODFREY, J. J., SYRDAL-LASKY, A. K., MILLAY, K. K., and KNOX, C. M. 1981. Performance of dyslexic children on speech perception tests. *Journal of Experimental Child Psychology, 32,* 401–424.

GOLDMAN, S. R., HOGABOAM, T. W., BELL, L. C., and PERFETTI, C. A. 1980. Short-term retention of discourse during reading. *Journal of Educational Psychology, 68,* 680–688.

GOLINKOFF, R. M. 1976. A comparison of reading comprehension processes in good and poor comprehenders. *Reading Research Quarterly, 11,* 623–669.

GOLINKOFF, R. M. 1978. Critique: Phonemic awareness skills and reading achievement. In F. B. Murray and J. J. Pikulski (eds.), *The acquisition of reading: Cognitive, linguistic and perceptual prerequisites*. Baltimore, MD: University Park Press.

GOLINKOFF, R. M., and ROSINSKI, R. R. 1976. Decoding, semantic processing, and reading comprehension skill. *Child Development, 47,* 252–258.

GOODMAN, K. S. 1967. Reading: A psycholinguistic guessing game. *Journal of the Reading Specialist, 6,* 126–135.

GOODMAN, K. S. 1970. Reading: A psycholinguistic guessing game. In H. Singer and R. B. Ruddell, R. B. (eds.), *Theoretical models and processes of reading*. Newark, DE: International Reading Association.

GORDON, B., and CARAMAZZA, A. 1982. Lexical decision for open and closed class items: Failure to replicate differential frequency sensitivity. *Brain and Language, 15,* 143–160.

GOSWAMI, U. 1986. Children's use of analogy in learning to read: A developmental study. *Journal of Experimental Child Psychology, 42,* 73–83.

GOUGH, P. B. 1972. One second of reading. In J. F. Kavanagh and I. G. Mattingly (eds.), *Language by ear and by eye*. Cambridge, MA: MIT Press.

GOUGH. P. B. 1985. One second of reading: Postscript. In H. Singer and R. B. Ruddell (eds.), *Theoretical models and processes of reading*. Newark, DE: International Reading Association.

GOUGH, P. B., ALFORD, J. A., and HOLLEY-WILCOX, P. 1981. Words and contexts. In O. L. Tzeng and H. Singer (eds.), *Perception of print: Reading research in experimental psychology*. Hillsdale, NJ: Erlbaum.

GOUGH, P. B., and COSKY, M. J. 1977. One second of reading again. In N. J. Castellan, D. B. Pisoni, and G. R. Potts (eds.), *Cognitive theory*. Hillsdale, NJ: Erlbaum.

GOUGH, P. B., and HILLINGER, M. L. 1980. Learning to read: An unnatural act. *Bulletin of the Orton Society, 20,* 179–196.

GRAESSER, A. C. 1981. *Prose comprehension beyond the word*. New York: Springer-Verlag.

GRAESSER, A. C., GORDON, S. E., and SAWYER, J. D. 1979. Recognition for typical and atypical actions in scripted activities: Tests of a script pointer + tag hypothesis. *Journal of Verbal Learning and Verbal Behavior, 18,* 319–333.

GRAESSER, A. C., HOFFMAN, N. L., and CLARK, L. F. 1980. Structural components of reading time. *Journal of Verbal Learning and Verbal Behavior, 19,* 135–151.

GROFF, P. 1975. Research in brief: Shapes as cues to word recognition. *Visible Language, 9,* 67–71.

GROLL, S. L., and ROSS, L. E. 1982. Saccadic eye movements of children and adults to double-step stimuli. *Developmental Psychology, 18,* 108–123.

GUTTENTAG, R. E., and HAITH, M. M. 1978. Automatic processing as a function of age and reading ability. *Child Development, 49,* 707–716.

HABER, R. N. 1983. The impending demise of the icon: A critique of the concept of iconic storage in visual information processing. *Behavioral and Brain Sciences, 6,* 1–54.

HABER, R. N., and HABER, L. R. 1981. The shape of a word can specify its meaning. *Reading Research Quarterly, 16,* 334–345.

HABER, R. N., and HABER, L. R. 1982. Does silent reading involve articulation? Evidence from tongue-twisters. *American Journal of Psychology, 95,* 409–419.

HABER, R. N., and SCHINDLER, R. M. 1981. Error in proofreading: Evidence of syntactic control of letter processing? *Journal of Experimental Psychology: Human Perception and Performance, 7,* 573–579.

HABERLANDT, K., BERIAN, C., and SANDSON, J. 1980. The episode schema in story processing. *Journal of Verbal Learning and Verbal Behavior, 19,* 635–650.

HABERLANDT, K., and BINGHAM, G. 1978. Verbs contribute to the coherence of brief narratives: Reading related and unrelated sentence triples. *Journal of Verbal Learning and Verbal Behavior, 17,* 419–425.

HALL, J. W., WILSON, K. P., HUMPHREYS, M. S., TINZMANN, M. B., and BOWYER, P. M. 1983. Phonemic-similarity effects in good vs. poor readers. *Memory & Cognition, 11,* 520–527.

HARDYCK, C. D., and PETRINOVICH, L. F. 1970. Subvocal speech and comprehension level as a function of the difficulty level of reading material. *Journal of Verbal Learning and Verbal Behavior, 9,* 647–652.

HARDYCK, C. D., PETRINOVICH, L. F., and ELLSWORTH, D. W. 1966. Feedback of speech muscle activity during silent reading: Rapid extinction. *Science,* 154, 1467–1468.

HAVILAND, S. E., and CLARK, H. H. 1974. What's new? Acquiring new information as a process in comprehension. *Journal of Verbal Learning and Verbal Behavior, 13,* 512–521.

HAWKINS, H. L., REICHER, G. M., ROGERS, M., and PETERSON, L. (1976). Flexible coding in word recognition. *Journal of Experimental Psychology: Human Perception and Performance. 2,* 380–385.

HEALY, A. F. 1976. Detection errors on the word *the:* Evidence for reading units larger than letters. *Journal of Experimental Psychology: Human Perception and Performance, 2,* 235–242.

HEALY, A. F. 1980. Proofreading errors on the word *the:* New evidence on reading units. *Journal of Experimental Psychology: Human Perception and Performance, 6,* 45–57.

HEALY, A. F., and DREWNOWSKI, A. 1983. Investigating the boundaries of reading units: Letter detection in misspelled words. *Journal of Experimental Psychology: Human Perception and Performance, 9,* 413–426.

HELFGOTT, J. 1976. Phonemic segmentation and blending skills of kindergarten children: Implications for beginning reading acquisition. *Contemporary Educational Psychology, 1,* 157–169.

HENDERSON, L. 1982. *Orthography and word recognition in reading.* New York: Academic Press.

HENDERSON, L. 1984. *Orthographies and reading.* Hillsdale, NJ: Erlbaum.

HILLYARD, S. A., HINK, R. F., SCHWENT, V. L., and PICTON, T. W. 1973. Electrical signs of selective attention in the human brain. *Science, 182,* 177–182.

HINTZMAN, D. L., CARRE, F. A., ESKRIDGE, V. L., OWENS, A. M., SHAFF, S. S., and SPARKS, M. E. 1972. "Stroop" effect: Input or output phenomenon? *Journal of Experimental Psychology, 95,* 458–459.

HOCHBERG, J. 1970. Components of literacy: Speculations and exploratory research. In H. Levin and J. P. Williams (eds.), *Basic studies on reading.* New York: Basic Books.

HOGABOAM, T. W. 1983. Reading patterns in eye movement data. In K. Rayner (ed.), *Eye movements in reading: Perceptual and language processes.* New York: Academic Press.

HOGABOAM, T. W., and MCCONKIE, G. W. 1981. *The rocky road from eye fixations to comprehension.* Technical Report 207, Center for the Study of Reading, University of Illinois at Urbana-Champaign.

HOGABOAM, T. W., and PERFETTI, C. A. 1978. Reading skill and the role of verbal experience in decoding. *Journal of Educational Psychology, 70,* 717–729.

HOLDEN, M. H., and MACGINITIE, W. H. 1972. Children's conceptions of word boundaries in speech and print. *Journal of Educational Psychology, 63,* 551–557.

HOLENDER, D. 1986. Semantic activation without conscious identification in dichotic listening, parafoveal vision, and visual masking: A survey and appraisal. *Behavioral and Brain Sciences, 9,* 1–66.

HOLMES, J. M. 1973. *Dyslexia: A neurolinguistic study of traumatic and developmental disorders of reading.* Ph.D. thesis, University of Edinburgh.

HOLMES, J. M. 1978. Regression and reading breakdown. In A. Caramazza and E. Zurif (eds.), *Language acquisition and language breakdown.* Baltimore: Johns Hopkins University Press.

HOLMES, V. M., and O'REGAN, J. K. 1981. Eye fixation patterns during the reading of relative-clause sentences. *Journal of Verbal Learning and Verbal Behavior, 20,* 417–430.

HOLT, E. B. 1903. Eye-movement and central anaesthesia. *Psychological Monographs* (Vol. 4), 3–48.

HOMA, D. 1983. An assessment of two extraordinary speed-readers. *Bulletin of the Psychonomic Society, 21,* 123–126.

HOWELL, E. R., SMITH, G. A., and STANLEY, G. 1981. Reading disability and visual spatial frequency specific effects. *Australian Journal of Psychology, 33,* 97–102.

HUBEL, D. H., and WIESEL, T. N. 1962. Receptive fields, binocular interaction and functional architecture in the cat's visual cortex. *Journal of Physiology, 160,* 106–154.

HUEY, E. B. 1908. *The psychology and pedagogy of reading.* New York: Macmillan. (Republished: Cambridge, MA: MIT Press, 1968.)

HULME, C. 1987. Reading retardation. In J. R. Beech and A. M. Colley (eds.), *Cognitive approaches to reading.* Chichester: Wiley.

HUMPHREYS, G. W., and EVETT, L. J. 1985. Are there independent lexical and nonlexical routes in word processing? An evaluation of the dual-route theory of reading. *Behavioral and Brain Sciences, 8,* 689–740.

HUNG, D. L., and TZENG, O. J. L. 1981. Orthographic variations and visual information processing. *Psychological Bulletin, 90,* 377–414.

HUTTENLOCHER, J. 1964. Children's language: Word-phrase relationship. *Science, 143,* 264–265.

IKEDA, M., and SAIDA, S. 1978. Span of recognition in reading. *Vision Research, 18,* 83–88.

INHOFF, A. W. 1982. Parafoveal word perception: A further case against semantic preprocessing. *Journal of Experimental Psychology: Human Perception and Performance, 8,* 137–145.

INHOFF, A. W. 1984. Two stages of word processing during eye fixations in the reading of prose. *Journal of Verbal Learning and Verbal Behavior, 23,* 612–624.

INHOFF, A. W. 1987. Lexical access during eye fixations in sentence reading: Effects of word structure. In M. Coltheart (ed.), *Attention and performance 12.* London: Erlbaum.

INHOFF, A. W. 1988a. Lexical access during eye fixations in sentence reading: Are word access codes used to integrate lexical information across interword fixations. Manuscript submitted for publication.

INHOFF, A. W. 1988b. Parafoveal processing of words and saccade computation in reading. *Journal of Experimental Psychology: Human Perception and Performance,* in press.

INHOFF, A. W., POLLATSEK, A., POSNER, M. I., and RAYNER, K. 1988. Covert attention and eye movements in reading. *Quarterly Journal of Experimental Psychology.* In press.

INHOFF, A. W., and RAYNER, K. 1980. Parafoveal word perception: A case against semantic preprocessing. *Perception & Psychophysics, 27,* 457–464.

INHOFF, A. W., and RAYNER, K. 1986. Parafoveal word processing during eye fixations in reading: Effects of word frequency. *Perception & Psychophysics, 40,* 431–439.

JACKSON, M. D. 1980. Further evidence for a relationship between memory access and reading ability. *Journal of Verbal Learning and Verbal Behavior, 19,* 683–694.

JACKSON, M. D., and MCCLELLAND, J. L. 1975. Sensory and cognitive determinants of reading speed. *Journal of Verbal Learning and Verbal Behavior, 19,* 565–574.

JACKSON, M. D., and MCCLELLAND, J. L. 1979. Processing determinants of reading speed. *Journal of Experimental Psychology: General, 108,* 151–181.

JEFFREY, W. E., and SAMUELS, S. J. 1967. The effect of method of reading training on initial reading and transfer. *Journal of Verbal Learning and Verbal Behavior, 6,* 354–358.

JOHNSON-LAIRD, P. N. 1983. *Mental models.* Cambridge, MA: Harvard University Press.

JOHNSON-LAIRD, P. N., and STEVENSON, R. 1970. Memory for syntax. *Nature, 227,* 412.

JOHNSTON, J. C. 1978. A test of the sophisticated guessing theory of word perception. *Cognitive Psychology, 10,* 123–153.

JOHNSTON, J. C., and MCCLELLAND, J. L. 1974. Perception of letters in words: Seek and ye shall not find. *Science, 184,* 1192–1193.

JOHNSTON, R. S. 1983. Developmental deep dyslexia? *Cortex, 19,* 133–139.

JORM, A. F. 1979. The cognitive and neurological basis of developmental dyslexia: A theoretical framework and review. *Cognition, 7,* 19–33.

JORM, A. F. 1983. Specific reading retardation and working memory: A review. *British Journal of Psychology, 74,* 311–342.

JORM, A. F., and SHARE, D. L. 1983. Phonological recoding and reading acquisition. *Applied Psycholinguistics, 4,* 103–147.

JUEL, C., GRIFFITH, P. L., and GOUGH, P. B. 1986. Acquisition of literacy: A longitudinal study of children in first and second grade. *Journal of Educational Psychology, 78,* 243–255.

JUOLA, J. F., SCHADLER, M., CHABOT, R. J., and MCCAUGHEY, M. W. 1978. The development of visual information processing skills related to reading. *Journal of Experimental Child Psychology, 25,* 459–476.

JUOLA, J. F., WARD, N. J., and MCNAMARA, T. 1982. Visual search and reading of rapid serial presentations of letter strings, words, and text. *Journal of Experimental Psychology: General, 111,* 208–227.

JUST, M. A., and CARPENTER, P. A. 1980. A theory of reading: From eye fixations to comprehension. *Psychological Review, 87,* 329–354.

JUST, M. A., and CARPENTER, P. A. 1987. *The psychology of reading and language comprehension.* Newton, MA: Allyn and Bacon.

JUST, M. A., CARPENTER, P. A., and MASSON, M. E. J. 1982. *What eye fixations tell us about speed reading and skimming.* Eye-Lab Technical Report: Carnegie-Mellon University.

JUST, M. A., CARPENTER, P. A., and WOOLLEY, J. D. 1982. Paradigms and processes in reading comprehension. *Journal of Experimental Psychology: General, 111,* 228–238.

KAIL, R. V., CHI, M. T. H., INGRAM, A. L., and DANNER, F. W. 1977. Constructive aspects of children's reading comprehension. *Child Development, 48,* 684–688.

KAIL, R. V., and MARSHALL, C. V. 1978. Reading skill and memory scanning. *Journal of Educational Psychology, 70,* 808–814.

KAMEENUI, E. J., CARNINE, D. W., and FRESCHI, R. 1982. Effects of text construction and instructional procedures for teaching word meanings on comprehension and recall. *Reading Research Quarterly, 17,* 367–388.

KARLIN, M. B., and BOWER, G. H. 1976. Semantic category effects in visual word search. *Perception & Psychophysics, 19,* 417–424.

KATZ, J. J., and FODOR, J. A. 1963. The structure of a semantic theory. In L. A. Jakobovits and M. S. Miron (eds.), *Readings in the psychology of language.* Englewood Cliffs, NJ: Prentice-Hall.

KATZ, L. K. 1977. Reading ability and single-letter orthographic redundancy. *Journal of Educational Psychology, 69,* 653–659.

KATZ, L. K., and FELDMAN, L. B. 1983. Relation between pronunciation and recognition of printed words in deep and shallow orthographies. *Journal of Experimental Psychology: Learning, Memory, & Cognition, 9,* 157–166.

KATZ, R. B., SHANKWEILER, D., and LIBERMAN, I. Y. 1981. Memory for item order and phonetic recoding in the beginning reader. *Journal of Experimental Child Psychology, 32,* 474–484.

KEELE, S. W. 1972. Attention demands of memory retrieval. *Journal of Experimental Psychology, 93,* 245–248.

KEENAN, J. M., and BROWN, P. 1984. Children's reading rate and retention as a function of the number of propositions in a text. *Child Development, 55,* 1556–1569.

KEENAN, J. M., MACWHINNEY, B., and MAYHEW, D. 1977. Pragmatics in memory: A study of natural conversation. *Journal of Verbal Learning and Verbal Behavior, 16,* 549–560.

KENNEDY, A., and MURRAY, W. S. 1984. Inspection times for words in syntactically ambiguous sentences under three presentation conditions. *Journal of Experimental Psychology: Human Perception and Performance, 10,* 833–849.

KERTESZ, A. 1979. *Aphasia and associated disorders: Taxonomy, localization and recovery.* New York: Grune and Stratton.

KIMBALL, J. 1973. Seven principles of surface structure parsing in natural language. *Cognition, 2,* 15–47.

KIMURA, Y. 1984. Concurrent vocal interference: Its effects on Kana and Kanji. *Quarterly Journal of Experimental Psychology, 36A,* 117–132.

KIMURA, Y., and BRYANT, P. E. 1983. Reading and writing in English and Japanese: A cross-cultural study of young children. *British Journal of Developmental Psychology, 1,* 143–154.

KINTSCH, W. 1974. *The representation of meaning in memory.* Hillsdale, NJ: Erlbaum.

KINTSCH, W., and KEENAN, J. M. 1973. Reading rate and retention as a function of the number of propositions in the base structure of sentences. *Cognitive Psychology, 5,* 257–274.

KINTSCH, W., KOZMINSKY, E., STREBY, W. J., MCKOON, G., and KEENAN, J. M. 1975. Comprehension and recall of text as a function of content variables. *Journal of Verbal Learning and Verbal Behavior, 14,* 196–214.

KINTSCH, W., and MROSS, E. F. 1985. Context effects in word identification. *Journal of Memory and Language, 24,* 336–349.

KINTSCH, W., and VAN DIJK, T. A. 1978. Toward a model of text comprehension and production. *Psychological Review, 85,* 363–394.

KINTSCH, W., and VIPOND, D. 1979. Reading comprehension and readability in educational practice and psychological theory. In L-G. Nilsson (ed.), *Perspectives on memory research.* Hillsdale, NJ: Erlbaum.

KLEIMAN, G. M. 1975. Speech recoding in reading. *Journal of Verbal Learning and Verbal Behavior, 14,* 323–339.

KLEIN, G. S. 1972. Semantic power measured through the interference of words with color naming. *American Journal of Psychology, 77,* 576–588.

KLIEGL, R., OLSON, R. K., and DAVIDSON, B. J. 1982. Regression analyses as a tool for studying reading processes: Comments on Just and Carpenter's eye fixation theory. *Memory & Cognition, 10,* 287–296.

KOLERS, P. 1972. Experiments in reading. *Scientific American, 227,* 84–91.

KOSSLYN, S. M., and MATT, A. M. 1977. If you speak slowly, do people read your prose slowly? Person-particular speech recoding during reading. *Bulletin of the Psychonomic Society, 9,* 250–252.

KOWLER, E., and MARTINS, A. J. 1982. Eye movements of preschool children. *Science, 215,* 997–999.

KUTAS, M., and HILLYARD, S. A. 1980. Reading senseless sentences: Brain potentials reflect semantic incongruity. *Science, 207,* 203–205.

KUTAS, M., and HILLYARD, S. A. 1983. Event-related brain potentials to grammatical errors and semantic anomalies. *Memory & Cognition, 11,* 539–550.

LABERGE, D. 1972. Beyond auditory coding. In J. F. Kavanagh and I. G. Mattingly (eds.), *Language by ear and by eye.* Cambridge, MA: MIT Press.

LABERGE, D., and SAMUELS, S. J. 1974. Toward a theory of automatic information processing in reading. *Cognitive Psychology, 6,* 293–323.

LEAN, D. S., and ARBUCKLE, T. Y. 1984. Phonological coding in prereaders. *Journal of Educational Psychology, 6,* 1282–1290.

LENNEBERG, E. H. 1967. *Biological foundations of language.* New York: Wiley.

LEONG, C. K. 1973. Hong Kong. In J. Downing (ed.), *Comparative reading.* New York: Macmillan.

LESGOLD, A. M., and CURTIS, M. E. 1981. Learning to read words efficiently. In A. M. Lesgold and C. A. Perfetti (eds.), *Interactive processes in reading.* Hillsdale, NJ: Erlbaum.

LESGOLD, A. M., and RESNICK, L. B. 1982. How reading disabilities develop: Perspectives from a longitudinal study. In J. P. Das, R. Mulcahy, and A. E. Wall (eds.), *Theory and research in learning disability.* New York: Plenum.

LESGOLD, A. M., ROTH, S. F., and CURTIS, M. E. 1979. Foregrounding effects in discourse comprehension. *Journal of Verbal Learning and Verbal Behavior, 18,* 291–308.

LEVELT, W. J. M. 1978. A survey of studies in sentence perception: 1970–1976. In W. J. M. Levelt and G. B. Flores d'Arcais (eds.), *Studies in the perception of language.* Chichester, England: Wiley.

LEVIN, H. 1979. *The eye-voice span.* Cambridge, MA: MIT Press.

LEVIN, H., and KAPLAN, E. L. 1970. Grammatical structure and reading. In H. Levin and J. P. Williams (eds.), *Basic studies on reading.* New York: Basic Books.

LEVY, B. A. 1975. Vocalization and suppression effects in sentence memory. *Journal of Verbal Learning and Verbal Behavior, 14,* 304–316.

LEVY, B. A. 1977. Reading: Speech and meaning processes. *Journal of Verbal Learning and Verbal Behavior, 16,* 623–638.

LEVY, B. A. 1981. Interactive processes during reading. In A. M. Lesgold and C. A. Perfetti (eds.), *Interactive processes in reading*. Hillsdale, NJ: Erlbaum.

LEVY-SCHOEN, A. 1981. Flexible and/or rigid control of oculomotor scanning behavior. In D. F. Fisher, R. A. Monty, and J. W. Senders (eds.), *Eye movements: Cognition and visual perception*. Hillsdale, NJ: Erlbaum.

LEWKOWICZ, N. K. 1980. Phonemic awareness training: What to teach and how to teach it. *Journal of Educational Psychology, 72,* 686–700.

LIBERMAN, A. M., COOPER, F. S., SHANKWEILER, D. P., and STUDDERT-KENNEDY, M. 1967. Perception of the speech code. *Psychological Review, 74,* 431–461.

LIBERMAN, I. Y. 1973. Segmentation of the spoken word and reading acquisition. *Bulletin of the Orton Society, 23,* 65–77.

LIBERMAN, I. Y., LIBERMAN, M., MATTINGLY, I., and SHANKWEILER, D. 1980. Orthography and the beginning reader. In J. Kavanagh and R. Venezky (eds.), *Orthography, reading and dyslexia*. Baltimore: University Park Press.

LIBERMAN, I. Y., MANN, V. A., SHANKWEILER, D., and WERFELMAN, M. 1982. Children's memory for recurring linguistic and nonlinguistic material in relation to reading ability. *Cortex, 18,* 367–375.

LIBERMAN, I. Y., SHANKWEILER, D., LIBERMAN, A. M., FOWLER, C., and FISCHER, F. W. 1977. Phonetic segmentation and recoding in the beginning reader. In A. S. Reber and D. Scarborough (eds.), *Toward a psychology of reading*. Hillsdale, NJ: Erlbaum.

LIBERMAN, I. Y., SHANKWEILER, D., ORLANDO, C., HARRIS, K. S., and BERTI, F. B. 1971. Letter confusion and reversals of sequence in the beginning reader: Implications of Orton's theory of developmental dyslexia. *Cortex, 7,* 127–142.

LIDDLE, W. 1965. *An investigation of the Wood Reading Dynamics method*. Ann Arbor: University Microfilms, No. 60-5559.

LIMA, S. D. 1987a. Morphological analysis in sentence reading. *Journal of Memory and Language, 26,* 84–99.

LIMA, S. D. 1987b. *Stem representation for prefixed words: Effects of compositionality of meanings*. Paper presented at the Midwestern Psychological Association, Chicago.

LIMA, S. D., and INHOFF, A. W. 1985. Lexical access during eye fixations in reading: Effects of word-initial letter sequence. *Journal of Experimental Psychology: Human Perception and Performance, 11,* 272–285.

LIMA, S. D., and POLLATSEK, A. 1983. Lexical access via an orthographic code? The Basic Orthograhic Syllable Structure (BOSS) reconsidered. *Journal of Verbal Learning and Verbal Behavior, 22,* 310–332.

LUI, I.-M, CHUANG, C.-J., and WANG, S.-C. 1975. *Frequency count of 40,000 Chinese words*. Taiwan: Luck Books Company. (In Chinese.)

LLEWELLYN-THOMAS, E. 1962. Eye movements in speed reading. In R. G. Stauffer (ed.), *Speed reading: Practices and procedures*. Newark, DE: University of Delaware Reading Center.

LOCKE, J. L. 1971. Phonemic processing in silent reading. *Perceptual and Motor Skills, 32,* 905–906.

LOCKE, J. L. 1978. Phonemic effects in the silent reading of hearing and deaf children. *Cognition, 6,* 173–187.

LOFTUS, G. R. 1983. Eye fixations on text and scenes. In K. Rayner (ed.), *Eye movements in reading: Perceptual and language processes*. New York: Academic Press.

LOFTUS, G. R., and MACKWORTH, N. H. 1978. Cognitive determinants of fixation location during picture viewing. *Journal of Experimental Psychology: Human Perception & Performance, 4,* 565–572.

LOVEGROVE, W., BILLING, G., and SLAGHUIS, W. 1978. Processing of visual contour orientation information in normal and reading disabled children. *Cortex, 14,* 268–278.

LOVEGROVE, W., BOWLING, A., BADCOCK, D., and BLACKWOOD, M. 1980. Specific reading disability: Differences in contrast sensitivity as a function of spatial frequency. *Science, 210,* 439–440.

LOVEGROVE, W., and BROWN, C. 1978. Development of information processing in normal and disabled readers. *Perceptual and Motor Skills, 46,* 1047–1054.

LOVETT, M. W. 1987. A developmental approach to reading disability: Accuracy and speed criteria of normal and deficient reading skill. *Child Development, 58,* 234–260.

LUKATELA, G., POPADIC, D., OGNJENOVIC, P., and TURVEY, M. T. 1980. Lexical decision in a phonologically shallow orthography. *Memory & Cognition, 8,* 124–132.

LUKATELA, G., SAVIC, M. GLIGORIJEVIC, B., OGNJENOVIC, P., and TURVEY, M. T. 1978. Bi-alphabetical lexical decision. *Language and Speech, 21,* 142–165.

LUNDBERG, I., OLOFSSON, A., and WALL, S. 1980. Reading and spelling skills in the first school years predicted from phonemic awareness skills in kindergarten. *Scandinavian Journal of Psychology, 21,* 159–173.

LYLE, J. G. 1979. Reading retardation and reversal tendency: A factorial study. *Child Development, 40,* 832–843.

LYLE, J. G., and GOYEN, J. 1968. Visual recognition, developmental lag, and strephosymbolia in reading retardation. *Journal of Abnormal Psychology, 73,* 25–29.

MACKWORTH, J. F. 1972. Some models of the reading process: Learners and skilled readers. *Reading Research Quarterly, 7,* 701–733.

MACKWORTH, N. H. 1965. Visual noise causes tunnel vision. *Psychonomic Science, 3,* 67–68.

MACKWORTH, N. H., and MORANDI, A. J. 1967. The gaze selects informative details within pictures. *Perception & Psychophysics, 2,* 547–552.

MACLEAN, M., BRYANT, P. E., and BRADLEY, L. 1987. Rhymes, nursery rhymes, and reading in early childhood. *Merrill-Palmer Quarterly, 33,* 255–281.

MANDLER, J. M., and JOHNSON, N. S. 1977. Remembrance of things parsed: Story structure and recall. *Cognitive Psychology, 9,* 111–151.

MANELIS, L., and THARP, D. A. 1976. The processing of affixed words. *Memory & Cognition, 4,* 53–61.

MANN, V. A. 1984. Reading skill and language skill. *Developmental Review, 4,* 1–15.

MANN, V. 1986. Phonological awareness: The role of reading experience. *Cognition, 24,* 65–92.

MANN, V. A., and LIBERMAN, I. Y. 1984. Phonological awareness and verbal short-term memory. *Journal of Learning Disabilities, 17,* 592–599.

MANN, V. A., LIBERMAN, I. Y., and SHANKWEILER, D. 1980. Children's memory for sentences and word strings in relation to reading ability. *Memory & Cognition, 8,* 329–335.

MANN, V. A., SHANKWEILER, D., and SMITH, S. T. 1985. The association between comprehension of spoken sentences and early reading ability: The role of phonetic representation. *Journal of Child Language, 11,* 627–643.

MARCEL, T. 1974. The effective visual field and the use of context in fast and slow readers of two ages. *British Journal of Psychology, 65,* 479–492.

MARCEL, A. 1978. Unconscious reading: Experiments on people who do not know they are reading. *Visible Language, 12,* 391–404.

MARCEL, A. J. 1980. Surface dyslexia and beginning reading: A revised hypothesis of pronunciation of print and its impairments. In M. Coltheart, K. Patterson, and J. C. Marshall (eds.), *Deep dyslexia.* London: Routledge & Kegan Paul.

MARCEL, A. J. 1983. Conscious and unconscious perception: Experiments on visual masking. *Cognitive Psychology, 15,* 197–237.

MARCEL, T., KATZ, L., and SMITH, M. 1974. Laterality and reading proficiency. *Neuropsychologia, 12,* 131–139.

MARCEL, T., and RAJAN, P. 1975. Lateral specialization for recognition of words and faces in good and poor readers. *Neuropsychologia, 13,* 489–497.

MARCHBANKS, G., and LEVIN, H. 1965. Cues by which children recognize words. *Journal of Educational Psychology, 56,* 57–61.

MARCUS, M. 1980. *A theory of syntactic recognition for natural language.* Cambridge, MA: MIT Press.

MARGOLIN, C. M., GRIEBEL, B., and WOLFORD, G. 1982. Effect of distraction on reading versus listening. *Journal of Experimental Psychology: Learning, Memory, and Cognition, 8,* 613–618.

MARK, L. S., SHANKWEILER, D., LIBERMAN, I. Y., and FOWLER, C. A. 1977. Phonetic recoding and reading difficulty in beginning readers. *Memory & Cognition, 5,* 623–629.

MARKMAN, E. M. 1979. Realizing that you don't understand: Elementary school children's awareness of inconsistencies. *Child Development, 50,* 643–655.

MARKMAN, E. M. 1981. Comprehension monitoring. In W. P. Dickson (ed.), *Children's oral communication skills.* New York: Academic Press.

MARKS, C. B., DOCTOROW, M. J., and WITTROCK, M. C. 1974. Word frequency and reading comprehension. *Journal of Educational Research, 67*, 259–262.

MARSH, G., FRIEDMAN, M. WELCH, V., and DESBERG, P. 1981. A cognitive-developmental approach to reading acquisition. In T. G. Waller and G. E. MacKinnon (eds.), *Reading research: Advances in theory and practice*, Vol. 3. New York: Academic Press.

MARSHALL, J. C., and NEWCOMBE, F. 1966. Syntactic and semantic errors in paralexia. *Neurophychologia, 4*, 169–176.

MARSHALL, J. C., and NEWCOMBE, F. 1973. Patterns of paralexia: A psycholinguistic approach. *Journal of Psycholinguistic Research, 2*, 175–200.

MARTIN, M. 1978. Speech recoding in silent reading. *Memory & Cognition, 6*, 108–114.

MARTIN, S. E. 1972. Nonalphabetic writing systems: Some observations. In J. F. Kavanagh and I. G. Mattingly (eds.), *Language by ear and by eye*. Cambridge, MA: MIT Press.

MASON, J. M. 1980. When do children begin to read: An exploration of four year old children's letter and word reading competencies. *Reading Research Quarterly, 15*, 203–227.

MASON, M. 1975. Reading ability and letter search time: Effects of orthographic structures defined by single letter positional frequency. *Journal of Experimental Psychology: General, 104*, 146–166.

MASON, M., and KATZ, L. K. 1976. Visual processing of nonlinguistic strings: Redundancy effects and reading ability. *Journal of Experimental Psychology: General, 105*, 338–348.

MASSARO, D. W. 1975. *Understanding language: An information-processing analysis of speech perception, reading, and psycholinguistics*. New York: Academic Press.

MASSARO, D. W., and TAYLOR, G. A. 1980. Reading ability and utilization of orthographic structure in reading. *Journal of Educational Psychology, 72*, 730–742.

MASSARO, D. W., TAYLOR, G. A., VENEZKY, R. L., JASTRZEMBSKI, J. E., and LUCAS, P. A. 1980. *Letter and word perception: Orthographic structure and visual processing in reading*. Amsterdam: North-Holland.

MASSON, M. E. J. 1983. Conceptual processing of text during skimming and rapid sequential reading. *Memory & Cognition, 11*, 262–274.

MASSON, M. E. J., and MILLER, J. 1983. Working memory and individual differences in comprehension and memory of text. *Journal of Educational Psychology, 75*, 314–318.

MATIN, E. 1974. Saccadic suppression: A review and an analysis. *Psychological Bulletin, 81*, 899–917.

MATTINGLY, I. G. 1972. Reading, the linguistic process, and linguistic awareness. In J. F. Kavanagh and I. G. Mattingly, (eds.), *Language by ear and by eye*. Cambridge, MA: MIT Press.

MATTIS, S. 1978. Dyslexia syndromes: A working hypothesis that works. In A. L. Benton and D. Perl (eds.), *Dyslexia: An appraisal of current knowledge*. New York: Oxford University Press.

MATTIS, S., FRENCH, J. H., and RAPIN, I. 1975. Dyslexia in children and young adults: Three independent neuropsychological syndromes. *Developmental Medicine and Child Neurology, 17*, 150–163.

MCCAUGHEY, M., JUOLA, J., SCHADLER, M., and WARD, N. 1980. Whole-word units are used before orthographic knowledge in perceptual development. *Journal of Experimental Child Psychology, 30*, 411–421.

MCCLELLAND, J. L. 1986. The programmable blackboard model of reading. In J. L. McClelland, D. E. Rumelhart, and The PDP research group (eds.), *Parallel distributed processing: Explorations in the microstructure of cognition*, Vol. II. Cambridge, MA: Bradford Books.

MCCLELLAND, J. L. 1987. The case for interactionism in language processing. In M. Coltheart (ed.), *Attention and performance 12*. London: Erlbaum.

MCCLELLAND, J. L., and O'REGAN, J. K. 1981. Expectations increase the benefit derived from parafoveal visual information in reading words aloud. *Journal of Experimental Psychology: Human Perception and Performance, 7*, 634–644.

MCCLELLAND, J. L., and RUMELHART, D. E. 1981. An interactive activation model of context effects in letter perception: Part 1. An account of basic findings. *Psychological Review, 88*, 375–407.

MCCONKIE, G. W. 1979. On the role and control of eye movements in reading. In P. A. Kolers, M. E. Wrolstad, and H. Bouma, (eds.), *Processing of visible language (Vol. 1)*. New York: Plenum.

MCCONKIE, G. W., and HOGABOAM, T. W. 1985. Eye position and word identification in reading. In R. Groner, G. W. McConkie, and C. Menz (eds.), *Eye movements and human information processing*. Amsterdam: North-Holland Press.

MCCONKIE, G. W., and RAYNER, K. 1975. The span of the effective stimulus during a fixation in reading. *Perception & Psychophysics, 17,* 578–586.

MCCONKIE, G. W., and RAYNER, K. 1976a. Asymmetry of the perceptual span in reading. *Bulletin of the Psychonomic Society, 8,* 365–368.

MCCONKIE, G. W., and RAYNER, K. 1976b. Identifying the span of the effective stimulus in reading: Literature review and theories of reading. In H. Singer and R. B. Ruddell (eds.), *Theoretical models and processes in reading*. Newark, DE: International Reading Association.

MCCONKIE, G. W., RAYNER, K., and WILSON, S. J. 1973. Experimental manipulation of reading strategies. *Journal of Educational Psychology, 65,* 1–8.

MCCONKIE, G. W., UNDERWOOD, N. R., ZOLA, D., and WOLVERTON, G. S. 1985. Some temporal characteristics of processing during reading. *Journal of Experimental Psychology: Human Perception and Performance, 11,* 168–186.

MCCONKIE, G. W., and ZOLA, D. 1979. Is visual information integrated across successive fixations in reading? *Perception & Psychophysics, 25,* 221–224.

MCCONKIE, G. W., and ZOLA, D. 1981. Language constraints and the functional stimulus in reading. In A. M. Lesgold and C. A. Perfetti (eds.), *Interactive processes in reading*. Hillsdale, NJ: Erlbaum.

MCCONKIE, G. W., and ZOLA, D. 1984. Eye movement control during reading: The effects of word units. In W. Prinz and A. F. Sanders (eds.), *Cognition and motor processes*. Berlin: Springer-Verlag.

MCCONKIE, G. W., ZOLA, D., BLANCHARD, H. E., and WOLVERTON, G. S. 1982. Perceiving words during reading: Lack of facilitation from prior peripheral exposure. *Perception & Psychophysics, 32,* 271–281.

MCCONKIE, G. W., ZOLA, D., and WOLVERTON, G. S. 1980. *How precise is eye guidance?* Paper presented at the annual meeting of the American Educational Research Association, Boston, MA, April.

MCCUSKER, L. X., BIAS, R. G., and HILLINGER, M. L. 1981. Phonological recoding and reading. *Psychological Bulletin, 89,* 217–245.

MCCUTCHEN, D., and PERFETTI, C. A. 1982. The visual tongue-twister effect: Phonological activation in silent reading. *Journal of Verbal Learning and Verbal Behavior, 21,* 672–687.

MCGUIGAN, F. J. 1967. Feedback of speech muscle activity during silent reading: Two comments. *Science, 157,* 579–580.

MCGUIGAN, F. J. 1970. Covert oral behavior during the silent performance of language tasks. *Psychological Bulletin, 74,* 309–326.

MCGUIGAN, F. J. 1971. External auditory feedback from covert oral behavior during silent reading. *Psychonomic Science, 25,* 212–214.

MCGUIGAN, F. J., and BAILEY, S. C. 1969. Longitudinal study of covert oral behavior during silent reading. *Perceptual and Motor Skills, 28,* 170.

MCGUIGAN, F. J., KELLER, B., and STANTON, E. 1964. Covert language responses during silent reading. *Journal of Educational Psychology, 55,* 339–343.

MCGURK, H., and MACDONALD, J. 1976. Hearing eyes and seeing voices. *Nature, 264,* 746–748.

MCKEEVER, W. F., and HULING, M. D. 1970. Lateral dominance in tachistoscopic word recognition of children at two levels of ability. *Quarterly Journal of Experimental Psychology, 22,* 600–604.

MCKEEVER, W. F., and VAN DEVENTER, A. D. 1975. Dyslexic adolescents: Evidence of impaired visual and auditory language processing associated with normal lateralization and visual responsivity. *Cortex, 11,* 361–378.

MCKEOWN, M. G., BECK, I. L., OMANSON, R. C., and PERFETTI, C. A. 1983. The effects of long-term vocabulary instruction on reading comprehension: A replication. *Journal of Reading Behavior, 15,* 3–18.

MCKOON, G., and RATCLIFF, R. 1980. Priming in item recognition: The organization of propositions in memory for text. *Journal of Verbal Learning and Verbal Behavior, 19,* 369–386.

MCKOON, G., and RATCLIFF, R. 1981. The comprehension processes and memory structures involved in instrumental inference. *Journal of Verbal Learning and Verbal Behavior, 20,* 671–682.

MCKOON, G., and RATCLIFF, R. 1986. Inferences about predictable events. *Journal of Experimental Psychology: Learning, Memory, and Cognition, 12,* 82–91.

MCLAUGHLIN, G. H. 1969. Reading at "impossible" speeds. *Journal of Reading, 12,* 449–454, 502–510.

MCMAHON, M. L. 1976. Phonemic processing in reading printed words: Effects of phonemic relationships between words on semantic response categorization time. Unpublished Master's thesis, University of Massachusetts, Amherst.

MEHLER, J., SEQUI, J., and CAREY, P. 1978. Tails of words: Monitoring ambiguity. *Journal of Verbal Learning and Verbal Behavior, 17,* 29–36.

MELTZER, H. S., and HERSE, R. 1969. The boundaries of written words as seen by first graders. *Journal of Reading Behavior, 1,* 3–14.

MEYER, B. J. F. 1975. *The organization of prose and its effect on recall.* Amsterdam: North Holland.

MEYER, B. J. F., and MCCONKIE, G. W. 1973. What is recalled after hearing a passage? *Journal of Educational Psychology, 65,* 109–117.

MEYER, D. E. 1970. On the representation and retrieval of stored semantic information. *Cognitive Psychology, 1,* 242–300.

MEYER, D. E., and GUTSCHERA, K. 1975. *Orthograhic versus phonemic processing of printed words.* Paper presented at the annual meeting of the Psychonomic Society, Denver, CO, November.

MEYER, D. E., and SCHVANEVELDT, R. W. 1971. Facilitation in recognizing pairs of words: Evidence of a dependence between retrieval operations. *Journal of Experimental Psychology, 90,* 227–234.

MEYER, D. E., SCHVANEVELDT, R. W., and RUDDY, M. G. 1974. Functions of graphemic and phonemic codes in visual word-recognition. *Memory & Cognition, 2,* 309–321.

MEZRICH, J. J. 1973. The word superiority effect in brief visual displays: Elimination by vocalization. *Perception & Psychophysics, 13,* 45–48.

MICKISH, V. 1974. Children's perceptions of written word boundaries. *Journal of Reading Behavior, 6,* 19–22.

MILLER, G. A. 1956. The magical number seven, plus or minus two: Some limits on our capacity for processing information. *Psychological Review, 63,* 81–89.

MILLER, J. R., and KINTSCH, W. 1980. Readability and recall of short prose passages: A theoretical analysis. *Journal of Experimental Psychology: Human Learning and Memory, 6,* 335–354.

MINDELL, P. 1978. Dyslexia and sequential order errors in reading. *Bulletin of the Orton Society. 28,* 124–141.

MITCHELL, D. C. 1982. *The process of reading.* Chichester, England: Wiley.

MITCHELL, D. C., and GREEN, D. W. 1978. The effects of context and content on immediate processing in reading. *Quarterly Journal of Experimental Psychology, 30,* 609–636.

MITCHELL, D. C., and HOLMES, V. M. 1985. The role of specific information about the verb in parsing sentences with local structural ambiguity. *Journal of Memory and Language, 24,* 542–559.

MITTERER, J. O. 1982. There are at least two kinds of poor readers: Whole-word poor readers and recoding poor readers. *Canadian Journal of Psychology, 36,* 445–461.

MOHAN, P. J. 1978. Acoustic factors in letter cancellation: Developmental considerations. *Developmental Psychology, 14,* 117–118.

MORAIS, J., ALEGRIA, J., and CONTENT, A. 1987. The relationship between segmental analysis and alphabetic literacy: An interactive view. *Cahiers de Psychologie Cognitive, 7,* 415–438.

MORAIS, J., CARY, L., ALEGRIA, J., and BERTELSON, P. 1979. Does awareness of speech as a sequence of phones arise spontaneously? *Cognition, 7,* 323–331.

MORRIS, R. K. 1987. *Eye movement guidance in reading: The role of parafoveal letter and space information.* Unpublished master's thesis, University of Massachusetts.

MORRISON, F. J., GIORDANI, B., and NAGY, J. 1977. Reading disability: An information-processing analysis. *Science, 196,* 77–79.

MORRISON, R. E. 1984. Manipulation of stimulus onset delay in reading: Evidence for parallel programming of saccades. *Journal of Experimental Psychology: Human Perception and Performance, 10,* 667–682.

MORRISON, R. E., and INHOFF, A. W. 1981. Visual factors and eye movements in reading. *Visible Language, 15,* 129–146.

MORRISON, R. E., and RAYNER, K. 1981. Saccade size in reading depends upon character spaces and not visual angle. *Perception & Psychophysics, 30,* 395–396.

MORTON, J. 1964a. The effects of context upon speed of reading, eye movement and eye-voice span. *Quarterly Journal of Experimental Psychology, 16,* 340–354.

MORTON, J. 1964b. The effect of context on the visual duration threshold for words. *British Journal of Psychology, 55,* 165–180.

MORTON, J., and PATTERSON, K. E. 1980. Little words-no! In M. Coltheart, K. E. Patterson, and J. C. Marshall (eds.), *Deep dyslexia.* London: Routledge & Kegan Paul.

MORTON, J., and SASANUMA, S. 1984. Lexical access in Japanese. In L. Henderson (ed.), *Orthographies and reading.* London: Erlbaum.

MOUSTY, P., and BERTELSON, P. 1985. A study of Braille reading: Reading speed as a function of hand usage and context. *Quarterly Journal of Experimental Psychology, 37A,* 217–233.

MURPHY, L. A., POLLATSEK, A., and WELL, A. D. 1988. Developmental dyslexia and word retrieval deficits. *Brain and Language, 35,* 1–23.

MURRAY, F. B. 1978. Critique: Development of intellect and reading. In F. B. Murray and J. J. Pikulski (eds.), *The acquisition of reading: Cognitive, linguistic, and perceptual prerequisites.* Baltimore: University Park Press.

MURRELL, G. A., and MORTON, J. 1974. Word recognition and morphemic structure. *Journal of Experimental Psychology, 102,* 963–968.

MYERS, J. L., SHINJO, M., and DUFFY, S. A. 1987. Degree of causal relatedness and memory. *Journal of Memory and Language, 26,* 453–465.

MYERS, M., and PARIS, S. G. 1978. Children's metacognitive knowledge about reading. *Journal of Educational Psychology, 70,* 680–690.

NAVON, D., and SHIMRON, J. 1981. Does word meaning involve grapheme-to-phoneme translation? Evidence from Hebrew. *Journal of Verbal Learning and Verbal Behavior, 20,* 97–109.

NEELY, J. H. 1977. Semantic priming and retrieval from lexical memory: The roles of inhibitionless spreading activation and limited-capacity attention. *Journal of Experimental Psychology: General, 106,* 1–66.

NEISSER, U. 1967. *Cognitive psychology.* New York: Appleton-Century-Crofts.

NEWCOMBE, F., and MARSHALL, J. 1981. On psycholinguistic classifications of the acquired dyslexias. *Bulletin of the Orton Society, 31,* 29–46.

NEWMAN, E. B. 1966. Speed of reading when the span of letters is restricted. *American Journal of Psychology, 79,* 272–278.

NEWMAN, J. E., and DELL, G. S. 1978. The phonological nature of phoneme monitoring: A critique of some ambiguity studies. *Journal of Verbal Learning and Verbal Behavior, 17,* 359–374.

NODINE, C. F., and EVANS, D. 1969. Eye movements of prereaders to pseudowords containing letters of high and low confusability. *Perception & Psychophysics, 6,* 39–41.

NODINE, C. F., and LANG, N. J. 1971. Development of visual scanning strategies for differentiating words. *Developmental Psychology, 5,* 221–232.

NODINE, C. F., and SIMMONS, F. G. 1974. Processing distinctive features in the differentiation of letterlike symbols. *Journal of Experimental Psychology, 103,* 21–28.

NODINE, C. F., and STEUERLE, N. L. 1973. Development of perceptual and cognitive strategies for differentiating graphemes. *Journal of Experimental Psychology, 97* 158–166.

NOIZET, G., and PYNTE, J. 1976. Implicit labelling and readiness for pronounciation during the perceptual process. *Perception, 5,* 217–223.

O'BRIEN, E. J. 1987. Antecedent search processes and the structure of text. *Journal of Experimental Psychology: Learning, Memory, and Cognition, 13,* 278–290.

O'BRIEN, E. J., DUFFY, S. A., and MYERS, J. L. Anaphoric inference during reading. *Journal of Experimental Psychology: Learning, Memory, and Cognition, 12,* 346–352.

O'BRIEN, E. J., and MYERS, J. L. 1985. When comprehension difficulty improves memory for text. *Journal of Experimental Psychology: Learning, Memory, and Cognition, 11,* 12–21.

O'BRIEN, E. J., and MYERS, J. L. 1987. The role of causal connections in the retrieval of text. *Memory & Cognition, 15,* 419–427.

O'BRIEN, E. J., SHANK, D. M., MYERS, J. L., and RAYNER, K. 1988. Elaborative inferences during reading: Do they occur on-line? *Journal of Experimental Psychology: Learning, Memory, and Cognition, 14,* 410–420.

OLOFSSON, A., and LUNDBERG, I. 1985. Evaluation of long term effects of phonemic awareness training in kindergarten: Illustrations of some methodological problems in evaluating research. *Scandinavian Journal of Psychology, 26,* 21–34.

OLSON, M. E. 1973. Laterality differences in tachistoscopic word recognition in normal and delayed readers in elementary school. *Neuropsychologia, 11,* 343–350.

OLSON, R. K., DAVIDSON, B. J., KLIEGL, R., and DAVIES, S. 1984. Development of phonological memory in disabled and normal readers. *Journal of Experimental Child Psychology, 37,* 187–206.

OLSON, R. K., KLIEGL, R., and DAVIDSON, B. J. 1983. Dyslexic and normal children's tracking eye movements. *Journal of Experimental Psychology: Human Perception and Performance, 9,* 816–825.

OMANSON, R. C. 1985. Knowing words and understanding texts. In T. H. Carr (ed.) *The development of reading skills.* San Francisco: Jossey-Bass.

OMANSON, R. C., BECK, I. L., MCKEOWN, M. G., and PERFETTI, C. A. 1984. Comprehension of texts with unfamiliar versus recently taught words: Assessment of alternative models. *Journal of Educational Psychology, 76,* 1253–1268.

O'NEILL, G., and STANLEY, G. 1976. Visual processing of straight lines in dyslexic and normal children. *British Journal of Educational Psychology, 46,* 323–327.

ONIFER, W., and SWINNEY, D. A. 1981. Accessing lexical ambiguities during sentence comprehension: Effects of frequency, meaning, and contextual bias. *Memory & Cognition, 9,* 225–236.

O'REGAN, J. K. 1975. *Structural and contextual constraints on eye movements in reading.* Unpublished doctoral dissertation, University of Cambridge, England.

O'REGAN, J. K. 1979. Eye guidance in reading: Evidence for the linguistic control hypothesis. *Perception & Psychophysics, 25,* 501–509.

O'REGAN, J. K. 1980. The control of saccade size and fixation duration in reading: The limits of linguistic control. *Perception & Psychophysics, 28,* 112–117.

O'REGAN, J. K. 1981. The convenient viewing position hypothesis. In D. F. Fisher, R. A. Monty, and J. W. Senders (eds.), *Eye movements: Cognition and visual perception.* Hillsdale, NJ: Erlbaum.

O'REGAN, J. K. 1983. Elementary perception and eye movement control processes in reading. In K. Rayner (ed.), *Eye movements in reading: Perceptual and language processes.* New York: Academic Press.

O'REGAN, J. K., and LEVY-SCHOEN, A. 1983. Integrating visual information from successive fixations: Does transsaccadic fusion exist? *Vision Research, 23,* 765–768.

O'REGAN, J. K., LEVY-SCHOEN, A., and JACOBS, A. M. 1983. The effect of visibility on eye movement parameters in reading. *Perception & Psychophysics, 34,* 457–464.

O'REGAN, J. K., LEVY-SCHOEN, A., PYNTE, J., and BRUGAILLERE, B. 1984. Convenient fixation location within isolated words of different length and structures. *Journal of Experimental Psychology: Human Perception & Performance, 10,* 250–257.

ORTON, S. T. 1928. Specific reading disability—strephosymbolia. *Journal of the American Medical Association, 90,* 1095–1099.

OSAKA, N. 1987. Effect of peripheral visual field size upon eye movements during Japanese text processing. In J. K. O'Regan and A. Levy-Schoen (eds.), *Eye movements: From physiology to cognition.* Amsterdam: Elsevier.

PAAP, K. R., NEWSOME, S. L., McDONALD, J. E., and SCHVANEVELDT, R. W. 1982. An activation-verification model for letter and word recognition: The word superiority effect. *Psychological Review, 89,* 573–594.

PAAP, K. R., NEWSOME, S. L., and NOEL, R. W. 1984. Word shape's in poor shape for the race to the lexicon. *Journal of Experimental Psychology: Human Perception & Performance, 10,* 413–428.

PALINSCAR, A. S., and BROWN, A. L. 1984. Reciprocal teaching of comprehension and monitoring activities. *Cognition and Instruction, 1,* 117–175.

PALMER, J., MACLEOD, C. M., HUNT, E., and DAVIDSON, J. E. 1985. Information processing correlates of reading. *Journal of Memory and Language, 24,* 59–88.

PARIS, S. G., CROSS, D. R., and LIPSON, M. Y. 1984. Informed strategies for learning: A program to improve children's reading awareness and comprehension. *Journal of Educational Psychology, 76,* 1239–1252.

PARIS, S. G., and JACOBS, J. E. 1984. The benefits of informed instruction for children's reading awareness and comprehension skills. *Child Development, 55,* 2083–2093.

PARIS, S. G., and LINDAUER, B. K. 1976. The role of inference in children's comprehension and memory for sentences. *Cognitive Psychology, 8,* 217–227.

PARKIN, A. J. 1982. Phonological recoding in lexical decision: Effects of spelling-to-sound regularity depend on how regularity is defined. *Memory & Cognition, 10,* 43–53.

PATTERSON, K. E. 1979. What is right with "deep" dyslexic patients? *Brain and Language, 8,* 111–129.

PATTERSON, K. E. 1982. The relation between reading and phonological coding: Further neuropsychological observations. In A. W. Ellis (ed.), *Normality and pathology in cognitive functions.* London: Academic Press.

PATTERSON, K. E., and BESNER, D. 1984. Is the right hemisphere literate? *Cognitive Neuropsychology, 1,* 523–541.

PATTERSON, K. E., and KAY, J. 1982. Letter-by-letter reading: Psychological descriptions of a neurological syndrome. *Quarterly Journal of Experimental Psychology, 34A,* 411–422.

PATTERSON, K. E., and MARCEL, A. 1977. Aphasia, dyslexia, and the phonological code of written words. *Quarterly Journal of Experimental Psychology, 29,* 307–318.

PATTERSON, K. E., MARSHALL, J. C., and COLTHEART, M. 1985. *Surface dyslexia: Neuropsychological and cognitive studies of phonological reading.* Hillsdale, NJ: Erlbaum.

PAVLIDIS, G. T. 1981. Do eye movements hold the key to dyslexia? *Neuropsychologia, 19,* 57–64.

PAVLIDIS, G. T. 1983. The "dyslexia syndrome" and its objective diagnosis by erratic eye movements. In K. Rayner (ed.), *Eye movements in reading: Perceptual and language processes.* New York: Academic Press.

PAVLIDIS, G. T. 1985. Eye movement differences between dyslexics, normal, and retarded readers while sequentially fixating digits. *American Journal of Optometry & Physiological Optics, 62,* 820–832.

PENFIELD, W., and ROBERTS, L. 1959. *Speech and brain mechanisms.* Princeton, NJ: Princeton University Press.

PERFETTI, C. A. 1985. *Reading ability.* New York: Oxford University Press.

PERFETTI, C. A., BELL, L. C., and DELANEY, C. 1988. Automatic phonetic activation in silent word reading: Evidence from backward masking. *Journal of Memory and Language, 27,* 59–70.

PERFETTI, C. A., BEVERLY, S., BELL, L. C., and HUGHES, C. 1987. Phonemic knowledge and learning to read: A longitudinal study of first grade children. *Merrill-Palmer Quarterly, 33,* 283–319.

PERFETTI, C. A., FINGER, E., and HOGABOAM, T. W. 1978. Sources of vocalization latency differences between skilled and less skilled young readers. *Journal of Educational Psychology, 70,* 730–739.

PERFETTI, C. A., and GOLDMAN, S. R. 1976. Discourse memory and reading comprehension skill. *Journal of Verbal Learning and Verbal Behavior, 14,* 33–42.

PERFETTI, C. A., GOLDMAN, S. R., and HOGABOAM, T. W. 1979. Reading skill and the identification of words in discourse context. *Memory & Cognition, 7,* 273–282.

PERFETTI, C. A., and HOGABOAM, T. W. 1975. The relationship between single word decoding and reading comprehension skill. *Journal of Educational Psychology, 67,* 461–469.

PERFETTI, C. A., and MCCUTCHEN, D. 1982. Speech processes in reading. Pp. 237–269 in N. Lass (ed.), *Speech and langauge: Advances in basic research and practice* (Vol. 7). New York: Academic Press.

PERFETTI, C. A., and ROTH, S. F. 1981. Some of the interactive processes in reading and their role in reading skill. In A. M. Lesgold and C. A. Perfetti (eds.), *Interactive processes in reading.* Hillsdale, NJ: Erlbaum.

PETERSEN, S. E., FOX, P. T., POSNER, M. I., MINTUN, W. and RAICHLE, M. E. 1988. Positron emission tonographic studies of the cortical anatomy of single word processing, *Nature, 331,* 585–589.

PIAGET, J. 1952. *The origins of intelligence in children.* New York: International Universities Press.

PICHERT, J. W., and ANDERSON, R. C. 1977. Taking different perspectives on a story. *Journal of Educational Psychology, 69,* 309–315.

PICK, A. D., UNZE, M. G., BROWNELL, C. A., DROZDAL, J. G., and HOPMANN, M. R. 1978. Young children's knowledge of word structure. *Child Development, 49,* 669–680.

PINTNER, R. 1913. Inner speech during silent reading. *Psychological Review, 20,* 129–153.
PIROZZOLO, F. J. 1979. *The neuropsychology of developmental reading disorders.* New York: Praeger.
PIROZZOLO, F. J., and RAYNER, K. 1977. Hemispheric specialization in reading and word recognition. *Brain and Language, 4,* 248–261.
PIROZZOLO, F. J., and RAYNER, K. 1978. The normal control of eye movements in acquired and developmental reading disorders. In H. Avakian-Whitaker and H. A. Whitaker (eds.), *Advances in neurolinguistics and psycholinguistics.* New York: Academic Press.
PITMAN, J., and ST. JOHN, J. 1969. *Alphabets & reading.* London: Sir Isaac Pitman and Sons.
POLLATSEK, A., BOLOZKY, S., WELL, A. D., and RAYNER K. 1981. Asymmetries in the perceptual span for Israeli readers. *Brain and Language, 14,* 174–180.
POLLATSEK, A., and RAYNER, K. 1982. Eye movement control in reading: The role of word boundaries. *Journal of Experimental Psychology: Human Perception and Performance, 8,* 817–833.
POLLATSEK, A., RAYNER, K., and BALOTA, D. A. 1986. Inferences about eye movement control from the perceptual span in reading. *Perception & Psychophysics, 40,* 123–130.
POLLATSEK, A., WELL, A., and GOTT, R. 1978. *Searching through words and non-words.* Paper presented at Psychonomic Society Nineteenth Annual Meeting.
POSNANSKY, C. J., and RAYNER, K. 1977. Visual-feature and response components in a picture-word interference task with beginning and skilled readers. *Journal of Experimental Child Psychology, 24,* 440–460.
POSNER, M. I. 1980. Orienting of attention. *Quarterly Journal of Experimental Psychology, 32,* 3–25.
POSNER, M. I., and BOIES, S. W. 1971. Components of attention. *Psychological Review, 78,* 391–408.
POSNER, M. I., and SNYDER, C. R. R. 1975. Attention and cognitive control. In R. Solso (ed.), *Information processing and cognition: The Loyola symposium.* Hillsdale, NJ: Erlbaum.
POTTER, M. C., KROLL, J. F., and HARRIS, C. 1980. Comprehension and memory in rapid, sequential reading. In R. S. Nickerson (ed.), *Attention and performance* (Vol. 8). Hillsdale, NJ: Erlbaum.
POULTON, E. C. 1962. Peripheral vision, refractoriness and eye movements in fast oral reading. *British Journal of Psychology, 53,* 409–419.
PRIOR, M., and McCORRISTON, M. 1983. Acquired and developmental spelling dyslexia. *Brain and Language, 20,* 263–285.
PRITCHARD, R. M. 1961. Stabilized images on the retina. *Scientific American, 204,* 72–78.
PYNTE, J. 1974. Readiness for pronunciation during the reading process. *Perception & Psychophysics, 16,* 110–112.
QUINN, L. 1981. Reading skills of hearing and congenitally deaf children. *Journal of Experimental Child Psychology, 32,* 139–161.
RADER, N. 1975. *From written words to meaning: A developmental study.* Unpublished doctoral dissertation, Cornell University, Ithaca, NY.
RANKIN. E. F. 1970. How flexibly do we read? *Journal of Reading Behavior, 3,* 34–38.
RAYNER, K. 1975a. The perceptual span and peripheral cues in reading. *Cognitive Psychology, 7,* 65–81.
RAYNER, K. 1975b. Parafoveal identification during a fixation in reading. *Acta Psychologica, 39,* 271–282.
RAYNER, K. 1976. Developmental changes in word recognition strategies. *Journal of Educational Psychology, 68,* 323–329.
RAYNER, K. 1977. Visual attention in reading: Eye movements reflect cognitive processes. *Memory & Cognition, 4,* 443–448.
RAYNER, K. 1978a. Eye movements in reading and information processing. *Psychological Bulletin, 85,* 618–660.
RAYNER, K. 1978b. Foveal and parafoveal cues in reading. In J. Requin (ed.), *Attention and performance VII.* Hillsdale, NJ: Erlbaum.
RAYNER, K. 1979. Eye guidance in reading: Fixation locations within words. *Perception, 8,* 21–30.
RAYNER, K. 1983. *Eye movements in reading: Perceptual and language processes.* New York: Academic Press.
RAYNER, K. 1984. Visual selection in reading, picture perception, and visual search: A

tutorial review. In H. Bouma and D. Bouwhuis (eds.), *Attention and performance X*. Hillsdale, NJ: Erlbaum.

RAYNER, K. 1985. Do faulty eye movements cause dyslexia? *Developmental Neuropsychology, 1,* 3–15.

RAYNER, K. 1986a. Eye movements and the perceptual span in beginning and skilled readers. *Journal of Experimental Child Psychology, 41,* 211–236.

RAYNER, K. 1986b. Eye movements and the perceptual span: Evidence for dyslexic typology. In G. T. Pavlidis and D. F. Fisher (eds.), *Dyslexia: Its neuropsychology and treatment.* New York: Wiley.

RAYNER, K. 1988. Word recognition cues in children: The relative use of graphemic cues, orthographic cues and grapheme-phoneme correspondence rules. *Journal of Educational Psychology.* In press.

RAYNER, K., BALOTA, D. A., and POLLATSEK, A. 1986. Against parafoveal semantic preprocessing during eye fixations in reading. *Canadian Journal of Psychology, 40,* 473–483.

RAYNER, K., and BERTERA, J. H. 1979. Reading without a fovea. *Science, 206,* 468–469.

RAYNER, K., CARLSON, M., and FRAZIER, L. 1983. The interaction of syntax and semantics during sentence processing: Eye movements in the analysis of semantically biased sentences. *Journal of Verbal Learning and Verbal Behavior, 22,* 358–374.

RAYNER, K., and DUFFY, S. A. 1986. Lexical complexity and fixation times in reading: Effects of word frequency, verb complexity, and lexical ambiguity. *Memory & Cognition, 14,* 191–201.

RAYNER, K., and DUFFY, S. A. 1987. Eye movements and lexical ambiguity. In J. K. O'Regan and A. Levy-Schoen (eds.), *Eye movements: From physiology to cognition.* Amsterdam: Elsevier.

RAYNER, K., and FISHER, D. L. 1987. Letter processing during eye fixations in visual search. *Perception & Psychophysics, 42,* 87–100.

RAYNER, K., and FRAZIER, L. 1987. Parsing temporarily ambiguous complements. *Quarterly Journal of Experimental Psychology, 39A,* 657–673.

RAYNER, K., and HAGELBERG, E. M. 1975. Word recognition cues for beginning and skilled readers. *Journal of Experimental Child Psychology, 20,* 444–455.

RAYNER, K., INHOFF, A. W., MORRISON, R. E., SLOWIACZEK, M. L., and BERTERA, J. H. 1981. Masking of foveal and parafoveal vision during eye fixations in reading. *Journal of Experimental Psychology: Human Perception and Performance, 7,* 167–179.

RAYNER, K., and MCCONKIE, G. W. 1976. What guides a reader's eye movements? *Vision Research, 16,* 829–837.

RAYNER, K., MCCONKIE, G. W., and EHRLICH, S. F. 1978. Eye movements and integrating information across fixations. *Journal of Experimental Psychology: Human Perception and Performance, 4,* 529–544.

RAYNER, K., MCCONKIE, G. W., and ZOLA, D. 1980. Integrating information across eye movements. *Cognitive Psychology, 12,* 206–226.

RAYNER, K., and POLLATSEK, A. 1981. Eye movement control during reading: Evidence for direct control. *Quarterly Journal of Experimental Psychology, 33A,* 351–373.

RAYNER, K., and POLLATSEK, A. 1987. Eye movements in reading: A tutorial review. In M. Coltheart (ed.), *Attention and Performance 12.* London: Erlbaum.

RAYNER, K., and POSNANSKY, C. 1978. Stages of processing in word identification. *Journal of Experimental Psychology: General, 107,* 64–80.

RAYNER, K., SLOWIACZEK, M. L., CLIFTON, C., and BERTERA, J. H. 1983. Latency of sequential eye movements: Implications for reading. *Journal of Experimental Psychology: Human Perception and Performance, 9,* 912–922.

RAYNER, K., WELL, A. D., and POLLATSEK, A. 1980. Asymmetry of the effective visual field in reading. *Perception & Psychophysics, 27,* 537–544.

RYANER, K., WELL, A. D., POLLATSEK, A., and BERTERA, J. H. 1982. The availability of useful information to the right of fixation in reading. *Perception & Psychophysics, 31,* 537–550.

READ, C., ZHANG, Y., NIE, H., and DING, B. 1986. The ability to manipulate speech sounds depends on knowing alphabetic spelling. *Cognition, 24,* 31–44.

REICHER, G. M. 1969. Perceptual recognition as a function of meaningfulness of stimulus material. *Journal of Experimental Psychology, 81,* 275–280.

REITSMA, P. 1983a. Printed word leaning in beginning readers. *Journal of Experimental Child Psychology, 36,* 321–339.

REITSMA, P. 1983b. Word-specific knowledge in beginning reading. *Journal of Research in Reading, 6,* 41–56.

REITSMA, P. 1984. Sound priming in beginning readers. *Child Development, 55,* 406–423.

REISBECK, C., and SCHANK, R. 1978. Comprehension by computer: Expectation-based analysis of sentences in context. In W. J. M. Levelt and G. B. Flores d'Arcais (eds.), *Studies in the perception of language.* New York: Wiley.

RODGERS, B. 1983. The identification and prevalence of specific reading retardation. *British Journal of Educational Psychology, 53,* 369–373.

ROSINSKI, R. R. 1977. Picture-word interference is semantically based. *Child Development, 48,* 643–647.

ROSINSKI, R. R., GOLINKOFF, R. M., and KUKISH, K. 1975. Automatic semantic processing in a picture-word interference task. *Child Development, 46,* 243–253.

ROSINSKI, R. R., and WHEELER, K. E. 1972. Children's use of orthographic structure in word discrimination. *Psychonomic Science, 26,* 97–98.

ROTHKOPF, E. Z. 1970. The concept of mathemagenic activities. *Review of Educational Research, 40,* 325–336.

ROTHKOPF, E. Z. 1971. Incidental memory for location of information in text. *Journal of Verbal Learning and Verbal Behavior, 10,* 608–613.

ROTHKOPF, E. Z. 1978. Analyzing eye movements to infer processing styles during learning from text. In J. W. Senders, D. F. Fisher, and R. A. Monty (eds.), *Eye movements and the higher psychological functions.* Hillsdale, NJ: Erlbaum.

ROTHKOPF, E. Z., and BILLINGTON, M. Z. 1979. Goal-guided learning from text: Inferring a descriptive processing model from inspection times and eye movements. *Journal of Educational Psychology, 71,* 310–327.

ROZIN, P., BRESSMAN, B., and TAFT, M. 1974. Do children understand the basic relationship between speech and writing? The Mow-Motorcycle test. *Journal of Reading Behavior, 6,* 327–334.

ROZIN, P., and GLEITMAN, L. R. 1977. The structure and acquisition of reading II: The reading process and the acquisition of the alphabetic principle. In A. S. Reber and D. L. Scarborough (eds.), *Toward a psychology of reading.* Hillsdale, NJ: Erlbaum.

ROZIN, P., PORITSKY, S., and SOTSKY, R. 1971. American children with reading problems can easily learn to read English represented by Chinese characters. *Science, 171,* 1264–1267.

RUBINSTEIN, H., LEWIS, S. S., and RUBENSTEIN, M. H. 1971. Evidence for phonemic recoding in visual word recognition. *Journal of Verbal Learning and Verbal Behavior, 10,* 645–647.

RUGEL, R. P. 1974. WISC subtest scores of disabled readers. *Journal of Learning Disabilities, 7,* 57–64.

RUMELHART, D. E. 1975. Notes on a schema for stories. In D. G. Bobrow and A. M. Collins (eds.), *Representations and understanding: Studies in cognitive science.* New York: Academic Press.

RUMELHART, D. E. 1977. Toward an interactive model of reading. In S. Dornic (ed.), *Attention and Performance VI.* Hillsdale, NJ: Erlbaum.

RUMELHART, D. E., LINDSAY, P., and NORMAN D. 1972. A process model for long-term memory. In E. Tulving and W. Donaldson (eds.), *Organization of memory.* New York: Academic Press.

RUMELHART, D. E., and MCCLELLAND, J. L. 1982. An interactive activation model of context effects in letter perception: Part 2. *Psychological Review, 89,* 60–94.

RUTTER, M., TIZARD, J., and WHITMORE, K. 1970. *Education, health, and behavior.* London: Longman.

RYAN, E. B. 1982. Identifying and remediating failures in reading comprehension: Toward an instructional approach for poor comprehenders. In G. E. MacKinnon and T. G. Waller (eds.), *Advances in reading research (Vol 3).* New York: Academic Press.

SACHS, J. S. 1967. Recognition memory for syntactic and semantic aspects of connected discourse. *Perception & Psychophysics, 2,* 437–442.

SACHS, J. S. 1974. Memory in reading and listening to discourse. *Memory & Cognition, 2,* 95–100.

SAFFRAN, E. M., BOGYO, L. C., SCHWARTZ, M. F., and MARIN, O. S. M. 1980. Does deep dyslexia reflect right hemisphere reading? In M. Coltheart, K. Patterson, and J. C. Marshall (eds.), *Deep dyslexia*. London: Routledge & Kegan Paul.

SAILOR, A. L., and BALL, S. E. 1975. Peripheral vision training in reading speed and comprehension. *Perceptual and Motor Skills, 41,* 761–762.

SALTHOUSE, T. A., and ELLIS, C. L. 1980. Determinants of eye fixation duration. *American Journal of Psychology, 93,* 207–234.

SAMUELS, S. J. 1979. The method of repeated readings. *Reading Teacher, 32,* 403–408.

SAMUELS, S. J., LABERGE, D., and BREMER, C. D. 1978. Units of word recognition: Evidence of developmental change. *Journal of Verbal Learning and Verbal Behavior, 17,* 715–720.

SANFORD, A. J., and GARROD, S. C. 1981. *Understanding written language: Explorations in comprehension beyond the sentence*. New York: Wiley.

SATZ, P., RARDIN, D., and ROSS, J. 1971. An evaluation of a theory of specific developmental dyslexia. *Child Development, 42,* 2009–2021.

SATZ, P., TAYLOR, H. G., FRIEL, J., and FLETCHER, J. M. 1978. Some developmental and predictive precursors of reading disabilities: A six year follow-up. In A. L. Benton and D. Pearl (eds.), *Dyslexia: An appraisal of current knowledge*. New York: Oxford University Press.

SAVIN, H. B. 1972. What the child knows about speech when he starts to learn to read. In J. F. Kavanagh and I. G. Mattingly (eds.), *Language by ear and by eye*. Cambridge, MA.: MIT Press.

SCHANK, R. C. 1972. Conceptual dependency: A theory of natural language understanding. *Cognitive Psychology, 3,* 552–631.

SCHANK, R. C. 1975. *Conceptual information processing*. Amsterdam: North-Holland.

SCHANK, R. C., and ABELSON, R. P. 1977. *Scripts, plans, goals, and understanding: An inquiry into human knowledge structures*. Hillsdale, NJ: Erlbaum.

SCHINDLER, R. M. 1978. The effect of prose context on visual search for letters. *Memory & Cognition, 6,* 124–130.

SCHUBERTH, R. E., and EIMAS, P. D. 1977. Effects of context on the classification of words and nonwords. *Journal of Experimental Psychology: Human Perception and Performance, 3,* 27–36.

SCHUSTACK, M. W., EHRLICH, S. F., and RAYNER, K. 1987. The complexity of contextual facilitation in reading: Local and global influences. *Journal of Memory and Language, 26,* 322–340.

SCHWANTES, F. M. 1981. Effect of story context on children's ongoing word recognition. *Journal of Reading Behavior, 13,* 305–311.

SCHWARTZ, M. F., MARIN, O. S. M., and SAFFRAN, E. M. 1979. Dissociation of language function in dementia: A case study. *Brain and Language, 7,* 277–306.

SCHWARTZ, M. F., SAFFRAN, E. M., and MARIN, O. S. M. 1980. Fractionating the reading process in dementia: Evidence for word specific print-to-sound associations. In M. Coltheart, K. Patterson, and J. C. Marshall (eds.), *Deep dyslexia*. London: Routledge & Kegan Paul.

SEIDENBERG, M. S. 1985a. Constraining models of word recognition. *Cognition, 20,* 169–190.

SEIDENBERG, M. S. 1985b. The time course of information activation and utilization in visual word recognition. In D. Besner, T. G. Waller, and G. E. MacKinnon (eds.), *Reading research: Advances in theory and practice* (Vol. 5). Orlando, FL: Academic Press.

SEIDENBERG, M. S., TANENHAUS, M. K., LEIMAN, J. M., and BIENKOWSKI, M. 1982. Automatic access of the meanings of ambiguous words in context: Some limitations of knowledge-based processing. *Cognitive Psychology, 14,* 489–537.

SEIDENBERG, M. S., and VIDANOVIC, S. 1985. *Word recognition in Serbo-Croatian and English: Do they differ?* Paper presented at Psychonomic Society Meeting, Boston.

SEIDENBERG, M. S., WATERS, G. S., BARNES, M. A., and TANENHAUS, M. K. 1984. When does irregular spelling or pronunciation influence word recognition? *Journal of Verbal Learning and Verbal Behavior, 23,* 383–404.

SEIDENBERG, M. S., WATERS, G. S., SANDERS, M., and LANGER, P. 1984. Pre- and post-lexical loci of contextual effects on word recognition. *Memory & Cognition, 12,* 315–328.

SELKIRK, L. 1982. *The syntax of words*. Cambridge, MA: MIT Press.

SEYMOUR, P. H. K., and MACGREGOR, C. J. 1984. Developmental dyslexia: A cognitive experimental analysis of phonological, morphemic and visual impairments. *Cognitive Neuropsychology, 1,* 43–82.

SEYMOUR, P. H. K., and PORPODAS, C. D. 1980. Lexical and nonlexical processing of spelling in developmental dyslexia. In U. Frith (ed.), *Cognitive processes in spelling.* London: Academic Press.

SHALLICE, T., and WARRINGTON, E. K. 1977. The possible role of selective attention in acquired dyslexia. *Neuropsychologia, 15,* 31–41.

SHALLICE, T., and WARRINGTON, E. K. 1980. Single and multiple component central dyslexic syndromes. In M. Coltheart, K. Patterson, and J. C. Marshall (eds.), *Deep dyslexia.* London: Routledge & Kegan Paul.

SHALLICE, T., WARRINGTON, E. K., and MCCARTHY, R. 1983. Reading without semantics. *Quarterly Journal of Experimental Psychology, 35A,* 111–138.

SHANKWEILER, D., LIBERMAN, I. Y., MARK, L. S., FOWLER, C. A., and FISCHER, F. W. 1979. The speech code and learning to read. *Journal of Experimental Psychology: Human Learning and Memory, 5,* 531–545.

SHARE, D. L., MCGEE, R., MCKENZIE, D., WILIAMS, S., and SILVA, P. A. 1987. Further evidence relating to the distinction between specific reading retardation and general reading backwardness. *British Journal of Developmental Psychology, 5,* 35–44.

SHARKEY, N. E., and MITCHELL, D. C. 1985. Word recognition in a functional context: The use of scripts in reading. *Journal of Memory and Language, 24,* 253–270.

SHARKEY, N. E., and SHARKEY, A. J. C. 1987. What is the point of integration? The loci of knowledge-based facilitation in sentence processing. *Journal of Memory and Language, 26,* 255–276.

SHEBILSKE, W. L., and FISHER, D. F. (1983). Understanding extended discourse through the eyes: How and why. In R. Groner, C. Menz, D. F. Fisher, and R. D. Monty (eds.), *Eye movements and psychological functions: International views.* New Jersey: Erlbaum.

SHEN, E. 1927. An analysis of eye movements in the reading of Chinese. *Journal of Experimental Psychology, 10,* 158–183.

SIEGEL, L. S. 1985. Deep dyslexia in childhood? *Brain and Language, 26,* 16–27.

SIMON, D. P., and SIMON, H. A. 1973. Alternative uses of phonemic information in spelling. *Review of Educational Research, 43,* 115–137.

SINGER, H., and BALOW, I. H. 1981. Overcoming educational disadvantagedness. In J. T. Guthrie (ed.), *Comprehension and teaching: Research review.* Newark, DE: International Reading Association.

SINGER, M. 1979. Processes of inference in sentence encoding. *Memory & Cognition, 7,* 192–200.

SINGER, M. 1980. The role of case filling inferences in the coherence of brief passages. *Discourse Processes, 3,* 185–201.

SINGER, M., and FERREIRA, F. 1983. Inferring consequences in story comprehension. *Journal of Verbal Learning and Verbal Behavior, 22,* 437–448.

SKINNER, B. F. 1957. *Verbal behavior.* New York: Appleton-Century-Crofts.

SLAGHUIS, W. L., and LOVEGROVE, W. J. 1985. Spatial-frequency-dependent visible persistence and specific reading disability. *Brain and Cognition, 4,* 219–240.

SLOWIACZEK, M. L. 1983. What does the mind do while the eyes are gazing? In K. Rayner (ed.), *Eye movements in reading: Perceptual and language processes.* New York: Academic Press.

SLOWIACZEK, M. L., and CLIFTON, C. 1980. Subvocalization and reading for meaning. *Journal of Verbal Learning and Verbal Behavior, 19,* 573–582.

SLOWIACZEK, M. L., and RAYNER, K. 1987. Sequential masking during eye fixations in reading. *Bulletin of the Psychonomic Society, 25,* 175–178.

SMITH, E. E., SHOBEN, E. J., and RIPS, L. J. 1974. Structure and process in semantic memory: A featural model for semantic decisions. *Psychological Review, 81,* 214–241.

SMITH, F. 1971. *Understanding reading: A psycholinguistic analysis of reading and learning to read.* New York: Holt, Rinehart and Winston.

SMITH, F. 1973. *Psycholinguistics and reading.* New York: Holt, Rinehart and Winston.

SMITH, F., and GOODMAN, K. S. 1971. On the psycholinguistic method of teaching reading. *Elementary School Journal, 71,* 177–181.

SMITH, F., LOTT, D., and CRONNELL, B. 1969. The effect of type size and case alternation on word identification. *American Journal of Psychology, 82,* 248–253.

SMITH, P. T., and GROAT, A. 1979. Spelling patterns: Letter cancellation and the processing of text. In P. A. Kolers, M. E. Wrolstad, and H. Bouma (eds.), *Processing of visible language* (Vol. 1). New York: Plenum.

SMITH, P. T., and STERLING, C. M. 1982. Factors affecting the perceived morphemic structure of written words. *Journal of Verbal Learning and Verbal Behavior, 21,* 704–721.

SNOWLING, M. J. 1980. The development of grapheme-phoneme correspondence in normal and dyslexic children. *Journal of Experimental Child Psychology, 29,* 294–305.

SNOWLING, M. J. 1981. Phonemic deficits in developmental dyslexia. *Psychological Research, 43,* 219–234.

SNOWLING, M. J. 1983. The comparison of acquired and developmental disorders of reading. *Cognition, 14,* 105–118.

SNOWLING, M. J., and FRITH, U. 1981. The use of sound, shape, and orthographic cues in early reading. *British Journal of Psychology, 72,* 83–88.

SOKOLOV, A. N. 1972. *Inner speech and thought.* New York: Plenum.

SPERLING, G. 1960. The information available in brief visual presentations. *Psychological Monographs, 74* (No. 498).

SPERLING, G. 1963. A model for visual memory tasks. *Human Factors, 5,* 19–31.

SPRAGINS, A. B., LEFTON, L. A., and FISHER, D. F. 1976. Eye movements while reading and searching spatially transformed text: A developmental examination. *Memory & Cognition, 4,* 36–42.

STANLEY, G. 1975. Visual memory processes in dyslexia. In D. Deutsch and J. A. Deutsch (eds.), *Short-term memory.* New York: Academic Press.

STANLEY, G. 1976. The processing of digits by children with specific reading disability (dyslexia). *British Journal of Educational Psychology, 46,* 81–84.

STANLEY, G., and HALL, R. 1973. Short-term visual information processing in dyslexics. *Child Development, 44,* 841–844.

STANLEY, G., and MOLLOY, M. 1975. Retinal and visual information storage. *Acta Psychologica, 39,* 283–288.

STANLEY, G., SMITH, G. A., and HOWELL, E. A. 1983. Eye movements and sequential tracking in dyslexic and control children. *British Journal of Psychology, 74,* 181–187.

STANNERS, R. F., NEISER, J. J., HERNON, W. P., and HALL, R. 1979. Memory representation for morphologically related words. *Journal of Verbal Learning and Verbal Behavior, 18,* 399–412.

STANNERS, R. F., NEISER, J. J., and PAINTON, S. 1979. Memory representation for prefixed words. *Journal of Verbal Learning and Verbal Behavior, 18,* 733–743.

STANOVICH, K. E. 1980. Toward an interactive-compensatory model of individual differences in the development of reading fluency. *Reading Research Quarterly, 16,* 32–71.

STANOVICH, K. E. 1986. Matthew effects in reading: Some consequences of individual differences in the acquisition of literacy. *Reading Research Quarterly, 4,* 360–406.

STANOVICH, K. E., CUNNINGHAM, A. E., and CRAMER, B. 1984. Assessing phonological awareness in kindergarten children: Issues of task comparability. *Journal of Experimental Child Psychology, 38,* 175–190.

STANOVICH, K. E., NATHAN, R. G., and VALA-ROSSI, M. 1986. Developmental changes in the cognitive correlates of reading ability and the developmental lag hypothesis. *Reading Research Quarterly, 21,* 267–283.

STANOVICH, K. E., and WEST, R. F. 1979. Mechanisms of sentence context effects in reading: Automatic activation and conscious attention. *Memory & Cognition, 7,* 77–85.

STANOVICH, K. E., and WEST, R. F. 1983. On priming by a sentence context. *Journal of Experimental Psychology: General, 112,* 1–36.

STANOVICH, K. E., WEST, R. F., and FREEMAN, D. J. 1981. A longitudinal study of sentence context effects on second-grade children: Tests of an interactive-compensatory model. *Journal of Experimental Child Psychology, 32,* 185–199.

STEIN, J. F., and FOWLER, S. 1982. Ocular motor dyslexia. *Dyslexia Review, 5,* 25–28.

STEIN, J. F., and FOWLER, S. 1984. Ocular motor problems of learning to read. In A. G. Gale and F. Johnson (eds.), *Theoretical and applied aspects of eye movement research.* Amsterdam: North Holland Press.

STEIN, N. L., and GLENN, C. G. 1979. An analysis of story comprehension in elementary school children. In P. O. Freedle (ed.), *New directions in discourse processing.* Norwood, NJ: Ablex.

STERN, J. A. 1978. Eye movements, reading, and cognition. In J. W. Senders, D. F. Fisher, and R. A. Monty (eds.), *Eye movements and higher psychological functions*. Hillsdale, NJ: Erlbaum.

STERNBERG, S. 1969. The discovery of processing stages: Extensions of Donders' method. In W. G. Koster (ed.), *Attention and performance II, Acta Psychologica, 30*, 276–315.

STEVENSON, H. W., PARKER, T., WILKINSON, A., HEGION, A., and FISH, E. 1976. Longitudinal study of individual differences in cognitive development and scholastic achievement. *Journal of Educational Psychology, 68*, 377–400.

STROOP, J. R. 1935. Studies of interference in serial verbal reactions. *Journal of Experimental Psychology, 18*, 643–662.

SUN, F., MORITA, M., and STARK, L. W. 1985. Comparative patterns of reading eye movement in Chinese and English. *Perception & Psychophysics, 37*, 502–506.

SWINNEY, D. A. 1979. Lexical access during sentence comprehension: (Re)consideration of context effects. *Journal of Verbal Learning and Verbal Behavior, 18*, 645–659.

SWINNEY, D. A., and HAKES, D. T. 1976. Effects of prior context upon lexical access during sentence comprehension. *Journal of Verbal Learning and Verbal Behavior, 15*, 681–689.

TAFT, M. 1979. Lexical access via an othographic code: The Basic Orthographic Syllable Structure (BOSS). *Journal of Verbal Learning and Verbal Behavior, 18*, 21–39.

TAFT, M. 1981. Prefix stripping revisited. *Journal of Verbal Learning and Verbal Behavior, 20*, 284–297.

TAFT, M. 1985. The decoding of words in lexical access: A review of the morphological approach. In D. Besner, T. G. Waller, and G. E. MacKinnon (eds.), *Reading research: Advances in theory and practice* (Vol. 5). New York: Academic Press.

TAFT, M. 1986. Lexical access codes in visual and auditory word recognition. *Language and Cognitive Processes, 4*, 297–308.

TAFT, M. 1987. Morphographic processing: The BOSS re-emerges. In M. Coltheart (ed.), *Attention and Performance XII*. Hillsdale, NJ: Erlbaum.

TAFT, M., and FORSTER, K. I. 1975. Lexical storage and retrieval of prefixed words. *Journal of Verbal Learning and Verbal Behavior, 14*, 638–647.

TAFT, M., and FORSTER, K. I. 1976. Lexical storage and retrieval of polymorphemic and polysyllabic words. *Journal of Verbal Learning and Verbal Behavior, 15*, 607–620.

TALLAL, P. 1980. Auditory temporal perception, phonics, and reading disabilities in children. *Brain and Language, 9*, 182–198.

TANENHAUS, M. K., LEIMAN, J. M., and SEIDENBERG, M. S. 1979. Evidence for multiple stages in the processing of ambiguous words in syntactic contexts. *Journal of Verbal Learning and Verbal Behavior, 18*, 427–440.

TARABAN, R., and MCCLELLAND, J. L. 1988. Constituent attachment and thematic role assignment in sentence processing: Influences of content-based expectations. *Journal of Memory and Language*. In press.

TAYLOR, I. 1981. Writing systems and reading. In G. E. MacKinnon and T. G. Waller (eds.), *Reading research: Advances in theory and practice* (Vol. 2). New York: Academic Press.

TAYLOR, I., and TAYLOR, M. M. 1983. *The psychology of reading*. New York: Academic Press.

TAYLOR, S. E. 1962. An evaluation of forty-one trainees who had recently completed the "Reading Dynamics" program. In E. P. Bliesmer and R. C. Staiger (eds.), *Problems, programs, and projects in college adult reading. Eleventh yearbook of the National Reading Conference*. Milwaukee, WI: National Reading Conference.

TAYLOR, S. E. 1965. Eye movements while reading: Facts and fallacies. *American Educational Research Journal, 2*, 187–202.

TEMPLE, C. M. 1985. Developmental surface dysgraphia: A case report. *Applied Psycholinguistics, 6*, 391–405.

TEMPLE, C. M., and MARSHALL, J. C. 1983. A case study of developmental phonological dyslexia. *British Journal of Psychology, 74*, 517–533.

THIBADEAU, R., JUST, M. A., and CARPENTER, P. A. 1982. A model of the time course and content of reading. *Cognitive Science, 6*, 157–203.

THOMSON, M. 1984. *Developmental dyslexia*. London: Arnold.

THORNDYKE, P. W. 1977. Cognitive structures in comprehension and memory of narrative discourse. *Cognitive Psychology, 9*, 135–147.

TINKER, M. A. 1939. Reliability and validity of eye-movement measures of reading. *Journal of Experimental Psychology, 19*, 732–746.

TINKER, M. A. 1955. Perceptual and oculomotor efficiency in reading materials in vertical and horizontal arrangement. *American Journal of Psychology, 68,* 444–449.

TINKER, M. A. 1958. Recent studies of eye movements in reading. *Psychological Bulletin, 55,* 215–231.

TINKER, M. A. 1963. *Legibility of print.* Ames, IA: Iowa State University Press.

TINKER, M. 1965. *Bases for effective reading.* Minneapolis: University of Minnesota Press.

TORGESEN, J. K., and GOLDMAN, T. 1977. Rehearsal and short-term memory in reading disabled children. *Child Development, 48,* 56–60.

TORGESEN, J. K., and HOUCK, D. G. 1980. Processing deficiencies of learning-disabled children who perform poorly on the digit span test. *Journal of Educational Psychology, 17,* 141–160.

TORNEUS, M. 1984. Phonological awareness and reading: A chicken and egg problem? *Journal of Educational Psychology, 76,* 1346–1348.

TORREY, J. W. 1969. Learning to read without a teacher: A case study. *Elementary English, 46,* 550–556.

TRABASSO, T., ROLLINS, H., and SHAUGHNESSY, E. 1971. Storage and verification stages in processing concepts. *Cognitive Psychology, 2,* 239–289.

TRABASSO, T., and SPERRY, L. L. 1985. Causal relatedness and importance of story events. *Journal of Memory and Language, 24,* 595–611.

TRABASSO, T., and VAN DEN BROEK, P. 1985. Causal thinking and the representation of narrative events. *Journal of Memory and Language, 24,* 612–630.

TREIMAN, R. A. 1984. Individual differences among children in reading and spelling styles. *Journal of Experimental Child Psychology, 37,* 463–477.

TREIMAN, R. A., and BARON, J. 1983. Phonemic analysis training helps children benefit from spelling-sound rules. *Memory & Cognition, 11,* 382–389.

TREIMAN, R. A., BARON, J., and LUK, K. 1981. Speech recoding in silent reading: A comparison of Chinese and English. *Journal of Chinese Linguistics, 9,* 116–124.

TREIMAN, R. A., FREYD, J. J., and BARON, J. 1983. Phonological recoding and use of spelling sound rules in reading of sentences. *Journal of Verbal Learning and Verbal Behavior, 22,* 682–700.

TREIMAN, R. A., and HIRSH-PASEK, K. 1983. Silent reading: Insights from second-generation deaf readers. *Cognitive Psychology, 15,* 39–65.

TREIMAN, R. A., and HIRSH-PASEK, K. 1985. Are there qualitative differences in reading behavior between dyslexics and normal readers? *Memory & Cognition, 13,* 357–364.

TULVING, E. 1972. Episodic and semantic memory. In E. Tulving and W. Donaldson (eds.), *Organization and memory.* New York: Academic Press.

TULVING, E., and GOLD, C. 1963. Stimulus information and contextual information as determinants of tachistoscopic recognition of words. *Journal of Experimental Psychology, 66,* 319–327.

TULVING, E., MANDLER, G., and BAUMAL, R. 1964. Interaction of two sources of information in tachistoscopic word recognition. *Canadian Journal of Psychology, 18,* 62–71.

TURVEY, M. T. 1977. Contrasting orientations to a theory of visual information processing. *Psychological Review, 84,* 67–88.

TURVEY, M. T., FELDMAN, L. B., and LUKATELA, G. 1984. The Serbo-Croatian orthography constrains the reader to a phonologically analytic strategy. In L. Henderson (ed.), *Orthographies and reading.* London: Erlbaum.

TZENG, O. J. L., and HUNG, D. L. 1980. Reading in a nonalphabetic writing system. In J. G. Kavanagh and R. L. Venezky (eds.), *Orthography, reading and dyslexia.* Baltimore: University Park Press.

TZENG, O. J. L., HUNG, D. L., and WANG, W. S.-Y. 1977. Speech recoding in reading Chinese characters. *Journal of Experimental Psychology: Human Learning and Memory, 3,* 621–630.

UNDERWOOD, G. 1980. Attention and the non-selective lexical access of ambiguous words. *Canadian Journal of Psychology, 34,* 72–76.

UNDERWOOD, G. 1981. Lexical recognition of embedded unattended words: Some implications for reading processes. *Acta Psychologica, 47,* 267–283.

UNDERWOOD, N. R., and MCCONKIE, G. W. 1985. Perceptual span for letter distinctions during reading. *Reading Research Quarterly, 20,* 153–162.

UNDERWOOD, N. R., and ZOLA, D. 1986. The span of letter recognition of good and poor readers. *Reading Research Quarterly, 21,* 6–19.

UTTAL, W. R., and SMITH, P. 1968. Recognition of alphabetic characters during voluntary eye movement. *Perception & Psychophysics, 3,* 257–264.

VAN DER WISSEL, A., and ZEGERS, F. C. 1985. Reading retardation revisited. *British Journal of Developmental Psychology, 3,* 3–9.

VAN DIJK, T. A., and KINTSCH, W. 1983. *Strategies of discourse comprehension.* New York: Academic Press.

VAN ORDEN, G. C. 1987. A rows is a rose: Spelling, sound, and reading. *Memory & Cognition, 15,* 181–198.

VAN ORDEN, G. C., JOHNSTON, J. C., and HALE, B. L. 1987. Word identification in reading proceeds from spelling to sound to meaning. *Journal of Experimental Psychology: Learning, Memory, & Cognition, 14,* 371–386.

VAN PETTEN, C., and KUTAS, M. 1987. Ambiguous words in context: An event-related potential analysis of the time course of meaning activation. *Journal of Memory and Language, 26,* 188–208.

VELLUTINO, F. R. 1979. *Dyslexia: Theory and research.* Cambridge, MA: MIT Press.

VENEZKY, R. L. 1970. *The structure of English orthography.* The Hague, Netherlands: Mouton.

VONK, W. 1984. Eye movements during comprehension of pronouns. In A. G. Gale and F. Johnson (eds.), *Theoretical and applied aspects of eye movement research.* Amsterdam: North-Holland.

VURPOILLOT, E. 1968. The development of scanning strategies and their relation to visual differentiation. *Journal of Experimental Child Psychology, 6,* 632–650.

WAGNER, R. K., and TORGESEN, J. K. 1987. The nature of phonological processing and its causal role in the acquisition of reading skills. *Psychological Bulletin, 101,* 192–212.

WALKER, R. Y. 1938. A qualitative study of the eye movements of good readers. *American Journal of Psychology, 51,* 472–481.

WALTON, H. N. 1957. Vision and rapid reading. *American Journal of Optometry and Archives of American Academy of Optometry, 34,* 73–82.

WANAT, S. F. 1971. *Linguistic structure and visual attention in reading.* Newark, DE: International Reading Association.

WANG, F. C. 1935. An experimental study of eye movements in the reading of Chinese. *Elementary School Journal, 35,* 527–539.

WANG, W. S-Y. 1973. The Chinese language. *Scientific American, 228,* 50–60.

WANNER, E. 1974. *On remembering, forgetting, and understanding sentences.* The Hague, Netherlands: Mouton.

WASON, P. C. 1965. The contexts of plausible denial. *Journal of Verbal Learning and Verbal Behavior, 4,* 7–11.

WATERS, G. S., KOMODA, M. K., and ARBUCKLE, T. Y. 1985. The effects of concurrent tasks on reading: Implications for phonological recoding. *Journal of Memory and Language, 24,* 27–45.

WATERS, G. S., SEIDENBERG, M. S., and BRUCK, M. 1984. Children's and adult's use of spelling-sound information in three reading tasks. *Memory & Cognition, 12,* 293–305.

WEBER, R. 1970. A linguistic analysis of first grade reading errors. *Reading Research Quarterly, 5,* 427–451.

WEINSTEIN, R., and RABINOVITCH, M. S. 1971. Sentence structure and retention in good and poor readers. *Journal of Educational Psychology, 62,* 25–30.

WEST, R. F., and STANOVICH, K. E. 1978. Automatic contextual facilitation in readers of three ages. *Child Development, 49,* 717–727.

WHEELER, D. D. 1970. Processes in word recognition. *Cognitive Psychology, 1,* 59–85.

WILLIAMS, J. P. 1979. Reading instruction today. *American Psychologist, 34,* 917–922.

WILLIAMS, J. P. 1980. Teaching decoding with an emphasis on phonemic analysis and phoneme blending. *Journal of Educational Psychology, 72,* 1–15.

WILLIAMS, J. P., BLUMBERG, E. L., and WILLIAMS, D. V. 1970. Cues used in visual word recognition. *Journal of Educational Psychology, 61,* 310–315.

WILLIAMS, J. P., TAYLOR, M. B., and DECANI, J. S. 1984. Constructing macrostructure for expository text. *Journal of Educational Psychology, 76,* 1065–1075.

WILLOWS, D. M., BORWICK, D., and HAYVREN, M. 1981. The content of school readers. In G. E. MacKinnon and T. G. Waller (eds.), *Reading research: Advances in theory and practice* (Vol. 2). New York: Academic Press.

WITTROCK, M. C., MARKS, C., and DOCTOROW, M. 1975. Reading as a generative process. *Journal of Educational Psychology, 67,* 484–489.

WOLFORD, G., and FOWLER, C. A. 1984. Differential use of partial information by good and poor readers. *Developmental Review, 4,* 16–35.

WOLVERTON, G. S., and ZOLA, D. 1983. The temporal characteristics of visual information extraction during reading. In K. Rayner (ed.), *Eye movements in reading: Perceptual and language processes.* New York: Academic Press.

WOODWORTH, R. S. 1938. *Experimental psychology.* New York: Holt.

WURTZ, R. H., GOLDBERG, M. E., and ROBINSON, D. L. 1982. Brain mechanisms of visual attention. *Scientific American, 246,* 124–135.

YEKOVICH, F. R., and WALKER, C. H. 1978. Identifying and using referents in sentence comprehension. *Journal of Verbal Learning and Verbal Behavior, 17,* 265–277.

YENI-KOMSHIAN, G. H., ISENBERG, D., and GOLDBERG, H. 1975. Cerebral dominance and reading disability: Left visual field deficit in poor readers. *Neuropsychologia, 13,* 83–94.

YIK, W. F. 1978. The effect of visual and acoustic similarity on short-term memory for Chinese words. *Quarterly Journal of Experimental Psychology, 30,* 487–494.

YULE, W. 1973. Differential prognosis of reading backwardness and specific reading retardation. *British Journal of Educational Psychology, 43,* 244–248.

YULE, W., RUTTER, M., BERGER, M., and THOMPSON, J. 1974. Over and under achievement in reading: Distribution in the general population. *British Journal of Educational Psychology, 44,* 1–12.

ZANGWILL, O. L., and BLAKEMORE, C. 1972. Dyslexia: Reversal of eye movements during reading. *Neuropsychologia, 10,* 371–373.

ZECHMEISTER, E. B., and MCKILLIP, J. 1972. Recall of place on the page. *Journal of Educational Psychology, 63,* 446–453.

ZIFCAK, M. 1981. Phonological awareness and reading acquisition. *Contemporary Educational Psychology, 6,* 117–126.

ZOLA, D. 1984. Redundancy and word perception during reading. *Perception & Psychophysics, 36,* 277–284.

AUTHOR INDEX

Eimas, P.D.   222, 228
Eldridge, M.   199
Elkind, D.   334, 339
Ellis, A.W.   361, 406, 408, 415, 425–426, 428
Ellis, C.L.   176
Ellis, N.C.   420
Ellsworth, D.W.   192
Erdmann, B.   6
Erickson, D.   211
Erickson, T.D.   254
Eskenazi, B.   418
Evans, D.   337
Evans, M.A.   357
Evett, L.J.   80, 88, 90

Farnham-Diggory, S.   402
Feitelson, D.   334, 347, 367
Feldman, L.B.   99
Ferguson,H.B.   416
Ferreira, F.   250, 258–261, 271–272, 284
Ferres, S.   184
Fillmore, C.   242
Findlay, J.M.   176
Finger, E.   401
Fischler, I.   222, 228
Fisher, D.F.   182, 388, 421, 451, 470
Fisher, D.G.   454
Fisher, D.L.   451
Fisher, V.L.   366
Fleisher, L.S.   391
Fletcher, C.R.   298, 311
Fodor, J.A.   220, 244–245, 253, 313
Fodor, J.D.   246–247
Ford, M.   246
Forster, K.I.   75, 102–109, 220, 223
Foss, D.J.   217, 227, 231, 243, 285
Fowler, C.A.   70, 402
Fowler, S.   419, 431
Fox, B.   343, 345
Francis, W.N.   68
Frankfurter, A.   421
Franks, J.J.   303
Frazier, L.   158, 185, 215, 246–252, 258–261
Fredricksen, J.R.   458
Freeman, D.J.   385
Freeman, R.   80
French, J.H.   429–430
Freschi, R.   391
Freyd, J.J.   94, 205, 207–208
Friedman, A.   307
Friedman, R.B.   408
Friedrich, F.J.   375
Frith, U.   368, 400
Funnell, G.   409

Garnham, A.   217, 300
Garrett, M.F.   101, 244–245
Garrity, L.I.   194
Garrod, S.   272, 277, 280–281

Gelb, I.J.   30, 32, 37, 40, 42
Gerrisen, J.F.   129, 133, 441
Gibson, E.J.   25, 99, 190, 338, 366, 375
Gilbert, L.C.   183
Giordani, B.   421
Glass, A.L.   256–257
Gleitman, L.R.   51, 331, 343
Glenberg, A.M.   316
Glenn, C.G.   390
Glock, M.D.   447
Glucksberg, S.   233
Glushko, R.J.   88–90
Godfrey, J.J.   421
Gold, C.   222
Goldberg, H.   423
Goldberg, M.E.   172
Goldman, S.R.   385, 402
Goldman, T.   402
Golinkoff, R.M.   344, 380–381, 390, 401
Goodman, K.S.   25, 61, 69, 181, 221, 350–351, 462–468
Gordon, B.   101
Gordon, S.E.   306–307
Goswami, U.   333, 370–371, 376, 416
Gott, R.   73
Gough, P.B.   17, 25, 76, 92, 104, 221, 226, 343, 351, 359–360, 376, 465–468
Goyen, J.   411
Graesser, A.C.   268, 306–307, 458
Green, D.W.   185
Gregg, L.W.   402
Griebel, B.   200
Griffith, P.L.   343
Groat, A.   450
Groff, P.   365
Groll, S.L.   339
Gutschera, K.   94–95
Guttentag, R.E.   382

Haber, L.R.   206, 365
Haber, R.N.   16, 206, 365, 450
Haberlandt, K.   309, 311
Hagelberg, E.M.   366
Haith, M.M.   382
Hakes, D.T.   217, 231, 243
Hale, B.L.   96
Hall, J.W.   383
Hall, R.   420–421
Halle, M.   54
Hanson, D.   420–421
Harding, L.M.   402–403
Hardyck, C.D.   192–193
Harris, C.   75, 183, 213
Hasher, L.   279, 305–306
Haviland, S.E.   266, 275, 278
Hawkins, H.L.   78, 84–85
Hayvren, M.   353–354
Healy, A.F.   450
Helfgott, J.   343
Henderson, L.   407
Herse, R.   341

SUBJECT INDEX

	DATE DUE		